C000244525

LIQUID EMPIRE

Liquid Empire

WATER AND POWER IN THE COLONIAL WORLD

Corey Ross

PRINCETON UNIVERSITY PRESS
PRINCETON & OXFORD

Copyright © 2024 by Princeton University Press

Princeton University Press is committed to the protection of copyright and the intellectual property our authors entrust to us. Copyright promotes the progress and integrity of knowledge. Thank you for supporting free speech and the global exchange of ideas by purchasing an authorized edition of this book. If you wish to reproduce or distribute any part of it in any form, please obtain permission.

Requests for permission to reproduce material from this work should be sent to permissions@press.princeton.edu

Published by Princeton University Press
41 William Street, Princeton, New Jersey 08540
99 Banbury Road, Oxford OX2 6JX

press.princeton.edu

All Rights Reserved

ISBN 978-0-691-21144-2
ISBN (e-book) 978-0-691-26123-2

British Library Cataloguing-in-Publication Data is available

Editorial: Ben Tate and Josh Drake
Production Editorial: Jenny Wolkowicki
Jacket design: Chris Ferrante
Production: Danielle Amatucci
Publicity: William Pagdatoon and Charlotte Coyne
Copyeditor: Maia Vaswani

Jacket image: Khadi Ganiev / Shutterstock

This book has been composed in Miller Text

Printed in the United States of America

10 9 8 7 6 5 4 3 2 1

CONTENTS

ILLUSTRATIONS

ACKNOWLEDGMENTS

I NEVER COULD have written this book without the help and support of many other people and institutions, and had I tried, it certainly would be a lesser book. One of the pleasures of finishing it is the opportunity to thank everyone who helped bring it to fruition. First of all, I am extremely grateful to the Leverhulme Trust for awarding me a Major Research Fellowship over 2018–21, which gave me the time to complete most of the research and writing. I likewise owe a debt of gratitude to the National Endowment for the Humanities for awarding me a fellowship in 2018, which was crucial for getting the project off the ground. Since then, the book was further supported by the College of Arts and Law at the University of Birmingham, which provided not only financial assistance but also a very supportive place to work. For nearly twenty-five years, my colleagues at Birmingham (especially but not exclusively in the History Department) have been wonderful to work with, and since my recent move to the University of Basel, I have continued to be fortunate in this respect.

I am indebted to many other colleagues and friends for their generous advice and encouragement along the way. A special word of thanks goes to Andrew Denning, who read and critiqued sizeable chunks of the manuscript and who has been an extremely engaging conversation partner on the history of empire and environmental history over the past several years. He, Paul Betts, Debjani Bhattacharyya, Daniel Haines, Simon Jackson, Giacomo Parrinello, Julia Adeney Thomas and Frank Uekötter all read parts of the manuscript in some form or other, and are owed a favour for sharing their valuable time and expertise. Still others helped my thinking in various ways as the book progressed, among them Peter Coates, Sabine Lee, John McNeill and Chris Wickham. Some of the ideas and arguments were road-tested at seminars, workshops, or conferences in Amsterdam, Berlin, Boston, Bristol, Chicago, Munich, Oxford, Paris, Warsaw and Zürich, and I am grateful for the suggestions that I received there.

I would also like to thank the editors of *Contemporanea* for permission to reproduce material that first appeared in 'Confluent Narratives: Writing the History of Water and Empire' (*Contemporanea* vol. 25, no. 2 (2022), 162–67), and the editors of the *International Journal of Asian Studies* for permission to reproduce material that first appeared in 'Constrained River, Constrained Choices: Seasonal Floods and Colonial Authority in the Red River Delta' (*International Journal of Asian Studies* (2023), 1–19, https://doi.org/10.1017/S1479591423000190). These sections are acknowledged in the chapters where they appear. Illustrations are reproduced courtesy of the Nationaal Museum van Wereldculturen; the National Archives Image Library;

the British Library; the Archives nationales d'outre-mer; the École française d'Extrême-Orient; the Institution of Civil Engineers; past-india.com; the Tata Central Archives; the Centre for Environment, Fisheries and Aquaculture Science; and the Deutsches Museum. Every reasonable effort has been made to contact all copyright holders, and any omissions will be rectified in subsequent printings if notice is given to the publishers.

As ever, my biggest thanks go to my family: to Alex and Tessa for generally tolerating my interest in talking about history and always helping me keep the bigger picture in mind; to my parents Charles and Charlotte, my sister Candace and her family for their all-round support (and for spoiling us when we visit); and most of all to Deborah, for all of the above and much, much more.

Corey Ross
Basel, August 2023

LIQUID EMPIRE

INTRODUCTION

Water and Empire

THERE IS TROUBLE brewing in the world's waters.[1] Whether we consider its availability, quality, or the state of the life that lives within it, water is increasingly at the centre of a mounting global crisis. The lack of adequate fresh water amid rising economic pressures is causing widespread problems on every continent. Two-thirds of the world's population experiences severe water shortage at least one month of the year, with half a billion facing it year round. Throughout the 2010s and early 2020s, the World Economic Forum has regarded water scarcity as one of the greatest global risks over the coming decades.[2] While acute droughts and shortages often capture the bulk of media attention, the underlying problem of deteriorating water quality has simultaneously led to what the World Bank calls an 'invisible water crisis'.[3] In rich and poor countries alike, the combined impacts of industrial pollution, lax sanitation, agrochemicals and over-extraction pose a growing threat not only to human health and aquatic ecosystems but also to food security and efforts at poverty alleviation. Meanwhile, in the world's oceans it is estimated that almost 90 per cent of fisheries are fully to overexploited, depleted, or in a state of collapse, with many under additional strain from pollution, the loss of spawning habitats, or the effects of exotic species introductions. Unless urgent measures are taken, pessimistic predictions suggest that stocks of nearly all commercial seafood species could collapse by the middle of the twenty-first century (more conservative estimates suggest a similar outcome by the 2110s).[4]

The scope of these problems is worldwide, but the front line is undoubtedly in the Global South. Southern Asia, Africa and Latin America are where

1. Parts of the introduction are based on material first published in my 'Confluent Narratives', with the permission of the editor.
2. World Economic Forum, *Global Risks Report 2021*, 14, 87, 90.
3. World Bank, *Quality Unknown*.
4. Worm et al., 'Impacts of Biodiversity Loss'; Jaenike, 'Comment'; Wilberg and Miller, 'Comment'.

the human population is expanding fastest, infrastructure is least able to cope with extreme water and climate conditions, governance structures are often weakest, and food supplies are most precarious. Despite slow progress over the last two decades, in 2020 around 2 billion people still suffered from inadequate supplies of clean water, around half of them living in poor countries and four-fifths of them in rural areas. Meanwhile, sewage provision has improved even more slowly: 3.6 billion people still lack safe sanitation services, including 1.7 without even basic services, nearly half of them living in sub-Saharan Africa.[5] It is estimated that around 80 per cent of waste water worldwide is released untreated into the environment, a figure that climbs well over 95 per cent in many less developed countries. As a result, water pollution is increasing in most of the rivers of Asia, Africa and Latin America, causing hundreds of thousands of deaths annually, creating huge dead zones in coastal seas and adversely affecting around a quarter of a million square kilometres of marine ecosystems.[6] Fishery resources, both marine and freshwater, are in an increasingly parlous state owing not only to pollution but also to the effects of poor supervision, a lack of regulatory enforcement and financial pressures to boost seafood exports to wealthy markets, which create a direct linkage between consumption in the Global North and degradation in the Global South. And all the while, in parts of Asia and Africa in particular, tensions over the management of transborder rivers threaten to spark 'water wars'.[7]

The stakes are high, and climate change is set to raise them yet further. Among climate scientists, meteorologists and much of the general public, there is no doubt that rising global temperatures are leading to more extreme precipitation patterns. Because warmer air holds more water vapour, downpours and floods have become more frequent and more intense. Global economic losses from flooding are nowadays around four times what they were in the 1980s, and the upward trend is set to continue as storms intensify and more people move into cities.[8] Once again, the problem is especially acute in poorer parts of the world. The fifteen countries with the highest number of people at flood risk are all in the Global South, which is suffering from the effects of greenhouse gas emissions that have emanated primarily from the Global North. Urban areas are especially prone to flooding because of their limited storage capacity and the prevalence of impervious paved surfaces. Worst off are the coastal megacities of southern and eastern Asia, where the risks from extreme rainfall are compounded not only by rising sea levels and storm surges, but also – for example, in Dhaka, Manila, Bangkok and especially Jakarta – by the added challenge of subsidence due to excessive

5. World Health Organization and United Nations Children's Fund, *Progress*, 8, 9.
6. United Nations World Water Assessment Programme, *Wastewater*, v.
7. For an overview: Chellaney, *Water, Peace, and War*.
8. Marsh McLennan Ltd, *Sunk Costs*; see also R. Elliott, *Underwater*.

groundwater extraction.[9] Yet increased flooding is only part of the picture. Higher temperatures also lead to higher rates of evaporation, which increase the threat of drought. Indeed, many large rivers are shrinking as hotter, drier soils in catchment areas are absorbing more of the rain that falls on them, allowing less to run off into watercourses, lakes and seas.[10] To make matters worse, climate change is also rearranging the temporal availability of water by making periods of low precipitation drier than before, especially in warm climates. As wet regions (and wet seasons) become wetter and dry regions (and dry seasons) drier, the unequal distribution of water is set to exacerbate existing disparities of supply and access. Meanwhile, out at sea, rising atmospheric carbon dioxide concentrations have led to higher water temperatures and higher levels of acidity, causing widespread damage to reefs and the abundance of life they support, and prompting the migration of marine species into new waters as former haunts become less habitable.[11]

Despite the recent push to reduce global emissions, the response of governments and international agencies to this bundle of challenges has largely been to continue the long-standing quest for more effective technological solutions. Huge dams remain a favourite tool for dealing with floods, droughts and rising energy demands – despite the fact that they block the passage of the silt that keeps low-lying coastal areas above sea level. Throughout Asia and Africa, enormous canal schemes are being planned or built (often by Chinese or Western firms) to divert water flows hundreds of kilometres to arid lands. The Food and Agriculture Organization of the United Nations (FAO) has spent tens of millions of dollars helping cash-strapped governments acquire the necessary expertise and infrastructure to monitor and protect their fisheries, even as it has financially supported the mechanization of fishing fleets that deplete marine stocks further and the conversion of coastal land into fish farms that remove protective mangroves from low-lying coasts. A plethora of non-governmental organizations (NGOs) is engaged in efforts to improve access to clean water and sanitation, though municipal systems throughout the Global South continue to lag far behind the needs of rapidly growing urban populations.

All of these problems, and all of these purported solutions, have a long genealogy. They are the outcomes of a historic quest to conquer aquatic nature, one that has profoundly reshaped the societies and ecosystems of the developing world. If we wish to understand them, we must examine the earlier ideas, institutions and infrastructures from which they emerged and which still materially shape them today. Despite the unprecedented spike in water usage

9. Brecht et al., 'Sea-Level Rise'. For a detailed regional case study focusing on the temporary and mostly ineffective 'fixes' that state authorities and local residents have introduced, see Ley's *Building on Borrowed Time*.

10. A. Sharma, Wasko and Lettenmaier, 'Precipitation Extremes'.

11. Poloczanska et al., 'Responses of Marine Organisms', 62.

during the post-colonial era, tracing the origins of the various water-related crises that poor countries currently face requires us to look beyond the last few decades of acute shortages and collapsing fish stocks, beyond even the fixation of Cold War development experts and decolonizing elites on mega-dams, diversions and industrialized fishing fleets. We need to look at the history of water and Europe's modern empire, a history that we have too often neglected.

The dramatic spread of European power in the nineteenth century ushered in a far-reaching transformation of human relationships with the rest of nature. Across vast stretches of the globe, from the Americas to Africa and Asia, the rapid pace of Europe's imperial expansion marked an important environmental–historical watershed. These empires tied lands and peoples more closely into the global capitalist economy and exploited their resources on an unparalleled scale. The ravenous appetite for raw materials in industrial metropoles imposed huge demands on natural assets in the rest of the world, from soils and forests to energy, mineral deposits and water resources. At the core of European imperialism was an attempt to transform biophysical environments for human (above all, metropolitan) purposes, to render conquered territories into productive and legible spaces.

Controlling water was a crucial part of the process. At a material level, whatever the imperial powers sought to do by way of exploiting their colonies – whether by boosting agricultural output, generating power, improving health, enhancing fisheries production, or bringing swamps and arid 'wastes' under the plough – managing the hydrosphere was an absolute necessity. At a perceptual level as well, water and its availability lay at the heart of Europeans' understandings of the new territories they conquered. In the eyes of temperate-dwelling Europeans, the very challenge posed by nature in the 'torrid' and 'tropical' parts of the world was not only one of temperature but also a matter of water: that is, either too little or too much of it, in the wrong places at the wrong times, depending on the place and time of year. If one of the hallmarks of tropical regions was the relative lack of seasonal temperature fluctuations (which, according to contemporary theorists, reduced people's mental activity, work ethic and self-discipline), another was the highly seasonal nature of water, characterized by periods of heavy rainfall and flooding followed by long dry spells that saw little precipitation at all.[12] Wherever water was lacking, the prospects for economic development seemed dim. Wherever it was abundant, it was often considered a dangerous source of disease. Throughout Europe's empire, not only was water an object of material intervention, it also shaped contemporary understandings of colonial environments more generally. From

12. On Western ideas of 'tropicality', see Sutter's 'Tropics', Arnold's *Problem of Nature* (141–68) and *Tropics*, and Driver and Martins's *Tropical Visions*.

agriculture to transport and from public health to energy, the scope of efforts to subjugate water expanded accordingly.

Europe's empire builders were, of course, by no means the first or only rulers to regard water management as a source of wealth and power. Indeed, no other element of the natural world has been subjected to attempts at human control longer and more forcefully than water.[13] Across large parts of the premodern world, the quest to harness the seasonal flow of rivers reaches back millennia. Egypt's irrigation basins covered much of the lower Nile valley for thousands of years, and parts of what became China's Grand Canal (still the longest canal in the world) date back to the fifth century BCE.[14] South Asia was strewn with local tank systems long before Europeans arrived there, and early-modern Ottoman rulers built or sponsored extensive water distribution systems.[15] In addition to the control of water flows, stationary water bodies (seas, lakes, ponds) have likewise long attracted people's attention as a reservoir of goods and sustenance to supplement what their terrestrial habitats could provide.

Yet despite this long 'terraqueous' history, and notwithstanding the many continuities with premodern hydroengineering efforts, what was new in the empires of the nineteenth and twentieth centuries was the sheer scope and pace of transformation.[16] European imperialists transformed waterways into highways and fixed ever-shifting shorelines into serviceable ports on a literally industrial scale. Much like their Japanese or American imperial counterparts – with whom they exchanged many ideas about how to exploit water and aquatic spaces – they vastly increased both the number and size of barrages and irrigation systems in a bid to boost crop production and increase land revenues for state coffers. In their determination to tap the supposedly 'latent' resources of their colonies, they teamed up with land-hungry farmers to drain swamps, build flood defences and reclaim land on an unprecedented scale. They introduced entirely new water and sanitation systems for rapidly growing cities and eventually erected hydroelectric dams to illuminate their streets and power the industries located there. They sought to 'rationalize' marine fisheries off the coasts of their colonies and to enhance the catch from inland waters by deliberately altering their biological make-up. The global surge of European power in the nineteenth and twentieth centuries washed its way across the various elements of the hydrosphere, and the legacies it left behind for the post-colonial world persisted long after these empires had receded.

13. As emphasized by Tvedt in '"Water Systems"'.

14. On the long history of water control in China, see Mostern's *Yellow River*; Elvin's *Retreat of the Elephants*, 115–64; and Marks's *Tigers, Rice, Silk*.

15. For a panoramic, water-centred history of pre-colonial India, see S. Sen's *Ganges*. On the Ottoman Empire, see Husain's *Rivers of the Sultan*; Mikhail's *Nature and Empire*, 38–81, 242–90; and Joseph's 'Islamic Law'.

16. Bashford, 'Terraqueous Histories'.

Liquid Empire tells the intertwined stories of water and Europe's modern imperial enterprise. It examines the multifaceted efforts to exploit the waters of the colonial world, the constraints that moulded them and the consequences (intended or otherwise) that resulted. It recounts how new ideas, technologies and institutions transformed human engagements with water, and how aquatic ecosystems – understood here as interconnected biophysical networks located in or around bodies of water – were themselves reshaped through attempts to control, alter and manage them. It does this by approaching the story from a global and trans-imperial angle, and by emphasizing how colonial interventions in the hydrosphere fitted within the broader political and ideological agendas that framed them. By reconsidering the history of European empire from an aquatic standpoint, it argues that water was an essential part of the story, one that literally flowed through the entire project of modern imperialism.

This is a different perspective from the terra-centric outlook that usually frames our understanding of Europe's modern empire. Although rivers, lakes and oceans have often featured in historical accounts of imperial expansion, for the most part they have been confined to the margins or appear as little more than contextual background. Indeed, the very 'terrestriality' of Europe's nineteenth- and twentieth-century imperial venture is broadly regarded as one of its defining characteristics. Among the chief factors that distinguished Europe's modern empires from their maritime forerunners was the penetration of huge swathes of the African and Asian landmasses beyond the coastal trading outposts to which they had largely been confined in the past. By the turn of the twentieth century, a series of transport, military and medical innovations had enabled a handful of European states to extend the territory under their control (however uneven, sporadic and intermittent this control was) by no less than twenty-three million square kilometres, around one-sixth of the entire global land surface. For good reason, the 'new imperialism' of the late nineteenth century, however much it grafted on to longer-term political transformations within Asia and Africa, is widely regarded as the largest land grab in world history.[17]

Even in the burgeoning field of environmental history, studies of Europe's colonial empire have long tended to cluster around a handful of terrestrial themes: the rise of 'scientific' forestry, the emergence and legacies of colonial wildlife conservation, the production of tropical commodities for global markets, and efforts to 'improve' colonial agriculture.[18] But if this terrestrial emphasis is understandable, it is nonetheless incomplete, for it overlooks the

17. For a survey of the literature, see Butlin's *Geographies of Empire*; on the 'scramble' for Africa as part of a longer pattern of regional political change that European imperial powers exploited, see Reid's 'Africa's Revolutionary Nineteenth Century'.

18. For overviews: Ross, *Ecology and Power*; Beinart and Hughes, *Environment and Empire*; Beattie, Melillo and O'Gorman, *Eco-Cultural Networks*; Ax et al., *Cultivating the Colonies*.

extent to which imperial power was immersed in water. As European empires transitioned from maritime enclaves to territorial domination, they encompassed not only rich tropical forests, parched deserts and teeming savannahs but also many of the world's mightiest rivers, largest lakes, greatest wetlands and most prolific coastal seas. These waters were more than just blue patches on the expanding imperial map. They shaped the history of European empire in numerous ways: as natural capital from which colonizers and colonized alike sought to profit in different ways, as vital conduits of mobility, as an important realm of scientific research and knowledge generation, and as key sites of social and cultural contestation. Just like the vegetal and mineral resources of the colonies, their waters were valuable assets that people sought to understand, control and exploit. After all, managing water was crucial for harnessing the productivity of colonized landscapes themselves, whether for keeping people fed, powering industries, or mitigating losses from floods and erosion. In this sense, *Liquid Empire* aims to reveal hitherto neglected aspects of Europe's imperial engagement with the people and environments of the colonial world.

The attempt to conquer water in Europe's colonies was, of course, part of a worldwide story of escalating human intervention in the hydrosphere. Historians of the United States have long emphasized the centrality of water control for continental settlement, industrialization and urbanization; more recently, they have also brought the country's fisheries into sharper focus.[19] Over the past couple of decades, scholars of Europe, China, Australia and the Russian/Soviet empires have likewise explored how water flows sculpted political, socio-economic and cultural developments, placing particular emphasis on 'enviro-technical' hydraulic systems as building blocks of the modern state itself.[20] Seas, lakes and rivers have also featured in the historiography of European empire, though their coverage has been patchy and uneven. To date, the bulk of attention has centred on water as an agricultural resource. We know quite a lot about the social and economic dimensions of irrigation works – the paramount tool of colonial agricultural modernization – above all in India and Egypt, and to a lesser extent in Sudan, the Middle Niger and the Netherlands Indies.[21] By contrast, the many other imperial engagements

19. Worster, *Rivers of Empire*; R. White, *Organic Machine*; Pisani, *Water and American Government*; Melosi, *Water*; Hundley, *Great Thirst*; Steinberg, *Nature Incorporated*. On fisheries: McEvoy, *Fisherman's Problem*; Chiang, *Shaping the Shoreline*; J. Taylor, *Making Salmon*; Bolster, *Mortal Sea*; Reardon, *Managing the River Commons*.

20. Pritchard, *Confluence*; Cioc, *Rhine*; Blackbourn, *Conquest of Nature*; Pietz, *Engineering the State* and *Yellow River*; Peterson, *Pipe Dreams*; O'Gorman, *Flood Country*.

21. On India: D'Souza, 'Water in British India'; Gilmartin, *Blood and Water*; Haines, *Building the Empire*; Whitcombe, *Agrarian Conditions* and 'Irrigation'; I. Stone, *Canal Irrigation*; Mosse, *Rule of Water*. On Egypt and Sudan: Mitchell, *Rule of Experts*; Tvedt, *Economic, Political, Social* and *Age of the British*; Blocher, *Der Wasserbau-Staat*; Ertsen,

with water remain underexplored, despite some excellent works on particular topics and places. The impulse of colonial states to convert swamps and marshes into solid land has occasionally come into focus, most notably in southern Asia's river deltas.[22] Despite the propensity of monsoon-fed rivers to burst their banks, only a handful of studies (almost exclusively on India) examine efforts to mitigate, prevent or deal with the fallout from extreme flood events.[23] The history of colonial cities as nodes of exchange and cultural hybridization has been one of the liveliest areas of imperial historiography in recent years, but the fraught history of municipal water and sewage works has mostly remained local in scope.[24] Research on hydroelectric projects in Asia and Africa has focused overwhelmingly on the mega-schemes of the post-war period, to the detriment of colonial-era surveys and initiatives.[25] Meanwhile, the attempts of colonial states to improve the navigability of rivers for trade and communication purposes has remained a niche interest, and even less attention has gone to the transformation of coasts and marshes into modern port facilities.[26] With precious few exceptions, the history of colonial efforts to control fisheries, promote aquaculture and re-engineer aquatic ecosystems remains largely unwritten.[27] Rarest of all are studies that tackle the question

Improvising Planned Development; R. Collins, *Waters of the Nile*. On the Netherlands Indies: Ravesteijn, *De zegenrijke heeren*; Ertsen, *Locales of Happiness*. On the Middle Niger: Van Beusekom, *Negotiating Development*; Schreyger, *L'Office du Niger*; Filipovich, 'Destined to Fail'. On East Africa: Bender, *Water Brings No Harm*.

22. Bhattacharyya, *Empire and Ecology*; Iqbal, *Bengal Delta*; Biggs, *Quagmire*; Brocheux, *Mekong Delta*; Adas, *Burma Delta*.

23. D'Souza, *Drowned and Dammed*; C. Hill, *River of Sorrow*; Mishra, 'Bihar Flood Story'; T. Ghosh, 'Floods and People'; Kingsbury, *Imperial Disaster*.

24. The best overview is Broich's 'Engineering the Empire'. The bulk of work on urban water systems focuses on India's main conurbations: Arnold, *Colonizing the Body*; M. Harrison, *Public Health*; McFarlane, 'Governing the Contaminated City'; Gandy, 'Landscapes of Disaster'; Prashad, 'Technology of Sanitation'; Mann, 'Delhi's Belly'; Klein, 'Urban Development and Death'; Dossal, 'Henry Conybeare'. For studies of colonial cities beyond India: Yeoh, *Contesting Space*, 177–89; M'Bokolo, 'Peste et société urbaine'; Ngalamulume, 'Coping with Disease'; Gandy, 'Planning, Anti-planning'; Nilsson, 'Unseeing State'; Ismail, 'Epicures and Experts'; Kooy and Bakker, 'Splintered Networks' and '(Post)Colonial Pipes'.

25. For overviews: McCully, *Silenced Rivers*; Adams, *Wasting the Rain*. On colonial-era hydroelectricity: Hoag, *Developing the Rivers*, 135–72; Lanthier, 'L'électrification de Bombay'; Kale, 'Structures of Power'; Isaacman and Isaacman, *Dams, Displacement*; Hart, *Volta River Project*.

26. On river navigation: Bernstein, *Steamboats on the Ganges*; Dewey, *Steamboats on the Indus*; Lacroze, *Les grands pionniers*; Lederer, *Histoire de la navigation*; Huybrechts, *Transports et structures*; Headrick, *Power over Peoples*, 177–225. On ports: N. Mukherjee, *Port of Calcutta*; Headrick, *Tentacles of Progress*, 32–35; Powell, 'Singapore's Lost Coast' and 'Harnessing the Great Acceleration'.

27. The few exceptions are Butcher's *Closing of the Frontier*; Medrano's 'Edible Tide'; C. Jennings's 'Unexploited Assets'; Reeves's 'Inland Waters'; and Reeves, Pokrant and McGuire's 'Auction Lease System'.

of how the circulation of water and its multiple uses connected such histories together.[28] This book accordingly follows a twofold rationale: to investigate some of the less familiar aspects of colonial water history, and to integrate them into a broader account of the multidimensional entanglement of water and Europe's imperial power.

Doing so requires us to break some long-standing historiographical habits. One is the tendency to focus mainly on the surface. Historians have long recognized the importance of waterways for imperial expansion; during the nineteenth century, steam-driven gunboats and ocean liners were among the key technologies that made the extension of European power into the Asian and African landmasses possible in the first place. Over the last two decades, a growing body of work on seas and oceans – sometimes referred to as the 'maritime turn', or 'new thalassology' – has recovered long-forgotten patterns of interconnection and exchange across vast nautical spaces. Partly inspired by earlier work on Mediterranean and Atlantic history, such histories have taught us to appreciate how water bodies of varying sizes – whether the Indian Ocean or the Suez Canal – can serve as useful categories of historical analysis. Yet in nearly all of these accounts, water itself features as no more than a medium of transport for the goods, people and ideas that drive history, a surface to move across between various pieces of land.[29]

Another habit to overcome is treating water mainly as an input. Clearly, water supplies were critical for agricultural production, urban growth and various colonial industries. During the droughts and famines that straddled the late nineteenth and early twentieth centuries, they were literally a matter of life and death for millions of people in colonial Asia. Previous work on the history of dams and irrigation schemes shows how the availability or absence of water in particular places was a key constraint that shaped human welfare, political calculations and economic activity.[30] But the relationship between imperial power and the hydrosphere was much broader than that. Water was not only a substance to divert and re-channel but also constituted a vast ecosystem itself, one that contained a multitude of potential resources as well as a host of microscopic dangers that threatened human life. Moreover, human actions and ideas also had profound effects on water, which in turn had far-reaching

28. The outstanding exception is Amrith's *Unruly Waters*, which focuses primarily on modern India through the lens of the monsoon. See also Heather Hoag's *Developing the Rivers* and Beattie and Morgan's 'Engineering Edens'.

29. Bose, *Hundred Horizons*; Huber, *Channelling Mobilities*; Tagliacozzo, *In Asian Waters*; Hofmeyr, Dhupelia-Mesthrie and Kaarsholm, 'Durban and Cape Town'; Armitage, Bashford and Sivasundarum, *Oceanic Histories*; Miller, *Sea*; North, *Zwischen Hafen und Horizont*; Buchet, *La mer*; 'Forum: Oceans of History'. Two noteworthy exceptions that incorporate aquatic environments into their analyses are Cushman's *Guano* and Amrith's *Bay of Bengal*.

30. See notes 21, 25.

consequences for human activities. All throughout the colonial era, a series of new technologies and initiatives – ranging from urban sanitation to electricity generation to fishery development – altered not only the flow and distribution of water but also its composition, ecology, flora and fauna, along with the cultural meanings that people attached to it. Although many of these issues have attracted scant consideration, they too were deeply enmeshed in the fabric of imperial power and became an integral part of its aqueous legacy.

Water is a unique substance, and its distinctive attributes make it a remarkably useful object of study for historians.[31] For one thing, its critical importance for human life and economic activity render it an ideal vehicle for examining the 'political ecology' of modern empire at large. The basic premise of political ecology is that the production and distribution of wealth and power are based not only on the social construction of human activities but also on the ability to transform the material world – not least the hydrosphere – and control it for particular purposes.[32] In many ways, the idea that water and power are interlinked is far from new. In the 1950s, the sociologist Karl Wittfogel famously argued that 'hydraulic societies' such as ancient Egypt, China, Mesopotamia or India were fundamentally organized around the control of water for irrigation, which in turn gave rise to highly centralized bureaucracies and decidedly 'despotic' forms of government. Ever since then, scholars have questioned and criticized Wittfogel's thesis, noting that the formation of centralized states often preceded large-scale irrigation works, that many of the absolutist tendencies he described were apparent in areas without irrigation, and that the day-to-day maintenance of irrigation networks was frequently organized on a local or communal basis.[33]

But regardless of such debates, we do not need to accept Wittfogel's deterministic theories – or, for that matter, restrict our gaze to irrigation and agriculture – to recognize that human interactions with water are intimately bound up with questions of hierarchy, inequality and power. Who controls the flows and distribution of water both reflects and (re)produces social difference. Who defines how it is perceived, measured and valued is rooted in distinctions between different forms of knowledge. Who controls access to rivers, lakes and seas is best placed to profit from the resources living within them and to use them for religious or recreational purposes. Who gets to use water as a waste dump – and, consequently, who has to live with the detritus carried downstream or washed up

31. For a stimulating recent discussion, see T. Fernando, Physioc and Rider's 'Flows of History'.

32. P. Robbins, *Political Ecology*; Bryant, *International Handbook*; Peet, Robbins and Watts, *Global Political Ecology*; Stott and Sullivan, *Political Ecology*; Loftus, 'Rethinking Political Ecologies'; Holt, *Water and Power*.

33. Wittfogel, *Oriental Despotism*; Ulmen, *Society and History*. On critiques of Wittfogel's thesis: Peet, 'Karl Wittfogel'; Ley and Krause, 'Ethnographic Conversations'.

on shore – is shaped by social status. In brief, water and power are interrelated in a multitude of different ways and in a variety of different aquatic settings: from fresh to salt water; from surface to groundwater; from drainage, flood control and urban sanitation to navigation, irrigation and fisheries.

By weaving together a new fabric of infrastructures, rights and entitlements, and by regulating the conflicts that continually arose over them, modern states – including colonial states – did more than just govern the manipulation of water; they governed *through* the manipulation of water. Although these dynamics were by no means new to the modern era or unique to the history of European empire, in many ways Europe's imperial heyday presents us with an unusually illustrative case, a kind of historical exemplar of the deep and multifaceted interconnectedness of water, political power and social difference. Whether we look at the glaring disparities of water access in colonial cities, the deliberate displacement of traditional waterworks by expert-controlled megaschemes, or the skewed distribution of costs and benefits from colonial flood defences and reclamation projects, the inequalities on display were in each case amplified by the stark racial and civilizational hierarchies that structured colonial societies. The 'politics of difference' in Europe's modern empires gave them a somewhat distinct dynamic in comparison to other political entities characterized by asymmetrical power relationships.[34] Furthermore, the enormous scale of environmental change that modern colonialism wrought in the areas that it conquered ensured that these disparities have continued to suffuse the waterscape of the Global South well into the twenty-first century.

Water thus furnishes a powerful lens for examining the socioecological dynamics of imperial power. But to turn the perspective around, it also provides insights into the limits of this power. Water is a notoriously contradictory substance. It is at once the stuff of life and a purveyor of deadly disease. It is an indispensable necessity for human sustenance but also a destroyer of property and human life. It provides a cheap and efficient means of transport but also threatens communications infrastructure and can pose a major barrier to the mobility of people, goods and information. On a cultural level, it is simultaneously an object of veneration, subjugation and anxiety. And to complicate matters further, water also operates on multiple, overlapping timescales: the recurrent annual cycle of the seasons; the intermittent chronology of catastrophic floods or droughts; and the slow, creeping nature of long-term changes such as the silting up of rivers, sinking river deltas, falling groundwater levels, or the biochemical alteration of lakes and oceans.[35] For all the colonial assertions about 'mastering' water, it was never fully tamed – perhaps least of all in the volatile hydrographic regimes of Europe's tropical colonies. In this sense, water was both a source of imperial power and a challenge to it.

34. Burbank and Cooper, *Empires in World History*, 8–11.
35. A point eloquently highlighted by Amrith in *Unruly Waters* (9–10).

After all, the claim to conquer nature through superior know-how and technology was both a cornerstone of colonial rule and a crucial means of justifying it. Consequently, the failure (or perceived failure) to control water served to undermine European authority and open up spaces for opposition, whether from indigenous people who resented the threat to their economic interests and cultural sensibilities or from budding nationalist political movements that demanded a more rapid and thorough development of water resources than colonial states appeared willing or able to achieve.

A further benefit of focusing on water is that it reflects historical changes in so many different spheres. Schemes to channel and exploit water provide a measure of a state's political priorities, social ambitions and technological capabilities. How people use and abuse water, how they allocate and conserve it, tells us a lot about their relations with each other and with the rest of the natural world. Water is the lifeblood of a whole array of modern social and economic systems, from the circulatory networks of cities to agricultural development projects, electrical grids and mechanized fishing industries. Although water is, in a strictly chemical sense, a unitary substance (notwithstanding the different minerals, nutrients or contaminants that might be mixed with it), in the social world it comes in a variety of different guises. It sloshes through the imperial past as a resource for farmers, as a commodity for urban consumers, as a threat to floodplains and coastlines, and as a habitat in which living resources could be caught or cultivated.

The basic aim of *Liquid Empire* is to survey the breadth and diversity of imperial encounters with water. Tackling such a wide array of themes poses challenges, which helps explain why water-related histories to date have tended to focus on single topics or regions. It also entails certain drawbacks; it is no exaggeration to say that each of the following chapters could be turned into many books. But stepping back to take in the bigger aquatic picture also presents significant opportunities, because the various forms and uses of water were ultimately intertwined. The construction of vast irrigation systems unavoidably affected river navigation since their flow requirements often contradicted one another. Capturing run-off behind dams or using watercourses as refuse dumps impacted fisheries and other users downstream. Promoting industrial modes of fishing or draining swamps for agricultural use commonly had an adverse effect on artisanal fishers. Building flood controls or irrigation works in one area raised the risk of catastrophic inundation, waterlogging or water shortages in others. The world of water is literally awash with such interconnections and trade-offs.

My starting point is that all of these different 'waters' formed part of a single integrated hydrosphere, and that the period of European global dominance was one of momentous and enduring change in the long history of human interactions with it. Consequently, the chapters that follow not only cover a broad range of themes – water-based transport, irrigation, swamp reclamation, marine and inland fisheries, lake stocking, aquaculture, flood control, municipal sanitation, hydropower – but also seek to tease out some of the linkages between them. Water connected upland farmers with lowland cities, the fisherman with the irrigator, the riverside cultivator with the electricity consumer. The basic rationale for placing water at the centre of the narrative is that we can gain new insights by looking at these topics together rather than focusing merely on one or the other. After all, any water that is 'wasted' or that escapes human control is never truly lost; whatever leaks, drains or evaporates away always ends up somewhere else. In this sense, *Liquid Empire* is a book about the fundamental interconnectedness of things – not only different parts of the hydrosphere but also the manifold ways in which humans are interwoven with the biophysical environment.

Exploring these interdependencies requires us not only to consider a variety of aqueous spaces but also to look across political boundaries. Water, like many other elements of the natural world, shows little respect for borders. Although there are sound political and geographic reasons to study water on a local or regional scale – whether at the level of a single river, state or physical watershed – taking a wider spatial view enables us to see how changes in particular places were linked to much broader processes, both natural and historical. Rivers link mountain rain and snow with drylands, deltas and the global sea. Water currents carry sediment, nutrients and contaminants from one place to another. Consequently, water challenges conventional understandings of territoriality.[36] The (rather arbitrary) lines that Europe's imperial diplomats drew on the map were intended to delineate fixed domains of land. But flows of water across these frontiers muddled any neat distinction between different spheres of influence, and the concept of 'international waters' further confounded them when dealing with matters offshore. Moreover, the boundaries between land and water were themselves often indistinct and changeable. Deltas, littorals and low-lying river plains were mutable, half-liquid spaces characterized by the continual movement of mud and silt; in ecological parlance, they were 'ecotones', in which different biological communities meet and mix. Much to the frustration of state officials, engineers and investors, water had a way of turning firm territorial settlements into a physical and political mire.[37] To be sure, political boundaries affected the movement and uses of water (indeed, increasingly so as colonial and post-colonial states imposed new claims on it), but ideas about water and its exploitation travel as much as water itself does. So, too, did many of the people (engineers, administrators, hydrologists) who sought to control, regulate and re-channel it. To study water is to follow these currents.

36. See Maier, *Once within Borders*.
37. Von Hardenberg, 'Knowing the Littoral'; Bhattacharyya, 'Fluid Histories' and 'River Is Not'; O'Gorman, *Wetlands in a Dry Land*.

Liquid Empire therefore adopts a fluid sense of geography. Its primary focus is on colonial Asia and Africa, especially (though not exclusively) non-settler colonies, but it treats these regions as spaces whose edges were blurred by flows of water as well as by the circulation of ideas, technologies and practices associated with it. Tracing these cross-currents sometimes takes us beyond the bounds of European colonies and protectorates, whether to the fisheries of Japan, the watersheds of North America, or back to the rivers and harbours of the metropole. In this sense, our focus on the empires of Western European states is by no means intended to downplay the importance of other imperial projects (Japanese, American, Russian, Ottoman), which often pursued similar water-control aims, or to ignore the cross-border exchange of ideas, technologies and political impulses that bound them together. Rather, it is a reflection of Europe's dominant collective power throughout much of the period and the need to impose some practical limits on the subject.

Even within the spatial confines of European empire, studying water requires us to adopt a trans-imperial perspective that transcends the boundaries of individual colonies or regions of influence. One benefit of this approach is that it opens up areas that have attracted relatively little scholarly attention. Like so many aspects of the imperial past, histories of water control have hitherto centred predominately on the British Empire. Although British-ruled colonies feature prominently in the pages that follow, the story also encompasses the less familiar water histories of the other major European colonial empires, drawing on material in French, German, and Dutch. Another advantage of this trans-imperial viewpoint is that it allows us to draw comparisons and trace commonalities across frontiers. In spite of – and to some extent because of – their rivalries, Europe's empires are best understood in connection with one another. There were, to be sure, different ways of 'doing' colonialism: direct or indirect forms of rule, overriding or upholding local 'customs', private versus state-led resource exploitation. Colonial authorities also set somewhat different political and economic priorities, not least around the questions of profitability versus 'native welfare' or gradual change versus rapid economic development. As we will see, these various governing strategies and policy decisions influenced both the conception and consequences of hydrological interventions in different colonial territories, from irrigation to fishing and from flood control to hydropower. Nonetheless, administrators, engineers and scientists faced many common challenges in their encounters with the waters of the colonial world. As a result, ideas about how to exploit them were the subject of imitation, adaptation and sometimes coordination across imperial boundaries and beyond.[38]

38. Hedinger and Heé, 'Transimperial History'; Kamissek and Kreienbaum, 'Imperial Cloud?'; V. Barth and Cvetkovski, *Imperial Co-operation and Transfer*; Adelman, 'Mimesis and Rivalry'; Streets-Salter and Getz, *Empires and Colonies*; Singaravélou, *Les empires coloniaux*; Jerónimo and Pinto, *Ends of European Colonial*.

Examining the interconnections and interdependencies of water also demands a fluid chronological framework. Our main focus will be on the nineteenth and twentieth centuries, starting with the consolidation of European power in southern Asia and early forays up Africa's rivers, and continuing through the age of decolonization after the Second World War. These temporal parameters will vary from one subject to another and will flex at both ends. From the very beginning, colonial waterworks in parts of Asia and Africa were powerfully shaped by pre-colonial practices and infrastructures, and are therefore best viewed as part of a longer trajectory of human hydraulic interventions. The same point holds true for the latter stages of the story: given the huge aquatic transformations over which Europe's empire builders presided, we will also explicitly consider the hydraulic legacies of European empire for the post-colonial world.

Although tackling two centuries inevitably involves a high degree of compression, taking a long view has significant benefits when dealing with the history of water. For one thing, most large-scale water management systems took decades to come to fruition. Schemes that began as colonial infrastructure projects often ended up being inaugurated as symbols of national independence by post-colonial governments. Moreover, a long temporal framework allows us to consider discontinuities within the colonial era itself, whether due to changing attitudes and political constellations, technological innovations or as a result of crisis moments such as famines, war or economic depression. By looking across this time span we can trace the gradual transition from a phase of improvisation and experience gathering in the early and mid-nineteenth century towards a more expert-based, scientifically oriented mode of water exploitation that became increasingly dominant in the twentieth century. Finally, the multilayered temporalities of water meant that the full environmental effects of hydrological interventions often took decades to manifest themselves, which meant that contemporaries frequently underestimated the long-term implications of what they were doing. This is, of course, a problem of more than just historical interest. In the twenty-first century, we still struggle to understand how our current uses and misuses of the hydrosphere will play out in the future.

Our focus on the era of 'modern colonialism' thus does not posit any neat historical breaks. As recent histories of empire have emphasized, there were many continuities and parallels between the imperial projects of modern Europe and empire-building processes in other times and places. Certainly there was little new in the basic idea that supposedly more advanced or 'refined' groups had a right to propagate or even force their own norms and institutions on to those whom they regarded as backward or brutish. Such notions were rooted in long-standing discourses of imperial providence, and informed Chinese notions of state-building as much as European self-imagination.[39]

39. Harrell, *Cultural Encounters*; B. Barth and Osterhammel, *Zivilisierungsmissionen*; Pagden, *Lords of All*.

Since ancient times, deploying the latest technologies to construct large-scale waterworks had been a favourite tool of imperial elites eager to demonstrate their beneficence, extend their influence and bolster the resources at their command. In these and many other ways, the colonial regimes of the nineteenth and twentieth centuries drew on a multitude of older ideas, methods and strategies to fashion their own 'imperial repertoires'.[40]

But even so, there are several factors that make this period somewhat distinctive. At the most basic level, Europe's modern empires were collectively larger; more populous; and more geographically, culturally and economically variegated than anything that earlier imperial powers had managed to assemble. Over time, the global supremacy of these empires was amplified by the 'Great Divergence' of economic growth between the Western powers and the rest of the world after around 1800, which meant that they were able to deploy more resources than ever before for the domination of subject lands and peoples.[41] In turn, this widening economic differential also reflected the unprecedented technological discrepancy that opened up over the course of the nineteenth century, which eventually furnished the 'tools of empire' that made it possible to penetrate large parts of Asia and Africa that had previously lain beyond European grasp.[42] Finally, these new industrial-era technologies did more than just enable imperial conquest; they also encouraged the deployment of European knowledge, capital and administrative practices for mobilizing the natural wealth and labour of subjugated territories on an extraordinary scale.

The overall result was a markedly interventionist approach to empire-building. Although the notion that Europeans should guide and educate what they regarded as more 'primitive' peoples had long formed the cornerstone of the so-called 'civilizing mission', over time their incursions were increasingly animated by visions of an enlightened form of colonialism spearheaded by engineers and scientists rather than by conquering armies, and geared more towards mutual benefit and moral advancement than coercion and suppression. It was an approach that resonated with other imperial projects in the nineteenth- and twentieth-century world, whether the extension of Japanese supremacy in East Asia, Russian expansion in central Asia, or the 'internal colonization' efforts of federal agencies in the western and southern United

40. See especially Burbank and Cooper's *Empires in World History* (1–22, 287–329). I make no neat distinction in the text between 'colonial' and 'imperial', but rather use them as overlapping (but not identical) terms. On the advantages and disadvantages of the terminological options, see Kumar's 'Colony and Empire'.

41. Pomeranz, *Great Divergence*; Parthasarathi, *Why Europe Grew Rich*; Osterhammel, *Die Verwandlung der Welt*; E. Jones, *European Miracle*.

42. Headrick, *Tools of Empire*. On the importance of non-military over military factors, see Sharman's *Empires of the Weak*.

States.[43] By and large, the results rarely matched the rhetoric. In the case of Europe's colonies, the 'shoestring' budgets of most colonial states were hardly conducive to progressive social reform, and nor was their heavy reliance on indigenous elites for the purpose of governing conquered territories. The introduction of new technologies often benefitted investors and merchants more than local people, and was often used to direct and control their activities more effectively. Nonetheless, from the late nineteenth century onwards, and especially after the fallout of the two world wars generated mounting pressures to justify the continuation of colonial rule, the core responsibility of European colonial states was (at least ideally) not merely to tax and exploit subjugated societies but rather to 'develop' their economies through the application of modern science and technology.[44]

The control of nature was critical to this undertaking. The markedly technocratic impulse of modern colonialism meant that subject territories were no longer viewed merely as spaces to govern but as places to be managed and improved – 'living laboratories' for social and environmental experimentation.[45] In this context, mastering flows of water and harnessing the productivity of aqueous spaces represented more than just a material means of exerting imperial authority (though it certainly was that). It also had a profound symbolic importance: in the eyes of Europeans, it justified their claims to colonial stewardship over natural resources that subject peoples were less capable of capitalizing on themselves.[46] Whether through the irrigation of farmland, the draining of swamps, the expansion of fisheries or the improvement of sanitation, the management of water lay at the heart of the colonial development agenda and indeed has remained a central focus of development initiatives ever since.

Yet for all the emphasis on developing colonial water resources, the imperial conquest of water was more than just a matter of imposing external power over subjugated territories and disseminating technologies from metropolitan 'centres' to colonial 'peripheries'. As the following chapters show, it often involved a lot of trial and error, adapting technologies to unfamiliar environments, importing ideas and practices from other colonies or national settings,

43. Peterson, *Pipe Dreams*; Mizuno, Moore and DiMoia, *Engineering Asia*; A. Moore, *Constructing East Asia* and 'Yalu River Era'; M. Jansen, *Making of Modern Japan*, 436–41; Beasley, *Japanese Imperialism*, 198–219; B. Barth and Osterhammel, *Zivilisierungsmissionen*; Downs, *Transforming the South*, 73–180; Worster, *Rivers of Empire*; Pisani, *Water and American Government*.

44. The most programmatic contemporary statements were Leroy-Beaulieu's *De la colonisation* and Kidd's *Control of the Tropics*. On interventionist colonialism and development: Cooper and Packard, introduction to *International Development*, 6–9; Hodge, *Triumph of the Expert*; Conklin, *Mission to Civilize*.

45. Tilley, *Africa*.

46. Adas, *Machines as the Measure*; MacLeod, *Nature and Empire*; Bennett and Hodge, *Science and Empire*; Marsden and Smith, *Engineering Empires*; Fischer-Tiné and Mann, *Colonialism as Civilizing Mission*.

and occasionally adopting or absorbing indigenous techniques that had been refined over generations to take advantage of local hydrological conditions. Colonial engineers and their projects will feature prominently, but large-scale hydraulic tinkering always involved a high degree of negotiation and alignment of interests between different social groups. This very much included colonized people themselves, who in some cases were among the primary drivers of transformation and who variously supported, opposed or repurposed imperial water designs for their own ends. In this respect, the story diverges from older diffusionist narratives of technology transfer, in which Europeans conveyed their own practices to seemingly passive colonized societies and territories.[47] Taking its cue from recent work on colonial infrastructures, knowledge and environmental history, it instead seeks to paint a more complex picture of mutual interaction, the circulation of ideas and practices within and beyond imperial boundaries, selective appropriation, unintended consequences, and the emergence of resistance to imperial innovations.[48] Such an approach not only has the advantage of capturing a broader spectrum of human agency beyond European colonizers. It also helps us to comprehend modern empire as the franchise venture that it was, a system of rule that forcibly bound places and peoples together, but one that could function on the ground only by opening up opportunities and incentives for non-Europeans as well. Despite all of the violence and the stark power asymmetries that characterized European imperialism, the actual exercise of colonial rule – including the management of water – fundamentally depended on practical compromises.[49]

As the following chapters will show, such accommodations extended well beyond the diverse social interests that had to be negotiated, for water was itself a powerful force to be reckoned with. Rivers, lakes and seas, like the rest of nature, were by no means merely a blank slate on which engineers and administrators could cast their designs, but rather played an active part in the story of modern empire. Although this book is very much a work of history rather than hydrology, one of its premises is that it is insufficient to focus solely on ideas about water or on the various things that people marshalled in order to control and profit from it (all of which feature prominently in any case). It is also important to pay attention to the water itself. After all, the various purposes that water systems were intended to serve were possible in the first place only because of the movements and properties of the actual fluid, which in turn affected how all of the other elements of such systems functioned. This becomes all the more apparent when we consider that flows and bodies of water often seemed to have ideas of their own about how to behave

47. Headrick, *Tentacles of Progress* and *Power over Peoples*.

48. For a recent overview, see Van der Straeten and Hasenöhrl's 'Connecting the Empire'.

49. Cooper, *Colonialism in Question*, 153–203.

and where to move, and these inanimate actions frequently ran counter to human designs.

In short, water had its own form of agency. Its currents, movements, absences and overabundances powerfully moulded human activity, even as humans reconfigured the waterscape in a reciprocal process of transformation. To borrow from Bruno Latour, water was an 'actant' within a wider, co-evolving set of arrangements that bound together water, people, technologies, cultural practices, socio-economic structures, legal–political institutions and the wider biophysical environment, all for the human-led purpose of capitalizing on the productive potential of aqueous spaces.[50] Viewed from this perspective, modern imperialism was (among many other things) a 'hydro-social' enterprise, a process of expansion and subjugation that reordered relationships between water and human societies across large swathes of the globe, and that helped set the overall course of water management for decades to follow.[51]

Over the past two centuries, and especially since the twilight years of empire in the middle of the twentieth, modern societies have become an elemental part of the Earth's water cycle. According to the UN, global water use has risen roughly sixfold over the past century (far faster than the rate of population growth), such that the vast majority of the world's major rivers have already been dammed and diverted for various human uses.[52] Of course, the technological hold we now have on the hydrosphere has in many ways been a massive boon to human welfare, allowing us to produce more food, generate more power and contract fewer diseases than ever before. Yet as more and more of the planet's waters have been transformed into artefacts of human engineering, people – especially poor people with the least ability to move from low-lying areas or to buy their way out of the effects of drought – have simultaneously grown more vulnerable to changes in the hydrological cycle itself. Although the challenge of striking a balance between the risks and rewards of hydrological tinkering is in many respects an age-old problem, in recent years its scale and implications have become ever-more alarming as demands on water resources have skyrocketed and as the disruptive effects of climate change have begun to take hold.

In this sense, our dealings with water in the modern era epitomize our changing relationship with the global environment at large during the age of the Anthropocene. Stripped down to its essentials, the overarching story is one of escalating human needs generating greater dependencies on nature's assets, and greater dependencies in turn giving rise to increasingly elaborate

---

50. Latour, *Reassembling the Social.*

51. Linton and Budds, 'Hydrosocial Cycle'; Schmidt, 'Historicising the Hydrosocial Cycle'; Boelens et al., 'Hydrosocial Territories'.

52. Kooncagül, Tran and Connor, *United Nations World Water*, 1–3.

attempts to harness the resources on which we rely. As geoscientists have been warning us for some time, this spiralling pattern of human intervention can be observed across the entire biophysical environment: land, sea and atmosphere, as well as the nitrogen and carbon cycles that link them together. Yet nowhere are the inherent limitations of this perpetual growth strategy more apparent than in the hydrosphere. Water is arguably the ultimate constraint on economic growth. Directly or indirectly, fresh water is necessary for everything we do, but supplies are finite and already under severe strain from overuse and pollution, and there are no substitutes. In turn, the fact that freshwater supplies also pose a constraint on the productivity of land has prompted us to direct more of our attention to the oceans, though here too we have begun to push (and in some areas exceed) the limits of what marine ecosystems can provide.[53]

And so states around the world today find themselves bound by their own water histories, their hydrological options circumscribed by the visions and choices of previous generations. This is, with few exceptions, a global dilemma, one that applies as much to China, Australia or the American West as to post-colonial Asia and Africa. Yet for many states and societies in the Global South, it is important to recognize that their options are bounded not only by their own previous choices but also by those of European imperial powers that, for much of the modern era, took it upon themselves to make such decisions on their behalf. As things turned out, these choices had momentous social and environmental consequences, and their legacies continue to shape the fortunes of billions of people.

53. My thanks to Julia Adeney Thomas for highlighting to me the importance of these water-related limits.

CHAPTER ONE

Fluid Networks

WATER, MOBILITY AND THE
INFRASTRUCTURE OF EMPIRE

EMPIRE BUILDERS HAVE often had a special fondness for maps, and not just as navigational devices. During the heyday of Europe's global power, cartographic depictions of the vast expanse of colonial territories were among the most widely disseminated artefacts of imperial iconography, gracing atlases, textbooks and schoolrooms on nearly every continent. Invariably placing Europe at the top and centre of the world, and often embellished by idealized images of conquered peoples and landscapes, such maps were more akin to propaganda posters than visual reference tools. But even apart from their ideological distortions, their cartographic depiction of space also obscured as much as it revealed. The practice of colouring in areas according to political rule was an effective means of portraying the formal conquest of colonial territories, but it masked the relationship of imperial power with other features of subjugated spaces. Unlike terrestrial areas, rivers generally appeared as neutral black lines, or as mere boundaries between different swathes of colourcoding. Seas and lakes tended to be blue spaces seemingly devoid of political or military power. Maps of empire obscured the fact that water bodies were themselves both objects and vehicles of imperial conquest.[1]

Such depictions reflected the static view of states and polities that prevailed at the time. The zenith of European power from around the 1860s to 1960s broadly coincided with what historians regard as the era of 'modern territoriality', a period when the control and development of politically delineated territory was considered the essential basis of state power. One of the factors that distinguished the 'new imperialism' from Europe's maritime expansion in previous centuries was the attempt to control large swathes of territory in

---

1. See Harley, *New Nature of Maps*; Black, *Maps and History*, 58–63.

Southeast Asia and sub-Saharan Africa, where the European presence had previously been confined mainly to ports, coastal trading posts and shipping lanes. Contemporary world maps neatly expressed this 'grounded' conception of imperial might.[2]

Yet the great paradox of modern territoriality is that it relied on a dramatic acceleration of mobility – of goods, money, people and information. The consolidation of power over a bounded territory required a huge expansion of transport and communications infrastructure (railways, roads, shipping, telegraph) to integrate centres of production with their hinterlands, to assemble far-reaching markets, and to assimilate people and resources under a unified administrative structure. The proliferation of movement that these infrastructures made possible brought both risks and rewards. On the one hand, it was regarded as a motor of modernization and a sign of progress; on the other hand, as a centrifugal force that threatened order and control. As historians have recently emphasized, the key task for modern states and empires alike was to strike a balance between these two dynamics, to regulate and 'channel' mobility in ways that served their political and economic interests. Territorial states thus functioned also as 'circulatory states', political constructions that sought to encourage but also control the rapid acceleration of movement, generally through the creation of immobile infrastructures that both enabled and contained this fluidity.[3]

Waterways and coastlines played a crucial role in augmenting and channelling the mobilities of modern empire. Before the nineteenth century, the geography of Europe's overseas expansion was shaped more by wind than by water per se. In the age of sail, ships navigated where prevailing airstreams and currents allowed them to go.[4] Seasonal trade winds governed travel on the high seas, limiting voyages to certain parts of the year. Sailing up rivers or navigating coastal shallows was challenging year round. On inland and near-shore waters, sailing vessels were not only subject to currents and tides but also vulnerable to attack by local people who did not want them there. For centuries, these technological limitations were among the chief obstacles to the expansion of European power in Africa, Asia and parts of the Americas. Indeed, the challenges were particularly formidable in tropical areas because of their volatile and highly seasonal hydrographic regimes.[5]

The advent of steamships greatly expanded the scale and scope of movement on the water. By making maritime conveyance cheaper, faster and more

2. On territoriality: Maier, 'Consigning the Twentieth Century' and *Once within Borders*; on the evolution of modern 'geo-epistemologies': Rankin, *After the Map*.

3. I draw here on Huber's *Channelling Mobilities*; the 'circulatory state' is taken from Denning's 'Life Is Movement', esp. 1482–83; see also T. Cresswell's *On the Move* and Ballantyne's 'Mobility, Empire, Colonisation'.

4. Bankoff, 'Aeolian Empires'.

5. Headrick, *Power over Peoples*, 177–79; *Tools of Empire*, 17–57.

predictable, the new fossil-fuelled shipping lines connected distant places and economies more tightly than ever before. Unlike the 'aeolian empires' of the past, the spatial framework of Europe's global influence was no longer based on wind and sea currents but could be stretched as far as coal and oil allowed.[6] Moreover, the enhanced ability of steamers to navigate up rivers made it far easier for Europeans to penetrate inland regions hitherto beyond their grasp. Even after the advent of railways, rivers continued to function as highways to the interior, vital thoroughfares for the projection and consolidation of territorial power. Throughout the nineteenth and twentieth centuries, waterways and coastal ports were – just like the far more heavily studied imperial railways – key conduits for the trade networks that integrated colonized lands and peoples into an increasingly global economy. They served as fluid 'pathways of empire'.[7]

But if modern transport technologies signified the human mastery of time and space, they still had to contend with the vicissitudes of water. Throughout much of Asia and Africa, the extreme seasonality of tropical rains and rivers posed a major challenge. Depending on the time of year, rivers could become impassable as a result of too much water, or too little. Coastal navigation was likewise threatened by seasonal storms, irregular tidal currents and shifting submarine channels. Even when conditions were favourable, waterways harboured all manner of hidden dangers (snags, rocks, bars and the like). Although the expansion of roads and railways promised to bypass such hazards, they, too, were affected by rains, floods and droughts.

Navigating the waters of empire thus required know-how. Rivers regularly altered course, coastlines constantly shifted, channels closed and opened as sediments moved. The ability to transit through these oozing and intrinsically unstable environments often rested not only on mapmakers' charts but also on local knowledge that had been acquired through decades of familiarity with ever-changing surroundings. Making waterscapes amenable to the needs of transport also meant modifying them. Along the major rivers, engineers removed obstacles, created bypasses, and deepened or straightened channels to render them more navigable. In the absence of passable rivers, new waterways were sometimes constructed from scratch, often as a part of larger water control schemes. On the coasts, the need to accommodate larger ships and greater trade flows required the 'fixing' of mutable boundaries between land and sea, the dredging of channels, and the creation of breakwaters and

6. Bankoff, 'Aeolian Empires'.

7. Ahuja, *Pathways of Empire*. On technological changes: Headrick, *Tools of Empire*, 129–49, 165–79. On ocean-going ships as sites of knowledge and experience, see the articles in the *Journal of Global History* vol. 11, no. 2 (2016), esp. Dusinberre and Wenzlhuemer's 'Being in Transit'. For an overview of railways: B. Davis, Wilburn and Robinson, *Railway Imperialism*.

jetties to diminish the effects of waves and swell. Yet despite all these efforts to contain the natural dynamics of rivers and coastlines, the inherent fluidity of these environments meant that attempts to fix them in place never ceased. The modern mission to regulate mobility thus required states to control not only movements of people, goods and information, but also movements of water, sediment and mud that perennially threatened to clog, disrupt or destroy the routes along which they travelled.[8]

In short, the waterways and coastlines of Europe's colonies formed a distinctive type of infrastructure. They facilitated the expansion of imperial power not least because so much of Asian and African life was already oriented around them, which allowed Europeans to graft on to long-standing patterns of mobility and trade. Yet if indigenous societies already made extensive use of rivers and coasts on the basis of centuries of local knowledge and navigational experience, imperialists regarded the existing conditions of water transport as ripe for 'improvement' through the application of European initiative and know-how. In a sense, rivers, bays and estuaries represented a kind of infrastructural 'windfall' provided by nature, but using them for large-scale transport nonetheless came at a cost. The waterways of empire required constant maintenance and investment, and their natural changeability often confounded European visions of smooth, regulated mobility. If infrastructure works best when it is reliable, secure and stable, water infrastructures were particularly unreliable, insecure and unstable owing to the unruliness of riverine and coastal environments.[9]

In all of these ways, the expansion, territorialization and spatial integration of European empire was a process immersed in water. This chapter explores some of the changes that were involved and their effects on colonial waterscapes. It starts along the rivers of colonial Asia and Africa, and considers how watercourses shaped the very formation of imperial space. It then turns to the relationship between water- and land-based communication networks and how they influenced each other. The focus then shifts to the coasts, where swelling volumes of trade spurred major alterations both above and below the surface. For Europe's empire builders, the waterscapes of the colonial world posed both opportunities and challenges.

8. There is an increasingly rich literature exploring the fluctuating, half-liquid nature of littoral spaces and societies: see esp. Bhattacharyya, *Empire and Ecology*; Bashford, 'Terraqueous Histories'; M. Pearson, 'Littoral Society'; Gillis, *Human Shore*. See also the special issue of *Isis*, vol. 112, no. 1 (2021), including von Hardenberg's 'Knowing the Littoral', plus da Cunha's *Invention of Rivers*, McLean's 'Black Goo', Schlichting's *New York Recentered*, Zimring and Corey's *Coastal Metropolis* and Kelman's *River and Its City*.

9. I am grateful to Andrew Denning for suggesting some of these thoughts on waterways as infrastructure. On infrastructure and empire more generally, see van Laak's *Imperiale Infrastruktur*.

Channels of Empire

Rivers are not just physical entities; they have social, cultural and economic lives too. They carry not only water but also goods, people and ideas. They have long functioned as byways of exploration and as arteries of human commerce. When Europeans began to frequent the shores of Africa and Asia, they often situated their coastal trading enclaves at or near the mouths of major rivers that already served as forums of exchange. For centuries they rarely ventured far upriver; a combination of disease and hostility among inland traders generally kept them confined to the continental fringes. But in the late eighteenth and nineteenth centuries, and especially after the advent of steam navigation, rivers became veritable channels of empire. Across southern Asia and much of Africa, Europeans looked to the rivers as the principal avenues by which they could expand their commercial reach, spread their 'civilization' and extend their military hold over new territories.

On the Indian subcontinent, the spatial extension of British power closely followed the geography of its waterways. Ever since the early seventeenth century, British, Dutch, Portuguese and French companies had competed for influence around the fringes of India, lured by the profits to be made from its textiles, spices, salt, indigo, tea and opium. European power was concentrated in a sprinkling of coastal trading posts, which depended on carefully forged alliances with local rulers who controlled the flow of goods and money between the coasts and the interior. Trade was as brisk as it was lucrative, fuelled by a long period of economic expansion under centralized Mughal rule. As Mughal power declined in the eighteenth century, European companies proved highly adept at forging new commercial and military alliances with the various regional elites who stepped into the political vacuum. Gradually, their interests shifted from trade to territory. The decisive military victory of the East India Company at Plassey in 1757 gave it control over most of Bengal and the rich stream of revenues that it generated. Over the following century, the Company's foothold in the fertile plains of the lower Ganges furnished much of the money and manpower required to subjugate the bulk of the subcontinent. From its headquarters in Bengal, British power gradually extended up the Ganges valley before moving into southern India and the western Maratha lands. Even after the consolidation of this vast terrestrial domain, the Ganges valley remained, in the words of Christopher Bayly, 'the main axis of Britain's Asian Empire'. While vast quantities of cotton, opium and indigo flowed downstream for shipment to China and Europe, a growing current of British goods travelled upriver to the huge interior market.[10]

10. Bayly, *Rulers, Townsmen and Bazaars*, 1–2, quote at 1; *Indian Society*, 79–105; J. Richards, *Mughal Empire*, 225–81.

Throughout the early nineteenth century, the rivers of northern India formed a vital natural communications network. The Ganges, Jumna and Brahmaputra provided what one naval officer called 'an uncertain and an insufficient, yet the principal, and at particular seasons the only means of conveyance for persons or goods, between the presidency of Bengal and the principal cities and military stations of Hindostan and Assam'.[11] In total, they gave access to an area of over two hundred thousand square miles (half a million square kilometres). Yet before the 1830s, transport conditions on India's waterways differed little from how they had been in the days of the Mughal emperors. All along the main rivers and their meandering deltas, a variety of boats of different sizes and shapes could be found hauling goods to and fro. Most river traffic comprised local 'country boats', fairly simple craft decked with bamboo, equipped with thatched cabins and propelled by oars or small sails. Vessels ranged in size from under five to around sixty tons, and were generally specialized for navigating on particular stretches of water. Regional differences in boat design closely reflected local transport needs and water conditions, though many of these craft ranged quite far nonetheless. Whereas the flat-bottomed boats of northern India could operate in as little as eighteen inches (forty-five centimetres) of water, the deep-hulled craft of Dhaka drew up to five feet (1.5 metres).[12]

Working a riverboat was a slow and often perilous business. The extreme seasonality of India's rivers made navigation difficult. Normal seasonal rises at Allahabad (the highest navigable point on the Ganges) usually ranged from twenty-five to thirty-five feet (7.6 to 10.7 metres), though floods as high as forty-five feet were not unknown (by way of comparison, a rise of 8.6 metres, or twenty-eight feet, on the Seine resulted in the 1910 'Great Flood' of Paris). Even the tidal waters at Calcutta rose around seven feet (2 metres) in the rainy season.[13] Strong currents during the annual monsoon meant that it was often necessary to tow craft from the riverbanks, many of which were prone to collapse as they were undermined by swift-moving floodwaters. When large chunks of riverbank broke away, they could sometimes cause a wave large enough to swamp small craft; indeed, mooring at night was considered too dangerous wherever nearby riverbanks had been undermined. During the rainy season there was also the constant danger of tow ropes breaking, subjecting boats to the 'impetuosity of the current'. Such accidents were reportedly 'of frequent occurrence', and loss of life was common: 'It rarely happens that a movement of troops by water is unattended by casualties of this nature.' The risks caused by crumbling riverbanks were also the main reason why insurance rates for

11. James Johnston, *Précis of Reports*, 23.
12. Bernstein, *Steamboats on the Ganges*, 12–15; Saikia, *Unquiet River*, 92–124, 202–46.
13. J. Johnston, *Inland Navigation*, 18; de Moncan, *Paris inondé*.

FIGURE 1.1. 'Country boat' landing at Serampore, near Calcutta, 1870s.
By permission of akg-images/British Library, photo 682(18).

a river voyage were roughly the same as for freight passage all the way from
England to India.[14]

Even when collapsing riverbanks posed no immediate hazards, they
caused other problems in the form of silt and snags. As millions of tons of
suspended soil made their way downstream, they filled slow-moving channels and piled up into an ever-shifting maze of mudbanks and shoals that
could confound even the most experienced local river pilot. Trees that fell into
the rivers from eroded banks added to the tally of obstructions. Some spots
along the Ganges were notoriously treacherous to navigate during the rains.
At its confluence with the Kosi River, the latter deposited so much material
into the riverbed 'that long islets are heaped up and swept away', and boats
could be 'caught in whirlpools formed without a moment's warning'.[15] The
Hooghly, the main thoroughfare to Calcutta from the Bay of Bengal, likewise

14. James Johnston, *Précis of Reports*, 11, 24–25 (all quotes from Johnston); Bernstein,
Steamboats on the Ganges, 19.

15. Joseph Dalton Hooker, *Himalayan Journals* (London: Murray, 1854), quoted in
Amrith, *Unruly Waters*, 39.

had its danger areas. Near the mouth of the river, the combined waters of the Hooghly and Damodar were held up by the confluent waters of the Rupnarain, whose flow cut across the main current at right angles and thereby caused an enormous amount of suspended silt to drop into sandbanks that were 'extremely unstable and subject to almost daily change'.[16] Locally called the James and Mary Sands (after the name of a vessel that foundered on them in 1694), these shoals were the main reason for the establishment of the Bengal Pilot Service, one of the oldest institutions in British-ruled India.

As British officials and entrepreneurs sought to expand commerce up the Gangetic plain, the Company was determined to improve the conditions of river transport. One means of doing so was to dredge channels, build small dams or screens to encourage the flow along particular passages, and remove submerged obstacles. Given the sheer scale of the river system, this was a gargantuan undertaking. To give a sense of scale, from 1830 to 1833 the superintendent of the Nadia district rivers in western Bengal (a small snippet of the Gangetic plain comprising several arms of the main channel of the Ganges) reported the construction of 359 screens as well as the removal of 118 sunken boats, 219 sunken trees or timbers, and 1,731 trees along the riverbanks that threatened to fall into the rivers as they ate into the banks. Despite spending significant sums on these interventions, he concluded that there could be 'no assurance that the measures adopted for mitigating or repairing the evils of one season would be of the least avail in the ensuing one'.[17] Keeping the rivers navigable was always going to be an arduous and never-ending task.

The other key measure in the eyes of officialdom lay in the introduction of steam vessels, which promised to enhance the volume, speed and predictability of trade. As it happened, the first steam vessel in India had a less utilitarian purpose: it was a pleasure yacht built in 1819 for the nawab of Oudh, powered by a small engine brought from England. Shortly thereafter came two vessels from the Kyd shipyards at Kidderpore: the *Pluto*, built in 1822 as a steam dredge for removing silt from the channels of the Hooghly, followed by the *Diana* in 1823, a large side-wheeler originally designed as a ferry but which ended up being used as a rather unprofitable tugboat. In 1825 they were joined by the *Enterprise*, the first steamer to navigate around the Cape to India (partly under sail), which was likewise employed mainly as a tug.[18]

From a commercial perspective, these early steamers were a disappointment. All of them lost money and were eventually deployed for other purposes. From a military perspective, however, they were far more successful. Their usefulness in overcoming some of the obstacles to inland navigation was soon confirmed by the Company's military expedition against the kingdom of Burma.

16. J. Johnston, *Inland Navigation*, 17.
17. D'Souza, 'Mischievous Rivers', 134.
18. Gibson-Hill, 'Steamers', 126–39.

After years of mounting tensions over British expansion into north-eastern India, in 1825 Governor-General William Pitt Amherst launched what became known as the first Anglo-Burmese War. The main theatre of the campaign was the Irrawaddy valley, where the winding river made navigation difficult and rendered British ships more susceptible to attack by fireboats and Burmese galleys. The deployment of the Company's steamers gave British forces a new technological edge. The dredger *Pluto* was equipped with cannons and joined the attack on Arakan on the eastern coast of the Bay of Bengal. The *Diana* was armed with explosive rockets and took part in the main advance up the Irrawaddy, where it proved highly effective at transporting troops and capturing enemy craft. As soon as the *Enterprise* arrived in Calcutta, the government bought it for £40,000 and used it to move troops and supplies to Burma. By the time the Burmese king surrendered in February 1826, the strategic value of steamboats was clear. The Company soon took possession of two more armed steamers – the *Ganges* and *Irrawaddy* – to maintain communications with its newly acquired territories on the Arakan and Tenasserim coasts.[19]

After the war with Burma, attention quickly shifted back up the Ganges. In 1828, one of the first acts of the new governor Lord William Bentinck was to commission a survey of the river for use by steamers.[20] From the early 1830s onwards, a growing fleet of ironclad steamers plied the river, nearly all of them designed with shallow draughts and capable of moving at least six miles (ten kilometres) per hour to fight the strongest currents. Shortly afterwards, officials also surveyed the Brahmaputra and introduced steamers there in the 1840s. In the meantime, a string of new steamboat stations began to line the two rivers at various intervals to provide them with fuel and supplies and to supervise the loading and unloading of cargo. This network of river stations was very much a British creation designed to serve British ends, but it is worth emphasizing that it could function only with the benefit of local input. For the agents who staffed the stations, one of their most important jobs was the recruitment of local fishers and boatmen as pilots for particular sections of the river. Ideally, a *manjhee* (steersman) and two or three *dandees* (oarsmen) were placed every twenty to thirty miles to row out to the steamers and guide them around the various submerged obstacles on their respective stretches of water. However detailed and hydrographically sophisticated the Company's charts became, the capricious nature of the river meant that they were no match for the intimacy of local knowledge and the skills gained by lifelong experience.[21]

With the establishment of regular steam services, the Ganges in particular became a kind of mainline for the communications of the Indian state. Boats heading downriver carried the all-important tax revenues of Hindustan to

19. Gibson-Hill, 130, 136–37, 142; Bernstein, *Steamboats on the Ganges*, 28–37.

20. See generally James Johnston, *Précis of Reports*.

21. Bernstein, *Steamboats on the Ganges*, 84; Saikia, *Unquiet River*, 190–91.

the Company coffers in Bengal, along with a steady stream of administrators, magistrates and official documents. Boats heading upriver carried a counter-flow of state agents, correspondence, arms and supplies. Given the slowness and irregularity of land travel before the 1850s and 1860s, the relatively reliable transit service provided by river steamers was crucial for the exercise of British rule and the expanding presence of the colonial state throughout northern India.[22]

At the same time, rivers were also a vital thoroughfare for integrating the Indian landmass with the increasingly global economy. The boats that moved up the Ganges, Brahmaputra and their navigable tributaries carried not only the materials of state but also large sums of money from Calcutta-based merchants eager to buy the rights to the next season's crops. After harvest, these goods then flowed back to Calcutta for trans-shipment overseas. Given the high freight prices charged by steamboats, they tended to carry only the most valuable goods. Cotton, silk, opium, shellac and indigo dominated the commodity traffic on Ganges steamers. On the Brahmaputra, the main item was tea from the expanding plantation frontier in Assam.[23] Bulkier items like grains, salt, coal or sugar were mainly moved overland or were carried on the huge fleet of 'country boats' that continued to dominate life on the rivers. Despite the introduction of steamers, most waterborne freight was still carried by so-called 'native craft'. At Calcutta alone, 125,000 country boats passed its toll point in 1844, carrying a total of around 1.25 million tons – well over twice the total sea traffic to and from Calcutta at the time. By way of comparison, that same year steamers from the major upstream port of Mirzapore carried a mere 24,000 tons of freight to Calcutta, most of it cotton, indigo and shellac, with a similar amount of metal goods and packages going the other way.[24] Like many technological innovations, the coal-fuelled steamer supplemented rather than displaced existing modes of wind- or muscle-powered river transport, and allowed for a greater degree of specialization in their uses and functions.

Even so, steamers enabled a quickening of the pace of exchange. Country boats took on average two to three months to travel the twelve hundred kilometres from Calcutta to Allahabad, descending in around twenty days during the rains or one to two months during the dry season. By contrast, steamers required only three weeks upstream, and one or two weeks to return.[25] Yet in spite of this speed advantage, seasonal variations in depth and flow continued to make steamboat navigation difficult, as did the countless snags and

22. Arnold, *Science, Technology and Medicine*, 104.

23. Bernstein, *Steamboats on the Ganges*, 90–100; J. Johnston, *Inland Navigation*; Arnold, *Science, Technology and Medicine*, 104–5; Saikia, *Unquiet River*, 165–201.

24. A. Robertson, *Recent Improvements*, 18–19. 'Native' craft also remained dominant for paddy and jute transport in Assam: Saikia, *Unquiet River*, 184–85.

25. A. Robertson, *Recent Improvements*, 15; Arnold, *Science, Technology and Medicine*, 104; Bernstein, *Steamboats on the Ganges*, 56.

ever-shifting sandbanks that lurked beneath the surface. Even experienced local pilots could not always avoid these obstacles, occasionally leaving boats stranded for long periods when water levels were low. Refloating stranded steamers was no easy task. In 1838, a year of unusually poor rains, the *Megna* ran aground in shallow water near Revelganj, around three hundred kilometres below Allahabad. When the decision to unload part of the cargo failed to solve the problem, 150 men were recruited to dig a canal from the boat to the main channel. Their numbers proved to be far from adequate, so they eventually had to be joined by hundreds more men and a team of elephants, who worked for several weeks before finally floating the *Megna* free. Company directors could breathe a sigh of relief, but not for very long. A few days later, the 120-foot (thirty-seven-metre) sternwheeler *Lord William Bentinck* ran aground near Barh, requiring around a thousand men to relaunch her.[26] Ironically, although steam transport was often celebrated for saving labour, it occasionally required huge injections of human and animal toil to function properly.

Another problem was the tendency of rivers in the Ganges and Brahmaputra basins to change their course because of the seasonal scouring of riverbanks and deposition of silt. This posed challenges not only to river pilots but also to the network of steamboat stations. A particularly notorious example was Goalundo, a port at the confluence of the Padma and Brahmaputra Rivers, which served as a terminus for a spur of the Eastern Bengal Railway. Although the Bengal government spent large amounts of money to protect it from erosion, the constant shifting of the river mouth rendered this a hopeless task. In 1875, flooding washed away the railway spur, and from that point onwards the railway terminus had to be repeatedly relocated to keep up with the movement of the rivers. By 1913, the terminus was no less than eleven kilometres south of its original location. That year, a handbook published by the Eastern Bengal Railway declared that:

> Goalundo has the wandering habits of the prodigal son and constantly evinces a strong desire to escape from doing its duty in that state of life to which it has pleased an imperious trade to call it. It is the unstable water which has misled it, as it has misled many another Eastern town, into these ways.[27]

If the nature of the Ganges and Brahmaputra posed numerous challenges, many of the subcontinent's other rivers were even more recalcitrant. In southern India, the pronounced seasonality of the main rivers meant that almost none were suited to year-round navigation. During the rains, the strong

26. Bernstein, *Steamboats on the Ganges*, 89.

27. Eastern Bengal State Railway, *From the Hooghly to the Himalayas: Being an Illustrated Handbook to the Chief Places of Interest Reached by the Eastern Bengal State Railway* (Calcutta: the author, 1913), 15, quoted in Saikia, *Unquiet River*, 190–91.

currents hampered movement upstream; in the dry season, boats were blocked by extensive shallow stretches. Although engineers hatched plans to top up dry-season river levels through the construction of huge storage reservoirs, such schemes never made it off the drawing board owing to the enormous costs they entailed.[28] Meanwhile, in the north-west, the Indus River utterly confounded steam captains ever since the first voyage was attempted in 1835. Its powerful currents demanded heavy engines to move upstream, but the additional weight of such engines made vessels far more likely to run aground on the river's numerous shoals. Although lighter, smaller engines could lessen a boat's draught, they were unable to make headway against the flow. On the Indus, steamers thus faced a 'technological trap', which explains why only a handful ever operated on the river, and quite unsuccessfully at that.[29]

When the first steamboats were launched on Asia's rivers in the 1820s, Europeans still knew very little about the African interior. Despite a long-established trade presence along the West African coast, a combination of factors prevented them from venturing very far inland. One reason was disease, especially falciparum malaria, which earned West Africa the label of the 'white man's grave'.[30] Another was the resistance of African traders against outside interference in their commercial affairs. A third was the very topography of the continent itself. Much of the African coastline is bereft of natural harbours and is flanked by mangroves or barrier islands that block access to the mainland. Most of the continent's major rivers plunge down cataracts close to the coast, and even those that do not (Nile, Niger) are prone to extreme seasonal variations of flow. As one contemporary lamented, despite the 'great magnitude' of Africa's rivers, 'it is remarkable that not one of them can be used as a highway to the interior on account of the numerous obstructions in their courses'.[31] Well into the nineteenth century, these obstacles continued to hamper European penetration.[32]

Yet when European influence began to spread in Africa, it did so largely via its rivers. The Niger was of particular significance, both for commercial and humanitarian reasons. It had long served as a principal transport route for the slave trade, which made it a target of interest for abolitionists in the late eighteenth century. With the decline of the slave trade after 1807, commercial activity along the river was redirected towards other goods. Palm oil was in high demand in industrializing Europe, both as a lubricant for machinery and for the production of soap. Trade was brisk, especially in the Niger delta, so

28. Cotton, *Public Works in India*, 89–110.
29. Dewey, *Steamboats on the Indus*; Arnold, *Science, Technology and Medicine*, 105.
30. Curtin, '"White Man's Grave"', 88.
31. Mackenzie, *Flooding of the Sahara*, vii.
32. See generally Headrick, *Tools of Empire*; also *Power over Peoples*, 206–7.

much so that the winding labyrinth of channels was commonly referred to as the 'Oil Rivers'. From the 1820s to the end of the century, palm oil was the principal trade good between West Africa and Britain, most of it flowing down the Niger from palm groves along its banks.[33]

Although the Niger had long fascinated Europeans, before 1830 its course was a matter of conjecture. Some geographers believed that it flowed into the Nile; others that it emptied into the Congo; still others that it flowed further inland before evaporating in vast desert lakes. A series of early expeditions failed to answer the question. Mungo Park's travels along the upper Niger in 1795–97 and again in 1805–6 confirmed that the river flowed to the east – and that local authorities were unlikely to welcome outside traders – but his death at Bussa, in what is today northern Nigeria, ended his second exploratory venture hundreds of kilometres above the coast. In the early 1820s, Hugh Clapperton's journeys from Libya to Lake Chad and Sokoto ruled out an eastward linkage with the Nile. Rival expeditions led by Gordon Laing and René Caillié reached Timbuktu in 1826, but added little to Park's earlier findings. It was only in 1830 that the course of the Niger was finally established. After landing west of Lagos and walking north to Bussa, Richard and John Lander floated down the Niger in canoes before finally arriving at its outlet in the 'Oil Rivers'.[34]

With the course of the river now roughly mapped out, the question for European traders and officials was how to put this knowledge to profitable use. The Lander brothers' voyage confirmed two important things: that the Niger emptied into the Atlantic, and that it was navigable for shallow-draught boats hundreds of miles inland. The Niger – in conjunction with its tributary the Benue – was the only river in sub-Saharan Africa that afforded such an uninterrupted waterway into the distant interior. In theory, then, it was possible to navigate directly up the mouth of the river to the palm oil producers of the Niger valley, thus bypassing local intermediaries, securing a lucrative flow of trade goods and denying them to other European rivals.

It was an alluring prospect. Among the many who were attracted by it was the young shipbuilder Macgregor Laird, who began planning a trade expedition soon after hearing about the Lander brothers' exploits. In 1832, he and a group of Liverpool merchants formed the African Inland Commercial Company, whose aims were to expand trade in the region and to facilitate what they called 'the amelioration of uncivilized man'.[35] At the centre of Laird's plans was the use of steam vessels, which promised to free commercial traffic from the river's seasonal fluctuations and thus make trade more predictable.

33. J. Robins, *Palm Oil*, 42–74; Lynn, *Commerce and Economic Change*, 'From Sail to Steam' and 'Change and Continuity'.

34. Hoag, *Developing the Rivers*, 62–76.

35. Laird and Oldfield, *Narrative of an Expedition*, inscription.

The idea was to head upriver towards the Benue to trade for palm oil and other commodities during the dry season, then return to the coast to transfer goods on to a waiting brig for transportation to Britain.

The plan faced two main obstacles. One was the absence of steamers suited to conditions on the Niger, which prompted Laird to build two shallow-draught vessels specifically designed for the purpose: the *Quorra*, a 120-foot (thirty-seven metre) wooden paddlewheeler, and the *Alburkah*, a 70-foot iron-hulled vessel and the first iron steamer to make the ocean voyage to West Africa. The other impediment was the river environment itself. The maze of channels and invisible shoals in the delta made for an accident-prone start to the journey, so much so that Laird was 'not without suspicions of the pilot's intentions'.[36] Further upriver the boats repeatedly ran aground on sandbanks. On one occasion the *Quorra* was grounded for eighteen days, on another instance for thirteen. Eventually the frequent encounters with the riverbed wore off part of the copper sheathing on the hull, which exposed it to the depredations of *Teredo navalis*, the naval shipworm.[37] But apart from these challenges, the biggest problem was disease, which Laird attributed to the 'poisonous miasma' from the surrounding swamps.[38] Of the forty-eight men who began the journey, only nine survived. All in all, it was a calamitous expedition, both medically and commercially. But it did yield new knowledge about the river and its inhabitants, who of course knew the river best of all. Laird's extended stay on the Niger enabled him to assemble far more information – about its width, depth, currents, and minor tributaries – than previous expeditions.[39] Even if the value of this information was limited by the ever-changing nature of the river, it nonetheless proved useful for others who were determined to pick up where Laird left off.

Although the slave trade had been banned in 1807 and the institution of slavery formally abolished throughout the British Empire in 1833, many British observers shared Laird's view that its persistence within West Africa continued to hamper trade and development throughout the region. In an attempt to rectify the situation once and for all, in 1841 a coalition of merchants and abolitionists persuaded the British government to provide direct backing for a major expedition up the Niger. Led by two naval officers with experience in the region, and comprising a trio of new steamships, its aims were more comprehensive than those of earlier voyages. While the main objective was to sign new trade treaties with African leaders (in exchange for their agreement to cease all involvement in slave trafficking), the mission was also

36. Laird and Oldfield, 76.
37. Laird and Oldfield, 148, 269, 292, 296.
38. Laird and Oldfield, 53.
39. As emphasized by Hoag in *Developing the Rivers* (81–82).

tasked with collecting scientific data, studying the problem of fever and setting up a model farm at the confluence of the Niger and Benue.[40]

Overall, the expedition was far better equipped than its forerunners. The improved accuracy of charts made navigation easier. Two of the three steamboats, the HMS *Albert* and HMS *Wilberforce*, were much larger and more powerful than anything that had ascended the Niger before. Indeed, the smoke and noise they emitted often provoked fear and astonishment among riverine villagers, who reportedly sometimes fled at the sight of the 'devil ships'.[41] The boats were even outfitted with relatively spacious living quarters expressly designed to limit the exposure of European crew members to the 'bad air' that was still thought to be the cause of fevers. Yet despite such precautions, familiar problems awaited. Finding sufficient fuel for the ravenous boilers was a constant headache, which sometimes required delicate negotiations with local leaders. Snags, shallows, and submerged sandbanks continued to pose a threat; on one occasion the *Wilberforce* had to offload its contents and even its anchors before it could get back afloat. High floodwaters in the rainy season lessened the dangers of running aground, but they brought other risks – not least an invasion of snakes that sought to escape the floods by climbing into the boats. But the biggest problem, as before, was disease (mainly malaria), which claimed the lives of 53 of the 303 crew members, nearly all of them (48) Europeans. Chastened by the high mortality rate, the government withdrew its support for the venture in 1842.[42]

For the next decade, British traders in the delta were left to their own devices, but in 1854 the government once again provided funding for a major expedition. The immediate trigger was the disappearance of two German explorers, but the underlying motive was the ever-increasing interest in the palm oil trade. Once again, Macgregor Laird supplied a vessel, the *Pleiad*, a 260-ton iron-sided ship driven by a propeller (the first in Africa) rather than a paddle. And once again, the plan was to steam upriver to explore the Niger and the Benue for trade and navigation purposes. The expedition was to be led by a veteran of the Niger region named John Beecroft, British consul on the island of Fernando Po and one of the most experienced traders in the delta. In the event, Beecroft died before the *Pleiad* even arrived at Fernando Po, so the command passed to the ship's physician, William Baikie, a novice in West Africa. Baikie was acutely conscious of his lack of experience, but as a physician he was equally attuned to the challenges that awaited upriver, above all malaria. On the voyage to the Gulf of Guinea he ensured that the twelve European crew members took two daily doses of quinine – which was rapidly gaining use as a prophylactic in the 1850s – and he continued the prescription

40. Hoag, 83–87.
41. Allen and Thomson, *Narrative of the Expedition*, 184, 188.
42. Allen and Thomson, 330–32, 342; Headrick, *Power over Peoples*, 210.

throughout the entire expedition. The result was remarkable: during 118 days of travel, which saw the *Pleiad* navigate 400 kilometres farther up the Benue than any steamer had ever gone before, not one crew member died. Although some suffered from fevers, all recovered fairly quickly. As Baikie subsequently reported, despite the need to go ashore frequently, which often involved landing 'in swamps and other unhealthy spots', he himself enjoyed 'constant health'. 'I mention these circumstances to show, that under proper precautions, Europeans may not only live quietly, but even commit with impunity what, some years ago, would have been considered as terrible indiscretions.'[43]

Once malaria no longer posed an existential threat, Europeans certainly pursued their interests in West Africa with greater impunity and less discretion than before. In the 1850s, Laird's company was providing monthly steamer services between Britain and the West African coast, and by the end of the decade it maintained three steamers on the Niger under contract with the British government. As more and more British traders arrived on the river, the outbound flow of palm oil swelled. Ship tonnage in the palm oil trade rose from under twenty-two thousand in 1850 to nearly sixty thousand in 1870 before peaking at just over ninety thousand in 1885.[44] What were once periodic expeditions became regular trade voyages, and the resulting competition with African palm oil traders soon led to violence. As steamers came under more frequent attack, they armed themselves with cannons and rockets. And as clashes with local people along the Niger and Benue intensified throughout the 1880s and 1890s, the Navy sent punitive missions upriver to bombard towns that attacked British boats or trading posts.[45] As in other parts of the world, the expansion of British influence in the region was based largely on gunboat diplomacy.

In the meantime, as the British were forcefully tightening their hold on the lower Niger, French boats were doing much the same on the river's upper reaches. In 1880, Joseph Gallieni (later governor of French Sudan) led an expedition from Senegal to the upper Niger to map out a possible railway route linking the river with the port of Dakar. Over the following two years, gunboats were hauled in pieces from Senegal to the Niger and reassembled into a small flotilla for controlling trade along the river. After the capture of Bamako in 1883, French boats rapidly extended their influence downstream, reaching as far as Timbuktu by 1887. In 1894, they took part in the occupation of Timbuktu itself, which thereafter served as a base for the extension of French commercial and military presence further downstream.[46] In the second half of the nineteenth century, the Niger thus became the corridor for

43. Baikie, *Narrative*, 328.
44. Lynn, 'From Sail to Steam', 233.
45. Hernon, *Britain's Forgotten Wars*, 405–24; Home, *City of Blood Revisited*.
46. For a contemporary account, see Bory's *La conquête du Soudan* (63–100).

a vast imperial pincer movement that eventually encircled the bulk of West
Africa. From the French outposts of the western Sudan region to the British
trading posts of the delta, the race to control the waterway was the key to
subjugating the land.

Such riverine rivalries were by no means confined to Africa. In Asia, the expansion of British shipping – both maritime and inland – was viewed with envy
by the other colonial powers. By the early nineteenth century the British blue-
water fleet had long since overtaken its Spanish, Portuguese and Dutch rivals
in the Indian Ocean, and the advent of steam underpinned a growing brown-
water fleet on the rivers as well. French officials in particular eyed these developments with concern. Their worry was that France would fall irretrievably
behind in the race to expand commercial trade with Asia – a trade that became
all the more lucrative after the Opium Wars of the 1840s and 1850s forcibly
opened Chinese markets.

The Opium Wars themselves offered a vivid illustration of the importance
of river navigation for the projection of imperial power. Before the nineteenth
century, European trade with China was markedly unbalanced. While a steady
stream of tea, silk and fine porcelain went to Europe, only silver travelled in
the opposite direction. All this changed after 1800 as Chinese demand for
Indian-grown opium began to surge. Although Chinese authorities sought to
prohibit imports of what they regarded as a dangerous product (foreshadow-
ing subsequent British and French attempts to stop the spread of opium use
across colonial Southeast Asia),[47] opium was enormously profitable for the
East India Company, which accordingly permitted British merchants to smug-
gle it into China. For the next several decades, the two sides remained dead-
locked over the issue. All the while, illegal imports continued to grow. Tensions
came to a head in 1839 when Chinese authorities tried to shut down the trade
by force, which prompted the British government to respond with gunboats.
In the ensuing war, British steamers played a crucial role in defeating Chinese
forces in the shallow coastal waters and rivers that had long rebuffed seagoing
men-of-war.[48] The resulting 'unequal treaties' forced new trade terms on Chinese markets, but ongoing tensions again led to war in 1857. In many ways, the
second Opium War was a repeat of the first. This time, however, French ships
joined the attack as well, ostensibly in response to the execution of a French
missionary priest in 1856, but fundamentally driven by a desire to strengthen
France's commercial and military presence in Asia and ensure that the British
did not monopolize the spoils of victory.

As French attention subsequently shifted to Indochina, the conquest of
the region was shaped by many of the same factors that characterized France's

47. Kim, *Empires of Vice*.
48. Headrick, *Power over Peoples*, 197–206.

involvement in China: Anglo-French geostrategic rivalries, the protection of French missionaries as a pretext for intervention and the centrality of rivers as communication corridors. Indochina was very much a naval colony, and its subjugation largely took place on the water. French colonial rule began after a series of gunboat attacks on Da Nang and Saigon in 1858–59, once again triggered by disputes over the treatment of Catholic priests by local officials. For the next two years, the swampy waterways of southern Indochina proved to be more a hindrance than a help to French forces encamped at Saigon. But after the arrival of additional forces in 1861, steam-powered gunboats were crucial for penetrating the Mekong delta and opening a route to Cambodia. With the signing of the 1862 Saigon Treaty, the Hue court not only legalized Catholicism and ceded much of the south-eastern delta to France; it also gave French ships freedom of navigation on all branches of the Mekong, thus opening the rest of the delta to trade. Over the following years, French and dissident Vietnamese forces continued to fight a muddy, amphibious war in the swamps of southern Vietnam. In the meantime, French influence extended further inland when the small kingdom of Cambodia requested protectorate status in 1862 in an attempt to deter further encroachments by Siam (now Thailand).[49]

From this small toehold on the waterlogged fringe of Southeast Asia, French colonizers looked to expand their presence up the Mekong – partly to establish trade links, partly to deny the neighbouring territory to rivals, and partly to justify continued French efforts in the region to a rather sceptical metropolitan public. The great hope was that the Mekong would provide a direct link to the enormous markets of central China, thus transforming Saigon into a second Shanghai.[50] After all, the British were already ensconced on the banks of the Irrawaddy – thought at the time to be another possible river route to China – and controlled the main sea lanes to the Chinese coast. From a geostrategic and commercial perspective, the Mekong had the potential to do for the French in Indochina what the Ganges did for the British in India.

In 1866, the French government launched a major expedition up the river, led by the naval officers Ernest Doudart de Lagrée and Francis Garnier. The main objectives were to map the Mekong's course, catalogue the mineral and forest resources of its hinterlands, and most importantly establish the river's navigability as a trade thoroughfare. For the next two years the Mekong Exploration Commission – or at least those who survived the constant malaria and dysentery – surveyed the river over some two thousand kilometres, additionally exploring its tributaries and their environs for another five thousand kilometres. After eventually reaching China's Yunnan province, they proceeded

49. Brocheux and Hémery, *Indochina*, 21–27; Biggs, *Quagmire*, 23–30.
50. Lacroze, *Les grands pionniers*, 11–13.

to the upper reaches of the Yangtze River before finally descending it to the Chinese coast.[51]

By any measure, it was an extraordinary feat. Upon his return to Europe, Garnier – who took command of the expedition after Doudart de Lagrée's death en route – was celebrated on a par with the great African explorer David Livingstone, even by London's Royal Geographical Society. But on the specific matter of the Mekong's navigability, the expedition was a bitter disappointment. The two small steam-driven gunboats that set off from Saigon did not get very far. After reaching Phnom Penh and taking a detour through the Tonlé Sap (the great inland lake of Cambodia) to the ruined temples of Angkor, the crew set off further upstream in a single steam-powered gunboat. A few days later, they had to abandon it at the first set of rapids just above Kratié, where the current proved too powerful for the boat's engine. After re-embarking on pirogues (long canoes), they soon reached the Khône falls in southern Laos, where the river splits into a tangle of channels and islets scoured by powerful currents and stacked into a series of impassable waterfalls.[52] So formidable was the barrier at Khône that even portaging canoes around the falls was difficult. As Doudart de Lagrée had long suspected, there was a good reason for the lack of any river trade descending from Laos. By contrast, Garnier refused to accept the idea that no channel around the Khône falls could be found, or at least that none could be made navigable with the application of French engineering genius. Yet despite his optimism the evidence was overwhelming. The Mekong was, as one chronicler has put it, 'more suited to white-water adventuring than merchant shipping'.[53]

Although the Mekong Exploration Commission could not find a navigable route to China, it did raise the prospect of the river functioning as an artery of expansion for the Indochinese colony itself. In 1870, the Messageries à Vapeur de Cochinchine started a regular trading service between Saigon and Kratié, followed by the much larger Messageries fluviales de Cochinchine in 1881, which soon reached upriver as far as the falls at Khône. In the 1890s, steamers were disassembled below the falls and hauled up a small railway for reassembly on the middle Mekong, where they ferried goods and passengers between Khône and Vientiane. After 1900, engineers made numerous alterations to the river both above and below the falls to minimize the need for trans-shipment in the dry season and to assist ascending vessels during the flood. By the 1920s, traffic on the Cambodian stretch of the Mekong had reached half a million tons per year.[54]

51. Keay, 'Mekong Exploration Commission' and *Mad about the Mekong*.

52. Lacroze, *Les grands pionniers*, 14–20; Keay, 'Mekong Exploration Commission', 289–96.

53. Keay, 'Mekong Exploration Commission', 294.

54. Pouyanne, *Les travaux publics*, 146; Lacroze, *Les grands pionniers*, 154–56; Brocheux and Hémery, *Indochina*, 128.

But before all this happened, the Mekong Exploration Commission also opened up other prospects. As expected, it found a wealth of silk, tea and textiles in Yunnan, which soon came to be regarded by colonial traders and officials as a kind of El Dorado for French commerce. More surprisingly, it also found a river that Yunnan locals called the Yuán Jiāng, which could only be the headwaters of what the Vietnamese called the Sông Hồng or Sông Cái (Red River). Most importantly, it found that this river appeared to be navigable all the way to Hanoi and the coast. From this moment on, the Red River rather than the Mekong was viewed as the long-sought thoroughfare to China.[55]

The French 'discovery' of the Red River's headwaters triggered a sudden shift of interest from Cochin China in southern Vietnam to Tonkin in the north. In 1872, the colonial government in Saigon ordered a full reconnaissance of the Red River, and in 1873 Francis Garnier himself led a small expeditionary force to plant the tricolour at Hanoi and capture strategic parts of the Red River delta. It did not end well from a French perspective: local Vietnamese forces put a swift end to this initial expedition, Garnier himself was killed, and the French soon had to withdraw. For around a decade afterwards this debacle precluded any further French forays into Tonkin. But in the early 1880s, amid talk of British plans to build a railway up the Irrawaddy valley to Yunnan, the French returned in force to 'pacify' the delta and accelerate the flow of trade along the river. As one contemporary bluntly put it, 'the main reason for our intervention in Tonkin was to possess the Red River and use it as a route for penetrating into China'. Like the Mekong some fifteen years earlier, its main value in the eyes of French colonizers lay not in its importance for local agriculture or fishing, but rather in the 'advantages that it can offer us to get ahead of England in the immense markets of Yunnan, Szechuan, Guizhou, and Guangxi'.[56]

As it turned out, the Red River was indeed much more navigable than the Mekong. The French colonial government quickly established a subsidized steamer service between upriver trading posts and the port of Haiphong. Nonetheless, when initial reconnaissance surveys were carried out in 1876–77, they established that the river required various 'improvements' if it were to become a serviceable conduit to China. The colonial administration had precious little money to spend on amelioration works, so it tended to focus on inexpensive measures such as signage and the removal of obstacles in the hope that they would suffice for future transport needs.[57] To some extent they did, at least in the delta portion of the river up to Vietri. The areas farther upstream were a different matter. The first rapids lay around 150 kilometres above Vietri, followed by around 185 kilometres of stony banks to Lào Cai on the frontier with Yunnan. These upper reaches of the Red River were often too shallow for

55. Keay, 'Mekong Exploration Commission', 301–2.
56. Franquet, *Importance du fleuve Rouge*, 5.
57. Ibos, *Le chemin de fer*, 7–8

steamers during the dry season, forcing trans-shipment on to sampans (small, flat-bottomed wooden boats). The most treacherous segment of all was the middle section between the delta and the first rapids, which was riddled with sandbanks that continually moved. Here the constant shifting of navigable channels meant that finding one was essentially a matter of trial and error, even for boats regularly making the journey. The *Moulun*, one of the steamers used to survey the river, discovered this the hard way. Shortly after its first mission upstream, it carefully retraced its course back down the river, only to run into a bank that had formed in the intervening weeks just above the rapids of Tach-Van-Cai. Adding insult to injury, it was eventually pushed sideways by the current and hit previously uncharted rocks.[58]

The challenge, then, lay in maintaining navigable channels. One possible means of doing so was continual dredging, though the costs were prohibitive. Another possibility, blasting, was cost-efficient for removing rocks but not for moving silt. Given the colonial government's chronic lack of funds, the conventional river-training techniques of local people proved to be a remarkably attractive alternative. Despite French surveyors' penchant for dredging and blasting, they found much to admire in the methods that riverside villagers used for keeping channels open in the winter dry season. Every year in October or November, Tonkinese farmers planted bundles of reeds at the head of any sandbanks to direct the flow around them and thereby prevent the banks from spreading into adjacent channels and joining together. What impressed French observers was not only the low cost of the technique, but also the way in which it let the natural river currents do most of the work. The necessary raw material (reed bundles) was free and abundant, and the way it was deployed mimicked natural obstacles like fallen trees that create channels around themselves.[59] Not for the first time, working with rather than against the nature of the river appeared to be the most sensible move, and European colonizers were quite willing to adopt local techniques when they proved superior to their own.

Yet in the end, no amount of human modification could entirely overcome what one contemporary called the 'obvious inadequacies of the river as a transit route'.[60] Navigating the Red River was slow even when water levels were high, and slower still in the dry season owing to the need for additional transboarding. It was also expensive, and became more so the further one moved above Hanoi.[61] Altogether it was little wonder that French investors and officials increasingly turned to railways, much like their counterparts elsewhere in the colonial world.

58. Escande, *Navigabilité du fleuve Rouge*, 16; Robequain, *Economic Development*, 106–7.
59. Escande, *Navigabilité du fleuve Rouge*, 7–8, 10–17.
60. Ibos, *Le chemin de fer*, 9.
61. Franquet, *Importance du fleuve Rouge*, 28–29.

Waterways and Railways

Before the mid-nineteenth century, travel was constantly subject to the caprices of nature, especially the nature of water. A powerful storm or an abrupt change of seasons could turn solid roads into sticky mires and gentle streams into unfordable torrents. Rivers that were too swollen to navigate during the rains became too shallow for boats during dry periods. Roads could be washed out or blocked; bridges could be damaged or carried away. All of these factors made transportation unpredictable, on the roads as on the rivers. Railways promised a revolutionary solution. Their ability to overcome geographic obstacles and to function regardless of the weather brought about a radical collapse of space and time. By liberating human activities from the tyranny of distance – so the argument goes – railways created a fundamentally new relationship to the landscape.[62] To what extent did they also forge a new relationship to the waterscape? The question is universally applicable, but has particular significance in the humid tropics. In regions where life – including transport – was governed by the annual rhythms of the rains, the railways' conquest of space equally implied the subjugation of water.

Among the many supposed 'achievements' of colonial rule, none were so lauded by imperial enthusiasts as the railways. This was especially the case in India, which had the first and by far the largest railway network in the colonial world. Construction began in the 1850s and gradually accelerated over the following decades, financed by private companies whose profits were backed by state guarantees. By the end of the century, India possessed over forty thousand kilometres of track, the fourth largest network in the world.[63] Railways quickly expanded elsewhere in Europe's colonies, though on a smaller scale. The East Indies rail network, begun in the 1860s, was concentrated almost solely on Java and Madura until after 1900. Construction began in Indochina in the 1890s with a programme designed to connect inland plantation or mining areas with existing centres of trade and industry. From 1904 to 1910 the French built a line from Haiphong to Kunming in Yunnan province to supplement the traffic along the Red River, and in 1905 began work on the trans-Indochinese railway, a 1,860-kilometre line linking Hanoi and Saigon, which was only fully completed thirty-one years later.[64] In Africa, Egypt had the continent's first railway in the 1850s, followed by South Africa in the 1860s. Railway construction boomed after the 1880s as rival colonial powers raced to exploit the resources of their newly acquired African possessions, though the

62. See esp. Schivelbusch, *Railway Journey*; Cronon, *Nature's Metropolis*, 63–93; Aparajita Mukhopadhyay, *Imperial Technology*.
63. Headrick, *Tentacles of Progress*, 55.
64. Reitsma 'De overwinning'; Brocheux and Hémery, *Indochina*, 128–29.

overall length and density of Africa's railways were never more than a fraction of India's.[65]

All throughout Europe's colonies, railways functioned mainly to evacuate goods as quickly and cheaply as possible from interior producer areas to ports on the coast. The mobility of export goods, capital and information took clear priority. The integration of regional economies and the expansion of passenger traffic were secondary considerations, where they were considered at all. Wherever railways were built, the effects rippled throughout the countryside. More than any other piece of colonial infrastructure, railways expanded the reach of the state, transmitted the signals of global markets to producers, and integrated lands and people into the cash economy.

Railways profoundly rearranged imperial space. Writing in 1894, a prominent civil engineer in India reckoned that they had 'reduced the effective size of that continent to one-twentieth of its former dimensions, so that places situated 400 miles [650 kilometres] from the home of an intending traveller or producer of goods for the market, are now as practically near to him as others only 20 miles [30 kilometres] distant formerly were'. Journeys that had previously taken a month 'can now, with ease, comfort, and economy, be performed within the compass of a day'.[66] Yet such calculations, however appealing to railway boosters, were by no means universally valid. The reordering of colonial space proceeded unevenly and created new patterns of social and economic difference through new patterns of mobility and immobility. Whereas the Ganges plain was criss-crossed by a dense network of railway lines, parts of central and north-western India were barely touched as late as the 1910s. Even in Bengal, many people found themselves 'stuck' in regions that suffered from chronic 'network poverty'.[67] In Indochina, whose primary trade axis had long run north–south, the railways superimposed a new network of east–west traffic that widened the socio-economic gap between the deltas and the uplands and that altered the relationship between the export-oriented south of Vietnam and the more subsistence-based economy of the north.[68]

Despite the spatial transformations brought about by railways, rivers continued to shape colonial patterns of mobility and transport planning. When railway fever spread in India in the 1850s and 1860s, not everyone was infected by it. Arthur Cotton, one of the country's most prominent engineers, instead dreamed of turning the waterways of the subcontinent into its principal arteries of communication. Brimming with confidence from a series of celebrated irrigation schemes in the Madras deltas (see chapter 2), he calculated that a

65. Baltzer, *Die Kolonialbahnen*; Wiener, *Les chemins de fer*; B. Davis, Wilburn and Robinson, *Railway Imperialism*; T. Roberts, 'Republicanism, Railway Imperialism' and 'Trans-Saharan Railway'.

66. MacGeorge, *Ways and Works*, 221.

67. Chatterji, 'Being Stuck in Bengal', 517f.

68. Brocheux and Hémery, *Indochina*, 131.

system of river improvement and canal construction would not only be far less expensive than a railway network but would also be completed more quickly and generate far higher returns. As a poor country 'as yet almost wholly unimproved by Public Works', India needed, he argued, 'cheap food and cheap transit before it requires high speed'.[69] The key to creating his waterway network was to cheat the seasons, and the means to do so was by deepening riverbeds and creating vast storage ponds to top up river levels in the dry season.

The scale of Cotton's vision was gargantuan, equalling or indeed surpassing any such inland navigation plans in the industrial world. He reckoned that there were at least five thousand miles (eight thousand kilometres) of rivers in India that could be 'improved' for navigation purposes. He also planned a series of canals linking the main rivers into a network stretching the length and breadth of the subcontinent.[70] For Cotton, there was 'very little hope at present of any plan, by which a greater extent of very cheap transit can be obtained in a short time, than by improving the rivers'.[71] Yet despite his supreme confidence, hindsight proved him wrong. The few river improvement ventures he managed to launch failed on account of unexpectedly high costs, the difficulties of combining navigation with irrigation and, above all, the stiff competition from newly built railways.[72]

The advent of railways certainly dampened the prospects for new inland navigation ventures, but by no means did they necessarily displace river traffic. In fact, in some areas the railways struggled to make headway because of the low costs and extensive geographic reach of water-based transport networks. Southeast Asia's vast river deltas, for instance, had long functioned (and were perceived) very much as a network of rivers separated by land rather than landmasses interspersed with rivers, and this remained the case throughout the entire colonial era.[73] In Burma (Myanmar), the Irrawaddy and its tributaries continued to serve as a vital conduit of trade. After 1867, the Irrawaddy Flotilla Company presided over a growing flow of goods between Lower and Upper Burma, despite the construction of a parallel railway in 1877. Throughout much of Lower Burma, even roads were considered a luxury before the spread of the motor vehicle in the interwar period. According to John Furnivall, the renowned Burma-based scholar and administrator, 'for most purposes the waterways were good enough'.[74] When the construction of roads and

69. Cotton, *Profits upon British Capital*, i–ii.

70. Cotton, *Public Works in India*, 96–103.

71. Cotton, 122.

72. Deakin, *Irrigated India*, 264–69; Sandes, *Military Engineer in India*, 27–28; Headrick, *Tentacles of Progress*, 181–83.

73. As Donald Pisani has argued, the same description can be applied to the United States in the early nineteenth century: Pisani, 'Beyond the Hundredth Meridian', 468.

74. Furnivall, *Colonial Policy and Practice*, 48 (quote), 77–78, 185; see also Baillargeon, 'Road to Mandalay'.

railways accelerated in the interwar period, they were still designed to work in conjunction rather than in competition with the waterways. In Indochina too, the thousands of small craft plying the maze of canals in the Mekong and Red River deltas posed a serious challenge to the financial viability of the colony's railways. Even in the late 1930s most of the bulky cargo flowing out of Tonkin, Cochin China, and Cambodia – rice, corn, charcoal – was carried on the waterways.[75] Unlike in France, where rail companies made most of their income from freight haulage, the continuing importance of waterway traffic meant that the railways in Indochina carried more passengers than cargo, the vast majority of them 'natives' segregated into cramped fourth-class wagons 'specially reserved for Asiatics of little wealth'.[76]

On a more general level too, colonial railways were profoundly affected by flows of water. Year after year, seasonal floods posed a serious challenge to railway construction projects. On Easter Sunday 1885, while constructing a railway near the Punjab town of Narrai, the engineer George Scott-Moncrieff awoke to 'a sight such as I never saw before and hope never to see again – a truly awful flood. Huge brown waves leaping and roaring, whirling timber and corpses, spreading over everything'. Before the rains eased, they washed out a culvert under the railway causing a two-engine train to derail and kill three people.[77] In early 1900, engineers building the East African line between Mombasa and Nairobi were similarly caught out by the volatility of the local climate. That year, the 'short' rainy season in Kenya (generally between October and December) brought unusually heavy downpours that melted earthworks, washed away newly built segments of line, and turned the heavy soils into such a quagmire as to make un-ballasted sections impassable. Small, dry stream beds that engineers had initially deemed harmless suddenly became rushing torrents. In one place workers had to replace an eighteen-inch (half-metre) pipe with a forty-foot (twelve-metre) bridge; at another they had to construct a sixty-foot bridge where they had previously seen no need for any additional infrastructure at all.[78] The ferocity of monsoon rains literally washed away many European engineering assumptions.

Even after bridges and embankments were completed, they still proved vulnerable to the erosive power of unruly rivers. It took decades for European engineers to understand how deep they had to build bridge foundations to withstand seasonal floods on monsoon waterways. Piers and supports were often toppled or tilted as powerful currents scoured away the sand and rock in which they stood. The bridge across the Narmada River for the Bombay, Baroda and Central India Railway was particularly ill-fated in this respect.

75. Gourou, *Le Tonkin*, 242–44; Robequain, *Economic Development*, 112.

76. Ibos, *Le chemin de fer*, 13 (quote); Brocheux and Hémery, *Indochina*, 129.

77. Scott-Moncrieff, *Canals and Campaigns*, 132.

78. M. Hill, *Permanent Way*, 160, 192–93.

Almost immediately after completion, it suffered severe flood damage in 1857–58. No sooner were essential repairs finished than it suffered further damage in 1860. After reopening for traffic in 1861, it was repeatedly damaged by floodwaters in 1864, 1865, and 1867, before finally losing three entire piers in 1868.[79] Such problems were by no means unique to India. In Indochina too, engineers continually struggled against the soft subsoils in the main river deltas and 'the ravages of annual inundations that carry off walls or embankments'.[80] Over the years, pier foundations got deeper and deeper, some going as far as 150 feet (forty-six metres) beneath the riverbed. Despite the deployment of steam pumps and dredges, pier wells in India often penetrated strata that required manual digging, most of which was carried out by highly skilled indigenous divers. It was difficult and dangerous work. Air supply systems were still rudimentary, and some divers who reascended too quickly were crippled or killed by the 'bends', whose causes and treatment were not yet well understood.[81]

More generally, the natural mobility of waterways – especially those in seasonal monsoon climates – posed major challenges to inherently immobile pieces of railway infrastructure. Wherever topographical gradients were gentle and watercourses tended to meander, flood-swollen rivers occasionally bored through their banks to change course altogether, thereby threatening to bypass a bridge and render it obsolete. To prevent this from happening, engineers sought to train the main channels underneath newly built bridges to ensure that the rivers stayed where they were deemed to belong. A prime example was the Hardinge Bridge, a formidable steel-truss construction spanning nearly a mile of water over the lower Ganges. To keep the river on its current course, the bridge was equipped with two stone-clad guide banks extending more than half a mile (nearly a kilometre) upstream and more than three hundred yards (three hundred metres) below. These embankments were themselves massive pieces of infrastructure; it was reckoned that the stone they required would have filled a train stretching from Calcutta to Darjeeling, a distance of around three hundred miles (nearly five hundred kilometres). Additional embankments were required for the approach roads to the bridge – four miles on the left bank and three miles on the right – to ensure safe passage when the river plain was flooded. Although this straitjacketing of the Ganges was necessary for guaranteeing the utility of the bridge, over the long term it had a range of unforeseen consequences. Soon after its completion in 1912, it became clear that the massive structure was altering the hydrology of the entire region. The millions of cubic metres of water that banked up along the approach roads and against the enormous piers not only caused extensive flooding in the paddy fields above the works; it also triggered an accelerated deposition

79. Kerr, *Engines of Change*, 48.
80. Ibos, *Le chemin de fer*, 9.
81. Kerr, *Engines of Change*, 47–51.

of silt. Eventually so much sediment accumulated at the bridge as to render it scarcely necessary in the dry season: vehicles nowadays pass underneath it on the newly formed land.[82] The Hardinge Bridge is just one of many examples of how rivers and railway infrastructure mutually shaped each other. The result was a new hybrid waterscape, the product of natural flows of water and human efforts to straddle them.

If railways and waterways often competed as transport arteries, in certain circumstances they worked very much in tandem. Nowhere was this more evident than in the Congo basin. The Congo is a giant of a river. Though surpassed by the Nile for length, it ranks second in the world (behind the Amazon) in overall discharge. Rising in the highlands and great lakes of East Africa, it descends generally westward through one of world's largest rainforests before emptying into the Atlantic. The lands drained by the Congo and its tributaries cover around four million square kilometres, an area larger than India.

In theory, this enormous river system promised access to a staggering wealth of trade goods, but its geography made access from the sea impossible. Seagoing vessels can navigate only around 80 miles (130 kilometres) up the Congo to the port of Matadi, above which lies a series of cataracts extending another 220 miles (350 kilometres) inland, many of them flanked by craggy, impassable terrain. For centuries, these obstacles confined Europeans to the lower stretches of the river. It was only in 1876 that Henry Morgan Stanley became the first European to travel through the higher reaches of the Congo, and even then he approached it from the east coast of Africa. Hoping to locate the source of the Nile, Stanley and his team set off northwards down the Lualaba River, following it for several hundred miles as it veered to the west away from the Nile to become the Congo (the river name changes at the Boyoma Falls). After portaging around a set of rapids they christened as Stanley Falls, the crew floated for another thousand miles (1,600 kilometres) downriver, occasionally coming into conflict with riverside villagers who marvelled at their 'sticks which sent forth thunder and lightning'.[83] Eventually they reached a large inland lake, which Stanley once again humbly named after himself (Stanley Pool), and from there embarked on a treacherous overland journey to the coast after establishing that the roaring cascades below were completely unnavigable.

Stanley's voyage down the Congo not only made him a Victorian household name; it also prompted King Leopold of Belgium to recruit him for the newly founded Association Internationale pour l'Exploration et la Civilisation de l'Afrique Centrale, a front organization designed to pursue Leopold's goal of acquiring African territories of his own. What bound the two men together was a desire to use the Congo as a route into the heart of Africa. In 1879,

82. Iqbal, *Bengal Delta*, 134–37; Kerr, *Engines of Change*, 54.
83. Quoted in Hochschild, *King Leopold's Ghost*, 54.

Stanley ordered four steamboats to be brought to Matadi on the lower Congo. The only way to reach the navigable upper stretch of the river was to carry the disassembled boats overland to Stanley Pool. In March 1880, hundreds of press-ganged African workers began building a four-metre-wide road for this purpose. Difficult terrain and constant bouts of illness severely hampered their progress; it took nearly a year to transport the first two boats eighty-seven kilometres above the lower falls. After delicate negotiations with local leaders, who could have stopped the entire enterprise in its tracks, the first of the four steamboats, the *En avant*, was finally launched on Stanley Pool in December 1881. The three others soon followed, and were joined in 1884 by a small steamer brought upriver by an English missionary group.[84] When Leopold officially established the Congo Free State in May 1885, this fledgling political entity essentially comprised little more than a small handful of steamers. As the king himself wrote to the association president Maximilien Strauch shortly thereafter, 'it is imperative that our small navy is kept in good condition', for it constituted nothing less than 'the basis of our entire enterprise'.[85]

Over the following years, the main aim of this miniature flotilla-state was to boost commerce along the river. As the steamers probed the commercial potential of the region, the cataracts below Stanley Pool were increasingly regarded as an intolerable hindrance to trade. Porterage from Matadi to Léopoldville (the main trading post on the Pool) took roughly three weeks and cost around a thousand francs per ton, which severely hampered bulk exports from the region. This raised the question of whether the value of upstream trade justified the construction of a railway between Matadi and Léopoldville. In 1888, the Belgian military engineer Alexandre Delcommune set off to find out, captaining a purpose-built steamer, the *Roi des Belges*, to the navigable limits of the river's main tributaries, altogether covering nearly twelve thousand kilometres in a single year. Further exploratory missions soon followed, one involving the young merchant mariner Joseph Conrad, who in 1890 signed on as second captain of the *Roi des Belges* for a reconnaissance trip to Stanley Falls. Although the journey inspired Conrad's most celebrated novel (*Heart of Darkness*) and eventually brought him fame, it also gave him such a severe case of dysentery that he had to be repatriated to England in January 1891 and never fully recovered. Many other Europeans who ventured upriver suffered a similar fate, but their reports of ivory and rubber were promising enough to convince investors of the commercial viability of a railway around the Congo's cataracts.[86]

When construction of the railway finally commenced in March 1890, the narrow-gauge line from Matadi to Léopoldville was one of the most challenging rail projects ever undertaken. Although it measured only 366 kilometres in

84. Lederer, *Histoire de la navigation*, 11–29.
85. Letter of 2 November 1885, quoted in Lederer, *Histoire de la navigation*, 72.
86. Batchelor, *Life of Joseph Conrad*; Lederer, *Histoire de la navigation*, 71–72.

length, it took over eight years to complete. Much of the difficulty stemmed from the hydrology of the region. The route passed through a series of tortuous canyons and ravines, requiring no fewer than ninety-nine bridges, which together spanned around twenty kilometres. The most challenging stage was the initial ascent up the M'Pozo Valley, a deep gorge punctuated by falls and rapids that earned it the grim nickname 'valley of despair'. It took over two years to build the first nine kilometres. To make matters worse, sudden rains and flash floods frequently wreaked havoc on the construction sites. In December 1891, the upper M'Pozo River rose an astounding seven metres within the space of several hours, carrying off a sixty-metre Eiffel-style bridge and depositing it 100 metres downstream. The descent from the heights down the Lukaya Valley to Stanley Pool presented similar dangers. When engineers began work on a bridge across the N'Kissi River, locals warned them that no one had ever managed to maintain a walkway across it owing to its exceptionally volatile floods. The engineers were sceptical of such local wisdom, but the advice proved to be entirely justified: their first wooden support bridge was annihilated in a single night when a torrent of brown water tore off a huge chunk of riverbank that crashed through the structure. Having learned their lesson, engineers built a second support bridge that was far more robust than the initial one, though it only barely survived long enough to allow workers to complete the steel span above the floodwaters. The instant the weight of the 460-ton steel bridge was lifted off the wooden structure, it was swept away by the torrent in a 'horrible fracas'.[87]

Completing the Matadi–Léopoldville railway was an engineering triumph, but it was also a humanitarian calamity – both directly and indirectly. On an immediate level, working conditions on the railway were horrendous. The thousands of men who built it – most of them forcefully or deceptively recruited from West Africa, China, and the West Indies – constantly suffered from malaria and dysentery, whose effects were exacerbated by poor food provisions and brutal treatment by overseers. Death rates were high; the steep valleys along which the line ran were likened to 'vast tombs'. Only coercion could keep the workforce on site. As the number of casualties rose, the increasing desperation among workers led to frequent revolts and occasional fights between different ethnic groups, all of which were brutally suppressed. Although the official death toll was 132 whites and 1,800 non-whites, the real figure was almost certainly much higher.[88]

On a more general level, the suffering of the railway workers was closely linked to the widespread misery that was inflicted on Africans above the falls.

87. Cornet, *La bataille du rail*, 207–11, 343–44; Baltzer, *Die Kolonialbahnen*, 231–38; Hochschild, *King Leopold's Ghost*, 170.

88. Cornet, *La bataille du rail*, 207, 209; Hochschild, *King Leopold's Ghost*, 171. Some three decades later in neighbouring French Congo, the construction of the Congo–Océan Railway was scarcely less brutal: Daughton, *Forest of No Joy*.

From the mid-1880s to the 1900s, the forests of the Congo basin were swept by a rubber boom. The prospect of huge profits from the rubber trade was a crucial factor behind the decision to build the railway in the first place. As the 'bicycle craze' in Europe and North America sent demand for latex soaring, concessionary companies bought up huge tracts of jungle interspersed with latex-bearing trees and vines. To acquire cheap supplies, they imposed a lethal system of compulsory delivery quotas that required local people to scour the forest for latex. Beatings and kidnapping were common. Where such methods failed to produce the desired level of compliance, militias cut off people's hands or massacred entire villages to convey the message. Although it became harder and harder for local people to meet their quotas as nearby latex sources were tapped out, the sheer level of violence meted out by company militias was sufficient to keep supplies flowing. By the time the railway was finished in 1898, rubber already far surpassed ivory as the principal export commodity from the Congo. With the completion of the line, the thousands of tons of rubber arriving at Stanley Pool no longer had to be carried for three weeks on men's heads to reach Matadi. By unclogging the flow of goods between the upper and lower Congo, the railway greatly amplified the stream of latex pouring down the river, along with the wave of violence that sustained it. Despite mounting criticism of the atrocities back in Europe, it took ten more years before the notorious 'red rubber' regime in the Congo finally came to an end.[89]

After the opening of the railway, the main constraint on commercial traffic was the capacity of the Congolese river fleet. Far from displacing river transport, the railway multiplied it. For one thing, it was now much easier to transport boats up to Stanley Pool. In the first three years after the railway was completed, the number of steam vessels on the upper river more than doubled from 43 in 1898 to 103 in 1901. At the same time, the boats also got bigger. To mark the railway's opening, the government launched a new forty-five-metre sternwheeler called the *Brabant*, which could carry twenty-four passengers in considerable comfort and which dwarfed all of the other boats on the river. Soon afterwards came the *Hainault*, whose 350-ton capacity was more than half the combined tonnage of the entire pre-railway fleet. With the advent of larger boats, the small 20-ton launches that had previously made up the backbone of the river flotilla were redeployed to boost commercial traffic along the Congo's tributaries.[90]

This proliferation of boats stimulated a rapid expansion of commercial traffic, but it also led to an increase in accidents. Despite the refinement of maps and signage, navigating the rivers of the Congo basin was still a matter of trial and error, of groping one's way along. When vessels ran aground, which they

89. Harms, 'End of Red Rubber'; Morel, *Red Rubber*; Hochschild, *King Leopold's Ghost*, 150–66.

90. Lederer, *Histoire de la navigation*, 134–37.

FIGURE 1.2. Rails and rivers in synergy: Léopoldville, view of the port and railway station, c.1910.
Source: Historical Railway Images, Congo Railways. CC-PD-Mark.

frequently did, African crew members were often ordered into the water to push them off snags. If that did not work, they often passed a chain under the hull and moved it back and forth in a sawlike motion to clear the soft debris underneath.[91] In response to the rise in accidents, the government commissioned the German hydroengineer Ludwig Franzius – renowned for having recently supervised the so-called 'Weser Correction', which enabled modern seagoing ships to reach the harbours of Bremen – to report on the best means of improving navigability on the Congo. Of particular concern were the maze-like stretches where the main stream divided into numerous channels that snaked around a multitude of small islands. Franzius's advice was straightforward: fighting nature was futile. Controlling the Congo River was a Sisyphean task at best. Unlike the lower Weser, whose deepened channels were kept open by a strong daily tidal flow, there was little point in dredging the shifting sands of the upper Congo. A more sensible approach in his view was to keep it under continuous observation in order to notify boats of changing navigational hazards. Following Franzius's report, this became the job of the Congolese Hydrographic Service, founded in 1910. Modelled on the system that guided boats on the Mississippi, its main purpose was not to 'map' the river as a fixed entity but rather to keep its dynamic nature under constant surveillance.[92]

91. Lederer, 146–49.
92. Huybrechts, *Transports et structures*; 21–23; Lederer, *Histoire de la navigation,* 157–60.

Over the following decades, this close synergy between railways and waterways continued to characterize Congolese communications. In many respects, the transport network of the region was a classic example of mutually dependent infrastructures that had to develop jointly for either to function effectively. After the completion of the Matadi–Léopoldville line, subsequent railway schemes were similarly designed to supplement the main water routes; for example, the 1906 Stanleyville–Ponthierville line, which linked with the river service from Ponthierville to Kindu, and the Kindu to Kongolo railway around the falls of Sendwe and Porte d'Enfer, which was completed in 1911.[93] In the interwar years, the rapid growth in commerce spurred an even tighter coordination of river and rail transport. Between 1920 and 1930, traffic through the port of Matadi grew fourfold. From 1924 to 1937, the overall capacity of the upper Congo fleet grew from 10,500 to 46,150 metric tons.[94] As the signage and surveillance of the river steadily improved in the 1920s and 1930s, the Congo basin was widely regarded as 'the finest network of navigable routes in the entire world'. As one contemporary observer fittingly put it, the railways of the Congo did not replace river traffic at all, but rather functioned essentially as 'tributaries of the navigable watercourses'.[95]

Coastlines and Commerce

The rivers of Europe's colonies drained the land in two senses. Physically, they conveyed rainfall and snowmelt to the sea. Commercially, they carried a stream of commodities to trade hubs located near the coast. As the volume of exports grew, and as traffic on the high seas multiplied, the coastlines of the colonial world witnessed a parallel set of changes. While long-established colonial ports such as Calcutta, Bombay and Jakarta grew beyond all recognition, a string of new ports – Saigon, Singapore, Dakar, Karachi – were built to serve as outlets for recently conquered hinterlands.[96] Most colonial ports were located at the intersection of sea lanes and overland trade routes, often on sites where rivers joined the sea. In many respects, they functioned as frontiers, two-way interfaces that linked terrestrial interiors with markets overseas.[97]

In recent years, historians have become increasingly interested in the role of colonial port cities as centres of imperial exchange – crucial nodes in the networks that carried people, ideas and other things across vast oceanic spaces.[98] Yet despite all the attention they have received, the emphasis on long-

93. Baltzer, *Die Kolonialbahnen*, 238–39.
94. Huybrechts, *Transports et structures*, 35–37.
95. Wiener, *Les chemins de fer*, 276.
96. See also Headrick's *Tentacles of Progress* (32–35).
97. See the discussion in Amrith's 'South Asia's Coastal Frontiers'.
98. Bose, *Hundred Horizons*; Metcalf, *Imperial Connections*; S. L. Lewis, *Cities in Motion*; Amrith, *Migration and Diaspora*; Arsan, *Interlopers of Empire*; Hofmeyr,

distance connections has tended to detach the ports themselves from their immediate amphibious surroundings. What did the surge of imperial commerce mean for coastal and estuarine environments, and for the people who lived there?[99]

In the age of sail, nature dictated not only how swiftly ships could travel but also where they could land. The key feature of a port was the existence of a natural harbour that afforded sufficient protection from storms and surges, yet also provided adequate depth to accommodate ocean-going vessels. In the age of steam, the most important factor was not topography but trade. The combination of steam, steel and concrete meant that wherever a sufficient flow of goods and material required an outlet to the sea, harbours could be expanded, dredged, bulk-headed or even built from scratch in order to create a port if the costs were justified. To accommodate modern ocean steamers, a port needed breakwaters to dampen the swell, channels for reaching the waterfront, and a depth of around ten metres at dockside. Where nature did not provide these features, it could be modified to do so.

The expansion of ocean-going trade in colonial Asia certainly required extensive natural modification. Few ports in the world are blessed with both a commercially advantageous position and a capacious, deep natural harbour (e.g., Rio de Janeiro, San Francisco, Durban). In colonial Asia, such fortunate coincidences of physical and economic geography were especially hard to come by. Singapore occupied an ideal maritime location at the eastern end of the busy Malacca Strait, but it sat on a rise in what was otherwise a shallow mangrove swamp. As port cities go, it was not unlike New Orleans or Rotterdam: a prime example of the 'tension between an optimal situation (a city or state's relationship to other places) and a problematic site (its physical environment)'.[100] By contrast, Manila had a magnificent natural harbour but, unlike Singapore, was located on the eastern edge of the region's network of maritime commerce and serviced a hinterland with a less dynamic export economy. Saigon was closer than Manila to the busy sea lanes that rounded Singapore between the Straits and the South China Sea, but the muddy river that gave admittance to its port limited its accessibility, especially for large ships. Similar problems affected

Dhupelia-Mesthrie and Kaarsholm, 'Durban and Cape Town'; Ballantyne, *Between Colonialism and Diaspora*; Markovits, *Global World*; Tagliacozzo, *In Asian Waters*, 191–248.

99. For a brief discussion of port cities and surrounding environments, see S. Mosley's 'Coastal Cities'. For the colonial world, the best environmental–historical treatment to date focuses on Singapore, though the most dramatic changes there came after the colonial era: Powell, 'Singapore's Lost Coast' and 'Harnessing the Great Acceleration'. It is worth noting that the emphasis on the connectedness of port cities has also tended to overlook the ways in which they relied on fixed regulatory boundaries that delineated them from their surroundings: J. Ehrlich, 'Port City Boundary'.

100. Powell, 'Singapore's Lost Coast', 638.

the ports of Haiphong and Batavia, which were connected to the sea by narrow, winding estuarine rivers.[101]

Farther west, India's overall size, strategic location and wealth of resources might have made it the envy of Britain's colonial rivals, but it was no 'jewel in the crown' when it came to ports. Despite its 3,600 miles (5,800 kilometres) of coastline, the subcontinent was remarkably lacking in good natural harbours. In the late nineteenth century, as the railway boom peaked and exports surged, the ports and anchorages of India remained 'singularly few in number'.[102] Despite the fact that India's seas were seasonally among the most tempestuous in the world, its port facilities received little attention before the 1870s. Apart from Calcutta, the entire east coast of the peninsula afforded little shelter for ocean-going ships. On the west coast too, harbours were generally unsuitable for large craft. Bombay was the main exception, with Karachi ranking a distant second, and even these two havens needed radical alteration to accommodate the big steamers. For the colonial export economy to grow, it was imperative to make the boundary between land and sea more suitable for trade – above all by making it less ambiguous and fixing it firmly in place.

Calcutta had long been South Asia's foremost port, though it enjoyed this status more in spite of than because of its location. Situated some ninety miles (145 kilometres) up the winding Hooghly River, it took sailing vessels as much as three weeks to reach it from the coast; even steamboats required one or two days. Well aware of Calcutta's shortcomings, colonial officials and Bengali business leaders made numerous proposals to enhance the flow of trade through the city, though little came of their efforts until the 1880s. Even after a pair of ferocious cyclones destroyed much of the existing port in 1842 and again in 1864 (see chapter 4), plans to construct new wet docks downriver went nowhere.[103] Local merchants complained that the existing facilities were nothing short of 'a reproach to a commercial city . . . We have no wharves, jetties or landing stages, no steam or hydraulic cranes.'[104] Although officials and merchants alike recognized the need for more capacity, there was disagreement over where to site it. Government officials generally favoured the construction of new facilities at Diamond Harbour, fifty miles (eighty kilometres) below Calcutta on the coast, which would avoid the problems associated with navigating the Hooghly. But merchants successfully opposed any plans that would divert commerce away from the city.[105] In the end, it was agreed to build new enclosed moorings at Kidderpore, two miles below Calcutta, where a ten-acre

101. De Rouville, *L'amélioration des ports*, 8–25; Agard, *La navigation maritime*, 6–24; Ministère des Colonies, *Les ports autonomes*, 3–52; Putri and Rahmanti, 'Jakarta Waterscape'.

102. MacGeorge, *Ways and Works*, 508.

103. N. Mukherjee, *Port of Calcutta*, 34–35.

104. Bengal Hurkaru, *Great Bengal Cyclone*, 38.

105. *Report of the Calcutta Port Commissioners*, 1–2.

(four-hectare) tidal basin and a hundred acres of docks were carved out of the swamps by 1892. Soon afterwards came a new petroleum wharf at Budge-Budge twelve miles (nineteen kilometres) downriver, followed in 1929 by the King George's Dock at Garden Reach just below Kidderpore.[106]

The completion of these works created more space for large ships, but it did nothing to mitigate the main problem for Calcutta's port authorities: namely, the mutable nature of the Hooghly River. Part drainage channel for the Ganges and part tidal creek, it was far from an ideal navigation channel. There is good reason why the River Hooghly Survey Department, founded in 1668, was the oldest public service in all of British-controlled India.[107] Seasonal floods along the Ganges can change its water level by over six metres. When these oscillations interacted with the tides, they occasionally created powerful bores that were funnelled up the mouth of the river into a two-metre head-wave that could affect navigation as far upstream as Calcutta itself. Seasonal floodwaters also brought silt, and the volumes of sediment they carried only grew over time as land clearance and erosion progressed upstream. Colonial officials were constantly worried about what they called the 'deterioration' of the river, all the more so as ocean-going ships grew larger. In the mid-nineteenth century, a special committee was charged with examining whether the Matla River should be developed as an alternative route to the sea, but the idea was dumped in favour of redoubling efforts to dredge the Hooghly's channel. In the early 1890s, following a series of particularly high floods, the government hired a team of experts to advise on danger spots, such as the James and Mary Sands and the shoals at Moyapur. Whereas some advocated vast works to 'train' the river, others saw little need for such a radical intervention. The lack of consensus even among experts prompted the government to revert to its usual policy of buying more dredgers as a supposedly interim measure. In the 1930s, the same arguments were rehearsed yet again when shipping firms warned that it was uneconomical to continue sending large boats up the river if port authorities could not guarantee safe passage at 30 feet (nine metres) draught. Simply put, the problems caused by the Hooghly's oozing silt and mudbanks resisted any lasting solution. The overall result was an endless war of attrition between the river and an ever-growing fleet of dredgers.[108]

In many ways, the prospects for Bombay were considerably brighter. In the late nineteenth century, it had two big advantages over Calcutta. One was its western location. After the completion of the Suez Canal in 1869, the opening of the Red Sea trade route had the effect of moving Bombay much closer to markets in Europe – an effect that was amplified by the geographic layout of

---

106. Stuart-Williams, 'Port of Calcutta'. On the legal and physical fixing of terra firma in Calcutta, see Bhattacharyya's *Empire and Ecology*.

107. Stuart-Williams, 'Port of Calcutta', 893.

108. N. Mukherjee, *Port of Calcutta*, 36–37, 101–2, 158.

India's railways, which channelled an increasing proportion of trade through Bombay. The other advantage was its natural harbour. Measuring around twenty miles long and four to six miles wide (thirty by eight kilometres), and protected from the sea by the barrier of Bombay Island itself, it was the finest natural haven of the entire subcontinent. In the enthusiastic words of one engineer, 'the hand of God had fashioned the wide reaches of Bombay Harbour, the hand of man had merely to adapt them for shipping'.[109] Yet here, too, the fluid nature of the estuarine environment continually challenged such adaptations.

Given the unique merits of Bombay harbour, its transformation into a modern port was remarkably slow. As late as 1860, the *Times of India* still complained that 'the want of wharfage and pier accommodation thrusts itself so prominently before us that the apathy of our merchants thereon is past belief. Every man who reclaims a foot of land or gives a new foot of pier room to Bombay deserves to be looked upon as a public benefactor.'[110] In this swampy environment, the clear separation of land and water was a costly undertaking that required strong political backing. It was only after the establishment of the Bombay Port Trust in 1873 that the pace of construction quickened. The Prince's Dock, built in 1875–80, provided over a mile (1.6 kilometres) of solid quayside. In 1891 came the Victoria Dock, followed by the Merewether Dry Dock, the Hughes Dry Dock and finally the Alexandra Dock, which included a mile-long sea wall and nearly two miles of quayside. During the 1890s and 1900s, extensive reclamation projects in the northern parts of the island added hundreds of hectares of land and several kilometres of wharf frontage to the city. The mucky foreshores of Bombay Island were gradually being hardened; the boundary between land and sea became increasingly distinct.[111]

All around Bombay Harbour, imperial technology was deployed to convert the half-liquid estuarine environment into solid port infrastructure. But maintaining this new arrangement between land and water was a colossal task, for the very same processes that created the harbour in the first place – the movement and accumulation of suspended sediment – were also its biggest challenge. Bombay Island was formed from seven small natural islets where coastal currents piled up the mud that was carried downstream from the Western Ghats by the rivers that emptied into the harbour. Even as these islets were linked together through reclamation work, heavy monsoon rains on the Western Ghats continued to deliver enormous quantities of silt to the coast. The key to creating the modern port was to ensure that this sediment stayed in the right places. But the more the harbour was modified, the harder this task became. While some of the main channels cleared themselves through natural tidal action, many did not, and nor did the new dock basins. Every

109. Sandes, *Military Engineer in India*, 172.
110. Quoted in Sharpe, *Port of Bombay*, 18.
111. Everatt, *Maintenance Dredging*, 6–9.

year around one foot (thirty centimetres) of sediment had to be removed from the Alexandra Dock, and around twice that amount from its approach channel. Siltation at the Prince's and Victoria Docks was far worse: two feet per year from the quayside, and around five feet from the channels and their flanks. Maintaining adequate depth thus required the removal of an enormous amount of mud, which required the deployment of a fleet of state-of-the-art dredgers. By the 1920s, some of Bombay's dredgers were capable of lifting and depositing nearly ten thousand cubic yards (7,500 cubic metres) per day, much of which ended up as fill for reclaiming yet more land and wharf space from the sea.[112] Like their counterparts on the Hooghly, port officials in Bombay were locked in a continuous battle against silt – quite literally a kind of submarine 'trench warfare'. Stabilizing the inherently dynamic coastal environment required a massive input of energy and resources, and even then the effects were, by their very nature, only temporary.

By contrast, in Madras the difficulty was not shifting marsh and mud, but the absence of any harbour at all. Despite being the oldest British trading post in India (1639), as a port Madras left nearly everything to be desired. Unlike Bombay or Calcutta, the shoreline at Madras was a straight, open beach pierced by only a handful of small stream outlets, which afforded no sanctuary whatsoever from the pounding surf. For around two and half centuries after the city was founded, ships had to anchor a quarter mile (four hundred metres) offshore, where they were serviced by surfboats that ferried cargo to and from the beach. When seas were calm, the surfboats could take loads of up to one and a half tons at a time; in heavy weather less than half that amount. Navigating them took considerable skill, and was the sole preserve of local oarsmen. The permission to work the surfboats was strictly regulated by caste privilege, so those who did it were able to charge exorbitant fees. Altogether the process was slow, unpredictable and costly. Although matters improved somewhat with the construction of a pier in the 1860s, ships that moored there still had no protection from ocean swell.[113] To enhance the flow of goods through Madras, the city desperately needed a barrier to calm the seas.

The idea of building an artificial sea wall, first mooted in the late eighteenth century after a massive cyclone hit the Madras coast in 1787, finally gained traction with the creation of a special 'Breakwater Commission' in 1868. The commission debated various proposals for a full eight years before work finally began on an enclosed harbour. Starting in 1876, work crews gradually built two sea walls situated just over half a mile (about a kilometre) apart from each other, each extending 1,200 yards (1,100 metres) straight out from the shoreline and connected at their ends by a perpendicular breakwater with a 150-yard (140-metre) opening in the centre. It was a colossally expensive

112. Everatt, *Maintenance Dredging*, 9–20.
113. MacGeorge, *Ways and Works*, 514–15.

undertaking that took some five years to complete, but as the secretary of state remarked upon approving the plans:

> the question is too large to be dealt with only on financial grounds. Many human lives are sacrificed in the tempests which annually ravage the Coromandel coast, and it is possible that a large proportion of these might be saved if vessels which are now surprised in the roadstead could seek the shelter of a harbour.[114]

As events soon showed, the ferocity of the local climate could also catch harbour engineers by surprise. On 12 November 1881, when work on the structure was nearly completed, an unusually violent cyclone ravaged the new sea walls. In the course of a single day, the heavy rolling waves off the Bay of Bengal wrecked much of the outer breakwater, undermining its foundations at depths of over twenty feet (six metres). The scale of the damage was beyond anything that British engineers had deemed possible. Unaccustomed to the severity of Asian cyclones, they had erroneously assumed that even the largest waves had little effect on the seabed at depths of over fifteen feet. In the wake of the disaster, there were various proposals to alter the harbour's design in order to withstand such cyclones in the future, but in the end the walls were simply reinforced at greater depths on a broadly similar layout.[115]

When it was finally completed in 1890, the Madras port had ended up costing nearly £1.25 million, around twice its original budget.[116] Many deemed the price worth paying, given the uptick in the city's commercial fortunes, but the harbour eventually brought with it other costs as well. When the 1868 Breakwater Commission submitted its original report, it recommended the creation of a simple two-thousand-yard (1,800-metre) barrier running parallel with the shore to calm the waters behind it. Although the commission members recognized that a fully enclosed harbour would be preferable for shipping, many feared that the creation of solid structures projecting outward from the shoreline would disrupt the strong southerly currents along the Madras coast, block the natural movement of sand northward, and therefore raise the risk of shoaling. When colonial officials eventually rejected a simple barrier in favour of a closed harbour, they did so in the knowledge that they were creating a long-term problem. Nonetheless, they reckoned that sand accumulation would pose little threat to the harbour itself, which was their primary concern. By contrast, they showed little interest in the effects it might have on other groups who lived or fished along the coast. As it turned out, they were correct about the lack of sand accumulation in the harbour, which never became a major problem. Beyond the harbour, however, the long-term impact on the

114. MacGeorge, 516.

115. Sandes, *Military Engineer in India*, 169–71; MacGeorge, *Ways and Works*, 517–18.

116. MacGeorge, *Ways and Works*, 518.

FIGURE 1.3. Looking towards the newly built Madras Harbour, 1880. Courtesy of past-india.com.

surrounding shoreline was even greater than the Breakwater Commission members ever imagined. Over the century after the construction of the sea walls began (1876–1976), the beach north of the artificial harbour receded by over half a kilometre, threatening local residents, shrinking the coastal aquifer and adversely affecting local fishermen. Over the same period, the shoreline to the south correspondingly advanced to form what is now the broad Marina Beach. By halting the northerly flow of sand along the Madras coast, the artificial harbour has completely remade the oceanfront in unintended but not entirely unforeseen ways. Despite a series of conservation efforts since the 1970s to halt the further erosion of the northern beach, it has continued to retreat at a rate of around eight metres per year, with no end in sight.[117]

As the examples of Madras and Bombay show, altering the coastline on such a scale is a risky, expensive, and often never-ending business. As a general rule, it is undertaken only where strong commercial incentives or military requirements appear to justify it, as was the case in both of these cities. Along the African coast, especially south of the Sahara, relatively few spots fulfilled either of these criteria. On the eve of the Second World War, it was reckoned that the continent's entire sixteen-thousand-mile (twenty-six-thousand-kilometre)

117. Mani, 'Coastal Conservation Programme'; MacGeorge, *Ways and Works*, 516.

coastline boasted only eighty-eight serviceable harbours – that is, havens well protected from wind and currents, sufficiently spacious to accommodate several ships at once, and providing a minimum depth of about fifteen feet (4.5 metres) for the smallest steamers. Of these eighty-eight harbours, only half could handle average-size steamboats, and a mere sixteen could cope with large vessels drawing up to thirty feet.

The spatial distribution of Africa's ports was of course partly a reflection of economic geography. Whereas the Cape and the Mediterranean coast at either end of the continent were studded with modern ports designed to handle their large volumes of trade with Europe, ports were few and far between along the shores of tropical Africa, where trade flows tended to be smaller. Yet at the same time, the prevalence and location of ports also mirrored Africa's physical geography. Whereas some stretches of the African coast provided an abundance of natural harbours (e.g., from Mozambique to Kenya), others offered only hundreds of kilometres of featureless beach or barrier islands separated from the mainland by shallow lagoons (e.g., between Nigeria and northern Liberia). Where coastlines offered no shelter, the adjacent hinterlands were, as one geographer put it, 'obviously . . . confronted with a distinct handicap'.[118] For colonial 'development' to happen in such areas, ports were essential.

French officials were particularly conscious of this problem. Although France's vast African empire encompassed nearly a quarter of the continent's coastline, it boasted only nine natural harbours. As a result, French authorities built more artificial harbours in Africa than all the other colonial powers combined. Most were constructed along the shores of the Maghreb, where engineers 'completely remade the coastline . . . changing it from one almost devoid of shelter for large, modern vessels to one of the two most accessible stretches of coast on the continent'.[119] Algeria alone had six entirely artificial harbours, which accounted for all of its 'first-class' ports. The situation was very different in French West Africa, whose busiest port, Saint-Louis, was scarcely accessible by large steamers owing to the existence of a shallow mud bar across the mouth of the Senegal River. Yet as the volume of trade with West Africa grew, the dearth of natural harbours eventually spurred changes there as well.

The port of Dakar was in every sense an imperial creation. Perched on the westernmost tip of Africa, it occupied an exceptional strategic spot. Not only was it located on the main sea lanes between Europe and all points south; it was also one of the few places on the West African coast that was free of barrier islands. Thanks to the Cap Vert peninsula, which projects westward into the Atlantic and hooks southward to Cap Manuel, the bay of Dakar is protected from the strong westerly swells that batter the rest of the West African coast and pile the sand into offshore bars. Though long ignored by

118. Deasy, 'Harbors of Africa', 325–27, quote at 327.
119. Deasy, 327–28.

French ships, Dakar eventually came into use in the 1860s as a coaling station for refuelling steamers on their way to West Africa and South America. Dakar grew slowly at first on account of the shallow waters alongside the two jetties that initially composed the port. Traffic began to accelerate as the harbour was successively deepened in the 1870s and 1880s, and especially after the arrival of the railway to Saint-Louis in 1885. It grew even more rapidly with the decision to build a major naval base on the eastern section of the bay after the Fashoda Incident of 1898, the climax of Anglo-French disputes over the upper Nile. Shortly after the transfer of the French West African capital from Saint-Louis to Dakar in 1902, a new commercial port was built just to the west of the naval base to handle the growing volume of trade goods from the Senegal and Niger valleys. By 1910, the two original jetties were joined by a pair of larger piers and an entirely new waterfront measuring a kilometre long and one to two hundred metres wide, all of it built on land reclaimed from the sea. During the First World War, the naval base was expanded yet further, and after the war the flow of groundnuts and other export commodities more than trebled from 82,000 tons in 1919 to 288,000 tons in 1928. All the while, dredgers cleared sand from the main channels to maintain the necessary nine metres depth for naval vessels. By 1930, Dakar ranked among the busiest French-controlled ports anywhere in the world, handling more ships and cargo than Bordeaux, Nantes, or Cherbourg.[120]

But Dakar was an outlier. As one merchant described it, 'on the entire seaboard from Port-Etienne in Mauritania to the mouth of the Congo, there is truly only one single French port worthy of the name, and that is Dakar'.[121] For French officials, changing this situation became an integral part of their self-styled 'civilizing mission' in West Africa.

Côte d'Ivoire was of particular interest in this respect, for it was here that the perceived gap between economic potential and port facilities was most glaring. The humid forests in the south of Côte d'Ivoire contained a wealth of valuable timber and were well suited to the production of export crops such as cocoa, coffee, and palm oil. In the drier savannahs to the north, officials pressured farmers to grow cotton for metropolitan markets.[122] As production and exports rose, the absence of a working port on the coast was viewed as an irksome brake on the territory's 'development'. Like most of the Gulf of Guinea coast, the Ivorian shoreline was low, sandy, and lined with barrier islands and lagoons that separated the mainland from the sea. The only way to load

120. Afrique Occidentale française, *Le port de Dakar*, 25–35; Gouvernement général de l'AOF, *Le port de Dakar*, 17–24, 29–30; Ribot and Lafon, *Dakar*, 113–20; Barrès, *Les ports*, 53–88; Arbelot, *Les ports*, 2–3.

121. Barrès, *Les ports*, 29.

122. Bassett, *Peasant Cotton Revolution*, 58–59, 66–80.

and unload ocean-going ships was via small surfboats, much like the situation in Madras before its artificial harbour was built.

For many years, the only maritime infrastructure on the Ivorian coast was the single pier built in 1900 at Grand-Bassam, around twenty kilometres south-east of Abidjan, the principal railhead on the mainland. The pier faced problems from the start, and soon had to be lengthened to keep ahead of the seaward expansion of the beach brought on by the faster-than-expected accumulation of sand around its pylons. A similar fate was very likely in store for the two piers that were built several years later at Petit-Bassam, immediately south of Abidjan across the Ebrié lagoon, though neither of them survived the pounding surf and storm surges long enough to suffer from the problem of sand accumulation. After the First World War, the colonial government built another pier at Grand-Bassam to provide much-needed additional wharf capacity, though in the event it ended up merely compensating for the loss of the original pier to a violent storm in 1922. It took another decade for engineers finally to ease the infrastructural bottleneck on the Ivorian coast. A new wharf at Port-Bouët, completed in the early 1930s, not only multiplied the colony's dock space but also provided a direct rail link to Abidjan across two sections of lagoon and the marshy Ile de Petit-Bassam that lay between the mainland and the coast.[123]

All of these installations sought to make the best of the coastal geography as it was, which was far from ideal for maritime commerce. There were, however, also more ambitious attempts to transform the coastline itself in such a way as to turn Abidjan into a proper seaport. Although the city lacked direct access to the sea, its lagoon was naturally deep and its railhead provided plenty of traffic. With a direct route to the ocean, Abidjan could potentially handle more traffic more cheaply than any other port between Lagos and Freetown.

Even as the first coastal piers were being built at Grand- and Petit-Bassam, engineers dreamed of piercing the barrier island to allow ships to pass into the lagoon behind it. The location they chose was midway between Port-Bouët and Vridi, where the island was at its narrowest (about eight hundred metres) and where a deep undersea valley leading up to the coast – the so-called *trou-sans-fond* – promised to swallow the tons of sand migrating along the coast and thereby keep them from clogging the opening. In 1904, suction dredgers began work on a channel designed to measure sixty metres wide and seven metres deep, which involved the removal of well over a million cubic metres of earth. For three years, colonial engineers struggled to keep the shifting sands from closing the channel's mouth, but in 1907 they eventually gave up. Although it proved possible to keep the canal open during the rainy season (when high lagoon waters flushed it clear on their way to the sea), as soon as the floods subsided, the westerly currents along the coast clogged it again,

---

123. See generally *Les installations maritimes*; Berron, 'Le littoral lagunaire', 359; Arbelot, *Les ports*, 4; Barrès, *Les ports*, 107–26.

despite the vast quantities of sand that spilled down into the *trou-sans-fond*. The canal thus turned out to be a big waste of time and effort, but this did not deter the colonial government from making a second attempt to dig a seaway in the same spot in 1933, this time with a much wider mouth designed to funnel the daily tidal flows through the channel to flush out any accumulating sand. Although engineers were once again confident that the scheme would work, the result was the same as in 1907. The remnants of the canal, now a small arm of the lagoon, are still visible today.[124]

Despite these repeated failures, the dream of piercing the barrier island persisted. This was partly due to the limitations of the existing wharves, which could barely handle current volumes of traffic, let alone the kind of increase that French officials hoped for and anticipated. It also stemmed from a sense of rivalry with British engineers, who had already managed to maintain a navigable channel across the shallow mouth of the lagoon leading to Lagos in Nigeria, and had even built an artificial harbour at Takoradi on the neighbouring Gold Coast.[125]

As France's plans for developing its African colonies ballooned after the Second World War, colonial authorities in Côte d'Ivoire gave it one last try. In 1950, after enlisting the help of Dutch engineers from the technical university of Delft, they finally succeeded in building a permanent canal at Vridi, just west of the site of the earlier projects. Although the French press hailed the Vridi Canal as a heroic achievement, suspicions of future problems and unintended consequences were rife in view of the chequered history of attempts to alter the topography of the Ivorian coast. Indeed, for several years after the canal had been completed, such scepticism appeared to be more than justified. In the early 1950s, the beaches east and west of the opening suffered an abrupt and unexpected retreat, threatening to wash away coconut farms near the shore and eliciting widespread criticism of the project. Once again, the vagaries of the coastal currents threatened to avenge all efforts to remake the Ivorian shoreline for human purposes. Before long, however, the process of erosion suddenly reversed, and the area affected by the canal's interference with littoral currents remained small.[126] In the end, for reasons that were unclear, the canal did not turn into the disaster that doubters feared it would be, and that it initially looked like it might be. Although coastal engineers could eventually celebrate it as a major accomplishment, it was ultimately a lesson in humility for all concerned. As ever, the coastal environment proved to be volatile and unpredictable – not just for those who sought to modify it but also for their critics.

124. Houdaille, *Le chemin de fer*, 32–34; Berron, 'Le littoral lagunaire', 359–60; Barrès, *Les ports*, 120–22; Bourdillon, *Les travaux publics français*, 47–48.

125. Olukoju, 'Development of the Port'; Plageman, 'Colonial Ambition'.

126. Berron, 'Le littoral lagunaire', 360–61.

FIGURE 1.4. Canal de Vridi, 1955.
Photographed by Jacques Gonthier. Courtesy of the Archives nationales d'outre-mer,
FR ANOM 30Fi49/68.

The waters of Asia and Africa played a central role in the expansion and consolidation of Europe's imperial power. From the Mekong to the Congo and
from the Ganges to the Niger, European efforts to chart rivers, mark out or
remove hazards, and improve or maintain their navigability reflected the
significance of waterways as conduits of imperial authority and commercial
expansion. On the coastlines too, projects to drain estuaries, deepen natural
channels and create new harbours likewise testified to the importance of controlling water for exploiting the land.

But the transformation of colonial waterscapes was about much more than
just transport and communications. Mastering water flows was crucial for
moving goods and people, but it also made it possible to generate more goods
in the first place. Making water supplies more predictable and more widely
available was indispensable for producing more of the necessities of life and
more of the commodities that overseas markets coveted. Wherever insufficient or irregular water supplies were the principal threat to subsistence, and
wherever droughts or floods constituted the chief brake on economic growth,
officials and engineers sought to remedy such inconveniences of nature. As the
next three chapters show, smoothing out the spatial and temporal unevenness
of water, getting it to the right places at the right time in the right amount, was
at the heart of the imperial project.

CHAPTER TWO

Mastering the Monsoon

SEASONALITY AND THE RISE
OF PERENNIAL IRRIGATION

THE MANIPULATION OF water has long been a cornerstone of political power. For thousands of years, elites have prized the merits of public water-works as symbols of their beneficence and as tools for maintaining their authority. For autocratic governments and state officials, the construction of vast irrigation systems served a variety of useful purposes: laying claim to territory, making lands more productive and winning the loyalty of grateful cultivators. It is no coincidence that many of the oldest and most long-standing civilizations – Egyptian, Chinese, Mesopotamian, Indic – were based on the regulation of rivers, nor that many other societies from the Andes to Cambodia and from Central America to Java likewise built themselves on watery foundations. In all of these places, social, political and economic structures were deeply entangled with flows of water.

As Europeans extended their influence around the globe, they gained control over many of these cradles of hydraulic civilization. In the process, they too were drawn to grand water projects as a means of mobilizing natural resources and enhancing their wealth and power. In several respects, their forays into the art of irrigated despotism followed long-established precedent. As ever, the motivation behind large-scale water control schemes was to boost state revenues, dampen social unrest and legitimate their own authority. Like their Asian and African predecessors, European imperialists also mobilized huge armies of labourers to build and maintain their waterworks. Yet in other ways, their particular version of hydraulic imperialism was distinctive. By and large Europe's empire builders turned to irrigation projects not merely to augment their authority or to demonstrate their benevolence, but to reshape their colonial possessions along modern commercial lines: more specifically, to increase their agricultural exports and make them profitable on world markets. Furthermore, they deployed a variety of new techniques to achieve this end. Coal and steam – and eventually steel and concrete – enabled engineers to construct waterworks on a scale that earth, rock and human muscle scarcely allowed. Irrigation was crucial for making agriculture more productive, for exploiting the soils and labour of conquered territories more effectively.

Wherever they were built, modern irrigation systems profoundly rearranged the relationships between people and the rest of nature. In many parts of the nineteenth- and twentieth-century world – from the western United States to Australia to central Asia – they served primarily to bring water to arid regions and open them up to farming and settlement. By contrast, in the tropical and subtropical parts of Europe's colonial empire, the main problem that irrigation systems were designed to solve was, as Sunil Amrith has recently emphasized, not so much the absence of water as its unevenness.[1] Wherever water supplies were governed by the seasonal rhythms of monsoon rains, at any given time there was usually too much or too little of it. Such was the case in the bulk of colonial Asia and most of sub-Saharan Africa. Although the drier northern and southern fringes of Africa have a different pattern of precipitation, even Egypt depended on monsoon rains that flowed down the Nile from wetter regions to the south. In all these areas the bulk of rainfall or floodwaters came within a period of four or five months of the year, either in a single rainy season (as in Southeast Asia and West Africa) or in long and short rainy seasons at opposite ends of the calendar (as in East Africa). Some years were of course wetter than others, and when the annual rains failed then crops and people invariably suffered. When two or more dry years occurred in succession – as repeatedly happened in the late nineteenth century – the results could be catastrophic. As one observer noted at the time, 'nothing in such circumstances can stand between millions of people and starvation, except irrigation'.[2]

For most people living in the colonial world, the stakes of this annual cycle could hardly be higher. For colonial officials too, the arrival of the rains or seasonal floodwaters was a matter of the utmost importance. The oscillations of the monsoon were thought to determine much more than just a good or bad harvest. European observers widely regarded these cyclical variations as the very basis of social and economic life across much of Asia and Africa. Even in areas where irrigation stretched back centuries, the seasonal fluctuation of water supplies fundamentally structured planting and harvest schedules, thereby constraining the choice and productivity of crops. In European eyes, this elemental dependence on the caprices of the monsoon reflected the technological inferiority of subject peoples; it was a measure of their continued vulnerability to the

---

1. Amrith, *Unruly Waters*.
2. Deakin, *Irrigated India*, 59. On definitions, causes and impacts of droughts generally, see Cook's *Drought*.

forces of nature. The task of irrigation engineers was therefore to smooth out these periodic peaks and troughs, to 'correct' the natural variability of water into more predictable flows that could better serve human ends. After all, the duty of enlightened government – and one of the principal justifications of colonial rule – was to help supposedly backward societies overcome such natural constraints through the application of superior knowledge and technology. Making water available at the right time and in the right amount would enable farmers to adopt new cultivars, optimize their use of the land and crop their fields more frequently. In the minds of colonial officialdom, perennial irrigation promised nothing less than to free colonial subjects from the generations-old curse of living 'at the mercy of the monsoons'.[3]

The aim, in short, was to master the monsoon. But the way in which this aim was pursued shows that irrigation was always about much more than just growing crops. Europe's hydraulic imperialists had a distinct fondness for large, centrally managed irrigation systems. One of the main attractions of such projects was that they appealed to so many different interest groups: state bureaucrats, indigenous landowners, metropolitan investors and agricultural modernizers alike. By and large, they were designed to serve several different purposes at once: revenue generation, famine relief, sedentarizing itinerant groups, transport and security. Many were primarily geared to the production of exports rather than subsistence crops. Equally important, their design and operation reflected an underlying shift in how the hydrosphere was understood in the nineteenth and twentieth centuries. Colonial-era irrigation projects were part of an increasingly worldwide discourse of water engineering that sought to distil rivers and canals into mathematical models that could be comprehended, calculated and controlled for the purpose of maximizing distribution, productivity and income generation. In the process, the hydraulic environment itself became the object of a distinct form of 'scientific' water knowledge – one that bolstered colonial domination through a claim to superior efficiency and that simultaneously devalued indigenous knowledge and traditional techniques.[4]

Colonial irrigation projects were, in this sense, both symbols of European power and a means of exerting it. In some places the attempt to master the seasons became a cornerstone of the colonial state itself.[5] This chapter will focus on the three most prominent cases: India, the Netherlands Indies and Egypt. In all of these territories irrigation systems had long supported exceptionally dense farming populations, and under European rule the

3. Deakin, *Irrigated India*, 55.

4. On hydraulic science and colonial knowledge regimes, see esp. Gilmartin's *Blood and Water*, 'Models' and 'Scientific Empire'.

5. On the relationship between water control and state-making more generally, see Pritchard's *Confluence*.

manipulation of water remained instrumental for transforming landscapes and economies. By the late nineteenth century, each of these countries boasted vast perennial irrigation works that represented the state of the art in water control. Over the course of the colonial era they served as laboratories of hydraulic engineering, which furnished models and practices of worldwide hydrological significance. In all three regions, modern perennial irrigation works created a new set of relationships among many different things: soils, topography, farmers, merchants, the state and water itself. As we will see, the precise nature of these relationships differed significantly from place to place and evolved over time depending on the priorities and overall political aims of colonial administrations. Yet wherever they were built, for colonial rulers they represented a potent tool for extracting revenue and governing local populations. For the millions of people directly affected by them, they were a much more mixed blessing. And for everyone concerned, these new socio-hydrological arrangements were difficult to disentangle once they were established.

Irrigation, Improvement and Improvisation in Colonial Asia

Long before Europeans built their colonial administrations in southern and south-eastern Asia, the region was home to a multitude of different irrigation systems. In the fertile river valleys of northern India, earlier rulers had built a series of canals and barrages to harness the seasonal run-off and glacial meltwater flowing down from the Himalayas. In the coastal deltas of Tonkin, Annam, Madras and Bengal, a network of channels and dykes criss-crossed the alluvial plains to supply water to rice fields. Throughout the foothills of Java, Bali and Madura, farming communities built exquisitely contoured *sawah* terraces fed by extensive channel systems. Across the Deccan Plateau of central India, villagers built tens of thousands of tanks and reservoirs to capture the monsoon run-off and carry them through the dry season. All of these systems had been around for centuries, some for millennia. Many displayed a sophisticated understanding of hydraulics, and most were supported by an elaborate assemblage of rights and/or religious practices that governed their usage and maintenance.[6]

By contrast, colonial officials travelling to India or the East Indies in the early nineteenth century brought with them little knowledge of irrigation. Some of the officers of the East India Company were familiar with the transport canals back in Britain, but these networks had little in common with the

---

6. A. Agarwal and Narain, *Dying Wisdom*, 11–23; Booth, *Agricultural Development in Indonesia*, 73–81; Hardiman, 'Small-Dam Systems'.

irrigation systems they found on the subcontinent. Even Dutch engineers, masters in the art of drainage and land reclamation, were mere apprentices in the field of irrigation. Nonetheless, their faith in the superiority of European know-how convinced them that the application of Western science to colonial waterways would provide an effective means of guarding against drought, increasing agricultural production and boosting the government's tax receipts. In the eyes of European empire builders, the deployment of European technology was nothing less than a sacred duty of Christian government, an instrument of economic betterment and civilizational 'uplift'. As they soon discovered, however, 'modern' hydrology did not have all the answers, and 'traditional' knowledge sometimes proved to be remarkably well suited to local environmental conditions. For this reason, viewing the early development of irrigation from an environmental history perspective challenges conventional interpretations of technology transfer to the colonies.[7] By and large, irrigation technologies were developed within Europe's colonies and travelled elsewhere from there. For all the confidence that was placed in what we might call 'colonial water knowledge', for many decades the need to adapt to unfamiliar environments made it remarkably tentative and unstable. This peculiar combination of missionary zeal and practical inexperience meant that the development of colonial irrigation in Asia was in many respects a story of improvisation.

When the British first encountered the multitude of existing waterworks in India they could not help but be impressed by their size and sophistication. Among the most striking was the ancient anicut (weir) that for centuries had regulated the flow of water through the fertile delta of the Cauvery River, which empties into the Bay of Bengal on the south-eastern coast. Like much of India's pre-colonial hydraulic infrastructure, the anicut on the Cauvery had fallen into disrepair over the previous century as decades of political turmoil and warfare had taken their toll. The British attempt to restore this grand work of their predecessors marked the beginning of their irrigation efforts in Peninsular India.

Located near the southern tip of the subcontinent, the Cauvery delta is fed by two main channels, the Coleroon (now Kollidam) and Cauvery (Kaveri), whose waters were diverted into an intricate network of smaller canals that wound through the alluvial landscape. The most important piece of infrastructure was the Grand Anicut, a low, three-hundred-metre barrage of massive granite blocks that held up the Cauvery's flow during the rainy season and pushed it into various offtake channels. Originally built by Chola rulers in the first century CE, and enlarged around a thousand years later by the Tanjore kings, it had fallen into a state of advanced decay when the East

7. E.g., Headrick, *Tentacles of Progress* and *Power over Peoples*.

India Company took control of the region in 1803. The following year, the first British surveys of the delta found that the Cauvery just above the anicut was choked with silt, sending most of the river's water down the Coleroon directly to the sea. Many of the canals in the basin below were likewise clogged with silt, which deprived the previously fertile land of water supplies and continually shrank the area that could be irrigated.

Little was done about this situation until 1828, when the Company dispatched the twenty-five-year-old engineer Arthur Cotton, recently promoted to captain after surveying the maritime passage between India and Ceylon, to investigate the problem. He began by organizing the manual removal of silt by labourers, but since this did little to alleviate the mounting distress of local farmers – and the accompanying decline in tax revenues for the Company – he soon developed a more ambitious approach. In 1834, Cotton proposed a radical solution: a massive half-mile (780-metre) masonry barrage across the Coleroon, which would divert its water into the Cauvery, reverse the process of siltation and preserve a portion of the summer floodwaters for the dry season. Work began almost immediately, and in 1836 the new 'Upper Anicut' was finished. Its effects, both hydrological and financial, were quickly felt. By the end of the decade not only had it allowed a major expansion of irrigation throughout the delta; its low construction costs also made it exceptionally profitable.[8]

Almost immediately, the new hydraulic works on the Cauvery established Cotton's reputation as one of India's foremost hydraulic engineers. Yet such acclaim was premature, for it soon became apparent that the effects of the new anicut were not altogether beneficial. The twenty-two sluices that regulated the flow of the Coleroon proved inadequate, causing the river to slow and dump large amounts of silt into the riverbed just above the barrage (eventually the sediment built up to the top of the barrage itself). This meant that more water was diverted into the Cauvery than had been expected, which in turn caused severe erosion of its banks and its bed, and which threatened the surrounding region with even worse floods than before. Moreover, far from mitigating the problem of sedimentation, the new barrage actually exacerbated it, especially around the ancient Grand Anicut itself, whose peculiar hydraulic design – involving a curved shape and sloping crest, which had proved effective for well over a millennium – was not well understood by British engineers at the time. As it turned out, many of the 'traditional' design features of the ancient anicut were quite sound from a 'modern' hydroengineering perspective (as hydrologists later recognized), which blurred any neat distinction between these different types of knowledge. By the early 1840s, engineers had to enlarge the sluices of the new weir, lower its crest, and build a

8. Sandes, *Military Engineer in India*, 20–22; R. Smith, *Cauvery, Kistnah, and Godavery*, 3–6; Whitcombe, 'Irrigation', 678–81.

whole additional barrage across the Cauvery branch to control its flow as well. Alterations continued over the following decades, such that Cotton's original design was eventually 'changed almost out of recognition'.[9]

The Cauvery works thus taught British engineers some difficult lessons, but the fact that they remained profitable encouraged the Madras government to replicate the project in the two major river deltas to the north, the Godavari and Krishna. Originating in the Western Ghats, these two rivers drain the bulk of the Deccan Plateau and Northern Madras, both of which suffered from a series of famines and food shortages in the 1830s. Even as drought and crop failure plagued the region, the waters of these rivers flowed unchecked into the Bay of Bengal. Although a small number of inundation canals carried their seasonal floodwaters to fields, they could do so only for around two months of the year when river levels peaked, and they covered only a tiny fraction of the potentially irrigable land.[10]

In 1844, Cotton submitted a proposal for an immense set of waterworks on the Godavari delta. The area itself, he reported, 'can scarcely be surpassed by any part of the world' with respect to its soil, climate and overall irrigability. He calculated that no less than one million acres (four hundred thousand hectares) of land was eminently suited to the cultivation of rice or sugar, which at current prices would earn as much as £5 million per annum. Accomplishing this would require more than the 'repair (of) old, partial, and radically defective works'. What was needed, he insisted, was a coordinated series of dams, embankments, channels and roads that would collectively revolutionize the delta and its fortunes. The centrepiece of the proposal was a set of four huge masonry weirs across the various branches of the Godavari at Dowleswaram, which together measured over 4,000 yards (3,600 metres) long and were flanked by another 2,600 yards (2,400 metres) of embankments.[11]

The construction of these works promised to free the entire district from the vagaries of the rains. In Cotton's view, it would be 'unworthy of the Government of a civilized nation' to allow such a waste of a potential benefit 'when we have it in our power to construct a complete and general set of works, which will bring the last drop of water to the surface of the lands, and put it all under complete control'.[12] The government agreed: work began in 1847 and the barrage was completed in 1852. Once again, many mistakes were made. Despite being able to draw on the experience of the Upper Anicut on the Cauvery, the original weirs were too low, caused the current to scour

9. Sandes, *Military Engineer in India*, 21–22, quote at 22. On the effectiveness of the design of the original anicut, see Bijker's 'Dikes and Dams' (111–14).

10. Headrick, *Tentacles of Progress*, 180.

11. Hope, *General Sir Arthur Cotton*, 96; Sandes, *Military Engineer in India*, 23.

12. Hope, *General Sir Arthur Cotton*, 98.

the riverbed, and soon had to be raised. In addition, Cotton overestimated the area they were capable of irrigating, while grossly underestimating the total costs.[13]

Yet the accuracy or otherwise of engineering decisions was ultimately less important than the financial bottom line. The Godavari works still promised to be sufficiently remunerative for the Madras government to approve a similar project across the Krishna River at the head of its delta. In 1851, Cotton's lieutenant Charles Orr began the construction of a 1,200-yard (1,100-metre) barrage that was designed to hold up the powerful flow of the Krishna, which could – according to Orr's calculations – rise over thirty feet (10 metres) when in flood. Designing a barrage for such an immense seasonal rise represented an extremely cautious measure by European standards. Nonetheless, it soon proved inadequate. Halfway through the building work on the Krishna barrage, an exceptional flood of forty feet topped all of the river's embankments, covered the entire delta under several feet of water, forced inhabitants in many villages to seek refuge on the roofs of houses or in trees, and drowned large numbers of cattle. Chastened by the experience, Orr scaled up the project accordingly. After a series of design amendments to raise the barrage, it finally began operations in 1855.[14]

Ever since their completion, the hydraulic works on the Cauvery, Godavari and Krishna have been objects of acclaim. For the Madras government, their 'phenomenal contribution' to public revenues prompted officials to establish the first department of public works in British India in 1852, with irrigation its core concern.[15] For the farming communities of the deltas, the barrages were likewise venerated for bringing prosperity to previously stricken lands. In the Godavari delta in particular, Arthur Cotton achieved a kind of sacred status that endures to this day.[16] For merchants and traders, the newly built canals even managed to improve the prospects of navigation as well as irrigation, carrying over half a million tons of freight and over 1.8 million passengers per year by the early 1880s.[17] Despite the subsequent need to fix initial design mistakes, this trio of works entered the annals of colonial engineering as renowned triumphs.

Against this backdrop of (qualified) success, it is worth noting that other projects in the river deltas of Madras turned out quite differently and attracted more censure than celebration. The ill-fated anicut across the Penner River, located between the Cauvery and Krishna, demonstrated the enduring ability

---

13. Cotton, *Profits upon British Capital*, 1; Sandes, *Military Engineer in India*, 24; B. Rao, 'Taming "Liquid Gold"'.

14. Walch, *Engineering Works*, 65–66.

15. Whitcombe, 'Irrigation', 684.

16. Schmitthenner, 'Colonial Hydraulic Projects', 197–98; Amrith, *Unruly Waters*, 17–20.

17. Public Works Department, *Godavari, Kistna and Cauvery*, 20.

of India's monsoon to surprise European engineers who sought to tame it. Within a few months of the dam's completion in May 1856, a thirteen-foot (four-metre) flood breached the apron on one of its flanks. Although the damage was soon repaired, in November 1857 the barrage itself suffered a rupture when a severe cyclone struck the district, followed by another breach ten months later. The *coup de grâce* finally came in October 1858 when floodwaters rose some thirteen feet above the anicut's crest, carrying away two-thirds of the entire structure. With no more than a wrecked dam to show for its efforts, the Madras Public Works Department turned to the now-legendary Arthur Cotton, who recommended a stronger anicut based on the design of the Krishna barrage. Work on this anicut commenced in 1861 and finished a year later after going severely over budget. Even after the completion of this second structure, a number of further modifications were still required. In late 1862, the new barrage sustained minor damage from seasonal torrents, and in 1869 its central sluices had to be closed off to strengthen the structure. These alterations probably rescued the anicut from complete destruction during the floods of October 1870 – the highest in nearly two decades – which once again caused significant damage and necessitated various reinforcements. Finally, on 26 October 1874 came the highest flood ever recorded on the Penner. As the waters rose to twenty-six feet (8 metres) – a full eighteen feet (5.5 metres) above the crest of the dam, far beyond anything that Cotton had calculated for – they spilled across the land and gouged out a new river channel seventy-five yards (70 metres) wide just to the north of the anicut, rendering the structure largely obsolete.

If the renowned works on the Cauvery, Godavari and Krishna furnished engineers with important lessons, so too did the ill-fated enterprise on the Penner. At one level, the story of the Penner barrage was a classic example of engineering hubris and the failure to understand local hydrological conditions. At a more fundamental level, it was also an object lesson in false economizing. Ultimately, the litany of misfortunes suffered by the barrages on the Penner stemmed from the government's determination to minimize the construction costs. In order to keep the anicut as short and inexpensive as possible, the barrages were built at an abnormally narrow point of the river. At 527 yards (482 metres) long, the second, larger anicut measured less than half the mean width of the river (1,200 yards, or 1,100 metres). The purpose of this design choice was to save money, but in the end it was a costly decision. For one thing, the funnelling effect caused by the narrowing of the river led directly to the flooding problems that continually plagued the structures. Moreover, the selection of the site was too far down the river to command a large irrigation area, which precluded high returns on the investment. According to an 1883 report, 'the history of this work is a warning against the selection, in the absence of rock foundations, of sites for weirs which afford much less than the normal width of waterway of the river'. With the benefit of hindsight, public works officials concluded that it would have been technically and financially preferable to build a 1,000-yard anicut at an altogether different site. By that time, however, the sunk costs were too high to entertain such notions. In the end, officials had to content themselves with an improvised 147-yard (134-metre) extension of the existing barrage, and hope that it lasted longer than its predecessors did.[18]

It would be easy to assume that the early hydraulic projects in the Netherlands East Indies might have avoided many of the problems that plagued British waterworks in India. After all, the Dutch colonizers brought with them centuries of experience with floods, water channelling and drainage. Soon after regaining control of the East Indies from the British in 1815, one of the first acts of the Dutch colonial government in Batavia was to establish a civil engineering corps to make improvements to rivers, harbours, canals, weirs, bridges and the like. After 1842, many of these engineers received a formal education at the Royal Academy based in Delft, which effectively served as a training ground for officials bound for the East Indies. Yet Dutch hydraulic knowledge, extensive though it was, had little to do with irrigation, and nothing whatsoever to do with monsoon settings. Dutch engineers were keenly aware of the very different hydraulic and topographical conditions of Java, and some visited mountainous areas of Switzerland, Germany and Austria to learn more about how their watercourses worked. Such study tours were no doubt enlightening, but there was no way to prepare themselves entirely for the distinctive challenges of Java's hydrology: the extreme fluctuations of river flow, the enormous silt loads they carried, the steep terrain and proneness to flash flooding. Here, too, the attempt to tame the monsoon was a slow and sometimes painful learning process.[19]

The Dutch colonial government became increasingly immersed in Java's hydrology after the introduction of the so-called Cultivation System (*cultuurstelsel*), the very epitome of a colonial extraction regime. In order to raise much-needed funds for the metropolitan government, in 1830 Governor General Johannes van den Bosch forced Javanese farmers to plant a fifth of their fields with a variety of export crops, which were to be handed over to the state. The main focus was on sugar and to a lesser extent indigo; other crops such as coffee and pepper followed later. Up until the abolition of the Cultivation System in the early 1870s, this coercive planting regime made Java one of the most lucrative colonies in world. At its peak during 1840–60 it generated around 20 million guilders per year, around a third of the Netherlands' entire state revenue.[20]

18. Public Works Department, *Godavari, Kistna and Cauvery*, 200–201.

19. Ravesteijn, *De zegenrijke heeren*, 306–9; Ertsen, *Locales of Happiness*, 16; 'Waterstaat', 707–10; de Vos, 'De strijd', 277–78.

20. Fasseur, *Politics of Colonial Exploitation*, 149–50.

Producing all of this wealth required a major reorganization of existing social and environmental arrangements. Above all, it demanded the careful regulation of water, principally for the cultivation and processing of sugar. The sugar cane itself needed a steady, controlled water supply, especially during its first six months of growth. In addition, water power drove the scores of mills where the harvested cane was crushed and processed. All villages within roughly four to seven kilometres of a sugar factory – which accounted for much of the land in east Java and along the north central coast – were obliged to plant sugar cane under the supervision of local regents and village headmen.[21]

The first Dutch irrigation works in the East Indies, a weir across the Sampean River in east Java, was built primarily to encourage the cultivation of cane in the area. Its history demonstrates not only how little experience Dutch engineers had with the hydrological conditions of Java but also how long the process of trial and error lasted.

For generations, local people along the Sampean River had sought to control its unruly waters by building barrages of wood and earth. Few of these structures lasted very long; most were severely damaged or entirely washed away by the first big flood (*banjir*) of the rainy season. Dutch officials were dissatisfied with such 'temporary' works and were convinced that they could do better. In 1832, the engineer C. van Thiel was dispatched to the Sampean delta to construct a modern weir across the river. Like most of the early works constructed by colonial authorities, Van Thiel's new overflow dam was built with the same basic materials and the same forms of coercive labour that Javanese rulers had long deployed. As was also typically the case in the first half of the nineteenth century, it was built on the same site as an older Javanese dam in order to make use of the existing canal network. What set the modern weir apart from its predecessor was its larger size (forty-five metres long and eight metres high) and its reinforced teakwood frame, which engineers thought was designed to last.[22]

In the event, Van Thiel's creation was only marginally more 'permanent' than the indigenous-built barrage it replaced. Though sturdier than earlier structures, it needed so much maintenance and renovation after every rainy season that it soon exhausted local teak supplies. Furthermore, it suffered from basic design flaws that caused the formation of a deep hole in the riverbed just below the overflow. In the end, it lasted only until 1857, when it was finally breached by a flash flood that gouged a deep channel down the middle of the river as it burst through.

For over a decade after the demise of Van Thiel's dam, Dutch engineers essentially abandoned their ambitions to modernize the waterworks on the

21. Bosma, *Sugar Plantation*, 88–129; Fasseur, *Politics of Colonial Exploitation*, 149–50.

22. Ravesteijn, *De zegenrijke heeren*, 53–76; 'Waterstaat', 710.

Sampean, opting instead to revert to indigenous practice by building a series of temporary barrages that closely resembled the previous Javanese structures across the river. The problem was that each had to be larger and longer than the last one in order compensate for the constant undermining of the river's banks by the water they held up. As successive iterations of the barrage were washed away, the river continued to widen. Finally, in 1875 engineers attempted to solve the problem once and for all by building a new masonry weir a full kilometre in length (over twenty times longer than the original weir built by Van Thiel). But as it turned out, even this structure was incapable of taming the Sampean's seasonal flash floods. When floodwaters began to form another large hole in the riverbed, engineers resorted to digging flash-flood canals around the entire dam complex, but even these channels proved inadequate as the seasonal torrents increased in severity (likely caused or at least exacerbated by deforestation and agricultural expansion in the watershed above).[23]

Altogether, the history of the Sampean works was a classic case of a 'nature-technology spiral', a process in which one technological intervention generated effects that necessitated a series of further interventions.[24] At the root of the problem was a lack of understanding of the Sampean River itself. According to one Dutch contemporary, the difficulties stemmed from a habit of 'precipitate working, without preceding study of water levels and discharges', which invariably led to a 'gross underestimation of flash flooding capabilities'.[25] This remained the case even after the massive masonry barrage was built in 1875. When engineers dug the first flash-flood canals around the dam, they assumed a maximum flow rate of 1,000 m³/second. Work on these canals had scarcely finished when, in 1878, heavy rains caused the river to swell to 1,788 m³/second, followed in 1887 by a peak flow of 2,075 m³/second. On both occasions, the flood canals suffered serious damage, though it was only after the 1887 floods that a supposedly more 'permanent' system of sluices, weirs and bypasses was finally built. As it turned out, even these works were overwhelmed in 1916 when the Sampean's floodwaters reached a record 2,700 m³/second.[26]

In view of this catalogue of errors, it is scarcely surprising that observers derided the Sampean barrage as the 'works without a plan'. But the experience at Sampean was by no means unique in this respect.[27] Throughout the nineteenth century, maps of most areas of Java were poorly researched, and

23. Ravesteijn, *De zegenrijke heeren*, 74–75.

24. Ravesteijn, 74.

25. C. W. Weijs, *Schets van de ontwikkeling van technische bemoeienis met irrigatie in Indië* (Delft: Waltman, 1913), 8, quoted in Ertsen, *Locales of Happiness*, 16.

26. Ravesteijn, *De zegenrijke heeren*, 74–76, 98–99; Ertsen, *Locales of Happiness*, 16.

27. H. H. van Kol, 'Een allgemeen irrigatie-plan voor Java', *De ingenieur* vol. 16 (1901), 343, quoted in Ravesteijn, *De zegenrijke heeren*, 101.

data on river flows and watersheds were sketchy. As a result, trial and error remained the chief modus operandi until the end of the 1800s. Sometimes engineers got lucky. A few projects like the irrigation works in the Brantas delta or at Bagelen in central Java proved to be more or less successful in spite of the guesswork they involved. Others schemes were less fortunate. For instance, in 1849 a new framework dam at the bottom of the Menenteng gorge in western Java was wrecked by a flash flood just before its completion. For the next three decades local administrators had to settle for a Javanese-style dam above the gorge, which had to be rebuilt every year. Similar problems plagued the new weir at Glapan on the Tuntang River. Soon after its completion in 1859 its overflow surface was so badly damaged that engineers considered giving up on the structure and building another one in a different place altogether.

Such experiences help explain why the vast bulk of Java's nineteenth-century waterworks were not 'modern' structures at all, but were still built in the traditional fashion by Javanese farmers using locally available labour and material. As one engineer later noted, the early years of 'technical' hydraulic works were marked by 'so much adversity that it was difficult to have confidence in engineers in this field, and many thought that it would be better to let the native go his own way'.[28]

But there was by no means consensus on this issue. In fact, many officials at the time drew the opposite conclusion: what the situation required was more modern engineering, not less. J. J. Rochussen, governor-general of the East Indies from 1845 to 1851, firmly believed that 'no major irrigation works should be constructed which have not been surveyed and designed by experts'.[29] The hydraulic engineers in the colony naturally agreed, and sought to use such sentiments to their advantage. They increasingly resented the 'quiet power' of the East Indies Civil Service (Binnenlands Bestuur), which effectively governed all infrastructural works in the colony and showed little desire to relinquish control over the all-important state purse strings.[30] H. de Bruyn, who twice directed the Public Works Department in the 1860s and 1870s, was scathing about the hydraulic amateurism of Binnenlands Bestuur civil servants and indigenous farmers alike. 'Coming as they did from their low, flat and marshy country', most of the Dutch bureaucrats in the Indies were, he said, 'amazed to see how the Javanese provided their rice fields every year with water that came down from the mountains. Every defective weir, every defective lock, every small dyke along the rice fields seemed to them a masterpiece of hydraulic

28. C. W. Weijs, *Schets van de ontwikkeling*, 8, quoted in Ravesteijn, *De zegenrijke heeren*, 103, and see also 83, 93, 100–102; 'Waterstaat', 714–15.

29. J. J. Rochussen, *Toelichting en verdediging van eenige daden van mijn bestuur in Indie* ('s-Gravenhage [The Hague]: Van Cleef, 1853), 210, quoted in Ravesteijn, 'Controlling Water, Controlling People', 95.

30. Van den Doel, *De stille macht*.

engineering'. The Javanese themselves, despite their presumed aptitude for water control, had 'not the faintest idea' of engineering principles and were capable of building only 'extremely primitive' structures. Their weirs 'cannot withstand a sudden surge of water or overflow due to the lack of protection against scouring. Every rainy season most of these works are swept away by the force of the current, only to be built again with the same lack of know-how'.[31]

De Bruyn's critique was soon echoed by other public works engineers such as C.L.F. Post, whose 1879 book *On Water Management in the Netherlands Indies* (*Over den waterstaat in Nederlandsch-Indië*) amounted to an extended denunciation of civil servants' role in the realm of irrigation. Not only did their hydraulic 'dabbling' lead to a 'useless waste' of time and effort, but their admiration of Javanese water management techniques was also profoundly misplaced: 'the way in which the Javanese – as well as the administrative officials imitating their masters – build dykes can be seen as an answer to the question of how a dyke should *not* be built'.[32] The problem with this argument was, of course, that engineers had been guilty of a fair amount of 'amateurism' themselves. As one civil servant put it in response to Post's book: 'just go to Panaroekan [in the Sampean delta] to see what sums of money technicians have literally thrown into the Sampean River for no practical purpose whatsoever'.[33]

These skirmishes between East Indies engineers and civil servants reflected more than just the dynamics of a bureaucratic power struggle. They were also rooted in current ideas about knowledge, technology and the wider colonial mission itself. Even among those who admired the ingenuity of 'traditional' irrigation methods on Java, few if any doubted the inherent superiority of 'modern' Western technology. The notion that non-European societies were letting their resources run to 'waste' through an inability to harness them effectively was a near-universal assumption among colonial administrators and technicians alike. Equally widespread was the belief in the right, even duty, of Europeans to rectify these shortcomings through enlightened government. By the late nineteenth century, the task of the modern colonial power was not merely to govern such 'backward' areas, but to 'develop' them proactively through the application of science and technology.[34] As we will see below, it was not until the 1890s that Dutch hydraulic engineers were finally given the chance pursue this task at scale. When the opportunity came, their grand designs did not work out entirely as planned.

---

31. Quotes from Ravesteijn, *De zegenrijke heeren*, 90–91; see also 'Waterstaat', 722–23.

32. Quoted in Ravesteijn, *De zegenrijke heeren*, 96.

33. H. van Gijn, *De verwaandheid van de technici contra de kommiezerij*, quoted in Ravesteijn, 106.

34. Bloembergen and Raben, *Het koloniale beschavingsoffensief*; Adas, *Machines as the Measure*; Hodge, *Triumph of the Expert*.

While colonial engineers remoulded the rivers of Java and coastal Madras, their counterparts in northern India were equally eager to harness the great flows of water that streamed across the Gangetic plain. Although the soils, topography and climate of northern India were quite distinctive from these other regions, the overall waterscape presented many of the same opportunities and challenges for hydraulic engineers. Just as in Madras and Java, initial efforts to replumb the waterscape of northern India involved the restoration or replacement of existing hydraulic works. Here, too, the experience acquired from these renovations was later deployed for new and more ambitious endeavours. Despite numerous mishaps and miscalculations, by the 1850s colonial irrigation projects had gone a long way towards transforming the sacred river into the 'Ganges water machine' of today.[35]

The earliest British hydraulic interventions in the Gangetic plain focused on a pair of ancient canals that ran for several hundred kilometres along either side of the Jumna (now Yamuna) River above Delhi. The first to be restored was the Western Jumna Canal. Initially built in the fourteenth century, it was repeatedly extended under the Mughals to provide water for Delhi and to irrigate the fields along its banks. Like its Eastern sibling, the Western Jumna Canal drew its water from headworks that diverted a portion of the Yamuna's flow just above the point where the river enters the Gangetic plain. By the 1750s, much of the canal had silted up or collapsed, but when the British arrived in Delhi in 1803 lengthy stretches were still salvageable. Work began on the canal in 1817, and by 1820 British engineers had restored the 185-mile (300-kilometre) channel that supplied water to the city. Over the following years, a team of young military officers extended the irrigation network and rebuilt the parallel canal running just east of the river. Although both of the main Jumna canals were based on Mughal precedents, the restorations more than doubled their original length and more than tripled their overall capacity.[36]

These waterworks along the Jumna were an important testing ground for British engineers, for it quickly became clear just how much they needed to learn. None of the officers who constructed the canals had any prior training or experience in irrigation, so they unsurprisingly made serious errors. On the Western canal, some stretches were given too steep a slope, which caused the formation of rapids that scoured the bed and threatened to destroy bridge supports and embankments. Discrepancies in flow rates along the canal meant that water distribution was uneven, providing some areas with too little water and some too much. Whereas the former areas suffered from parched fields, in the latter areas extensive waterlogging smothered crop roots and created

35. Revelle and Lakshminarayana, 'Ganges Water Machine'; Acciavatti, *Ganges Water Machine*.

36. Whitcombe, 'Environmental Costs of Irrigation', 242–43.

malarial swamps wherever the natural drainage of the land was blocked. Such problems were even worse along the Eastern canal, where engineers had to realign entire stretches and build a series of masonry falls to reduce its slope and velocity. On top of all these technical difficulties, engineers also became mired in local disputes between landlords and farmers over land tenure, water rights and distribution privileges.[37]

All in all the Jumna canals meted out harsh lessons, significantly more so than the works in the Madras deltas. Yet in the process, they taught a small cadre of British officials the fundamentals of hydraulic engineering. One of them, a young Bengal Artillery officer named Proby Cautley, soon applied this knowledge on a whole new scale.

Like many of the East India Company's officers, Cautley had little formal education. After training as a cadet for less than a year, he arrived in India in 1819 as an artilleryman. In 1825, he was reassigned to assist with the reconstruction of the Eastern Jumna Canal, and over the following years he learned the art of hydraulic engineering largely by practising it. In 1831, he was put in charge of the canal, and five years later he was asked by Superintendent Colonel John Colvin to determine whether it would be possible to irrigate the long, drought-prone *doab* (interfluvial land) that stretched between the Jumna and the Ganges. It was clear from the outset that this would be a gargantuan task, larger than any irrigation project ever attempted. Initial surveys concluded that it would be too costly and difficult to build. But outlooks changed in 1837–38 when the summer rains almost entirely failed across the central and lower *doab*, unleashing a severe famine that claimed the lives of around eight hundred thousand people (and cost the East India Company over a million pounds sterling in lost revenue and relief work). In 1841, the project was provisionally approved. After several years of exhaustive investigation – including a visit by Cautley to northern Italy to study what were then regarded as the most advanced waterworks in the world – the project started in earnest in 1848.[38]

This seven-year delay between the approval and commencement of the Ganges Canal is noteworthy in itself, for it highlights the tensions between rival claims on waterways: in this case the trade-offs between irrigation and navigation. Cautley originally designed the canal primarily as an irrigation duct that could also be navigated, at least for part of the year. Soon after design work commenced in 1843, Governor-General Lord Ellenborough abruptly decided that it should instead serve chiefly as a navigation channel, and that all water not required for this purpose could be used for irrigation. The problem was that this involved a complete redesign of the entire project, for the requirements

37. Sandes, *Military Engineer in India*, 4–5; Whitcombe, 'Irrigation', 687–89.
38. Cautley, *Ganges Canal Works*, 17–19; MacGeorge, *Ways and Works*, 147–48; S. Sharma, '1837–38 Famine in U.P.'; Amrith, *Unruly Waters*, 44.

of navigation and irrigation were not the same; indeed, they were often diametrically opposed to each other.

Whereas irrigation canals are designed with a significant slope to allow
large quantities of water and silt to flow through, navigation channels have
a low water intake and ideally no slope. In addition, irrigation canals run
through agricultural areas; navigation canals tend to connect trading towns.
Even where waterworks can accommodate both uses, canal operators frequently have to choose one purpose over the other at any given time. During
rainy periods, an irrigation canal often has to maintain a low water level to
minimize the problem of waterlogging. By contrast, a navigation canal should
always be full to allow heavily laden boats to pass. The same countervailing
tensions are present during dry periods, when irrigation canals often have
to let out as much water as possible to water crops, thus reducing canal levels especially at their lower reaches. In the case of the Ganges Canal, those
who prioritized navigation often pointed out that the great waterworks in the
Madras deltas managed to combine irrigation and navigation, but this was
of little relevance since physical conditions and agricultural practices there
were very different. Whereas the demand for irrigation water in the deltas fell
principally during the monsoon when water was abundant, thus allowing the
maintenance of navigable water levels in the canals more or less year-round,
in the *doab* the demand for water was highest during the dry season when
river and canal levels were already low. It took some time for these trade-offs
to be fully appreciated, and in the end the navigation scheme was dropped.[39]

Even without the complications of combining irrigation and navigation, the
technical challenges of the Ganges Canal were immense. No one had yet tried
to channel such enormous volumes of water over such vast distances. The canal
was in effect an artificial river. It began just below the sacred town of Haridwar,
where the Ganges exits the Himalayan foothills. To give a sense of scale, the headworks at Haridwar were designed to divert 191 m^3/second, which was more than
twice the flow of the two Jumna canals combined, around 80 per cent more than
the nominal discharge of the Cavour Canal in Italy (which was yet to be actually
built), and roughly equivalent to the entire Ganges flow at low ebb. From there
a single channel ran southwards for 180 miles (290 kilometres) before splitting
into two parallel canals, each 170 miles long, one running to Cawnpore on
the Ganges and the other to Hamirpur on the Jumna.[40] The first 20 miles
(30 kilometres) were by far the most difficult, for along this initial stretch
the canal ran perpendicular to the natural drainage slope of the country.
Moreover, before the canal could reach the Gangetic plain, it had to cross (at
right angles) a series of natural ravines and mountain streams that annually

39. Cautley *Ganges Canal Works*, 33–35; Sandes, *Military Engineer in India*, 7–8.

40. Figures from Cautley, *Ganges Canal Works*, 93, 197, 236; MacGeorge, *Ways and
Works*, 149; Deakin, *Irrigated India*, 182.

FIGURE 2.1. The Solani Aqueduct on the Ganges Canal, Roorkee, c.1866.
By permission of akg-images/British Library, photo 42(193).

swelled into torrents during the summer rains. The infrastructure required to
achieve this was immense. Two of the natural watercourses that intersected
with the canal were eventually carried above it on broad aqueducts; one was
allowed to pass its waters perpendicularly through the channel via an inlet
and escape dam. The most celebrated piece of engineering along the canal was
the massive aqueduct over the Solani River. At 338 metres long and 50 wide,
and flanked by nearly five kilometres of embankments, the Solani Aqueduct
dwarfed any of the hydraulic structures that had hitherto been built in Italy.
For decades after its completion, civil engineers regarded it as the 'most inter-
esting and remarkable modern structure' in India, 'the greatest indeed of its
kind in the world'.[41] Only after passing over the Solani River could the canal
finally flow unhindered down the gently sloping plain, gradually diminishing
in size as its waters were diverted into side branches.

It was a startlingly novel undertaking. No hydraulic project had ever
been attempted on anything like so large a scale or had to contend with so
many topographical obstacles. Yet like most of the waterworks in nineteenth-
century India, the Ganges Canal was nonetheless a mixture of the old and
the new. The techniques used to build it differed little from those of bygone
eras. The canal itself was excavated mainly by hand. Tens of thousands of
labourers toiled on its embankments and cuttings, most of them recruited
from surrounding areas by local contractors. Thousands more moulded and

41. MacGeorge, *Ways and Works*, 156; more generally, R. Smith, *Short Account* , 9,
33–34.

fired the millions of bricks for the masonry structures or cut the wood that fuelled the kilns. Unlike the British engineers who are remembered for having 'built' the canal, little is known about these people who did the physical work. Much of what we know comes from reports about a series of strikes in 1848–49 when brickmakers working on the upper stretches of the canal downed tools and destroyed equipment in protest over attempts to cut their wages.[42]

When the Ganges Canal began operation in April 1854, it was the largest project of its kind in the world, measuring over 650 miles (1,100 kilometres) in length. Yet at this stage it still was not entirely 'complete'. Once again, engineers found themselves forced to improvise. For all the technical prowess on display, it was several years before they could operate the canal at full capacity, and once they did they still encountered a series of problems. Soon after the canal opened, it became clear that its slope was too steep, causing the water to scour its bed and banks. The fundamentals of hydroengineering that Cautley and his officers had learned on the Jumna, and the design formulas that they applied from more recently built canals in Europe, proved a poor guide for constructing such an enormous waterway. In 1863, none other than Sir Arthur Cotton was called in to inspect the works and make recommendations. His report was so critical of the design as to propose the construction of an entirely new headwork for a new canal further downriver (a proposal that eventually led to the construction of the Lower Ganges Canal, completed in 1880, in addition to the original project). Only after costly corrective works had been carried out in the 1860s and 1870s was the flow sufficiently decelerated to avoid scouring of the canal bed.[43]

For the time being, however, none of these problems detracted from the grand inauguration ceremony of the Ganges Canal on 8 April 1954 at Roorkee, the site of the new College of Civil Engineering, the first of its kind in the British Empire. Although some officials feared that the prior release of water from the headworks at Haridwar might elicit a violent reaction from devout priests or pilgrims, who regarded the diversion of the sacred river as a profanity, in the event there were no serious incidents. The ceremony had been heavily publicized beforehand, and in the days leading up to it thousands of officials, dignitaries, army troops, workmen and ordinary civilians flooded into Roorkee, eventually forming a crowd estimated at around half a million people. As one American correspondent excitedly wrote, 'in no other land is a great throng of people so picturesque as in India, and even India herself has seen few more striking assemblies than this; for in it are gathered the representatives of a hundred tribes, distinguished as well by differences of form and feature, as by the gay and motley varieties of dress'. The canal, he went on to claim, marked the beginning of 'a new era . . . for India, – an

42. Lucassen, 'Brickmakers' Strikes'.
43. Sandes, *Military Engineer in India*, 10–11; Headrick, *Tentacles of Progress*, 179.

era of intelligent and liberal government, – of government which regards and cherishes the interests of the governed, and finds its own interests correlative with theirs'.[44] Certainly this was how British officials liked to present it. In his speech, Lieutenant-Governor John Russell Colvin proclaimed that 'here at least we have an answer, which no detractor can gainsay, to the old reproach, that the British have left no permanent mark upon the soil of India to attest the power, the wealth, and the munificence of their nation'.[45] According to the official brochure published to mark the occasion, 'the great leading motive . . . by which the British Government was led to sanction the Ganges Canal . . . was to secure to its people, in the country between the rivers Ganges and Jumna, an immunity from the pains and losses that famine brings with it'.[46]

But this was only half of the story. For all the emphasis on humanitarian impulses, there was no hiding the fiscal deliberations that also underpinned large-scale hydraulic works like the Ganges Canal. So long as these two factors could be made to align, water projects tended to be approved. Where they could not it was a different matter, even in places where the humanitarian need for water was acute. As the inauguration brochure itself conceded, the government was 'bound to consider how its own resources would be affected; for on these depends its power of continuing in the same course of progress, and of finding in one such work encouragement to proceed onward to the execution of others'.[47] For colonial states, the poetry of improving nature was seldom as compelling as the prose of monetary considerations.

Water, Welfare and the Costs of Irrigation

All throughout colonial Asia, hydraulic policy was shaped by two different imperatives: financial profitability and sociopolitical stability. Behind every investment decision lay the desire to extract wealth, but in order to sustain this arrangement it was necessary to prevent social unrest and maintain a basic level of public order. The vicissitudes of the monsoon challenged both of these aims. Whenever rains failed and crops died, governments fretted not only about the loss of life but also about the loss of revenue and the more general prospect of riots, crime and turmoil. Just as the provision of water helped underpin European power in Asia, the lack of water threatened to undermine it.

The famine that ravaged northern India in 1837–38 – and which helped pave the way for the Ganges Canal – was merely one of around a dozen famines to strike colonial Asia in the nineteenth century. In the context of recurring drought and food shortage, the expansion of irrigation seemed like an

44. 'Short Account of the Ganges Canal', 537, 540–41.
45. MacGeorge, *Ways and Works*, 158.
46. R. Smith, *Short Account*, 3.
47. R. Smith, 3.

obvious means to unite the fiscal needs of the state and the economic needs of the people.

As scholars have repeatedly shown, the prospect of finding a technical fix for various social, political and economic problems is something that most modern governments have found well-nigh irresistible.[48] Europe's colonial administrations were no exception, and nor was the attractiveness of irrigation. But like most would-be technical panaceas, the actual creation of irrigation projects raised a host of tricky issues. For starters, there was a balance to be struck between what came to be known as 'productive' versus 'protective' works – that is, those geared mainly towards revenue generation and those designed primarily as a safeguard against famine. There were also choices to be made about the appropriate scale of hydraulic schemes, about the distribution of limited resources between different regions, and about the relative benefits of investment in new or existing works. Insofar as irrigation was intended to advance the cause of 'native development', there were likewise questions about what this term actually meant. Moreover, irrigation systems had their own social and ecological impacts that needed to be addressed. In short, the effort to combine the interests of rulers and ruled by improving the control of water involved a multitude of difficult decisions. The rigidly hierarchical nature of colonial rule ensured that almost none of the people directly affected had much say in them.

In 1847, the governor-general of the Netherlands Indies J. J. Rochussen wrote to the Dutch minister of colonies to highlight what he saw as the fundamental importance of hydraulic works on Java:

> Artificial irrigation is the basis of the fertility of the Indies soil, without which rice cultivation can be neither *guaranteed* [verzekerd] nor expanded. I emphasize here the term *guaranteed* because the reliance on a regular change of the seasons, upon which rice cultivation originally depended, seems to be increasingly questionable because the rain no longer falls so regularly and in central Java is no longer as abundant as it used to be. (Naturalists attribute this to the disappearance of the forests, which have gradually had to make way for the cultivation of different crops and to provide construction material and fuel for our fortifications, our civil buildings, for sugar and indigo factories, tobacco sheds and many other agricultural and industrial needs). We can therefore no longer leave rice cultivation dependent on the rains, but should instead ensure it on the above-mentioned solid foundation of *artificial irrigation.*[49]

48. See esp. Scott, *Seeing like a State.*
49. Quoted in Ravesteijn, *De zegenrijke heeren,* 87; 'Waterstaat', 714.

Rochussen's remarks reflected a mixture of long-term and short-term concerns. His fears about the slow, creeping effects of land clearance on Java's climate echoed the prevailing 'desiccationist' discourse of the era, which posited a direct link between large-scale forest loss and a decline in precipitation. As was also the case in India, by the 1840s such ideas formed the scientific rationale for an increasingly coordinated campaign to conserve Java's forests.[50] At the same time, his comments were also linked to more immediate anxieties about food and water shortages. From 1844 to 1847 a series of crop failures drove rice prices – which were already alarmingly high owing to the use of so much *sawah* land for sugar and indigo cultivation – to critical levels across much of the island. Prices were especially high in Surabaya, the centre of sugar cultivation, but the most severe food shortages emerged in the Cirebon residency, the rice bowl of West Java, which suffered an acute spell of famine and depopulation in 1844. Worse was soon to come. From 1848 to 1850 successive droughts in the Semarang residency triggered a widespread famine across central Java. Worst affected were the Demak and Grobogan Regencies, where more than a hundred thousand people died of starvation and around twice that many fled to other areas to escape the same fate.[51]

None of these disasters was entirely due to 'natural' causes. Like most food crises in colonial Asia, they resulted as much from a failure of policy as a failure of the rains. In Cirebon, the food situation was already adversely affected by the commercialization of the rice market, which disrupted existing credit and sales arrangements. In Semarang, high levels of forced labour and taxation had rendered an increasingly landless and cash-strapped peasantry extremely vulnerable to poor harvests.[52]

In the aftermath of the 1848–50 famine, Governor-General Rochussen introduced a raft of measures to reduce the burden on Javanese farmers, including new limits on the enforced planting of cash crops (especially indigo, whose cultivation was particularly arduous).[53] Over the following years, he and his successors also set about improving the island's hydraulic infrastructure, above all in the districts recently ravaged by drought-induced famine. In Demak they drew on a previously rejected proposal for a new weir and drainage system drawn up by C. van Thiel, the engineer who had been in charge of the ill-fated Sampean works. In 1852, Van Thiel's plan was dusted off and put into effect at Glapan on the Tuntang River, though the resulting weir was nearly abandoned after suffering severe damage in 1859, and it ultimately did little to improve

50. Grove, *Green Imperialism*; Peluso, *Rich Forests, Poor People*.

51. On Cirebon: M. Fernando, *Famine in Cirebon Residency*. On Semarang: Ravesteijn, 'Irrigatie en koloniale staat'; Elson, 'Famine in Demak'.

52. Bosma, 'Integration of Food Markets'; Fernando, *Famine in Cirebon Residency*. On Semarang: Ravesteijn, 'Irrigatie en koloniale staat'; Elson, 'Famine in Demak'.

53. Bosma, *Sugar Plantation*, 106.

FIGURE 2.2. Ploughing rice fields in the repeatedly famine-struck Demak Regency, Java, c.1910.
By permission of the Nationaal Museum van Wereldculturen, coll. no. TM-33005495.

local welfare even after it was salvaged.[54] Somewhat more successful were the concurrent efforts in the east of the island, where the engineer H. de Bruyn oversaw the construction of a moveable weir and canal system on the Surabaya River in a bid to improve water provision for sugar mills and alleviate the risk of food shortages. Capable of irrigating twenty-eight thousand hectares, it was the largest set of waterworks in the East Indies when it was completed in 1857.[55] To provide expertise for such projects, the government also established a new Bureau for Public Works in 1854 staffed by Delft-trained engineers, whose job was to carry out improvements on the colony's growing portfolio of irrigation works.[56]

The mid-century famines on Java not only prompted a series of hydraulic interventions; they also sparked a broader debate about the Cultivation System and its harmful effects on food security. News about the crises was quick to make it into metropolitan newspapers, and in the 1850s the famines took

54. Ravesteijn, *De zegenrijke heeren*, 83; 'Irrigatie en koloniale staat'; 'Waterstaat', 714–15.

55. Ravesteijn, *De zegenrijke heeren*, 88.

56. Ravesteijn, 'Controlling Water, Controlling People', 96; Ersten, *Locales of Happiness*, 17.

centre stage in the growing chorus of attacks by reformers in the Netherlands on the forced planting regime. Following the Dutch constitutional reforms of 1848 (which limited the powers of the Crown in favour of an elected parliament), it was inevitable that the Cultivation System would be significantly modified, but the famines undoubtedly added to the momentum. In effect, the compulsory cultivation of crops no longer expanded after 1850, and over the following decades the various elements of the regime were dismantled piece by piece. Although the Cultivation System was officially abolished in 1870, it was not until 1915 that the last remnant – the compulsory cultivation of coffee – finally disappeared.[57]

Yet despite the dismantling of the Cultivation System, one important holdover remained intact: food crops and commercial crops continued to be grown in the same fields. Even though commercial growers now had to pay Javanese farmers for the use of their land, the colony was still expected to make a profit. Irrigation was viewed as an ideal tool for boosting the production of export crops and subsistence crops alike, and irrigation systems on Java were almost invariably designed to serve both purposes within the same area. What made this possible was the fact that the main food and commercial crops – rice and sugar – did not directly compete for water. Wet rice and sugar cane both needed irrigation, but at different times of the year: rice mainly during the west monsoon from October to March/April, and cane mainly during the east monsoon from May to September. The main problem was that farmers' *polowidjo*, or dry-season crops (beans, ground nuts, root crops), required water at the same time as sugar cane, but irrigation technicians tried to resolve this by delivering water from the same canals to different fields at different times of day: sugar during the day, *polowidjo* at night. Most canal systems in the East Indies were specially designed for this rhythm. It was an unusual feature that reflected not only the specific environmental circumstances on Java but also the particular socio-economic priorities of the Dutch colonial government.[58]

As Clifford Geertz argued in his famous work *Agricultural Involution*, the social and economic history of colonial Java was fundamentally shaped by this 'mutualistic' relationship between rice and sugar.[59] Because sugar cane did not lend itself to long-term monoculture on the same land, it had to be grown in rotation with other crops, mainly rice. Initially this meant that cane tended to undermine food production by displacing rice on existing fields. Over time, however, the expansion of irrigation for the sugar industry increased both the acreage and productivity of *sawah* plots as well, enabling Javanese farmers to boost their rice yields through increasingly labour-intensive cultivation methods. In many ways irrigation thus seemed like the best way to develop the

57. See, generally, Fasseur, *Politics of Colonial Exploitation*.
58. For a detailed description: Ertsen, *Locales of Happiness*, 34–35.
59. Geertz, *Agricultural Involution*, 55–57.

colonial economy while at the same time enhancing the welfare of indigenous subjects. In the words of I. D. Fransen van de Putte, a former sugar planter who served two terms as Dutch minister of colonies: 'Not only for the income but to meet the economic needs of the people, there is, according to all experts and all journal articles only one means: improvement of irrigation.'[60]

Nonetheless, there were limits to how far the control of water could effectively straddle the needs of export and subsistence economies. For one thing, the diurnal division of water supplies between rice and sugar fields was often neater in theory than in practice. In order to take full advantage of the west monsoon rains, rice had to be planted as soon as cane-growing lands became available at the end of the dry season. If, however, cane was harvested late – owing to the timing of the rains, labour shortages or other factors – it compromised rice production. Another problem was that the sugar industry required water not just when the cane was growing but also to drive the processing mills where it was crushed. Despite the common practice of alternating day- and night-time supplies to different fields, there were still tensions during those parts of the year when both sugar plantations and village *polowidjo* crops required water.[61]

All of these issues generated frequent disputes over the distribution of water. Although farmers and planters had a shared interest in the expansion of the water supply, they nonetheless competed for its use. With the abolition of the Cultivation System, the government attempted to strike a balance between these different interests. In 1870, it took steps to decrease water use by sugar mills, and a year later it sought to limit the cropping dates of sugar cane by ordering that all irrigation water should be devoted to rice after 15 October (the beginning of the rainy season). In 1872, it created a special commission to ensure that water distribution between the two sectors was as equitable as possible. The commission's report, which clearly reflected the administration's overriding concern with the 'bottom line', criticized the current arrangements as woefully inefficient, and concluded that the aim of water management should be to maximize its economic value. Given the profitability of sugar, its cultivation represented a highly 'economic' use of water. Rice production was far less 'economic' in this sense, though concerns about food security meant that it inevitably remained a core aim as well.[62]

The key question of how far irrigation policy should prioritize the production of food or export crops was therefore left unanswered. It remained unanswered even after the state undertook a major expansion of irrigation in the 1890s. In 1885, much to the delight of the engineers in the colony, a new public

60. Quoted in Moon, *Technology and Ethical Idealism*, 25–26.

61. Furnivall, *Netherlands India*, 317–18, 323; Ertsen, *Locales of Happiness*, 35–36, 59–60.

62. Ertsen, *Locales of Happiness*, 36–37.

works regulation radically upgraded the role of technical experts in relation to civil service officials and paved the way for a more 'modern' approach to irrigation. At the same time, it explicitly stipulated that the improvement of existing works (many of them small and geared to rice cultivation) was to be favoured over the construction of new projects. Engineers conveniently ignored this latter provision when they drew up their plans for a massive rearrangement of Javanese waters, favouring instead the construction of large, centrally managed systems. In 1890 they managed to convinced the government to launch an ambitious new 'General Irrigation Plan', which encompassed nineteen different projects covering over four hundred thousand hectares of land. Yet, even then, proposals for new schemes almost invariably had to justify themselves on the basis of improving food production in order to gain formal approval.[63]

The issue came to a head around the turn of the century as a series of events prompted a more thorough reconsideration of large-scale irrigation schemes as a vehicle for 'native development'. The failure of the enormous Solo Valley project in central Java was a watershed moment of sorts. The Solo is Java's longest river, and the attempt to control its waters constituted by far the biggest hydraulic scheme ever planned in the East Indies. Like most large projects, it was designed to serve multiple purposes: flood control, the provision of perennial irrigation for one of the island's poorest regions and the prevention of silt blockages in the navigation channels of the Surabaya Straits. The main canal was to be 165 kilometres long with 900 kilometres of secondary canals, and would be capable of supplying water to a vast irrigation network covering around 160,000 hectares. The Solo scheme was the showpiece of the General Irrigation Plan, dwarfing all the other projects and consuming nearly half of its entire budget. Launched with great fanfare in 1893, it quickly ran into difficulty.[64]

Criticism of the project arose on a number of levels. One objection was that there was little evidence that it would increase agricultural yields. Indeed, many officials were concerned that it might actually diminish the fertility of the land by inhibiting the deposition of rich volcanic silt from Java's uplands.[65] There were also doubts about the technical risk and feasibility of some of the structural works, in particular the main weir and the aqueducts that would carry the canal over the river's lower tributaries. Engineers familiar with the chequered history of dam construction in the East Indies feared the catastrophic damage that would result if such large pieces of infrastructure were to fail. Most fundamentally, there were deep misgivings about its cost. In order to ensure that funds were spent effectively, the government insisted that new

63. Ravesteijn, *De zegenrijke heeren*, 148–54.

64. For a detailed contemporary account: Van der Heide, *Beschouwingen*.

65. Edelman, *Studiën over de Bodemkunde*, 290; Ravesteijn, 'Controlling Water, Controlling People', 101–2.

schemes should be profitable, and established a new Rentability Commission in 1897 to monitor expenditure. In 1898, the prospect of huge cost overruns prompted colonial minister J. T. Cremer to call a temporary suspension of work on the Solo scheme. When it subsequently became clear that construction would cost over twice the original estimate and take many more years than originally foreseen, Cremer's successor A.W.F. Idenburg finally terminated the project in 1903, much to the annoyance of the colony's water engineers.[66]

Financial and technical concerns were clearly key factors behind the decision to halt the Solo Valley works, but the current political context in Netherlands Indies was also crucial. After 1901, the introduction of the so-called 'Ethical Policy' – a new approach championed by Dutch liberals that emphasized indigenous well-being as the foremost responsibility of the government – made it increasingly difficult to justify such lavish expenditure on a single project, and especially one whose social benefits were still speculative. Hovering over all of these doubts was a growing recognition that, in practice, colonial irrigation systems tended to benefit the sugar industry more than rice cultivation, and had thus far done little to improve the welfare of ordinary farmers.

In 1902, this fact was brutally highlighted by another bout of severe famine in Semarang, once again centred on the Demak region and once again triggered by a combination of drought, floods and disease. In the aftermath of the disaster, a Semarang Famine Commission was tasked with devising long-term measures against future food crises. The resulting report, based on a wealth of data and scientific analysis, prompted a major shift in the government's approach towards 'native welfare'. Rather than viewing periodic food crises as the result of unpredictable rains, it instead began to understand them as the outcome of broader systemic inadequacies involving agricultural technique, irrigation provision and land availability. Henceforth the key to improving indigenous welfare was to support small farming, and the key to achieving this was – as the Ethical Policy slogan went – irrigation, education (training peasants in better cultivation techniques) and emigration (encouraging population movement to the 'Outer Isles' to reduce land pressure on Java).[67]

Irrigation thus remained a core objective of the colonial government. The main question was how to do it, and for whom. In this context, the enormous scale and cost of the Solo Valley works represented a dubious extravagance. Even the director of public works J. E. de Meyier came to regard it as an example of 'irrigation fanaticism'.[68] This is not to say that the 1903 demise of the engineers' flagship scheme discredited irrigation as a tool for economic

66. For a contemporary critique of the suspension of the project: Van der Heide, *Beschouwingen*, 219–47, 255–59; more generally, Ravesteijn, *De zegenrijke heeren*, 173–206.

67. Moon, *Technology and Ethical Idealism*, 22–23; Bosma, 'Integration of Food Markets', 149–52.

68. Ravesteijn, *De zegenrijke heeren*, 192, 207–42, quote at 192.

FIGURE 2.3. Main canal, Pekalen irrigation works, Probolinggo Regency, Java, c.1917.
By permission of the Nationaal Museum van Wereldculturen, coll. no. TM-60056558.

development. Far from it: between 1910 and 1940 the area of land in the East Indies serviced by what contemporaries referred to as 'fully technical irrigation works' rose from around 100,000 hectares to over 1.3 million hectares, which equated to around two-fifths of the entire surface of the Netherlands.[69] It did, however, signal a move to prioritize indigenous welfare and to 'hou het klein' (keep it small) in the conception of irrigation schemes after the turn of the century.[70] In the aftermath of the Solo Valley project's closure, even A. G. Lamminga, the founding father of modern irrigation on Java, acknowledged that the proponents of large-scale engineering works often exaggerated their cost–benefit ratio.[71] Although the construction of large-scale, centralized irrigation projects made something of a comeback in the interwar period, the twin criteria of profitability and welfare remained intact.[72]

69. De Vos, 'De strijd', 284.
70. Ravesteijn, *De zegenrijke heeren*, 193–95; Ravesteijn, 'Controlling Water, Controlling People', 104–5; Moon, *Technology and Ethical Idealism*, 26–28; Ertsen, *Locales of Happiness*, 187.
71. Lamminga, Beschouwingen, 24.
72. Ravesteijn, *De zegenrijke heeren*, 245–93; Ertsen, *Locales of Happiness*, 57–58.

Overall, the story of irrigation in the Netherlands Indies is a useful reminder that the relationship between water and welfare, and the extent to which local ways of managing resources were overridden or incorporated by centralized schemes, was not merely driven by the seemingly ineluctable momentum of 'high-modern' technological systems and expert knowledge.[73] Ultimately, it was a matter of priorities; that is to say, a political choice.

In India, colonial authorities faced similar issues, held similar debates and deployed similar techniques to harness water flows for the sake of food security. In much of northern and central India the threat of famine was even greater than in the East Indies, and the question of how far irrigation could or should help mitigate this threat was all the more pressing. But some of the challenges they faced and the political choices they made were markedly different than in the East Indies – partly due to the sheer scale of India's watercourses, partly to the remarkable power of public works officials in India, partly to the enduring adhesion to Smithian principles of liberalism and partly to a different understanding of how government should pursue 'native welfare'.

The overall direction of travel was established in the immediate aftermath of the biggest crisis the British had yet faced in India. The Indian Rebellion of 1857, though brutally suppressed, brought an end to Company rule and forced a major reorganization of the entire administration under the direct control of the British government. In 1858, one of the first acts of the new colonial government was to devise a new policy framework for state investment in public works. A committee chaired by Major Richard Strachey, who later served as director general of irrigation, drew a clear distinction between 'state works' and 'works of internal improvement'. Whereas the former were defined as facilities that were essential to the functioning of government and were generally not remunerative (courts, schools, etc.), the latter should be 'essentially based on the idea of their being *profitable* in a pecuniary point of view . . . to the entire body politic of the State (both government and community, as partners). If it cannot reasonably be predicted that such a work will be *profitable* in this sense, it should not be undertaken'.[74]

In essence, these guidelines defined the central thrust of irrigation policy from the beginning to the end of the Raj. For every decision that involved significant public expenditure, the overriding concern of the government was to generate revenue. Consequently – and in contrast to the Netherlands Indies during the period of 'Ethical Policy' – the irrigation programme in colonial India was about providing water less where it was needed than where it was

---

73. Scott, *Seeing like a State*.

74. *Report of a Committee . . . on the Classification of Public Works Expenditures* (Calcutta, 1858), quoted in Whitcombe, 'Irrigation', 692; see also Headrick, *Tentacles of Progress*, 183–84.

potentially lucrative. Waterworks were built to make money, both indirectly – by boosting agricultural exports and justifying higher land rates – and directly through the levying of water charges and transit tolls, the sale of wood or grass from canal banks, or the issuing of fines for violating canal regulations.[75] Ultimately, the costs of building and maintaining these irrigation systems were passed on to ordinary Indians.

Against this policy backdrop, it is remarkable just how *unprofitable* much of India's irrigation system was. Even after a whole new generation of canal schemes was completed in the 1860s and 1870s – centred mainly on the Punjab and on the extension of existing works in the North-Western Provinces – India's canal network as a whole continued to operate in the red. In 1876–77, only seven of the forty-four supposedly 'remunerative' works in operation actually merited the label. What's more, all seven were works 'of native origin' whose profitability derived from the fact that they required relatively little restoration to bring into good working order, and for this reason earned more than they had cost.[76]

From a financial perspective, the results of government support for so-called 'productive' irrigation works were therefore disappointing. Tragically, they were even less successful at protecting people from the scourge of famine. For two years from 1876–78, an intense and protracted drought caused massive crop failure across the Deccan Plateau and parts of central and north-western India. Caused by an exceptionally powerful El Niño event, the drought was part of a much broader pattern of weather disturbance and food shortage that likewise affected parts of China, South America and Africa. But if the drought itself was an act of nature, the resulting famine was due to more than the failure of the rains. As Mike Davies in particular has argued, it was also clearly a product of government policy: namely, the long-term reluctance to invest in public works designed to safeguard against food shortages; and, more immediately, the failure to provide adequate relief to millions of starving people owing to a dogmatic devotion to the doctrine of free markets and the determination of officials such as Sir Richard Temple, a special envoy to the famine-struck regions, to minimize the scale of relief expenditure.[77]

By the time the rains returned in summer 1878, around 5.5 million people had perished. In the wake of the calamity, the government appointed a commission to investigate the causes of India's recurrent famines and to make recommendations on measures to prevent them. The most important administrative outcome was the introduction of new Famine Codes that instructed local officials on how to respond to food shortages, mainly through a combination of employment, income support and direct relief for those unable to

75. Whitcombe, *Agrarian Conditions*, 134–36.
76. Whitcombe, 'Irrigation', 704.
77. M. Davis, *Late Victorian Holocausts*.

work. Beyond such emergency measures, the commission also recommended the construction of two different types of public works: 'famine railways' linking drought-prone areas to the rest of the transport network, and 'protective' irrigation works designed primarily to provide security against drought rather than to generate revenue. According to the commission, among all the means of protecting India against drought-induced famine, 'the first place must unquestionably be assigned to works of irrigation'. Instead of measuring the value of such works 'only with reference to the net return to Government on the capital invested in them', their 'true value', the commission concluded, lay first and foremost in 'the direct protection afforded by them in years of drought, by the saving of human life, by the avoidance of loss of revenue remitted, and of the outlay incurred in costly measures of relief'.[78]

In response, the government sanctioned a raft of 'protective' works whose construction was to be supported by the new Famine Relief and Insurance Fund established in 1881–82. But despite these good intentions, there were limits to what state finances and natural physiography would allow. Some parts of India offered far better prospects than others for 'productive' and 'protective' works alike. In the north, there were still a few places where the local topography made large-scale irrigation technically possible, but financially unprofitable: alluvial plains not far from snow-fed rivers that guaranteed a minimum supply of water regardless of seasonal rains. By contrast, throughout the Deccan and central India the rough, rocky terrain made canals expensive to build, and the lack of snow-fed rivers required the construction of large reservoirs to store water from one rainy season to the next. As a result, only a handful of the government's new protective schemes qualified as 'major' works; for example, the Betwa Canal in the North-Western Provinces, the Rushikulya reservoir system in coastal Madras and the Nira Canal in the Bombay Presidency. Most consisted of 'minor' improvements to village tanks and irrigation channels in the Deccan and Madras hinterlands, which drew their water from seasonal rivers nearby. As welcome as such minor works were, they nonetheless left these regions defenceless in the face of severe drought. The lack of meltwater in central and southern India meant that when the rains failed and the rivers ran dry – precisely when irrigation was most needed – so too did the works that relied on them. Moreover, the modest budget for such improvements meant that the vast majority of local waterworks across these vulnerable areas remained untouched in any event.[79]

Despite this political upgrading of 'protective' works, it was not long before famine struck again. For the second time in two decades, the inadequacy of the government's approach was brutally exposed when a renewed succession of droughts ravaged the countryside at the close of the nineteenth century.

78. *Report of the Indian Famine Commission*, 150–68, quotes at 150.
79. Buckley, *Irrigation Works of India*, 314–16; Whitcombe, 'Irrigation', 717.

From 1896 to 1898, the repeated failure of the summer rains alternated with successive outbreaks of epidemic disease to cause mass starvation and misery throughout central and southern India. After a brief respite, in 1899–1900 the same regions were hit by the driest year on record, once more causing colossal crop failure and widespread starvation. Although the activation of the Famine Codes undoubtedly helped keep the death toll much lower than it had been twenty years earlier, all in all the famines of the 1890s claimed at least a million lives.[80]

Once again, a humanitarian catastrophe prompted a re-evaluation of the government's irrigation policy. In 1901, a special Irrigation Commission chaired by Colin Scott-Moncrieff – previously a senior water engineer in India but best known for replumbing the Nile in the 1880s – was tasked 'to Report on the Irrigation of India as a Protection against Famine'. After two years of investigation covering the length and breadth of India, its report provided a *tour d'horizon* of irrigation across the subcontinent. The commissioners surveyed the 'extraordinary variations' of rainfall across the seasons and from one region to another. They charted the many options for irrigating the 'innumerable' varieties of soil throughout India. They calculated that about a fifth of India's cultivated land was irrigated, and that well over half of the irrigated surface was still served by private rather than state-owned hydraulic works. Out of a total of 353,000 square miles (91.5 million hectares) of cropland in India, 24,000 (6.3 million) were watered by state-run canals, another 4,600 (1.2 million) by minor state works, and just under 39,000 (10 million) by private tanks, wells and other sources.[81] The commission also estimated that some 87 per cent of the available surface water still 'passes to waste in the sea', but equally recognized that capturing more for irrigation purposes would be difficult and costly given that the most suitable localities for hydraulic works were fast becoming exhausted. While the expansion of well irrigation was promising, the prospects for large-scale projects were tightly limited by factors such as climate, physiography, soils, and not least the jurisdictional boundaries that divided watersheds and created a potential source of conflict over rights and access.[82]

In short, the commission's report showed that India 'can never be protected from famine by irrigation alone'. The most that waterworks could realistically do was 'to restrict the area and to mitigate the intensity of famine'.[83] The task for government was to decide how best to accomplish this within the existing geographic and (perhaps especially) financial constraints, for public works were still invariably expected to pay. This raised the question of whether

80. M. Davis, *Late Victorian Holocausts*.
81. *Report of the Indian Irrigation Commission*, 3–7.
82. *Report of the Indian Irrigation Commission*, 14–16.
83. *Report of the Indian Irrigation Commission*, 125.

such tight financial constraints were themselves acceptable, and many thought they were not. The distinguished Bengali economist and civil servant Romesh Chunder Dutt spoke for many in the growing Indian nationalist movement when he wrote that 'what India wants now is an extensive system of irrigation' based on social utility rather than profitability alone.[84] In some ways echoing the concurrent Dutch emphasis on indigenous well-being, he argued that the government's fixation on a narrow conception of value for money was blinding it to the broader potential of irrigation as a tool for economic development and social improvement.

For the Irrigation Commission, however, this question lay beyond its remit. Taking the existing financial framework as a given, it concluded that the bulk of funding should go to those areas with the highest potential for profit – namely the drylands of the Punjab and Sindh, which the monsoon rains did not reach. At the time, two large projects were already reclaiming several hundred thousand hectares of arid 'wasteland' in the northern Punjab. Soon after receiving the commission's report, the government embarked on a truly gigantic hydraulic transformation of the entire Indus River basin. As we will see in chapter 3, by the early 1900s irrigation in colonial India was less about mastering the monsoon than conquering the desert.

Unlike the East Indies, where the rise of the Ethical Policy led to calls to 'keep it small' when it came to irrigation projects, in colonial India the recurrent drought crises of the late nineteenth century therefore reinforced rather than undermined the prevailing attachment to large, centrally run irrigation systems. At one level, this was simply a matter of administrative practicality. Understandably, perhaps, the government preferred to concentrate its limited resources on a small number of large-scale projects that could be more effectively overseen by its slim cadre of public works officials than a large number of small-scale projects ever could be. But there was more to it than that, for the partiality towards big engineering schemes also reflected the technocratic ideologies, sociocultural hierarchies and exclusionary politics of colonial rule in India more generally.

By the end of the nineteenth century, India had become the world's leading showcase for hydraulic technology. Its irrigated surface of nearly seventy thousand square miles (eighteen million hectares) was by far the largest in the world.[85] Its canal systems were unparalleled in scale and ranged across the full spectrum of soils and topographies, making it an ideal laboratory for testing different techniques. As such, India was not only the key training ground for British irrigation experts but also a site of pilgrimage for the worldwide fraternity of hydraulic engineers. Visitors from North America, Australasia or

84. Dutt, *Famines and Land Assessments*, 82.
85. *Report of the Indian Irrigation Commission*, 11.

Russia were invariably impressed, and often awestruck, by the technological feats they saw.[86] They were equally captivated by the immense power and prestige that such grand systems bestowed upon their British peers. Throughout much of the Indian countryside, hydraulic engineers became the very embodiment of the state, combining the roles of tax collector, law enforcer and judge. 'In northern India the engineer is a ruler of men,' remarked the Australian lawyer (and subsequent prime minister) Alfred Deakin. 'To him are directed the manifold complaints of irrigators, and the appeals in village disputes; into his hand pour complaints against his subordinates, reports of his officials on petty contractors and labourers, and the thousand and one pleas by which all alike seek to make the State their prey.'[87]

Deakin was an unusually astute observer of India's hydraulic regime. His perspective differed somewhat from that of the standard irrigation tourist; he was not an engineer by training but rather a lawyer-politician who had become something of a water expert during extended stints as commissioner for public works and water supplies in his native Victoria. He was also remarkably well travelled, having already studied the water infrastructures of the western United States, Italy and Egypt before finally travelling around India in the early 1890s. Like the other hydraulic tourists who went there, Deakin was impressed by the hydraulic infrastructure he saw. Yet unlike most of them, he was also keenly alert to its broader social and political implications. Everywhere he went he was struck by the extraordinarily top-down nature of India's irrigation systems: 'the Indian ryot . . . is never consulted in any way or at any stage in the construction. Government initiates designs and executes the work, offering him the water if he likes to take it, and relying only upon his self-interest to induce him to become a purchaser'. Deakin's own experience of water management was based on the very different political context of Victoria, a settler colony and soon-to-be federal state of the self-governing Commonwealth of Australia, where water projects were generally initiated by – and required the explicit approval of – the (white) farmers who would use them. By contrast, in India the government 'acts of its own motion, at its own responsibility, and acknowledges no title in those who use the water to criticise its proposals'. Furthermore, it even 'ignores riparian rights, or makes but small compensation for actual injury done or land taken'.[88]

India's water regime was thus a microcosm of the political system as a whole. Although Deakin condemned this system as 'anti-democratic in every respect', he also acknowledged 'the advantages of a despotic rule . . . , where the officers of the department are perfectly free to choose the best scheme

---

86. Teisch, *Engineering Nature*, 28–33; Worster, *Rivers of Empire*, 147–54; Peterson, *Pipe Dreams*, 124, 144.

87. Deakin, *Irrigated India*, 229.

88. Deakin, 233–34.

possible, and to execute it without regard to the individual wishes or interests of their constituents'. Despite the 'excellent motives' that inspired India's irrigation works, he concluded that 'the net result is a benevolent tyranny, leaning a little towards unnecessary officiousness. The tyrant has not been content to offer what he believed to be advantages, but sometimes has gone so far as to thrust them upon his subjects'.[89] India's hydraulic bureaucrats did not merely govern the use of its waters; they governed through the use of its waters.

Just how 'benevolent' this hydraulic tyranny was has long been a matter of debate. Many would agree with the conclusions reached by Elizabeth Whitcombe half a century ago, that 'the local population paid for the progress bestowed upon them in a variety of ways': not just financially, but also in the form of disease and soil deterioration.[90] Others have argued that the effects were broadly positive for the material well-being of the peasantry, or that the outcomes were mixed as a result of the inherent tensions between boosting economic growth and seeking to constrain the ensuing social changes within a framework of antiquated indigenous institutions and colonial political hierarchies.[91] Still others, especially those focusing on the south of India, have emphasized rather the continuities of water control between the pre-colonial and colonial periods, not least because the design and effects of many pre-colonial waterworks were anything but socially egalitarian.[92]

Clearly, the effects were not uniform. India's irrigation systems, like most major public works, created winners and losers. Although perennial water supplies allowed farmers to grow more lucrative crops, most of the additional income went on water fees and higher land rents, which primarily benefitted other groups. For many peasants, the growing dependency on state waterworks and the consequent need to grow export crops in order to pay for water and other basic needs actually made them poorer and less food secure than before. By and large, the greatest benefits accrued to local landowners, who were able to charge their tenants more for irrigated tracts and who often controlled water distribution off the main canals. On balance, large-scale irrigation schemes tended to polarize wealth in the Indian countryside, especially in the northern plains.[93]

In addition to widening social clefts, state-run waterworks created regional winners and losers too. The emphasis on revenue generation and on large, technocratic schemes excluded huge swathes of Indian countryside where

89. Deakin, 21.

90. Whitcombe, *Agrarian Conditions*, 273.

91. For the more optimistic view: I. Stone, *Canal Irrigation*. On countervailing tensions: Gilmartin, *Blood and Water*. For a brief historiographic overview: D'Souza, 'Water in British India'.

92. Mosse, *Rule of Water*; Hardiman, 'Small-Dam Systems'; Bijker, 'Dikes and Dams', 114–18.

93. Whitcombe, *Agrarian Conditions*, 119.

irrigation was deemed unlikely to be profitable, however socially desirable it might have been. As money was poured into the massive works in the Madras deltas and North-Western Provinces, many traditional systems for harnessing the monsoon rains – the small dams of South Bihar, the ancient inundation canals in Bengal, the myriad wells and tanks scattered across the Deccan – were ignored and fell further into disrepair. Not everyone in the colonial administration shared this sense of priorities. In the 1850s, district officials from across Madras bemoaned the derelict state of village tanks and highlighted the resulting lack of water as a fundamental check on prosperity. In the more drought-prone parts of central India, local officers reported how once-flourishing villages with fertile soils had been abandoned because of broken tanks and channels. Even Arthur Cotton himself, the creator of Madras's great hydraulic monuments, was scathing about the near-total disregard of indigenous waterworks: 'The fact is that the neglect of these noble native works has been one of the most grievous and most astonishing defects in our government.'[94] In Bengal, the renowned hydrological engineer William Willcocks was equally critical of the disregard shown towards the ancient inundation canals that criss-crossed the landscape. Whereas these channels had for centuries brought an annual supply of nutrient-rich silt to the cultivated delta plain – along with a beneficial influx of fish, which devoured harmful mosquito larvae and provided a valuable source of dietary protein – decades of inattention had left them stagnant and clogged with sediment. The failure of colonial authorities to maintain these canals turned them from an agricultural blessing into a public health curse.[95] As these examples clearly demonstrate, colonial officialdom by no means spoke with one voice on these matters.

Perhaps the biggest drawback of India's perennial irrigation systems were the environmental changes they caused. Here, too, the fixation on revenue brought hidden costs, for much of the damage stemmed from the systematic emphasis on the delivery of water over adequate drainage. The reason was simple: whereas the expansion of water supplies generated income, investment in drainage did not quickly pay for itself. These financial incentives were reflected in the very design of most canal systems, few of which were lined to prevent seepage or equipped with adequate drainage, because of the additional expense involved. Furthermore, the problems they caused were often exacerbated by the operation of the smaller distributaries by local *zamindars*, who were generally more interested in maximizing their own incomes than in avoiding unnecessary water loss. Much of the water that the distribution channels carried ended up seeping out and collecting in low-lying areas, with no place to go once it got there. The result was extensive waterlogging that smothered crops, sterilized fields by drawing up salts out of the subsoil, and

94. Hope, *General Sir Arthur Cotton*, 191–95, quote at 240.
95. Willcocks, *Ancient Irrigation of Bengal*, 3–8.

created an ideal habitat for malarial mosquitoes and other waterborne disease vectors.

The two Jumna canals were among the worst offenders in this respect. By the early 1840s, their lower reaches were already afflicted by chronic water-logging, saline efflorescence and persistent outbreaks of malaria. Following a major epidemic along the Western Jumna in 1843, an investigative committee found that the incidence of 'fever' was noticeably higher and more severe in canal-irrigated areas, especially within half a mile of a canal. In the early 1850s, engineers carried out corrective works to realign parts of the channel and to improve surface drainage, but most of the man-made swamps remained, and so did the prevalence of malaria. In the late 1860s, infection rates were as high as they were two decades earlier, and in the early 1880s the same litany of problems – soil saturation, salinization, high rates of malaria – still plagued the canal districts. Characteristically, efforts to remedy the problems continued to centre on the same technical fixes – canal alignment and surface drains – rather than a restriction of irrigation itself. It was only in the 1890s that conditions in the worst-affected areas bordering the Western Jumna showed signs of improvement. And even then, groundwater levels and malaria rates along the Eastern Jumna Canal remained as high as ever.[96]

The situation was scarcely better along the Ganges Canal. Cautley's celebrated engineering feats on the canal's upper reaches were not matched lower downstream, where silting, seepage and waterlogging soon appeared. Here too, basic design flaws were at the root of the problems. Quite apart from the difficulties caused by the main canal's improperly steep slope, its distributaries were laid out in a gridiron pattern rather than conforming to the natural contours of the land, which immediately gave rise to standing water in low-lying areas. To fix the problem, engineers dug dozens of drainage cuts to allow the excess water to escape, though even then it took only slightly above average rainfall to cause widespread waterlogging and a spike in malaria rates. In wet years much of the lower *doab* lay 'soaked and sodden', its worst affected villages left to 'cry for drainage' that was difficult to provide owing to 'the objection of those below to receive more water in such seasons, when they themselves already have too much'. Once again, engineers opted to double-down on the same solutions that had proven inadequate in the past. Although more drainage ditches were cut, malaria rates remained stubbornly high. It was only after another serious epidemic in 1908 that officials finally turned towards quinine distribution and the oiling of surface waters as a means of combatting malaria in the irrigated districts.[97]

96. Whitcombe, 'Environmental Costs of Irrigation', 250–52; 'Irrigation', 689; Headrick, *Tentacles of Progress*, 187.
97. Deakin, *Irrigated India*, 189; Whitcombe, 'Environmental Costs of Irrigation', 252–54.

The problems along the Ganges and Jumna canals illustrate a more general point: the more a hydraulic project altered an area's natural hydrology, the more detrimental its environmental effects tended to be. At base, perennial irrigation sought to 'correct' the local shortcomings of nature by providing water wherever insufficient or unpredictable supplies were the chief brake on agricultural production. More often than not, however, the attempt to even out these natural disparities ended up creating new ones. As a general rule, perennial irrigation enhanced productivity wherever soil conditions and surface topography permitted sufficient drainage. It failed to do so – and often reduced productivity – wherever circumstances were unfavourable; for instance, where soils were heavy and impermeable or in flat, low-lying tracts. Irrigation therefore had markedly different effects in different places. It is telling that the major works in the Madras deltas caused few of the salinization or disease problems associated with their equivalents in the Gangetic plain. The anicuts across the Cauvery, Godavari and Krishna raised river levels just enough to supply a reliable source of water to the alluvial plains below, and the associated reduction of siltation actually improved drainage in many areas. Unlike the major irrigation works in northern India, which radically altered local hydrology, these schemes by and large sought to enhance rather than transform natural flood conditions (though, as we will see in chapter 5, they nonetheless had a severe impact on aquatic life within the rivers themselves).[98] As ever, working with nature rather than against it tended to yield better results.

Whereas in some parts of India irrigation works resulted in 'oases of good soils, well-watered and attended by the benefits of the optimum in natural resources', in others they led to 'saline deserts and bald patches of alkalinity, the swamps and waterlogged tracts, the erosion of riverine areas'.[99] As so often happens when humans try to control their surroundings, the attempt to correct one environmental problem – in this case unpredictable water supplies – ended up causing a host of others. It was a conundrum that hydraulic engineers in Egypt found equally challenging.

The Rhythm of the Nile

According to an oft-quoted aphorism, 'the Egyptian question is the Irrigation question'.[100] The phrase is attributed to Nubar Pasha, Egypt's prime minister on three occasions during the 1870s to 1890s, but its sentiment was wholeheartedly shared by the European officials who de facto ruled the country in the late nineteenth and early twentieth centuries. Egypt was, after all,

98. Schmitthenner, 'Colonial Hydraulic Projects', 196–97; Whitcombe, 'Environmental Costs of Irrigation', 239–41, 258–59.

99. Whitcombe, *Agrarian Conditions*, 275.

100. Willcocks, *Sixty Years*, 88.

almost entirely reliant on water that fell as rain elsewhere. It was also a country of enormous geopolitical significance after the opening of the Suez Canal in 1869. For the leading imperial powers of the era, the key to controlling Egypt was to make it more productive and prosperous. And the key to making it more prosperous was to make the most of its critical water supplies while they were readily available – or, better still, to make them more readily available in the first place.

Ever since farming began in Egypt some seven millennia ago, the seasonal ebb and flow of the Nile governed the basic rhythms of life. Every year, late summer monsoon rains in the Ethiopian highlands streamed down the Blue Nile towards Khartoum, where they met the more regular flow of the White Nile. In the valley below, water levels generally rose in August, peaked in early September and subsided once again in October. As the river fell, farmers planted their winter staple crops – mainly wheat or barley – in the moist alluvial soil left behind. After harvesting in the spring, most fields were left fallow until the floodwaters returned. All along the lower Nile the arrival of the annual flood was an object of anxious observation, even preoccupation. 'The period of the flood is the crisis for the country', noted the German physician-traveller Carl Klunzinger in the 1870s. 'The populace is in a state of excitement; "how much has the Nile risen today?" is the daily question of everyone who thinks about the future'. If the floodwaters were too meagre, the result was scarcity 'or even famine'. If they were too plentiful, then the outcome was burst dams, ruined fields, and the drowning of people and livestock. 'If, however, the river god filled his horn of plenty precisely to the brim . . . then everybody is in a joyful state,' for a good harvest was more or less certain.[101]

The yearly floodwaters of the Nile constituted both an opportunity and a risk, a recurrent gamble for those who lived along its banks. They were, in this sense, a crucial historical agent every bit as important as the people who conquered, ruled or farmed the valley. As Alain Mikhail has argued, 'it would not be an over-exaggeration to say that rainfall in the Ethiopian highlands that created the annual flood had more of an impact on Egypt's history than any political entity that controlled the territory over its millennia of documented history'.[102]

Nubar Pasha's 'irrigation question' was indeed as old as Egyptian civilization itself. For thousands of years farmers employed an ingenious system of basin irrigation designed to capitalize on the cyclical rise and fall of the Nile's waters. The basic technique was to construct low dykes around fields and to excavate canals through the riverbanks to allow the seasonal floods to inundate them. The silt-laden waters then stood on the fields for around forty to sixty days, depositing a layer of rich volcanic sediment before being released

---

101. Klunzinger, *Bilder aus Oberägypten*, 123–24.
102. Mikhail, *Nature and Empire*, 22.

FIGURE 2.4. Men working a *shaduf* in Upper Egypt, 1860–70.
Source: Library of Congress Prints and Photographs Division, LOT 13549-15,
no. 2 [P&P].

back into the river or into an adjacent field-basin. By and large, the system
was maintained and operated by the farmers who directly benefited from it,
at least up until the formation of a more modernizing and centralized Egyptian administration in the early nineteenth century.[103] Moreover, it brought
numerous agroecological advantages. It required little additional fertilization
beyond the yearly silt subsidy; it reduced labour demands by allowing farmers to sow crops on soft, moist fields; it avoided the build-up of salts in the
soil through the annual flushing of the basins; and it even aided soil aeration
by allowing the soil to heat up and crack during the hot summer months just
before the flood.

Overall, Egypt's basin agricultural system was not only highly productive;
it was arguably the most ecologically sustainable irrigation scheme in world
history. William Willcocks deemed it 'the most efficacious method of utilising
existing means of irrigation which the world has witnessed'.[104] It did, however, have one major drawback: its reliance on the annual flood meant that it

103. Mikhail, 22.
104. Willcocks and Craig, *Egyptian Irrigation*, vol. 1, 299.

was ill-suited to raising summer crops. Although farmers could use a *saqiya* (bucket chain) or *shaduf* (a pole with a bucket and counterweight) to lift low summer waters on to their fields, this was possible only along the banks of the main river or in areas with high water tables, and even here the additional effort and expense meant that summer cropping was rare. For centuries this limitation had posed a natural check on what cultivars Egyptian farmers could grow – mainly winter crops such as wheat, barley and beans – and how much they could produce. It became an unacceptable constraint only when Egypt's rulers wanted to transform the country's agricultural economy to grow crops in all seasons, and to specialize on one crop in particular: cotton.[105]

Europeans were by no means the first to try to overcome the seasonality of the Nile. The earliest efforts started decades earlier under the arch-modernizer Muhammad 'Ali. After seizing power in 1805 and brutally eliminating his Mamluk rivals in 1811, 'Ali quickly set about reorganizing the economy, establishing a professional bureaucracy and building a modern army in a bid for independence from Ottoman rule. All of this required more revenue, but since most of Egypt's commerce was with the Ottoman Empire it was vital to reorient trade towards Europe. Cotton was by far the most promising means for doing so. The central role of textile manufacturing within a rapidly industrializing European economy meant that cotton was the chief moneymaker behind 'Ali's modernization strategy.[106]

The fundamental problem was that the growing season of cotton, stretching from February to October, mapped awkwardly onto the rhythms of the Nile. On the one hand, the fact that cotton was harvested after the summer floodwaters began to rise meant that it had to be planted on high ground to avoid being drowned. On the other hand, it also needed copious amounts of water – approximately one vertical metre per crop in Egypt's dry climate – during the preceding growing season, from early spring to summer, precisely when river levels were at their lowest and the effort required to raise water on to fields was correspondingly highest.[107] The overall result was a seemingly unbridgeable temporal disjunction, for the needs of large-scale cotton cultivation simply did not accord with the rhythms of the Nile. If cotton were to become the leading export crop in Egypt, perennial irrigation was an absolute necessity.

'Ali and his successors accordingly took a number of steps to make water available even when river levels were low. One method was to dig deeper canals into which summer waters could flow. This was the initial focus in

---

105. For an excellent recent analysis of the 'perennial Nile River', see Derr's *Lived Nile*.
106. Owen, *Cotton*; Marsot, *Egypt*.
107. Willcocks and Craig, *Egyptian Irrigation*, vol. 2, 768–73; A. Richards, *Egypt's Agricultural Development*, 15–19.

the 1820s, but it quickly proved impractical. For one thing, it was a Sisyph-ean task: the hundreds of thousands of labourers who were drafted in had to repeat their work each year after silt-laden floodwaters refilled the canals with mud.[108] Moreover, lifting the necessary volumes of water from the canals dur-ing the summer required an enormous amount of effort; according to one esti-mate, around 480 man-days per feddan (over 1,000 man-days per hectare).[109] The other option was to raise the water level itself, which greatly reduced the effort required to irrigate fields during the summer. Towards this end, 'Ali's government drew up plans to build two barrages at the upper end of the Nile delta on the two main branches of the river, the Rosetta and Damietta. The purpose of the barrages was much like that of Cotton's anicuts in Madras – namely, to hold up a portion of the annual flood and distribute it to the chan-nels below in order to keep them topped up. To supply the necessary building materials, 'Ali ordered the pyramids at Giza to be dismantled, but fortunately this aspect of the plan was abandoned when the lead engineer Louis Maurice Adolphe Linant de Bellefonds convinced him that it would be possible only to extract stone from the tops of the pyramids downwards, making it more costly than using new quarries near the river. In 1833, Linant began work on the two barrages about ten kilometres below the river's bifurcation, one on each branch, but work was abandoned just two years later following a massive out-break of plague among the workforce. In 1843, another French engineer, E. Mougel, resumed work at the bifurcation itself, about twenty-five kilometres below Cairo, but progress was painfully slow owing to disease outbreaks and an understandable lack of enthusiasm among the thousands of peasants who were forcibly conscripted on to the site.[110]

In his eagerness to boost cotton production, 'Ali forced the pace of con-struction by hounding the engineers and setting unrealistic daily targets. Predictably, his impatience proved to be counterproductive. 'Ali's constant interference led to serious construction flaws in the underwater foundations, parts of which were built on shifting sand or loose stone that had been laid on the river bed. Although the supervising engineers were acutely aware of these problems, work continued after 'Ali's death in 1848, first under Mougel and then under the Egyptian engineer Mazhar Bey. In 1861, the Delta Barrage was finally completed, but because of the defects in its foundation it was two more years before engineers dared to close the gates and hold up the Nile's flow. When they finally did so, it took only 1.40 metres of water to force the sand out from below the Rosetta barrage and to cause 'ominous cracks' in the masonry. After that, the engineers never raised the water more than 0.5 metres, but

108. Estimated at the rate of around 13 million m^3 per year: Brown, *History of the Barrage*, 2.
109. A. Richards, *Egypt's Agricultural Development*, 19.
110. Brown, *History of the Barrage*, 6–8; Headrick, *Tentacles of Progress*, 197.

even with this precaution, an entire segment of ten arches sagged perceptibly downstream in 1867. In short, the massive Delta Barrage – measuring over two kilometres long and costing around £4 million – was, for the time being, of little use for irrigation. As Linant himself put it in 1872, 'the barrage is like a gangrenous body. It looks healthy on the outside but the sickness plagues it within. . . . It requires major intervention and not palliatives, which could only make matters worse'.[111]

The Delta Barrage was initially a fiasco, but this did not stop perennial irrigation from expanding rapidly. The onset of the worldwide 'cotton famine' in the early 1860s, caused by a disruption of exports from the southern United States during the American Civil War, marked a defining moment for modern Egypt – economically, politically and hydrologically. As European textile manufacturers scrambled to find alternative supplies, soaring prices gave a powerful stimulus to cotton cultivation, effectively cementing its status as Egypt's principal commercial export. In 1861, when the Civil War began, cotton already covered a little over 100,000 hectares of land, which together yielded around 25,000 tons of raw cotton per year. By the time the war ended in 1865, Egyptian cotton production had risen fourfold and acreage nearly fivefold, covering around 40 per cent of the entire cultivable area of Lower Egypt. Over the same period cotton exports to Europe roughly trebled, the bulk of it going to Britain with the remainder mainly sent to Marseille and Trieste.[112]

Such was the momentum of this shift that not even the sudden return of the United States as the world's dominant exporter caused more than a brief halt to cotton expansion. After suffering a short-term decline, Egyptian exports surpassed their 1865 peak in the early 1870s and proceeded to grow steadily to around 150,000 tons in 1880. All the while, irrigation expanded accordingly. Under the khedive Isma'il Pasha, who ruled Egypt during 1863–79, some 13,500 kilometres of new canals were excavated. During the quarter-century after the end of his reign, cotton exports more than doubled again, reaching 340,000 tons by 1914, most of it destined for British spinneries.[113] By the early twentieth century it was, as one contemporary put it, 'not exaggerated to say that Egypt has become a land of monoculture'.[114]

111. De Bellefonds, *Mémoires*, 468–77, quote at 474; Brown, *History of the Barrage*, 6–18; Barois, *Les irrigations en Égypte*, 291–96; Willcocks and Craig, *Egyptian Irrigation*, vol. 2, 633–34.

112. Figures from Todd, *World's Cotton Crops*, 421; Owen, *Cotton*, 89–90, 92–95, 103, 161–66; A. Richards, *Egypt's Agricultural Development*, xiii. See more generally Beckert's *Empire of Cotton*, 135–51, and 'Emancipation and Empire'.

113. Todd, *World's Cotton Crops*, 421–26; A. Richards, *Egypt's Agricultural Development*, 29–33; Owen, *Cotton*, 105–6.

114. Charles-Roux, *La production du coton*, 329.

Egypt's conversion into a global centre of cotton production entailed a bundle of interrelated changes. For one thing, it required a major expansion of the country's physical and scientific infrastructure, including railways, port facilities and cotton breeding programmes. It likewise relied on new systems of land tenure and contract law, as well as new credit and marketing facilities largely backed by European capital. Such innovations were all part of a broader reorganization of social and economic life, which brought greater prosperity to merchants and landowners but led to mounting debt, landlessness, forced labour and penury for much of the Egyptian peasantry. As Timothy Mitchell has remarked, 'no other place in the world in the nineteenth century was transformed on a greater scale to serve the production of a single industry'.[115]

What underlay all of these changes was the replumbing of the Nile valley. The river's waters were the ultimate source of Egypt's wealth, but controlling them on the envisaged scale was beyond the means of the state itself. Under 'Ali and his successors the bulk of hydraulic works – like Egypt's other infrastructural investments – were funded by foreign loans. This strategy of importing large amounts of capital in order to export large amounts of cotton set up a race of sorts, whereby the inward flow of profits had to exceed the outward flow of credit payments. In the end, the Egyptian government lost the race. Not even the enormous growth of cotton exports after the start of the American Civil War was able to cover the state's spiralling debts. In 1876, the government finally defaulted on its loans. It managed to avoid economic implosion only by selling its shares in the Suez Canal to the British government and by allowing European (mainly French) creditors to control the state treasury through the independent Caisse de la dette publique. Such blatant foreign dominance of Egyptian affairs was bound to stoke political tensions. When these tensions finally boiled over in the 'Urabi Revolt of 1882, the resulting turmoil provided the British and French governments with the perfect pretext for military intervention. By the end of the year Egypt was effectively a British protectorate, a status that was to last, in various forms, until after the Second World War.[116]

Water development was at the top of the agenda throughout the entire British occupation of Egypt. For Consul-General Lord Cromer, the Nile was critical for servicing Egyptian debts and for helping Lancashire industrialists reduce their dependence on US cotton. For the khedival government, which essentially had to administer Cromer's policies, the river's water was a vital means of maintaining living standards and maximizing state revenue from the collection of export duties and the sale of state land to prominent notables. Despite all of the canals and barrages that had been built to date, the control of the Nile was nowhere near its potential. In all but the driest years the vast bulk of its annual floodwaters flowed unused into the sea. For nearly

115. Mitchell, *Colonising Egypt*, 16.
116. The classic study is Landes's *Bankers and Pashas*.

everyone concerned – landowners, the government, the Caisse de la dette publique, British banks and manufacturers alike – all of this unexploited water
was increasingly viewed as an intolerable 'waste' of a valuable asset, literally a
stream of liquid wealth passing them by.[117]

As Cromer and his officials were well aware, the control of this flow was a
vital political and economic asset. Indeed, mastering the Nile was all the more
important for an occupying power that justified its presence by claiming to
bestow the technological and scientific benefits of a more 'advanced' civilization. One of Cromer's first acts as consul-general was to hire a team of experienced hydraulic engineers from India. They were led by Colin Scott-Moncrieff,
who had previously worked on the Jumna and Ganges canals and had taught
at Thomason Civil Engineering College in Roorkee. Among his assistants was
the thirty-one-year-old William Willcocks, who had grown up along the
banks of the Western Jumna Canal, studied at Thomason College, and eventually rose to become one of the most influential – and unorthodox – water
engineers of his generation. As inspector general of irrigation, and then as
under-secretary of state for public works, Scott-Moncrieff was given a generous budget and exceptional discretionary powers to extend perennial irrigation throughout Egypt. His team of hydraulic engineers enjoyed a remarkably
privileged position in the Egyptian occupation regime owing to the perceived
importance of their work for domestic political stability. Cromer himself put
them on a par with the army in respect of their overall political importance.
As he wrote shortly after leaving Egypt in 1907, the water engineers 'justified
Western methods to Eastern minds' and arguably did more than anyone else
to demonstrate the 'good results of European administration'.[118]

Their first major initiative was to put the ill-fated Delta Barrage into working order. Although a detailed investigation officially condemned the entire
structure in 1883, Willcocks and Scott-Moncrieff asserted – against prevailing opinion – that it could be repaired and eventually used for its intended
purpose. From 1884 to 1886, Willcocks made provisional improvements to the
barrage and experimented with water levels during the summer ebb, though
his attempt to hold up ten feet (three metres) on the Rosetta branch in 1885
caused yet more structural damage, which had to be urgently mended. Systematic repair work on the foundation and gates finally began in 1887 and
was completed in 1890, allowing the water to rise thirteen feet (four metres)
behind the dam and fill the feeder canals with five times more water than they
previously carried in the summer. The benefits were significant and immediate. For the first time, farmers in the delta could dispense with costly steam
pumps or onerous *shadufs* in the dry season, thus enabling them to raise

117. Tvedt, *Age of the British*, 21–22.

118. Quoted from Tvedt, *Age of the British*, 30; on the political status of water expertise
in Egypt, see also Derr's *Lived Nile* (15–43).

FIGURE 2.5. The completed Delta Barrage, 1867–99.
Source: Library of Congress Prints and Photographs Division, LOT 13550,
no. 150 [P&P].

cotton and other summer crops independently of the summer water supply.
Equally important for farmers, the elevation of water levels also contributed
to the abolition of the hated *corvée*, which had mainly mobilized work gangs to
clear mud from the shallow summer canals.[119]

Thanks to the repaired barrage, by the early 1890s perennial irrigation
was possible throughout the entire cultivated area of the delta. Meanwhile,
in middle and upper Egypt, farmers remained beholden to the fluctuations
of the river. Unusually low summer waters – which occurred frequently in
the late 1880s and early 1890s – still adversely impacted the cotton trade
and reportedly provoked popular discontent against the government.[120] By
the same token, abnormally high autumn floods (1878, 1887, 1892) could be
equally damaging, not only for cotton yields but also for summer food crops
like maize and rice, both of which were becoming more important for feeding
the growing population. Perceptions of the river were subtly changing among
state officials and ordinary farmers alike. The once 'natural' variations in its
flow became an unacceptable problem that had to be solved.[121]

119. Brown, *History of the Barrage*, 38–40, 47–51, 59–60.
120. Tvedt, *Age of the British*, 23.
121. Cookson-Hills, 'Aswan Dam', 67.

But 'fixing' the flow of the Nile involved certain trade-offs, for its natural fluctuations affected more than just agriculture. Ironically, some of the most difficult dilemmas were unwittingly worsened by the engineers themselves. In their determination to repair the Delta Barrage for irrigation purposes, they overlooked the river's other uses, including its importance as a source of drinking water for villages and cities. During periods of low flood, there was simply not enough water in the Nile to provide adequate supplies to both delta branches while also allowing for an increase of the cultivated area. Whereas the holding up of summer water by the barrage raised water levels in some areas, it also lowered levels in the deep canals of the delta, which allowed sea-water to run into channels from which people drew their water supplies. At the same time, the diminished flow in the summer also caused upstream waste water to collect in the delta canals, along with sewage from delta settlements. During the unusually low floods of 1888–89, Alexandria itself was faced with an acute water crisis. One possible solution was to allow more summer water to flow to the sea, but this would have jeopardized the all-important summer crops. The only way to expand irrigation without causing a sanitary crisis was to supply more water altogether.[122]

In short, the Nile 'needed to be made as regular as the railway and as reliable as clockwork'.[123] This required not only an altogether different type of waterworks from the Delta Barrage but also a set of interventions much farther upstream. In 1890, Willcocks was dispatched to survey the Nile's upper reaches, and in 1893 Scott-Moncrieff launched an enquiry into possible sites for a large reservoir. Soon thereafter Willcocks submitted a detailed report on 'perennial irrigation and flood protection', which estimated the future need for summer water to be 4.7 billion cubic yards (3.6 billion m^3) per year, and which recommended the construction of a dam at Aswan measuring eighty feet high and a mile and a quarter long (twenty-five metres by two kilometres) as a first step towards meeting this need.[124] Although the proposed dam would be the world's largest at the time, it was clear from the very beginning that it would not suffice over the long term. No sooner was Willcocks's report submitted than officials in Cairo began to examine the possibilities for additional dams in the Sudan, which was then still an independent state.

The decision to build a dam at Aswan was taken in 1894, but construction had to wait until several other problems were solved. On a technical level, it turned out that the dam's planned storage capacity of 3.3 billion cubic yards (2.5 billion m^3) would have to be reduced in order to avoid high rates of sedimentation. On a political level, archaeologists in Britain and France launched a vocal campaign against the foreseen inundation of the ancient temples of

122. Cookson-Hills, 68.
123. Grinsell, 'Mastering the Nile?', 111.
124. Willcocks, *Report on Perennial Irrigation*.

FIGURE 2.6. The first Aswan Dam under construction, 1901.
Courtesy of the Institution of Civil Engineers Library and Archive (ID66).

Philae, eventually forcing the government to lower the dam height to sixty-five feet (twenty metres) and reduce the capacity of the reservoir to a mere 1.3 billion cubic metres (1 billion m³). It was a major disappointment for government officials, whose annoyance was tersely captured by the young Winston Churchill: 'The state must struggle and the people starve in order that professors may exult and tourists find some place to scratch their names.'[125] Finally, on a geostrategic level it was clear to officials in London that Britain's hold over Egypt and Suez could be secured only by placing the entire Nile under a single – British-controlled – jurisdiction. The invasion of Sudan was already a firm intention in Whitehall, but British officials insisted that the costs of the dam and the military expedition upstream should be covered by the Egyptian treasury. For this reason, it was only after the 'reconquest' of Sudan in 1898 that work on the Aswan Dam began in earnest.

Directed by Willcocks himself and employing a workforce of over eight thousand men, the construction of the first Aswan Dam was completed in 1902. The design was closely tailored to the natural character of the river.

125. See Gange, 'Unholy Water'; Andersen, 'Philae Controversy'; quote from Tvedt, *Age of the British*, 25.

Its key feature was a system of large under-sluices that allowed the silt-laden autumn floodwaters from the Blue Nile to pass through without clogging up the reservoir (estimates suggested that one year's worth of Nile silt would fill a volume twenty-five times that of the pyramid of Cheops).[126] Once the annual flood had passed, the gates were closed and the lake allowed to refill with the clearer water from the White Nile. The dam proved its value almost immediately, bringing irrigation water to around a thousand square miles (a quarter of a million hectares) of land. Because of the enforced reductions in its height, however, it still captured only a fraction of the water that could theoretically be harnessed. To make the most of its existing capacity, supplementary dams were built at Assiut in middle Egypt in 1902, at Zifta in the delta in 1903, and at Esna in Upper Egypt in 1909. But even these coordinated measures were insufficient to meet Egypt's needs, so from 1908 to 1912 the government finally faced down the archaeologists and raised the height of the Aswan Dam to 90 feet (27 metres), inundating the temples at Philae. As Egypt's population and water needs continued to grow, it was raised once again to 125 feet (38 metres) in 1929–34, creating a reservoir over 200 miles (350 kilometres) long with a total capacity of 7.5 billion cubic yards (5.7 billion m^3).[127]

By this time, the horizons of the water engineers in Cairo extended far beyond Egypt's borders. Hydrologists had been carrying out upstream studies since the late 1890s, and in 1904 the Anglo-Egyptian government established the Sudan Irrigation Service as a subsection of the Egyptian Service. For the British government, securing control over the flow of the upper Nile became even more important after Egypt's declaration of independence in 1922. As a British official in the finance ministry noted in 1923, 'it is indeed not too much to say that Great Britain . . . exercises a Hydrographical Protectorate over Egypt, which is far less assailable and may well prove to be more important than the Political Protectorate abolished in February 1922'.[128] British engineers soon completed a pair of dams upstream in Sudan: one at Sennar on the Blue Nile in 1925, and another in 1937 at Jebel Aulia on White Nile. These dams were intended to serve multiple purposes within Sudan itself, including the creation of a vast irrigation project at Gezira above the confluence of the Blue and White Niles at Khartoum.[129] But the fundamental motive was the decades-old desire to control the Nile before it entered Egypt, a goal that was shared by the Egyptian government. Both of these works formed part of a broader conception of the Nile as a single hydraulic unit, one that included plans to impound its waters even further upstream in Ethiopia and

126. Tvedt, *Age of the British*, 25.

127. Blocher, *Der Wasserbau-Staat*, 74–80; Derr, *Lived Nile*, 45–73; Tvedt, *Age of the British*, 25–38.

128. Quoted in Blocher, *Der Wasserbau-Staat*, 167.

129. On Gezira: Ertsen, *Improvising Planned Development*; Bernal, 'Cotton and Colonial Order'; *Notes on the Gezira Irrigation Project*; *Sennar Dam and Gezira Irrigation Works*.

Uganda. The dams in Sudan also reflected the clear prioritization of Egyptian interests over those of upstream riparian states. They were, quite literally, concrete manifestations of Egypt's economic and geostrategic importance in British imperial thinking. In 1929, the British government enshrined these thoughts in law. The Nile Waters Agreement of that year, drawn up by Britain on behalf of its colonies, gave Egypt the vast bulk of the Nile's annual flow and complete control over its waters during the dry season, as well as the power to veto any upstream waterworks that might threaten its supplies.[130] It was a hydro-political arrangement ideally crafted for pursuing British and Egyptian interests – and also, as we will see in chapter 8, for generating interstate tensions in the future.

The upshot of all these hydraulic works was a huge expansion of year-round water supplies throughout the lower Nile valley. By the eve of the First World War, over six thousand square miles (1.6 million hectares) had been converted from seasonal to perennial irrigation, leaving only two thousand square miles (522,000 hectares) under traditional basin irrigation. Farmers grew a number of summer crops on these lands, including sugar cane, rice and especially maize. But cotton was undoubtedly the main impetus behind the changes, accounting for over three-quarters of the total summer acreage in the early 1900s. The reason for its dominance was simple: on average, no alternative cultivar earned more than half the gross returns that cotton achieved.[131] Indeed, it was not so much a matter of irrigation serving to promote cotton cultivation as the other way around. As contemporaries clearly recognized, 'the increasingly important role of cotton in Egyptian agriculture is the cause of the unremitting advance of irrigation'.[132]

The rapid spread of perennial irrigation in the 1890s and early 1900s marked an epochal watershed for the land and people of the lower Nile valley. Fields that had been cultivated for millennia according to the rhythm of the annual floodwaters could now grow crops year-round. Wherever summer waters were available, multicropping soon followed. From 1882 to 1907, the overall cultivated area of Egypt increased only marginally from 7,700 to 8,700 square miles (2–2.25 million hectares), but the cropped area (which counts the same land twice for two crops in the same year) grew a full third from 9,300 to 12,400 square miles (2.4–3.2 million hectares).[133] This sudden intensification of land use was mirrored in a corresponding reduction of the annual fallow period. From 1886 to 1913, the average annual period during which land was

130. Blocher, *Der Wasserbau-Staat*, 210–18, 268–73.

131. Willcocks and Craig, *Egyptian Irrigation*, vol. 1, 303, 366; vol. 2, 770; Owen, *Cotton*, 188, 247.

132. Charles-Roux, *La production du coton*, 210.

133. Waterbury, *Hydropolitics*, 36.

being cultivated rose from six months to eight. As year-round water supplies expanded, crop rotations that had been followed for generations were modified to accommodate summer crops, above all to grow as much cotton as possible. Instead of planting cotton every four years, many cultivators began to plant it every three or even two years, with maize or *birsim* (Egyptian clover, a fodder crop) often following the harvest instead of a period of fallow. As more and more farmers shifted from triennial to biennial cotton rotations, the main casualties were the traditional cereal crops, especially barley and beans, which could be grown only every other winter rather than two years out of every three. By 1908, over half of the cotton crop in the Nile delta was on two-year rotations, including most of the land in the leading cotton-producing districts of Daqahliyah, Buhaira, Sharqiya, and Gharbiya.[134]

In the short term this intensification of land use achieved impressive results. During the 1890s alone, cotton yields increased from around 330 to nearly 520 kilograms per hectare. But the figures soon began to decline. Whereas the average cotton yield in 1895–99 was 520 kilograms/hectare, it fell to 445 in 1900–1904 and to a mere 379 in 1905–9.[135] After decades of steady growth, this productivity slump caused widespread consternation. Agronomists advanced several possible explanations for the problem: pest attacks, the unwanted hybridization of cotton cultivars, overcropping and rising groundwater levels. Establishing a clear chain of causality was challenging, for there were 'so many influences affecting the yield of cotton that it is difficult to decide which has predominated in any particular year'.[136] Certainly, the much-favoured Mit Afifi cotton variety had suffered genetic deterioration, and the increasing depredations of the boll worm and cotton worm took a significant toll as well. In addition, the spread of multicropping itself caused problems. By the early 1900s, there were indications that the reduction of fallows was damaging soil fertility by depleting nutrients and eliminating any period during which the ground could heat up and crack, which agronomists later discovered was highly beneficial both for aerating the soil and for killing off protozoa that competed with nitrifying bacteria.[137] The rise in cotton yields through the 1890s was based, in other words, not only on better water supplies but also on the extraction of fertility reserves that were being depleted. Although a few wealthy cultivators began to apply chemical fertilizers to compensate for declining fertility (totalling a mere seventy-two tons in 1913), the bulk of poorer farmers continued to rely on the annual silt delivery and on the dwindling supply of livestock manure.[138]

134. Owen, *Cotton*, 149, 186, 248–49.

135. Owen, 191.

136. Brown, introduction to Willcocks and Craig, *Egyptian Irrigation*, vol. 1, xxii.

137. A. Richards, *Egypt's Agricultural Development*, 70–76; Schanz, *Cotton in Egypt*, 25–26.

138. Owen, *Cotton*, 253–55.

While all of these factors played a role in lowering yields, researchers eventually singled out rising groundwater levels as the main culprit. Subsoil measurements showed that water tables in the middle delta had risen from approximately twenty to twenty-five feet (six to eight metres) below the surface in the early 1800s to around half that in the mid-1880s, before climbing to only three feet (one metre) by 1908.[139] Rising groundwater not only suffocated plant roots, it also led to the familiar problem of soil salinization – a problem that, for a thirsty summer crop like cotton, was amplified by the high evaporation rates of summer irrigation water. Moreover, the constant presence of water promoted other problems such as pest infestation, both directly by producing more succulent and rank-growing cotton plants that attracted boll-worms, and indirectly by supporting the intensive cropping systems that ensured a steady supply of uniform host plants for pests to feed on (a common problem of monocultures nearly everywhere).[140]

The fact that most of these problems were linked to perennial irrigation was obvious, but the idea that continuous water supplies could depress yields was difficult for many to accept. Irrigation was, after all, long regarded as 'the source of everything in Egypt'.[141] Average annual rainfall along the lower Nile is less than eighty millimetres, and since most of it falls in the winter months, irrigation was crucial for summer crops such as cotton. Ever since the reign of Muhammad 'Ali in the early nineteenth century, the provision of year-round water supplies formed the basis of what appeared to be a winning package, one that intensified the use of land, raised the proportion of cropped area to cultivated area, and enabled farmers to grow more (and more lucrative) crops. For many years, the potential drawbacks were small enough to be ignored, but in 1908–9 they were thrust into the spotlight by a pair of exceptionally high and early Nile floods. Although most observers assumed that such plentiful waters would beget correspondingly plentiful crops, the result was a miserable cotton harvest of only 250,000 metric tons (well below recent averages), mainly due to the protracted elevation of subsurface water tables caused by the unusually high floodwaters. Whereas 'the idea that too much water was possible would have been laughed to scorn' before the floods of 1908–9, afterwards it soon became accepted wisdom.[142]

Viewed over the longer term, the declining cotton yields after 1900 resulted not from the spread of perennial irrigation per se, but from how it was practised. More specifically, it stemmed from an abiding overemphasis on

139. Ferrar, *Subsoil Water*, 9–15.

140. Balls, *Cotton Plant in Egypt*, 176–78; Schanz, *Cotton in Egypt*, 76–77; Charles-Roux, *La production du coton*, 270–72; A. Richards, *Egypt's Agricultural Development*, 72–76; Owen, *Cotton*, 190–94.

141. *Pall Mall Gazette*, 23 March 1888, quoted in Hollings, *Sir Colin C. Scott-Moncrieff*, 210.

142. Todd, *World's Cotton Crops*, 255–57, quote at 257; Schanz, *Cotton in Egypt*, 25–26.

supplying water at the expense of removing it. As we have seen above, this was a familiar problem in India, but unlike the drainage and salinization problems that had previously plagued engineers on the subcontinent, the difficulties in Egypt arose not so much from a lack of knowledge as from a failure to act on it. Most British irrigation officers working on the Nile had first-hand experience of waterlogging in India and sought to avoid a recurrence in Egypt. When they first tackled the Delta Barrage in the early 1880s there were already concerns about the risk of land 'infiltration' without a correspondingly extensive system of drainage canals and extra storage capacity to wash out accumulated salts.[143] By the early 1890s, Scott-Moncrieff cautioned that 'as irrigation without drainage always tends to injure the soil, and as drainage had been quite neglected, it had to be taken in hand'. William Willcocks became so critical of the effects of high summer waters as to advocate a wholesale return to traditional basin irrigation.[144] For most critics, however, the purpose of better drainage was to improve the perennial irrigation works themselves.[145]

Just as in colonial Asia, this habitual emphasis on water supply over drainage stemmed mainly from financial considerations. Whereas irrigation works promised relatively quick returns, investment in drainage was a long-term commitment with little immediate payback. Indeed, the incentives for privileging supply over removal were even stronger in Egypt than elsewhere, for the desire to ensure the speedy repayment of its loans was among the main factors that prompted the British occupation in the first place. Finding money for drainage works was problematic in several ways. While the imperative of financial self-sufficiency precluded major subsidies from London, the policy of 'pacification' within Egypt gravitated against the raising of domestic taxes. The French government, too, resisted the diversion of Egyptian revenues from the Caisse de la dette publique into works that would not quickly pay for themselves. The overall result, as one contemporary observer put it, was that millions were spent each year on irrigation but only thousands on drainage.[146]

It was only on the eve of the First World War that large-scale drainage works got underway, but this hardly brought an end to the problems caused by perennial irrigation. Decades of waterlogging had already done their damage. By the 1920s, soil salinization in the provinces around Cairo had turned large areas into 'veritable man-made salt wastes'. In the worst affected districts cotton yields sank by as much as 75 per cent, mostly owing to the failure, as the German soil scientist Paul Vageler put it, to 'consider these entirely self-evident pedological consequences in the quest for large profits'.[147] Signs of soil

143. Brown, *History of the Barrage*, 62.

144. Hollings, *Sir Colin C. Scott-Moncrieff*, 205 (quote); Willcocks and Craig, *Egyptian Irrigation*, vol. 1, 410–11.

145. Balls, *Cotton Plant in Egypt*, 176–78; Todd, *World's Cotton Crops*, 259–64.

146. Todd, *World's Cotton Crops*, 255.

147. Vageler, *Koloniale Bodenkunde*, 10–11; see also Owen, *Cotton*, 253.

exhaustion also began to proliferate. By the early 1920s, yields of every major crop apart from maize were well below 1913 levels. At the end of the 1930s total agricultural production was still only a quarter above 1909–13 levels, despite huge expenditures on pest control, irrigation, drainage improvements and the import of six hundred thousand tons of chemical fertilizer per year, the highest per-hectare rate of fertilizer use in the entire world at the time.[148] To make matters worse, the fertility-depressing effects of waterlogging and overcropping were compounded by the reduction of silt deliveries by the ever-growing barrage at Aswan. Although the design of the dam included extensive under-sluices to minimize this problem, it still substantially slowed the flow of the river. Whereas the Nile at Aswan was nearly a mile wide, the sluice openings measured only 360 yards (330 metres) across. What's more, as the original dam was repeatedly heightened, the sluices were not correspondingly enlarged, causing yet further disruption to the river's annual flood regime and reducing the downstream delivery of sediment that had long rejuvenated the valley's riverine soils. More alarming still, the Aswan Dam also stopped – and in some places reversed – the millennia-long process of land formation that had created the Nile delta, the main breadbasket of the country.[149]

Perhaps the gravest unintended consequence for the people living along the river was the rapid upsurge in waterborne diseases, above all malaria, hookworm and bilharzia. *Falciparum* malaria was unknown in Egypt before the early 1940s, arriving in the gut of *Anopheles gambiae* mosquitoes that thrived in the new perennial irrigation canals of Sudan and Egypt. From 1942 to 1945 the arrival of these migrants from equatorial Africa coincided with the effects of wartime food shortages to cause a major epidemic that killed as many as two hundred thousand people.[150] As devastating as the malaria outbreak was, bilharzia was an even bigger menace over the long term. Although the schistosome parasites that cause the disease had always existed in Egypt, the expansion of perennial irrigation created an ideal habitat for their snail hosts, making it the country's foremost health problem for most of the twentieth century. Although figures for early decades are sketchy, the evidence suggests that the shift from basin to perennial irrigation in the nineteenth century increased the prevalence and morbidity of bilharzia at least tenfold. By the early 1920s, infection rates surpassed 75 per cent in many areas, and by the late 1930s an estimated seven million Egyptians (out of a total population of fifteen million) had schistosomiasis, with rural villagers suffering significantly more than city dwellers. The link with perennial irrigation was unmistakable. Whereas

---

148. Mitchell, *Rule of Experts*, 26; Owen, *Cotton*, 254–55; A. Richards, *Egypt's Agricultural Development*, 120–28.

149. Cookson-Hills, 'Aswan Dam', 74; Stanley and Warne, 'Nile Delta'; McNeill, *Something New*, 171–73.

150. Mitchell, *Rule of Experts*, 25–31.

infection rates in areas with year-round canals hovered around 60 per cent, they were only 5 per cent in the few tracts south of Assiut where basin irrigation was still practised. Bilharzia was thus the very epitome of a 'man-made disease'. As the historian John Farley has put it, 'cotton first tied bilharzia and Egypt together in a knot that has yet to be untangled'.[151]

Over the long term, the rise of perennial irrigation moulded Egypt's fortunes in many other ways as well. Ever since the inception of the 'water-engineering state' under the British,[152] Egypt has been locked in a spiralling trajectory of hydrological interventions. Eliminating the adverse effects of irregular floods contributed to a rapid expansion of Egypt's population, which rose from just under five million in 1850 to ten million in 1900 to over twenty million by 1950. It was also critical for growing the export crops that balanced government books. By the 1930s, cotton alone constituted four-fifths of Egypt's exports. Together, these demographic and financial pressures placed additional demands on water, which necessitated ever-larger modifications of the Nile's hydrology. We can track the scale of intervention on several different measures: in the continuous extension of the canal network, in the growing prevalence of two-year cropping rotations and in the successive enlargements of the Aswan Dam. Beyond Egypt too, we can see it in the increasingly complex engineering plans for Sudan, Ethiopia and equatorial Africa, which sought to hold enough water to even out the Nile's floods over several years (what engineers dubbed the 'century storage' scheme).[153]

Indeed, the hydraulic systems built by the British continued to shape Egypt's fate long after imperial power faded. When General Gamal Abdel Nasser and his nationalist officers seized power in 1952, they faced the same demographic and economic pressures that their predecessors had confronted. While they were convinced that further hydroengineering works were unavoidable, they were wary of plans to store Egypt's precious water supplies in foreign countries upstream. In this sense the enormous High Dam at Aswan, built during 1960–71, represented a 'territorial' solution to the problem of Egyptian water sovereignty by creating a reservoir that initially held thirty times more water than its 1934 predecessor.[154]

Unfortunately for Egypt, the High Dam also multiplied all of the environmental problems caused by its earlier incarnations. With the near-elimination of annual flooding, Egypt's stagnant irrigation canals became an ideal habitat for water hyacinth, which clogged the flow of waterways and furnished a perfect environment for the proliferation of the snails that carried

151. Farley, *Bilharzia*, 47, 114–15, 298; see also Gallagher, *Egypt's Other Wars*; Derr, *Lived Nile*, 99–156.

152. Blocher, *Der Wasserbau-Staat*, 12.

153. Blocher, 277–89.

154. Blocher, 330–44.

bilharzia-inducing schistosomes, thus compounding the already acute public health problems caused by the disease. The High Dam also stopped nearly all of the river's silt delivery, which not only made Egypt overwhelmingly dependent on chemical fertilizers but also rapidly filled the reservoir with sediment and dramatically accelerated the ongoing shrinkage of the Nile delta. Furthermore, whereas the enlarged reservoir (dubbed Lake Nasser) was confined mainly within Egypt's borders, the dam's social and ecological effects were not. Out at sea the reduced nutrient subsidy and dwindling supply of fresh water from the Nile raised the salinity of the south-eastern Mediterranean, thereby facilitating the influx of species from the salty Red Sea via the Suez Canal (hence the label 'Lessepsian migration', after Ferdinand de Lesseps, the engineer who built the canal). Before long this bio-invasion of Indo-Pacific fauna began to reorder aquatic ecosystems and food webs in the eastern Mediterranean, and the irreversibility of the incursion means that there is now no way to turn back the clock. If the Aswan High Dam was intended to alter Egypt's fortunes in the here and now, its consequences for the Mediterranean will persist for millions of years to come.[155]

For Egypt, as for India and Java, the decades-long attempt to even out seasonal water supplies imposed heavy environmental, social and health costs. In view of all the problems that it caused, to what extent were the associated benefits worth it? There is, of course, no simple answer to this question. Any attempt to reach a verdict first needs to address a host of additional issues: which scheme or which social group one is talking about; what arrangements such schemes replaced; how irrigation systems interacted with local soils, topographies and disease ecologies; not to mention the relative weight one attaches to short- versus long-term consequences. To complicate matters further, it also needs to indulge in at least some speculation about how things would have turned out if perennial irrigation projects had not been built, and what the realistic alternatives would have been.

Pondering such counterfactual scenarios may not get us very far, but it does suggest another way of putting the question: what were the historical (or 'sunk') costs of shifting to perennial irrigation, and how did they influence future actions? Here we are on somewhat firmer ground, for despite the many ill effects of perennial irrigation systems, over time they became a cornerstone of socio-economic life in the agricultural heartlands of Egypt, India and Java, all of which came to depend heavily on these systems for their basic requirements. Regularizing water supplies allowed their populations and economies to grow at an unprecedented rate, which in turn generated yet more pressure to expand perennial irrigation even further. As we will see in chapter 8,

---

155. A point emphasized by McNeill in *Something New* (171–73). For recent studies: Arndt and Schembri, 'Common Traits'; Goren et al., 'Invading'.

decolonization did not alter this basic trajectory; indeed, from the 1940s onwards nationalist governments embarked on a spree of dam and canal building that simultaneously built on and surpassed the activities of their European predecessors. Throughout much of the post-colonial world, irrigation lay at the heart of efforts to solve the so-called 'food problem' and develop rural economies. Despite mounting concerns about the costs and long-term sustainability of large irrigation projects, it was only towards the end of the twentieth century that the momentum behind them began to slow, and even then only for a while. Gradually, almost imperceptibly, this self-reinforcing dynamic – and the coalition of interests that benefitted from it – rendered certain regions so reliant on perennial irrigation as to make any major course alteration all but unthinkable. Ironically, then, one of the main outcomes of trying to deal with the monsoon's volatility was a profound political and institutional rigidity, one that stored up a multitude of problems for future generations.

When the German travel writer Emil Ludwig first saw the Aswan Dam in 1924, what struck him most of all was its Faustian implications:

> Its symbolic significance thrust itself upon me with such force that I could grasp the life of the Nile forwards and backwards from this crucial point in its course. A mighty element had been tamed by human ingenuity so that the desert should bear fruit, an achievement which the centenarian Faust had attempted as the highest act of manliness for his fellow-men.[156]

In the German legend, Faust's limitless pursuit of knowledge and power brings him great success, but only for a time and at great cost. In Europe's colonies, the determination to master the rhythms of the monsoon was driven by immediate political and economic interests, but the repercussions have shaped life ever since.

156. Ludwig, *Der Nil*, 9.

CHAPTER THREE

Wastelands and Water

HYDRAULIC FRONTIERS AND THE
EXPANSION OF IMPERIAL POWER

NINETEENTH-CENTURY EUROPEANS WERE remarkably confident in their
ability to shape the world around them. Since the early 1800s, the extraordinary accomplishments of modern science and industry had enabled them to
overcome many of the constraints – energy, food, distance – that had previously
restricted their endeavours. During this period, a wave of technological innovations altered Europe's place in the wider world, creating an unprecedented divergence of wealth between Western and non-Western economies and permitting
the rapid expansion of European power across large swathes of Africa and Asia.[1]

Yet science and technology were more than just tools of conquest; they fundamentally defined a broader mode of empire-building. The claim to have mastered
nature was a core legitimatory tenet of colonial rule, one that was inextricably
entwined with contemporary ideas about racial hierarchy and social evolution.
It reinforced the notion that some civilizations had advanced farther along
the universal spectrum of progress than others, and in the process it nurtured
among Europeans a belief in their right, even responsibility, to govern people
whom they deemed less capable of controlling their biophysical surroundings.
As scholars have exhaustively shown, the ambition to control colonized territories presented vast opportunities not only for entrepreneurs and investors but
also for an army of technical experts. At the core of modern imperialism was
the desire to use European knowledge, capital and expertise to subjugate unruly
environments and to develop supposedly 'underused' resources.[2]

1. See Pomeranz, *Great Divergence*; Osterhammel, *Die Verwandlung der Welt*; E. Jones,
European Miracle; Parthasarathi, *Why Europe Grew Rich*.
2. See, e.g., Hodge, *Triumph of the Expert*; Cooper and Packard, *International Development*, esp. 6–9; Adas, *Machines as the Measure*; Headrick, *Tentacles of Progress* and
Tools of Empire.

In many respects, the greatest challenge to this mission of technological domestication were the vast 'wastelands' of the colonial world: the impenetrable swamps and marshlands, the barren expanses of desert, the arid and uncultivated steppes. These hostile and inaccessible landscapes had resisted the incursions of pre-colonial states and people for centuries. Long after the arrival of European colonizers, most of their resources remained untapped and their inhabitants scarcely governed. Over time, however, a combination of rising population pressures and new trade and economic opportunities drew more and more people into areas that were previously considered too remote or marginal to attract much attention in the past. In the late nineteenth and early twentieth centuries, many of these erstwhile backwaters of colonial Asia and Africa became frontiers of empire – zones of exploration, interaction and pioneer colonization on the margins of imperial power. They were spaces in which environmental transformation and the extension of colonial authority were inseparably intertwined.[3]

In nearly all of these imperial frontier zones, the control of water was the key to unlocking their economic potential. Obvious though it may seem, it is seldom explicitly recognized that what made them 'wastelands' in the first place, and what hindered large-scale settlement in the past, was generally the problem of extreme wetness or dryness. European colonizers, armed with their modern technologies, sought to overcome such obstacles once and for all in the name of 'development'. Along the coasts, state administrators designed sprawling new canal systems to drain thousands of square kilometres of soggy marshland. In the parched savannahs and scrublands, officials drew up plans to divert mighty rivers to irrigate otherwise barren soils. In the scorching deserts of the colonies, engineers dreamed of altering entire regions by flooding vast tracts of land. In each case, the manipulation of water was a means to extend cultivated settlement, and with it the reach of state power.

This chapter considers the interplay between water control and imperial expansion on three such 'hydraulic frontiers': the river deltas of Southeast Asia, the northern edges of the Sahara, and the drylands of north-western India. Like frontiers of pioneer expansion the world over, all of these areas were, in the words of one historian, 'places . . . where empire strives to incorporate people into orderly peripheries'.[4] Nonetheless, each of these frontiers presented its own set of problems and challenges, elicited its own set of responses and solutions, and developed its own internal dynamics, which evolved over time. As we will see, the hydrological conquest of the wastelands of empire enjoyed widespread support both within and beyond colonial

3. For a stimulating global analysis of late nineteenth-century frontiers, see Hopkins's *Ruling the Savage Periphery*.

4. Ludden, 'Process of Empire', 147. On frontiers more generally, see Redclift's *Frontiers*; also J. Richards's *Unending Frontier*, esp. 1–14.

officialdom. For rulers and farmers alike, few changes were regarded with such unalloyed approval as the conversion of wetlands and deserts into productive fields and pastures. Yet like any attempt at large-scale water control, this process had its limits and its drawbacks. In the event, none of these places proved to be as manageable as engineers initially hoped, and for the people and other organisms that had long inhabited them the changes were by no means entirely welcome.

Swamps and Settlers

For good reason, environmental histories of colonialism often revolve around the blatant exploitation of conquered lands and peoples: the compulsory cultivation of export crops; the expansion of foreign-owned plantations; or the dispossession of local communities for state forests, reservoir dams, or nature reserves. All of these changes certainly had extensive effects on landscapes and rural communities, but in terms of sheer scope and scale – that is, the extent of territory and overall number of people affected – the most far-reaching driver of socio-environmental change in the colonial world was the outward expansion of agricultural settlement. Compared with the sudden traumas of forced eviction or land alienation, it was admittedly a rather mundane and gradual phenomenon, and in many respects there was nothing especially novel or 'colonial' about it. For many centuries before European conquest, land-hungry farmers and revenue-hungry states had sought to enhance their prosperity through the spread of cultivation. What was new in the colonial period was the sharp acceleration of this longer-term process. Naturally, the pace of change varied greatly from region to region, as did the main factors driving it: demographic pressures in some areas, improved communications or new commercial cropping opportunities in others. Yet generally speaking, wherever large-scale land conversion took place, the principal impetus was usually the rise of human numbers and the escalating demand for food.

The centrifugal dynamics of demographic expansion were particularly strong in parts of colonial Asia. According to the best estimates we have, the net cultivated area of South Asia (India, Bangladesh and Sri Lanka, but excluding modern Pakistan) grew by some twenty-five million hectares between 1880 and 1950 (an area slightly larger than that of the United Kingdom), mainly due to a rapid increase in human population from 253.1 million to 412.2 million. In mainland and island Southeast Asia (Myanmar, Cambodia, Laos, Vietnam, Thailand, Malaysia, Brunei, Singapore, Indonesia, Philippines) the changes were even more dramatic, at least in relative terms. Here the cultivated area grew by thirty million hectares while the population more than trebled from 57.4 million to 177.1 million.[5] What these figures illustrate is not only the sharp

5. Figures from Richards and Flint, 'Century of Land-Use Change', 20, 34, 36.

demographic uptick that occurred during the colonial period but also the decidedly land-extensive character of agricultural growth throughout most of the colonial world. Despite ongoing efforts to raise yields per hectare through crop breeding, the use of fertilizers and the construction of irrigation works, most of the growth in agricultural production resulted from the diffuse, often uncoordinated, yet cumulatively colossal efforts of millions of pioneer farmers to convert forests, scrub and marshes into farmland.

One of the greatest frontier migrations in the nineteenth- and twentieth-century world occurred in the boggy river deltas of Southeast Asia. In some respects, the deltaic plains of the Irrawaddy River in Burma and the Mekong in southern Indochina (as well as the Chao Phraya in central Thailand) were ideally suited for agriculture. Created over millions of years by the prodigious deposition of silt from upstream, their deep alluvial soils were fertile, well-watered and partly shielded from the sea by a thicket of coastal mangroves. In other ways, however, they were distinctly less alluring. Like all of the world's great river deltas, the southern reaches of the Irrawaddy and Mekong were amphibious environments, spaces in which the distinction between land and water was blurred. Much of the land was waterlogged or at least seasonally flooded, and most was still blanketed by thick swamp grasses or dense tropical forests when the British and French first arrived there. Despite the formidable challenges these wetlands posed, they soon became the site of one of the most dynamic agricultural frontiers in the entire world. Over the course of half a century they were cleared, drained and collectively transformed into the world's greatest rice-exporting region.[6]

The process began in the lower reaches of the Irrawaddy delta. When the British first annexed Lower Burma in 1852, only around 1,200 of its 15,000 square miles (3,200 of 40,000 square kilometres) were cultivated. The officials who notionally governed the delta viewed it as an 'interminable and notorious waste land', a low-lying plain 'covered with elephant grass, scrub and jungle which is waist deep for more than six months in the year'. Despite the forbidding conditions in the delta, its agricultural potential was recognized early on. The most obvious obstacles were environmental. Even apart from the hard graft of clearing the forests, settlers would have to contend with seasonal monsoon floods, waterborne diseases, and a host of wild animals (crocodiles, tigers, snakes, insects) that posed a serious danger to people, livestock and crops. In the eyes of British officialdom there were also various cultural obstacles to overcome; namely, 'the difficulty in raising the masses from the sloth of ages'. If local 'Asiatics' were unable to develop the region themselves,

---

6. On the frontier characteristics of agricultural expansion in these areas: Adas, 'Continuity and Transformation'. On the emergence of the region as a major rice exporter: Coclanis, 'Southeast Asia's Incorporation'.

then the more enlightened and capable British would need to take the lead. As one settlement officer put it in 1865, 'we are dealing with a semi-civilized race; we should assist them in advancing themselves . . . our superiority as a nation warrants us to do this'.[7]

Towards this end, the British administration in Burma introduced a range of inducements to attract peasant pioneers into the delta, the most important of which was the establishment of new land tenure arrangements that gave farmers title to the land they reclaimed. Despite the prevalence of laissez-faire doctrines within colonial government, administrators in Lower Burma took an unusually interventionist approach to ensure that the delta's development would be pursued mainly by smallholders rather than wealthy property owners. Their aim was to create a new export economy based on peasant proprietors, who would not only be allowed to sell their produce as they saw fit but also be free from the ill effects of landlordism and indebtedness that plagued much of rural India. It was a paternalistic yet comparatively progressive vision, and it proved a powerful magnet for land-poor peasants across the region. What's more, its pulling power was further enhanced by push factors upstream. In the drier and more densely populated region of Upper Burma, mounting land pressures and periodic food shortages generated a steady stream of migrants southwards. In the early 1880s the number of emigrants swelled amid a series of poor rice harvests. In 1884 alone nearly a quarter of a million people left the southern Mandalay provinces for the delta, and the flow of migrants rose still further after the British annexation of Upper Burma in 1885–86.[8]

The key to settling the delta was to transform its existing maze of creeks and channels into a new hydraulic network. Rivers had always been the primary conduits of transport in the region, and they remained so throughout most of the colonial era. Despite the gradual construction of railways connecting the main rice-growing provinces to coastal ports, the bulk of cargo and passenger traffic was still carried on the water (see chapter 1).[9] The Irrawaddy Flotilla Company, founded in 1868 with strong state support, operated over six hundred vessels by the early 1930s. To supplement the natural waterways, engineers excavated a series of major canals designed to facilitate the movement of people, rice and consumer goods into and out of the delta. At the same time, the colonial government built a multitude of secondary waterworks to serve more strictly agricultural purposes and oversaw the excavation of hundreds of kilometres of smaller channels to extend the reach of the seasonal floodwaters. It also built a series of major embankments to protect those parts of delta most at risk from high seasonal floods. By the 1920s,

7. Quotes from Adas, 'Colonization'. 101–3.
8. Keeton, *King Thebaw*, 143; more generally Adas, *Burma Delta*.
9. On railways, see Baillargeon's 'Road to Mandalay'.

state-sponsored embankments had converted some fifteen hundred square miles (four hundred thousand hectares) of uncultivated swamp into rice paddies.[10] In contrast to the vast hydrological works in Egypt or the Gangetic plain, the primary purpose of hydraulic infrastructure in the rain-abundant Irrawaddy delta was not to promote artificial irrigation per se, but rather to channel the annual floods and ensure that the main transit canals remained navigable.

Farmers soon streamed into the delta, swelling its population from around 1.5 million in 1852 to over 4 million by the turn of the century. Most of the migrants came from Upper Burma and the east coast of India, and were disproportionately drawn from districts with high land pressures and recurrent food shortages. As one might expect, the ebb and flow of migrants varied as conditions in these exodus districts fluctuated. Periodic water crises were a major cause of migration into the delta. Droughts and attendant harvest failures were a perpetual push factor from the dry zone of Upper Burma, though they struck with particular frequency in the 1860s and again in the 1890s. In 1896–97, the worst affected areas saw around a third of their entire population depart for the delta. Similar events influenced net migration flows from eastern India. The widespread floods that occurred there in the late 1880s, along with the severe cyclone that struck eastern Bengal in 1897 and the devastating series of droughts in the late 1890s and early 1900s, all coincided with spikes in the number of people crossing the Bay of Bengal to Lower Burma.[11]

Contrary to official rhetoric, much of the land that the migrants were moving into was not an empty 'wilderness'. Like other agricultural frontiers in the nineteenth-century world, the mass colonization of the Irrawaddy delta displaced people who already lived there. Its inhabitants were mostly fishermen, small farmers or traders who made a living from forest products. Far from being isolated by the watery nature of the landscape, many used the creeks and rivers of the delta to sell rice, fish or tropical wood in the dense commercial networks that criss-crossed the Bay of Bengal. A large proportion of delta occupants were Mons, who traditionally regarded the Burmese as adversaries, and who responded to the influx of pioneer farmers by moving from customary areas of settlement to more remote regions. This tactic worked as long as there was sufficient land to do so, yet in the end most Mon groups became culturally 'Burmanized' and lost their language in the process.[12]

By the early twentieth century, the spongy expanses of the Irrawaddy delta had been fundamentally transformed. From 1852 to the early 1930s the area

10. On public works: Nisbet, *Burma under British Rule*, 239–43; Adas, *Burma Delta*, 35–36.

11. Adas, *Burma Delta*, 45–47, 95–97, 162. On Indian migration to Burma (and elsewhere in Southeast Asia), see Amrith's *Bay of Bengal* (101–43).

12. See Coclanis, 'Metamorphosis', 38–41; Adas, *Burma Delta*, 50, 56.

of rice paddy grew more than tenfold from approximately one thousand to over thirteen thousand square miles (284,000–3.4 million hectares). The boom years were the 1890s, during which the frontier moved so fast in some areas as to cause local land shortages by the close of the decade. Although the pace of land conversion subsequently slowed as the most accessible sections of the delta were cleared, the overall cropped surface continued to expand. Rice exports rose in line with the area of cultivation, increasing from 162,000 to almost 3 million tons annually.[13]

Lower Burma thus became one of Asia's main surplus food producers and a key supplier for world markets. Yet even as the agricultural frontier expanded, the limits of further growth were already hovering into view. The dramatic development of the delta's rice economy was almost entirely extensive rather than intensive; that is, it was based on the conquest of swamps and forested wetlands rather than on any significant innovations in planting methods or agricultural technologies. It was only in the interwar years that experiments with improved rice strains or new ploughs made much headway, and even then they had little effect on the ground. Farmers made almost no use of fertilizers, and throughout most of the delta the control of water was largely confined to flood protection.[14]

Over time, this lack of agricultural intensification had profound social implications. As uncultivated lands became scarcer in the early twentieth century, the result was a rising tide of peasant indebtedness, land loss and poverty. From 1914 to 1918, wartime dislocations exacerbated all of these problems, and over the following years social and ethnic tensions mounted as economic growth began to slow and smallholders lost more and more land to creditors and to large estates – precisely what the initial smallholder-first policy in Lower Burma was intended to avoid.

The onset of the Depression was a major turning point. With the sudden collapse of rice prices in the early 1930s, the delta finally lurched into a full-blown agrarian crisis. In essence, the Depression multiplied the problems and tensions that had been building up over previous decades. These tensions soon boiled over into a series of violent uprisings that were directed mainly against landlords and merchants (especially non-Burmese), who, alongside the colonial administration, were blamed for the deepening misery among Burmese labourers and tenants. Although colonial security forces managed to suppress the most serious rebellion by 1932, the ongoing economic distress continued to feed sporadic outbreaks of ethnic violence for the remainder of the decade. Well before the Japanese invasion fatally crippled British authority in Burma in 1942, the intermingling currents of economic distress, Burmese nativism

13. Adas, *Burma Delta*, 35, 128–29; 'Continuity and Transformation', 195.
14. Adas, 'Colonization', 106.

and anti-colonial sentiment that swirled throughout the Irrawaddy delta proved even more difficult to control than the water that flowed through it.[15]

In the meantime, around 1,400 kilometres to the south-east, a parallel agrarian frontier swept across the wetlands of the lower Mekong River. Long before French forces occupied the Mekong delta in the 1860s, Khmer and Vietnamese rulers had built a series of canal systems to encourage the settlement of Vietnamese peasants and to bolster their authority in the region. Soon after the French took over, they began to expand on these pre-colonial waterworks. From these early beginnings, French engineers gradually carved their way into the western and southern parts of the delta, initially by mobilizing thousands of unpaid Vietnamese labourers to dig canals, and after 1900 by deploying a flotilla of huge mechanical dredges as well. All throughout the period of French rule, the waterways of the Mekong delta – the natural rivers and creeks, the 'improved' channels and the entirely man-made canals – were the principal means of communication and the key to making the deltaic plain more economically productive. As David Biggs has felicitously put it, colonial power in the lower Mekong rested on a 'floating state', a waterborne polity whose core task 'had less to do with enforcing its vague boundaries . . . than with grafting [itself] on to the existing Vietnamese landscape and Chinese-controlled economy'. Ever since the first French incursions into the region in 1859, 'the water's edge in Cochinchina had been the primary site for colonial encounters', whether military, scientific or commercial.[16]

Just as in Lower Burma, the main purpose of the Mekong delta's waterworks was to facilitate transport and control the seasonal floods, both of which were crucial to the expansion of rice cultivation. Surveillance and security concerns initially outweighed economic considerations, but once the delta was 'pacified' most of the canals built by the French served both transport and agricultural functions.[17] Drainage and storm protection were also important – considerably more so than on the Irrawaddy – because the western Mekong delta scarcely rises more than two metres above sea level, which is roughly the level of the highest tides on the South China Sea. Consequently, many of the waterworks in Cochin China were designed to protect croplands from periodic storm surges and to drain salt water from low-lying areas. For French engineers the two central aims were to channel the seasonal flows of the Mekong into an ever-expanding grid of paddy fields, and to manage the action of sea tides on the region's waterways.

---

15. On the effects of the Depression in the delta, see Montesano and Brown's 'Colonial Economy in Crisis'; on land alienation, Furnivall's *Colonial Policy and Practice* (85–87, 110–11); see also Adas's *Burma Delta* (127–53, 185–208).

16. Biggs, *Quagmire*, 48–51, 59–70, quote at 50.

17. Brocheux, *Mekong Delta*, 17–18, 52–54.

The initial attempts to do so were fraught with difficulty, for the creation of permanent canals in the Mekong delta was essentially an attempt to stabilize an inherently unstable and fluid environment. The fate of the flagship Duperré Canal – by far the largest hydraulic project of the 1870s, which the colonial governor Victor Auguste Duperré humbly named after himself – demonstrated the challenges that lay ahead. Built to connect Saigon with the delta port of My Tho, it took twenty-five thousand conscripted labourers well over a year to excavate. Inaugurated with great pageantry in 1877, it became unnavigable within only a few months owing to the accumulation of large silt bars across the main channel. These *dos d'âne* (donkey backs), as the French called them, were formed wherever tidal currents flowing from different directions into canals or creeks met one another, resulting in 'dead points' where the currents halted and deposited their sediment. Engineers found them extremely hard to eradicate, so much so that the government temporarily halted further canal construction in favour of railways and roads. Over the following years, officials in the Department of Public Works continued to study the *dos d'âne* and eventually developed a system of flushing basins to regulate water flows and minimize silt deposition along major canals such as the Duperré. From a technical point of view, the problem appeared to be solved. The social implications, however, were more complicated, for the attempt to eliminate 'dead points' was not cost-free. Around a year after a flushing system was constructed on the similarly afflicted Saintard Canal, local farmers pierced the dam that blocked its connection with a tidal creek in order to restore the circulatory tidal flows on which their fields and villages had long relied. With the dam gone, it was only a matter of weeks before the *dos d'âne* returned. Whereas the natural fluctuations of the tides were detrimental to canal transport, they were a benefit for the delta's paddy farmers.[18]

Such trade-offs highlight both the competing uses of the delta environment and the conflicts that resulted from the disruption of the existing pre-colonial hydrological regime. All throughout the colonial period, French hydraulic infrastructure in the Mekong delta tended to serve the interests of navigation and frontier expansion over the desire to boost productivity on existing farmland. Although the excavation of artificial canals was crucial for opening new lands to cultivation, most of the resulting channels were of little use for agricultural water management. In fact, many canals actually exacerbated the hydrological challenges of farming in a swampy environment. In those parts of the delta affected by both the tides and seasonal river flooding, the construction of canals running parallel to the main river actually hindered drainage and raised the risk of catastrophic inundations. In low-lying tidal areas, canals leading to the sea desiccated the soil in the dry season and allowed the incursion of salt water far inland. The control of water for specifically agricultural

18. Biggs, *Quagmire*, 30–34, 40–41.

purposes was largely left to farmers themselves, who pursued it with little coordination and quite often with contentious side-effects – for example, by channelling sought-after water away from neighbours' fields or, conversely, diverting excess water on to other people's land. As a result, the least powerful farmers – mostly those with small or second-rate plots – remained particularly vulnerable to the vagaries of floods, tides and seasonal rains (a theme to which we will return in chapter 4).[19]

Rather than resolving such hydro-political difficulties, the colonial government instead sought to escape them altogether by expanding the frontier ever farther across the delta. After 1900 a new generation of gigantic steam-powered dredges chewed their way through the region's swamps, forests and fields, most of them operated under contract by the Société française industrielle d'Extrême-Orient (renamed Société française d'entreprises de dragages et de travaux publics in 1910). While the dredges excavated the main canals, many of the smaller connecting channels were dug by hand at the expense of local landowners or provincial authorities. Altogether, the creation of this new grid of waterways in the Mekong delta constituted one of the greatest earthmoving exercises in world history. From 1900 to 1930 French dredgers excavated 165 million cubic metres of mud and soil, a volume exceeded at the time only by the construction of the Suez and Panama Canals. By the 1930s, around four thousand kilometres of primary and secondary canals connected the paddy fields of the delta to the rice mills at Cholon and the main port at Saigon.[20] It was an expensive undertaking, but the state managed to recoup its outlays many times over through the export of rice and the public auction of newly 'opened' land. From 1880 to the 1930s, the paddy area of Cochin China grew from 522,000 to 2.2 million hectares, and its rice exports from 284,000 to over 1.5 million tons.[21]

French officials naturally liked to credit themselves for the 'improvement' of these previously 'unproductive' lands. In a speech to mark the opening of the Rach Gia-Ha Tien Canal in 1930, Governor-General Pierre Pasquier extolled the beneficent ingenuity of 'l'œuvre française' in converting the 'dismal, vast solitudes' of the deltaic plain into 'rich patchworks . . . in which are set as far as the eye can see the gold and emerald of peaceful fields'.[22] Yet in fact the transformation of the delta owed at least as much to peasant initiative as to colonial development policies. Like most agricultural frontiers the world over, there was a convergence of interests between state officials eager to expand

19. Brocheux, *Mekong Delta*, 52–55; Brocheux and Hémery, *Indochina*, 121.

20. Robequain, *Economic Development*, 110–11; Biggs, 'Managing a Rebel Landscape', 456. On canal-building and dredging: Biggs, *Quagmire*, 30–48, figure p. 71.

21. Gourou, *L'utilisation du sol*, 284–95; Brocheux, *Mekong Delta*, 18–21; Robequain, *Economic Development*, 220.

22. Inspection des travaux publics, *Dragages de Cochinchine: Canal Rachgia-Hatien* (Saigon, 1930), 7–8, quoted in Biggs, *Quagmire*, 89.

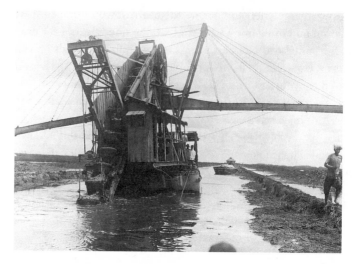

FIGURE 3.1. Grand Picanon dredge digging a canal in the Plaine des Joncs, Mekong delta, 1919–26.
Courtesy of the Archives nationales d'outre-mer, FR ANOM 30Fi107/37.

their revenue base and ordinary farmers keen to improve their own fortunes. Most of the actual work was done by settlers from the densely populated lowlands of central and northern Vietnam, which had long been the main sources of peasant migration into the Mekong delta (see chapter 4). As the French-built steam dredgers carved their watery corridors across the landscape, they were followed by a fleet of sampans carrying would-be settlers eager to claim a parcel alongside the new canals. The demand for land was such that some settlers took the risk of clearing and farming plots before acquiring legal title. From 1886 to 1928 the total population of the western delta grew from 391,000 to 1.45 million.[23]

There were many similarities between the processes of frontier expansion in Cochin China and Lower Burma, but there were also significant policy differences that shaped how agricultural colonization developed. Like their British counterparts in Burma, French authorities tried to attract migrants into the Mekong delta through low taxes and promises of land. But unlike the British prioritization of small-scale landowner-farmers, they also granted large concessions to French *colons* and wealthy Vietnamese or Chinese investors, especially as the frontier moved into the southern and western sections of the delta (where the bulk of rice exports were produced). The social consequences of this decision were substantial. Over the years, the constant volatility of rice prices favoured the expansion of large estates as more and

23. Brocheux, *Mekong Delta*, 22–25; Biggs, *Quagmire*, 70–71.

more smallholders – who could not as easily weather price drops – fell into debt and lost their land. The result by the early twentieth century was an increasingly polarized social hierarchy in which a rising number of tenant farmers worked on vast rice-producing *latifundia* for little more than subsistence wages. By 1930, 4 per cent of the population owned just under half of the delta's cropland, while nearly three-quarters of rural households possessed no land at all.[24]

The social disparities on the delta were, then, already stark before the Depression hit Indochina in late 1930, but the situation soon went from bad to worse. Here, as in Burma, the Depression effectively turbocharged processes of land loss and polarization that had gradually been unfolding for many years. From 1930 to 1934 rice prices fell by roughly three-quarters, forcing farmers to work harder simply in order to pay their taxes. As ever, the price collapse hit poor smallholders the hardest, but the actions of the colonial government made their situation even more difficult. Whereas large plantations were provided with financial assistance – following a kind of 'too big to fail' logic driven by concerns about the effect that insolvent estates might have on future inward investment – smallholders were left on their own to face a surge of bankruptcies and foreclosures. For the first time since the 1860s, the delta's rice acreage shrank as a result of land abandonment, declining from 2.2 million hectares in 1929 to 1.85 million hectares in 1933. To make matters worse, the devastating economic problems caused by the Depression were compounded by exceptionally high floods in 1929 and 1937, which destroyed the homes and crops of thousands of people and caused many others to take on additional debt. It was not long before this social and ecological malaise sparked a succession of localized strikes, demonstrations and riots. Although the uprisings in Cochin China were smaller and more sporadic than the violent revolts that broke out in the northern and central parts of colonial Vietnam in the early 1930s, the Mekong delta was nonetheless a fertile recruiting ground for the various secret societies and political movements that increasingly challenged French colonial authority during the Depression years. Despite the partial economic recovery in the mid-1930s, the resentments fuelled by the crisis showed little sign of abating in the near future. By the close of the decade, as war loomed in Europe, French authorities along the lower Mekong were no more able to stabilize its volatile sociopolitical environment than they could its fluid physical environment.[25]

In both the Irrawaddy and Mekong deltas, the social upheavals of frontier settlement intersected with a similarly dramatic set of ecological changes.

24. Le Coq, Trébuil and Dufumier, 'History of Rice Production', 169, 172; Gourou, *L'utilisation du sol*, 269–83.

25. Brocheux, *Mekong Delta*, 152–85; Biggs, *Quagmire*, 91–98, 113–14; Adas, 'Continuity and Transformation', 197.

Perhaps the most obvious was the rapid destruction of mangrove and forest. Woodland clearance was essential for growing more food crops, but it also had numerous downsides. For one thing, it denied farmers access to timber, fuel and other resources that had previously been freely obtainable. As the wetland forests shrank, and as colonial governments reserved for themselves any remnants of woodland containing commercially valuable species, settlers were increasingly forced to purchase building materials and even firewood on the market. Over time, the need to pay for products that had once been freely gathered in the forests had a decidedly negative effect on peasant living standards, further aggravating the social polarization and agrarian unrest that swept across the deltas in the interwar years.[26]

A further consequence of deforestation was a sharp rise in disease. Malaria was endemic throughout much of the Irrawaddy and Mekong deltas, but it frequently reached epidemic proportions on recently cleared land – especially areas with numerous canals – whose stagnant, sunlit waters proved to be ideal breeding grounds for some of the chief mosquito vectors in the region, such as *Anopheles hyrcanus* and *A. minimus*. New settlers often became so ill as to be unable to cultivate their fields, forcing them either to abandon their land or to go into debt. Outbreaks in recently cleared areas were occasionally so severe as to wipe out entire households or even villages. Gradually, the incidence of malaria tended to decline as survivors developed a degree of immunity and as the spread of cultivation left fewer standing pools for mosquito larvae. Yet even then, other maladies such as typhus and cholera continued to strike the delta settlements, and disease problems were by no means confined to the settlers themselves. The bullocks and buffaloes that played a critical role as draft animals in the deltas likewise suffered from high mortality rates, and occasionally perished en masse from epizootics of rinderpest or foot-and-mouth disease.[27]

Furthermore, the ecological consequences of agricultural colonization were by no means limited to the initial effects of forest clearance and swamp drainage. They soon led to problems for the newly established agroecosystems themselves. The hundreds of kilometres of new embankments may have been crucial for flood control and navigation, but over the long term they also compromised soil fertility by diminishing the delivery of nutrient-rich silt from upstream. As a result, the disruption of the natural flood regime served to compound the yield-depressing effects of the lack of fertilizer applied to delta fields.[28] By reducing the natural ebb and flow of the rivers, man-made flood-works also prevented farmers from promptly draining away stagnant water on their paddies, which could severely stunt plant growth by encouraging the build-up of

26. Adas, 'Colonization', 107; Coclanis, 'Metamorphosis', 46.

27. Saha, *Colonizing Animals*, 74–77; Coclanis, 'Metamorphosis', 49–50; Adas, 'Continuity and Transformation', 199; *Burma Delta*, 62.

28. Murray, *Development*, 444; Adas, *Burma Delta*, 131.

alum salts in the soil.[29] And to top it off, all of these problems were further exacerbated by pests and diseases. The rice fields of the Irrawaddy and Mekong deltas were perennially prone to attack by birds, deer, elephants and rats. Farms along the littoral were also periodically ravaged by swarms of crabs, which devoured young rice shoots or seeds. Worst of all, the creation of vast expanses of homogeneous rice monocultures presented a veritable smorgasbord for insects such as caterpillars, larval worms and beetles. In total, between 15 and 30 per cent of the annual rice crop in the Mekong delta was lost to pests and disease, with stem borers alone claiming around 10 to 15 per cent.[30]

While some animals posed a threat to rice paddies, the expansion of agriculture also took a heavy toll on the region's wildlife. Although the effects of land clearance and swamp drainage on historic fauna populations are impossible to quantify, there is every reason to assume that the displacement of some of the world's most biodiverse wetlands and forests by millions of hectares of rice paddy destroyed the habitat of countless creatures, ranging from large mammals such as elephants and tigers to birds, reptiles and numerous other species.[31] Whereas some of these stricken creatures were reviled as pests and targeted for eradication by the payment of bounties, others were prized as resources, above all those that lived in the water.[32]

Indeed, the tensions between fishing and agriculture in Southeast Asia's river deltas provide yet another example of how the interconnectedness of the hydrosphere provided ample grounds for conflict among different user groups. The destruction of mangrove and the drainage of wetlands eliminated large areas of protective habitat for fish and crustaceans.[33] With the spread of cultivation, farmers and fishermen regularly clashed over the management of creeks and floodwaters. Whereas fishermen often blamed upstream hydraulic works for declining catches, farmers occasionally suffered from the construction of fish screens and traps that slowed the movement of creeks, causing them to silt up and flood cultivated areas downstream. 'Agriculture and inland fisheries are in many respects antagonistic', wrote the colonial forester John Nisbet in 1901. 'And, of course, in the struggle that must ultimately ensue, the former is bound to maintain itself as the supreme interest'.[34] As we will see in more detail in chapter 5, the privileging of agriculture over fisheries was by no means unique to the deltas of Southeast Asia, but was a common phenomenon throughout the colonial world.

29. Biggs, *Quagmire*, 95–96; Murray, *Development*, 446.

30. Murray, *Development*, 446; Adas, *Burma Delta*, 61–62.

31. Coclanis, 'Metamorphosis', 46–47.

32. On efforts to eradicate 'vermin': Saha, *Colonizing Animals*, 83–106.

33. Generally: Brocheux, *Mekong Delta*, 81–83; Biggs, *Quagmire*, 75; Adas, 'Continuity and Transformation', 199.

34. Nisbet, *Burma under British Rule*, 358.

Despite all of these problems, the dramatic refashioning of the Irrawaddy and Mekong deltas was almost universally applauded at the time. Few contemporaries gave much thought to the ecological changes that it entailed, and fewer still saw much reason for concern. Colonial rhetoric enthusiastically celebrated the conversion of dank and murky 'wastes' into productive farmland. For the thousands of pioneer settlers streaming in from Upper Burma, India or central Annam, the displacement of swamp and forest by carefully cultivated rice paddies likewise marked the advance of orderly and civilized village life, and none of these farmers were particularly saddened to witness the decline of wild animal populations that posed a threat to their crops and indeed their lives.

By any standard, the drainage and colonization of Southeast Asia's river deltas constituted a momentous transformation. Few other parts of the colonial world witnessed such a far-reaching reconfiguration of their social and biophysical landscape. Although the settlement of the Irrawaddy and Mekong deltas has attracted less attention from historians than the 'neo-European' frontiers of the Americas or Australasia, it nonetheless displayed a number of basic similarities to these other agricultural frontiers. For one thing, it was impelled by many of the same basic factors: land shortages in population centres, the establishment of tenure systems that encouraged settlement, rising commercial demand and a growing communications network that connected farmers to distant markets. Moreover, many of the social and economic consequences paralleled those on the frontiers of neo-European settlement. The colonization of Southeast Asia's deltas furnished a useful outlet for demographic pressures. In the process, it marginalized indigenous peoples and created a major food-exporting region for the global capitalist economy. Even the ecological effects were broadly analogous. The delta frontiers, like their counterparts elsewhere, involved a massive incursion of people, cultivars and domesticated animals into areas that were hitherto lightly populated and relatively undisturbed by the effects of sedentary agriculture – even if they were hardly the empty 'wastes' they were claimed to be.

Nonetheless, when viewed in global perspective the replumbing and replanting of Southeast Asia's river deltas appears to have been less environmentally or socially disruptive than the contemporary settlement frontiers in the Americas or Australasia. As Michael Adas has suggested, the spread of wet-rice cultivation involved a relatively high degree of adaptation to – rather than reconfiguration of – the existing social and biophysical landscape.[35] Although the deltaic plains were extensively deforested during the late nineteenth and early twentieth centuries, the massive spread of rice cultivation did not always displace tropical woodland or mangrove. In certain areas, it essentially amounted to the replacement of existing species of marsh grass

---

35. This argument is based on Adas's 'Continuity and Transformation' (201–5).

with a different, domesticated species of marsh grass. Despite the alteration of the existing hydrological regime, the new networks of embankments and canals were broadly designed to channel, extend or moderate the natural flood cycles rather than abrogate them entirely. As a result, they only partially disrupted the process of silt accumulation that had created the deltas in the first place and that made them so fertile. In turn, this continuation of basic geomorphological processes helps explain why the predominant farming methods in the deltas were themselves relatively sustainable. The wet-rice cultivation techniques that prevailed throughout the colonial era (until the 'Green Revolution' of the 1960s and 1970s, to which we will return in chapter 8) had been practised in Southeast Asia for thousands of years. They required few if any exogenous inputs from commercial firms or scientific 'experts', and they were capable of maintaining soil fertility almost indefinitely if well managed and not deprived of silty floodwaters.[36] Finally, although the huge influx of Upper Burmese, Indian or Tonkinese peasants certainly altered the fortunes of the deltas' indigenous inhabitants, the overall consequences were not as traumatic as they were for the displaced and mistreated indigenous peoples of the Americas and Australasia. In all of these ways, the pioneer settlement of the Irrawaddy and Mekong deltas differed significantly from the ploughing up of North America's grasslands, the conversion of Australia's outback to livestock farms or the obliteration of Brazil's coastal forests by commercial plantations.

The colonization of Southeast Asia's deltas thus presents us with a peculiar type of frontier: one that involved a partial rather than thorough alteration of the existing waterscape; one that combined local farming methods with hydraulic interventions from outside; and one that, for all the socio-economic asymmetries and inequalities involved, was driven as much by peasant initiative as by the political imperatives of a modernizing state. Meanwhile, in other remote corners of Europe's empire, the efforts of colonial states to develop unproductive 'wastelands' through the manipulation of water followed a very different pattern. Fortunately, some of the most ambitious schemes never made it off the drawing board.

Making the Desert Bloom

If the fluid delta landscapes of tropical Asia proved difficult to control, the vast deserts of Europe's empire posed an even greater set of hydrological challenges. It was here that the high-modernist impulse to dominate nature encountered perhaps its most formidable foe. From the Kalahari in southern Africa to the arid borderlands of western India, the scarcity of water was the key determinant of human activity. In such regions, the physical distribution of water had long structured patterns of settlement and trade, and it imposed

36. Generally: Bray, *Rice Economies*, 8–19.

tight limits on colonial designs as well. Arid climates tended to make for a sparse and highly mobile local population, difficult to police or to integrate into the colonial economy. Wherever water supplies were extremely scant or unreliable, large-scale development and infrastructural investment were completely unfeasible. In the driest parts of Africa, the Middle East and central Asia, the lack of water meant that all activities were subordinated to the search for this most basic element for human survival. Here, the project of rendering territories more 'legible' – let alone more productive – hinged almost entirely on overcoming their hydrological constraints.

Nowhere were the limitations greater than in the Sahara, and nowhere were the dreams of overcoming them more ambitious. If we discount the frozen poles of the planet, the Sahara is by far the largest desert in the world. Covering over nine million square kilometres, its surface area is larger than the entirety of non-Russian Europe, dwarfing all the world's other major drylands. The sheer size of the Sahara made it an object of fear and fascination alike. Of all the alien environments in the colonial world, none exerted a more powerful grip on the European imagination than the vast, unforgiving wastes in the heart of the African continent. For nineteenth-century Europeans the Sahara was the very epitome of a pristine 'wilderness', a timeless and untamed space whose extraordinary physical hostility repelled all but the most intrepid. It formed a seemingly impassable barrier dividing the Mediterranean world from the riches of the African interior, and it retained this image long after explorers had sent back reports of the cities and trade routes that connected the northern and southern 'shores' of this ocean of sand. As European influence spread throughout Africa, the Sahara acquired a somewhat paradoxical perceptual status. On the one hand, it was the epitome of a hostile and forbidding environment beyond human control; on the other, it was the ultimate proving ground for demonstrating heroic fortitude and ingenuity.[37] On both a metaphorical and a practical level, it was a space in which to test the capacity of European technological civilization to master even the most intractable parts of the natural world.

Although the Sahara had long been an object of European fantasy, it took some time for this desert frontier to come into view. For several decades after French expeditionary forces invaded Algeria in 1830, the main focus of successive administrations was to extend their authority throughout the colony, quell periodic outbursts of indigenous opposition, and open up supposedly 'vacant' or 'underused' lands to European settlers. French expansion in Algeria accelerated markedly in the 1870s after the humiliating defeat in the Franco-Prussian war and the consequent loss of Alsace-Lorraine. In the wake of the debacle, dreams of revitalizing French prestige focused largely on the *mise*

---

37. See McDougall and Scheele, *Saharan Frontiers*, esp. 1–22; Lehmann, *Desert Edens*, 13–37.

en valeur (enhancing or developing the value) of its colonial territories. The new Republican government faced mounting pressure to colonize more land in North Africa as a means of both compensating for lost territory at home and restoring France's battered reputation abroad. Over time, as settlement expanded and fertile land along the coastal strip became scarcer, attention gradually turned towards the arid regions of the interior. For French planners, the conquest of the Sahara was envisioned as a 'pénétration pacifique', an incremental process to be led by scientists and commercial traders rather than European settlers, and characterized more by persuasion than by brutal coercion (in the event, it proved to be extremely violent). In French eyes, here was a vast and seemingly empty territory that could be opened for exploitation – if only sufficient water could somehow be made available.[38]

The extreme aridity of the Sahara posed an enormous problem, and it spawned a commensurately grand solution. In the 1870s and 1880s, a team of French engineers and surveyors devised a scheme to create a vast inland sea by flooding parts of the desert. More specifically, the plan involved the diversion of water from the Mediterranean into low-lying depressions in Tunisia and Algeria by means of an artificial canal. The leading advocate of the scheme was François Élie Roudaire, an army surveyor whose job was to create accurate topographic charts of the desert for use by the French military. As a graduate of Saint-Cyr (France's top military academy), a freethinker and a freemason, he was an archetypal representative of the milieu of adventurers, geographers and politicians who formed the backbone of the French colonial lobby. For a while, his proposal enjoyed widespread public and official support. Although the project ultimately failed, both its emergence and its demise give us a useful insight into the nature, mentality and limits of imperial water engineering at the time.[39]

The project first took shape in 1872–73 while Roudaire was carrying out a topographical survey of the depressions, or 'chotts', that line the northern reaches of the desert. These barren, low-lying plains stretch some 375 kilometres between the desert province of Biskra (known as the province of Constantine during the colonial era) in north-eastern Algeria to the outskirts of Gabès on the Tunisian coast. It had long been surmised that these depressions were once part of the ancient Sea of Triton, a large inland gulf that periodically appeared in classical writings ever since the days of Herodotus, but which had apparently dried out over the centuries. The idea gained a measure of scientific credence in the 1840s when French geological surveys suggested that the

38. For general background: McDougall, *History of Algeria*, 89–100; Sessions, *By Sword and Plow*. On the role of violence in the French conquest of the Sahara: Brower, *Desert Named Peace*.

39. For detailed accounts: Marçot, *Une mer au Sahara*; Létolle and Bendjoudi, *Histoires d'une mer*. For a concise but insightful analysis: Lehmann, *Desert Edens*, 38–52; Heffernan, 'Bringing the Desert'.

three main chotts of Melrhir, el Gharsa and el Djerid lay below sea level. By the 1860s a handful of geologists in the colony began to muse about the possibility of piercing through the ridge behind Gabès and refilling the inland sea, thus creating what one geologist described as a 'Baltic of the Mediterranean'.[40] The most immediate problem was that altitudinal measurements of the area were still hampered by a considerable degree of uncertainty. The specific purpose of Roudaire's survey in 1872–73 was to dispel any ambiguities. After a series of careful measurements, he determined that the lowest point of the Chott Melrhir was twenty-seven metres below sea level.[41]

Armed with this crucial piece of data, Roudaire pored over existing surveyors' maps and the writings of ancient chroniclers to find out more. He soon became convinced that the chotts were indeed remnants of an inland sea that had disappeared around the beginning of the Christian era following the formation of an isthmus that separated it from the Mediterranean. He published his findings in 1874 in the *Revue des deux mondes*, a leading French current affairs magazine, and suggested that the construction of a series of canals between the depressions and the Gulf of Gabès could recreate the long-lost Sea of Triton.

Roudaire extolled what he saw as the multiple virtues of such an undertaking. Economically, the submergence of the region would open up the interior to commerce by facilitating navigation from the Mediterranean to Biskra. Militarily, it would block the way northward for the unruly desert tribes that still opposed French rule. Politically, it would not only demonstrate France's beneficent intentions to the water-stressed North African population but also serve as a dramatic display of French technological prowess in the forum of international public opinion. Perhaps the most important effects would be environmental. Restoring such a large water surface, he surmised, would significantly increase humidity and rainfall throughout the region, thus re-establishing the climatic conditions that had once made North Africa the 'granary of Rome'. It was, as one contemporary put it, undoubtedly a 'grandiose project'. In Roudaire's own words, it constituted one of 'the most important conquests of nature ever made through the intelligence and energy of humankind'.[42]

Roudaire's proposal certainly made a big impression, but opinions were mixed. By and large, it was well received among the general public, and perhaps more importantly by a powerful group of commercial and technical backers, including the highly influential Ferdinand de Lesseps, the renowned builder of the Suez Canal, who had been inducted into the French Academy of Sciences in 1869. Among other members of the academy, however, Roudaire's vision met with considerable scepticism. Some critics doubted that the chotts had ever been connected to the sea. Others thought that the scheme would

40. Quote from Martins, 'Le Sahara', 314; see also Lavigne, *Le percement*.
41. Roudaire, *La mission des chotts*, 3–12.
42. Roudaire, 'Une mer intérieure', 350.

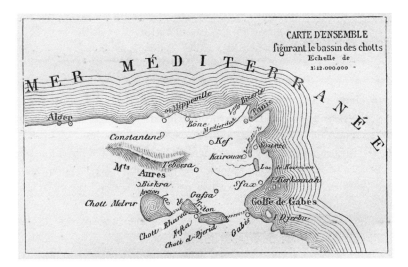

FIGURE 3.2. Roudaire's plan for inundating the basin of chotts in Algeria and Tunisia, c.1881.
Source: http://www.profburp.com/tunisie/biblio/roudaire.jpg. Public domain.

create nothing more than a vast inland marsh while unnecessarily flooding productive oasis land near the chotts. Still others thought that the high evaporation rates would quickly cause the sea to dry out once again. In the end, Roudaire's explanations and de Lesseps's strong backing were enough to convince the academy to establish an investigation committee. In the summer of 1874 the French government sponsored a major expedition to study the project further, placing it under the direction of Roudaire himself.[43]

The mission proved to be a major success, both scientifically and politically. From December 1874 to April 1875 the group surveyed the chotts of Melrhir and Gharsa to determine the extent and depth of the water body that an inundation canal would create. Though well equipped and well funded, the expedition proceeded very much in the 'heroic' mode of nineteenth-century African exploration. Each day the men walked over twenty kilometres as they made their measurements, often in blazing heat, and each night they were allowed only four hours sleep, usually in freezing temperatures. After two months, several members suffered from acute fatigue and fever. For Roudaire, at least, the results were worth it. The survey indicated that around 6,700 square kilometres of desert could be transformed into an inland sea up to thirty-one metres deep, and that only three small oases would be sacrificed in the process.[44]

43. Marçot, *Une mer au Sahara*, 249–63.
44. Marçot, 263–79; Heffernan, 'Bringing the Desert', 99.

Upon his return to Paris, Roudaire's work was warmly received by the Academy of Sciences and met with general acclamation at the 1875 Congrès international des sciences géographiques. Buoyed by his success, Roudaire quickly managed to acquire funding for a follow-up mission to survey the long Chott el Djerid that stretched across the Regency of Tunis, which was still an independent state at the time. From February to May 1876, he and a group of companions compiled sufficient hydrological and altitudinal data to create a detailed report on the feasibility of the project. Although the scheme was still viewed with suspicion among many scientists, the findings of the second expedition were widely publicized and struck a chord among politicians and the general public alike. What made the proposal so appealing was its audacious scale. As outlined in Roudaire's final report of 1877, the plan was to inundate some 13,000 square kilometres of desert by the staged construction of around 240 kilometres of canals that would link the three chotts together and traverse the 16 kilometres that separated the eastern end of el-Djerid from the Mediterranean.[45] Like the Suez Canal, this was environmental engineering on a mind-boggling scale, a classic example of the 'technological sublime'.[46]

Of all the purported benefits of the project, the most sensational – and controversial – were its supposed climatic effects. For critics, one of the key questions surrounding the viability of the scheme was whether enough water could be delivered to the chotts to prevent the inland sea from evaporating in the hyper-arid climate. Roudaire insisted that it could be done and that the effects would be nothing but beneficial for the region and its inhabitants. After all, according to de Lesseps himself, the much smaller 'bitter lakes' that had been created by the construction of the Suez Canal – and which existed under analogous climatic conditions – were already credited with an increase in rainfall around the Isthmus of Suez. Based on a submersible surface area of over thirteen thousand square kilometres, Roudaire calculated an average daily evaporation rate of just over thirty-nine million cubic metres of water, doubling to over seventy-eight million cubic metres whenever hot, dry 'sirocco' winds blew up from the south. During such periods this enormous volume of water would be carried northward to the Aurès Mountains, whose high altitudes and relatively cool temperatures would act as a great 'condensator' to turn the water vapour into clouds and eventually into rain. Much of the rain would fall on the south-facing slopes of the massif, covering them in vegetation and turning their infrequent torrents into perennial streams that would drain back into the inland sea in a completely new hydrological cycle. At the same time, higher humidity and precipitation would turn the alluvial soils along the shores of the sea into an 'immense oasis' ideal for growing cotton and other export crops. A final benefit of moderating the torrid climate of the region was that it would

45. Roudaire, *La mission des chotts*, 129.
46. The term is borrowed from Nye in *American Technological Sublime*.

supposedly improve the health of local inhabitants. As Roudaire put it, the inland sea would give a 'new impulse to the industry of this magnificent country', one that would be all the more transformative for 'modifying climate at the same time'. Altogether, his project would allow 'fertility and life to take the place of sterility and death, civilization to drive back fatalism'.[47]

As visionary as such assertions may sound, they in fact reflected a broader set of contemporary theories about climatic change in general and about the environmental history of North Africa in particular. Ever since the eighteenth century, scientists working in the British, Dutch and French maritime empires became convinced that the destruction of forests caused a decline in precipitation and thereby posed a serious threat to agricultural production in island colonies. With the expansion of European power in the nineteenth century, this 'desiccationist' discourse powerfully shaped perceptions of land use and climate in the continental empires of Asia and Africa. By the 1860s the concept of anthropogenic desiccation – that drier climates were principally the consequence of human action – was widespread within colonial officialdom.[48] In North Africa these ideas intersected with a dominant historical narrative of environmental decline, which held that centuries of environmental mismanagement under Arab and Turkish rule had transformed this ancient 'granary of Rome' into a dry and degraded pastoral landscape. The idea that local populations had ruined the region's previous fertility emerged soon after the French conquests of 1830, was in full force by the 1850s, and served as a key justification for colonial rule and French settlement throughout the Third Republic. According to this narrative, modern France was the historical heir of Roman civilization, and its duty was to restore the supposedly 'natural' environmental conditions of the region that had pertained before the Arab invasions.[49] For Roudaire and his backers, there was no better way to extend cultivable land and forest than to re-establish the ancient climate that supported them.

Despite the popular appeal of the project, many scientists and officials remained unconvinced by Roudaire's report. While even doubters recognized its strategic and security benefits, few thought that the volume of trans-Saharan trade would justify the creation of sizeable inland ports. Bold claims about improving the regional climate were treated with considerable scepticism, and there were also well-founded misgivings about whether the geology of the proposed canal route from Chott El-Djerid to the Mediterranean would allow the construction of a large channel. Although some government

47. Roudaire, *La mission des chotts*, 73–75, 81–82; see also Lehmann, *Desert Edens*, 49–52.

48. Generally, Grove, *Green Imperialism* and 'Historical Review', 160–66.

49. See generally D. Davis's *Resurrecting the Granary*, which notes the irony that in fact soil degradation appears to have begun mainly with the Romans and their farming techniques, and was followed by soil regeneration under the less intensive land-use practices of Arab pastoralists.

ministers shared such reservations, they nonetheless granted Roudaire's request for a third expedition to study the bedrock between the Chott El-Djerid and Gabès. From November 1878 to May 1879 his team collected a sufficient amount of survey data and drill samples to produce a full and final report, which was published in early 1881.[50] In the meantime, however, more and more officials began to doubt the wisdom of investing so heavily in a speculative overseas venture, especially in the light of recent evidence from other researchers indicating that the chotts were never connected to the sea and that inundating them ran the risk of doing little more than creating a useless and unhealthy swamp in the middle of the desert.[51]

Finally, in 1882 the French government established a special enquiry commission to conduct a definitive examination of the proposal. Despite strong support from de Lesseps (who served as one of its senior members), the commission concluded that the overall costs would be more than eight times higher than the optimistic estimates provided by Roudaire (1.3 billion francs as opposed to 160 million), and that such enormous expenditure was out of proportion to any expected benefits that the scheme might provide. From that moment on, the dream of creating a Saharan sea was effectively dead. Although de Lesseps tried to maintain interest in the scheme through a newly established Société d'études de la mer intérieure, which in early 1883 paid for Roudaire to complete his drilling survey in Tunisia, even he was soon forced to accept an end to the controversy.

There were many different factors that contributed to the demise of Roudaire's audacious plan, which collectively show how many different interests had to be aligned to carry out major hydraulic works in the colonies. One was the fact that 'le Grand Français' (as the Republican politician Léon Gambetta dubbed de Lesseps) who had masterminded the Suez Canal and had long backed the plan was losing credibility in the 1880s amid the unfolding fiasco of his company's ill-fated attempt to build a Panama canal.[52] Another was the mounting stack of scientific evidence that the plan's publicity generated and that increasingly threw Roudaire's claims into question. Meanwhile, the broader political context was also shifting, especially after the French conquest of Tunisia in 1881, which rendered the scheme obsolete as a lever for boosting French influence there (hitherto one of its primary geostrategic attractions). As it turned out, the commission's decision not to fund the scheme almost

50. Roudaire, *Dernière expedition des chotts*.

51. E.g., Martins and Désor, 'Observations sur le projet'; Marçot, *Une mer au Sahara*, 326–35; Heffernan, 'Bringing the Desert', 106.

52. De Lesseps's Panama Canal Company began work in 1881, soon ran into difficulties from engineering problems and eye-watering mortality rates due to malaria and yellow fever, and eventually went bankrupt in 1888. The United States government, through the Isthmian Canal Commission, resumed work in 1904 and completed the canal in 1914: Carse, *Beyond the Big Ditch*; Greene, *Canal Builders*.

certainly prevented a financial disaster for French investors and the state, as well as a pointless loss of resources for the people who used the oases that would have been inundated. For Roudaire, however, it was a personal tragedy. Embittered by the rejection of his vision, he withdrew from public life, turned increasingly to alcohol, and died in 1885 aged only forty-nine.[53]

At one level, it would be easy to disregard the Saharan sea project as nothing more than the relic of a history that never was. Yet in several ways it repays closer attention, for it offers a glimpse into the changing beliefs, attitudes and visions that shaped imperial engagements with colonized environments during the rapid expansion of European power in the late nineteenth century. Roudaire's scheme bore testament to the remarkable technological optimism of colonial engineers and officials, and also to the resulting gigantism that so often characterized their plans to remedy what they viewed as nature's shortcomings. It demonstrated both their steadfast belief in the superiority of European knowledge and civilization, and their corresponding tendency to overlook or blatantly disregard the interests of subject peoples and the peculiarities of local environments. It stemmed from a widespread perception of conquered territories – especially 'wastelands' – as a blank canvas for European designs. It reflected the contemporary belief in an enlightened form of colonialism driven not by military subjugation but rather by mutual benefit and civilizational uplift through the gifts of modern science. And finally, it was rooted in the conviction that major engineering works represented a 'peaceful' means of conquest, even if they meant flooding land on which other people lived.[54]

The attempt to create a Saharan sea thus offers a window on to the ideas, hopes and 'imaginary futures' that shaped the emergence of a distinctly technocratic form of colonialism during the heyday of empire.[55] As such, it illustrates broader patterns of thought and behaviour that underlay colonial visions for the re-engineering of environments more generally. Despite its unusual grandiosity, it was by no means unique in this respect. Indeed, it was not even the only contemporary scheme designed to inundate African deserts.

While Roudaire was first fleshing out his plans in the 1870s, the Scottish engineer Donald Mackenzie was busily drumming up support for a project to flood what he thought was a large desert depression in the western part of French Sudan. His aim was to create a navigable waterway deep into the heart of West Africa as a means of opening trade and facilitating the 'civilization' of the region. The basic idea was similar to Roudaire's: namely, to pierce through a coastal sand ridge that appeared to have cut off the influx

53. Marçot, *Une mer au Sahara*, 375–418.

54. On these themes more generally, see Adas's *Machines as the Measure* and B. Barth and Osterhammel's *Zivilisierungsmissionen*.

55. Goswami, 'Imaginary Futures'.

of seawater from a long, low-lying plain called El Djouf. The canal would start roughly midway between Cape Bojador and Cape Juby on the coast, a mere 1,500 miles (2,400 kilometres) from Britain's shore. By 1875, the project enjoyed significant support from a group of distinguished British traders and engineers, among them none other than the renowned authority of Indian hydraulic engineering Sir Arthur Cotton. In the summer of that year it even got a hearing with Colonial Secretary Lord Carnarvon. According to the *Times*, the ingeniousness of the project 'dazzles the imagination' and radiated an 'irresistible attraction'. But Mackenzie's scheme, unlike Roudaire's, got no further with British officialdom owing to a deep scepticism about its feasibility from the very start – which was just as well, given that the depressions he focused on were, in fact, mostly well above sea level.[56]

Just as plans to flood the Sahara reflected the fantasies and preoccupations of the time, their eventual failure also mirrored how the contemporary intellectual and political landscape was evolving. During the late nineteenth century, the gradual professionalization of the colonial science and engineering community created a far less favourable climate for the inspirational enterprises of scientific adventurers such as Roudaire, de Lesseps or Mackenzie. As research capacity became increasingly university based and discipline focused, the romantic designs of 'men on the spot' became less and less convincing among politicians and investors. And as the list of failed macro-engineering projects grew longer, this trend was increasingly reinforced by the benefits of hindsight. Certainly the abandonment of the French trans-Saharan railway project in 1881 (initially proposed in 1879, and eventually built in the early 1940s) did little to help Roudaire, and the subsequent French failure to build a Panama canal in the 1880s only added to this sense of suspicion. By the early twentieth century, such grandiose visions for the transformation of nature were even a bit too much for the science-fiction pioneer Jules Verne, whose last novel, *L'invasion de la mer* (1905), tells the story of a twentieth-century scientist's heroic efforts to resurrect Roudaire's project against the fierce opposition of local people, only to see it end in complete disaster when an earthquake causes an uncontrolled inundation of the entire region.[57]

Yet despite the changing political and ideological context, dreams of flooding Africa's desert wastelands continued to capture the imagination of scientists and political leaders for decades. In 1911–12, a French professor named Etchegoyen tried to revive Roudaire's project, proposing an even larger set of canals to flood a more extensive area of desert. Opponents warned that the displacement of such an enormous volume of water might tip the Earth's axis, or

56. Mackenzie, *Flooding of the Sahara*, 267–70, *Times* quotes at 283; Figuier, *Les nouvelles conquêtes*, 807–8.

57. Verne, *L'invasion*. On the changing political and intellectual context, see Heffernan's 'Bringing the Desert' (106–8) and Marçot's *Une mer au Sahara* (402–9).

potentially cause catastrophic climate change for Europe itself.[58] Several years later, at the other end of the African continent, the geologist Ernest Schwarz proposed a scheme to divert the Chobe and Kunene Rivers into the heart of the Kalahari desert in order to counter the effects of 'desertification' that were threatening white South African farmers with ruin. Although the South African government deemed the project impractical, his 'Kalahari Redemption Scheme' enjoyed strong backing from farmers, politicians and scientists well into the 1940s.[59] In 1927, Doctor John Ball, the director of the Survey of Egypt, suggested that it might be possible to flood the vast Qattara Depression in western Egypt (much of which is well below sea level) to generate hydroelectricity, humidify the regional climate and create new agricultural land.[60] As we will see in chapter 7, Herman Sörgel's 'Atlantropa' scheme of the 1930s was a variation on this very theme, only on a far grander scale.[61] Following the discovery of Saharan oil in the mid-1950s, a group of mainly French engineers founded the Association de recherche technique pour l'étude de la mer intérieure saharienne (ARTEMIS) to revive Roudaire's inundation plans, even in the midst of the Algerian War of Independence. Enthralled by the new potential of nuclear power, they went so far as to propose that a string of fifteen twenty-megaton hydrogen bombs could be used to blast a canal thirty miles long and a mile wide (50 kilometres long and 1.6 wide) from the Gabès barrier to the Chott Djerid.[62] As late as the 1980s, the Algerian and Tunisian governments commissioned yet another study of the idea by a Swedish engineering firm, which firmly concluded that the environmental and socio-economic benefits would be negligible or nonexistent in relation to the costs.[63]

In the end, none of these proposals to flood Africa's deserts ever came to fruition. Yet the reasons were mainly financial rather than technical, and in no way reflected a lack of confidence in the power of modern hydraulic engineering to remedy the defects of nature. After all, from a technical point of view there was no shortage of other, more practical ways to bring water to desert environments. And from an economic and strategic point of view, there were plenty of other 'wastes' that water engineers could help incorporate into the socio-ecological order of empire.

58. G. Thompson, 'Converting the Sahara', 114, 124–25; see also 'Proposes to Turn Sahara into a Sea; French Engineer's Scheme – He Declares It Not Difficult of Accomplishment', *New York Times* (October 15, 1911), 1; Fleming, *Fixing the Sky*, 205.

59. Schwarz, *Kalahari*. For an excellent discussion of the scheme, see McKittrick's 'Empire of Rivers'.

60. Ball, 'Problems', 35–38.

61. Gall, *Das Atlantropa-Projekt*; Lehmann, 'Infinite Power'.

62. See E. Ward, *Sahara Story*, 181–84.

63. Ghassemi and White, *Inter-basin Water Transfer*, 382.

Canals and Colonies

Around the same time that Roudaire's plans in North Africa were unravelling, British officials in India began to undertake one of the largest dryland reclamation schemes the world has ever seen. Its purpose was twofold: to create cropland in hitherto uncultivated areas, and to shore up state authority in places where its influence was weak. Since the mid-nineteenth century, the arid steppes and deserts of north-western India marked the frontier of British power in Asia. Just beyond the colonial provinces of Sindh and Punjab lay a dry mountainous region inhabited by Baloch and Pashtun groups who successfully resisted imperial subjugation and who frequently conducted raids across the border. Even inside the western provincial boundaries, the combination of water scarcity and a mobile pastoral population meant that state control remained tenuous. In British eyes, the entire area was little more than an unstable and unproductive wasteland. In the late nineteenth century, the attempt to domesticate it through a massive programme of agrarian settlement ushered in a fundamental transformation of the land, its people and their relations to the colonial state.[64]

The entire enterprise hinged on the control of water. As we saw in chapter 2, water availability was the primary constraint on agricultural production across much of South Asia, but it was particularly critical in the few parts of India that received little or no monsoonal rainfall – namely, Sindh and the western reaches of the Punjab. Lying at the edge of the monsoon, this belt of dryland formed a climatic frontier as much as a territorial one. In many ways it was quite distinct from the rest of India. Officials working there regarded it as 'really part of the great desert extending from the Western Sahara to Manchuria'.[65] Thanks to its snow-fed rivers, however, the alluvial floodplains of the region were among the oldest centres of crop cultivation in all of southern Asia; along the Indus, farmers have channelled its annual floodwaters for over four thousand years. The Indus is fed by a group of five tributaries – the Jhelum, Chenab, Ravi, Beas and Sutlej – which originate in the western Himalayas and descend roughly parallel to one another in a south-westerly direction through the Punjab (the 'land of five rivers') before converging just above the Sindh province. Together they form one of the great river systems of the world, draining over one million square kilometres and stretching all the way from the Tibetan plateau to the Arabian Sea.

Harnessing these waters was the key to both farming and governing the region. Long before the arrival of the British, the Mughal emperors and the Sikh rulers of the Punjab had dug wells and seasonal inundation canals in an

---

64. On the drylands of north-western India as a frontier: Haines, 'Constructing State Power'.

65. Douie, 'Punjab Canal Colonies', 612.

attempt to extend settled cultivation and bolster their power. For the most part such works did not seek to alter natural drainage channels so much as expand them in order to allow the annual floods to spread across adjacent fields and raise local groundwater levels. After annexing the Punjab in 1849, the British initially followed a similar approach, focusing on the repair or enlargement of existing works that channelled the seasonal floodwaters into fields immediately adjoining the rivers. They had little interest in the scrubby and sparsely inhabited drylands that lay between these narrow, fertile riverine tracts. Unlike the productive and densely populated districts of central and eastern Punjab, rainfall in the west was simply too scarce to permit cultivation, averaging under ten inches (twenty-five centimetres) per year in most places. It was noted, however, that the region's deep alluvial soils were by no means intrinsically poor. What made the land in the western Punjab barren was not its infertility but its aridity.[66]

In the decades following the annexation of the Punjab, British officials gradually began to look beyond the floodplains towards the extensive *doabs*, slightly elevated lands that stretched between the five tributary rivers beyond the reach of inundation canals. In many respects these interfluvial expanses were ideal for irrigation, offering not only good soils and close proximity to large perennial rivers, but also gentle gradients that facilitated the steady flow of water across the region. Furthermore, they had the great advantage of being largely unused, at least in British eyes. For colonial officials the western Punjab was a region with 'no resident population, beyond a few nomads who eked out a precarious existence as graziers'.[67] Its legal classification as Crown Waste Land allowed canal builders to avoid the thorny ownership issues that complicated such projects elsewhere in India. In sum, the western Punjab had all the ingredients for large-scale irrigation. In the 1880s, British engineers began building a huge network of weirs and channels to convey a perennial supply of water to millions of hectares of previously uncultivated land. By the early twentieth century it had become the largest irrigation system in the entire world, covering roughly fifty thousand square kilometres by 1918 and around seventy-five thousand by the 1940s.[68]

This colossal system of hydraulic works opened colonial India's greatest agrarian frontier. From 1886 to 1940, it allowed the settlement of over a million people on land that had previously been scrub and desert. At the core of the transformation were nine canal colonies, planned townships built to house

66. Gilmartin, 'Scientific Empire', 1143; Ali, *Punjab under Imperialism*, 5; Agnihotri, 'Ecology', 39–44.

67. Harris, *Irrigation in India*, 48.

68. Ali, *Punjab under Imperialism*, 10; Gilmartin, 'Scientific Empire', 1143n.; *Blood and Water*, 144–81.

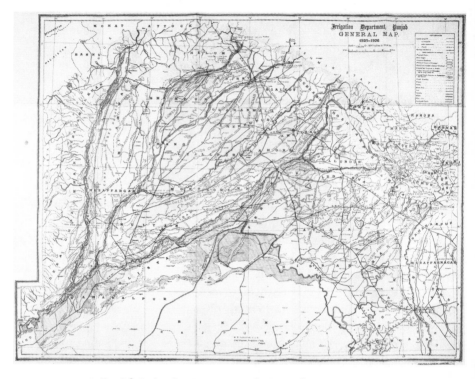

FIGURE 3.3. Punjab Irrigation Department's General Map, 1925–26.
By permission of akg-images/British Library, IOR/X/12099.

an influx of peasant migrants from the more crowded districts of eastern and central Punjab. The first of these settlements were the Sidhnai and Sohag Para colonies on the Bari Doab, situated between the Ravi and Beas Rivers, which began in 1886 and soon demonstrated that canal colonies could be made to work both for cultivators and for the government. The last one was the Nili Bar colony, where colonization began in 1926. The largest and most important was the Chenab colony, which commenced in 1892 on the Rechna Doab between the Chenab and Ravi Rivers in the north of the Punjab, and which eventually covered around 2,900 square miles (7,500 square kilometres). The Lower Chenab Canal that fed it was the largest hydraulic undertaking since the construction of the Ganges Canal. Measuring 430 miles (690 kilometres) long, with 2,200 miles (3,600 kilometres) of secondary channels, it had the greatest discharge of any canal in India (303 m³/second, or around six times the non-tidal flow of the Thames on the western outskirts of London).[69] Before the colony was built, the tract it occupied was described as one of 'extreme desolation': an arid plain 'extraordinarily devoid of animal life' and covered

69. Sandes, *Military Engineer in India*, 14; Harris, *Irrigation in India*, 55.

FIGURE 3.4. The massive Chenab under-sluices and weir, March 1892.
By permission of akg-images/British Library, photo 593(6).

in 'dusty shrubs, some of a certain value as fuel but others of no use to either
man or beast'. Its only inhabitants were described as a 'spare and hardy race'
of indigenous nomads who lived off the rearing of goats and camels. Within a
decade the area was transformed 'from a wilderness into a garden', making the
Lower Chenab Canal the most lucrative waterworks in all of India. By 1920 it
was outperforming even the most optimistic forecasts, irrigating crops worth
some £16 million (five times more than the costs of construction). Overall,
the Chenab Colony was widely regarded as the 'most extensive and successful
irrigation system in India and probably in the world'.[70]

The stunning financial success of the Lower Chenab Canal paved the way
for even larger waterworks after the turn of the century. In 1905, in the wake
of Scott-Moncrieff's Irrigation Commission report (see chapter 2), the government launched the so-called Triple Canals Project, whose basic purpose was to
irrigate the lower portions of the Bari Doab between the Sutlej and Ravi Rivers. The problem that engineers sought to overcome was that the Ravi did not
carry enough water to support a colony on the scale envisaged, and the waters
of the Sutlej were the only means of eventually extending irrigation to the adjacent *doab* that lay south of its valley. The solution was to integrate the region's
rivers by tapping the two northernmost rivers of Punjab, the Jhelum and the
Chenab, and conveying a portion of their flow to the Bari Doab. The first of
these interfluvial links was the Upper Jhelum Canal, which diverted water to
the Chenab just above the headworks of the existing Lower Chenab Canal.
Since the Chenab colony could thereafter be supplied in large part by the Jhelum, this allowed the second link, the Upper Chenab Canal, to transfer Chenab

70. Figures from Michel, *Indus Rivers*, 77; Harris, *Irrigation in India*, 57. Quotes from
Harris, *Irrigation in India*, 52, 54–55.

water south to the Ravi, where it crossed the river at Billoki to become the Lower Doab Canal, the third link in the trio. In essence, the flow of the Ravi was left intact thanks to the addition of water from the Chenab, which in turn was replenished by the Jhelum. The main canals were finished in 1915 and once again set new records; the Upper Chenab Canal had the greatest discharge in the world (331 m³/second), and the Billoki Barrage was the largest in all of India. They also constituted a landmark in the history of irrigation by transcending the flow of a single river to encompass an entire river basin. The Triple Canals project was the world's first such integrated transfer system, establishing a pattern that other countries would soon follow. As we will see in chapter 8, it also eventually became the source of bitter disputes between the different political entities that shared the Indus basin's water.[71] But regardless of its political implications, from an engineering perspective the project was a major triumph, commanding around six thousand square miles (sixteen thousand square kilometres) by 1920 and feeding three major canal colonies: the Upper Chenab, Upper Jhelum and Lower Bari Doab (the second largest in the Punjab).

The canal colonies of the Punjab formed the nuclei of a multifaceted process of ecological and social change. The availability of water profoundly transformed the physical environment, replacing sparse scrubland with verdant fields of wheat, cotton and sugar. It also brought a sudden demographic shift, as sedentary farmers displaced the scattered pastoralist groups that had previously roamed the area. For the British officials who planned them, the canal colonies were an opportunity to create a whole new kind of village, one specifically designed to optimize the agricultural 'development' of the region. In a lecture at the Royal Society of Arts in 1914, James Douie, an officer who spent several decades in the Punjab, declared that the aim was nothing less than to create 'a model settlement in every respect'.[72]

In many ways the canal colonies epitomized the 'high modernist' vision of a regimented, rationalized and geometrically planned landscape. Village boundaries were determined by the track of the artificial watercourses, generally in such a way as to ensure that they did not have to share the same distribution canal with another village. Each village was then methodically mapped out into squares or rectangles of between twenty-two and twenty-eight acres (8.9 to 11.3 hectares), which were further subdivided into fields of around one acre. Most households received one and a half or two squares, though larger parcels were sometimes granted to better-off 'yeomen' or landowners of a 'higher class'. Once the village and parcel boundaries were determined, the settlements themselves were configured into a pattern of streets, residential areas and communal facilities (tanks, schools, etc.). Most of this planning was done in advance and without any input from colonists; all that was left

71. Michel, *Indus Rivers*, 90–93; Harris, *Irrigation in India*, 73.
72. Douie, 'Punjab Canal Colonies', 617.

for settlers to do was to build their houses and work the land. In his address to the Royal Society of Arts, Douie conceded that such a systematic layout of the land may appear dull and unpleasing to those who 'love the irregular fields of the homeland, with their hedges of black and white thorn or wilding rose'. Nonetheless, he contended that the system had several big advantages: it helped avoid the problem of scattered holdings, it facilitated the equitable distribution of irrigation water, and it allowed for the easy and accurate subdivision of holdings in a society where each son inherited an equal share of his father's land. A final benefit that officials often highlighted was the 'marked sanitary advantages over the ordinary Indian homesteads'.[73]

Officials like Douie had the power to determine not only the physical arrangement of the colonies but also their demographic makeup. The selection of colonists was a central part of the process, and was generally carried out by revenue officers in the congested districts from which the settlers came. The aim was to select only those with ample capability but insufficient land, and to assemble groups of colonists of similar descent in order to foster social cohesion. The key challenge was to 'weed out' various categories of undesirables: the 'dotards and mere boys' who were simply trying to gain an extra parcel for the family, the greedy landowner who wanted to add to his already ample holdings, the overstretched farmer trying to escape his debts, as well as 'the physically and mentally unfit, the village loafers and the like'.[74] Officials developed their own selection techniques, some of them decidedly eugenic in nature. One popular method was to look at candidates' hands to determine 'the real workers in the community'. Douie himself judged them by their chests, and illustrated the process to his London audience by showing slides of several bare-chested Punjabis.[75]

By the early 1900s, the previously barren *doabs* of the western Punjab had become the breadbasket of the Raj. For the remainder of the colonial period they yielded prodigious crops of wheat, sugar and cotton for export, while also providing herds of horses and camels for the army. The replumbing of the Punjab enabled it to generate more tax revenue than any other province of India. Its peasantry was among the most prosperous in the entire empire, and repaid the Crown by providing around half of the manpower for the Indian Army. The plan to irrigate the arid lands of the Punjab thus served British interests on multiple levels. Economically, it was major boon for the colonial treasury. Strategically, it shored up colonial authority in a sensitive frontier zone. And militarily, it helped secure the Raj against foreign and domestic opponents alike.[76]

73. Douie, 'Punjab Canal Colonies', 614, 617; Scott, *Seeing like a State*; Harris, *Irrigation in India*, 49–51.

74. Harris, *Irrigation in India*, 50.

75. Douie, 'Punjab Canal Colonies', 615–16.

76. Generally: Ali, *Punjab under Imperialism*; Islam, *Irrigation*; Gilmartin, *Blood and Water*, 27–68.

For all these reasons, the Punjab canal colonies were long praised as models of agricultural development and showpieces of enlightened colonial rule. The hydraulic works themselves were of worldwide engineering significance, and the villages served as prototypes for the large-scale settlement of irrigated dry-lands elsewhere. British officials saw them very much as part of an expanding global frontier of agricultural settlement. 'When one speaks of colonisation', Douie remarked, 'the mind turns at once to new countries. We think of the prairies of the United States, or the pampas of Argentina, of the broad plains of Western Canada, or the Australian bush.' Here, too, the mass conversion of 'wastes' into settled farmland was closely bound up with the search for water, just as it was 'in so old a country as the land of the five rivers'.[77]

But along with these changes came a new set of challenges and problems. As ever, large-scale colonization brought advantages to some and disadvantages to others. The first casualties were the pastoral communities who already lived in the western Punjab. The expansion of the canal colonies into these suppos-edly 'empty' lands threatened not only their livelihoods but their entire way of life. The state classification of the arid *doabs* as unowned 'wastes' amounted to a massive expropriation of their customary grazing lands. Officials like Douie clearly recognized that such an infringement of inhabitants' rights would not be possible in Britain itself. If land on any of the metropole's great estates were fit for the plough 'the English Government could not settle communities of peasant farmers upon it without making a fair composition with the landlord for the surrender of his rights'. By contrast, most of western Punjab was 'cov-ered with scanty grass and scrub-jungle, over which certain families or clans asserted a loose sort of dominion'. The lack of what British administrators rec-ognized as clear proprietary claims allowed them to declare the land as state property 'held in trust for the common good'.[78] Of course, the matter looked very different to the herding communities themselves. When work began on the Lower Chenab Canal, the nomads in the area reportedly 'neither desired nor expected the canal to be a success' and were 'determined to do all in their power to prevent its being so'. Their opposition was hardly surprising given that officials granted them only small areas for grazing, usually on the worst soils. Yet over time, the clashes with colonist settlers slackened, partly as a result of 'vigorous repressive measures' but also from a growing recognition that the canal was there to stay. Eventually many of the original inhabitants sought to make the best of the situation by taking up irrigated parcels themselves.[79]

The canal colonies also brought similar drawbacks for the long-established riverine cultivators of the region. The enormous water withdrawals from the

77. Douie, 'Punjab Canal Colonies', 611; see also Amrith, *Unruly Waters*, 122–23.
78. Douie, 'Punjab Canal Colonies', 613; Agnihotri, 'Ecology', 43. On village and pastoral rights: Gilmartin, *Blood and Water*, 69–103.
79. Harris, *Irrigation in India*, 56–58.

region's rivers impaired the functioning of the older inundation canals, making seasonal flood cultivation – an economically precarious undertaking in any event – significantly less viable than before. It also affected the water level in wells, prompting many cultivators to abandon the riverside villages altogether. As district officials recognized, the existing farmers along the rivers effectively suffered a double injustice: not only were they left out of the land bonanza in the colonies, they were also materially harmed in the process. To make matters worse, few of them were given much by way of compensation, and many had little choice but to move to the fringes of the canal colonies or to work there as farm labourers.[80]

It did not take long for tensions to rise within the canal settlements themselves. In the early 1900s, events in the Chenab colony became a serious concern for the provincial government, which found it difficult to enforce the regulations that underpinned the entire developmental vision of the scheme. Some settlers erected buildings on plots designated for crops. Others tried to avoid the colony's strict residence requirements for landholders, used water inefficiently or failed to observe what colonization officers regarded as proper sanitary habits. Most importantly for the government, many settlers fragmented their parcels by dividing the land between numerous heirs, an action that they considered to be their customary right. In 1906, the government responded with a new Colonization Bill that gave district officials sweeping powers to regulate land use. The following year, the resulting tensions boiled over into the biggest protests yet witnessed in colonial Punjab. One source of the setters' resentment was the failure – as they saw it – of the Irrigation Department to supply adequate water for their fields. As the colony grew in size, engineers found it necessary to reduce deliveries at some outlets in order to improve supplies elsewhere, especially at canal tails where deliveries had always been problematic. In the eyes of many colonists the state was not living up to its commitment to control the hydraulic environment as it had promised. Another grievance was the widespread corruption among the lower-level bureaucrats who were responsible for measuring local water flows and levying fines on violators. Their propensity to abuse their powers in order to extort bribes from farmers only added to the antipathy towards the tightening of rules on inheritance, land use and sanitation measures. In the end, the provincial government backed down over the issue of inheritance in order to avoid further unrest, though this hardly resolved all of the contradictions between the settlers' language of 'rights' and the state-led vision of scientific 'development' that underlay the design of the canal colonies.[81]

In sum, the colonists did not behave how planners expected them to – and nor did the re-engineered environment itself. By the early 1900s, the social

80. Agnihotri, 'Ecology', 44–47.
81. Gilmartin, *Blood and Water*, 173–81; Ali, *Punjab under Imperialism*, 66–68.

strains within the colonies were exacerbated by a worsening set of ecological problems. One was the spread of malaria, whose prevalence increased more or less in line with the expansion of the irrigation network. What was once a seasonal health problem became a persistent scourge. Local petitioners complained that 'the mosquito has made a permanent home with damp soil', turning malaria into 'a perennial disease of our village'.[82] In 1908, a major epidemic swept through the Punjab, and by the early 1920s endemic malaria had become so serious as to raise questions about the overall wisdom of expanding irrigation any further. Other waterborne diseases only added to the death toll. Cholera epidemics repeatedly ravaged the canal colonies, sometimes killing more than half the population in the most acutely stricken villages.[83]

Meanwhile, the menace of soil salinization quickly assumed alarming proportions, just as it had done decades earlier along the canals of the Gangetic plain. By the early 1900s the struggle against waterlogging was one of the principal tasks of the Punjab Irrigation Institute in Lahore, and by 1918 it had become so severe as to prompt the Punjab government to establish a special Drainage Board (superseded in 1925 by a Waterlogging Enquiry Committee) to devise solutions.[84] While some officers advocated a reduction in supplies of irrigation water in the hope that this would encourage colonists to sink more wells, most preferred technical tweaks to the existing system, such as altering water distribution rates or lining the channels in order to reduce seepage. As it turned out, the most effective remedy was the excavation of tube wells designed to facilitate vertical drainage wherever local conditions allowed. But despite such measures, the problems of waterlogging and salinity continued to spread. By the final years of the colonial period they reduced yields by as much as 75 per cent in the most severely affected parts of the Punjab, and annually took around seventy-five square miles (two hundred square kilometres) out of cultivation altogether.[85]

Once again, we can see here the familiar problem of short-term versus long-term financial returns on irrigation infrastructure – a problem that dogged farmers and water engineers in Egypt and in other parts of India as well. In all of these areas, the provision of irrigation water was always more immediately profitable than the creation of adequate drainage. For Punjab as for other arid lands, ensuring adequate water supplies was crucial for making agriculture work. But there could always be too much of a good thing.

In many respects, the Punjab canal colonies thus illustrated a familiar pattern of boom and decline that characterized most settlement frontiers throughout

82. Agnihotri, 'Ecology', 54.

83. Whitcombe, 'Environmental Costs of Irrigation', 254–57; Agnihotri, 'Ecology', 54.

84. N. Singh, *Irrigation and Soil Salinity*, 159–63.

85. Whitcombe, 'Environmental Costs of Irrigation', 255; Agnihotri, 'Ecology', 48–52; Gilmartin, *Blood and Water*, 235–40.

the nineteenth- and twentieth-century world. Just as in Australia, the American West or indeed the river deltas of Southeast Asia, the newly cleared land initially paid a handsome dividend, but returns steadily declined as land became more scarce, the fertility windfall was depleted, and the effects of mismanagement began to bite. This global pattern is clearly discernible with hindsight, but it was by no means lost on contemporaries. Writing in the early 1920s, Albert Howard – an agronomist at the Institute of Plant Industry in central India who went on to become one of the pioneers of the organic farming movement – argued that 'when the engineers, by means of perennial canals, enabled the surplus population of the congested areas of the Eastern Punjab to conquer the desert, a system of exploitation of the virgin soil took place not unlike that in North America when the great Western movement occurred'.[86] As Howard rightly pointed out, the eventual result was slumping yields, soil exhaustion and in some cases even the contraction of the agricultural frontier as land once again became uncultivable. But as serious as such problems were, they hardly brought an end to plans for bringing dry or marginal land into cultivation. In South Asia, a combination of political and population pressures ensured that the hydraulic conquest of the region's drylands continued apace, indeed long after the end of the colonial era. As was also the case on many of the world's other agricultural frontiers, only outward expansion could disguise the internal losses, at least before the era of synthetic fertilizers (see chapter 8).

More importantly, perhaps, Punjab's canal colonies were also a harbinger of things to come. For many observers both within and beyond British officialdom, they provided a clear demonstration of how scientific planning and large-scale hydraulic works could turn even barren desert environments into productive farmland, 'underpopulated' districts into prosperous agrarian heartlands and nomadic pastoralists into sedentary farmers. Spearheaded by an interventionist state, and specifically designed to transform both the land and the people who worked it, they were forerunners of the large-scale, expert-led settlement schemes that became such a common feature of agricultural development efforts throughout the twentieth-century world. By the interwar years they helped inspire schemes to settle sparsely populated drylands in colonial Africa, most notably the irrigation colonies of the vast Gezira Plain just above the confluence of the Blue and White Nile in Sudan, and the Office du Niger project surrounding the inland delta of the Niger River in French Sudan.[87] In turn, these two African mega-projects provided models and practical know-how for a series of agricultural schemes during the final years of colonial rule – for example the Richard Toll Rice Project in Senegal,

86. Howard, *Crop Production in India*, 36–37.

87. Ertsen, *Improvising Planned Development*; Gaitskell, *Gezira*; van Beusekom, *Negotiating Development*; Filipovich, 'Destined to Fail'.

the *paysannat* settlements of the Belgian Congo, or the Mwea Development and Reclamation Scheme in Kenya.[88] Over the longer term, the construction of irrigation systems for the settlement of supposedly vacant or underused lands remained a favourite policy of modernizing post-colonial governments as well, from the Kano River Project of northern Nigeria to the Kirindi Oya scheme in southern Sri Lanka, and from Kenya's Bura settlements to the Dumoga transmigration project in northern Sulawesi.[89]

Throughout the colonial period and beyond, the control and provision of water were a crucial tool for conquering 'wildernesses', extending state authority and expanding the frontiers of human control over nature. Given the political, cultural and economic allure of transforming forests, swamps or deserts into productive gardens, the persistence of such ideas is easily understandable. But there was always a darker side to these continuities. For a variety of reasons, the numerous social and ecological drawbacks they entailed (displacement, conflict, disease, land degradation) have proven to be just as persistent. In part, the many problems associated with the hydro-settlement of marginal lands are attributable to the inherent complexities of managing water. They are also partly due, no doubt, to the many pitfalls and perils of social engineering. Fundamentally, they stem from the fact that the myths of empty wastelands that animate such visions remain just that.

88. Malengreau, *Vers un paysannat indigène*; Bonneuil, 'Development as Experiment'; Chambers and Moris, *Mwea*; Ertsen, 'Controlling the Farmer'; R. Dumont, *False Start in Africa*.

89. Adams, *Wasting the Rain*, 155–88; Nijman, *Irrigation Decision-Making*; Hoey, 'Nationalism in Indonesia'.

CHAPTER FOUR

Deluge and Disaster

THE COLONIAL POLITICS OF FLOOD CONTROL

AS THE PRECEDING chapters have shown, colonial authorities spent a great deal of time and effort to get water to the right places at the right times.[1] All throughout Europe's overseas colonies, the extension of irrigation into drylands and the provision of year-round supplies to drought-prone areas were a key tool for enhancing agricultural production, 'civilizing' wastelands, and boosting the power and wealth of the state. Yet the colonial reordering of the hydrosphere was about more than delivering water to where it was wanted; it was also about keeping it out of places where it was not.

Seasonal torrents and floods were a regular occurrence in tropical monsoon territories, where the bulk of annual rainfall – in many places over four-fifths of it – falls over the course of only four to five months. In most years, these periodic inundations were a boon to farmers in the deltas and floodplains, who specifically designed their agricultural systems to maximize the benefits that the floodwaters conferred. As swollen rivers spilled over their banks they not only watered crops at crucial times in the growing cycle; they also brought fertile silt to riparian fields, filled village tanks, replenished wells and often provided an abundance of fish. Nonetheless, there could be too much of a good thing. Whereas normal levels of seasonal flooding were beneficial, above a certain level the effects were harmful. And every so often – whether ten, fifty, or a hundred years, depending on the locality – exceptionally high water levels along rivers and coastlines could be downright disastrous, destroying homes, crops and livestock; unleashing famine and epidemics; and claiming dozens, hundreds or thousands of human lives.

---

1. Parts of this chapter, above all the section 'Deluges, Dikes and Dependency in Colonial Indochina', are based on material first published in my 'Constrained River', with the permission of the editor.

It is common to regard such extreme flood events as 'natural' phenomena, the products of freak weather incidents over which people have no control. It is an understandable conclusion to reach when confronted with the spectacle of submerged fields, inundated towns, and thousands of refugees stranded on rooftops or paddling their way to safety along flooded roadways. But in order to understand the wider causes and consequences of such events, we must also recognize them as social phenomena, products of human decisions and behaviours.

Over the past couple of decades researchers have increasingly highlighted how we create 'disasters' through what we do: living in risky areas, doing risky things (disturbing catchment areas, eliminating buffer zones, ignoring warnings), failing to invest in safeguards, all of which are generally done in the pursuit of material benefits of one sort or another. To borrow the terminology of Ulrich Beck, who did perhaps more than anyone else to highlight the problem, so-called natural disasters are generally the result of both 'external risks' and 'manufactured risks'.[2] Instead of focusing on particular disasters as key historical moments, more recently scholars have tended to emphasize the longer-term temporalities that are involved. From this perspective, disasters appear not so much as singular occasions but rather as continuing processes of decision-making, of learning to cope with and/or recover from unpredictable events. On an immediate level, natural forces such as cyclones, deluges, droughts or earthquakes can of course cause enormous disruption to human activities, but how societies prepare for and deal with these uncontrollable but not entirely unforeseeable events is very much a reflection of prevailing ideas, economic priorities and political choices. Fertile, flood-prone bottomlands and coastal deltas can be prized or avoided as places of settlement. Erratic rivers or flood-prone shorelines can be left to their own devices or 'tamed' to various degrees by technological works of different sizes, shapes and levels of sophistication.

Furthermore, when droughts, cyclones or floods occur, the effects are rarely distributed equitably. Susceptibility to natural forces tends to reflect and reproduce inequalities of power and privilege. Social and biophysical vulnerability generally go hand in hand. In the aftermath of such events, the process of dealing with the effects also tends to create new forms of knowledge and expertise that empower some groups more than others. Learning from disasters, like preparing (or not preparing) for them, is a consummately political act, and policies of recovery and mitigation are much more apt to preserve existing social relations than overturn them.[3]

When viewed in this light, the efforts of officials, engineers, landowners and ordinary farmers to deal with the threat of flood disasters tell us more

2. Beck, *Risk Society*.

3. Walter, *Catastrophes*; van Bavel et al., *Disasters and History*; Mauch and Pfister, *Natural Disasters, Cultural Responses*; Bankoff, Frerks and Hilhorst, *Mapping Vulnerability*; Steinberg, *Acts of God*; Bankoff, *Cultures of Disaster*; Courtney, *Nature of Disaster*; Ayalov, *Natural Disasters*; Segalla, *Empire and Catastrophe*.

about colonial societies than first meets the eye. For one thing, they furnish insights into state priorities and how they clashed or meshed with competing interests within subject societies. They also demonstrate how human activities in one place could have major consequences for those living elsewhere, and how structures of power and privilege determined who bore most of the risk. Moreover, they show how attempts to put an end to flooding often had the opposite effect of drawing states and communities into an escalating spiral of ever-larger technological interventions. In this sense, they highlight the different timescales at work in the history of disasters: creeping geomorphological changes, long-term patterns of settlement, seasonal mitigation measures and periodic moments of acute crisis. Although floods and other calamities may seem to come out of the blue, in many ways their histories begin long before the event and reverberate long after it.[4] In theory, the task of the colonial hydraulic engineer was to keep water in its place, to create and maintain a hydrological regime that served the imperial agenda of improvement and economic development. In practice, the ability to do so was invariably shaped by local ecologies, topographies and social contexts – and it was constantly challenged by the sheer force of the waters themselves.

Although we tend to think of floods as exceptional events, on a non-human timescale they are a normal occurrence. Sooner or later, all rivers burst their banks and submerge surrounding lands. But not all rivers are equally liable to do so, and depending on local topography and patterns of settlement, not all floodplains are equally susceptible to the risks of catastrophic inundation. This chapter focuses on two major hotspots: north-eastern India and northern Vietnam. Both were home to large and densely settled populations that lived close to volatile rivers and coastlines and were therefore highly exposed to floods. Before, during and indeed after the colonial era, destructive inundations were a depressingly regular occurrence in these regions, each of which exacted a heavy toll on lives and property, as well as household and state finances. We will analyse the problem of flooding through two interrelated lenses: the history of disasters as social and political phenomena, and the history of technology – or, more specifically, the ways in which the technologies that were employed to prevent or cope with destructive floods were constrained by the political, economic and environmental contexts in which they were embedded. As we will see, in both regions flood control played a crucial role in the maintenance of the colonial order, as well as an important part in its undoing.

Floods, Property and Protection in Colonial India

The fertile plains of north-eastern India have long been – and remain – among the most flood-prone areas in the world. The entire region is criss-crossed by a network of river systems that drain enormous volumes of monsoon run-off

4. See, e.g., Oliver-Smith's 'Peru's 500-Year Earthquake'.

and snowmelt from vast upland catchment areas. As these waters surge down tributaries to converge in the lowlands, they regularly spill over river-banks to inundate extensive swathes of land. All throughout the colonial period, flooding was common along the Ganges and Tista (the largest rivers in North Bengal) as well as the Karatoya, Lish, Ghish and a host of smaller water-courses. To the south, the three great rivers of Orissa – the Mahanadi, Brah-mani and Baitarani – regularly submerged their lower floodplains and coastal deltas. Perhaps most unruly of all was the Kosi River in Bihar, whose unusual combination of a large catchment area (sixty-two thousand square kilometres, the biggest Himalayan watershed apart from the Ganges and Brahmaputra) and relatively short length (thirteen hundred kilometres) made it especially prone to violent flooding. Capable of rising nine metres in twenty-four hours, this 'river of sorrow' (as it was aptly named) regularly devastated crops, drove farmers from their homes, and covered fields with so much sand and stone as to leave some areas uncultivable for up to fifty years. Along all of these rivers, inundations were a key element of hydrological and geomorphological pro-cesses, an integral part of the natural order.[5]

Living in the floodplains of north-eastern India was therefore an inher-ently hazardous business, but most of the time the benefits of cultivating moist, fertile bottomland soils compensated for the risks. For centuries, large farming populations sought to profit from the seasonal inundations as best they could, tailoring their agricultural practices to the annual rise and fall of the waters. The silt-laden waters of these rivers regularly replenished soil nutrients. In pre-colonial Bengal, cultivators maintained a vast network of inundation channels to carry them on to their fields at appropriate times of the flood cycle. According to the influential hydraulic engineer William Willcocks, the ancient system of inundation channels traversing the lower reaches of the Ganges and Damodar Rivers was ideally designed for spreading floodwaters and maintaining soil fertility. At the same time, it allowed the rivers to per-form the natural geomorphological task of gradually building up the elevation of the deltas, which in turn reduced the threat of severe floods.[6] In order to minimize the risks of farming the floodplains, cultivators planted different crops at different times in different locations – some at low elevations, some high, some in between – as a hedge against the possibility of total crop failure. In the Mahanadi delta in Orissa, for instance, farmers grew rice in a stag-gered cropping cycle that ensured that the arrival of floodwaters at any given time (usually between late July and early September, but could be any time between mid-June and late October) could not harm all of their rice crops and would likely benefit at least one of them. Even if an exceptionally prolonged

5. Mishra, 'Bihar Flood Story'; T. Ghosh, 'Floods and People'; D'Souza, *Drowned and Dammed* and 'Event, Process and Pulse'; C. Hill, *River of Sorrow*.
6. Willcocks, *Lectures*, 1–28.

inundation damaged most of the summer-sown rice, farmers could usually capitalize on the additional moisture and silt in the form of good winter crops of millets, pulses and oilseeds.[7]

Crucially, farmers' strategies to cope with the region's inherent hydrological instability were mirrored in the administrative practices of its pre-colonial rulers. The tax and revenue systems of the Mughals and their immediate successors were designed to flex with the vagaries of the annual floods, allowing collectors to negotiate higher tributes in years of surplus and lower levies – even full remissions – when harvests were poor. Like the floodplain farming systems themselves, these political arrangements accepted intermittent inundations as a fact of life, and they recognized that floods were part of a wider process in which crop losses one year often turned into plentiful harvests the next.[8]

By contrast, British colonial authorities did not see things this way at all. Instead, the floodwaters that occasionally damaged fields and settlements were a part of nature that had to be controlled. The underlying reason was the specific way in which the East India Company rearranged relations between the land and the state. With the introduction of the so-called 'Permanent Settlement' of 1793, revenue collection was no longer a matter of annual negotiation but was instead based on a regular set of fixed payments owed by local landlords (zamindars) according to their level of income at the time of the Settlement. Any amount that they made above this level was theirs to keep, but if they failed to pay the required sum in time their land would be confiscated and sold at auction. The basic rationale behind the new system was both political and economic. Bolstering the ownership rights of zamindars would not only create a powerful landed client class supportive of British rule; it would also encourage them to invest in the productivity of their estates in the knowledge that they would directly reap the dividends. By incentivizing 'improvement' in this way, the new agrarian order based on private property would supposedly benefit the Indian economy and thereby boost revenues for the Company itself.[9]

In many ways, this arrangement made good sense for the colonial state, not least in view of its weak presence on the ground and its consequent reliance on zamindars as a crucial basis of political stability. But the problem with this rigid form of revenue collection was that it was distinctly ill-suited to the unstable hydrology of north-east India's river valleys. For one thing, it meant that the colonial administration struggled to deal with irregularities in the flow of annual tax payments due to the continued occurrence of crop

7. D'Souza, *Drowned and Dammed*, 32–39.

8. J. Richards, *Mughal Empire*, 79–93; Habib, 'Agrarian Relations'; D'Souza, *Drowned and Dammed*, 51–85.

9. Guha, *Rule of Property*; Bose, *Peasant Labour*, 112–15; Travers, 'Real Value'; Stein, *Making of Agrarian Policy*, 1–33; Iqbal, *Bengal Delta*, 18–26.

losses caused by inundations. Indeed, the terms of the Permanent Settlement formally ruled out tax remissions in the case of flood losses, though in practice officials sometimes had to accept them as a necessity. Whenever flood damage occurred, landlords who risked the immediate loss of their property for failing to pay the expected amount duly passed this financial pressure on to their tenants just when they were least able to afford it.

If the disruption of the revenue stream was one problem, the disturbance to private property itself was an even more fundamental challenge. When shifting river channels caused existing land to disappear and new land to form elsewhere – as often happened in so-called *diara* lands, or fluctuating riparian tracts – they made a mockery of the fixed proprietary rights that administrators brought with them from Europe, which formed the very basis of the taxation system itself. Nowhere was the problem more acute than along the erratic Kosi River, where fields that were perfectly cultivable one year might be completely submerged – or even swept away – the next. Mapping people and settlements in *diara* areas was therefore no easier than mapping the land itself, since both frequently shifted with the patterns of the river. Systems of tenancy rights designed for stable landscapes were of little use there, and so were systems of administration and tax collection that relied on them.[10] In the most volatile *diara* lands, colonial officials had little choice but to adapt their standard property-based revenue systems by persuading cultivators to accept shorter-term leases.[11] Elsewhere, however, the imposition of a static revenue system onto a highly fluid agroecological setting meant that floods were regarded as a disruption that had to be avoided. What had once been treated as a natural hydraulic process gradually became a natural disaster.[12]

Rather than adapting their administrative practices to the nature of India's rivers, British authorities instead sought to adapt the rivers to their administrative practices. For the Permanent Settlement to work, cultivated land itself needed a degree of 'permanence'. In practice, this usually meant the construction of protective embankments. From the early nineteenth century onwards such *bandhs*, as they were locally called, proliferated throughout the river valleys of Bengal, Orissa and Assam. The initial focus was mainly on repairing or improving dilapidated embankments that had long been used for flood defence or irrigation purposes, but attention soon shifted towards the construction of newer, larger works that would protect more land from the threat of inundation. This multiplication of flood defences was not solely a top-down process. While the colonial government actively encouraged the construction of levees, they

10. C. Hill, 'Water and Power', 13–16; *River of Sorrow*, 49–50; Mishra, 'Bihar Flood Story', 2208–9.

11. Sinha, 'Fluvial Landscape'.

12. C. Hill, 'Water and Power'; D'Souza, *Drowned and Dammed*, 51–96; Cederlof, *Founding an Empire*, 117–61.

were also eagerly built by landowners who faced the prospect of confiscation if they defaulted on their taxes. In this sense, India's flood defences epitomized the practices of indirect rule that formed the very scaffolding of the colonial state. Over time, there emerged a kind of division of labour whereby the largest and most costly works were undertaken by public authorities, while the construction and maintenance of secondary defences were generally the responsibility of zamindars who drew the most direct financial benefit from them. By the late nineteenth century, the embankments flanking the region's rivers formed a vital part of the colonial infrastructure, one that signified a distinct shift from the more reactive relationship between floodwaters and the pre-colonial state to one in which volatile rivers were a danger that had to be managed. By insulating landed property from the depredations of water, they enabled state authorities to pursue their primary imperative: the systematic collection of land revenue.[13]

Throughout the colonial period India thus witnessed a rapid proliferation of flood defences. One of the chief reasons for this was that they appealed to so many different interests: revenue officials, zamindars, European planters, and anyone else whose property or income was exposed to the risk of flood damage. Yet this new hydrological order did not go unchallenged, especially as its various drawbacks became more apparent.

As Willcocks forcefully argued in the 1920s and 1930s, one of the main disadvantages of constraining rivers between solid embankments was to deprive nearby fields of irrigation water and fertile silt.[14] It was a problem that most cultivators throughout Bengal and Orissa recognized long before Willcocks did, and often sought to rectify by taking matters into their own hands. Instead of simply allowing the silt-laden floodwaters to pass them by, they commonly dug small breaches in the embankments to cover their fields at particular points of the cropping cycle, much as their ancestors had done under the older system of inundation canals. It was a dangerous thing to do, both legally and practically. The excavation of unauthorized 'cuts' in flood defences was a prosecutable offence in colonial India, punishable by hefty fines and substantial periods of imprisonment. Moreover, piercing an embankment always carried the risk that a small opening could, owing to the erosive power of the current it created, become much larger than intended and in the worst cases even uncontrollable.

Yet despite the dangers involved, dyke breaching was a widespread and well-organized practice among farming communities. Controlling the release

13. H. Harrison, *Bengal Embankment Manual*, 1–30; P. Singh, 'Flood Control', 161–64; 'Colonial State', 244–46; D'Souza, *Drowned and Dammed*, 97–120; 'Mischievous Rivers', 135–38; Saikia, *Unquiet River*, 407–57. On how the same propertizing principles applied to urban land, see Bhattacharyya's *Empire and Ecology*.

14. Willcocks, *Ancient Irrigation of Bengal* and *Lectures*.

of floodwaters and channelling them on to fields – and, just as importantly, concealing the act from state authorities – could not be done haphazardly, but rather involved the cooperation of entire villages, local zamindars and even dike inspectors, who were occasionally paid to turn a blind eye. Colonial authorities, for their part, condemned any such tampering with embankments as an act of 'sabotage' and insisted that complete flood protection was crucial for boosting agricultural productivity. But the matter looked very different to those familiar with conditions on the ground.[15] Just as in the Punjab or the Irrawaddy and Mekong deltas, the new colonial hydraulic order in north-eastern India was not imposed on to a blank canvas, but rather disturbed an older set of socio-ecological arrangements that had its own advantages and disadvantages. Seen in this light, temporary embankment breaches were not so much an act of vandalism as a pragmatic attempt to reintroduce some of the key benefits provided by the previous hydraulic regime.

Furthermore, the drawbacks of embankments went well beyond the questions of silt delivery and irrigation water. Over time, the straitjacketing of rivers actually intensified the problem of flooding itself. Diverting floodwaters away from some areas inevitably made matters worse elsewhere. The protection of floodplains on the upper reaches of rivers removed their crucial buffering effect in periods of high run-off. Instead of holding up floodwaters by allowing them to spread and slowly drain away, diked rivers channelled them rapidly downstream where they often overwhelmed defences. The effects of such hydraulic meddling were particularly severe in the deltaic plains, where the creation of solid, watertight embankments on these shifting and dynamic landscapes was based on a fundamental 'misreading' of the different types and causes of flooding in the deltas, which included not only monsoon floods from upstream but also the complex ways in which they interacted with coastal flooding and tides. The upshot was that the prevention of natural flooding often caused rivers to silt up and become shallower, which ultimately reduced their capacity to carry water from the land to the sea.[16] By hindering drainage out of the delta in this way, the embankments had the effect of actually raising the flood level and increasing the risk of catastrophic inundation. As a 1928 report on the Orissa delta bluntly put it, 'every square mile of country from which spill water is excluded means the intensification of floods elsewhere; every embankment means the heading up of water on someone else's land'.[17]

By the middle of the nineteenth century, colonial engineers themselves began to recognize the deleterious effects of all the embankment building of previous decades. In Bengal, their main concern was the 'haphazard' manner

15. See D'Souza, *Drowned and Dammed*, 40–42, 106–8; Willcocks, *Lectures*, 22–23; Dewan, *Misreading the Bengal Delta*, 33–34.

16. Dewan, *Misreading the Bengal Delta*, 21–47.

17. Willcocks, *Lectures*, 40–41; quote from *Report of the Orissa Flood Committee*, 13.

in which zamindars and other private parties were building dikes, which often had the effect of obstructing drainage and exacerbating the flood risk for their neighbours. In 1882, the provincial government in Bengal passed legislation enabling it to prevent the unauthorized construction of embankments in any areas where it might have a detrimental effect. In the Orissa delta, where a succession of floods continued to destroy large swathes of cropland, some engineers even began to call for the partial dismantling or total abandonment of embankments as the only way to solve the problem. The seemingly interminable work of repairing breaches and improving sections of embankment was the responsibility of the military engineers, and by the 1850s and 1860s they increasingly regarded it as an exercise in futility. Restoring the previous regime of 'natural inundations', so the argument went, would allow the rivers to deposit their silt-loads on surrounding lands, raise their level in relation to riverbeds, and thereby reduce the effects of exceptionally high floodwaters.[18] However sensible such proposals were from a strictly hydrological perspective, it was an unorthodox view, and not everyone in the colonial administration – especially those responsible for tax collection – shared this aversion towards embankments. Calls for their removal remained the exception rather than the rule within official circles. Despite widespread recognition of the problems they caused, flood defence dikes were generally regarded as a practical necessity, and as a result their construction continued apace.[19]

By the early twentieth century, flood control policy had thus become enmeshed in a tangle of conflicting interests and competing imperatives, both within and beyond the state bureaucracy. For most colonial engineers, the key was to take a wider view of flooding and drainage to ensure that flood defence systems as a whole functioned in a more 'scientific' manner. This was the basic rationale behind a series of new regulations that empowered the government to prohibit any embankments that would aggravate flooding elsewhere. By contrast, for colonial revenue officers the main concern was to take a wider view of the overall political economy of flood control. In order to ensure political stability and the smooth flow of tax proceeds, it was crucial to recognize the needs of indigenous elites to protect their property by whatever means were most effective. After all, keeping local elites on side was vital for enabling colonial rule to function on the ground. Far from following a coordinated, top-down plan, British flood policies in India were – like their early irrigation initiatives – largely a product of messy negotiations and short-term improvisation.[20]

18. Inglis, *Review of the Legislation*, 44–46; *Report of the Orissa Flood Committee*, 12–16; P. Singh, 'Colonial State', 244–46; Willcocks, *Ancient Irrigation of Bengal*; D'Souza, *Drowned and Dammed*, 113–20.

19. On the debates about drainage: D'Souza, 'Mischievous Rivers', 138–42.

20. See esp. P. Singh, 'Colonial State', 246–48.

Meanwhile, for the bulk of colonial subjects who actually made a living on the floodplains, the construction of embankments was a major source of conflict between different villages and neighbouring landowners. The determination of individual zamindars to safeguard their lands from inundation or to reclaim additional land along the rivers generated a chain reaction of sorts. As soon as a dike was completed along one stretch of a river, it was followed by the construction of opposing dikes by other landowners whose property had become more flood-prone owing to the diversion of water by the first dike. The result was a spree of embankment building, which soon led to a series of lawsuits and countersuits over alleged property damage. The disputes could drag on for years, and when the justice system failed to satisfy complainants, people often took matters into their own hands by organizing gangs to breach their opponents' dikes. Such actions often led to violence, especially during periods of high floodwaters, when people would go to extreme lengths to protect their crops and homes from inundation. As one experienced official in Gondwara remarked in 1935:

> There were great armies of *lathials* [hired strongmen equipped with batons] to guard the bandhs on each side of the Kosi, to make sure that no one from the other side would break the bandh on your side to cause flooding when the river rose. Every year the bandhs rose higher and higher, and so the river did also.[21]

Colonial authorities introduced a range of measures to bring some semblance of order to flood defences and the conflicts surrounding them. At a local level, they formed various boards to manage the different interests of competing landowners. At higher levels of administration, they also established embankment committees and advisory bodies to coordinate measures across district boundaries and across different interest groups within the colonial bureaucracy itself. In the 1920s and 1930s, provincial governments set up standing committees to advise on flood problems, while interprovincial conferences tried to hammer out more comprehensive strategies of flood control across larger areas. Yet despite all of these organizational efforts, the flooding situation merely continued to worsen. Powerful landowners in protected areas were unwilling to cede their advantages from current flood defences, and proved quite adept at resisting any attempts to curtail them. Meanwhile, administrators found it difficult to prohibit the construction of new dikes in less protected areas where flooding had grown worse because of previous alterations of the river elsewhere. In short, decades of embankment building created a morass of competing interests in which some groups

---

21. Quoted in C. Hill, *River of Sorrow*, 14–15. On embankment building more generally: P. Singh, 'Flood Control', 164–71; 'Colonial State', 248–53.

FIGURE 4.1. Rescue teams aiding people into boats during a flood near
Lucknow in northern India, September 1923.
By permission of akg-images/British Library, photo 10/8(5).

were determined to safeguard their property by diverting the flood risk to
others.[22]

The colonial enthusiasm for revenue collection and agricultural 'improvement'
altered the flood risk not only along the rivers of north-eastern India; it also
created new vulnerabilities on the coast – a coast that was characterized by
exceptionally high levels of natural flood vulnerability. Indeed, the shoreline of
the Bay of Bengal is more prone to cyclones and storm surges than any other
place on Earth. There are several reasons why it earns this dubious distinction. One is the very topography of the bay itself, whose concave shape and
shallow coastal shelf allow strong winds to funnel water towards its northern
coastline, which is low, flat, and stretches far inland. A second factor is the
lack of a large continental landmass between the bay and the Pacific, which
leaves it open to cyclones from far afield as well as those generated over the

22. P. Singh, 'Colonial State', 247–48; 'Flood Control', 170–71; D'Souza, *Drowned and
Dammed*, 166–71.

bay itself. This points towards a third reason – namely, the high humidity and unusually warm surface waters of the bay, both of which aid the formation of cyclones and enhance their strength. On average, around five to six tropical cyclones form in the Bay of Bengal each year (a far higher frequency than the global mean, and several times higher than in the Arabian Sea off India's west coast), roughly a third of which can be classified as severe. The strongest cyclones tend to form after the end of the south-west monsoon in October and November, though storms also form at the beginning of the monsoon in May and June. Together, these three characteristics made (and continue to make) the seaboard of Bengal a hazardous place to live.[23]

Nonetheless, the perennial threat of storms and flooding did not deter people from living there. The fertile alluvial soils along the coast of the Bengal delta made for excellent farmland, and more of it was being created all the time by the enormous volumes of silt carried downstream by the two great rivers of eastern India, the Ganges and Brahmaputra. In the eastern part of the delta in particular, where the bulk of discharge from these river systems empties into the bay, the accumulation of sediment meant that land was continually appearing, disappearing and reforming as channels and currents altered their course. While the great rivers brought millions of tons of sand and soil downstream, the cyclones that regularly swept the coast pushed them from the tidal mudflats back on to the land. The result of all this fluvial and tidal action was a ragged-edged, ever-shifting alluvial plain fringed by numerous islands, which represented a kind of vanguard of the land formation process – the 'trailing threads of India's fabric', as Amitav Ghosh describes them. These newly formed islands and sandbanks, known locally as *chars*, were initially visible only at ebb tide, but gradually emerged from the water as more sediment accumulated on top of them. Once they rose high enough to be colonized by grasses, it was not long before they were colonized by people and livestock too.[24]

For a variety of reasons, the spread of European power in Bengal brought more and more people to the hazardous coastal fringes of the delta. One important factor was the impact of British import and production policies on several of the region's major industries. For many centuries, Bengal was home to a thriving textile industry and was especially famous for the fine cotton cloth that it exported all around the world. Up until the early nineteenth century, the cotton industry underpinned the livelihoods of many different groups, from merchants and weavers to spinners and farmers. The industrialization of textile manufacturing in Britain, coupled with a punitive tariff regime that opened Indian markets to cheap British goods, had a devastating effect on the local industry. Thousands of spinners and weavers were effectively forced

23. Hossain and Shafeem, 'Bengal Cyclonic Storms'.

24. A. Ghosh, *Hungry Tide*, 6; Lahiri-Dutt and Samanta, *Dancing with the River*. For a contemporary description: Faulkner, *Sundarbans of Bengal*.

on to the land by poverty, and many of them settled the newly formed *chars* in Bengal's estuaries. A similar fate befell the regional salt-making industry, which occupied extensive stretches of coastline all the way from Orissa in the west to Chittagong in the east. When the East India Company (which held a monopoly on salt manufacture) reduced its salt production in the 1830s to allow British manufacturers into the Indian market, it forced thousands of people in north-eastern India out of work. Soon the British imports outcompeted the Company's expensive monopoly-made salt, and by the 1850s the Company stopped producing salt altogether in order to focus on the collection of import duties instead. Like the impoverished weavers and spinners, a large proportion of the salt makers who lost their livelihoods turned to farming or cattle herding along the coastal frontier.[25]

As it happened, the demise of two of Bengal's traditional industries roughly coincided with a second factor that brought more people to the coast: government efforts to encourage agricultural settlement in the delta. The aim, as ever, was to generate more revenue. Although the Permanent Settlement had fixed the tax rates of landed estates in 1793, the Company soon found itself in need of more money to cover the costs of military expansion. As financial pressures rose, it looked to the revenue-generating potential of areas that lay outside the boundaries of existing domains, which for the most part meant the mangrove forests fringing the coast and the new *char* land that had been created since the 1790s. Bringing such tracts into cultivation would increase the state's income in two different ways. Not only would it expand the very base of the land revenue itself (i.e., the extent of cultivated acreage); it would also, more importantly, enable the administration to impose a much higher rate of taxation on new lands than on those that were regulated by the Permanent Settlement. According to new 'resumption' laws introduced in the 1820s, any *chars* that formed as islands (which most initially did) were government property, and any that formed on the boundaries of an existing tenure were subject to higher rates than previously cultivated land. The same principle was not, however, applied in reverse; zamindars whose property was washed away by river or tidal currents were still liable for the same tax payments as before.[26]

As Benjamin Kingsbury argues, the government essentially took advantage of the very hydrology of the delta itself, 'using the process of erosion and deposition to increase its land revenue'. The more tenants it could entice to the *chars*, the more revenue it could generate. The problem was that this policy also rendered more people acutely susceptible to the dangers of cyclones and storm surges. It was a risk that was recognized by farmers and officials alike,

25. Ray, *Bengal Industries*, 52–87; 'Imperial Policy'; Kingsbury, *Imperial Disaster*, 8–15.

26. On hydrological processes and property law generally: Bhattacharya, 'Fluid Histories', 73; on the east Bengal coast specifically: Kingsbury, *Imperial Disaster*, 16–24.

but little was done about it. Building sea walls along the low-lying coastal plains was an expensive undertaking, and neither landlords nor officials – few of whom actually lived there – were prepared to pay for them. Even when cultivators offered to cover part of the costs, the prioritization of profits over security – and literally over people's lives – left them vulnerable to the sea.[27]

In the meantime, this vulnerability was further compounded by the conversion of the delta's mangrove forests into tax-paying agricultural land. In 1800, the Sundarbans (the largest continuous mangrove wetland in the world) stretched along the entire head of the Bay of Bengal, from the Hooghly River in the west to the Meghna estuary in the east. Composed of a maze of creeks and rivers and infested with tigers, snakes and crocodiles, it had long resisted the advance of the plough. The revenue-hungry colonial state saw big profits to be made from 'improving' these supposedly unproductive 'wastelands'. After declaring the Sundarbans as state domain – and thus subject to the same 'resumption' laws that governed the newly created *chars* – the government sold land parcels on highly advantageous terms and offered numerous tax incentives to lure investors and tenants. The frontier expanded most rapidly in the eastern half of the delta, where the huge amounts of fresh water and silt carried down the Ganges and Brahmaputra built up the land and kept salinity levels low. By contrast, in western and central parts of the Sundarbans, where the waterways had lost their connection to the main rivers, land subsidence and salt intrusion meant that expensive embankments and drainage works were required for agriculture to work. It was no coincidence that the Indian Forestry Department focused almost entirely on these less cultivable areas when it began gazetting parts of the Sundarbans as reserved forests in the 1870s. By this time there was far less tidal woodland left in the eastern Sundarbans in any event owing to inward migration and government-sponsored land conversion. Fatefully, as it turned out, much of the forest around the Meghna estuary was cleared all the way to coast, leaving most of the *char* land completely exposed to the Bay. Although some officials warned about the dangers of removing this natural breakwater between cultivated lands and the sea, their admonishments went unheeded, just like the various proposals for sea walls.[28]

The indifference that the colonial government showed towards coastal defences was certainly not due to a lack of evidence about the risks that were involved. Cyclones and storm waves posed a constant menace to settlers in low-lying delta lands and repeatedly destroyed lives and property. Any sceptics who still needed proof about the scale of these risks got it in abundance on 5 October 1864, when a vicious cyclone struck the coast just south of Calcutta.

27. I draw here on Kingsbury's *Imperial Disaster* (19–28, quote at 19).

28. J. Richards and Flint, 'Long-Term Transformations'; Amites Mukhopadhyay, *Living with Disasters*, 27–35; Kingsbury, *Imperial Disaster*, 33–40; Pargiter, *Revenue History*.

Considered at the time to be India's worst storm in decades, the cyclone dev-astated large swathes of lower Bengal, including parts of the capital city itself. All across Calcutta, noted one observer, 'the scene of devastation could only be faintly imagined'.[29] Of the 195 ships in the city's port at the time, only 23 escaped intact; over half suffered severe damage and 36 were 'totally lost'.[30] Although high winds were partly to blame, most of the destruction was caused by an immense storm wave that surged up the Hooghly. Worst hit were the low-lying districts along the main channel and its principal feeders, where the wave rose sixteen feet (five metres) above the highest spring tide, 'sweeping away the villages and submerging their inhabitants with their cattle and dwell-ings'. 'The violence of the wave may be realized', noted one eyewitness, by the fact that it 'scooped out and carried away the terraced floor' of a brick-and-mortar tollhouse at the mouth of the Rupnarayan River. Although estimates of the death toll were somewhat speculative, it was calculated that the cyclone alone killed over forty-eight thousand people. Over the following days and weeks, another twenty-five to thirty thousand people died from the ensuing outbreak of cholera and dysentery caused by the fouling of water supplies and the 'putrid vegetation and unburied bodies and carcasses which for many weeks lay strewn over the country'. To make matters worse, the cyclone season of 1864 was not yet finished. Precisely one month later, on 5 November, another unusually fierce storm struck the coast further south in Orissa, killing around thirty-three thousand people.[31]

Appalled by the scale of the losses, the government responded by estab-lishing a new weather service, the Indian Meteorological Department. Headquartered in Calcutta, its main purpose was to track storms in the Bay of Bengal through the collection of weather observations and shipping reports, and to telegraph the information to a network of warning stations along the coast. Though ill-equipped and poorly staffed, the system soon proved its worth. In November 1867, it gave authorities in Calcutta several hours' notice before the arrival of yet another powerful cyclone. Unfortunately, however, this was as far as the government was prepared to go. Apart from the estab-lishment of the Meteorological Department, its response was negligible. It built precious few protective embankments in the wake of the disaster, and even the new storm-warning system achieved only limited coverage. This was especially true in the coastal districts of eastern Bengal, far removed from the capital of British India. Although these areas were more prone to cyclones than anywhere else, they enjoyed little if any protection from sea defences and

29. Bengal Hurkaru, *Great Bengal Cyclone*, 9.

30. Gastrell and Blanford, *Calcutta Cyclone*, 143–44; Bengal Hurkaru, *Great Bengal Cyclone*, 42–52.

31. All quotes and figures from Gastrell and Blanford's *Calcutta Cyclone* (107–16, 125–40).

none whatsoever from the storm-warning system (which focused mainly on the protection of commercial ports and shipping).[32]

It was only a matter of time before disaster struck, and when it did, it struck with a vengeance. On 31 October 1876, the Meghna estuary – the main outlet of the Ganges and Brahmaputra – was hit by one of the deadliest cyclones in modern history. After forming at the southern end of the bay, the storm intensified on its trek northward, eventually reaching wind speeds of 147 miles per hour (237 kilometres per hour). As it moved along, it brought with it a huge volume of water that had piled up underneath its low barometric pressure and rotating winds. When this surge reached the shallow mouth of the river, it rose into a huge storm wave that ran headlong into the great countervailing flow of freshwater seeking an outlet down the Meghna. John Elliott, who later became the director of the Indian Meteorological Department, described how 'these two vast and accumulating masses of water opposed each other over the shallows of the estuary', each vying for supremacy and causing a 'very considerable piling up of the waters'. Ultimately, it was 'the larger and more powerful mass of waters forming the storm-wave' that prevailed, 'driving back the river water and advancing first in the form of a wave, carrying all before it'.[33]

The devastation was awful. Many of the alluvial islands along the coast were completely submerged under a thirty-foot (nine-metre) wave, which carried off three-quarters of the human population and nearly all of the cattle. On the mainland too, village after village was reported to have lost nearly half of its inhabitants and the bulk of its livestock. Touring the Bakerganj coastline (immediately west of the Meghna's outlet) two weeks after the event, the commissioner of the Dacca Division reported that 'three storm waves of from 15 to 20 feet high have swept over the place, literally levelling it with the ground. Not a single hut and hardly a post was left standing'. Agricultural communities suffered worst, though many of the larger settlements in the region were also swept away. Daulatkhan, a prosperous trading town and subdivisional headquarters, was 'a complete wreck', its administrative buildings, school, jail, distillery and bazaar literally 'levelled with the ground'. The situation was scarcely better east of the river in the Noakhali district, where officials reported a landscape 'strewn with the dead bodies of human beings and cattle'. All in all, it was estimated that 215,000 people – over one-fifth of the entire regional population – were drowned by the flood, most of them poor cultivators who had recently migrated to the area, and a disproportionate number of them women who had never been taught how to swim.[34]

32. On the early development of meteorology in India: K. Anderson, *Predicting the Weather*, 250–82, here 257. On eastern Bengal: Kingsbury, *Imperial Disaster*, 159–60.

33. J. Elliott, *Vizagapatam and Backergunge Cyclones*, 158–59; see also Amrith, *Unruly Waters*, 91–92.

34. J. Elliott, *Vizagapatam and Backergunge Cyclones*, 162–71, 180. On the disproportionate effects on different groups: Kingsbury, *Imperial Disaster*, 75–76.

As dreadful as the losses were, the disaster did not stop there, and nor did the death toll. Relief efforts in the stricken districts were slow and scanty, and clearly reflected colonial priorities. The administration's determination to minimize expenditure, combined with its dogmatic adherence to market principles, left hundreds of thousands of survivors without adequate food or water in the immediate wake of the disaster. Over the mid-term, the fact that it also left them without adequate numbers of livestock with which to prepare their fields for the next harvest only compounded the problems. The only thing that was not in short supply was corpses. For several weeks after the storm, survivors were still pulling bodies from fields, riverbanks, and the remains of wrecked buildings. 'The atmosphere is in many places simply poisonous', noted one official. 'Most of the tanks are full of decaying matter, animal and vegetable, and it is hard to conceive anything more sickening than the smell arising from them'.[35] It was not long before the area was in the grip of a full-blown cholera epidemic, the worst ever witnessed in Bengal. Hunger and destitution exacerbated the poor sanitary conditions, leaving people weakened and highly susceptible to illness. Yet in spite of the dire need on display, the government's provision of medical relief was no more generous than its food relief, and the few medical personnel who were dispatched into the countryside could do little to stop the spread of the disease. By the time the epidemic finally subsided around six months later in April 1877, another hundred thousand people had died.[36] Perversely, the architect of the botched relief operation, Lieutenant-Governor Richard Temple, was promoted to higher office for his sterling services to state finances. Soon he would adopt a similarly parsimonious approach to the millions suffering from drought in Madras (see chapter 2). Both before and after the storm, state finances were prioritized over the safety of poor communities.

If the 1876 storm wave was itself a chance event, the pattern of death and disease that it caused was far from arbitrary. As so often happens when disaster strikes, the suffering was overwhelmingly concentrated among those at the bottom of the social hierarchy. Decades of 'reclamation' and 'resumption' policies along the delta coast had ensured that the poor cultivators who were pushed there by poverty bore most of the risks of extreme weather, while absentee landlords and the colonial treasury reaped most of the rewards. After the flood, a combination of official miserliness and indifference among indigenous elites hindered the region's recovery and claimed tens of thousands more lives. Ultimately, the divisions of wealth, power and privilege that shaped the settlement of the Sundarbans coast became the dividing lines that 'separated the living from the dead'.[37]

35. J. Elliott, *Vizagapatam and Backergunge Cyclones*, 167.
36. For a detailed discussion of the epidemic: Kingsbury, *Imperial Disaster*, 79–131.
37. Kingsbury, 77.

Over the longer term, the horrible death toll from the storm did nothing to narrow these social disparities. If anything, the government's post-disaster policies served to widen the divisions yet further. Instead of providing cultivators with advances to buy new cattle and ploughs, it left them at the mercy of the zamindars and moneylenders. Tenants who had lost all their possessions became further indebted to their landlords, many of whom took advantage of the situation by increasing rents. As rural resentment grew, the administration beefed up its police presence in the region to ensure that these rents were collected, thereby enhancing the power of the landlords yet further. What was a traumatic calamity for poor peasants was by no means a tragedy for the state or for local social elites, whose control over the land and those who worked it was strengthened by all of the upheaval. Most importantly, perhaps, the government did almost nothing to avoid such a disaster in the future. Despite the fact that revenues continued to flow in, the administration calculated that ample protective measures would simply cost too much. Landlords had no desire to pay for the construction of sea walls, and nor did the government. Although some officials eventually recommended embanked tanks as places of refuge in coastal settlements that were vulnerable to storm-waves, in practice this initiative came to nothing. Nor was anything done to reforest the coastal belt as a breakwater, or to build up the storm-warning system for eastern Bengal. In the end, the colonial fixation on maximizing income and minimizing expenditure meant that millions remained as vulnerable to flood disaster as before.[38]

It was a pattern all too familiar in flood-prone areas the world over: as long as the powerful could shift the risk on to others, they had little incentive to change things. Along much of north-eastern India's coast, the ability of elites to escape the consequences of catastrophic inundation impeded the construction of flood defences where they were sorely needed. Meanwhile, along the region's rivers, the same set of factors also made it extremely difficult to fix the problems caused by flood defences that were already in place.

By the early twentieth century, the attempt to constrain north-eastern India's flood-prone rivers was in a quandary. On the one hand, the administration continued to encourage the building of embankments as the most practical form of defence against inundation. On the other hand, it recognized that doing so merely exacerbated the flood problem over the longer term. Resolving this fundamental contradiction would not be easy.

All across Bengal, Bihar and Orissa, decades of uncoordinated embankment and canal construction had raised river levels and clogged drainage channels. The combined effect was to build up enormous hydraulic pressures that periodically exploded in a succession of catastrophic inundations: 1892,

38. Kingsbury, 133–64.

1899, 1902, 1906, 1918, 1922, 1927.[39] With each successive disaster, it became more and more evident that the current policy approach could not continue. During the interwar years, there was growing opposition within engineering circles against meddling with the lower reaches of rivers in general, and against the use of embankments in particular. While some advocated upriver dams as an alternative measure, others argued that it was ultimately useless to try to hinder the natural process of flooding and land creation in deltaic and *diara* lands. Given the heavy silt loads of most of the region's rivers, which would quickly fill storage reservoirs with sediment, some engineers contended that floods should be recognized as an inevitable and natural occurrence in riverine tracts. From their perspective, it was the decades-long failure to acknowledge this fact that led to the current predicament.[40]

It was a supreme irony that the intensifying flood problem throughout much of the region was caused mainly by efforts to prevent it. In the words of an official report on the devastating Orissa floods of 1927:

> The problem in Orissa is not how to prevent floods, but how to pass them as quickly as possible to the sea. And the solution lies in removing all obstacles which militate against this result. . . . To continue as at present is merely to pile up a debt which will have to be paid, in distress and calamity, at the end.[41]

Such arguments ran directly counter to a century of conventional hydroengineering wisdom. By advocating an approach that worked more in tandem with natural hydrological processes rather than against them, it contradicted the strategy that had prevailed ever since the introduction of the Permanent Settlement in India. Yet despite this growing condemnation of existing canal and embankment systems, engineers rarely called for their outright removal. Even Willcocks, perhaps the most outspoken opponent of what he called the 'Satanic chains' that bound eastern India's rivers, recognized that some existing structures would have to stay and that they could even be beneficial if provided with openings.[42] There was, in other words, an apparent incongruity between the diagnosis of the problem and prescriptions to remedy it. If the solution was to remove impediments to the evacuation of floodwaters, why retain embankments at all?

The answer lay in the paradoxical situation that colonial flood policies had created. In spite of the unsuitability of the existing flood-works, for a number

39. For a description of the series of major floods in north Bengal, see T. Ghosh's 'Floods and People'.

40. See, e.g.: *Report of the Orissa Flood Committee*, 12–16; *Report of the Floods Enquiry Committee*, 205. Tt was also evident at the Patna Flood Conference of 1937: Mishra, 'Bihar Flood Story', 2209, 2214; P. Singh, 'Colonial State', 247–48; 'Flood Control', 171–75.

41. *Report of the Orissa Flood Committee*, 13.

42. Willcocks, *Lectures*, 40–41; *Ancient Irrigation of Bengal*, 9.

of reasons it was no longer realistic to revert to the previous flood regime. On a political level, such a move would quickly fall foul of the vested interests of indigenous landholding elites. From an administrative standpoint, it would undermine the coherence of the all-important colonial land and revenue settlement. Most fundamentally, it would expose too many people to the risk of catastrophic inundation, given the extent to which flood levels had risen after a century of embankment construction and the associated elevation of riverbeds in relation to surrounding fields caused by the restriction of silt deposition. As a result, engineers ultimately had to content themselves with various stopgap measures designed to improve the efficacy of the dike system and enhance drainage from the most congested parts of the floodplains.[43]

All in all, it was a textbook example of path dependence. The range of available choices for controlling floodwaters was tightly circumscribed by the decisions and developments of the past. Since it was impossible to turn back the clock, the only apparent solution was an 'escape forwards'; that is, to double down on existing methods. As seasonal torrents periodically breached embankments to find new (or former) channels, the task of flood control demanded ever-higher levels of intervention and expenditure. Over time, the ensuing spiral of embankment and canal construction drew the colonial state and its taxpayers into a kind of 'arms race against nature'.[44] With each new engineering measure, the rivers became yet more volatile, raising local flood risks even further. And as the floodwaters became increasingly dangerous, people in the floodplains – and the revenues they paid – became more and more dependent on the embankments to protect them. Despite the rising financial and environmental costs of flood control, and despite the growing risks, officials saw little alternative but to raise the ante yet further. Such was the situation until the final years of colonial rule in India, when the pressures of the Second World War finally opened a new phase in this ongoing arms race.

On 16 October 1942, a ferocious cyclone slammed into the coast of western Bengal. With winds reaching as high as 140 miles per hour (225 kilometres per hour), it uprooted trees, flattened crops, and wrecked houses and communications all along the littoral. In the Midnapore district south of Calcutta, a trio of tidal waves estimated at sixteen feet (nearly five metres) in height swept over coastal embankments, obliterating entire villages and flooding around 400 square miles (1,000 square kilometres). By the time it was over, the combination of wind, storm surge, and torrential rain ruined over 1,000 square miles (2,500 square kilometres) of some of the best paddy land in Bengal, and severely impaired 3,000 more. Some 7,400 villages were damaged or destroyed, including 527,000 houses and 1,900 schools. Although official figures put the death

---

43. The discussion here is based on D'Souza's *Drowned and Dammed* (158–60).
44. Beattie and Morgan, 'Engineering Edens', 56.

toll at 14,443 people and roughly 190,000 cattle (around 10 per cent of the region's livestock), some estimated that the storm surge alone killed as many as 40,000 people and 75 per cent of all the livestock in the most heavily affected districts. Altogether, around 2.5 million people lost their homes, livelihoods or lives to the cyclone.[45]

The people of coastal Bengal were (as we have seen) certainly no strangers to floods and cyclones, even violent ones such as this. Nonetheless, the storm of October 1942 struck at a moment of exceptional vulnerability. For one thing, the productivity of Bengal's croplands had been in decline for decades, and with it the incomes and food security of millions of poor people in the countryside. Much of the decline was due to recent hydrological changes. While the proliferation of embankments led to waterlogging and reduced soil fertility, from the early twentieth century onwards the rapid spread of water hyacinth (an invasive Amazonian import) obstructed water channels, smothered extensive swathes of paddy land and diminished freshwater fish stocks.[46] By the 1920s and 1930s, these long-term ecological problems were compounded by growing economic pressures. Rising taxes and mounting debts weighed heavily on Bengali smallholders, many of whom lost their land during the Depression because of an inability to repay their loans. Matters came to a head with the outbreak of war in Southeast Asia. The Japanese invasion of Burma in early 1942 cut off the hitherto substantial rice imports from the Irrawaddy delta and sent over half a million hungry refugees to India. As Bengal became the new front line in the war with Japan, British 'denial' policies caused further disruption to regional food markets by seeking to prevent rice, transport vessels or other potential assets from falling into enemy hands in the event of an invasion. To make matters worse, government agents forcibly requisitioned rice stocks in the countryside to ensure sufficient food supplies for Calcutta and the war industries based there. Wartime priorities, together with the higher purchasing power of affluent urban markets, served to drain yet more rice out of rural areas that could ill afford to lose it.[47]

The food situation in rural Bengal was therefore precarious before the storm hit, but the effects of the cyclone helped pitch the region into an acute food crisis. As rice prices soared, millions of poor and marginalized people – mostly wage labourers, women and children – began to starve. Apart from a small trickle of aid from charitable donations, little help was forthcoming. Despite forceful calls for more relief in both India and Britain, the government continued to export rice to other theatres of war and refused to divert scarce transport

45. J. Mukherjee, *Hungry Bengal*, 78–79; Greenough, *Prosperity and Misery*, 93. The estimate of 40,000 human deaths and 75% livestock losses is from the Ramakrishna Mission's *Bengal and Orissa Cyclone* (1–2); see also Amrith's *Unruly Waters* (168–69).

46. On the longer ecological prehistory of the famine, see Iqbal's *Bengal Delta* (140–83).

47. J. Mukherjee, *Hungry Bengal*, 23–83; Greenough, *Prosperity and Misery*, 52–92; A. Sen, *Poverty and Famines*, 52–85.

and food resources to alleviate the suffering in Bengal. Indeed, for around ten months after the October 1942 cyclone, it tried to deny the very existence of a food crisis. It was only in August 1943, after the Calcutta-based *Statesman* published photos of starving people in the streets, that the government was forced to acknowledge the scale of the disaster. Nationalist political leaders in Bengal were quick to criticize the government for rural food shortages, but – beholden as many of them were to domestic industrial interests – they did little to oppose the policy of funnelling supplies to Calcutta for the sake of the war effort, which undoubtedly intensified the famine. All the while, rampant profiteering by greedy speculators and hoarders only made matters worse. Although the government finally mounted an extensive relief effort in late 1943, which led to premature claims of an end to the crisis, starvation and disease continued to haunt the countryside for at least another two years. Overall, it is estimated that a staggering three to five million people lost their lives, at least 5 per cent of the entire Bengali population.[48]

The Bengal famine was by far the worst humanitarian catastrophe to befall India since the drought-induced famines of the early 1900s, shattering the complacent assumption that such calamities were a thing of the past. One of its main consequences was to generate a pervasive sense of the need for change. For many observers, and especially for adherents of the growing nationalist movement, the unexpected reappearance of mass starvation marked the beginning of the end of colonial rule. The spectacular failure to safeguard the basic welfare of millions of people amplified calls for self-government as the best way to prevent a recurrence. Moreover, beyond the divisive question of colonial versus home rule, the famine also engendered a broad consensus that India could not rely on imports and open markets to supply its basic food needs. Indian leaders and British nutritionists alike argued that greater self-sufficiency and market regulation were necessary to make India's food supply more secure.[49] As everyone recognized, the attainment of self-sufficiency was an ambitious goal, all the more so against the backdrop of rising population pressures. Achieving it would require far more investment and proactive government intervention than the colonial state had ever mustered in the past. Crucially, it would also require the adoption of bigger, better technologies to reshape the Indian hydrosphere.

It was in this political context that a whole new approach to the problem of flooding and river control emerged. Spurred into action by mounting political pressures, and inspired by new models of hydraulic management in

48. On relief campaigns: Simonow, 'Great Bengal Famine'; on responses (and lack thereof) among Indian elites: J. Mukherjee, *Hungry Bengal*, 85–114. Death estimates vary substantially; this figure is for 1943–46 and follows Mukherjee (251). For a detailed discussion of mortality, see A. Sen's *Poverty and Famines*, appendix D.

49. I draw here on Greenough's *Prosperity and Misery* (253–60), Amrith's *Unruly Waters* (170–71) and Vernon's *Hunger* (147–50).

the United States, government planners and administrators started thinking big. In the Damodar basin – where a severe bout of flooding in the summer of 1943 further aggravated the already acute food shortages in the area – a team of British and Indian engineers drew up plans to build a quartet of barrages across its main waterways (at Maithon and Tilaiya on the Barakar River, at Panchet on the Damodar and at Konar on the Konar River) to regulate their seasonal fluctuations once and for all. Meanwhile, on the Mahanadi River in Orissa the government approved plans for a massive dam at Hirakud to impound its floodwaters long before they reached its flood-prone delta. Both of these schemes were unprecedented in scale: the main Hirakud Dam would reach three miles (4.8 kilometres) long and two hundred feet (61 metres) high, and the Maithon Dam was of similar proportions. These projects numbered among a handful of huge new water storage works – including the Tungabhadra Dam in Deccan and the gargantuan Bhakra Nangal scheme in Punjab – whose planning and execution spanned the transition to Indian independence in 1947. Though dreamt up in the 1940s under the slogan of colonial modernization, at their completion in the 1950s they were hailed not as legacies of British beneficence but as monuments to the technical prowess and developmentalist resolve of the new Indian state.[50]

Both the Hirakud Dam and the Damodar valley projects exemplified the ethos of 'multi-purpose river valley development' pioneered in the United States in the 1930s by the Tennessee Valley Authority. Though primarily conceived for flood control, they were also designed to provide a range of other benefits – electricity, transport, irrigation – that together promised to jumpstart the economic development of the region. In the words of Ajudhiya Nath Khosla, the Roorkee-trained engineer (and later governor of Orissa) who led the planning and construction of the Hirakud Dam after a study tour of the latest dam designs in the United States, 'the only cure for the many troubles of Orissa, namely floods, droughts, poverty and disease lay in the control, conservation and utilization of the enormous water wealth of its rivers by means of storage dams'.[51] In the event, the results of both projects fell well short of expectations. Electricity generation was limited by the rapid accumulation of silt in the reservoirs, and most of the electricity bypassed local communities on its way to power the new industrial complexes that the post-colonial state was so keen to promote (a theme that we will explore in more detail in chapter 8). Although the reservoirs were used to feed sizeable irrigation networks, local farmers complained that too much of the impounded water was allocated to mines, power plants and other industries rather than going to

50. On the Damodar project: Klingensmith, 'One Valley'; on Hirakud: D'Souza, Drowned and Dammed, 182–205.

51. A. N. Khosla, Mahanadi Valley Development Hirakud Dam Project (Simla, 1947), 10, quoted in D'Souza, Drowned and Dammed, 192.

nearby croplands. As for the tens of thousands of people who were forcibly displaced by the new reservoirs, a disproportionate number of them 'tribals' with little political clout, few received much assistance by way of resettlement, which actually deepened poverty for many in the region. Indeed, financial compensation for the loss of submerged homes and fields fell well below what the government initially promised.

Most disappointing of all, perhaps, the projects did not even put an end to the perennial problem of flooding. The lower Damodar valley continued to experience severe inundations (e.g., in 1959, 1978, 1995, and 2000) because of the siltation of reservoirs, the clogging of river channels, the failure of embankments and even the deliberate release of water in order to keep the dams from overflowing. In the Orissa delta too, hydrographic analyses showed that dangerously high floods actually became more rather than less frequent after the completion of the Hirakud Dam.[52]

Like so many of India's hydraulic prestige projects – both before and after 1947 – these schemes ultimately did little to improve the prospects of most ordinary people in the immediate vicinity. In fact, they entailed heavy social and environmental costs that fell disproportionately on the rural poor, just as earlier flood defences had done. However powerful the new technologies appeared to be, the erratic rivers of Bengal and Orissa continued to defy human attempts to contain them. And however much they promised to enhance people's living standards and security, their actual effects remained an ongoing source of conflict.[53]

Deluges, Dikes and Dependency in Colonial Indochina

The history of technology has conventionally been a narrative of novelty and innovation, of original ideas and inventions that enhance humans' capacity to control the world around them. In recent years, however, it has also come to be written as a story of continuity, stasis and persistence. As David Edgerton has argued at length, understanding how existing technologies are used is just as important as studying how new technologies come into being.[54] Indeed, many technologies large and small remain in widespread use long after the cutting edge has moved on, even long after seemingly superior alternatives are available. There are many reasons why this is so. From an economic perspective, the desire to get a return on prior investment tends to gravitate in favour of existing ways of doing things, especially when they involve large and otherwise irrecoverable 'sunk' costs. Social and political inertia likewise plays a role in

52. On the longer-term effects of the dams: S. Ghosh and Mistri, 'Geographic Concerns'; D'Souza, Mukhopadhyay and Kothari, 'Multi-purpose River Valley Projects'.

53. Lahiri-Dutt, 'Large Dams'; Nayak, 'Big Dams and Protests' and 'Development, Displacement and Justice'.

54. Edgerton, *Shock of the Old*.

the form of vested interests that try to hold on to the benefits that a prevailing technology gives them. On a more general level, there are also the mutually reinforcing interactions between technologies, knowledge and institutions, which gradually create a mesh of rules, regulations and ways of thinking that favour incumbent technologies over newcomers. Over time, these dynamics can eventually lead to technological 'lock-in': a situation in which a firm, group or society becomes so reliant on a particular technology as to impede its ability to switch to a different one.[55]

As technologies go, flood control has a history that boasts more than its share of examples. Technological and institutional lock-in was a common problem wherever societies sought to keep wayward rivers from bursting their banks. From China to Germany and from India to the Mississippi Valley, the creation of hydraulic defences was often a fateful step. By attracting more people and investment into the floodplains, they created a new set of threatened assets and raised the stakes if anything should go wrong. By preventing the spread of floodwaters on to fields and wetlands, they often raised river levels within the restricted channels and thus created a need for further hydraulic interventions in the future. Once this positive feedback loop was established, it was difficult to break the cycle. The more that political elites and local residents depended on flood defences to safeguard lives, livelihoods and property, the less capable they were of making a decisive break from prevailing methods.[56]

Perhaps nowhere was this predicament more intractable than in the Tonkin delta, where French engineers became enmeshed in a decades-long struggle to contain the capricious waters of the Red River. With an overall gradient ten times steeper than the Mekong, the Red River (Sông Cái in Vietnamese) is notorious for its powerful current, huge seasonal fluctuations and violent floods. It rises in the Yunnan province of south-west China and flows in a generally south-eastward direction towards Vietnam, entering at the mountainous Lào Cái Province before descending to the delta and emptying into the Gulf of Tonkin. It is fed by a multitude of tributaries (the largest of which are the Black River and Lô River) and acquires its name from the reddish, heavily silt-laden water that it carries.

The Red River watershed receives around three-quarters of its rainfall between May and September, much of it in the form of downpours that run swiftly off the sloping upland relief. From July to September, the delta itself is regularly lashed by typhoons that dump up to a metre of rainfall in several days and that simultaneously threaten coastal areas with storm surges. The

55. For a general discussion: Arthur, 'Competing Technologies'. As applied to water technologies: Elvin, *Retreat of the Elephants*, 123–24, 155–70; Pietz, *Yellow River*, 40, 61.

56. Barry, *Rising Tide*; Doyle, *Source*, 59–111; Zhang, *Coping with Calamity*; Perdue, *Exhausting the Earth*, 164–96; Cioc, *Rhine*.

Red River's floodwaters typically rise in June and subside in October, but they do so in a remarkably erratic pattern that makes flood management difficult. Rather than following a single upward and downward curve, water levels often spike on multiple occasions throughout the summer and early autumn in line with heavy rainfalls and variable run-off times from its tributaries. At the peak of the flood season in late July and early August, water levels at Hanoi often rise by eight to nine metres compared with dry months, and occasionally by up to eleven metres. Altogether, the exceptional volatility, frequency and amplitude of flooding made life in the Tonkin delta a risky enterprise.[57]

Despite these dangers, the fertile soils of the delta had long supported a dense farming population. Rice cultivation began some four thousand years ago, and dike construction in certain regions in the second century BCE. State-led hydraulic works reach back a millennium under the Ly and Tran dynasties, and most were periodically destroyed and either rebuilt or abandoned over the centuries.[58] Subsequent rulers, including the Nguyen dynasty of the nineteenth century, built on this long-standing legacy of embankments and sea walls to protect croplands from inundation and to distribute waters more evenly across the delta. As a general rule, irrigation and flood control works were handled separately. Whereas the former was normally the responsibility of villages and individuals, only state institutions were capable of mobilizing the enormous labour and financial resources required to build and maintain dikes that could contain the river's flow. Over time, the layout of dikes and canals determined the location of towns, villages and cultivated fields, many of which lay well below the river level (some by as much as six metres) and were therefore wholly reliant on the embankments for their very existence.[59]

The construction and reinforcement of embankments was, then, a constant preoccupation of state authorities and colonizing farmers long before the French colonization of Tonkin in 1885. As Tana Li has emphasized, the long-term history of dike building in the region was by no means a linear, cumulative process of humans gradually conquering nature. Rather, it was a more fluid and cyclical story of expansion, retreat, occasional abandonment and reconstruction. Indeed, many of the dikes or sea walls that appear in records in the fifteenth and sixteenth centuries no longer existed by the beginning of the nineteenth; and many of those that were documented in the early nineteenth century were gone by the early part of the twentieth.[60] The levees flanking the Red River and its main channels at any given time therefore hardly brought an end to flooding in the region, and in fact they actually exacerbated the problem in certain ways. Moreover, many of the pre-colonial dikes

57. Gourou, *Les paysans*, 57–80; Bruzon, *Le climat de l'Indochine*.

58. Li, 'Sea Becomes Mulberry Fields', 61–65.

59. Gourou, *Les paysans*, 83–88; Tessier, 'Outline of the Process'.

60. Li, 'Sea Becomes Mulberry Fields', 55–56, 70–71.

FIGURE 4.2. Aerial view of the summer rise of the Red River near Hanoi, 1926. Note the relative level of the floodwaters and surrounding fields protected by dikes.
Cliché École française d'Extrême-Orient, Fonds Vietnam réf. EFEO_VIE04098.

were not high enough to contain more than average summer flood levels, and in the late nineteenth century the network as a whole was still riddled with salients and choke points that held up the flow and encouraged the erosion of the embankments themselves. Built of packed earth, they were often too thin and steep-sided to withstand the huge pressures of a sudden surge, and once the waters spilled over the top, the levees were quickly gouged out by the strong current. As a result, breaches of various magnitudes were a common occurrence, the largest of which inundated crops, livestock and settlements across large swathes of the delta. In the province of Hung Yen, for instance, there were at least twenty-six dike ruptures between 1806 and 1900 that were severe enough to destroy the entire seasonal rice crop.[61]

French administrators were convinced that they could improve the flooding situation with modern know-how. French engineers were already well versed in the art of flood control along metropolitan rivers, especially in the Alpine and southern parts of France. As we saw in chapter 3, they also commenced large-scale land reclamation and canal-building operations in

61. Gourou, *Les paysans*, 83–87.

the Mekong delta following the conquest of southern Vietnam in the 1860s.[62] After a series of military campaigns against Vietnamese and Chinese forces in 1883–86, motivated largely by a desire to open a Red River trade route into China (see chapter 1), French forces formally established a protectorate over Tonkin, though it would take another decade before the region was fully 'pacified'.[63] Like their imperial counterparts in India and elsewhere, the newly established French authorities in Tonkin regarded hydraulic control as a means of both developing the colonial economy and displaying the benefits of their rule. From 1893 onwards, the problem of flooding – especially around Hanoi and the lower parts of the delta – was examined by a series of dike commissions whose task was to propose remedies for the various 'defects' of the existing system. Engineers noted that although Vietnamese rulers, especially the Nguyen, had already built a system of dikes reaching some 1,200 kilometres in length (up from merely 124 kilometres in 1803), its overall layout was uncoordinated and many of the embankments were acutely prone to scouring.[64]

But revamping the entire network was a daunting task. Just as we have seen in the case of north-eastern India, the sheer scale of the challenge gave rise to serious suggestions that it might be better to remove the dikes altogether. This unorthodox idea, shared by numerous district officials in Tonkin as early as the 1890s, assumed that the suppression of embankments would allow the floodwaters to dissipate their energies across a larger surface of low-lying land rather than channelling them towards particular points where breaches caused catastrophic flooding. An additional benefit of allowing the floodwaters to flow unhindered would be the delivery of fertile silt to bottomland fields. Engineers studied the proposal for several years and noted some of the benefits that it could offer. Yet in the end, they concluded that such a measure, however sound from a strictly hydraulic perspective, could not be carried out owing to the enormous disruption it would cause for agriculture and settlement in the region. As the eminent geographer Paul Vidal de la Blache remarked in his *Principles of Human Geography*, Tonkinese settlements were fundamentally

> circumscribed by the natural *casiers* formed by the banks of the rivers. Between the dikes raised against the floods, small compartments are inscribed where the water accumulates with the summer rains in arroyos, pools, partly artificial ponds. This is where the Annamese of the delta have set up their village; with its adobe houses, its ponds, its vegetable gardens and bamboo enclosure interrupted by doors, which serves as its shelter or defense, it forms a whole.[65]

62. Biggs, *Quagmire*, 23–90; Brocheux, *Mekong Delta*, 1–50.
63. For an overview: Brocheux and Hémery, *Indochina*, 28–64.
64. Gunn, *Rice Wars*, 37–38; Li, 'Sea Becomes Mulberry Fields', 55.
65. De la Blache, *Principes de géographie humaine*, 192–93.

In this sense, French authorities in Tonkin – like British administrators in India – tended to approach pre-colonial infrastructures as quasi-'natural' parts of the landscape, ones whose shortcomings could be overcome only by the modernizing impulse of the colonial state.[66]

Simply put, it was impossible to execute such a fundamental recasting of the region's hydrography, given that the entire way of life in the delta – the layout of fields, the location of villages and the calendar of agricultural work – had for generations been predicated on the protection afforded by dikes. Just as the Red River dikes confined the seasonal floods, they also restricted the options available to French hydraulic engineers.[67]

Over the following decades, officials in the public works department instead focused on reinforcing and raising the dikes where it was deemed most necessary, much as their Vietnamese predecessors had done. According to contemporary estimates, the overall volume of earth and other material contained in Tonkin's dikes was around 20 million cubic metres when the French first arrived. By 1915, the public works department had added another 12 million cubic metres of earth to the structures, an additional 13.5 million between 1917 and 1926, and a further 26 million by 1931, by which time the main dikes reached fifty metres in width. Much of the added volume reflected the attempt to reinforce existing embankments, but French engineers had also supervised the construction of around 840 kilometres of new dikes by the end of the 1920s.[68]

As in centuries past, the bulk of the actual work was carried out by Tonkinese villagers of their own accord as a customary communal duty. In this sense, dikes were both 'big technologies' and 'everyday technologies'; at once sponsored and supervised by the state and rooted in the patterns and practices of everyday life.[69] Each year thousands of local farmers gathered to dig out millions of clay blocks from nearby land, carry them in shoulder baskets or (for larger blocks) directly on their shoulders to the site, and tamp them in place – though as French officials were quick to point out, at least they paid labourers a few cents a day for their efforts. It was not uncommon for five or six thousand people to work on a single project for a week or more each year. For the eminent geographer Pierre Gourou, the 'evocative spectacle' of the dike-building sites was like a 'human anthill' of activity, one that recalled 'those immense collective works that one could only undertake thanks to abundant and cheap (if not free) labour: the pyramids of Egypt, the temples of Angkor'.[70]

66. See Ahuja, *Pathways of Empire*, 119–53.

67. Pierron, *Suggestion d'une solution*, 9; Robequain, *Economic Development*, 223; Gunn, *Rice Wars*, 37–38.

68. Gauthier, *Hydraulique agricole*, 97.

69. On 'everyday technologies' in colonial contexts: Arnold, *Everyday Technology*.

70. Gourou, *Les paysans*, 88–89.

FIGURE 4.3. Tonkinese farmers reinforcing and elevating dikes, Gia Lam district, undated.
Cliché École française d'Extrême-Orient, Fonds Vietnam réf. EFEO_VIE06801.

Expanding and maintaining the dike network was not, however, merely a long-term project; it had seasonal and more sporadic temporal dimensions as well. For much of the year dike improvement and construction were a habitual routine, one of the many chores that filled the regular work schedule of delta cultivators. Nevertheless, during the summer flood season thousands of villagers occasionally mobilized themselves, or were mobilized by the state, to raise dikes that were under imminent threat of submersion, often working day and night in a frantic effort to shore up or divert waters from failing sections. André Touzet, a French official who witnessed such a scene while on a study tour of Indochina in 1934, heaped praise on the 'genius' and determination of Tonkinese peasants in standing up to 'these instances of great danger that leave one speechless at the sudden buildup of the flood . . . it is necessary to witness the defense against this invading water, to have participated with these armies of courageous peasants who fight from *casier* to *casier*, desperately, to save life and possessions'.[71] The sheer unpredictability of the Red River required constant vigilance from public works officers and farmers alike. Earthen embankments, however large, are inherently fragile structures at high water. During the peak flood season, surveillance was the 'primordial'

71. André Touzet, *L'économie indochinoise et la grand crise universelle* (Paris: Marcel Giard, 1934), 239–41, quoted in Biggs, *Quagmire*, 106.

concern, as one official put it. It took little more than 'a rat hole, a hollow from a rotten root, a small infiltration in the sub-soil' to compromise the structure and cause an unstoppable rupture.[72]

Despite all the effort that went into improving the embankment system, floods continued to plague the Red River delta on a regular basis. After the turn of the century, there were major ruptures every other year on average: in 1902, 1903, 1904, 1905, 1909, 1911, 1913, 1915, 1917, 1918, 1923, 1924 and 1926. The worst flooding occurred in 1915, when exceptionally high river levels caused forty-eight breaches in total. Together, these 1915 ruptures inundated a quarter of the entire delta, threatened crops and villages across some 3,650 square kilometres, and left the worst affected districts around Hanoi (where many rice paddies lay seven to eight metres below the flood level) under as much as six metres of water. At Hanoi itself, whose surrounding dikes were designed to withstand a flood of 11.2 metres, water levels reached an unprecedented 12.92 metres. The only thing that saved the city from severe inundation was the mobilization of huge work crews to build emergency flood defences. But while Hanoi was successfully rescued, elsewhere in the delta life was disrupted for several months by disease outbreaks, labour requisitioning and relief works. Although official statistics registered only two hundred deaths from the floodwaters themselves, the ensuing cholera epidemic claimed around four thousand lives. Even after the disease surge subsided, some of the after-effects of the flooding lasted for years. Whenever dikes broke, the rushing current tended to gouge out deep channels, sometimes reaching twenty metres deep. The escaping torrent often carried enormous amounts of sterile sand onto nearby fields, depressing their fertility and reducing their agricultural value. In the worst cases, the effects of such ruptures could be so severe as to force some villages to be abandoned. Such was the fate of the highly flood-prone Ha Dong province near Hanoi, where it was estimated that the 1915 flood dumped around sixty-nine million tons of alluvium, the equivalent of a one-metre layer covering an area of sixty-six square kilometres.[73]

As the scale of the 1915 disaster became clear, it reportedly 'made a powerful impact on public opinion, both European and indigenous'. Many of those who lost their crops and homes blamed the authorities for failing to prevent it, though the official enquiry that followed a year later insisted that it was beyond human control, the 'inevitable consequence of an irresistible cataclysm against which all human efforts were powerless'.[74] But even within French officialdom not everyone accepted that such catastrophic inundations were

72. Normandin, *La question des inondations*, 10.

73. Peytavin, *Rapport sur la crue*, 18–20, 29, 35–36; Gauthier, *Digues du Tonkin*; R. Dumont, *La culture du riz*, 21–22; Gourou, *L'utilisation du sol*, 217–21; *Les paysans*, 87.

74. Peytavin, *Rapport sur la crue*, 18.

a mere 'act of God'. Although early dike commissions rejected the notion of suppressing embankments to allow the floodwaters to spread, the idea never entirely disappeared. Doubts about the wisdom of expanding the dike system were based on the so-called 'siltation hypothesis', which held that the construction of earthen embankments caused silt to accumulate in the riverbed and thereby raise the level of floodwaters above their crest. It was similar to various criticisms that were circulating in India at the time (and which informed river management in Europe since the early nineteenth century), though in Tonkin the main cause of silt accumulation was thought to be the gradual erosion of the dikes themselves rather than the disruption of natural flooding patterns through the initial construction of embankments, which was by then a centuries-old memory in many parts of the delta.[75] The idea was partly rooted in local wisdom, which held that flood levels had gradually risen over the long term, and it was regularly echoed in French reports ever since the 1880s. For those who subscribed to the theory, the elevation of dikes was a Sisyphean task. The bigger and more extensive the embankments became, the more they raised the floodwaters; and the more the floodwaters rose, the higher the dikes had to become. The result, as in India, would be a never-ending contest with the river that would ultimately make the surrounding countryside more rather than less prone to cataclysmic flooding.[76]

To avoid this scenario, sceptics put forward a variety of alternative solutions, yet none of them withstood sustained scrutiny. One suggestion was to reforest the upland sections of the river's watershed in order to reduce run-off in the rainy season and increase flows during the rest of the year (a common practice in Europe). Although it was generally acknowledged that woodland was more absorbent than cleared land, and that highland forest loss therefore exacerbated the flooding problem, studies suggested that reforestation in the upper Red River's watershed would have only a marginal effect on extreme flood levels, since the excessive rainfall that caused them would quickly saturate the ground and rapidly run off regardless of whether the surface was wooded. Another suggestion was to create reservoirs far above the delta to regulate the river flow at source. The problem was that such a move would be prohibitively expensive and would only make matters worse unless the water releases were timed perfectly. Moreover, previous experiments with using parts of the upriver Vinh-Yen province as an emergency flood reservoir met with fierce opposition from locals, which prompted the administration to abandon the practice after 1918. A third proposal, and the one deemed most sound from a technical point of view, was to create reservoirs or collection basins within the delta itself. But the social and political barriers to doing so were deemed completely insurmountable, mainly because, as one report

75. Li, ' Sea Becomes Mulberry Fields', 61–65.
76. Gunn, *Rice Wars*, 36–37.

succinctly put it, 'one will never manage to convince the populations of the provinces in question that their well-being would be served by intentionally inundating them'.[77]

A final suggestion was to build new canals and/or augment the capacity of existing rivers, especially the Day River and the Canal des Rapides, two of the main defluent waterways besides the Red River itself. But such a measure, which was seriously considered in the 1910s, entailed too many negative side-effects. The Day was too slow and winding to allow a significant increase in flow. And although the Canal des Rapides was capable of substantial enlargement, it would seriously threaten the already-shallow port of Haiphong with the huge silt load it would carry there. As ever, the fundamental interconnectedness of the hydrosphere ensured that tampering in one area would have serious consequences in others. Moreover, enlarging the Canal des Rapides posed the additional risk that the Red River might 'choose' this shorter and more direct path to the sea as its main channel, thus depriving other areas of water 'with consequences that are difficult to imagine but that . . . would probably be disastrous'.[78] Humans were by no means the only actors in the equation. Engineers were well aware that the river could have a mind of its own.

This left colonial authorities with little alternative other than the improvement and expansion of existing dikes. All in all, it was yet another textbook example of path dependence. Superior technologies were not readily available, and the heavy reliance of delta residents on the existing flood defences meant that it was extremely difficult to escape the dynamics of lock-in. The range of available choices for how to control flooding was firmly limited by the decisions and developments of the past. 'The dikes are a necessary evil', remarked the official report on the 1915 inundations. 'It is too late today to find another remedy'.[79]

Flood control measures in colonial Tonkin were shaped not only by such long-term hydrological and political considerations but also by more immediate pressures. In many respects, it was the trauma of extreme flood events such as 1915 that spurred the state into action. It was no coincidence that the public works department launched an unprecedented programme of dike construction in 1916–17. In 1926 – in the wake of another series of unusually bad flood seasons – it embarked on an even bigger series of projects, which received generous government funding well into the 1930s.[80]

Yet the decision to double-down on the existing system of defences was more than just a knee-jerk response to recent crises. Another important factor

77. Normandin, *La question des inondations*, 3–6, quote at 6; Peytavin, *Rapport sur la crue*, 42–43; Pouyanne, *L'hydraulique agricole*, 22.

78. Normandin, *La question des inondations*, 7–8.

79. Peytavin, *Rapport sur la crue*, 70.

80. Pouyanne, *L'hydraulique agricole*, 28–30.

was the gradual rejection of the long-lived 'siltation hypothesis'. Although some farmers and district officials still held the view that diked riverbeds would inevitably rise, by the early 1920s hydrographic studies had accumulated a sufficient amount of data to conclude that it was not a major problem for the Red River. While the studies confirmed the long-surmised correlation between dike expansion and higher flood levels, measurements showed that the riverbed itself was not rising. Instead, the higher floodwaters were due to the lack of flooding elsewhere as dikes were improved and ruptures were reduced, thus forcing all the water down the main river channel. This finding led engineers to conclude that the most practical way to control high water levels was not to get rid of embankments or to convert large areas into emergency reservoirs, but rather to ensure that the dikes themselves were sufficiently high and sturdy to withstand all but the most exceptional flood events.[81]

In this sense, the French-built flood-works in the Tonkin delta, like many of their counterparts in India, were a far cry from the 'high modernist' infrastructure schemes that engineers elsewhere in the colonial world (and beyond) were so fond of pursuing in the twentieth century.[82] To be sure, they shared many characteristics with such grandiose projects. They offered a technological solution to what was in reality a complex social and environmental problem, and they were designed and directed by a trained cadre of professional experts whose authority was based on their scientific credentials. To a significant extent, however, the French dike-building programme drew on local precedent and indigenous knowledge rather than overriding it entirely. Instead of a story of imposition and local appropriation of Western technology, in many respects it was a hybrid solution, an attempt to improve what was already in place.[83]

Moreover, unlike some of the more grandiose water projects of the era, it never promised to deliver a 'total fix' to the volatility of the Red River. On the contrary, officials openly acknowledged that the problem of flooding in the Tonkin delta was 'not very easy to resolve in an absolute fashion'.[84] By the early 1920s, French hydraulic engineers were under no illusions that their flood-works could entirely tame the river or make the delta completely safe. Although many voices understandably called for a definitive form of protection, the more realistic aim, in their view, was not to vanquish flooding altogether but to manage it in such a way as to minimize the risks of serious damage. Reducing the frequency of major flood events to every ten or twelve years rather than every two or three (as was previously the case) was hardly a utopian aim, but it nonetheless represented significant progress. For officials who were forced

81. Normandin, *La question des inondations*, 12; Gunn, *Rice Wars*, 36.
82. Scott, *Seeing like a State*.
83. On the complexities of technology appropriation, see Gelvin and Green's *Global Muslims*.
84. Peytavin, *Rapport sur la crue*, 70.

FIGURE 4.4. Hybrid dike-building technology: bamboo-framed dike on the Île de la Douane, designed to protect Hanoi from flooding, undated.
Cliché École française d'Extrême-Orient, Fonds Vietnam réf. EFEO_VIE08671.

to make tricky cost–benefit analyses and juggle competing sets of interests between farmers in different districts who would be variably affected by new hydraulic works, progress seemed a more realizable goal than perfection. As the director of public works himself put it in 1923, the dike improvement programme was 'not a very original' solution and 'possesses no miraculous character'. What it did have, however, was 'the merit of being effective', which in the circumstances seemed as much as one could hope for.[85]

And effective it was, at least up to a point. After the acceleration of the dike improvement programme in 1926, the frequency of severe inundations declined markedly. Although heavy summer rains continued to pose risks, from 1927 to 1935 the levees along the Red River managed to retain its floodwaters without a single rupture.[86] Even if definitive protection remained out of reach, officials became increasingly confident that cataclysmic flood incidents were a thing of the past. For the time being, at least, the vulnerability of both farmers and state revenues to environmental shocks appeared to be decreasing, even if it was not eradicated altogether. Yet the social vulnerability of millions of delta residents to acute hardship remained as severe as ever, and if anything was on the rise in the 1930s as the effects of the global economic downturn on incomes and prices intersected with steadily rising population pressures.

85. Normandin, *La question des inondations*, 3, 10–13.
86. Gourou, *Les paysans*, 92.

By the early 1930s, this newfound sense of flood security – along with a spate of violent 'rice rebellions' in northern Annam in 1930–31 – prompted the colonial government to direct its attention towards harnessing the river's waters for irrigation in order to boost food production, mitigate the risks of drought and thereby reduce the scope for widespread social discontent in the delta as economic conditions deteriorated. Although this was not the first time that Tonkin's rulers had sought to combine 'protective' flood-works and 'productive' irrigation works (the Nguyen court made limited efforts to do so in the 1820s and 1830s, and the French had carried out small-scale projects mainly in the upper part of the delta since the 1900s), the scope of the French 'agricultural modernization' programme of the 1930s nonetheless marked a new departure in the involvement of central state authorities (which had hitherto focused their attention overwhelmingly on flood protection) in the realm of irrigation, a kind of colonial-era upgrading of the hydraulic bargain between rulers and ruled that consciously built on and further cemented the existing flood defence system.[87]

As the menace of floods appeared to recede, the stated aim was nothing less than 'the complete hydraulic management' of the deltaic plain, where erratic river levels and typhoon-induced storm surges 'often render the cultivation of rice too precarious'.[88] From 1931 onwards – and especially under the left-wing Popular Front government in Paris from 1936 to 1938 – French authorities embarked on a programme to improve the chequerboard of dike-bordered partitions (which the French called *cloisonné*) that covered the delta. The immediate goal was to integrate the water flows of these hitherto isolated pieces of jigsaw to improve irrigation without raising the risk of flooding. The means to achieve it was a series of canals and dams designed to carry irrigation water from openings in the secondary dikes, to facilitate drainage from low-lying fields and to prevent seawater from moving upstream with the tides. Few of these hydraulic works were designed for the purpose of extending the cultivated surface, since nearly all of the delta was already covered in paddy. The principal object, as in other densely settled parts of colonial Asia (notably Java and much of the Gangetic plain, which French engineers had long studied when devising their own hydraulic plans), was rather to control water levels throughout the year and thereby enable farmers to harvest two rice crops annually rather than a single crop.[89] By the early 1940s, such irrigation systems covered around 250,000 hectares of the delta, roughly one-third of its overall surface area.[90]

87. Brocheux and Hémery, *Indochina*, 316–20; Gunn, *Rice Wars*, 26, 35–37.

88. Pouyanne, *L'hydraulique agricole*, 93.

89. For a contemporary example of this trans-imperial learning process, see Normandin's *Étude comparative*.

90. Robequain, *Economic Development*, 222–27. On the Popular Front era in Indochina: Brocheux and Hémery, *Indochina*, 328–35; Gunn, *Rice Wars*, 38–40.

Moreover, as the irrigation network expanded under the protection of the dike system, agronomists also experimented with different water levels on fields, the timing of water releases and drainage, and the interaction of various irrigation techniques with local cultivation practices.[91] To make the most of these improvements, the Office indochinois du riz was established in 1930 to develop higher-yield rice strains and distribute seed to farmers. Although the uptake of the new rice varieties among farmers was low, by the 1940s it was estimated that yields had increased by around five to six hundred kilograms per hectare for a single crop, and by as much as two thousand kilograms per hectare where the irrigation system allowed for two annual crops instead of one.[92]

But if better flood control, water management and crop breeding made rice cultivation in the delta more productive, it did not directly translate into better living standards or greater food security for the bulk of its residents. The incremental gains that these measures achieved were ultimately of little consequence in relation to the large, densely packed, and swiftly growing population. The problem of 'overpopulation' (*surpeuplement*) had long been a matter of concern among French officials in Tonkin, but by the interwar years it was widely regarded as 'one of the most serious problems that has ever confronted France in the course of its colonial project'.[93] In the mid-1930s, the delta was home to over 6.5 million people, with an average population density of around 430 per square kilometre (among the highest in the world). Land was extremely scarce, especially in the most tightly inhabited districts along the lower Red River. In 1937, there were between 2 and 3 million day labourers and over a million unemployed, which meant that half or more of the delta's population was virtually landless.[94] Even for those who possessed land, much of the paddy acreage was divided into tiny micro-holdings – in some areas as many as thirty-two per hectare – that were far too small to support a household. Labour was correspondingly abundant, and gave rise to an exceptionally intensive form of cultivation that French observers likened to horticulture rather than agriculture.[95]

In many ways, the dynamics in the Red River delta were not unlike those of densely populated Java, where, as Clifford Geertz famously showed, the attempt to intensify agriculture through irrigated double- or triple-cropping led to an increase in land productivity (more output per hectare) but not labour productivity (more output per capita), which meant that it did little to

91. R. Dumont, *La culture du riz*, 110–12, 298–332; Robequain, *Economic Development*, 222–25.

92. Carle, *Le riz en Cochinchine*; Caty, 'L'amélioration des plantes'; Robequain, *Economic Development*, 227; more generally, Brocheux and Hémery, *Indochina*, 266–80.

93. Bouvier, *Richesse et misère*, 65; see also Bernard, *Le problème économique indochinois*.

94. Gourou, *Les paysans*, 571–74; Brocheux and Hémery, *Indochina*, 262–66.

95. Bouvier, *Richesse et misère*, 24; Gourou, *Les paysans*, 381–94.

raise living standards. The overall result was 'agricultural involution', or the intensification of existing cultivation techniques.[96]

In stark contrast to the Mekong delta in southern Indochina, which became one of the world's great rice-exporting regions (see chapter 3), in Tonkin the rural population consumed nearly all of the food they produced. The anthropologist Nguyen Van Huyen, who carried out extensive studies of rural conditions at the time, noted in 1939 that rice production in the delta oscillated between 18 and 22 million quintals (1.8 to 2.2 billion kilograms), but that the minimum consumption level was 18.5 million quintals. These figures alone illustrate the precarity of the food supply, but what exacerbated the situation was the fact that 4 million quintals were either exported, used for distilling and seeds, or went into domestic trade. In short, without rice trans-shipments from Cochin China, there simply was not enough food to go around. Nguyen Van Huyen estimated that around 80 per cent of the population in poor villages had only one meal per day, and that it was only 'during a third of the year, in particular during the harvest, that they have enough to eat'.[97]

French efforts to encourage an efflux of emigrants from Tonkin to the south of the colony through a mixture of low taxes and promises of land certainly helped to extend the frontier of rice cultivation in the more sparsely populated Mekong delta, but in the event it did little if anything to alleviate the pressures of population growth and food availability in the north. The organized recruitment of Tonkinese villagers for the coal mines of the region or for European rubber plantations in the centre and south of Indochina had even less effect, especially once returnees were factored in.[98] Meanwhile, French efforts at social reform in the delta were even less effective. Although officials recognized that the 'rice rebellions' of 1930–31 were driven at least as much by sheer poverty as by revolutionary ideas, they dared not risk the ire of rural elites whose interests were served by the status quo and on whose tacit cooperation the colonial government heavily depended. The powerful landowners and families who dominated the countryside not only blocked poor farmers' access to communal land they sorely needed; they also engaged in ruinous lending practices (with rates sometimes as high as 400 per cent) that ensnared indebted peasants in a state of peonage. As Nguyen Van Huyen remarked:

> The peasant elite, the village notables, are opposed to all true and deep reform. . . . If anyone tries to push through any kind of reform whatsoever, he inevitably attracts merciless spite. Someone puts opium under

96. Geertz, *Agricultural Involution*.

97. Nguyen Van Huyen, 'Le problème de la paysannerie annamite au Tonkin', *Est* (Hanoi), February 1939, quoted in Brocheux and Hémery, *Indochina*, 274.

98. On emigration from the delta: Gourou, *Les paysans*, 213–20; Gourou, *Le Tonkin*, 91–98.

his roof, or some contraband alcohol in his pigsty or his stable. And nine times out of ten, the framed man is condemned.[99]

In effect, this social inertia served to reinforce yet further the dynamics of hydro-technical 'lock in'. At base, the colonial government was confronted with a difficult dilemma that presented no easy choices: on the one hand, the need to 'modernize' the colonial economy in order to break the cycle of poverty and ensure political stability; and on the other, the imperative of upholding the structures and institutions that enabled it to extract profit. Avoiding this dilemma was precisely what the government's 'complete hydraulic management' strategy was designed to do – namely, by offering a technological solution to the problem of poverty that did not upset existing hierarchies and agrarian structures in the delta countryside. By investing in new hydraulic infrastructure, the colonial administration aimed to 'improve' peasant agriculture – that is, achieve more food output per capita – without altering the social foundations on which it rested.[100] Reliable flood defences constituted the cornerstone of this entire endeavour, for without them it would be impossible to reap the full benefits of new irrigation works.

Yet despite all the effort and investment that went into this hydraulic program, and despite the great skill of Tonkinese farmers – which was clearly recognized by French agronomists – living standards were low at the best of times, and famine was always a threat. Among the poorest half of the population a combination of poverty and volatile weather left them highly vulnerable to social and biophysical shocks alike. Even in normal years the peasant population 'lives on the edge of scarcity and misery', noted Pierre Gourou. It took only 'slightly unfavourable circumstances' to cause widespread privation.[101]

It was only a matter of time before the floodwaters of the Red River once again generated such 'unfavourable circumstances'. In early August 1937, the delta was struck by a series of typhoons that lashed the Indochinese coast and dumped huge amounts of rainfall across the entire region. As tidal surges pushed up the rivers, torrential rains inundated nearly all of the low-lying paddy land. When the run-off from the highlands arrived over the following days, the floodwaters proved too much even for the improved dike network. Major ruptures occurred along the Canal des Rapides, the Canal du Song Cai and the Thong Ba Canal. Flooding caused major damage in several provinces, covering as much as three-quarters of the entire surface in the badly

99. Nguyen Van Huyen, *Recherches sur la commune annamite* (Hanoi, 1939), quoted in Brocheux and Hémery, *Indochina*, 274–75.

100. This broadly echoes the interpretation of Brocheux and Hémery in *Indochina* (276–80).

101. Pierre Gourou, *The Standard of Living in the Delta of the Tonkin (French Indo-China)* (New York, 1945), 14, quoted in Huff, 'Causes and Consequences', 290.

hit Bac Ninh and Bac Giang provinces. The losses affected nearly 750,000 people, many of whom had already been suffering from a poor spring harvest due to the unusually dry winter and spring of 1936–37. Mindful of the 'rice rebellions' of the early 1930s, colonial authorities rushed to procure food supplies for the afflicted areas and introduced a range of public works projects to absorb labour and thereby cushion the looming income crisis. In the end, the relief efforts narrowly managed to avert a major famine, but the events of 1937 nonetheless dented confidence in the state's ability to control the river's floodwaters. It was by far the worst flood disaster since the inundations of 1915 and 1926, and it sorely tested the tacit agrarian hydraulic pact that underpinned relations among the colonial state, local elites and the Tonkinese peasantry.[102]

Eventually, these precarious hydro-political arrangements proved incapable of withstanding the pressures of the Second World War. When the French Third Republic was defeated by Nazi Germany in the summer of 1940, the administration of Indochina was handed to the new Vichy regime in France. Soon thereafter, the Vichy state allowed Japan to use a selection of the colony's railways, ports and airfields to support its ongoing military operations against China, and in September 1940 it allowed a limited number of Japanese troops to be stationed there as well. In July 1941, the French colonial administration – which was increasingly concerned about the threat posed by the new Chinese-backed Viet Minh movement – signed a joint defence cooperation protocol with the Japanese government, which enabled Japan to expand its use of Indochina's transport infrastructure and increase the number of its troops stationed there. Through this accord, the Vichy regime effectively gave Japan control of French Indochina (which it used as a base for military operations elsewhere in Southeast Asia after the attack on Pearl Harbor in December 1941) in exchange for a modicum of administrative autonomy.[103]

All of these changes meant that investment in dike maintenance and upgrades plummeted. The Vichy-backed administration had little financial or political leeway to continue the hydraulic or agricultural improvement efforts of the 1930s. Quite the opposite: it essentially transformed Indochina into a supplier of food and raw materials for Japan. From 1942, a requisitioning system forced farmers to deliver a fixed proportion of the rice harvest according to the amount of land they cultivated. The new levies took little notice of rising production costs or the sharp increase in the cost of living, which trebled between 1940 and 1943 as more and more farmers were forced to buy food on the open market. The overall effect of these additional burdens was a fall in rice production and the further immiseration of a population that already lived on the margins of subsistence. The strict prioritization of Japanese

102. Gunn, *Rice Wars*, 117–21.
103. The most thorough account is Verney's *L'Indochine sous Vichy*; see also E. Jennings's *Vichy in the Tropics*.

exports and local military needs thus rendered the bulk of the populace even more socially and physically vulnerable than they already were.[104]

The stage was set for disaster, and it eventually came in autumn 1944. After a poor spring harvest across much of northern Vietnam, three successive typhoons dumped water over the delta. From August to October, rainfall at Hanoi was around 50 per cent higher than normal, exceeding even the deluges of 1937. Although the master dikes were by now capable of withstanding floods of up to thirteen metres, the combination of exceptionally high river levels and bombing damage caused by US airstrikes led to several major ruptures, which together devastated around 230,000 hectares of paddy in the coastal provinces of the delta. Local eyewitnesses recounted how the flooding had literally 'wiped out' the all-important November rice crop, which was even more crucial than usual since rice reserves were already exhausted following the spring harvest failures. Food shortages quickly became severe; in the worst affected provinces it was reported that people had 'absolutely nothing to eat'.[105] Tens of thousands of rural refugees streamed into the cities, where many of them died from hunger, disease or exhaustion soon after arrival. To make matters worse, the flood disaster of autumn 1944 was followed by an unusually cold winter that killed rice seedlings and ruined a large portion of the annual non-rice crop (maize, potatoes, taro). During the winter and spring of 1944–45, over one million people – more than 8 per cent of the entire population of Tonkin and North Annam – perished as a result of starvation and disease, most of them landless or land-poor cultivators with little to fall back on apart from their labour.[106]

Like the other wartime famines in Asia – in Bengal, Java and Henan province, all of which were triggered by flooding or drought – the Great Vietnam Famine was not an entirely 'natural' disaster.[107] Although the direct and immediate cause was the severe flooding of 1944, it was also the result of a succession of human actions – above all, decades of extractive colonial policies, followed by an even more extractive Japanese military regime – that rendered millions of people highly susceptible to the effects of extreme weather events. Over the longer term, the dynamics of 'lock-in' had made the delta more dependent than ever on dikes for flood protection – dikes that everyone knew were not foolproof. During the crisis itself, the French administration tried to provide emergency relief, but its efforts were ultimately dwarfed by the scale of the calamity. Indeed, its attempt to manage the rice market to prevent spiking prices probably made the situation worse in some localities by hindering the

104. Huff, 'Causes and Consequences', 291–95; Gunn, *Rice Wars*, 140–42; Brocheux and Hémery, *Indochina*, 346–48.

105. Huff, 'Causes and Consequences', 291.

106. See generally Huff.

107. Huff, 'Great Second World War'; Bose, 'Starvation amidst Plenty'; Muscolino, *Ecology of War*; J. Mukherjee, *Hungry Bengal*; Greenough, *Prosperity and Misery*.

movement of rice to stricken areas. The Japanese insistence on continued rice requisitioning likewise amplified the effects of the food shortages. After the Japanese military took what amounted to full political control over the colony in March 1945 (via a transparent puppet regime under Vietnamese emperor Bao Dai), they proved no better at responding to the disaster than their French predecessors. The determination of US military planners to disrupt supply lines for the Japanese army also exacerbated the situation. One of the chief reasons why both French and Japanese authorities were unable to alleviate acute local food shortages was the Allied interdiction on rail and sea traffic and the infrastructural damage caused by US bombing.[108]

The Great Vietnam Famine of 1944–45 was a profoundly convulsive event. It was the biggest humanitarian disaster in the history of modern Vietnam, and memories of it are still very much alive to this day. Like the devastating famine in Bengal in 1943 – which similarly resulted from a combination of catastrophic flooding and administrative failure – it played an important role in fatally undermining colonial authority in the region.[109] Here too, the experience of mass starvation generated a widespread sense of the need for change. It was a current of thought that the Indochinese communist movement was determined to augment and turn to its advantage.

As the war drew to a close, the Viet Minh wasted little time filling the power vacuum left by the retreating Japanese occupiers. After seizing power in August 1945, it faced a range of threats from rival domestic political movements (especially the Nationalist Party of Vietnam, or Viet Nam Quoc dan Dang, along with other militia-organizing nationalist movements and religious sects in the south), from Chinese designs, and from exceedingly violent French efforts to reassert control throughout late 1945 and much of 1946 (first in the south of the colony, and later in Tonkin). The complex political fault lines and brutal civil-war-like conditions that engulfed much of Indochina during this period are the stock-in-trade of most accounts of the gradual decolonization of the peninsula and the role of the Viet Minh as a key player in the process.[110] Yet one of the biggest immediate challenges that Ho Chi Minh and his followers faced was the erratic nature of the Red River.

In August 1945, the same month in which the Viet Minh declared Vietnamese independence, torrential rains and severe flooding once again raised the prospect of a major famine. During the latter half of August, the river rose to over fourteen metres in Hanoi, the highest level ever recorded.

108. Long, *Before the Revolution*, 122–33; Anh, 'Japanese Food Policies'; Huff, 'Causes and Consequences', 303–8.

109. A. Sen, *Poverty and Famines*; J. Mukherjee, *Hungry Bengal*; Greenough, *Prosperity and Misery*.

110. Marr, *State, War, and Revolution* and *Vietnam 1945*; Tønnesson, *Vietnamese Revolution of 1945*; Brocheux and Hémery, *Indochina*, 348–65; Bayly and Harper, *Forgotten Wars*, 140–57; Thévenet, *La guerre d'Indochine*.

Multiple dike failures inundated some 330,000 hectares of newly planted rice fields across the middle and lower delta, once again destroying much of the November harvest and forcing peasants to eat what little seed rice they had left. As Ho Chi Minh and his deputies were well aware, the key to legitimizing their movement as a governing power was to avoid another famine. Given that the last such calamity had occurred less than a year earlier, preventing a sequel was a matter of the utmost priority, both morally and politically. Viet Minh forces promptly began to seize grain stores and organized a remarkably effective relief operation. They urged farmers to plant yams, corn and beans to carry them through the following spring. They also enjoyed an element of luck as far as the weather and the river were concerned. In 1946 and 1947, a combination of favourable rains, good harvests, dike repairs and ceaseless Viet Minh propaganda convinced millions that the agro-hydraulic pact with France was at an end.[111] It was, of course, only in 1954, after the victory of Viet Minh forces at Dien Bien Phu, that the French government finally reached the same conclusion. Yet despite the continued presence of French troops in Tonkin (following a 1946 Chinese-brokered agreement between the French and Viet Minh), colonial authority never recovered from the ordeals of war and famine.[112]

It would, of course, be an exaggeration to claim that the floods and ensuing food crises of 1943–45 led directly to the fall of British power in the subcontinent or French colonialism in Indochina. Yet, for all the well-documented political ferment in colonial Asia, and despite the many administrative failures of colonial governments during the war, it is no overstatement to say that they helped channel the course of history in a new direction. The colonial officials who took charge of these territories insisted that they could deploy superior knowledge and technologies for controlling the errant waters that sporadically surged across them. But their degree of control was far from complete, and was recognized as such throughout the colonial period. As we have seen, the technological limitations of colonial hydraulic management in India and Indochina were powerfully moulded by social, political and environmental circumstances, which tightly constrained the parameters within which water engineers could work, and which effectively forced them to double-down on existing methods of flood prevention. In this sense, who or what exercised 'control' remained an open question. Engineers, officials, landlords and farmers were by no means the sole agents in the equation: rivers, seas and the hydraulic decisions of previous generations crucially shaped historical outcomes. Moreover, in their quest to tame the floodwaters of colonial Asia, most officials gave insufficient thought to the ways in which their hydraulic interventions could actually

111. Gunn, *Rice Wars*, 239–46; Huff, 'Causes and Consequences', 310–12.
112. Brocheux and Hémery, *Indochina*, 355–74.

worsen the problem of flooding, and even less thought to how poverty, dislocation and social discrimination amplified the risks that were involved. When things went wrong, the claim to control translated into the burden of responsibility. And when things went catastrophically wrong, as they did in the early 1940s, responsibility inevitably had political implications.

For this reason, the human calamities that were triggered by floodwaters could never be entirely blamed on Mother Nature, however much people tried to do so. Rather, they had a way of highlighting problems that lurked under the surface in less extreme circumstances. In colonial Asia, the flood disasters that periodically ravaged the river valleys and low-lying coasts laid bare the costs of prioritizing economic development over human lives, just as they brutally exposed the gaping inequalities of wealth, status and vulnerability that structured colonial societies. But if the myth of 'natural' disasters diverted attention away from these awkward issues, it could not entirely obscure the fundamental questions that such catastrophes always raised: about risk and resilience, about social marginalization and disenfranchisement, about the trade-offs of building protective works, about the distribution of their costs and benefits, and about who should have the power to decide. In colonial Asia, the answers to these questions were largely claimed as the preserve of European officials, and the decisions they made eventually helped undermine their authority in the crisis conditions of war, flooding and famine. Yet here as elsewhere, the end of colonial rule did not bring an end to the difficult questions posed by such disasters – or, for that matter, to the naturalizing myths that continued to distract people from them.[113]

113. See, e.g., Bankoff, Frerks and Hilhorst, *Mapping Vulnerability*.

CHAPTER FIVE

Under the Surface

FISHERIES AND COLONIAL DEVELOPMENT

IN PREVIOUS CHAPTERS, we have traced the relationship between imperial power and water in a number of different guises: as a means of transport and circulation, as a crucial resource for agriculture, and as a threat to infrastructure, people and property. In each case, the focus of attention was on the water itself – its flows or its interfaces with the land – and on human efforts to make it function in certain ways. This chapter looks instead at what was living within these waters, and how colonial states, scientists and administrators sought to capitalize on it.

This is not a very familiar story. Despite a growing literature on the exploitation of fishery resources in various parts of the world, few historians have taken much notice of what was happening under the surface of the waters of Europe's empire.[1] There are a handful of studies that delve into particular subjects such as the regulation of freshwaters in colonial India, late-colonial marine research in British-ruled Africa or the transfer of exotic fish in white settler colonies.[2] By far the most detailed and extensive work to date has focused on the marine fisheries of Southeast Asia.[3] Yet for most of the colonial world, the interactions between imperial power and aquatic life have scarcely been investigated.

To some extent this lack of historical attention reflects a contemporary neglect of the subject. For much of the nineteenth and twentieth centuries, fisheries were not at the forefront of the colonial mind. All throughout Europe's empire, officials regarded water more as a resource to be harnessed

---

1. For overviews: C. Roberts, *Unnatural History*; Finley, *All the Boats* and *All the Fish*. On the US: McEvoy, *Fisherman's Problem*; Chiang, *Shaping the Shoreline*; J. Taylor, *Making Salmon*; Bolster, *Mortal Sea*. On China: Muscolino, *Fishing Wars*.

2. Reeves, 'Inland Waters'; Reeves, Pokrant and McGuire, 'Auction Lease System'; C. Jennings, 'Unexploited Assets'; Minard, *All Things Harmless*, 72–84, 121–32.

3. Butcher, *Closing of the Frontier*; Medrano, 'Edible Tide'.

for agricultural production than as a realm of production itself. Compared with hunting, wildlife preservation and animal husbandry, managing the aquatic life of the colonial world attracted far less attention. By and large colonial states were slow to establish agencies to supervise the fisheries of subject territories. Investors likewise showed less interest in aquatic resources than in terrestrial assets such as forests, soils and mineral deposits. Although fishing constituted an important part of the food supply (including the bulk of animal protein) in many parts of colonial Asia and Africa, and although it underpinned the livelihoods of millions of people, it represented only a small part of the imperial economy, and indeed one with limited potential for exports – apart, that is, from a few high-value items such as pearls, trepang (sea cucumbers) and sponges.[4]

Yet as colonial administrations increasingly sought to 'develop' local economies, fisheries gradually became part of the wider effort to understand, control and exploit subjugated environments. Over time, the interventions of officials and scientists had a significant impact on aquatic environments and the people who relied on them. In many ways, the story of colonial fisheries was a classic example of developmental imperialism: top-down intrusions into poorly understood biophysical and social environments with little regard for the views or knowledge of colonized peoples who were supposed to benefit from them.[5] As the following pages show, indigenous fisherfolk and their techniques were widely dismissed as backwards and primitive, and attempts to modernize colonial fishing industries were frequently hampered by the tendency to underestimate the complexities of social and ecological systems. Yet not all aspects of the story follow this script. Some colonial officials consciously broke with convention by seeking to incorporate indigenous methods and know-how into their fisheries projects. By the interwar years, the emergence of ecologically oriented field research also led to a more holistic understanding of how aquatic environments worked and how they might be modified.

This chapter explores the chief aims and effects of colonial fisheries development and how they evolved during the late nineteenth and early twentieth centuries. It does so in three parts: first, by investigating how states sought to conserve and regulate the use of fish resources; second, by examining attempts

---

4. Cariño and Monteforte, 'Environmental History'; E. Cresswell, *Sponges*; T. Fernando, 'Seeing like the Sea' and 'Mapping Oysters'; Melillo, 'Making Sea Cucumbers'. For an overview of marine products and trade in Southeast Asia: Tagliacozzo, *In Asian Waters*, 255–81.

5. On development and empire: Hodge, *Triumph of the Expert*; Moon, *Technology and Ethical Idealism*; Bonneuil, 'Development as Experiment'; Havinden and Meredith, *Colonialism and Development*. On science and colonialism, see: Schiebinger, 'Forum Introduction' (part of a special forum in *Isis*); Bennett and Hodge, *Science and Empire*; Tilley, *Africa*; Singaravélou, *Professer l'Empire*; Poncelet, *L'invention des sciences*; Ruppenthal, *Kolonialismus*.

to modernize capture techniques and exploit new resources; and third, by looking at efforts to re-engineer aquatic ecosystems in order to make them more productive. Although no one could know it at the time, many of these initiatives set important scientific, technological and institutional precedents that shaped human interactions with aquatic environments long after the colonial period.

Control and Conservation

In 1906, a major survey of fisheries in the French empire conclusively declared that 'the administration in our various colonies should presently concern itself mainly with developing the fishing industry rather than hindering it'. In the interests of sound management, the report's authors highlighted the need 'to establish from the start a set of regulations as simple and untroublesome as possible' and to ensure that they were 'based on an exact understanding of the biology of useful species and geared towards preventing a reduction of their stocks'. Despite this recognition of the importance of regulation and research, the main recommendation was nonetheless that 'measures are taken to exploit the resources contained in the sea and freshwaters as intensively as possible'.[6]

In many respects, this survey reflected the fundamental aims of fisheries officials the world over: namely, to maximize the exploitation of aquatic resources in a manner that did not undermine their long-term viability. At the same time, it also pointed to some of the challenges this involved – in particular, the need to obtain sufficient data for setting appropriate limits and formulating workable regulations on that basis. As scientists and officials in Europe were already well aware, this was a notoriously difficult thing to do given the complexity of aquatic ecosystems, the challenges of studying underwater environments, and the problems involved in modelling the interactions between population dynamics and human activities such as fishing.[7] As their counterparts in the colonies were only just beginning to realize, the challenges they faced were in some ways even more formidable than those confronted in the metropoles. For one thing, acquiring an 'exact understanding' of useful species was all the more difficult in view of the sheer diversity of aquatic organisms in the tropics. Even in the closing years of empire, biologists were acutely conscious of how much they still had to learn about tropical water ecosystems.[8] As a result, it was impossible to know whether fluctuations in the catch were due to overfishing or to any number of other poorly understood factors. Determining limits on fishing was therefore little more than guesswork, and actually enforcing them was even more uncertain, given the thin presence of the state on the ground. At one level, such problems seemed less pressing for

6. Darboux et al., *L'industrie des pêches*, vol. 1, 24.
7. T. Smith, *Scaling Fisheries*.
8. See generally Hickling, *Production of Fish* (1949 and 1954).

colonial waters than for metropolitan fisheries, untouched as they were by the industrial fishing fleets that prowled the seas of northern Europe. Nonetheless, by the late nineteenth century it was increasingly difficult to ignore the effects of overexploitation, pollution and habitat alteration on certain fish populations.

Inland waters were particularly exposed to such pressures. Rivers and lakes not only served as refuse sinks, storage reservoirs and irrigation channels; they were often heavily fished. Indeed, in many parts of the colonial world the freshwater catch far exceeded the haul from the sea. Before the age of refrigerated transport, lakes, rivers and tanks were the only source of fresh fish for inland regions. Although dried or salted fish was widely traded in Asia and parts of Africa, it accounted for only a portion of overall fish consumption, and much of it originated from freshwaters in any event. What made the inland fisheries of the colonies so important was not only their proximity to internal markets but also their remarkable productivity. As a general rule, tropical freshwater ecosystems are capable of yielding significantly more fish biomass per hectare than tropical marine environments, and far more than temperate freshwater ecosystems (partly owing to high mean temperatures, which accelerate biological growth and nutrient cycling, and partly because of the relative abundance of plant-eating fish, which prop up the food web).[9] Yet despite their remarkable fertility, tropical inland fisheries are nonetheless acutely prone to overharvesting because of the relatively compact size of freshwater bodies and their susceptibility to habitat degradation caused by economic development on surrounding lands. The more severe these degradation effects are, the more urgent is the need to reconcile production and protection. Altogether, this combination of high productivity and ecological fragility meant that inland fisheries were the first to attract the managerial attention of colonial authorities.

As Europeans expanded their authority in Asia and Africa, they encountered a multitude of different types of freshwater fisheries. While most were based on natural rivers or lakes, fishing or fish cultivation was also commonly practised in reservoirs, irrigation canals and village tanks. Whereas some fisheries could be worked year-round, others were only seasonal. In colonial Asia and Africa alike, the most valuable freshwater fisheries were created by seasonal monsoon floods. Each year, annual rains transformed many low-lying river valleys into vast shallow lakes where an abundance of submerged vegetation provided rich feeding and breeding grounds for fish populations. In Africa, such 'flood fisheries' could be found in the Sudanese Nuerland along the Upper Nile, the Kafue Flats in Northern Rhodesia, and the inland delta of the Middle Niger (which yielded up to forty-five thousand tons of fish per year, more than the

9. Kolding and van Zwieten, *Improving Productivity.*

great marine fishery of Senegal). In colonial Asia, the most notable flood fisheries were along the Irrawaddy in Burma and on Cambodia's prolific Tonlé Sap
(or 'Grand Lac'), which formed each year when a combination of snowmelt
and seasonal rains caused the swollen Mekong to reverse the flow up the Tonlé
Sap River (the channel linking the lake with the Mekong Valley), enlarging
the lake's surface from around 2,500 to 10,000 square kilometres and creating a fishery that produced as much as a hundred thousand tons each year.
In essence, these seasonal floodwaters created vast growing ponds in which
natural stocks of fish were allowed to mature before being harvested as the
water subsided.[10]

The social organization of freshwater fisheries in the colonies was similarly
variegated. In Africa, some were open to all users (e.g., parts of the Kafue
Flats), whereas others were carefully regulated by systems of customary fishing rights for established communities (e.g., the Middle Niger). In pre-colonial
India, landowners typically sought to lease out fishing rights over the waters
on their estates to contractors, and in such cases fishing was generally subjected to the so-called *muhtarifa* tax (a levy on non-agricultural trades) that
was payable to landlords. On Java, access to fisheries was controlled by local
rulers who periodically auctioned off rights to users. Burma's fisheries were
divided into state waters, on which fishers paid both rent and tax, and private
heritable fisheries, where owners paid only tax. Fishing on the Tonlé Sap was
for many years unrestricted, though in the late nineteenth century the Cambodian Crown began to auction off fishing rights for sale to bidders. Many
(though not all) of these regulatory mechanisms stipulated which modes of
capture were permitted.[11]

Fisherfolk used a range of techniques and equipment to work these different waters. Fixed and cast nets were the most pervasive, though other common
devices included hooks and lines, spears, and fish traps of various shapes and
sizes. While some methods carefully selected certain species and sizes of fish,
others were entirely indiscriminate: for example, damming a segment of river
and bailing it out to catch its contents, or using poisons fashioned from local
plants to stun fish. In the seasonal flood fisheries the most important devices
were barrages made of bamboo (in Asia) or wattle and grass (in Africa) to prevent fish from returning to the main river as the floodwaters subsided, though
moveable nets were also used in some areas.[12] Such netting operations were
often remarkably sophisticated: on the Tonlé Sap they involved the use of a
special three-part net of varying depths and mesh sizes, which was carefully

10. Hickling, *Tropical Inland Fisheries*, 139, 150.

11. Lévêque, Lazard and Paugy, 'Pêche et pisciculture', 106; Darboux et al., *L'industrie
des pIeches*, vol. 2, 301; Furnivall, *Netherlands India*, 324; Hickling, *Tropical Inland Fisheries*, 146–50; Reeves, 'Inland Waters', 263–67; Reeves, Pokrant and McGuire, 'Auction Lease
System', 251; Cooke, 'Tonle Sap Processed Fish'.

12. Hickling, *Tropical Inland Fisheries*, 139, 152.

FIGURE 5.1. A fish trap situated in the current of the Congo River near Kinshasa, 1929–37.
By permission of the Nationaal Museum van Wereldculturen, coll. no. RV-A162-140.

pulled through the water by large teams of workers to encircle entire schools of fish.[13]

Colonial rule brought significant social and organizational changes to these fisheries. Although the outcomes varied from place to place, the alterations tended to fall into two broad categories. One was to loosen customary fishing restrictions in accordance with the doctrine of free trade. On Java, for instance, the gradual liberalization of economic policies after the mid-nineteenth century led to the abolition of controlled fisheries auctions in 1864. Across much of India, too, older controls were eroded in the name of minimizing governmental interference in economic life. As Devika Shankar has recently shown, however, over the second half of the nineteenth century a series of legal disputes pitting the private ownership of waters against the public right to the fish (as *ferae naturae*) within them gradually restricted public access.[14] The other approach was to adapt rather than replace pre-colonial systems of access and payment. As the British expanded their control over Lower Burma, the administration sought to boost its revenues by appropriating all private fisheries and altering the existing lease system through the

13. For a detailed contemporary description of methods: Gruvel, *L'Indochine*, 210–24; Darboux et al., *L'industrie des pêches*, vol. 2, 323–35.

14. Day, *Report on the Freshwater*, 44–48; Furnivall, *Netherlands India*, 324–25; Shankar, 'Water, Fish and Property'.

creation of larger and more expensive lots. French authorities in Indochina similarly opted to continue the practice of auctioning lots on the Tonlé Sap, most of which were sold to wealthy Chinese entrepreneurs who then sublet sections to local fishers in exchange for a share of the catch. Generally speaking, such leasing systems were much more beneficial for traders, moneylenders and state coffers than for artisanal fishermen.[15]

These organizational changes were substantial, but the ecological impact of imperial expansion was even more consequential, especially in the densely populated heartlands of colonial Asia. By the 1860s, officials in India were increasingly worried about the adverse effects of dams and other hydraulic works on fish stocks, and in particular for anadromous species (fish that spend most of their lives in saltwater but return to their freshwater breeding grounds to spawn), such as the commercially important *hilsa* (Indian shad). In Madras, none other than the legendary dam-builder Sir Arthur Cotton surmised that 'the injury to the coast fisheries must be very great' from the extensive irrigation works that he and his associates had built on seven of the main rivers of the province's eastern coast. Scientists at the Asiatic Society of Bengal voiced similar concerns, arguing that it was 'in the highest degree probable that the effects of anicuts or weirs across large rivers leads to a rapid destruction of many kinds of fish'. Such waterworks were deemed harmful to fish populations in multiple ways, both by 'interfering with their spawning in their accustomed localities' and by concentrating them below the barrages 'where they are not only captured in large quantities by man, but are exposed in an increased degree to the attacks of crocodiles and predaceous fishes'.[16] In addition to dams and weirs, embankments and flood controls likewise threatened inland fish populations by reducing or entirely eliminating the seasonal inundation of river valleys on which the valuable flood fisheries depended. When catches in Lower Burma declined in the 1880s, local flood-fishermen were quick to blame the construction of river works that prevented the waters from extending across valleys and up into small creeks and depressions. Two decades later, fishermen in East Bengal were equally convinced that the conspicuous decline in fish stocks over recent years was due to the slowing of water flows and the sedimentation of rivers caused by embankments upstream.[17]

Once again, the fundamental interconnectedness of the hydrosphere meant that hydraulic works on the rivers had a direct impact on aquatic life. More indirect, though probably no less extensive, was the damage caused by changes on the land. As we saw in chapter 3, the expansion of rice frontiers in

15. Darboux et al., *L'industrie des pêches*, vol. 2, 300–302; Reeves, Pokrant and McGuire, 'Auction Lease System', 257–59; Cooke, 'Tonle Sap Processed Fish', 367–72.

16. Quotes from Day, *Report on the Freshwater*, 1, 3.

17. De, *Report on the Fisheries*, 70; Hickling, *Tropical Inland Fisheries*, 145–46; Iqbal, *Bengal Delta*, 175–76.

Southeast Asia's river deltas posed a serious threat to local fish populations by choking streams, destroying critical nursery habitat, and allowing farmers to net huge amounts of small fry from their paddies.[18] By the early twentieth century, there was also mounting evidence that forest clearance around the Tonlé Sap was affecting the catch from the lake by shrinking the feeding and spawning grounds that had previously been provided by the tangle of submerged forest vegetation.[19] Pollution from plantations and industrial activities likewise took a toll on fisheries. On the coffee plantations of southern and southeastern Asia, the processing of raw beans dumped tons of harmful pulp into mountain streams, reportedly turning some of them 'literally as dark as porter, and as foetid as flax water'.[20] On Java, inland waters were reported to be 'increasingly defiled by refuse' from factories and sugar mills.[21] In Bengal, the centre of world jute production, the process of 'retting' (extracting the jute fibres from the other plant tissues by allowing them to decompose in water) caused severe eutrophication and anoxia in ponds and streams.[22] Along the western coast of Malaysia, the thousands of tons of tailings washed downstream from the peninsula's vast tin mines reportedly killed large numbers of shad 'apparently choked by silt in their attempt to ascend the rivers'.[23] Downstream from urban centres, sewage and other forms of pollution added to the damage. In the worst affected canals around Calcutta one could see 'countless numbers of cat-fish . . . struggling in a helpless condition'.[24]

Colonial officials were well aware of the vulnerability of freshwater fisheries to such pressures. After all, many lakes and rivers in Europe had long since suffered a collapse of fish stocks due to habitat alteration and overfishing. In many parts of Europe, regulations to halt the damage stretched back to the medieval period or even earlier.[25] The question that nagged many officials was whether a similar process was set to unfold in Europe's most populous colonies.

Some thought that it was, and none more strongly than Major Francis Day, a British army surgeon and amateur naturalist who spent much of his free time studying the fish species of South Asia. Day became interested in the subject soon after his arrival in Madras in 1852, and began publishing on it in the 1860s. In 1868, he was commissioned to investigate the fisheries of Madras. Three years later he was given the opportunity to expand his survey

18. Khin, *Fisheries in Burma*, 80–83; Nisbet, *Burma under British Rule*, 358.

19. Lemasson, 'Aperçu général', 8; Hickling, *Tropical Inland Fisheries*, 139, 145–46, 154; Cooke, 'Tonle Sap Processed Fish', 373–74.

20. Thomas, *Report on Pisciculture*, 6–8, quote at 6.

21. Furnivall, *Fisheries in Netherlands India*, 2; *Netherlands India*, 324.

22. De, *Report on the Fisheries*, 73; Iqbal, *Bengal Delta*, 176.

23. Maxwell, *Malayan Fishes*, 11; see also Butcher, 'Marine Animals', 75.

24. Khin, *Fisheries in Burma*, 84.

25. Hoffmann, 'Brief History'.

to the entire subcontinent in his new role as inspector-general of fisheries. His ensuing report, submitted in 1873, painted an alarming picture. According to Day, India's freshwater fish were in decline nearly everywhere. As human populations grew and food pressures intensified, he reckoned that over half of the country's inland markets had insufficient supplies of fish.[26]

Although it is impossible to determine how serious the problem really was at the time, the sheer volume of anecdotal evidence that Day gathered – which was echoed by the findings of other contemporary studies[27] – suggests that it was becoming increasingly acute. India's inland fish stocks were facing pressure from multiple directions: from heavy fishing, from the modification of rivers and swamps that blocked migrations and reduced habitat, and above all from what he called the 'wasteful destruction' of fry and breeding fish caught by fixed traps and fine-meshed nets. In the North-Western Provinces, Day reported that breeding fish and fry 'are destroyed in every division, in any way in which they can be procured'. In the Bombay Presidency and Hyderabad, juvenile fish were likewise caught wherever and however people could get them. In Madras, the trapping of small fry and breeding fish was unrestricted, and it was common to use poison to stun fish that collected below or above dams. Rules stipulating minimum mesh sizes were rare, and were not broadly observed even where they existed. Some nets reportedly had mesh that was fine enough to catch a 'black ant'.[28]

In many ways Day's report epitomized the broader colonial conservation discourse of the late nineteenth and twentieth centuries. His diagnosis of a steep decline of fish stocks echoed concurrent fears about the disappearance of forests and the slaughter of wildlife amid rapid population growth and economic expansion. His despair at the 'wasteful destruction' of fish by locals reflected widespread patriarchal assumptions about the need to restrain 'native profligacy' in order to safeguard the long-term interests of indigenous people themselves. Such concerns were part of a much wider contemporary pattern of conservationist activity, most of it spearheaded by scientist-officials and amateur naturalists such as Day who were increasingly alarmed at the decline of threatened resources or endangered species.[29]

Yet Day's report was more than just an example of authoritarian 'colonial science' pinning the blame on local ignorance. In fact, like many other conservationists of the period, he regarded colonial rule itself as the root of the problem. At a general level, the acceleration of economic activity and population growth under the *pax colonia* was partly to blame for what he called the

26. Day, *Report on the Freshwater*.

27. E.g., Thomas, *Report on Pisciculture*.

28. Day, *Report on the Freshwater*, 40–42.

29. See generally Grove, *Green Imperialism*; Ross, *Ecology and Power*, 239–347; Beinart and Hughes, *Environment and Empire*, 200–213.

'disastrous effect upon the fresh-water fisheries of the Indian empire'. But the main problem, according to Day, was the government's fixation on free trade: 'the British, with the most philanthropic intentions, have given to the people license in fishing that has been greatly abused, and is now destroying the fisheries'. Whereas earlier arrangements under 'native rule' tended to limit the overall catch through royalty charges, lease payments and restrictions on certain fishing methods, in India (as on Java) such provisions were abolished or eroded for the sake of a more liberal economic policy. In turn, the failure to introduce any new regulations on how the inland fisheries should be worked led to a situation that Day described as 'unlimited license'. In Madras, where people could effectively take as many fish as they wanted, the ideology of 'free industries' had led to a situation of 'free poaching'.[30]

The overall result was a variation on the so-called 'fisherman's problem'.[31] As Arthur McEvoy argued in his classic study of California's fishing industry, whereas the rational harvest of any living resource would limit the overall take to a level that would ensure continued exploitation in the future, fisheries often fail to do so owing to the treatment of fish stocks as 'common property' resources. Because any fish that one might leave in the water would simply land in the net of someone else, there is little inbuilt incentive to conserve the stock. Conservationists in colonial Asia saw the freshwater fishery situation very much in this light. Without controls, Day argued, 'it becomes simply a scramble on the principle – "Should I not catch them, somebody else will."' Liberalizing measures that were intended to benefit the rural economy had left the inland fisheries in a 'ruined state'.[32]

According to conservationists such as Day, the only way to avoid the 'utter annihilation' of freshwater fisheries was through stricter regulation. Most of the restrictions they proposed were analogous to existing bye-laws in Europe: minimum mesh sizes on nets, closed seasons for the placement of nets or traps, constructing fish-passes around weirs, and banning the use of poisons. Some of the recommended measures, however, were more specific to tropical contexts – for example, eradicating various 'vermin' that preyed on vulnerable stocks, especially crocodiles and to a lesser extent birds and otters.[33] Yet the extent to which these proposals were translated into actual regulations varied greatly from place to place. On Java, conservation and improvement measures that were introduced in the early twentieth century reported led to 'most gratifying results'.[34] By contrast, the French administration in Indochina imposed few restrictions at all apart from bans on the use of poisons and explosives.

30. Day, *Report on the Freshwater*, 44–48, quotes at 47 and 48.
31. McEvoy, *Fisherman's Problem*.
32. Day, *Report on the Freshwater*, 48, 55.
33. Day, 48, 80–84, 111–14.
34. Furnivall, *Netherlands India*, 324 (quote); *Fisheries in Netherlands India*, 2.

India displayed a patchwork of different approaches. During the 1870s to 1890s, conservation-minded officials made various attempts to introduce legislation on a provincial level, but little was achieved in most areas. The main exception was Burma's 1875 Fisheries Act, which codified a new auction-lease system based in part on pre-existing arrangements, but which had little practical effect on actual fishing methods. In Bengal too, the 1889 Private Fisheries Protection Act made it punishable for unauthorized persons to fish in 'private waters', but likewise did little to restrict fishing methods, since it was motivated primarily by a desire to avoid the erosion of private property rights rather than by conservation concerns per se.[35] It was only in 1897 that an All-India Fisheries Act was finally passed, though in the event it outlawed only the most egregious techniques such as dynamite and poisons, while leaving the rest to the discretion of provincial administrations. Despite widespread concerns about the deteriorating condition of inland fisheries, measures to regulate them were decidedly patchy.[36]

It is worth emphasizing that this sorry state of fisheries protection contrasted starkly with the elaborate set of laws and restrictions that governed many terrestrial resources. Over the second half of the nineteenth century, colonial forestry departments took control over huge areas of territory, especially in Asia. So rapid was the growth of forest conservation that state-controlled woodlands covered over one-fifth of India's entire land surface by 1900, and roughly a quarter of Java's by the 1920s. Within these reserved forests, all economic activities – logging, grazing, gathering, planting – were strictly controlled in the interests of maximizing the production of certain types of timber and firewood. Meanwhile, the protection of terrestrial wildlife from overhunting likewise became a major concern among many colonial officials, especially in the British- and German-ruled colonies of southern and eastern Africa. By the turn of the century, colonial states had created a patchwork of hunting legislation, game reserves, and even international agreements designed to halt the 'indiscriminate slaughter' of threatened animal species.[37] What made forests a focus of attention was their instrumental value: more specifically, their fiscal importance for state revenues and their strategic importance for activities such as shipbuilding and railway construction. What made the protection of certain game species such a popular cause was their emblematic value. Efforts to preserve colonial wildlife did not focus on endangered creatures per se but rather on charismatic megafauna – giraffes, elephants, rhinos – that served as iconic symbols of pristine tropical 'wilderness' (the very

35. See Shankar, 'Water, Fish and Property', 110–12.

36. Gruvel, L'Indochine, 231–33; Gourou, Le Tonkin, 141–42; Khin, Fisheries in Burma, 7–8; Reeves, Pokrant and McGuire, 'Auction Lease System'.

37. For an overview of colonial forestry and wildlife protection: Ross, Ecology and Power, 239–306.

characteristic that made them hunting targets in the first place). By contrast, fish were neither instrumental nor emblematic. They were mainly used for local subsistence rather than exports or strategic industries,[38] and they were distinctly less alluring in European eyes than rhinos and elephants. As a result, whereas wildlife preservation and 'scientific forestry' became cornerstones of land-use policy in the colonial world, fisheries management was sparse and comparatively ineffective.

The relative indifference that colonial governments showed towards aquatic conservation was reinforced by a bundle of doubts about whether it could, or even should, be pursued at all. One source of scepticism was the widespread aversion among officials towards the introduction of any measures that rural people would find irksome or detrimental to their economic well-being. Fisherfolk were understandably suspicious that any new regulations would be designed to enrich the state at their expense. Although conservationists countered that preventing the destruction of fisheries served to protect people's welfare, there was a sense among many colonial officials on the ground that the state should avoid regulating too many aspects of life, and that its interventions in areas such as forestry and agriculture had already exhausted the limits of what could be 'supported by the opinion of the country'.[39]

Another factor was scepticism about the seriousness of the problem. In India, many administrators deemed the situation in their own districts to be unproblematic and assumed that the sheer extent of the subcontinent's rivers and lakes meant that no amount of fishing could take more than a tiny fraction of the overall stock. French officials in Indochina similarly regarded the colony's fish supplies as well-nigh inexhaustible. Indeed, the Tonlé Sap was perceived as a 'veritable fish-tank' that was capable of producing 'incomparable yields'. Elsewhere – and in Africa in particular – such doubts were reinforced by the idea that indigenous fishing methods were too primitive to cause serious harm to fish stocks, not least because of the high fertility of tropical freshwaters.[40]

There were also practical issues to consider. Zoologically, it was difficult for fish wardens to distinguish between the fry of large fish species and adults of small fish species. Taxonomically, the multitude of different species – and of different local names for the same species – only added to the problem. Socially, many officials feared that corrupt local wardens might abuse their new powers for self-enrichment rather than conservation. And to top it all off, all of these problems were complicated by the lack of reliable information about what needed to be protected in the first place. In the ongoing debates about whether

38. Exceptions here included a proportion of Tonlé Sap fish destined for regional plantations or mines, and the lake fisheries that supplied the copper mining complexes of central Africa: Cooke, 'Tonle Sap Processed Fish'; Gordon, *Nachituti's Gift*, 115–40.

39. Day, *Report on the Freshwater*, 91 (quote); Thomas, *Report on Pisciculture*, 2.

40. Darboux et al., *L'industrie des pêches*, vol. 2, 279, 289; Gruvel, *L'Indochine*, 208–9; Day, *Report on the Freshwater*, 86–92; E. Worthington, *Science in Africa*, 236.

particular fisheries were declining, neither side had much more evidence than hearsay and preconceived ideas.[41]

But perhaps the most important source of ambivalence was the fiscal implications of fishery regulations. These implications tended to fall into two different categories, neither of which encouraged the introduction of conservation measures. On the one hand, wherever the sale of fishing leases constituted an important income stream, any further restrictions were unappealing in the absence of firm evidence of overfishing. In Cambodia, for instance, where the auctioning of fishing rights on the Tonlé Sap was the single largest source of state income (and a crucial supply of protein for mines, plantations and urban markets throughout the region), French officials were decidedly disinclined to intervene despite the insistence of 'old fishermen' that 'the fish are starting to become less abundant'.[42] On the other hand, wherever fishery revenues were fiscally insignificant, few officials attached much importance to fishing or to the needs of those who made a living from it. In India, where land revenue was the primary source of state income, it was even argued that a decline in fish populations (and therefore in fishing) would force more people into taxable agricultural activities. Unlike the valuable hardwoods in India's state-controlled forests, the licensing and leasing of fisheries offered slim prospects for generating revenue, especially once the costs of enforcement were factored in.[43] Both of these categories of scepticism point to the same conclusion: the official willingness to conserve a vulnerable resource went only as far as it promised to enhance rather than detract from state finances. In this sense, the neglect of fisheries serves to highlight the fundamentally extractive priorities of colonial regimes.

In the early twentieth century, as rising populations and ever-larger hydraulic works put more pressure on inland fisheries, there was little agreement on how – even whether – to conserve them. There was, however, a widespread desire to boost fish supplies, and an equally widespread recognition that many lakes and rivers could not produce more without depleting stocks further. Faced with these countervailing pressures, colonial administrations began to look for solutions offshore.

Modernization and the Marine Frontier

In contrast to inland fisheries, the perceived problem on the seas was not too much fishing but rather too little. Apart from the most heavily exploited coastal waters of South and Southeast Asia, the waters off colonial shores

41. Khin, *Fisheries in Burma*, 7; Day, *Report on the Freshwater*, 89–91.

42. Darboux et al., *L'industrie des pêches*, vol. 2, 289 (quote), 301–2, Lévêque, Lazard and Paugy, 'Pêche et pisciculture', 106;. On the commercial importance of the Tonlé Sap fishery: Cooke, 'Tonle Sap Processed Fish'.

43. Day, *Report on the Freshwater*, 48, 86–92; Reeves, 'Inland Waters', 283–85.

FIGURE 5.2. 'Primitive contrivances' for inshore fishing: fishermen using lift
nets in Semarang, Java, c.1900.
By permission of the Nationaal Museum van Wereldculturen, coll. no.
RV-A440-z-68.

were regarded as a gigantic storehouse of resources that were just waiting to
be exploited. Such cornucopian perceptions of the ocean were common nearly
everywhere in the late nineteenth and early twentieth centuries, but they were
especially prevalent in the colonial world in view of the widening technological
gap between the industrialized fisheries of northern waters and the perceived
deficiencies of 'native' fishing technologies. The general sentiment was typified
by a 1910 study of Bengal's fisheries, which regarded the sea as 'the source of
an enormous supply, practically inexhaustible, of the most wholesome, nutri-
tive and palatable varieties of fish', but one that was 'exploited only to a very
insignificant extent'. While most fishing was conducted close inshore and was
carried out 'by means of primitive contrivances only', trawling for demersal
(bottom-dwelling) species was non-existent and offshore waters remained all
but untouched owing to the lack of suitable boats and gear.[44] Altogether, marine
fish populations were viewed as the epitome of a latent colonial resource.

 The question was how best to exploit it, and for most contemporaries the
answer lay in the adoption of technologies from the industrial world. By the end
of the nineteenth century, mechanized deep-sea fisheries were already well
established in Europe, North America and Japan. Steam-powered vessels and

44. De, *Report on the Fisheries*, 5, 75.

modern gear allowed fishermen to operate independently of wind and tide, to reach waters farther offshore, to stay out for longer periods, and to catch more fish with less labour. For colonial officials, it stood to reason that the introduction of motorized trawlers and seine-netting vessels would make it possible to target stocks that traditional gear could not. It also seemed reasonable to assume that the prospect of catching more fish with less effort would entice 'native' fishermen into adopting the new methods. As they quickly found out, however, things were not that simple.

The main problem was that the mechanization of the fishing industry could not proceed on its own, but only as part of a much broader set of changes. It was a problem that colonial agricultural officers would likewise encounter in their attempts to mechanize various aspects of 'native agriculture'. Whether fishermen (or farmers) adopted new equipment was based on a variety of considerations: the availability of capital, the size of markets, prevailing prices and operating costs. It also crucially relied on an interlocking infrastructure of boatyards, port facilities, transport and preservation facilities. Landing more fish was pointless if they could not be adequately preserved or distributed to wider markets. Investing large sums in a new boat was equally pointless if it spent half its time idle because of a lack of spare parts. Furthermore, making such an investment entailed a new attitude towards speculation and risk. New boats and gear might enable a fisherman to catch more, perhaps even sell more, but not necessarily to earn more if market prices dipped too low to cover all of the additional costs. There was also the broader question of whether such equipment was actually necessary or all that more productive than some of the techniques already in use. After all, ethnic Chinese fishermen using a mixture of traditional Hokkien and Malay methods caught huge amounts of fish in Sumatra's Rokan estuary on the Straits of Malacca. In the early twentieth century, their main settlement Bagan Si Api Api ranked second in the world (behind Bergen) with respect to the overall tonnage of fish products it exported.[45] As a 1922 British survey of colonial fisheries concluded: 'from these and other considerations . . . it is evident that the development of fisheries in many parts of the tropics will not be easy'.[46]

In the circumstances, few fishermen had the means to acquire motorized boats in the first place, and the few who could afford them generally found them unremunerative once they factored in the high operating costs and limited market outlets.[47] From their perspective, the arguments against adopting such techniques were entirely rational. Colonial officials, however, often perceived such reticence through the patronizing lens of cultural 'backwardness'. It was an aquatic variation on a familiar theme. Little could be

45. Medrano, 'Edible Tide', 586–87.
46. Regan, *Report on the Fishes*, 2.
47. See, e.g., Butcher, *Closing of the Frontier*, 123–24.

FIGURE 5.3. The busy fishing port of Bagan Si Api Api in East Sumatra, before 1920.
By permission of the Nationaal Museum van Wereldculturen, coll. no. RV-A40-1-46.

expected from most 'native' fishermen, who were often dismissed as 'resistant to the use of new equipment which they disdain out of prejudice or ignorance', and whose traditional ways of working 'leave almost everything to be desired in the methods of capture, preservation, and distribution'.[48]

This combination of weak commercial incentives and strong cultural preconceptions meant that colonial states themselves took the main initiative in promoting new fishing technologies. But the extent to which they did so varied greatly from place to place. Some (such as Burma, or Britain's East African colonies) did little or nothing.[49] Others did significantly more, especially where food demand was high or where offshore waters were particularly promising.

In colonial Asia, most of the impetus came from the pressure to feed growing populations in the most densely settled parts of the region, such as Java and Bengal. The first step was to determine where large, untapped fish stocks could be found. In the East Indies, Dutch authorities began to experiment

48. Quotes respectively from Villarem, *Pêcheries du Tonkin*, 1; Nicholson, *Fisheries in Japan*, 88.
49. Khin, *Fisheries in Burma*, 2; E. Worthington, *Science in Africa*, 241.

with motorized trawling as a means of producing cheap food and reducing foreign fish imports. Gripped by the spirit of 'Ethical Policy', the East Indies government established a Fishery Station at Batavia in 1904 to conduct research
on marine stocks, fishing gear and preservation methods. From 1907 to 1911, it
also began surveying potential trawling grounds after converting an old barge
(the *Gier*) into a makeshift trawler. Apart from a couple of promising spots
in the Madura Strait and off the coast of Borneo, most of the survey grounds
failed to live up to expectations. Further research was halted for the time
being, but the investigations nonetheless raised the prospect that purpose-
built trawlers with better engines and larger nets could successfully fish along
commercial lines. Meanwhile, similar surveys were being conducted in India.
Off the coast of Ceylon (Sri Lanka), two motorized vessels (the *Violet* and *Mar-
garita*) began searching for new fishing grounds in 1907. Two years later, the
Bengal government acquired an old trawler from Britain (the *Golden Crown*)
to investigate its own offshore waters. Here, as in the East Indies, early surveys
were discontinued after only a few years because of funding problems and
inconclusive results. By 1912, the *Golden Crown* had been sold to a Chinese
entrepreneur who briefly tried his hand at trawling off the Straits Settlements,
only to give up after three months.[50]

   After a hiatus during the First World War, the search for new fishing grounds
in colonial Asia resumed in the 1920s on a much larger scale. Leading the way
was the Institut océanographique de l'Indochine, founded in 1922 at Cauda
on the coast of central Annam, which many regarded as the best-equipped
facility of its kind in the entire tropical world. The Institute's five-hundred-ton
research vessel (the *de Lanessan*) served as both an experimental trawler and
as a floating laboratory for studying the temperatures, currents, nutrient levels
and other factors that influenced the size and exploitability of fish populations.
Like oceanographic outfits elsewhere in the early twentieth-century world,
its scientific and practical aims were inextricably entwined. In the words of
one of France's leading fisheries experts, the institute would not only enable
scientists to catalogue 'the entire marine fauna from whales to sponges' but
also encourage the formation of 'metropolitan-style fishing companies . . . to
exploit this fauna methodically'.[51] The early signs were promising: by 1925
researchers found a seasonal abundance of fish near the mouth of the Mekong,
where winter monsoon rains washed huge amounts of nitrogenous material
and freshwater prey downstream. Surveys elsewhere, however, painted a very
different picture. Despite vast expanses of trawlable sea floor off Indochina,
the density of fish populations was found to be 'very low'. Such disappointing

   50. *Report of the Fish Sub-committee*, 8; Reeves et al., 'Mapping India's Marine
Resources'; Furnivall, *Fisheries in Netherlands India*, 7–8; Butcher, *Closing of the Frontier*,
137–38; Khin, *Fisheries in Burma*, 50, 102–3.
   51. Gruvel, *L'Indochine*, 277.

results broadly echoed earlier findings in the East Indies. They also paralleled concurrent studies underway in British Malaya, where surveys carried out in the Straits of Malacca and South China Sea concluded that European-style trawling was not commercially viable due to a combination of high operating costs, low prices for bottom-dwelling species, and disappointing catches.[52]

Overall, there was little immediate prospect of using motorized industrial trawlers to create a new demersal fishing industry anywhere in colonial Asia. But boosting the harvest of pelagic fish – species swimming or schooling in open offshore waters – was a different matter, whether by introducing European boats or mechanizing traditional craft. In the late 1920s, the Institute for Fisheries in Batavia began experimenting with small petrol and diesel motors on indigenous sail-powered *payang* (seine-netting) boats, which were common along the northern coast of Java. At first, the high costs of even small motors limited the uptake to only a handful of operators capable of selling their catch on the large Batavia market. But as more Javanese fishers recognized the benefits of staying out at sea longer (previously they fished only in the mornings in order to have sufficient time to sail back to market before the end of the day), and as marine motors became cheaper and more reliable, more and more 'domestic skippers' adopted them in the 1930s.[53] Developments in Malaya followed a similar pattern. Throughout the 1930s, the Malayan Fisheries Department surveyed offshore waters, demonstrated the use of modern purse seine nets, and promoted the use of diesel-powered boats in place of the traditional junks that had hitherto dominated the inshore fisheries of the Straits of Malacca. As motorized craft ventured farther offshore, they achieved record hauls: from 1931 to 1938, mackerel landings at the fishing hub of Pangkor rose from 860 to 5,700 tons. As the catch grew, the Fisheries Department eventually turned its attention to refrigeration, salting and canning facilities to preserve the surplus. In both Malaya and the East Indies, such experiences belied the myth of the innately conservative 'native' fishermen. Most were in fact quick to adopt new technologies when they saw a concrete advantage in doing so.[54]

Meanwhile, state efforts to develop offshore fishing in colonial Africa followed a different pattern. Unlike colonial Asia, the main emphasis was not on promoting industrial fishing to African fisherfolk, but rather on promoting African waters to industrial fishing. The most important regions were the south-western and north-western coasts of the continent, where vast upwellings of cold,

52. Gourou, 'Océanographie et pêche', 540–41; Butcher, *Closing of the Frontier*, 138–40.

53. Butcher, *Closing of the Frontier*, 160–62; Furnivall, *Fisheries in Netherlands India*, 7–8.

54. Firth, *Malay Fishermen*, 17, 300–303; Furnivall, *Fisheries in Netherlands India*, 7–9; Butcher, *Closing of the Frontier*, 139–40, 152–55, 160–62.

FIGURE 5.4. Javanese fishing boat, 1924–32.
By permission of the Nationaal Museum van Wereldculturen, coll. no.
RV-A440-bb-31.

nutrient-rich water sustained a profusion of marine life. The coast of southern Angola had long been home to Portuguese whaling and fishing enterprises centred on the ports of Sao Antonio, Mossamédès, Port-Alexandre and Bahia dos Tigres. In the early twentieth century, South African vessels also operated a modern fishery west of the Cape and along the coast of Namibia.[55] But by far the most promising new fishing grounds were off the coast of French West Africa, in particular Mauritania, Senegal and Guinea.

The richness of West Africa's seas had been known to European fishermen for centuries. By the 1700s, Spanish boats from the Canary Islands occasionally fished some of the most productive banks off the Saharan coast. With the spread of French influence in West Africa in the early nineteenth century, French naturalists began to study the region's ichthyofauna in the hopes of drawing the attention of fishers and investors to the opportunities awaiting them there. In the second half of the nineteenth century, Marseillais shipowners occasionally sent boats to explore the commercial potential of these waters.[56] But it was mainly after the turn of the twentieth century – as part of

55. Van Sittert, 'Handmaiden of Industry'; Borgström and Heighway, *Atlantic Ocean Fisheries*, 179–83.

56. Chauveau, 'Cinq siècles de pêche', 241–44; Lévêque, Lazard and Paugy, 'Pêche et pisciculture', 95–96.

the wider *mise en valeur* of France's colonies – that French officialdom became interested in West Africa's fish resources.

As was also the case in Asia, the first step was to determine the size and value of the resource itself. From 1905 to 1907 the zoologist Abel Gruvel was commissioned to compile a systematic catalogue of West Africa's ichthyofauna, and his report remained a standard work on the subject for decades afterwards. In 1908, Gruvel was put in charge of a newly established Office de recherches et d'organisation des pêcheries de l'Afrique occidentale française, and in 1910 he launched a survey of the entire Atlantic coast of Africa.[57] The explicit purpose of these investigations was to find fish stocks that could be exploited by industrial methods on an industrial scale. As Gruvel himself put it, 'a metropolitan-style fishing industry can and should become one of the most powerful and flourishing industries of our entire magnificent West African colony'.[58]

French officials assumed that the quickest way to create such an industry was not by modernizing indigenous canoe fisheries – which were highly developed along the Ivory Coast, Dahomey and especially Senegal – but rather by luring French boats into West African waters. They sought to do so in two ways: by offering French fishermen generous government subsidies, and by providing them with modern preservation facilities that would allow them to export their catch to the distant metropolitan market. Up to a point the policy was successful. In the early 1910s, the administration in French West Africa oversaw the construction of a semi-industrialized port and conservation facility at Port-Etienne (Nouadhibou) in Mauritania, and in the 1910s and 1920s it drew a series of French commercial ventures to the waters off Mauritania and Senegal in search of langoustines and any other marketable species they could find.[59] Overall, however, the results were modest. Only a handful of French vessels ever made the journey south, and nearly all of those that did suffered losses that discouraged them from returning. Metropolitan investors were reluctant to underwrite the expansion of conservation facilities in West Africa in view of the continual difficulties they experienced with labour procurement, equipment breakdowns and finding suitable market outlets. Despite these setbacks, the colonial administration persisted throughout the 1920s with the policy of prioritizing industrial fishing at Port-Etienne, while ignoring the large African canoe fishery that already existed along the coast. It was only after the sharp contraction of the colonial export economy in the 1930s that officials began to consider how indigenous fisheries might be included in their plans. In the event, this initiative took concrete shape only after the Second World

57. Gruvel, *Les pêcheries de la côte* and *Les pêcheries des côtes*; Lévêque, Lazard and Paugy, 'Pêche et pisciculture', 95–97.
58. Gruvel, *L'industrie des pêches*, 179.
59. Gruvel, 7–15.

War as part of the wider French campaign to develop the economies of its remaining colonies.[60]

Despite all the emphasis that governments placed on introducing industrial fishing methods to Europe's colonies, not everyone was convinced by this approach. To be sure, the rapid introduction of steam trawlers and motorized craft had many advocates, including some indigenous elites eager to 'modernize' their economies. But there were also dissenting voices within the colonial bureaucracy who favoured a more gradualist approach centred on the improvement of existing boats and artisanal methods. These competing visions for the fishing industry reflected much broader discussions about the appropriate pace – even the fundamental aims – of colonial 'development'. In many respects, they echoed arguments in other policy areas such as agriculture and irrigation, where debates about scale, indigenous collaboration and appropriate technologies were already underway.[61]

The evolution of different development approaches was particularly evident in Madras, where India's first fisheries department was established in 1907. Fishing first came into focus here in the context of India's devastating famines of the late nineteenth century (see chapter 2) and was regarded as a potential form of insurance against the ravages of drought-induced food shortages. The key figure was Frederick Nicholson, a senior Madras official and a member of the Indian Famine Commission, who eventually became the Fisheries Department's first director. For Nicholson, the horrifying experience of India's recent famines led him to believe that the resources of the sea must be used to supplement those of the land. In 1899, he contended that 'the development of our fisheries is now absolutely essential in connection, whether direct or indirect, with our food-supply'. Unlike agriculture and irrigation, which the colonial state had supported for decades, 'this all important subject has too long been neglected', for the ocean 'yields its harvests in enormous quantities wholly irrespective of droughts and seasonal catastrophes'. At base, Nicholson's goal was the same one that inspired India's vast irrigation works: to produce 'food independent of climate'. In the ongoing struggle to achieve this aim, 'we may thank God that we have yet got the fisheries to develop'.[62]

Nicholson's initial strategy was to industrialize fish production as quickly as possible. Notably, he did not look to Europe as a model for inspiration. Rather, in 1906 he embarked on a fact-finding tour of Japan, which over the previous several decades had managed to transform its traditional fishing sector into the largest fishing industry in the world. Nicholson's journey convinced him

60. Pavé and Charles-Dominique, 'Science et politique'; Chauveau, 'Cinq siècles de pêche', 244–48.

61. See note 5; generally, Ross, *Ecology and Power*, 307–47.

62. Madras Fisheries Bureau, *Papers from 1899*, 1.

that India had much to learn from Japan's success. He highlighted several key lessons in particular: the importance of strong government involvement, generous investment in scientific research, the need to learn from foreign countries about the best available gear, close cooperation between the state and private enterprise, and the benefits of fishery education and trade associations. India's fishing industry was, he argued, in a similar state to Japan's before the Meiji Restoration of 1867: important for the life of the people, but hobbled by 'primitive and customary methods'. Developing it would, he reckoned, be even more challenging than in Japan, owing to what he saw as the innate flaws of the Indian fishing population: being 'less numerous, less hardy, less adventurous, less adaptive, and more readily content with that which is; infinitely suspicious of Government interference yet almost incapable of initiative or of serious new departures without such intervention'.[63]

Nicholson's assessment of Indian fisherfolk as backward, isolated and hopelessly bound by caste and tradition was widely shared at the time. British and Indian elites alike tended to regard fishing groups as culturally inferior to agrarian communities, as classic examples of 'people without history'.[64] During his first few years in charge of the Madras Fisheries Department, Nicholson assumed that the techniques and way of life of India's fisherfolk would inevitably disappear as part of the wider capitalist reshaping of socio-economic life. It was only a matter of time, he thought, before the industry progressed 'from the independent fisherman with a single small boat and petty local trade to the capitalist-employer with his fleet of large boats and his wages-paid crew'.[65] In anticipation of this inevitable process of evolution, he sponsored two trawling expeditions as soon as the Department was established, and followed them up a year later with the creation of a new facility at Ennore (just north of Madras) to experiment with large boats and nets.[66] But the more Nicholson learned about the life of fishing villages, the more he concluded that such efforts were futile. Over time, he reached the view that the very backwardness of India's coastal communities severely limited their capacity to adopt new techniques and new ways of distributing their catch. In order to develop India's fisheries, it was therefore necessary to engage fisherfolk at least partly on their own terms. More out of pragmatism than principle, he soon adopted a more gradual approach. Instead of a full-blown shift towards industrial boats and wage labour, the department focused on incremental improvements to indigenous craft and the organization of fishermen's cooperatives. As Nicholson summarized it in 1915, 'we cannot jump at once from the catamaran to the steam trawler'.[67]

63. Nicholson, *Fisheries in Japan*, 2–3.

64. Wolf, *People without History*.

65. Madras Fisheries Bureau, *Papers from 1899*, 36

66. *Report of the Committee on Fisheries*, 6–7.

67. Quote from Madras Fisheries Bureau, 'Annual Report', 76; see also Christie, *Report on Madras Fisheries*, 22–23; Subramanian, *Shorelines*, 107.

Nicholson's two successors as director of fisheries embodied these two very different developmentalist impulses.[68] James Hornell, who had worked alongside Nicholson since 1908, approached Madras's fisheries more from an ethnographic than an economic perspective. His time in Madras was part of a much longer engagement with tropical seas and fisheries, and his work there reflected a decades-long fascination with indigenous fishing technologies.[69] Unlike Nicholson's dismissive view of traditional fishing methods, Hornell admired how they were carefully tailored to particular marine ecosystems. Throughout his tenure as director, Hornell's priorities were shaped by a genuine respect for indigenous fisherfolk and an acknowledgement of their interests. For Hornell, India's fishing communities were not stagnant and insular but adaptive and technologically outward-looking. Although he and Nicholson viewed coastal communities from diametrically opposed perspectives, in practice their developmental priorities converged in the promotion of artisanal methods over industrial fishing. It was an approach that in many ways presaged what would later be called 'participatory' forms of development.[70]

By contrast, B. Sundara Raj – the first Indian director of the department, who succeeded Hornell in 1923 – brought a change of emphasis. No sooner had he taken the helm than he requested a trawler and Danish cutter to survey Madras's offshore fish resources. Although his request was initially denied, by 1927 the department nonetheless began to search for potential trawling and seine-netting grounds that artisanal fishing methods had so far left untapped. Like many nationalist-minded Indian elites, Raj was impatient with the cautious approach of colonial development, which he increasingly regarded as a form of underdevelopment. In the late 1920s and 1930s, he adopted a more top-down approach towards changing the techniques of local fishermen. In part, this strategy expressed his pejorative view of fishing communities as backward, conservative and little more than a brake on the industry's progress. It also reflected his frustration at local fisherfolk's inability to exploit the offshore fishing grounds that the department's surveys had recently found. When the fisheries departments of Ceylon and Malaya initiated their own trawling surveys off Cape Comorin (on India's southernmost tip), Raj worried that 'other Governments will exploit the Madras fishing grounds' so long as local fishermen could not do so themselves.[71] Such concerns spiralled in the mid-1930s when Japanese trawlers arrived to haul thousands of tons of fish out of Madras's waters, some of which was shipped to distant markets and

68. See also Subramanian, *Shorelines*, 105–24; Reeves et al., 'Mapping India's Marine Resources'.

69. For an overview of Hornell's numerous works on the subject: Hornell, *Bibliography of Scientific Publications* and *Fishing in Many Waters*.

70. Subramanian, *Shorelines*, 116.

71. Quote from *Madras Fisheries Bulletin*, 1918–37 (Madras: Government Press, 1938), 34, quoted in Subramanian, *Shorelines*, 120.

some landed at Indian ports where it undercut the incomes of local fisher-men. In order to counter this 'menace of foreign exploitation', Raj called on the provincial government to help ensure 'the fullest exploitation of the natural resources of the country for the benefit of the people'.[72]

By the 1930s, disputes over water rights and borders (a theme we will explore in more detail in chapter 7) encompassed Asia's seas as well as its riv-ers. But as colonial authorities throughout the region were discovering, the attempt to halt the spread of Japanese trawlers and drift-netters into what they regarded as their territorial waters – an initiative that was driven as much by military as by economic concerns – could achieve only so much in the con-text of international legal norms upholding the freedom of the seas.[73] Ulti-mately, only the modernization of the industry would enable local fishermen to capture their 'own' fish resources first.

Although no one could know it at the time, the divergent approaches that were pursued by Madras's fisheries directors were early manifestations of a decades-long debate about how best to develop marine fisheries in tropical waters more generally. The key issues that framed these discussions – high-tech versus low-tech, top-down versus community-oriented approaches – reverber-ated for decades and echoed arguments in other realms of development policy. Ultimately, the incremental approach adopted by officials like Nichol-son and Hornell proved to be the exception. The main thrust of colonial fisheries development remained the displacement of older techniques and vernacular forms of knowledge by supposedly more 'efficient' and 'scientific' practices from the industrial world. As we will see in chapter 8, it was an approach that many post-colonial leaders championed every bit as eagerly as their colonial predecessors, as a means of both exploiting the natural resources off their coasts and demonstrating their modernizing credentials to newly enfran-chised voters.

Cultivating the Waters

Ever since the European conquest of the Americas in the 1500s and 1600s, efforts to improve nature by rearranging its constituent parts were a central feature of European expansion. For centuries, the transfer of useful crops and animal species from one part of the world to another was the stock-in-trade of planters, farmers and agronomists seeking to boost the productivity of newly subjugated lands. During the heyday of European global power in the nine-teenth and twentieth centuries, scientists and officials launched countless

---

72. Madras Fisheries Department, *Report for the Year 1931-32*, 1–2; *Report for the Year 1936-37*, 2 (quotes); *Report of the Committee on Fisheries*, 17–20, 210–12; Subramanian, *Shorelines*, 120–23.

73. Butcher, *Closing of the Frontier*, 166–67.

attempts to 'acclimatize' different crops and domesticated animals in new locations. The intercontinental movement of organisms such as cattle, coffee bushes or rubber trees not only spawned new export industries; it also created whole new 'creole ecologies', novel combinations of living organisms drawn from the distant environments that were connected by the sinews of empire.[74]

Over the past fifty years or so, starting with Alfred Crosby's pioneering work on the 'Columbian Exchange', scholars have charted the history of how these biotic transfers reordered terrestrial environments and agrarian societies around the globe.[75] Yet in the process, few have paid much attention to the parallel set of changes that was taking place underwater. Just as new trade links and transportation technologies enabled species to move or be transplanted more easily between land masses, so too did they serve to bridge previously separate aquatic spaces. Although the imperial transfer of aquatic species is far less well known than its terrestrial equivalent, it likewise fashioned new hybrid biophysical environments that were intended to be more valuable or productive than what nature itself had provided.

This reshuffling of aquatic organisms in Europe's colonies was all part of a larger global pattern of ecological exchange, an accelerating process of biotic standardization that has led some observers to declare a new phase of natural history: the so-called 'Homogocene'.[76] Although various fish species had been transplanted and cultivated since ancient times (especially in East Asia), both the pace and scale of such relocations rose markedly in the nineteenth and twentieth centuries. From the 1830s onward, European and Chinese carp were widely introduced into the waterways of the eastern United States. By the 1870s and 1880s, agencies in Europe and the United States were actively organizing a transcontinental traffic in fish species. While Atlantic salmon and brown trout were moved from Europe to North America, Pacific salmon and rainbow trout went in the other direction. Once these transplanted species became established in their new homes, they were often taken from there to other places. Canadian provinces imported European carp from the United States, while Mexican authorities acquired them from parts of the Caribbean. In Australia, acclimatization enthusiasts sought to introduce all manner of familiar sport and food fish from Europe: salmon, trout, char and carp, along with various marine species. Such efforts were so widespread and unrestrained that they even affected the world's first national park. Whereas officials in Yellowstone resisted the introduction of exotic terrestrial species such as reindeer and non-native fowl, they actively stocked Yellowstone Lake with non-native

74. Osborne, 'Acclimatizing the World; Minard, *All Things Harmless*; Kirchberger and Bennett, *Environments of Empire*.

75. Crosby, *Columbian Exchange*.

76. A term apparently coined by the ecologist Gordon Orians in the 1980s: Rosenzweig, 'Four Questions'.

brown, rainbow and brook trout from 1889 until almost 1960, reducing the numbers of native grayling and cutthroat trout in the process.[77]

Although many of these early exchanges took place in temperate latitudes, the waters of the tropical world were also deemed ripe for 'improvement'. From the 1890s to the 1940s, over thirty species were widely transplanted within Southeast Asia alone, some of them originating from within the region, others from China, and still others from Europe, Africa or North America.[78] Such transfers were carried out for a number of different reasons. One was to improve public health. In malaria-prone parts of Asia, larvicidal fish species were occasionally used to help control mosquito populations. In Indochina, Bengal and Madras, colonial fisheries officials sought to increase the numbers of such fish by actively stocking lakes, ponds and irrigation tanks with larvicidal fry. In order to make such introductions work, it was often necessary to remove most of the existing fish beforehand, especially the large predators. Although native species of larvicidal fish were generally preferred wherever they were available (on the assumption that they would be more likely to thrive in local conditions and posed less of a threat to other species), such assumptions did not stop officials from trying more exotic solutions. In India, colonial health authorities introduced the South American *Poecilia reticulata* in 1908 and the North American *Gambusia affinis* (commonly called the 'mosquito fish') in 1928–29. As it turned out, neither of these species proved any more effective at eating mosquito larvae than various indigenous fish. In fact, as so often happened with exotic introductions, it proved to be a counterproductive move: the American mosquito fish was soon regarded as a pest owing to its voracious appetite for the fry of indigenous carp populations.[79]

Alongside health concerns, there were also less utilitarian reasons for introducing fish, not least the passion for sport. In the 1860s and 1870s, a group of British anglers released American rainbow and European brown trout into the streams of India's Nilgiri Hills, which were home to a popular hill station in which British bureaucrats liked to pass the scorching summer months. By the 1910s, fishing enthusiasts had also released brown trout into the rivers of Kashmir, the Himalayan foothills and the southern princely state of Travancore.[80] The high mountain streams of eastern and southern Africa were an even bigger target for sport fish introductions. When British settlers

77. Courtenay, 'Biological Pollution', 42–44; Kinsey, 'Seeding the Water'; Baskin, *Plague of Rats*, 7, 33, 38.

78. Schuster, *Over de import* and 'Provisional Survey', 189–90.

79. In the early 2000s, the Global Invasive Species Programme included *Gambusia affinis* among the 100 most consequential bio-invaders in the world: Lowe et al., *Worst Invasive Alien Species*. This paragraph also draws on Houdemer's *Les poissons dulcaquicoles* (2–3), Morin's *Utilisation des poissons*, Hora's 'Use of Fishes', Chandra et al.'s 'Mosquito Control' (14) and Sreenivasan's 'Transfers of Freshwater Fishes'.

80. S. Agarwal, *History of Indian Fishery*, 92–93.

explored the rivers of Kenya's highlands, they found an abundance of aquatic insects and small crabs, but no fish that fed on them. In European eyes, the cool water temperatures, plentiful food supplies and scarcity of indigenous fish life 'very naturally suggested the introduction of trout'.[81] Brown trout were first brought from Loch Leven in Scotland to the upper reaches of the Gura River in 1905, where they quickly – indeed, too quickly – established themselves. With no natural predators around, the river was soon so 'thick with them' that they exhausted their own food supply. In 1912, the Kenyan Forest Department built a hatchery on the Gura River to transfer fry into other streams in the region, and several years later the Kenya Angling Association set itself the goal of introducing rainbow and brown trout in all of the colony's suitable rivers. In the mid-1920s, the Kenyan Game Department took control over the Association's fish-stocking operations, and by the early 1930s it had stocked no less than two thousand miles (3,200 kilometres) of Kenya's streams. Before long, European and American trout were swimming in virtually all of the suitable rivers of eastern, central and southern Africa.[82]

The most important motive behind fish transfers in Europe's colonies was the prospect of improving food supplies. In the words of one fisheries biologist, the principal aim was 'to increase the production of our waters' through 'the stocking or restocking with fish which under prevailing conditions are able to yield better than the original stock'.[83] Carp were a perennial favourite for this purpose. European carp arrived on the African Cape as early as 1859, and were gradually taken from there to other parts of southern Africa. In the late nineteenth century, they were released in India's Nilgiri Hills and in parts of Madagascar.[84] In the warmer waters of lower-lying tropical latitudes, a handful of Indian carp species were widely introduced for converting aquatic vegetation into protein. In the early twentieth century, as biologists learned more about tropical fish species, the list of globetrotting food fish expanded well beyond carp. The giant gourami (*Osphronemus goramy*), already an important food fish in Java, became a favourite for stocking warm, shallow ponds on account of its good taste, herbivorous diet and high fecundity. Various species of African tilapia were also widely introduced throughout colonial Asia and the Caribbean, sometimes with official authorization and sometimes without it.[85]

Such biotic tinkering was by no means confined to the enhancement of natural lakes, rivers and streams. All throughout the colonies, the construction

81. E. Worthington, *Science in Africa*, 232.

82. S. Worthington and Worthington, *Inland Waters of Africa*, 191–95, 201–2; Lévêque, Lazard and Paugy, 'Pêche et pisciculture', 84.

83. Schuster, 'Provisional Survey', 191.

84. S. Agarwal, *History of Indian Fishery*, 89–91; Mouranche, 'Le développement'; Jackson, 'Desirability or Otherwise'.

85. Schuster, 'Provisional Survey', 191; Khin, *Fisheries in Burma*, 64; Hickling, *Tropical Inland Fisheries*, 245–49.

of dams, irrigation works and flood defences provided numerous opportunities to capitalize on the hydrological changes underway – or, conversely, to
mitigate any detrimental effects they caused. On the one hand, the creation of
reservoirs invited attempts to augment the availability of desirable lacustrine
(lake-dwelling) species. On the other, many of the largest fish stocking initiatives were intended to alleviate the impact of newly built barrages on species
that ascended the rivers to breed. A key example were the hilsa (shad) fisheries
of India's eastern rivers, which furnished a crucial supply of protein to local
markets and were a major concern for the Madras Fisheries Department. As
noted above, the various barrages that had been built across the waterways of
Madras had been exerting a detrimental impact on shad stocks ever since the
mid-nineteenth century. When the construction of fish passes around Arthur
Cotton's Grand Anicut failed to halt the decline of hilsa shad in the Cauvery
River, the department set up a fish hatchery in 1909 to maintain the population artificially. Twenty-five years later, it had to step up its stocking activities
when the construction of the gargantuan Mettur Dam – briefly the largest
dam in the world – completely stopped the Cauvery's shad runs in 1934.[86]

Large reservoirs and waterworks were not the only target for such activities. Just as important was the stocking of thousands of village irrigation tanks
in colonial Asia, which officials regarded as a promising means of producing much-needed protein and fats in the countryside. In the interwar period,
as international health committees at the League of Nations bemoaned the
low intake of protein in rural Asia, authorities in the Netherlands Indies and
Indochina experimented with the cultivation of small carp in irrigated rice
paddies and encouraged farmers to raise fish in their fields as a kind of 'secondary crop'. Meanwhile, some Indian officials viewed small-scale fish rearing
as nothing less than the key to recovering the nation's virility. In Bihar and
Orissa, a local 'Grow and Eat More Fish' campaign was explicitly inspired by
the example of Japan, where, in the words of a promotion leaflet, the 'generous
addition of fish to the diet . . . serves to make up the deficiency of rice in the
most effective and complete manner and thus helps the nation to maintain
the physical and mental vigour of its manhood at a high level of perfection'.[87]

At one level, all of these fish transplantations were merely the aquatic
side of the 'acclimatization' coin, mirror images of the concurrent efforts to
introduce non-native organisms into new terrestrial environments. Both
represented a form of experimentation designed to create a more useful
(for humans) set of biological relationships, and both had the potential to

86. *Report of the Committee on Fisheries*, 22; Madras Fisheries Department, *Report for the Year 1938–39*, 3; Barber, *Cauvery-Mettur Project*, 184–90; Amrith, *Unruly Waters*, 161.

87. Department of Industries, Bihar and Orissa, *Eat More Fish*, quote at 1; Lemasson and Benas, *Essais de mise au point*; Benas, 'Note sur la pratique'; Buschkiel, *De teelt van karpers*; Khin, *Fisheries in Burma*, 64–68.

generate unintended consequences, perhaps especially in unfamiliar tropical surroundings.

But if European colonizers had a patchy understanding of the terrestrial environments they were altering, they knew almost nothing about the aquatic ecosystems they were meddling with. This was partly due to the inaccessibility of underwater spaces and the associated difficulties of studying them, but it also reflected the remarkable complexity of aquatic biomes in the tropics. Whereas Europe has a little over five hundred known species of freshwater fish, Africa alone has well over three thousand. Such diversity made it extremely hard to piece together the life histories and habits of many species, let alone their interrelationships. As a result, it was impossible to judge – let alone foresee – the impact of species introductions for want of any baseline for comparison. Moreover, once such a biological experiment commenced, people had even less control over the outcomes than they did on land. Unlike exotic crops or livestock, which could be confined at first to certain fields or enclosures for the purpose of observation, fish could not easily be kept in one part of a lake or river. For the most part it was a matter of letting them loose and seeing what happened. This combination of ignorance and irreversibility meant that the risk of unintended consequences – even serious ecological upheaval – was correspondingly high wherever non-native fish were introduced. It was especially acute in water bodies with high numbers of endemic species not found elsewhere.

The inland waters of Madagascar were a good example. The island's ichthyofauna, like its terrestrial creatures, had evolved in relative isolation ever since its separation from the Indian and Seychelles Plates around ninety million years ago. The result was a high level of endemism but a low level of diversity, which included only twenty-eight freshwater species in total. As European influence expanded on Madagascar in the nineteenth and twentieth centuries, the island was subjected to a series of non-native fish introductions that completely reordered its freshwater ecosystems.

For millennia, the waters of Lake Alaotra (Madagascar's largest freshwater body) had been dominated by one native tilapia species (*Paratilapia polleni*), two smaller endemic fish and two endemic eels. The first newcomer was the Asian goldfish (*Carassius auratus*), which was released into the lake in 1865 and gradually established itself. After the goldfish's introduction, the lake's faunal makeup slowly changed. By 1925, catches on Lake Alaotra comprised 75 per cent native tilapia, 20 per cent Asian goldfish, and 5 per cent other species. But this was only the start, for in the meantime French officials also introduced the omnivorous European carp, which multiplied far more quickly than the Asian goldfish. Within a decade of its introduction in the 1920s, the European carp constituted a significant part of the catch, and from this point on its numbers grew exponentially. In 1952, European carp accounted for no less than 80 per cent of the local haul, whereas native tilapia and Asian goldfish were no longer abundant. By this time the fauna of Lake Alaotra had already been changed beyond recognition, but the ecological upheaval only intensified over the following years. In 1954, officials brought in the central African redbreast tilapia (*Tilapia rendalli*), which multiplied rapidly owing to its high fecundity and its ability to fill an empty ecological niche as the only herbivorous species in the lake. Within the space of only three years it already composed 46 per cent of the catch. In 1958, it was joined by the greenhead tilapia (*Oreochromis macrochir*) – a native of the Zambezi basin, and another fast breeder that occupied an empty niche as a plankton-feeder – which quickly displaced the redbreast as the dominant species. In the wake of Madagascar's independence in 1960, the greenhead tilapia was soon joined by other exotic tilapia, black bass and carp, though none of these subsequent introductions changed the overall picture very much.[88]

The end result was a completely human-made aquatic community, and a highly unstable one at that. The story of Lake Alaotra is not unique. Lake Itasy, the third-largest freshwater body on Madagascar, met a similar fate. Indeed, the biotic mayhem inflicted on Lake Itasy was such as to produce an entirely new crossbred species – the so-called 'Tilapia 3/4' – a fecund hybrid of the greenhead and Nile tilapia. To this day, Madagascar remains unique in the world for the coexistence of so many exotic species in otherwise 'natural' water bodies.[89]

The transformation of Madagascar's lakes was, to borrow from Albert Crosby, a dramatic case of 'ecological imperialism'. Like the 'Columbian Exchange' of plants, animals and microbes across the Atlantic, the intercontinental transfer of fish connected aquatic ecosystems that had been geologically separate for millions of years, in this case since at least the break-up of the Gondwana supercontinent some 180 million years ago.[90] Both processes were the direct result of European conquest, though the overall patterns of biotic incursion differed. Unlike Crosby's 'portmanteau biota' that European colonizers brought from their homes to the Americas, most of the newcomers in Madagascar came from other colonized territories in Africa and Asia. This was typical for the late nineteenth and twentieth centuries as the effort to acclimatize organisms in sub-Saharan Africa, southern Asia and South America was based mainly on the exchange of species between different parts of the tropical world.[91]

Because of the long biogeographical isolation of Madagascar, the introduction of exotic ichthyofauna to the island was in many ways an extreme case. Nonetheless, it is worth emphasizing that the transplantation of non-native fish – especially freshwater fish – can also take place at very different

88. Lévêque, *Biodiversity Dynamics and Conservation*, 321–23; Mouranche, 'Le développement', 45–49; Reinthal and Stiassny, 'Fresh-Water Fishes'.

89. Lévêque, *Biodiversity Dynamics and Conservation*, 322.

90. Crosby, *Ecological Imperialism* and *Columbian Exchange*.

91. Minard, *All Things Harmless*.

geographical scales. Unlike most microbes and terrestrial creatures, freshwater biota did not have to travel great distances to be 'exotic'. Because of the long geological isolation of many lakes, even transfers between neighbouring waters could wreak considerable ecological havoc.

Events on East Africa's great lakes offer a vivid illustration. Lake Victoria is the largest lake in the tropical world, and its fisheries have long formed an important part of the local food economy. Traditionally, its most important species was the *Tilapia esculenta*, known locally as the *ngege* (in Kenya and Uganda) or *satu* (in Tanganyika), which inhabited mainly the shallow gulfs along the shores of the lake. Lake Victoria's fisheries first drew official attention in the mid-1920s, when a rapid decline in the tilapia catch caused severe hardship in lakeside communities and threatened the breakfast plates of British settlers in the surrounding territories. The trouble started in 1905 when a Norwegian fisherman named Aarup introduced flax gill nets from Europe. At the time, extensive areas of the lake were said to be 'teeming' with tilapia, though indigenous fishermen targeted only the small proportion that ventured close to shore. At first, the new gill nets were extremely successful at capturing shoals in deeper waters; it was not uncommon for a single sixty-yard (fifty-five metre) net to catch a hundred or more fish in one night. The nets soon reportedly spread 'like wild-fire', especially in Kendu Bay and the Kavirondo Gulf, and especially after immigrant Indian boat builders began to construct a fleet of small dhows specially designed for gill-netting.[92]

For a few years, the new boats achieved record hauls within one or two miles (1.5–3 kilometres) of the lakeshore, but as catches there declined they ventured farther out on the lake. Before long, the initial catches of fifty to a hundred fish per net fell to only ten to twenty fish per net – a steep decline, but still sufficiently profitable to keep the fishery going. When catches subsequently plummeted in the mid-1920s, the governments of Kenya, Uganda and Tanganyika commissioned Michael Graham, a marine expert based at Britain's Lowestoft fisheries laboratory, to lead an investigation into the problem. Unsurprisingly, Graham concluded that overfishing was the principal cause and recommended minimum mesh sizes to mitigate it. The sponsoring governments soon passed legislation to this effect, though the pressure on tilapia stocks remained intense. This raised the question of whether different species might be introduced to compensate for the recent decline of tilapia, but Graham firmly opposed the idea because of the unknown effects that exotic introductions might have. Although such measures could, he thought, be considered in the future, he warned they would entail the 'utmost danger' without extensive prior research.[93]

Most scientists studying African lakes in this period shared Graham's caution. They rightly recognized that introducing exotic species into poorly

92. S. Worthington and Worthington, *Inland Waters of Africa*, 170–72.
93. M. Graham, *Victoria Nyanza*, 9–11, 21–23.

FIGURE 5.5. Lake Victoria Fisheries Survey, SS *Kavirondo* and African canoe at Port Victoria, 1920s.
Source: Centre for Environment, Fisheries and Aquaculture Science (Cefas) Photo Archive. Open Government License.

understood aquatic ecosystems was like opening a Pandora's Box. Yet at the same time, they were also eager to put these ecosystems to productive use.

One of them was Edgar Worthington, who in the late 1930s compiled the influential compendium *Science in Africa*, and who eventually went on to become one of world's most prominent ecologists. Worthington began his career as a member of the Lake Victoria fishing survey that was headed by Graham. After the survey was completed, he used this experience to lead two subsequent expeditions exploring East Africa's inland waters in the late 1920s and early 1930s. Worthington was one of a growing number of scientists in the colonies whose work was strongly influenced by the integrative insights of ecology, at the time a relatively new academic discipline. Rather than focusing on the discrete life cycles and habits of particular fish species such as Lake Victoria's tilapia, he was convinced that the only way to understand them was to place them within their broader biophysical context. For several years, Worthington and his team examined the interdependencies of flora, fauna and water conditions in East Africa's lakes, drawing liberally on local knowledge wherever possible. Some of his most important insights about species distinctions and food webs in fact came from African fishermen and sailors who, according to Worthington, 'probably taught us more about the fish and fisheries . . . than we were able to teach them'.[94] He also drew on the experience of his British guide

94. E. Worthington, *Ecological Century*, 8 (quote); Tilley, *Africa*, 106–7; S. Worthington and Worthington, *Inland Waters of Africa*, 141–52.

Dick Dent, a coffee planter turned fisheries warden who in the 1920s had led efforts to create new aquatic food chains as a means of supporting exotic game fish in Kenya's high mountain streams and lakes. As Worthington's knowledge of Africa's lakes grew, so too did his confidence in the capacity of applied ecology to form the basis of a new economy of nature. Eventually this knowledge made its way back to the inland waters of the metropole. When Worthington returned to Britain in the late 1930s as director of the Freshwater Biological Association of the British Empire, he deployed the know-how he had gained in Africa to reconstruct the ecology of the fish-depleted Lake Windermere.[95]

Like many of his peers, Worthington's aim was to deploy ecological knowledge for the rational management of the biophysical environment. His principle foe was the so-called 'waste' of natural resources – which, in the parlance of the time, denoted not a failure to protect resources but rather to leave them 'idle' or 'untapped'. He noted that the combined water surface of Kenya and Uganda was roughly one-fifth that of the North Sea, but that landings were no more than one-hundredth and perhaps as little as one-thousandth the size, despite the fact that biological processes were faster in warm tropical freshwaters than in cold temperate seas. 'If, then, the productivity of the tropical waters is greater, the food-supply for fish is abundant, and all the water is shallow and suitable, surely there must be a great wastage somewhere.' What struck him, in other words, was the yawning gap between the current and potential output of these waters. For Worthington, this gap presented a 'great opportunity for someone not only to catch and use the present supply of fish to the best advantage, but also to *adapt* the waters in such a way as to increase that supply and to avoid waste'.[96]

In sum, 'farming the waters' and 'turning the exuberant life of the tropics to man's account' was an alluring prospect for Africa's inland waters. For scientists such as Worthington, these lakes served as microcosms for more global ambitions to utilize ecology as a tool for environmental management. Against the background of rapid population growth in the colonies, he and his peers thought that 'stretches of productive water cannot be left unfarmed any more than stretches of good arable land'.[97] Worthington himself carried out numerous studies towards this end. One of his first jobs in East Africa in the late 1920s was to examine the effects of a proposed dam (intended to improve the control of the Nile) that would raise the level of Lake Albert by around four metres, potentially creating valuable new fishing grounds on the submerged land. Shortly afterwards he was commissioned to study the potential

95. As shown by Anker in *Imperial Ecology* (211–14).

96. S. Worthington and Worthington, *Inland Waters of Africa*, 167–68, emphasis added.

97. S. Worthington and Worthington, 169; more generally Anker, *Imperial Ecology*, 208–14.

of Uganda's other lakes to the south. In many of these smaller lakes – Bunyoni, Kachira, Nakavali – he suggested the introduction of exotic species to improve their bioeconomic utility. For larger lakes such as Edward and George, he was more cautious about such measures, and he was especially hesitant about any such tampering with Lake Victoria, whose already-stressed tilapia fishery was too important to put at risk.[98]

Yet even on Lake Victoria, there was plenty of 'waste' on display. In the deeper parts of the lake, there were enormous stocks of small and bony *Haplochromis* (cichlid) fish, which were commonly caught by local fishermen but regarded by Europeans as little more than fertilizer. As Worthington noted, 'this great untouched supply of small fish could be used in a different way if only there was a good and easily caught predacious fish to feed upon them'. Although there were some native predators in the lake (mainly catfish species), they were not generally prized as food fish, especially by Europeans in the region's urban markets. It was against this backdrop that the introduction of the non-native Nile perch (*Lates niloticus*) – an excellent food and sporting fish – was often suggested, but the risks were substantial. Although it was possible that an artificially introduced perch population would strike a natural 'balance' with its new habitat, it was equally possible that it would prey too easily on native fish, breed too rapidly, exhaust its own food supply and eventually collapse after having also wrecked Lake Victoria's existing fisheries. Scientists insisted that much more research was needed before interfering with such an important food web, so Worthington suggested running an experiment in a nearby satellite lake, Nabugabo, which had a similar fauna profile. Using Nabugabo as a kind of aquatic laboratory would, it was thought, give a fairly clear indication of how the Nile perch would affect the ecology of Lake Victoria.[99]

The very idea of running such an experiment foreshadowed a growing debate between ecologists and colonial administrators over the re-engineering of East Africa's lake ecosystems. Worthington himself expressed the basic dilemma: while insisting that 'it is impossible to over-stress caution' when transferring exotic creatures (and especially predatory species) into different environments, he also conceded that 'civilisation cannot stand still'.[100] And it did not. During the 1930s and early 1940s, as the effects of economic depression and war pushed food supplies to the top of the colonial agenda, the introduction of the Nile perch to Lake Victoria once again came in for serious consideration. At the time, nothing was done about it. But the idea never went away, and during the colonial development drive that followed the Second World War many

98. E. Worthington, *Fishing Survey* and *Fisheries of Uganda*; Anker, *Imperial Ecology*, 212.

99. S. Worthington and Worthington, *Inland Waters of Africa*, 172–74; Anker, *Imperial Ecology*, 212–13.

100. S. Worthington and Worthington, *Inland Waters of Africa*, 178.

colonial administrations in the region strongly supported it as a means of bolstering local fisheries. By contrast, the scientific community – including those at the new East African Fisheries Research Organization, founded in 1947 primarily for the purpose of studying Lake Victoria – was broadly opposed, once again citing the need for more research. As it happened, by the time they finally launched a major study of perch biology in 1959, it was already too late. The Nile perch was already breeding and spreading throughout the lake, almost certainly as the result of a furtive introduction by officials in the Uganda Game and Fisheries Department in 1954.[101]

In the ongoing disputes over ecological caution versus rapid economic development, those who advocated the latter were clearly more in tune with policymaking circles during the final years of colonial rule in East Africa (and, for that matter, after these colonies became independent). They did not, however, have the last word on the subject. For around two decades after the Nile perch had been introduced in the mid-1950s, its numbers in Lake Victoria remained low, suggesting that a kind of natural 'balance' might have been struck. Then, in the mid-1970s, the perch population suddenly exploded for reasons that are not entirely clear. By the early 1980s, the Nile perch accounted for around 80 per cent of the fish biomass in the lake.[102]

From a macroeconomic point of view, this 'Nile perch boom' was a major fillip for the region, multiplying the annual catch from a hundred thousand to half a million tons and making Lake Victoria the most productive lake fishery in the world.[103] From a social point of view the results were more mixed. While it brought greater prosperity to fish-freezing firms and traders, it made life harder for many ordinary fishermen who could not join in on the bonanza. These mixed results were directly related to the broader ecological consequences of the arrival of the Nile perch, which proved to be little short of disastrous over the long term. As the numbers of perch increased, the population of most native fish collapsed, causing a severe strain on the local artisanal fisheries that still depended on them. The small haplochromine cichlids inhabiting Lake Victoria bore the brunt of these changes. Because of the huge number of different cichlid species in the lake – more than five hundred species not found anywhere else in the world – their abrupt decline from 80 per cent of its fish biomass to merely 1 per cent in little over a decade is widely regarded as the 'greatest vertebrate mass extinction in the modern era'.[104] Moreover, the ecological fallout soon rebounded on the perch population itself by undercutting its supporting food chain. By the 1990s, overall catches on Lake Victoria

101. Pringle, 'Origins'.

102. Goudswaard, Witte and Katunzi, 'Invasion'.

103. For an excellent analysis of events from a fisherfolk perspective: Pringle, 'Local Responses and Adaptations'.

104. Baskin, 'Africa's Troubled Waters', 477.

were in marked decline, partly as a result of heavy fishing pressure and a lack of effective regulation, and partly because, as Worthington had feared sixty years earlier, the perch had eaten out much of its prey.

The colonial determination to 'farm the waters' thus left a troublesome legacy for East Africa's lakes, and for the people living around them. By the 1990s, Lake Victoria was one of the world's paradigmatic examples of ecological mismanagement. Although it was a particularly extreme example of what could go wrong when humans meddle with ecosystems that they do not fully understand, the events that unfolded there were not entirely unique among the lakes of the region. Some hundred kilometres to the north, Lake Kioga suffered a similar fate after the Nile perch was introduced there in the mid-1950s; so too did the would-be 'laboratory' Lake Nabugabo, where perch were eventually released in the early 1960s.[105] Against this backdrop, it is worth noting that not all non-native fish introductions have turned out to be so ecologically disruptive or socially controversial, including in East Africa. A more fortunate example was Lake Kivu, where Belgian authorities introduced plankton-feeding sardines (*Limnothrissa miodon*) from Lake Tanganyika in the 1950s in an attempt to 'fill' an empty pelagic niche in the lake's ecosystem. By the late 1970s, the exotic sardines had become the basis of a substantial new artisanal fishery without causing major damage to native species.[106] On balance, however, the story of East Africa's lakes offers a stark lesson in the dangers of biotic tampering. This is why an international consortium of scientists has been hard at work since the 1990s to ensure that Lake Tanganyika (the second-most-species-rich freshwater body in the world behind Lake Baikal) avoids the kind of biological mayhem that its neighbouring waters have experienced.[107]

Only time will tell if we can avoid more problems like these in the future, but one thing is already certain: for Africa's lakes and rivers, the consequences of colonial-era efforts to enhance their utility by modifying their biological makeup were irrevocable. Despite ongoing efforts to preserve threatened endemic species for possible reintroduction in the future, it is impossible to restore these aquatic ecosystems to their pre-colonial state. Indeed, because so little was known about them when they were altered, we would not even know how to do so if we could.[108]

What happened in Lake Victoria was an extreme example of unintended consequences, but in many ways the events that unfolded there exemplified

---

105. Lévêque, *Biodiversity Dynamics and Conservation*, 316; Paterson and Chapman, 'Fishing Down'.

106. De Iongh, Spliethoff and Roest, 'Impact of an Introduction'; H. Dumont, 'Tanganyika Sardine'.

107. Hall and Mills, 'Exotic Species', 120–21; Baskin, 'Africa's Troubled Waters', 478–79.

108. Courtenay, 'Biological Pollution', 40, 55; see also Kinsey, 'Seeding the Water', 551–52.

European engagements with fisheries throughout its colonial empire. For one thing, it points to the diversity of views among scientists and officials about the need to manage aquatic resources and the best ways for doing so. The disputes in East Africa over the deliberate manipulation of aquatic ecosystems were unusually intense, but they echoed arguments about how (even whether) to conserve freshwater fish stocks in colonial Asia and how best to exploit marine resources offshore. In the waters as on the land, colonial officials were united by the common goal of strengthening the imperial enterprise, but they did not agree on how this should be pursued, and their scientific conclusions did not always conform to imperial policy agendas.

Second, the very persistence of such debates reflected the decidedly patchy and precarious state of knowledge about aquatic environments in the colonies. The inaccessibility of these underwater spaces, coupled with the remarkable diversity of life they contained, made it exceedingly difficult to understand how they worked, and even more difficult to predict how different types of interference might affect them. In this respect, the fisheries of the colonial world posed some unique challenges when compared with terrestrial resources such as forests, soils or wildlife. Indeed, it seems plausible to suggest that the relative ignorance of colonial administrations about the aquatic ecosystems of conquered territories is one reason why their management became so contentious and why so little was ultimately done to preserve them.

A third key aspect of the story – one that was by no means unique to the aquatic realm – was the colonial intolerance for 'waste' and 'inefficiency', however they might be defined. If the problem in East Africa was a perceived failure to utilize the biological productivity of tropical lakes, and the problem in Asian freshwaters was the overexploitation of fish stocks by 'profligate natives', in the offshore waters of the colonies it was the inability of 'primitive' indigenous fishing techniques to capitalize on latent marine resources. In all three cases, the supposed 'waste' on display furnished a powerful rationale for intervention. The ensuing attempts by colonial authorities to introduce what they regarded as more 'rational' modes of exploitation not only enabled governments to enhance their control over aquatic resources but also allowed scientists and officials to impose their own forms of knowledge on to them.

Finally, the history of fisheries development in Europe's colonies typified the general tendency of colonial states to favour modernizing, production-oriented policies over more cautious, gradualist approaches to social and environmental transformation. Between the desire for quick results and the urge to safeguard 'traditional' ways of life or certain elements of the natural world, the former nearly always prevailed in the end, especially whenever it promised to generate more revenue. While there were always dissident voices urging restraint, the deep-seated determination to 'improve' the social and natural world through the application of science and technology ultimately prompted most colonial officials to advocate the industrialization of marine fisheries wherever possible, just as it underlay the reckless introduction of exotic species into poorly understood aquatic ecosystems. This impulse was by no means unique to Europe's colonies, and nor were its effects on aquatic life and fishing communities. In fact, as we will see in chapter 8, it provided the basic framework for developing fisheries in Asia and Africa long after the formal end of empire.

CHAPTER SIX

Water, Colonial Cities and the Civilizing Mission

AMONG THE MANY consequences of Europe's imperial expansion was the rapid growth of colonial cities. Throughout the nineteenth and early twentieth centuries, urban centres served as critical nodes in the commercial, political and cultural networks that knitted together the very fabric of empire. Like cities the world over, those in Europe's colonies performed a variety of different functions, whether as administrative capitals, seats of culture and learning, or sites of manufacture and extraction. Above all, they functioned as centres of trade, as commercial hubs that drew in goods and raw materials from surrounding areas and linked rural hinterlands with the expanding global economy. Some of the foremost cities of empire had been major urban centres for a long time (Cairo, Algiers, Delhi, Hanoi). A few had been relatively modest settlements that rose to prominence under colonial rule (Saigon, Rangoon, Bombay). Still others were wholly new colonial creations located at commercially or militarily favourable sites (Hong Kong, Singapore, Calcutta, Dakar, Léopoldville). All of them grew in size and importance as the demand for urban services increased.[1]

Water was at the heart of this urbanization boom. As colonial cities grew, so too did the task of regulating their urban metabolism: ordering their populations, providing them with basic necessities and dealing with the ever-larger volumes of waste they generated. For this to happen, it was imperative that adequate volumes of passably clean water flowed in for cooking, washing and drinking, just as ample supplies were needed to carry off the detritus from dense concentrations of human activity. Water was thus critical for maintaining public health, one of the most difficult challenges that confronted

---

1. See generally Metcalf's 'Colonial Cities'; for a long view, see Keene's 'Cities and Empires'.

municipal governments. The influx of more and more people into cramped urban spaces created ideal conditions for the spread of disease. Many colonial cities, like cities the world over, were located next to rivers or streams that served as both sources of drinking water and natural sewers. In cities where such riverine arrangements were not practical, urban residents generally drank from shallow wells and relieved themselves in communal cesspits that were often situated in close proximity to one another. The smell emanating from drainage ditches was often overpowering, and the flies that buzzed around them eventually landed in kitchens and eating areas as well. Waterborne diseases were endemic. Typhoid, dysentery and cholera were a recurrent menace, interspersed by outbreaks of malaria or yellow fever. Epidemics were frequent and took a heavy toll on the residents of colonial cities, European and non-European alike.[2]

The solutions that colonial governments adopted closely mirrored those of urban reformers in the industrial world. Indeed, many of these sanitarians travelled between the colonies and European metropoles to spread what they regarded as proper sanitation practices. Over the second half of the nineteenth century, municipal authorities in Europe and the colonial world alike built sophisticated new systems to provide clean water and piped sewerage to their rapidly growing urban populations. Though primarily designed as a means of combatting disease, the creation of sanitary infrastructures was motivated by more than just public health concerns. They also promised a range of other benefits that rulers deemed desirable. For one thing, a healthier population was a more productive population, owing to increasing life expectancy and the reduction in work absenteeism caused by illness. In addition to these economic advantages, easy access to safe water would, it was thought, also encourage better standards of personal cleanliness and thereby diminish the scourges of political radicalization and 'moral corruption' among the lower orders of society. Sanitary systems were attractive to European social elites because they provided a technical solution to the problem of public health that did not call into question the broader patterns of social and political inequality that shaped it.

The same admixture of motivations underpinned sanitary works in the colonies, though here the targets of such socio-economic improvement were defined more by race than by class. By ameliorating the living conditions that kept colonial city dwellers in a supposedly 'primitive' condition, urban reformers hoped to transform their behaviour and expectations. And by adopting new norms of water use and cleanliness, colonized peoples could elevate themselves and their surroundings into a healthier and more modern state of existence.[3] By the late nineteenth century, sanitation had come to be regarded

---

2. For overviews: Curtin, *Death by Migration*; M. Harrison, *Disease*, 89–95, 122–23; Arnold, *Imperial Medicine*; Macleod and Lewis, *Disease, Medicine, and Empire*.

3. The most wide-ranging overview remains Goubert's *Conquest of Water*.

as nothing less than an 'index of civilization'.[4] For colonial authorities, centralized urban water systems were one of the many indisputable benefits of Western progress that European rulers had a duty to share with the more backward
societies in their charge.

In practice, however, replumbing the cities of empire involved more than
just the transplantation of European technology into colonized environments.
For one thing, the creation of these water systems was shaped by the fact that
local observers did not necessarily share the colonizers' notions of what constituted cleanliness or 'filth'. Many regarded the new sanitation systems as a
solution in search of a problem; even more opposed the disruptions that they
caused to customary water- and land-use practices or the additional financial
burdens they entailed. Moreover, methods and materials that performed well
in Europe did not necessarily work in the very different biophysical conditions
of the tropics. For this very reason, new hydraulic infrastructures were often
less effective than they promised to be, and at times they created unexpected
problems in the form of disease, waterlogging or flooding. Like the irrigation
schemes, transport canals and flood defences that channelled flows of water
in the countryside, the creation of new urban waterworks was in many ways a
process of learning, negotiating and repurposing.

Despite such challenges, the construction of new sanitary infrastructures
in Europe's colonies had profound social and environmental consequences.
Wherever they were put in place, they did far more than merely bring water
in and take waste out. By displacing traditional water sources, they made
urban residents more dependent on centralized, state-controlled services.
By privileging the needs of elites and commerce (mainly but not exclusively
European), they served to rearrange urban space and reinforce the hierarchies of colonial societies. Moreover, sanitation systems connected these social
transformations in the cities with physical changes in their hinterlands. In
order to provide cities with water and remove their wastes, engineers rerouted
rivers, flooded valleys, displaced villagers and fouled watercourses well beyond
the city limits. In many respects, modern sanitation infrastructures functioned
as a kind of circulatory system, channelling the city's in-flows and out-flows
and directing its relations with the surrounding environment. The pipelines,
reservoirs and drainage canals that governed urban metabolism connected
city and countryside in ways that link their stories together. Simply put, the
modern sanitary city was no less a part of nature than its rural surroundings.[5]

Ultimately, this hydrological reordering of colonial cities reflected the
inherent contradictions of the so-called 'civilizing mission': namely, between

4. M. Harrison, *Disease*, 117.

5. The classic work on urban–rural environmental linkages is Cronon's *Nature's
Metropolis*; see also Soens et al.'s *Urbanizing Nature*; on municipal waterworks as both
infrastructure and urban environment, see Kaika's *City of Flows*.

the duty to 'uplift' and the desire to dominate. Despite the proclaimed benefits for colonial subjects, the new water systems clashed with local customs and imposed behaviours that conformed to European conceptions of civilized conduct. In spite of the promise to improve living conditions, the sanitation networks effectively bypassed much of the urban population and forced others nearby to abandon their homes or live with the wastes washed downstream. Even as the new sanitary works sought to instil what Europeans regarded as a more modern, hygienic way of life, they also helped to reinforce, even widen, the social and racial disparities that characterized colonial societies.

The Origins and Emergence of Colonial Sanitation Works

By the nineteenth century, Europeans already had a long tradition of associating tropical cities with the threat of disease. At a general level, the 'tropics' were regarded as inherently unhealthy. Despite the persistence of various acclimatization theories – which held that people and other organisms could grow accustomed to different surroundings – the notion that European bodies were poorly suited to hot climates was widespread. Mortality rates were notoriously high among white traders and troops in Asia, the Caribbean and especially West Africa, the so-called 'white man's grave'.[6] In European eyes, the intrinsic health risks posed by tropical climates were all the more dangerous in urban environments, which were viewed as veritable breeding grounds for contagious diseases. According to contemporary medical theory, fevers and illness were caused by the 'miasmas' and 'killing vapours' given off by decaying matter, and few environments were as full of noxious smells and putrefaction as colonial cities. After all, these were not only places in which large concentrations of humans and domestic animals lived; they were also places whose hot temperatures ensured the rapid decomposition of correspondingly large amounts of refuse and ordure. For European residents, the most obvious solution was to escape such contaminated spaces by moving to the outskirts of town or by regularly retreating to hill stations as a means of protecting oneself during the hottest and most malodorous months of the year.[7]

It was only around the mid-nineteenth century that colonial governments embarked on a more systematic attempt to improve hygienic conditions in the main urban centres. The measures they introduced closely paralleled contemporary efforts to improve public health in Europe itself.[8] As Europe's industrial cities grew, they too were characterized by the increasing

6. Curtin, 'White Man's Grave'.
7. On tropical disease in general: M. Harrison, *Disease*, 89–95. On hill stations: E. Jennings, *Curing the Colonizers*; Curtin, *Death by Migration*, 47–50.
8. For an overview of measures in Europe: Goubert, *Conquest of Water*, 191–208.

concentration of people into cramped spaces with poor sanitation facilities, all of which created ideal conditions for diseases such as typhoid, dysentery and tuberculosis.

In most historical accounts, the sanitation movement that swept across the Western world in the nineteenth century appears primarily a response to the problems of domestic industrialization. It is less commonly recognized that it was also a response to the problems of empire. After the 1830s, concerns about public health were turbocharged by the spread of cholera, which travelled along the trade routes created by imperial expansion in colonial Asia. Before 1817, the disease was largely confined to Bengal, but because of the displacements caused by British military campaigns in central and western India, it soon covered most of the subcontinent. From there it spread westwards along the main routes of trade and migration to cover much of Europe, unleashing a series of epidemics from the early 1830s onwards.[9]

The sudden arrival of cholera in Europe sparked panic. In many areas, it prompted the wealthy to flee the cities and the devout to declare it a form of divine punishment for moral corruption. Among cooler heads, it stimulated a flurry of research into the links between epidemics, overcrowding and the lack of sanitation, which eventually led to a raft of new interventions to address the threat. The measures adopted by municipal authorities were based on a radical new understanding of the causes of illness. For urban reformers such as Edwin Chadwick in Britain, Louis-René Villermé in France or Georg Varrentrapp in Germany, the control of disease could not be achieved by administering only to the individual body but rather by altering the social and physical environment – specifically, by allowing in more light, encouraging the circulation of air, and above all improving water supplies and drainage systems. Health was no longer merely a personal concern but a public one, a matter for the administrator and the engineer as much as for the physician.[10]

This new approach to public health was closely tied to a new understanding of water itself. Up until the late eighteenth century, scientists still regarded water much as their ancient counterparts had done, as one of the four basic elements. The working assumption was that there were many different types of water with their own inherent properties, which formed the theoretical underpinning of popular remedies such as drinking or bathing in certain waters that were reputed to have unique benefits. With the rise of modern chemistry in the late eighteenth century – and in particular with the appearance of Antoine Lavoisier's landmark *Traité élémentaire de chimie* (1789) – water was itself

9. Hamlin, *Cholera*.

10. Goubert, *Conquest of Water*, 103–15; Hamlin, *Public Health*; M. Harrison, *Disease*, 116–22; R. Evans, *Death in Hamburg*; von Simson, *Kanalisation und Städtehygiene*. On the spread of cholera and responses to it: Huber, 'Unification of the Globe'; Zeheter, *Epidemics, Empire, Environment*.

shown to be made up of two elements, hydrogen and oxygen. This new chemical definition of water as H_2O transformed it from a plural into a singular substance, one that was always the same and one whose qualities varied only in the extent to which it contained other foreign contaminants.[11]

The emergence of 'modern', chemically defined water not only helped usher in a fundamentally new understanding of matter; it also had numerous practical implications for medicine, agronomy, industry and hygiene. For urban reformers and public health experts, the recognition of a standardized definition of unadulterated water formed the basic rationale for creating centralized systems of supply and drainage. Across Britain, the Public Health Act of 1848 created new boards of health that soon set about building new reservoirs, pipelines and filtration plants after 'municipalizing' the private water companies that had hitherto supplied the growing cities. Given that human or animal waste was generally the most dangerous water contaminant, efforts to provide safe drinking water were widely accompanied by new sewage-treatment systems designed to reduce the pollution of local water supplies. Following London's 'Great Stink' of 1858, when a spell of unusually hot weather so exacerbated the stench of untreated waste in the Thames as to disrupt business in the Houses of Parliament, nose-holding legislators quickly approved a proposal by Joseph Bazalgette to build some twelve hundred miles (two thousand kilometres) of new sewage conduits under London's streets. Engineers launched similar works in Paris, where Napoleon III took a personal interest in the ideas of Chadwick and other British sanitarians. The famous renovation of Paris under Baron Haussmann in the 1850s and 1860s not only replaced crowded, hard-to-police neighbourhoods with wide boulevards and squares but also involved the construction of new aqueducts, water mains and sewers underneath them. Over the following decades, most Western cities built similar supply and sewerage systems, which broadly relied on the same engineering standards and techniques.[12]

By and large the systems worked well. Over the final third of the nineteenth century, the benefits of piped water supplies to residences and underground sewerage networks contributed to falling urban mortality rates in many cities worldwide. Ironically, it was during this very period that breakthroughs in microbiology explained why these systems worked as well as they did. When the physician John Snow first drew a clear statistical link between water,

11. On the emergence of 'modern' water: Hamlin, '"Waters" or "Water"?'. On the evolution of water analysis: Goubert, *Conquest of Water*, 35–41; Hamlin, *Science of Impurity*. On the practical implications: Graber, *Paris a besoin d'eau*; Melosi, *Sanitary City*. On knowledge-making about water more generally: Parrinello, Benson and von Hardenberg, 'Estimated Truths', 5–6.

12. Graber, *Paris a besoin d'eau*; Büschenfeld, *Flüsse und Kloaken*; Eiden, *Versorgungswirtschaft*; Hamlin, *Public Health*; Halliday, *Great Stink*; Melosi, *Sanitary City*; Goubert, *Conquest of Water*, 58–67, 191–208.

FIGURE 6.1. After the 'Great Stink'" construction of sewer tunnels in
Wick Lane, East London, 1859.
Source: Wikimedia Commons. Public domain.

sewage and cholera deaths in south London in 1854, sanitary reformers still
assumed that decaying filth and the miasmas it produced were the source of
infection. By the 1870s and 1880s, a string of discoveries by the likes of Robert
Koch and Louis Pasteur had firmly established that microorganisms were the
actual cause of communicable disease, which ushered in a new bacteriological
approach among public health experts. Fortunately for urban residents, the
water and sewage systems that had already been built were a quintessential
example of 'how bad theory can lead to good technology'.[13] Despite the fact that
the medical principles behind them were wrong, the provision of clean water
and efficient waste removal were remarkably effective at reducing disease rates.

Improving public health was not the only motivation behind the creation of new urban water systems. They also promised a number of beneficial political and cultural effects. First of all, they appealed to elites whose
concerns about disease were closely linked to fears of disorder, sedition and
insurrection. Sanitary reform had the potential to improve the lives of urban
residents and thereby quell revolutionary tendencies without entailing any
radical change to the prevailing social and economic order. Second, they
spoke to a new ethos of cleanliness among the expanding middle class in the
industrial world. Hygiene was both a public issue and a private matter. As
municipal networks grew and house connections became more common, the

13. Melosi, *Precious Commodity*, 37.

mass production of baths, washbasins, soap and even flushing toilets made such items affordable for significant segments of the urban population. From the 1860s onwards, middle-class households in Europe and North America in particular could enjoy a level of personal comfort and cleanliness that their ancestors could scarcely have imagined.[14]

Yet such standards of individual hygiene were far more achievable for some than for others. Like everything else in the Victorian city, access to water and sanitary facilities was powerfully moulded by class and privilege. 'What is it to the poor that it has been proved how cleanliness is the secret of health?' asked the cleric and social reformer Samuel Augustus Barnett in 1889. 'They cannot have the latest sanitary appliances. They cannot take baths, or have a constant change of clothing . . . The poor, by bad air, by dirt, by accident, cannot live out half their days. The good news about health which science preaches to the rich is not preached to them.'[15] For social reformers and sanitary engineers alike, spreading the gospel of hygiene among the 'great unwashed' remained a core ambition well into the twentieth century.

From early on, colonial cities were very much part of this hydrological reordering of urban centres. The overwhelmingly middle- and upper-class officials who manned the colonial administrations sought to uphold, as far as possible, what they considered to be metropolitan standards of hygiene for the European communities based there, and many regarded the provision of modern sanitation facilities to the indigenous population as a key plank of the 'civilizing mission'.

After all, existing sanitary conditions left much room for improvement (as they still did in European cities). To be sure, colonial depictions of cities in Asia and Africa can hardly be taken at face value; as a general rule, they tended to paint a grimmer picture of sanitary conditions than actually pertained. Whereas European physicians were relatively open to Asian medical practices before the 1830s (in the belief that tropical conditions warranted the adoption of at least some local conventions, even if they were never regarded as equal to Western medicine), over the following decades the emphasis gradually shifted from climatic or environmental factors to the habits of indigenous people as the main cause of disease. As a number of scholars have shown, colonial health reports were regularly based on a selective use of evidence that made extreme cases of filth appear as the norm. The portrayal of native inhabitants as unaware of basic hygiene furnished a justification for imposing colonial urban improvement plans. In the words of Nabaparna Ghosh, the 'black town' was more a formation of colonial health discourse

---

14. V. Smith, *Clean*, 279–85; Goubert, *Conquest of Water*, 82–97; M. Harrison, *Disease*, 119. For the US context: Ogle, *All the Modern Conveniences*.

15. Barnett, *The Duties of the Rich to the Poor* (1889), quoted in Smith, *Clean*, 305.

than a physical space, 'a product of symbolic geography that shaped native space as a culture of pathology'.[16]

This symbolic geography helps to explain why colonial health reports regularly brimmed with disgust and alarm at the water-use practices they described. In cities such as Batavia, Calcutta and Saigon, local residents were castigated for drawing their drinking and cooking water either from shallow wells near cesspits or from tanks and nearby rivers in which people could also be found bathing or doing their washing. According to European observers, Africans regularly drank from rivers or pools that were 'contaminated with every imaginable form of refuse'.[17] Water quality was deemed suspect even when it was regularly replenished during the rainy season, and matters only got worse in dry months. During Bombay's dry season, the city's wells reportedly became so depleted and polluted that people had to scoop it out in semi-liquid form and strain it through dirty cloths, forcing thousands 'to drink a liquid which could only be regarded as sewage'.[18] The water was purportedly no better in the city's depleted tanks, where large numbers of dead and decaying fish had to be cleared each year during the dry season.[19]

Colonial observers denounced Asian and African waste disposal arrangements in similar terms. As one sanitation engineer remarked, the prevalence of diseases was 'probably as much due to the collections of putrefying faecal matter which disfigure most Eastern towns as it is to pollution of water supplies'. British officials regularly bemoaned the 'predilection which many of the inhabitants of India show for defecating on the banks of rivers or tanks'. Along the Hooghly in Calcutta, 'the grossest pollution takes place daily, whilst a few yards away numerous people may be seen bathing, drinking water, and even drawing it for domestic use'.[20] Before sewage works were built in Bombay, the city's main drain – much of which was uncovered and had a flat gradient – was effectively 'a vast elongated cess-pool' full of 'a large quantity of putrefying sewage'. In Singapore, roadside ditches carried a mixture of rainwater, sullage and raw sewage 'into the nearest body of water available'.[21]

Faecal matter was by no means the only source of concern. In the 1860s, the *Rangoon Chronicle* complained about the 'decaying wrecks of mortality, dead dogs in an advanced stage of decomposition, putrid carcases of cats and rats' that were strewn about parts of the town. It took several years before the

16. N. Ghosh, *Hygienic City-Nation*, 27. On the exaggerations of colonial health discourse, see also: Chattopadhyay, *Representing Calcutta*, 63–68; Bissell, *Urban Design*, 149–52. On the shift of perspective from the 1830s onward: Harrison, *Climates and Constitutions*; Arnold, *Science, Technology and Medicine*, 61–63.

17. Plehn, *Die Kamerun-Küste*, 323.

18. Tulloch, *Water Supply of Bombay*, 211.

19. MacGeorge, *Ways and Works*, 446.

20. G. Williams, *Sewage Disposal in India*, 45, 215.

21. James, *Drainage Problems* (1917), 344–45, 410.

35 King St. at junction of Sackville Street - shewing fish, vegts, & other provisions exposed for sale over stagnant drains.

FIGURE 6.2. Water and hygiene problems: goods for sale over open drains, Gold Coast, 1912.
By permission of the National Archives, coll. no. CO1069/41 pt9(8).

municipal authorities ordered that 'the carcases of dead dogs, bullocks, etc., found about the streets or floating about the harbour, shall be at once disposed of, either by sinking or burying them'.[22] In Zanzibar, a Public Health Department report of 1913 grumbled:

> A primitive population is content to throw out upon the streets its refuse, and, what is more, is by no means averse to allowing it to be left there . . . Dirt, filth and rubbish of all kinds was flung on the streets, and if one went out of one's house, one was compelled to wade through a dreadful mess.[23]

Similar complaints could be heard in nearly all colonial cities. 'It is generally into the sea, or the river, or into ponds adjacent to houses that most of the refuse is thrown', noted a widely used French manual for colonial hygiene.

22. Pearn, *History of Rangoon*, 217–18.
23. Bissell, *Urban Design*, 150.

'These barbaric practices have the effect of aggravating, if not outright creating, the notorious insalubrity of the towns'.[24]

Efforts to ameliorate conditions in colonial cities accelerated from the 1850s onwards, partly owing to the growing acceptance of the links between water, sewage and disease; partly to the growth of urban trade and population (including European residents); and partly to the eagerness of sanitary engineers to replicate their schemes in both colonial and metropolitan cities.

The first proposals for new waterworks came in Bombay and Calcutta. In 1854, Bombay's chief engineer Henry Conybeare proposed a gravitation scheme to supply water for the city. The resulting Vehar project, located just north of Bombay, was similar to water projects that were built or planned for various cities in Britain. The basic concept was to capture water within an elevated reservoir, from which it entered large water pipes that conveyed it by its own gravity to where it was needed, arriving under high pressure without any need for pumping. Echoing the justifications for such systems in Europe, Conybeare emphasized not only the economic and public health benefits of such waterworks, but also the social advantages that would result from ridding the city of 'the immoral influence of filth and discomfort' and from 'teach[ing] the inhabitants the value of cleanliness and decency'.[25] The plan was quickly approved, and by 1860 the Vehar reservoir provided Bombay with eleven million gallons (fifty million litres) of water per day (around fifteen gallons, or seventy litres, per capita). As Bombay continued to grow, the Vehar project was soon followed by a series of other waterworks, most notably the gigantic Tansa scheme located some fifty miles (eighty kilometres) north-west of Bombay. At its completion in 1892, the Tansa waterworks numbered among the largest in the world, comprising a two-mile dam, a fifty-five-mile aqueduct, and twenty-seven miles of four-foot iron pipes (forty-three kilometres of 1.2-metre pipes) capable of supplying the city with an additional seventeen million gallons per day.[26]

The Tansa project was celebrated as one of the most important engineering achievements in all of India – providing what many assumed was a 'final settlement of the question of water-supply for Bombay' – but its effects on the urban waterscape also highlighted the city's acute sewage and drainage problems, which were yet to be tackled.[27] Given that less than half of Bombay Island had any drains at all, the enormous quantity of water arriving from Tansa had little place to go once it got there. Many of the drains that existed were in such poor condition that they could carry water only a short distance

24. Reynaud, *Hygiène coloniale*, 225.

25. Conybeare, *Sanitary State*, 22, appendix H, 15; Dossal, *Imperial Designs*, 95–124; 'Henry Conybeare'. For an excellent overview of gravitation schemes in Britain's colonies: Broich, 'Engineering the Empire', 353–57.

26. Deakin, *Irrigated India*, 169–75; MacGeorge, *Ways and Works*, 445–54.

27. MacGeorge, *Ways and Works*, 452.

before it spewed out again. In the absence of adequate drainage, the completion of the Tansa project effectively saturated the city, causing its numerous cesspools and sewage ditches regularly to overflow, and forcing thousands of residents to live in uncomfortable proximity to their own wastes. In response to the problem, the local government supported a major expansion of the sewer mains in the 1890s, but the system functioned poorly because of the lack of house connections and branch sewers. To make matters worse, it was also unable to handle the huge volumes of rainfall and reservoir water during the monsoon. Ironically, the provision of municipal water supplies for Bombay, a city almost entirely reclaimed from coastal marshlands, temporarily threatened to turn it back into a swamp.[28]

In contrast to the situation in Bombay, the construction of new water and drainage works for Calcutta proceeded more in tandem than in sequence. In 1854 (four years before the 'Great Stink' triggered the overhaul of London's sewage disposal system), the municipal engineer William Clark proposed a combined system of underground drainage and sewage that was designed to pump the city's wastes and run-off to the saltwater lakes east of the city, where it was thought that the exchange of tidal water through the channels that fed the lakes would wash the sewage into the Bay of Bengal. Municipal authorities approved the plan in 1859, though work was slow and patchy. It took over a decade for the system to cover even a small part of the city (the wealthiest district, where Europeans and high-caste residents lived) and to prepare the outfall site and the lakes. Even after it was completed, the combined system proved incapable of coping with floodwaters during the rainy season, which caused sewage to back up throughout the city. By the 1890s, there was little doubt that Calcutta needed separate systems of sewerage and rainwater drainage, but by that time such a fundamental overhaul of the city's unitary drainage system was deemed too expensive. Although around half of Calcutta's buildings were connected to sewers by the turn of the century, there were still hundreds of municipal and private drains around Calcutta that continued to discharge large quantities of raw sewage directly into the Hooghly River.[29]

Fortunately for Calcutta's residents, the introduction of a piped water system in 1870 mitigated some of the health risks posed by the fouling of the river. Unlike Bombay, whose hinterlands provided sufficient elevation for a gravitation scheme, Calcutta's new system drew its water from the Hooghly around eighteen miles (thirty kilometres) west of the city at Pulta, where the river was less polluted. At the Pulta site, steam engines suctioned water into a series of state-of-the-art settling tanks and sand filters before sending it to

28. Klein, 'Urban Development and Death', 739–43; James, *Drainage Problems* (1917), 344–66; Dossal, *Imperial Designs*, 125–48.

29. Davis Smith, *Report on the Drainage*; Goode, *Municipal Calcutta*, 173–78; M. Harrison, *Public Health*, 202–6.

underground reservoirs on the outskirts of the city. From there, the water was finally pumped to street hydrants or into elevated cisterns that served individual residences. No sooner was the system finished than engineers drew up plans to double its capacity from six to twelve million gallons (twenty-seven to fifty-four million litres) per day. The first expansion was completed in 1888, followed by a further overhaul of the city's reservoirs and pumping equipment in the 1900s. By 1914, Calcutta's water system delivered nearly thirty-six million gallons of filtered water per day, enough to provide each resident with around thirty-three gallons (150 litres; which, as it happens, was slightly more than Kolkata's per-capita water provision of 123 litres a full century later).[30]

As the different water systems of Bombay and Calcutta show, the construction of sanitary infrastructures was invariably shaped by a city's geography and climate. In humid, low-lying conurbations such as these, the primary challenge was not water provision but rather the evacuation of excess water without contaminating nearby sources. By contrast, in many other colonial cities the main problem was not too much water but too little. This was most obviously the case in arid or semi-arid regions such as the Maghreb, where French authorities struggled to secure adequate water supplies for Algiers after allowing parts of the older Ottoman/Algerian system of aqueducts to go to ruin.[31] But water scarcity could also be problematic even for cities with plentiful rainfall.

Such was the situation in Hong Kong, whose peculiar geography was an economic blessing but a hydrological curse. The city's location on a small island off the South China coast made it an ideal place for conducting maritime trade with the mainland, but an exceptionally difficult place to supply with fresh water. Although it received an average of around two metres of precipitation per year, most of it came between May and September in the form of sudden deluges that quickly ran off the island's rocky surface into the sea. With no perennial streams and scant groundwater on which to draw, Hong Kong became wholly dependent on seasonal water storage. Its first reservoir, completed in 1864, contained only enough water to supply the port and the wealthy western districts of the city. In 1882, the engineer Osbert Chadwick, son of the British sanitarian pioneer Edwin Chadwick, proposed a large gravitation scheme that would be capable of supplying affordable water for the entire urban population. Following his recommendation, a second reservoir was soon built at Tai Tam, high in the hills above the city. As Hong Kong continued to grow, engineers proceeded to double the reservoir's original capacity, and eventually built a third artificial lake (also at Tai Tam) twice

30. Goode, *Municipal Calcutta*, 184–211; Chakrabarti, 'Purifying the River', 186–88; M. Harrison, *Public Health*, 204–6, 216. Recent water supply figures from Deb's *Kolkata, India* (7).

31. Goubert, 'La ville'; Cutler, 'Imperial Thirst'.

as large as the first one. By the time the Tai Tam complex was completed in 1917, Hong Kong's water catchment system covered no less than a third of the entire island. Yet still the city remained short of water. During the interwar years engineers built new reservoirs on the mainland to mitigate the shortfall, but even they were incapable of guaranteeing round-the-clock supplies outside the wet season. During protracted droughts – such as occurred in 1929 and 1938 – water was available for only one hour per day, and much of that had to be brought in by boat.[32]

In contrast to the extreme measures that were adopted in Hong Kong, most colonial cities could draw their water supplies from a nearby river, an aquifer or a combination of the two. For example, Batavia's municipal network initially relied on artesian (self-pressurized) wells, whose output was supplemented after the First World War by spring water piped from the city's hinterland.[33] Saigon's initial network likewise drew from wells located just outside the city, though the rapid drop in the level of the aquifer – coupled with fears of contamination by urban surface waters due to poor sewerage provision – soon prompted officials to build settling and filtration systems for treating river water from upstream.[34] As in Saigon, Delhi's municipal scheme also transitioned from groundwater to filtered river water as the city grew, though with an intermediate stage in which engineers topped up depleted wells by diverting water from the Yamuna River into trenches dug above them, effectively using the alluvial soil as a natural filter.[35] Meanwhile, most water projects in colonial Africa were based on rivers and reservoirs. Saint-Louis, Cairo and Accra all had small river-fed supply networks before 1900, followed by Lagos in 1916, Dar-es-Salaam in the 1920s and Kumasi in the 1930s. A few cities piped their water mainly from springs, such as Nairobi and Mombasa. Even at Dakar – which, like Hong Kong, lacked a ready supply of surface water – engineers could draw on substantial groundwater sources.[36]

The water provisioning systems of colonial cities were therefore adapted to a wide range of different hydrological circumstances. What all of them had in common, however, was a failure to keep pace with the needs of their rapidly growing populations. Despite dozens of special commissions and consultants' reports, urban authorities throughout the colonial world found themselves in a perennial game of sanitary catch-up.

32. Chadwick, *Sanitary Condition*; Chu, 'Combating Nuisance', 25–26; Headrick, *Tentacles of Progress*, 148–52.

33. Kooy and Bakker, 'Splintered Networks', 1846–50.

34. Bréaudat, *Les eaux d'alimentation*, 15–17; Montel, *La ville de Saigon*, 70–78.

35. Sharan, 'From Source to Sink', 433–37.

36. Brasseur, *Le problème de l'eau*, 78–82; Afrique Occidentale française, *Le port de Dakar*, 51; Hoag, *Developing the Rivers*, 216–28; Olukoju, *Infrastructure Development*, 47–50; McCaskie, 'Water Wars in Kumasi'; Nyanchaga, *History of Water Supply*, 33–34; Kjellén, *From Public Pipes*, 98–99.

FIGURE 6.3. Urban growth and the expansion of water provisioning schemes into metropolitan hinterlands: mains pipes conveying water from Johore on the Malaysian peninsula to Singapore, 1932.
By permission of the National Archives, coll. no. CO1069/561 (65).

Developments in Rangoon offer a vivid illustration of the problem. Like most colonial cities in Asia, it had a dense and burgeoning population. From 1863 to 1881, the number of inhabitants more than doubled from 61,138 to 134,176, and continued to rise from there. Before the 1880s, Rangoon residents drew their water mainly from public or private wells, some of which were contaminated by seepage from nearby cesspits. The first attempt to improve the situation came in 1873, when city authorities arranged to cart the contents of latrines to the river. It was a meagre measure, and was criticized by municipal engineers as an inadequate solution to the problem, but as officials remarked at the time, 'it is about the best that can be introduced until the soil can be carried away in drains underground: and this cannot be accomplished until drains are constructed and there is a sufficient supply of water at hand to flush the drains frequently'. Building a new water system was therefore crucial both for supplying the city and for transporting its sewage. Two competing schemes were put forward: one to enlarge the nearby 'Royal Lakes', and one to convey water from around forty miles (sixty-four kilometres) upstream in an open canal. The latter solution was clearly preferable with respect to both quality and quantity, but it was also far more expensive. As was so often the case, city authorities opted for the cheaper alternative and began work on the Royal Lakes in 1877. After the completion of a final feeder reservoir in 1884, many thought that the project would solve Rangoon's water problem for the foreseeable future.[37]

But foresight was evidently in short supply, for the system was already overtaxed within six years. During the dry season of 1890, Rangoon was 'dangerously near a water famine', which was averted only by a fortuitously early start of the rains. The shortages were partly due to continued demographic expansion; Rangoon's population reached 180,324 in 1891 and 248,060 in 1901. They were further compounded by the additional needs of the city's new sewage system, which began operating in the central districts in 1889 and which needed large amounts of water to flush wastes out of the city. In order to keep up with the spiralling demand for water, engineers dug tube wells and drew up plans to extend the feeder reservoir at the Royal Lakes, though even optimists reckoned that such measures would only provide breathing space until 1908 at the latest. In 1904, amid fears of another acute water shortage, engineers completed a whole new reservoir at Hlawga, seventeen miles (twenty-seven kilometres) from Rangoon, which was designed to supply a future population of 650,000 with twenty-five gallons (over a hundred litres) of water per person per day. As it turned out, serious construction flaws prevented the reservoir from being filled as high as expected (and eventually caused a serious breach in 1905 that threatened the entire structure). Consequently, the waterworks at Hlawga ended up providing less than a third of the amount that had been anticipated. By the time the reservoir began operation, it was already inadequate for the city's 250,000+ people, many of whom still had no access to the municipal distribution network in any event. Despite further improvements to Rangoon's water supply after the First World War, even in the late 1930s some residents still had to get their water by boat transport, and most of the city still lay beyond the reach of its sewage system.[38]

The problems faced by colonial authorities in Rangoon mirrored those that hindered sanitary improvements in many other colonial cities. Rapid population growth posed difficult challenges that were often compounded by grinding poverty in slum areas. As we will see below, another set of difficulties stemmed from a lack of familiarity among colonial engineers with

37. Pearn, *History of Rangoon*, 228–31, 255–60, quote at 230.
38. Pearn, *History of Rangoon*, 262–74.

environmental conditions in the colonies. Yet however important these factors were, the fundamental obstacles were not demographic or environmental, but political. One of the core tenets of colonial policy was that subject territories needed to finance themselves, even as their resources and markets were used to enrich the imperial metropoles. Ultimately, the resulting budgetary constraints meant that municipal authorities never committed sufficient funds to close the yawning gap between provision and need.

Despite the inadequacies of these urban water infrastructures, in the eyes of colonial officialdom they stood as monuments to the superiority of Western technology and the benefits of European rule. At the opening ceremony for Bombay's Tansa waterworks in 1892 – hailed by some contemporaries as 'the finest town water-supply scheme in the world' – the viceroy Lord Lansdowne proclaimed to the thousands of people in attendance:

> There will not be a resident in the city, from His Excellency at Malabar Point, to the dweller in the humblest native bazaar – who will not be a gainer by what you have done. There is no result of European civilisation in India, which I look upon with more unmixed satisfaction than I do upon the great water-works, which so many of our principal cities have lately called into existence. I never look at a stand pipe in a dusty street without feeling that here at least is something which our civilisation has done for the country, and which has conferred upon it an absolutely unmixed advantage.[39]

Yet as impressive as these engineering feats were, the advantages they brought were far from 'unmixed' in the eyes of many colonial subjects. And however lofty was the rhetoric of the common good, some city dwellers benefitted from them far more than others.

Environmental Adaptation and Social Opposition

The colonial sanitation schemes of the late nineteenth and twentieth centuries were part of an increasingly widespread understanding of piped water and subterranean waste disposal as essential components of urban modernity. From a technical and environmental perspective, the basic problems they set out to solve – how to 'decontaminate' cities with large, densely packed populations of people (and often domestic animals too) – were essentially the same ones that occupied municipal governments in other parts of the world. Although the need for such systems varied greatly,[40] the networks that engineers built and the technologies on which they were based were, in principle, universally

---

39. Quoted in MacGeorge, *Ways and Works*, 453–54.

40. Water provision and night-soil collection systems in pre-industrial Japan, for instance, were remarkably effective at suppressing disease among large urban populations: Hanley, 'Urban Sanitation'.

applicable. They drew on know-how and experience that circulated around the globe. Ever since the mid-nineteenth century, sanitary experts in the colonies justified their proposals as a means of attaining what Europeans regarded as appropriate water and sewerage 'standards'. Even the notion that sanitary reform would help reduce 'immorality' and crime echoed contemporary expectations in the industrial world.[41]

Yet despite all these parallels, the understanding of colonial cities was also coloured by the conviction that they were socially and environmentally quite distinctive from cities in the West.[42] 'Those who are familiar with tropical countries recognise at once that the conditions obtaining in Oriental towns cannot be said to resemble those of Western cities', wrote the former sanitary commissioner of Bengal William Wesley Clemesha in 1910. Like many of his peers working in the colonies, he emphasized not only the challenges posed by heat and heavy seasonal rainfall, but also 'the habits of the people themselves', which displayed a 'very marked difference from those of the inhabitants of Europe'.[43] Charles Carkeet James, whose tome on sewage disposal in the 'East' served as a standard work on the subject, likewise drew a fundamental distinction between circumstances in Europe and those in tropical colonies. While it was a truism that the basic principles of waste disposal were the same everywhere, 'in the East the sanitary engineer has to confront factors peculiar to the scene of his operations, and relating to material, labour, meteorological phenomena, not to forget social and religious prejudices, sometimes of an uncommonly perplexing nature'.[44]

At one level, such claims of tropical exceptionalism were part of the more general contemporary discourse of nature, race and civilization that permeated the project of European empire. But they were more than just a reflection of colonial ideologies of hierarchy and difference; they were also rooted in the practical, concrete difficulties that regularly confronted engineers on the ground. Like many other attempts to impose new policies or technologies on the colonies, the creation of modern sanitation infrastructures was often carried out with scant regard for local social and environmental conditions. As officials sought to construct such systems in the colonial world, neither the social nor the physical environment proved as easy to manipulate as they had anticipated.

One of the main obstacles was a lack of familiarity with local climates and soils. Engineers repeatedly found that many of the techniques that they applied in Europe were out of place. During the construction of Bombay's

41. Gandy, *Fabric of Space*, 117–18; McFarlane, 'Governing the Contaminated City', 420–22, 424.

42. See Arnold, 'Pollution', 128–29.

43. Clemesha, *Sewage Disposal*, 1–2.

44. James, *Drainage Problems* (1906), vi.

Vehar waterworks, engineers followed the widely used practice of burying distribution pipes in order to protect them from seasonal temperature fluctuations. Much to their surprise, within around a decade the large mains pipe that conveyed water to the city had been 'reduced to a state of graphite' by the saline soils around Bombay. In some sections the corrosion was so severe that 'the iron can be cut like the softest lead pencil with an ordinary pen knife', forcing engineers to cut off supplies repeatedly while they carried out repairs.[45] Meanwhile, engineers at Vehar also ran into unexpected problems within the reservoir itself. Although the initial quality of the water was considered to be very good, prolonged high temperatures in the summer soon stimulated the growth of enormous algal blooms unlike any they had experienced in Britain. As water quality deteriorated to the point of being undrinkable, engineers proposed a range of solutions. Some advocated periodic emptying of the reservoir as the only way to deal with the problem. The problem was that the design had been based on British models, which lacked any mechanism for allowing a full release of the lake's contents. Others suggested the introduction of oxygenating aquatic plants to clarify sewage-laden waters, but experts warned that this would ultimately only add more plant detritus without significantly affecting the algae. Even the fish in Vehar Lake caused unanticipated difficulties. Although the water tower that fed the mains pipe was equipped with screens to prevent fish from entering the conduit, it was clear that certain species were able either to pass through the screens as fry and grow within the pipe, or get into the system through small cracks in the tower. Freshwater eels were a particular nuisance, and occasionally worked their way down the system to foul supplies in parts of the city. On one especially gruesome occasion, engineers removed a dead eel measuring 4.5 feet (1.4 metres) long and over a foot (30 centimetres) in circumference.[46]

The Vehar project was but one of many instances in which a new sanitation scheme was plagued by the unruly behaviour of unfamiliar environments. At Saint-Louis in Senegal, French engineers struggled for decades with the hydrological conditions of the region. Soon after the completion of the city's first reservoir on the Kassack floodplain in 1866, seasonal floods destroyed the dam and turned the artificial lake once again into a stream. Even after a stronger barrage was built in 1886, during the dry season the reservoir water became too brackish and polluted with organic matter to be fit to drink.[47] In Ceylon, the construction of a gravitation scheme to supply water for Colombo likewise suffered from a lack of experience with the local climate. On three separate occasions, the reservoir dam failed as the lake filled owing to cracks in the concrete and masonry caused by summer temperatures that were far

45. Tulloch, *Water Supply of Bombay*, 23.
46. Tulloch, *Water Supply of Bombay*, 24–27.
47. Ngalamulume, 'Coping with Disease', 152–57.

higher than European engineers were accustomed to.[48] In Delhi too, the use of inappropriate construction materials for water and sewage systems was a major source of headaches. Here the problem of corroded pipes and cracked drains compromised more than just the functioning of the water delivery system. It also directly threatened public health. The fact that distribution pipes were often situated near sewage lines – and occasionally even passed directly through drainage pits – meant that sewage was actually seeping into the water supply. In the 1920s and 1930s, medical officers blamed periodic increases in the incidence of cholera, typhoid and enteric fever directly on the problem of leaky pipes.[49]

In addition to the problems posed by soils and climate, engineers also singled out the built environment of colonial cities as a hindrance, especially in the poorest and most cramped districts. In colonial discourse, the figurative 'native town' was not only inherently unsanitary but also physically hard to sanitize. As Charles Carkeet James remarked in 1906, 'the ancient practice of building houses in Indian cities so close together as to be detached only in name, adds enormously to the difficulties of house-drainage'. He complained that it was difficult, and occasionally impossible, to lay pipes or drains in such confined areas, 'teeming with a dense population, the houses huddled together along narrow alleyways rather than streets'.[50] In Bombay, the city's chief medical officer T. S. Weir likewise complained that the passageways between houses were often too narrow for deploying trenching machinery or draught animals, and too filthy even for the toughest workmen: 'the work was foul to the last degree, the walls of the houses on either side being besmirched with night-soil and filth . . . and the soil saturated with sewage'. In some alleys, he contended, the conditions were so revolting that contractors struggled to recruit labourers willing to work in them, and many of those who took the jobs could tolerate the 'stench and sickening sights' for only brief periods of time.[51] Although municipal authorities across Asia and Africa launched various slum-clearance programmes following a series of plague outbreaks in the 1890s–1910s, most were concerned primarily with the improvement of ventilation and traffic circulation rather than water and sewage services.[52]

To complicate matters further, the animals that made a home in colonial cities sometimes posed additional challenges. A telling example was the water and sewage system in Hanoi, which was built in the 1890s as part of a broader effort to renovate the soon-to-be capital of the Union of Indochina as a symbol of France's *mission civilisatrice*. As in other colonial cities, the water and sewer

48. Burnett, *Colombo Waterworks*, 71–72; Broich, 'Engineering the Empire', 358.
49. Sharan, 'From Source to Sink', 441–46.
50. James, *Drainage Problems* (1906), xxviii–xxix, xxxi.
51. Quoted in Klein, 'Urban Development and Death', 742.
52. M. Harrison, *Public Health*, 184–86; see also Chhabria, *Making the Modern Slum*, 113–40; Simpson, *First Survey*, 12–43.

lines centred mainly on the city centre and wealthiest residential areas and were intended to keep them free of the filth and disease that affected other parts of the city. But the new sewer lines led to an unexpected problem: an explosion in the city's rat population. The sewers not only gave Hanoi's plague-bearing rats a perfect breeding ground devoid of predators; they also afforded the rodents direct access to the most affluent residences in the city, where they could be seen scurrying along pipes or occasionally climbing out of toilets. Amid acute fears of a plague outbreak in spring 1902, French authorities launched a major rat eradication campaign. At first, they hired municipal rat-catchers to clear out the sewers, but the low pay and horrendous working conditions soon led to walkouts and strikes. In response, the administration enlisted the help of city residents by offering a one-cent (later four-cent) bounty for every rat-tail they turned in. But if the operation succeeded in exterminating hundreds of thousands of rats, it completely failed to reduce the rat population. In fact, it led to a further growth in the number of rats. As health inspectors soon realized, some enterprising Hanoi residents were cashing in on the bounty policy by cutting the tails off live rats (so they could continue to produce more potentially lucrative offspring), smuggling rats into the city from the countryside, and even building rat farms on the outskirts of town as quasi-rat-tail factories. Eventually French authorities saw little option but to cancel the bounty system, resign themselves to living with the rats, and resort to quarantine measures to combat the plague outbreaks that swept the city over the following years.[53]

By and large, sanitary engineers regarded the environmental challenges in the colonies as technical obstacles that had to be overcome. Yet in one important respect, tropical environments also seemed to present certain natural advantages. Most nineteenth-century cities, even those with piped sewers, disposed of their wastes in a nearby water body, usually a river, a stream or an arm of the sea. As urban areas grew, this time-honoured practice inevitably caused problems for other water users, and above all for the quality of drinking water downstream. With the discovery of pathogenic waterborne bacteria in the late nineteenth century, colonial authorities became increasingly concerned about the risks to public health caused by the discharge of sewage and industrial wastes into watercourses. In some ways, these concerns reflected contemporary anxieties in Europe, where many rivers had become so polluted as to be little more than waste conduits. Yet in the ensuing debates about how to deal with the problem, it was uncertain how far European understandings of river pollution should apply in the different environmental conditions of the colonies.

India in particular witnessed far-reaching debates about the comparability of its rivers to those in Europe, and specifically about their capacity to assimilate wastes and 'self-purify'. Although small, seasonally stagnant or dry rivers

53. Vann and Clarke, *Great Hanoi Rat Hunt*; Vann, 'Building Colonial Whiteness'. On the links between animals and urban sanitation in Western cities: C. Pearson, *Dogopolis*.

were generally thought to be unhealthy, many officials dismissed the risk of pollution in large rivers as insignificant. As the *Indian Medical Gazette* remarked in 1890:

> The immense volume of water, the sparseness and distances from each other of large towns and villages situated on the big rivers, the absence of sewage works, and of factories and other sources of chemical contamination, the scouring effect of the annual inundation: these and other considerations render it almost certain that, for the present, risk to health arising from contamination of the water of our large rivers is either infinitesimal or absent; because the conditions favouring self-purification and conversion of noxious additions into innocuous compounds are so grand and effective.[54]

Five years later, E. H. Hankin, a chemical examiner for the United Provinces in northern India, argued that the combination of strong sunlight and the presence of acidic compounds in the Ganges gave the river a remarkable 'germicidal action'.[55] In the 1910s, Clemesha's work on the bacteriology of tropical water bodies drew a clear distinction between England, whose small rivers and relative lack of sunshine required waste systems to discharge only 'scientifically purified waters', and India as 'a land where purification . . . is brought about by natural agencies'.[56]

As widespread as such ideas were, not everyone was convinced by them. Indeed, many sanitarians deemed them at best complacent and at worst downright dangerous. Along the Ganges, the discharge of sewage and industrial wastes from Benares and Cawnpore was a major source of downstream contamination. So, too, was the growing stream of human and industrial detritus from the jute and paper mills that lined the Hooghly above Calcutta. To render such effluents less harmful, sanitary officials sought to introduce the latest methods of waste disposal from Europe and North America. Septic tanks, first used in Exeter in 1896, promised a simple and economical means of sewage treatment. Although mill owners in India eagerly adopted them at first, the specific models they imported proved markedly less effective at destroying pathogens in India than in Britain. In the 1910s, engineers also experimented with sewage filters, which worked by aerating waste water in order to stimulate the growth of aerobic bacteria, but these systems proved too costly for widespread use. After the First World War, two state-of-the-art 'activated sludge' facilities were installed with considerable success at Calcutta and at the steel-mill town Jamshedpur, though they too were prohibitively expensive and were not deployed elsewhere. Overall, such innovations did little to reduce the amount of sewage and

54. 'River Pollution in India'.
55. Quoted in Arnold, *Toxic Histories*, 187.
56. Clemesha, *Bacteriology of Surface Waters*, 1, 3.

industrial waste entering India's rivers. In the early 1920s, the Hooghly River Pollution Enquiry (established in 1919 to investigate the quality of Calcutta's water supply) reported that the mills and factories flanking the river were still dumping tons of pollutants into it, quite apart from the excreta and other wastes that poured in from hundreds of municipal drains in and around the city.[57]

Environmental conditions were not the only thing that hindered the introduction of new water systems in colonial cities. They also encountered widespread resentment among many of the people whom they purported to benefit. From Dakar to Cairo and from Bombay to Batavia, local townspeople often chafed against the top-down manner in which colonial authorities sought to impose their vision of the modern sanitary city.

Opposition arose on a variety of different levels. Perhaps the most common source of anger was the additional financial burden caused by new sanitation schemes. In Calcutta, indigenous leaders vociferously opposed the plan to construct the city's first reservoir and distribution network in 1867, whose costs were to be covered by a new water levy. While a minority of Western-educated patricians was in favour of the plan, most of the city's elites were sceptical about the necessity of the project and protested against the additional rates they would have to pay. In Bombay too, the commencement of the Vehar project was deeply unpopular among many townspeople. Local ratepayers were not only concerned about its exorbitant cost but also resented the idea that so much public money should be spent on a project that would be devised and operated solely by engineers with no input from those who were paying for it.[58] In both cases, such protests were brushed aside and the water schemes went ahead anyway. Over the following decades, similar objections were raised in Batavia, Singapore, Colombo, Benin City and Lagos, with broadly similar results. Occasionally, however, popular opposition to new water charges was too strong and organized to ignore. In Accra, the passage of the Gold Coast Water Works Ordinance in 1934 – which imposed water rates on urban residents who had not asked for the new system in the first place – provoked intense public protest among indigenous elites, some of whom even travelled to London to petition the colonial secretary to revoke the measure. Although some officials – including the colonial governor – recommended the abandonment of the new levy out of fear that it might lead to widespread civil disorder, the Colonial Office remained focused on the question of cost recovery, even if this required 'drastic action' to be taken against riots.[59]

57. Chakrabarti, 'Purifying the River', 197–204; Sharan, 'From Source to Sink', 448; Arnold, *Toxic Histories*, 186–87; Headrick, *Tentacles of Progress*, 158–59.

58. M. Harrison, *Public Health*, 206; Ramanna, *Western Medicine*, 97–102; Broich, 'Engineering the Empire', 361.

59. Bohman, 'Water and Sanitation Challenge', 70–75; Hoag, *Developing the Rivers*, 224–27; Yeoh, *Contesting Space*, 185–86; Acey, 'Forbidden Waters', 220; Olukoju,

The underlying problem was that most urban sanitation schemes turned water into a commodity. However altruistic the intentions might have been, they ultimately charged residents for something that used to be free (or at least less expensive). Urban water thus became a site of governance for colonial authorities, one bound up in a new structure of regulations, fees and fines that served to order and discipline municipal populations. Prior to the extension of piped water supplies, most townspeople in the colonies and metropoles alike drew their water from private or public wells that were scattered across the city. Some took the chore upon themselves; others paid a fee for the services of water-carriers. Sanitary officers regarded such water sources as a serious danger to public health and were keen to close them once municipal supplies were available. In colonial cities, locals were often unconvinced about the need to do so. Indeed, many suspected that the sealing of wells was motivated less by a concern about public health than by a desire to boost municipal revenues by denying residents access to a free resource.

Some local residents complied quite willingly with orders to close existing wells, at least initially. One of the reasons why the disputes in Accra evolved into full-scale public opposition was that residents filled in their wells only on the clear understanding that they would not subsequently be charged for piped water in view of the expense and inconvenience they had incurred in doing so. The most common response, however, was a strategy of subtle non-compliance. In Singapore, for example, many residents quietly reopened their wells soon after closing them or dug new wells to replace those they had sealed. Even in the 1910s, health officers in Singapore still railed against the existence of suspect wells throughout the city, many of which 'could not be held as otherwise than merely more or less diluted cesspools'.[60] Some people also sought to make use of the piped supply without paying for it. In Batavia, the introduction of new charges at standpipes in the 1920s led to a spike in meter tampering and other forms of 'vandalism'. In Lagos too, the extension of piped supplies to districts previously served by wells resulted in a rash of illegal connections.[61]

If the new charges for water were a prominent source of popular resentment, many of the heaviest costs fell not on the urban population but on those living in the nearby hinterlands. The creation of municipal reservoirs invariably submerged large tracts of land and often led to the displacement of people living there. To take just one example, Bombay's Vehar project was named

---

Infrastructure Development, 47–79; Kooy and Bakker, 'Splintered Networks', 1850; Broich, 'Engineering the Empire', 362–63. It is worth noting that tensions over water rates, metering and everyday water practices were also 'political' matters in Europe: see V. Taylor and Trentmann, 'Liquid Politics'.

60. Simpson, *First Survey*, 46.

61. Yeoh, *Contesting Space*, 185–90; Kooy and Bakker, 'Splintered Networks', 1849–50; Olukoju, *Infrastructure Development*.

FIGURE 6.4. Woman and child collecting water at an urban well in Bombay, c.1905.
By permission of akg-images/British Library, photo 790/1(131).

after the village that was submerged on the site. Even in cases where homes were not directly inundated, people and livestock were frequently removed from the area surrounding the new reservoirs in order to prevent their run-off from entering the lake. The construction of waterworks for Hong Kong, Singapore and Colombo all resulted in the displacement of local inhabitants living within their catchment areas. At the Iju works north of Lagos, the hand-ful of inhabitants in the catchment were allowed to stay but were prohibited from washing or bathing in the streams. Schemes that relied on groundwater rather than surface water likewise involved the displacement of people from such protective zones. For example, the Punjab government removed the entire village of Chandrawal to safeguard the new wells that supplied Delhi, and authorities in Dakar removed an African settlement 'of doubtful cleanliness' from the vicinity of the municipal wells at Hann.[62]

Yet the social frictions caused by colonial water schemes stemmed from more than just their material impacts. In some cities, especially in India, they also clashed with religious beliefs and customs. The sealing of wells in Bombay in the 1890s sparked uproar among devout Hindus, who argued that 'their scriptures enjoined the use of well water, and well water only, in connection with divers [sic] ceremonies'.[63] Zoroastrians likewise insisted that various wells had supernatural powers. New restrictions intended to safeguard water quality also collided with religious sensitivities wherever they interfered with bathing or cremation rituals. Plans to build a new waterworks at a sacred site on the banks of the Ganges near Benares even sparked widespread rioting there in 1892.[64]

The basic problem was that the provision of what Europeans regarded as clean municipal water collided with conflicting notions of 'purity'.[65] Pollution carried a double meaning in India. On the one hand, it denoted a loss of sacredness through contact with defiling substances or lower-caste people; on the other, it signified physical contamination from waste or filth that could cause disease. When sanitary officers drew up plans for Calcutta's first modern waterworks at Pulta, which were designed to provide a scientifically 'clean' supply of water free from pathogens and physical impurities, high-caste Hindus considered mechanically purified water to be undrinkable and polluted since it passed through iron pipes underneath the houses of people from lower castes and other religions. Many refused to connect their houses or even to obtain water from public standpipes since lower caste Hindus and Muslims drew water from them as well, preferring instead to rely on neighbourhood tanks. In in the early 1870s, local religious leaders debated the suitability of piped water for use in Hindu households and eventually concluded that it was appropriate for drinking and bathing but not for ritual or ceremonial purposes. Although some residents were satisfied with this distinction, many remained unconvinced.[66]

Meanwhile, the development of sewage systems ran into similar problems. The creation of a subterranean sewer network in Calcutta clashed with

62. Ribot and Lafon, *Dakar*, 122–24; Jojot, *Dakar*, 11–12; Burnett, *Colombo Waterworks*, 63–64; Singapore Municipality Waterworks, *Opening of New Works*, 14; Sharan, 'From Source to Sink', 435; Broich, 'Engineering the Empire', 358–59; Olukoju, *Infrastructure Development*, 47–49.

63. On religious protest over well closures: Masani, *Folklore of Wells*, 3–8.

64. M. Harrison, *Public Health*, 173–74; Broich, 'Engineering the Empire', 360.

65. See the classic anthropological study by Douglas: *Purity and Danger*; also Arnold's 'Pollution' (128–29).

66. Simms, *Establishment of Water-works*, 25–26, 46–51; Chakrabarti, 'Purifying the River', 193–95; N. Ghosh, *Hygienic City-Nation*, 34.

customary caste and religious practices for dealing with filth: namely, by upholding a clear physical separation between privies and living quarters in order to avoid contact between sewage and the house. Underground sewers and house connections violated this principle of physical separation by raising the possibility that sewage could pass directly underneath residential quarters. It also raised the prospect that the waste from lower-caste groups or from households of other religions would run beneath upper-caste houses, which was regarded as polluting. In response, many Calcuttans flatly refused to connect their houses to the sewer network or to allow the installation of sewerage lines underneath their private property.[67]

Such opposition was by no means confined to Calcutta. When officials in Bombay considered proposals for a new waste disposal system in the early 1870s, high-caste groups objected to the removal of night soil via sewers on the basis that the caste system already provided a satisfactory means of sanitation. In the traditional 'halalcore' system, tasks considered 'polluting' – such as the removal of human waste and other noxious materials – were carried out by lower-caste 'Dalits' who collected night soil from dry privies and carried it in baskets on their heads to various stations where it was dumped into carts that hauled it out of the city. Since the middle of the nineteenth century, British health officers had sought to 'perfect' rather than supersede this disposal system by introducing sealable iron carts to reduce the smell nuisance and by building a central sewage depot at Chinch Bunder (just west of the Victoria Docks), where the contents of the carts were washed into an underground reservoir before being piped to an outlet in the harbour at ebb tide. By the 1870s, however, officials increasingly condemned these arrangements on sanitary, financial and moral grounds. Replacing the 'sweeper' with a water conveyance system would, they argued, not only pay for itself from the money saved on wages, but would also rid the city of a public health hazard and liberate some of the most disadvantaged members of society from an unconscionably vile and undignified activity.

In his proposal for a new drainage scheme, the engineer Hector Tulloch argued that few of the native justices who sought to uphold the halalcore system 'will be able to spend half an hour in the gullies, and not one of them ten minutes in the Chinch Bunder yard without feeling sick'. The mere fact that 'hundreds of men, and women too, shall be engaged for several hours of the day in handling the very filthiest matter that can be produced, is sufficient to condemn it. . . . Can it be necessary, in this age of mechanical skill, to employ human beings in this degrading occupation?'[68] In the event, such well-meaning arguments did little to sway local opinion. Even after Bombay's new

---

67. N. Ghosh, *Hygienic City-Nation*, 26, 34.

68. Tulloch, *Water Supply of Bombay*, 13–14 and (on the halalcore system more generally) 12–17; *Report of the Special Commission on the Drainage*, vii.

drainage system was completed, it continued to rely in large part on manual night-soil removal from residences to municipal disposal sites. As was also the case in other Indian cities, high-caste and middle-class residents showed little interest in replacing the sweepers apart from the few occasions when they went on strike in search of better wages or working hours. Furthermore, the sweepers themselves, far from welcoming the introduction of new sewage facilities, actively sought to protect their livelihoods against any policies that appeared to threaten them.[69]

Local opposition, whether based on cultural or economic grievances, was often exacerbated by the shortcomings of the new sanitation systems themselves. As we have already seen, the completion of municipal waterworks by no means guaranteed a plentiful supply of clean water, especially during the dry months when supplies ran short. Many services in colonial cities delivered water for only a few hours per day, and many people in poor neighbourhoods had to walk long distances to the nearest standpipe. In Dakar, for instance, nearly the entire municipal water supply went to its port and the three thousand or so inhabitants in the European quarter, whereas African neighbourhoods were equipped with public standpipes that often supplied water only for brief periods in the morning and evening. The resulting inconvenience and uncertainty prompted many to collect rainwater in barrels or cisterns. Although such containers in some ways functioned as 'humble technologies' that supported the larger water infrastructure of the city, health officials decried them as nothing more than 'vast reservoirs of mosquitoes'. After a series of yellow fever outbreaks in the 1900s, residents were occasionally fined for storing stagnant water in their homes.[70] All throughout the colonies, such deficiencies made it even more difficult to prevent people from reopening their wells or drawing from surface waters.

Furthermore, in many colonial cities the quality of the piped water itself only added to the problem. In Singapore, residents complained about the brown colour and unpalatable taste of the municipal water supply, despite assurances from sanitary officers that it was healthy to drink.[71] Bombay's municipal supplies were, as we have seen, notorious for their offensive smell during dry spells.[72] The most telling case occurred in Cairo, where the issue of water quality grew into a major public controversy. When the Cairo Water Company shifted its intake from the Nile to deep artesian wells in 1905 (mainly on the insistence of British health experts), city residents flatly refused

69. Masselos, 'Jobs and Jobbery'; Prashad, 'Marks of Capital'; Hosagrahar, *Indigenous Modernities*, 107–9.

70. Jojot, *Dakar*, 11 ('reservoirs of mosquitoes'); Afrique Occidentale française, *Le port de Dakar*, 51; Brasseur, *Le problème de l'eau*, 76–82; Headrick, *Tentacles of Progress*, 161–62; M'Bokolo, 'Peste et société urbaine'; Rijke-Epstein, 'On Humble Technologies'.

71. Yeoh, *Contesting Space*, 178–79; Simpson, *First Survey*, 66–78, 127–34.

72. Tulloch, *Water Supply of Bombay*, 212.

to drink it. The dispute centred primarily on the unpleasant taste of the well water (caused by high levels of iron and manganese), which ordinary people had long regarded as a sign of unwholesomeness. Their objections were, however, based on more than just physical repulsion. As Shebab Ismail has shown, they also reflected a clash between different ways of 'knowing' water, the social authority that such knowledge conferred, and a growing undercurrent of resentment against the high-handed manner in which British officials sought to modernize the city. Whereas European water experts embraced an understanding of water based on chemistry and bacteriology – a form of knowing accessible only to them – city residents of nearly all social strata insisted on the common-sense importance of sensory experience as a key indicator of drinkability. For several years after the shift to artesian well supplies, health authorities sought to bridge this divide by removing the offending minerals in order to make the water more palatable for Egyptian consumers. Despite their efforts, public dissatisfaction remained so intense that the government eventually had to give up. In 1910, the Cairo Water Company was forced to revert to the Nile as its main source of supply after installing new filtration systems for treating the river's water.[73]

The story of Cairo's water dispute highlights a more general point. Indigenous opposition to new sanitary systems, whether successful (as in this case) or not, did not necessarily signal a rejection of Western science or technology per se. Indeed, Cairo residents broadly welcomed the provision of piped water throughout the city.[74] Like millions of people across the colonial world, they gladly appropriated Western technologies when they seemed to improve their lives. As historians of empire have recently emphasized, this process of selective adoption undermines assumptions of an innate incompatibility between 'modern' and 'traditional' forms of knowledge, often to the point of blurring the distinctions between them.[75] Seen in this light, local resistance against colonial water and sewerage schemes did not always – or even predominately – stem from the irreconcilability of different epistemic traditions, but rather from the way in which colonial hierarchies of power placed them in an antagonistic relationship, one in which vernacular forms of knowledge were at best ignored and at worst scorned as primitive and defective. In an age of almost unshakeable European confidence in the superiority of their own science and civilization, colonial engineers and health officials routinely dismissed local opposition to sanitation projects as evidence of the hidebound 'conservatism' of indigenous societies and their inherent aversion to change. Yet, paradoxically, this very same sense of self-assurance also convinced them that subject

73. Ismail, 'Epicures and Experts'.
74. Ismail, 36–37.
75. See, e.g., Gelvin and Green, *Global Muslims*; Seth, 'Colonial History'.

peoples would eventually overcome their 'prejudices' and embrace the self-evident benefits that European sanitary practices would bring.

Sanitation, Fragmentation, Discrimination

Water and sewage systems are major engineering works that cost a lot of money. Wherever they are undertaken, they usually represent one of the largest items of the municipal budget. Because end users are normally expected to cover the costs, the historical development of sanitation works has long been shaped by urban economic geography. When centralized water and sewage systems were first built in the industrial world, they usually started in city centres and affluent residential areas where users could most easily afford them. As economies grew and average incomes rose, they also spread to poorer neighbourhoods so that all residents eventually had access to them.

In the colonial world, the construction of sanitary infrastructures initially followed the same pattern, though the process of geographic expansion tended to stall beyond the wealthier parts of town. As more and more people migrated to the cities, a combination of low per capita incomes, official parsimony and lack of democratic input into decision-making processes meant that the swelling ranks of the urban poor had little or no access to the sanitary services that colonial authorities proudly pointed to as evidence of their enlightened benevolence. Consequently, poor neighbourhoods were relatively insanitary neighbourhoods, and insanitary neighbourhoods were mainly inhabited by those who lacked the financial means to live in healthier areas with better services. Because income differentials in colonial cities were strongly skewed according to race, class and caste, the overall effect of new waterworks was to promote or entrench patterns of residency based on colour and ethnicity.[76]

The economic geography of colonial cities thus meant that new sanitation initiatives resulted in new forms of segregation. Far from acting as social levellers, municipal water and sewerage systems instead served to widen the gap between rich and poor, rulers and ruled, local elites and subaltern groups, European and non-European. The development of urban water infrastructures physically inscribed these divisions into the fabric of colonial cities. Whereas affluent districts were provided with mains water, and increasingly were offered household sewage connections too, most poor people had to draw their water from hydrants (or from suspect tanks and nearby watercourses) and relieve themselves in latrines whose contents sometimes wound up in open drains. Despite the ongoing public health risks, it often took decades for municipal authorities even to contemplate an extension of services into poorer districts, and few ever got around to doing it. In Lagos, where residents in the outlying 'native' areas requested an expansion of the piped network

76. Headrick, *Tentacles of Progress*, 147–48.

in the 1930s, the Public Works Department was adamant that its services would remain confined within the township boundaries. It was only in the mid-1950s, in the final stages of colonial rule, that plans for such an expansion were even drawn up.[77]

It is worth emphasizing that such outcomes bore little resemblance to the original vision of urban reformers, most of whom championed sanitation works as a universal good and a means of social uplift. Nor did it necessarily reflect a deliberate policy of racial or social segregation on the part of colonial authorities. Although the physical separation of different racial groups was actively pursued in some areas – especially in the wake of malaria or plague outbreaks, and especially in colonies with large numbers of white settlers – the fragmentation of urban sanitation infrastructures was more often an unintended consequence of public health efforts rather than an intentional aim.[78] After all, the logic of colonial 'development' held that Europeans had a duty to facilitate the advancement of subject populations along the continuum of social and economic progress.

But regardless of the principles behind colonial water schemes, in practice they created new divisions within urban society, new means by which to categorize urban subjects. As understandings of germs, water and health shifted, distinctions between the hygienic and the insanitary, between the clean and the contaminated, generated new ways of differentiating the 'modern' from the 'primitive', the European from the 'native'. White residents in Colombo, noted a contemporary manual on colonial Ceylon, 'are, as a rule, careful about their sanitation and food . . . , live in the better portions of the city, and under more sanitary conditions than the other races'.[79] These links between sanitation, economic disparities and urban space did more than merely reflect the fractures of colonial societies. They also served to reinforce and 'naturalize' the racial distinctions that underpinned colonial rule.

As one might expect, the inequalities of sanitary provision contributed to disproportionately high mortality rates in deprived neighbourhoods. Although piped water supplies and sewerage helped reduce the overall incidence of waterborne diseases like cholera and dysentery, the impact of such improvements was least marked in slum areas. Given the range of different factors that influenced mortality and morbidity rates (diet, population density, migration from different disease zones, etc.) it is difficult to isolate the effect of water and sewage systems. Nonetheless, the correlations between health and urban sanitary services were strong. To cite merely one example: whereas the affluent

77. Acey, 'Space vs. Race'; Olukoju, *Infrastructure Development*.

78. See, e.g., Curtin, 'Medical Knowledge'; Parnell, 'Sanitation, Segregation'. Sanitation and racial segregation were also tightly linked in the United States: Zimring, *Clean and White*.

79. Arnold Wright, *Twentieth-Century Impressions*, 872.

South Fort district of Bombay had a death rate of 8.6 per thousand inhabitants in 1892, in the crowded neighbourhood of Kamatipura the figure rose to 46.2 per thousand. For what it is worth, the city's health officer attributed the high mortality rates in such areas to rapid population growth and the lack of sewer connections.[80] The historical data suggest that providing water without accompanying sewage works (the former commonly preceded the latter by years or even decades, largely for cost reasons) was far less beneficial than building the two networks concurrently. In some cities where piped water supplies were introduced without adequate drainage facilities – for instance, in Rangoon and Singapore – their overall effect on morbidity and mortality rates was negligible.[81]

Instead of prioritizing poor, crowded areas where the risk of epidemics was most acute, sanitary infrastructures tended to create small islands of health and cleanliness in which elite groups could isolate themselves from the perceived 'breeding grounds' of disease that surrounded them. Although this was rarely the overt intention of sanitary officials, in some places (particularly settler colonies) it was done quite deliberately. Writing in the 1970s about the South African context, Maynard Swanson famously referred to this as the 'sanitation syndrome': a situation in which a perceived (or conjured) acute health threat to whites posed by disease-carrying Africans or Asians furnished a supposedly 'scientific' rationale for segregating populations and creating separate townships.[82] In his reading of events in the Cape Colony, the origins of apartheid could be found not only in the interests and orientations of conservative, Afrikaans-speaking, rural voters (the conventional wisdom at the time) but also in the actions of professedly liberal and often well-intentioned English-speaking urbanites. Although scholars have since questioned Swanson's generalizations about the motives of health officials and his lack of attention to the ways in which non-whites participated in this discourse for their own ends, studies from across Africa and Asia have repeatedly reinforced his central point that scientific knowledge was by no means immune to underlying racist assumptions, and indeed could furnish a potent justification for racial exclusion and separation.[83]

Although it was most often in settler colonies like South Africa that the creation of new townships underpinned the racial and sanitary division of urban space, similar outcomes occasionally cropped up in areas without large white minorities. When planning the construction of New Delhi (following

80. Ramasubban and Crook, 'Spatial Patterns of Health', 146–47. On cholera and mortality rates in India more generally: Arnold, *Colonizing the Body*, 165–68.

81. Pearn, *History of Rangoon*, 261; Simpson, *First Survey*, 43–44; Yeoh, *Contesting Space*, 189–90.

82. Swanson, 'Sanitation Syndrome'.

83. For insightful reassessments: Epprecht, 'Native Village Debate'; Rijke-Epstein, 'Politics of Filth'.

the 1911 decision to move the capital of British India from Calcutta), British officials initially envisaged a reorganization of water supply and sewerage for the entire municipal area, including the old walled city and its suburbs. But the government of India refused the requisite funding, which meant that New Delhi was instead designed as a completely separate enclave, a beacon of Western progress and civility replete with its own up-to-date water and sewage systems. Even after the capital was formally dedicated in 1931, New Delhi continued to be the chief focus of municipal improvement efforts, despite the fact that it was already much better served than the older parts of the city. Meanwhile, Old Delhi, as it was now called, was relegated to the status of an 'oriental town' without modern water and drainage facilities.[84] The old city of Rabat in Morocco met a similar fate. Here, Résident Général Louis-Hubert Lyautey and his urban planner Henri Prost were determined to preserve the picturesque 'native city' after moving the administrative centre of the protectorate from Fes to Rabat in 1912. The result was a sharply bifurcated urban landscape that separated the indigenous population in the old town from the modern and distinctly 'French' *ville nouvelle* that was built beside it.[85]

Such a conscious infrastructural segregation of urban space did not require the construction of a whole new town, but could just as easily proceed within an existing city. Batavia furnishes a telling example. Before the 1920s, its municipal water network was expressly designed to serve only those residents – mostly Europeans and indigenous elites with a European education – whom Dutch authorities deemed capable of appreciating the value of a hygienic water supply. By contrast, most of the indigenous population was left to rely on untreated surface water for drinking and washing purposes, which in the eyes of officialdom merely affirmed their 'insensitivity to cleanliness and order'. Once established, this categorization of the urban population into the modern and the primitive provided the framework within which the city's sanitary infrastructure developed over the following decades. Despite the rise of 'Ethical Policy' in the Dutch East Indies at the turn of the twentieth century (which emphasized the well-being of the indigenous population as the central moral duty of the colonial government), the expansion of Batavia's piped water network in the 1920s served to reinforce the original inequities of the system. Whereas the European quarter increasingly got house connections as a matter of course, indigenous communities were furnished only with hydrants. Officials expressly justified this decision as an appropriately gradual means of guiding the people towards a more 'civilized' way of life rather than forcing too much change at once. Following the contemporary logic of 'social evolution', neighbourhood hydrants represented a sort of transitional technology that the indigenous population would eventually grow out of at some point in the

84. Prashad, 'Technology of Sanitation', 123–25; Sharan, *In the City*, 22–65.
85. Abu-Lughod, *Rabat*.

future. Although Dutch authorities soon extended household connections into a handful of indigenous neighbourhoods (mainly those near the affluent city centre), even this improvement served to uphold existing social hierarchies by driving poor residents out to the peri-urban fringes. Better sanitation facilities led to higher rents, and as rents increased such districts steadily became a gentrified preserve for the minority of well-off, middle-class Indonesians who could afford to live there. Water provision thus served not only to distinguish Europeans from non-Europeans but also to accentuate the fissures within colonized societies themselves.[86]

This conceptual separation of colonial cities into modern and unmodern spaces illustrates how urban sanitation systems were shaped by a complex interaction of cultural, economic, and environmental factors. All throughout the colonial world, the inequitable expansion of water and sewerage utilities reflected not only funding shortages or technical difficulties but also contemporary ideologies of race and social development. Wherever municipal authorities replaced older water and sanitation arrangements with more 'modern' systems, they justified it on the basis of superior medical and engineering knowledge. In the event, however, the actual measures they implemented were based as much on notions of racial and civilizational difference as on strictly scientific principles.

The general hope – indeed, expectation – among colonial officials was that indigenous subjects would, in time, eventually embrace more 'modern' sanitary habits. The attempt to educate or discipline people into adopting such behaviours constituted a form of what has colourfully been called 'excremental colonialism'.[87] Yet this developmentalist assumption was always tempered by doubts about the suitability of new water technologies for 'native' peoples. It was often claimed that Asians and Africans had relatively modest needs for piped water in view of their low hygiene standards. Writing in 1893, Alfred Deakin deemed it perfectly natural that Bombay's waterworks provided only around a third as much water per capita (thirty-two gallons, or 145 litres, per day) as Melbourne's (ninety-two gallons per day). Whereas thirty-two gallons represented only a 'reasonable supply for Europeans', he thought it was 'magnificently lavish for natives' and would more than suffice 'for some years to come'.[88] Such assumptions frequently provided a justification for the grossly unequal distribution of water among different urban populations. In the 1910s, when officials in Batavia began to plan for the enlargement of the city's network, they openly argued that 'natives had less need' for piped supplies, owing to their habit of drinking from nearby surface waters. The new system

86. Kooy and Bakker, 'Splintered Networks', 1848–50; '(Post)Colonial Pipes', 67–75.
87. W. Anderson, 'Excremental Colonialism'; see also *Colonial Pathologies*.
88. Deakin, *Irrigated India*, 175.

that took shape after the First World War was accordingly designed to deliver 140 litres per day to 90 per cent of the city's European households, but merely 65 litres per day to only 33 per cent of native residents. As a result, in 1929 Europeans constituted only 7 percent of Batavia's population but consumed 78 per cent of its residential water supply.[89]

Even after local people made the transition to piped water, municipal officers often fretted about their 'carelessness', 'wasteful tendencies', and ignorance of modern technologies. 'The Asiatic consumer is no economist of what costs him nothing,' remarked the Singapore commissioner Alex Gentle in 1900. If subjected only to a fixed rate for water, 'he proceeds to build a bathing tank and use or waste water as he can, by way of getting the value of his money out of the Municipality'. Here, as in other colonial cities, such concerns focused mainly on crowded tenements where tenants were accused of making a 'prodigal misuse' of water, above all by furtively providing for multiple residences or 'supplying the water of 30 to 40 coolie lodgers' from a single tap.[90] The preferred solution was usually compulsory metering, which officials regarded as a means of educating locals in the true value of hygienic water supplies.

Colonial stereotypes of the backward and careless native were perhaps even more evident when it came to the problems of urban waste disposal. 'History shews that the evil effects of neglecting to remove the excremental and putrescible organic matter that tends to collect in the neighbourhood of any group of human habitations . . . are extremely difficult to impress upon minds not trained in the principles of modern sanitary science', noted a 1924 manual on sewage disposal in tropical colonies.[91] When debating the construction of sewage works in colonial Asia, British officials often questioned whether European water-carriage systems were either technically or culturally appropriate. One problem that sceptics cited was the lack of sufficient water in the dry season, which prompted many health officials to prefer the latrine-based 'dry conservancy' system. But it was also widely thought that water closets were too novel and culturally exotic to gain acceptance among the bulk of indigenous residents, at least apart from the 'better class of Native houses'.[92] As the sanitary commissioner for Bengal put it in 1869, 'a water-closet is or rather will be an altogether new thing to a Bengalee; and we all know what this means. He won't like it; and he won't take to it if it can be avoided'.[93] Furthermore, officials worried that people would use water closets to flush away all manner of unsuitable

89. Kooy and Bakker, '(Post)Colonial Pipes', 75.

90. Quoted in Yeoh, *Contesting Space*, 187–88.

91. G. Williams, *Sewage Disposal in India*, 1; see also Prashad, 'Technology of Sanitation', 124.

92. *Report of the Special Commission on the Drainage*, viii, 72, 82 (quote); James, *Drainage Problems* (1917), 1–3; Mann, 'Delhi's Belly', 13–14; Klein, 'Urban Development and Death', 741.

93. David Smith, *Report on the Drainage*, 84.

materials. Such assumptions lingered for decades. In Singapore, doubts about the ability of locals to manage the water-closet system delayed the transition from manual night-soil collection to piped sewerage until well after the First World War. 'Water-closets have been recognised by those best fitted to judge, as being the most advantageous form of privy possible for an educated and civilized community,' remarked the city's municipal health officer in 1890. The chief obstacle in his view was that 'our populace is neither fitted, nor even likely to be fitted, to be trusted with such a system, especially considering the grave dangers of an inefficient water-closet, dangers greater than those of our non-system'.[94]

Although such arguments were a blatant means of discriminating against non-European city dwellers, it is important to recognize that it was not only the colonizers who deployed them in debates about urban waterworks. Occasionally indigenous people themselves – especially urban elites – appropriated and repurposed them for their own ends. Two examples can serve to illustrate the kinds of motives and tactics that were involved. The first occurred in Hong Kong, where Chinese landlords adopted the rhetoric of innate cultural difference to challenge the application of European water-provision norms in parts of the city. In 1879, a property developer named Li Tak-cheong submitted an application to build seventy-nine houses on the new waterfront promenade that the government had recently reclaimed from the sea. After studying the plans, the surveyor general rejected them because the proposed dwellings lacked any water fixtures or privies and would therefore become, in his words, 'the most aggravated type of fever-den'. In response, Li organized a petition with other Chinese landlords to refute the surveyor general's arguments, claiming that Chinese people fundamentally differed from Europeans in their sanitary practices and ways of life. Given that crowded, back-to-back housing had long been common in Chinese cities, where epidemics were relatively rare, they contended that it was erroneous to apply Western notions of sanitation to Chinese residents. Of course, the primary aim of the petitioners was not to defend the rights of poor Chinese tenants to live as they wished, but to advance the economic interests of a small group of wealthy property owners. Yet their arguments nonetheless show how the discourse of racial and cultural difference could be co-opted in various ways, in this case to undercut the sanitary provisions dictated by 'Western science'.[95]

The second example, from Calcutta, highlights how the colonial discourse of water and sanitation could be appropriated by indigenous elites to

94. Yeoh, *Contesting Space*, 194, 205.

95. Chu, 'Combating Nuisance', 22–25, quote at 23. It is worth noting that in the early 1900s Chinese landlords conversely argued – successfully – for an understanding of clean water as a universal good when colonial administrators threatened to disconnect crowded tenements from the municipal network (Chu, 25–30). In northwest Madagascar, local residents also adapted colonial sanitary discourses to suit their own concerns – namely, as a means of distinguishing between different ethnic groups: Rijke-Epstein, 'Politics of Filth'.

demarcate themselves from other communities and to bolster their own power and prestige. As we saw above, high-caste Hindus in the city broadly resisted the construction of piped water networks and subterranean sewers in the late nineteenth century as a form of pollution. Over the following decades, as large numbers of lower-caste and non-Hindu villagers migrated to the city, many high-caste Hindus became increasingly concerned about the informal settlements, or 'bustees', that were springing up on the outskirts of town or on vacant plots of land adjacent to their own neighbourhoods. As the process of urban migration accelerated in the 1910s and 1920s, the wealthy and often Western-educated professionals living in higher-caste areas adopted the colonial trope of the filthy and insanitary 'black town' to describe the disorderly settlements that bordered on their own quarters. Deploying the colonial discourse of sanitary difference was a means of self-empowerment, indeed in two ways. First, it enabled them to reinforce their self-distinction from the lower castes and to undermine the colonial depiction of all Indian neighbourhoods as insanitary spaces. Second, it provided a justification for sanitizing the bustees by imposing their own Hindu hygienic practices on the lower-caste and Muslim residents living there. During the interwar years, the campaigns of higher-caste educated Hindus to clean up Calcutta's slums effectively promised a range of sanitary improvements (including better water and sewerage provisions) in exchange for a readiness on the part of the slum dwellers to refrain from habits that were regarded as non-Hindu, such as the consumption of meat or alcohol. Altogether, it was a classic illustration of an 'indigenous modernity', a selective fusion of European ideas and local customs that emerged from the continuous exchanges across the racial divides of colonial cities.[96]

As these examples indicate, Asian and African appropriations of Western ideas of water, sanitation and health were multifaceted and complex. They defied simple binaries such as acceptance versus opposition, and they transcended neat distinctions between the 'modern' and 'traditional', the European and non-European. Reordering the water and waste flows of colonial cities was in some respects a shared enterprise between colonial and local elites, a process of negotiation, contestation and partially overlapping interests.

In the end, these continuous debates about water use, culturally appropriate waste-management practices and their implications for urban improvement plans dragged on for decades and were never fully resolved during the colonial period. All across colonial Asia and Africa, disagreements about new water or sewage systems and disputes about what constituted appropriate sanitation technologies for indigenous people delayed, limited or redefined

96. This paragraph is based on N. Ghosh's *Hygienic City-Nation* (154–85). On 'indigenous modernities': Hosagrahar, *Indigenous Modernities*; Chopra, *Joint Enterprise*; Burton, 'Introduction'.

FIGURE 6.5. 'Native' latrine in Semarang, Java, undated.
By permission of the Nationaal Museum van Wereldculturen, coll.
no. TM-10010442.

the urban water infrastructures that colonial engineers sought to install. Even in the twilight years of empire, the bulk of African and Asian city dwellers still had little access to piped water and sewerage facilities. As a result, they had little choice but to adopt behaviours that urban administrators condemned as a nuisance to public health and a cause of environmental degradation, and that colonial rulers could simultaneously point to as evidence that subject peoples were not yet sufficiently 'civilized' to govern themselves.

The overall result was a glaring incongruity between the symbolic importance that was attached to new water and waste-disposal systems as hallmarks of a civilized way of life and the practical failure to translate it into a more universal reality. In short, poor urban residents were admonished for their unhygienic habits while simultaneously being denied easy access to the facilities that would enable them to abandon such practices. As Awadhendra Sharan has eloquently put it, 'infrastructure in the colonial city, it may be suggested, operated most powerfully in the symbolic realm, gesturing to an imminent modernity, even as that modernity was endlessly deferred'.[97] As we will see in chapter 8, poor urban residents in many parts of the post-colonial world are still waiting for it today.

97. Sharan, 'In the City', 4906.

CHAPTER SEVEN

Water and Energy

THE DEVELOPMENT OF COLONIAL HYDROPOWER

IN NOVEMBER 1907, WHILE on a tour of Africa, the youthful Winston Churchill, then under-secretary of state for the colonies, paid a visit to the spot where the waters of Lake Victoria spilled down a rocky cascade to become the White Nile. As he later recorded in his 1908 travelogue *My African Journey*, he was captivated by the sheer beauty of the place: 'At your very feet, literally a yard away, a vast green slope of water races downward. Below are foaming rapids, fringed by splendid trees, and pools from which great fish leap continually in the sunlight'. Yet what interested him most about the falls was not their scenic grandeur, but rather the practical uses to which they might be put. 'It would be perfectly easy', he surmised, 'to harness the whole river and let the Nile begin its long and beneficent journey to the sea by leaping through a turbine'. He reckoned that 'nowhere else in the world could so enormous a mass of water be held up by so little masonry', since it would require only two or three short dams linking the rocky islands of the falls to raise the level of the entire 150,000-square-mile (390-thousand-square-kilometre) Lake Victoria. 'We must have spent three hours watching the waters and revolving plans to harness and bridle them. So much power running to waste, such a coign of vantage unoccupied, such a lever to control the natural forces of Africa ungripped, cannot but vex and stimulate imagination'.[1]

Churchill was merely the first of many to be tantalized by the power-generating potential of the site. It caught the attention of British engineers shortly after the First World War, and in the 1930s it was formally surveyed for a hydropower scheme. Eventually, after the Second World War, concrete

---

1. Churchill, *My African Journey*, 120, 132–33.

plans were at last drawn up to capture the energy of the falls.[2] In 1954, during Churchill's second term as prime minister, his vision from 1907 finally came true. With the completion of the Owen Falls Dam, Uganda got its first major electrical plant, and Lake Victoria became the world's largest reservoir. At the inauguration of the dam on 29 April, Queen Elizabeth II celebrated it as a work 'of greatest importance to the future welfare of all dwellers in the Nile Valley', one that would 'enable the peoples – and above all the African people – to advance'. Shortly after the ceremony, she sent a message to the prime minister reminding him of the prophetic remarks he had made nearly half a century earlier.[3]

The events at Owen Falls are a reminder that Europe's colonial empire, like all social and political organizations, relied on the capture of energy and its conversion into various types of action. This is well understood by historians, but unlike the young Churchill, we seldom focus on water flows as a key ingredient in the imperial energy mix. For good reason, the conventional historical wisdom is that Europe's global supremacy was built on fossil fuels. After all, it was only the massive exploitation of coal that first allowed parts of Europe and North America to escape the age-old constraints of the so-called solar energy regime.[4] Over the first half of the nineteenth century, the windfall provided by millions of years of fossilized, concentrated solar energy enabled these societies to achieve otherwise unattainable levels of economic growth, which in turn helped open up a vast power differential between the industrial and non-industrial world.[5] Over the following decades, coal powered the ships and railways that extended Europe's military and economic clout throughout the tropics. By the turn of the century, the rise of petroleum furnished industrial societies with yet another energy windfall. The struggle for control over oil flows profoundly shaped the geography of European power in the early 1900s and became a key strategic priority during the two world wars.[6] From an energy perspective, the history of Europe's modern empire can in many ways be read as an overlapping progression from 'coalonialism' to 'oil imperialism'.[7]

2. Clerk and Gibson, *Water-Power*, 22; Wilson, *Owen Falls*, 2; Elkan and Wilson, 'Owen Falls Hydro-electric Project', 388; Shamir, 'Head-Hunters'; Hoag, *Developing the Rivers*, 151–52.

3. Quoted in 'The Queen at Owen Falls', *Times*, 30 April 1954.

4. See Malm, *Fossil Capital*; Sieferle, *Subterranean Forest*; Crosby, *Children of the Sun*; Smil, *Energy in World History*.

5. Pomeranz, *Great Divergence*; Wrigley, *Continuity, Chance, and Change*, 68–97.

6. Mitchell, *Carbon Democracy*; Podobnik, *Global Energy Shifts*, 49–57, 68–91; Ross, *Ecology and Power*, 199–236.

7. The term 'coalonialism' is taken from Barak's *Powering Empire* (3–5). See also Fischer, *Oil Imperialism*; Galpern, *Money, Oil, and Empire*; Shutzer, 'Energy' and 'Subterranean Properties'; de la Tramerye, *La lutte mondiale*; Zischka, *La guerre secrète*. On oil, decolonization and claims of sovereignty, see Shutzer's 'Oil, Money and Decolonization'.

Credible though it is, this fossil-fuelled narrative of imperial history none-theless omits some important aspects of the story. Most notably, it margin-alizes the dramatic expansion of electricity, arguably the most crucial tech-nology of the twentieth century. Even though the rise of electricity broadly coincided with the high point of Europe's global reach, historians have paid comparatively little attention to the links between imperial power and elec-trical power. One possible reason for this neglect is that electricity is not a source of energy but merely a form of it, indeed one that is often derived from burning coal, oil or natural gas. Another explanation is that it did not number among the various technologies of conquest – steamboats, railways, breech-loaders, quinine – that enabled Europeans to control territories that had previously repelled their advances.[8] A third factor is that colonial states were generally slow to encourage the spread of electricity and spent far less money on electrical infrastructures than on canals, irrigation systems and rail-ways.[9] But regardless of the reason, it is worth noting that electricity originally came to much of the Global South as part of the 'new imperialism', and that its early development was therefore marked by colonial interests and dynamics.

Water played a central role in this story, for nearly all forms of electricity generation (apart from wind and solar) rely on water in some form or another. Obviously, hydroelectric plants depend directly on flowing water as their 'fuel', and often involve radical modifications of the hydrosphere to optimize their ability to capture its energy. Less obviously, thermal plants powered by coal or other solid fuels also require large amounts of water for their steam-driven turbines and cooling systems. Wherever water supplies are a problem, so too are electricity supplies.[10] For this reason, the process of electrification inevi-tably created a new set of linkages between water, people, capital and technol-ogy, a tightly interlocking set of arrangements that historians increasingly like to conceive as an 'envirotechnical' system.[11] Wherever rivers are plentiful but fossil fuels are not – as was the case throughout much of the colonial world – these arrangements usually entail the damming and diversion of water flows.

Hydroelectric energy thus became an important source of imperial power, and not just in the physical sense of the term. It also enhanced the control of colonial states over people, territory and nature itself. On a practical level,

8. Headrick, *Tools of Empire*.

9. As Elizabeth Chatterjee has recently emphasized, throughout most of Asia the expansion of electrical grids and electricity consumption was driven mainly by post-colonial states: E. Chatterjee, 'Asian Anthropocene' and 'Climate of Scarcity'.

10. According to a 2018 study by the World Resources Institute, the biggest threat to thermal electricity generation in many parts of the world comes not from renewable energy competitors but from drought and water stress: Astesiano et al. 'Water Stress'.

11. See esp. Pritchard (*Confluence*, 19), who defines envirotechnical systems as 'inextri-cably embedded environments and technologies that continually reshape individual parts of the system and the whole'.

it provided a more efficient means of processing raw materials into sale-able goods: cotton into fabric, cane into sugar and mineral ores into metals. On a spatial level, it allowed colonial cities and industries to tap the energy resources of previously remote hinterlands, while at the same time binding them more tightly into long-distance imperial networks of trade and information. On a symbolic level, hydroelectric dams served as emblems of 'science' and 'pro-gress', artefacts of cutting-edge technology that promised to modernize suppos-edly 'backward' economies and societies. As things turned out, the expansion of hydropower brought much more than light and advancement to colonized societies. By primarily serving the needs of elites and commerce, it also created new forms of social and racial exclusion. By making it easier to extract mineral and agricultural resources, it reinforced the subservience of colonial econo-mies to metropolitan interests. By blocking rivers and altering their natural rhythms, it wrecked ecosystems and livelihoods throughout the affected flood-plains. For good and ill, millions of people in the post-colonial world are still living with the consequences.

The Roots and Rise of Colonial Hydropower

Despite their modernist aura, hydroelectric dams have an ancient genealogy. For thousands of years, people have used various technologies to convert the energy of flowing water into kinetic energy. In ancient Sumer, Egypt and India, water-wheels driven by river currents were used to lift water into irrigation ditches. Throughout the Roman Empire they were used to crush grain, and by the first century CE Chinese craftsmen were building waterwheels for forging and ham-mering iron. As the technology gradually spread, so too did the range of tasks to which it was applied. By the eleventh century, thousands of waterwheels across Europe and the Islamic world were used for pulping fibres, working leather, crushing mineral ores, forging steel, sawing wood, grinding grain and pumping water from mines.[12] Centuries of improvement to waterwheel design eventu-ally made them so versatile and efficient as to be capable of competing with the steam engine well into the industrial era. Even in Britain, whose abundant coal and meagre hydropower resources encouraged a particularly swift and deci-sive shift to coal, water nonetheless remained an important source of power throughout the nineteenth century. Although steam engines overtook water-wheels by the 1830s, industrial water use in Britain actually peaked in absolute terms in the 1870s. Meanwhile, in parts of Europe and North America where mechanical water power was more abundant, many industries relied on it as their principal energy source well into the early twentieth century.[13]

12. See generally Schnitter, *History of Dams*, chapters 1–5; N. Smith, *Man and Water*.

13. Kander, Malanima and Warde, *Power to the People*, 154–55, 271–72; Steinberg, *Nature Incorporated*; Reynolds, *Stronger than a Hundred*; Hunter, *Waterpower*.

The persistence of water power in the industrial era was based on two key technological innovations. The first was the development of compact, enclosed water turbines in the 1820s and 1830s. The main drawback with the traditional waterwheel was its size, which limited the rate of flow and the amount of 'head', or gravitational water pressure, that it could harness. Turbines were not only more versatile because of their small size; they also made it possible to exploit high-pressure flows at waterfalls, at the base of barrages or through feeder pipes placed at steep inclines. By the mid-nineteenth century, water turbines were widely used in Europe and North America to power machinery via belts, gears and crankshafts.[14]

The second vital innovation was electricity, for the spread of turbines per se did nothing to address the other main shortcoming of mechanical hydropower – namely, its geographic inflexibility. Like traditional waterwheels, the inseparability of turbines from rivers or streams meant that the mills or factories that relied on them often had to be located in remote areas far from population centres and transport hubs. It also meant that some of the most promising locations for deploying water turbines remained unexploited because they were simply too isolated to serve as industrial sites. The advent of electricity in the late nineteenth century completely revolutionized the geography of water power. The ability to transmit energy over sizeable distances made it possible to consume water power far away from the site of production. This newfound portability of water energy shattered the economic and spatial constraints that had previously limited its scope, opening a whole new horizon of water resources that had previously been too remote to be developed.[15]

All across the industrial world, hydroelectricity spread rapidly in the late nineteenth and early twentieth centuries. In 1882, just one month after Thomas Edison lit up parts of New York City with a coal-fired plant, the first commercial hydroelectric installation powered a paper mill in Appleton, Wisconsin. By 1886, there were fifty hydroelectric plants throughout the United States and Canada, and by 1890 there were over two hundred in the United States alone. Hydroelectricity stations simultaneously sprang up in the Alps and along the mountain ranges of Scandinavia, mainly for powering industrial or metallurgical plants. The big breakthrough came in the 1890s with the emergence of alternating-current systems capable of efficiently transmitting electricity over distances as great as two hundred kilometres. The completion of the Niagara Falls plant in 1895 in some ways marked the coming of age of large-scale hydroelectric generation. The first installation at Niagara not only generated an unprecedented fifteen thousand horsepower (eleven thousand kilowatts), but also sent a portion of its power to the city of Buffalo some twenty miles

14. Viollet, 'Water Wheel to Turbines', 572–76.
15. On the spatial implications of hydroelectricity, see C. Jones's *Routes of Power* (161–94, esp. 161–64), Parrinello's 'Systems of Power' and R. White's *Organic Machine* (13).

away. By the early twentieth century, 'white coal' (as hydropower was often called at the time) was increasingly hailed as a practical, even preferable, alternative to fossil fuels. 'Among all the great innovations of this last half-century so prodigiously rich in discoveries', exclaimed one observer, 'white coal is one whose success has been most rapid and most universal'.[16]

The enthusiasm for hydropower was based on its promise to solve a whole range of economic and social problems. Anxieties about the exhaustion of finite energy supplies had nagged European leaders ever since William Stanley Jevons penned his tome *The Coal Question* in 1865, and the increasing reliance on petroleum in the early twentieth century did little to assuage such concerns. Amid growing fears about future energy shortages, hydropower offered the prospect of an inexhaustible energy supply. For countries that wished to industrialize but lacked significant coal deposits, hydropower was regarded as the key to revolutionizing their economies.[17] At the same time, it also presented itself as a clean, hygienic, 'modern' alternative to fossil fuels, one that produced no soot or grime and that consequently would reduce the burden of air pollution in industrial areas. Hydropower supporters even celebrated it as a remedy for the labour disputes that periodically interrupted coal supplies. Unlike mines, hydroelectric stations required only a small number of employees under centralized supervision, which presented little opportunity for political organization or strike action. Finally, it was widely thought that the spatial distribution of hydropower could help level out the inequities of economic geography. For isolated rural regions, and especially for hard-to-reach mountainous areas, it offered a means of developing their economies without the need for costly coal imports.[18] In this respect, the colonies of Asia and Africa seemed like a promising forum for the expansion of hydroelectricity. In an age in which economic development was a cornerstone of colonial policy, the mighty water flows of Europe's tropical empire beckoned as a resource to be exploited.

It did not take long for hydroelectricity to spread within Europe's colonies as well. Just as in the industrial world, it initially began with small-scale installations that serviced isolated enclaves of electrification. In India, the first hydropower facility was the Sidrabong power station in Darjeeling, built in 1896 to supply electricity to nearby tea plantations. The following year, Africa's first hydroelectric installation supplied parts of Cape Town from the Woodhead Reservoir on Table Mountain. In Malaysia, the first hydropower plant was built by an Australian mining company in 1900, followed five years later by

---

16. Cavaillès, *La houille blanche*, 214 (quote); see also T. Hughes, *Networks of Power*, 132–39, 264–65; Jakobsson, 'Industrialization of Rivers'; Landry, 'Europe's Battery', 50–69.

17. See, e.g., Montaño, *Electrifying Mexico*.

18. Cavaillès, *La houille blanche*, 212–13, 215; P. Lewis, *Romance of Water-Power*, 115–17; Lehmann, 'Infinite Power', 79–80.

a small hydroelectric station nineteen kilometres north-east of Kuala Lumpur. Hydroelectric generators soon appeared on neighbouring Java, mainly for powering Dutch sugar and tea factories. In East Africa, a hydropower plant on the Ruiru River supplied Nairobi from 1908 onwards, followed by two more plants in German East Africa on the Pangani River. By the early 1910s, hydroelectric stations began to proliferate across India, from Srinagar, Patiala and Mussoorie in the north to Wellington, Munnar and Gokak in the south.[19]

Most of these early hydropower plants were run-of-the-river installations that captured the energy of moving water without impounding it. Instead of storing water in a reservoir, they typically drew it off above a fall or headworks and conveyed it through a pipe, flume or open channel to a turbine station situated at a lower elevation in order to increase its pressure. Unlike hydroelectric dams, such stations caused relatively little disruption to riverine ecosystems since they merely tapped a part of their flow. From an ecological perspective this was clearly advantageous, but the drawback was that their productive capacity remained subject to the seasonal fluctuations of rivers. Variations in river flow meant variations in the supply of electricity, which did not conform to the ups and downs of energy demand.

The uneven temporal flow of watercourses was a problem for hydroelectric development in the industrial world too, but it was especially troublesome in tropical colonies where rainfall regimes were more volatile and where data on flow rates and hydro-climatic variability were scanty. Most rivers in India, for instance, were too seasonal to produce more than a small amount of electricity during dry months, forcing many users to install thermal or diesel generators as backups to avoid costly downtime.[20] Along the coast of Angola, a promising hydroelectric site on the Katumbela River remained only 'partially developed' owing to the large fluctuations in its generating capacity (which ranged from four thousand to twenty thousand horsepower, or three thousand to fifteen thousand kilowatts). In Kenya, the above-mentioned Ruiru hydropower plant that began operation in 1908 was, in the words of a 1947 report, 'a typical example of the construction of a hydro station based on inadequate hydrological data'. In 1933 it was abandoned and superseded by a steam-powered plant because dry-season flows were insufficient. In Algeria, where the bulk of rainfall came during a short winter season, the small 130-horsepower (100-kilowatt) installation built in 1911 on the Bou Sellam River demonstrated the limits of 'what can be done to develop water power in Algeria without storage'. Although rainy season floods could reach ten thousand cusecs (cubic feet

19. Rutnagur, *Electricity in India*, 4–5; Hausman, Hertner and Wilkins, *Global Electrification*, 89–90; Showers, 'Electrifying Africa', 197; Kinloch, 'Growth of Electric Power', 220–21; Donald Smith, 'Electrical Equipment Market', 10–11; J. Robbins, *Hydro-electric Development*, 11–13, 19–20; E. Richards, *Hydro-electric Resources*, 9, 22, 24.

20. Dickinson, 'Water Power in India', 424.

per second, one cusec being a little over twenty-eight litres per second), which was far more than the generator could handle, summer flows dropped well below fifty cusecs, not even enough to turn the plant's turbine.[21]

Dry seasons and droughts were by no means the only obstacle to hydropower development. Floods, too, posed a major challenge in many parts of the colonial world. J. W. Meares, the electrical adviser to the government of India in the 1910s and 1920s, had extensive experience with the problem. During the construction of the hydroelectric plant at Mussoorie, a hill station in the Himalayan foothills near Dehradun, he warned that the pipeline from the river to the plant was at risk of being washed away by floodwaters where it crossed a stream. Although he was mildly reprimanded for annoying the civil engineers with his unsolicited advice, his prophecy about the doomed pipeline came true only a few weeks later when the rains began and the stream carried it away. On several other occasions, Meares himself was nearly caught out by the vagaries of the monsoon. While planning the electrification of the Nilgiri Railway, he initially selected what he thought was a safe site for the power station based on rainfall records over the previous thirty years. His choice was criticized, however, by an old tea planter who had lived in the area for forty-five years and claimed that the river once rose six feet (nearly two metres) above where the power station would stand. Although friends of the planter teased him for exaggerating, the very next year an exceptional flood proved him right – fortunately for Meares, before any work on the power station had been carried out. Having learned his lesson, Meares adopted an even more cautious approach when conducting a hydroelectric survey at Narbada. This time he selected a power-station site based on a maximum flood level that had occurred fifty years earlier when no less than 10.5 inches (27 centimetres) of rain fell in just eighteen hours. But despite what he regarded as a very conservative decision, he was once again confronted by an old resident who told him of a much higher flood that had occurred before the one that determined his choice of site. Meares was sceptical about the old man's memory, but for the sake of certainty he set off to search for the signs of this alleged flood on nearby cliffs. It did not take him long to find them, a full thirteen feet (four metres) above the elevation that he had regarded as safe.[22]

The seasonality and unpredictability of rivers were problems that only storage dams could solve. The creation of reservoirs allowed hydroelectricity producers to smooth out the variations in power supply by storing water during periods of plenty and releasing it in times of scarcity. The chief impediment was that hydroelectric dams were expensive to build and required huge investment long before power generation would provide a return – assuming

---

21. United States Geological Survey, *World Atlas*, 31–33; E. Richards, *Hydro-electric Resources*, 9; see also Showers, 'Electrifying Africa', 197.

22. Meares, 'Development of Water Power', 61.

it ever would, which was less clear to investors than the financial promise of colonial railways. Consequently, the main obstacle to hydropower expansion in the colonial world was a shortage of capital rather than a shortage of promising sites. In addition, this dearth of capital for hydroelectric projects was closely related to – and exacerbated by – two other problems: the lack of reliable markets for the large amounts of electricity they would produce, and the relative cost per kilowatt provided in comparison to other forms of electricity generation. As the Indian Industrial Commission noted in 1918, storage works were usually necessary for hydroelectric projects because of the country's highly seasonal rainfall, but it was difficult to keep the price for hydroelectricity competitive unless the impounded water could also be used for irrigation. The overall result of these interlocking problems was, as the *Hydro-electric Survey of India* put it in 1919, a 'vicious circle of industries that require power and power looking for an assured outlet'.[23]

In practice, there were two possible ways to develop hydropower on a large scale. One was to leave it to private enterprise. Although this option was broadly favoured by frugal and liberal-minded colonial administrations, it required the existence of a large industrial market for energy to attract the required investment, and there were few places in the colonies where such a concentrated market existed. The other option worked in the opposite direction: providing state support for cheap hydropower as a means of stimulating industrial development. State involvement in hydroelectric projects, whether through direct public ownership or favourable loans, was becoming more common in Europe and North America by the 1910s. For the colonial world it promised an exit from the 'vicious circle' that slowed the growth of hydropower and the adoption of electrical machinery.

In the early twentieth century, the most far-reaching efforts along both of these lines emerged in India. Given the number and size of its rivers, as well as the growing demand for power, hydroelectricity promised to spur the 'industrial awakening' of the subcontinent.[24] It was by no means only British officials and technicians who saw hydroelectricity in this light. Indian entrepreneurs, engineers and political leaders were equally if not more enthralled by its potential.

Indeed, India's first major hydroelectric station was not built within the British Raj, but rather in the semi-autonomous princely state of Mysore in the south-western part of the peninsula. The fact that this small 'Native State' was so quick to take the initiative was no fluke. Although many of British India's jute, cotton and paper mills switched to electricity in the early 1900s,

23. Barlow and Meares, *Hydro-electric Survey of India*, 26; *Report of the Indian Industrial Commission*, 60; 'Water Power Resources'; Showers, 'Electrifying Africa', 197–98.

24. Dickinson, 'Water Power in India', 422.

the colonial government used electricity mainly for military and administrative purposes and did not regard it as a tool for industrial modernization until the latter stages of the First World War. By contrast, the government of Mysore was far more proactive in its approach to electricity in general and water power in particular. Ever since the return of its royal family to the throne in 1881 (following a half-century of direct rule), successive Mysore administrations used their limited autonomy to plot a rather different course of industrial development from the neighbouring British-ruled provinces, one that was less bound to the doctrine of laissez-faire and instead emphasized the strategic use of state support as a means of fostering economic growth. For the modernizing *dewans* (prime ministers) of Mysore, and for the British and Indian technicians who worked for them, state investment in hydroelectricity seemed an ideal vehicle to expand and diversify the state's industries, and ultimately to increase its revenues and autonomy vis-à-vis the Raj.[25]

Mysore's first hydropower plant was situated on the Cauvery River near Sivasamudram, where the river splits into several channels before plunging a hundred metres over a cliff. The idea of using the Cauvery Falls to generate electricity dated back to the 1880s and was strongly backed by the early *dewans* and British Residents in Mysore. In 1899, after years of surveying and planning, the Mysore government commissioned General Electric to build a hydroelectricity plant and distribution system. In essence, the project was a scaled-up run-of-the-river scheme. It drew water from the river around two miles (three kilometres) above the falls and conveyed it through a channel to a powerhouse around one mile below, thus obtaining a head of 405 feet (123 metres). Upon its completion in 1902, the six-thousand-horsepower (4,500-kilowatt) Cauvery Falls plant was by far the most powerful hydroelectric station in India – and, with a price tag of 5 million rupees, the most costly as well. The bulk of its power was transmitted via high-voltage lines to the Kolar goldfields about ninety miles (145 kilometres) to the north-east. Coming just seven years after the completion of the hydropower station at Niagara Falls, the transmission line to the Kolar mines was for a brief period the longest in the entire world.[26] To the delight of the Mysore administration, demand for the plant's electricity was such as to prompt engineers to boost its capacity to thirteen thousand horsepower (10,000 kilowatts) by 1908. At the same time, two new powerlines conveyed electricity to the cities of Bangalore and Mysore. In sum, the Cauvery Falls scheme showed what could be accomplished through a state-led

25. Nair, *Mysore Modern*; Hettne, *Political Economy*; Kale, 'Structures of Power', 457–59; S. Sarkar, *Let There Be Light*, 167–68.

26. J. Robbins, *Hydro-electric Development*, 27; Hettne, *Political Economy*, 237; Dickinson, 'Water Power in India', 420; *Report of the Indian Industrial Commission*, 61; Sandes, *Military Engineer in India*, 47–49; Kale, 'Structures of Power', 459–60.

FIGURE 7.1. Cauvery Power Works generating station, Sivasamudram, 1920s. By permission of akg-images/British Library, photo 10/29(23).

hydroelectricity initiative. It soon served as a model of public infrastructure investment for electrification advocates elsewhere.[27]

Meanwhile, the concurrent development of hydropower in Bombay followed an entirely different route. Instead of being led by the state, it was based entirely on private investment. And rather than serving as a means of stimulating industrialization, it was designed to provide much-needed power for an existing industrial centre. It was a model that more closely mirrored the contemporary domination of private electrical companies in the industrial world, and it also reflected prevailing views within British officialdom about the proper roles of colonial government and private enterprise.[28]

Electricity was first introduced in Bombay in the 1880s, but for around two decades its uptake was limited by the high cost of fuel and the financial instability of local utility firms. The problem was very much a lack of supply rather than demand. During these years Bombay's textile mills were booming, and they were eager to convert more fully to electrical machinery. By the turn of the century, there were growing calls to harness the region's water resources to

27. S. Rao and Lourdusamy, 'Colonialism', 44.
28. Kale, 'Structures of Power', 462.

supply the necessary power. In 1899, an editorial in the *Indian Textile Journal* noted that 'the progress made in the economy of transport of electric current brings us each year nearer the time when the power of falling water in the Ghauts [*sic*] on the other side of Bombay harbour will be utilised in our city for industrial purposes'. Whereas electricity had 'hitherto led a rather precarious existence in Bombay', it seemed likely that 'with the enormous resources of force that are wasted within sight of our city, the electrical engineer may look forward to a period of intense activity and of prosperity'.[29]

These 'wasted' resources were enormous indeed. Annual rainfall on the nearby Western Ghats averaged eighteen to twenty feet (5.5–6 metres) per year, rarely dipping below twelve feet and occasionally reaching twenty-six feet. The problem was that it fell almost entirely within four months of the year (June–September), often in the form of deluges that dropped twelve inches (thirty centimetres) – and sometimes as much as twenty inches – within twenty-four hours. In the mountains east of Bombay, valleys that contained torrents during the monsoon ran completely dry for most of the year.[30] The only way to harness these colossal flows was to store them, and the attempt to do so spawned one of the largest hydroelectric complexes in the world at the time.

The project was the brainchild of Jamsetji Tata, founder of India's biggest industrial firm, Tata and Sons. After making a fortune in the Chinese opium trade, from the 1860s onward the Tatas invested heavily in cotton manufacture and were constantly in search of cheap power to drive their mills. In 1899, Tata formed a syndicate with a British engineer and a Bombay merchant to explore the possibility of flooding several valleys in the Ghats to produce electricity. After his death in 1904, his sons ultimately brought the scheme to fruition.[31]

Like all nascent hydroelectric projects, the venture promised numerous benefits for the region. For starters, its backers emphasized the financial advantages for local industry. With a purchase price of only 0.55 anna (around a thirtieth of a rupee) per BTU (1,055 joules), its electricity would be significantly cheaper than using coal and steam. The scheme was also extolled for its environmental benefits. The fact that its output would be equivalent to burning six hundred tons of coal per day promised to reduce the severe smoke nuisance in the city.[32] The purported benefits were large, and captured the attention of Bombay's officials and industrialists alike. But not everyone was convinced by the plan, especially many of the engineers working in the region. Some warned that the catchment area was too small to fill the envisaged lakes; others regarded the whole idea as little more than a fairy tale. Friends of the

29. John Wallace, *Indian Textile Journal* (September 1899), quoted in Rutnagur, *Electricity in India*, 4.

30. Lanthier, 'L'électrification de Bombay', 219; Dickinson, 'Water Power in India', 418.

31. Lanthier, 'L'électrification de Bombay', 217–20.

32. Rutnagur, *Electricity in India*, 38; *Report of the Indian Industrial Commission*, 61; Dickinson, 'Water Power in India', 420.

chief consulting engineer Alfred Dickinson advised him not to risk his reputation on 'such a perfectly absurd engineering proposition'.[33] Yet despite such misgivings, the Tata Hydro-Electric Power & Supply Company was formally established in 1910, and construction work began the following year.

At the heart of the scheme were three masonry dams spanning the Lonavla, Valvan, and Shirawta valleys south-east of Bombay. Ranging in length from 0.7 to 1.4 miles (1.2 to 2.3 kilometres), the dams created a trio of reservoirs with a combined surface area of around 9 square miles (23 square kilometres). The accompanying power plant, built by General Electric some 580 yards (530 metres) below at the foot of the mountains, was fed by steel pipes from the reservoirs. When the plant commenced operations in 1915, it supplied 30,000 horsepower (22,000 kilowatts; more than twice the output of Cauvery Falls) to Bombay's cotton mills 43 miles away. Given the high demand for electricity, its capacity was increased two years later to 50,000 horsepower, but even this amount of power covered the needs of only twenty-six of the city's eighty-three textile mills. The Tatas were eager to fill this gap in the market and soon proceeded with plans to build two more hydroelectric schemes in the Ghats: a 60,000-horsepower project in the Andhra Valley just north of Lonavla (whose reservoir was larger than the three existing ones combined), followed by a 150,000-horsepower (112,000-kilowatt) scheme in the Pune district at the confluence of the Mula and Nila Rivers. By the mid-1920s, the water flows of the western Ghats provided the bulk of Bombay's power.[34]

The Tatas' hydroelectric venture was at once a global, imperial and self-consciously 'national' undertaking. The engineers who built the schemes brought with them a wealth of experience from around the world. H. P. Gibbs, the general manager of the Tata Hydro-Electric Company, had previously worked for General Electric in Mexico before coming to India and initially taking charge of the Cauvery Power Scheme in 1903. The technology that underpinned the Tata projects came from US, German and British electrical companies. In London, the heart of Britain's imperial power, the secretary of state for India Lord Hamilton gave strong backing to the initial trio of hydropower dams, and in Bombay the governor Sir George Clarke, himself an engineer, took a keen interest from early on.[35]

Yet, unlike other major infrastructure projects in colonial India, the necessary capital – 20 million rupees – was raised entirely within India itself. While touring the subcontinent in search of financial backers, the eldest Tata son Dorabji deliberately presented the venture as a patriotic symbol of India's

33. Dickinson, 'Water Power in India', 418.

34. Lanthier, 'L'électrification de Bombay', 224–29; Rutnagur, *Electricity in India*, 7, 17, 50; *Report of the Indian Industrial Commission*, 61.

35. Lanthier, 'L'électrification de Bombay', 225–26; Rutnagur, *Electricity in India*, 20–21.

FIGURE 7.2. Lonavla Dam, early twentieth century.
Courtesy of the Tata Central Archives.

industrial vitality. The message fell on fertile soil, for it was not long before the
supposed 'natural caution' of Indian investors reportedly 'gave way to national
pride'. Indeed, when the company was launched in 1910, its financial basis was
reflected in a predominantly Indian board of directors. The Tata scheme thus
became an early symbol of industrial 'self-rule' in India. As Governor Clarke
declared in 1911: 'Here is a great *swadeshi* project rendered possible by the
trust of Indians in the future of their own country. That is surely a political
object lesson of real importance.' Seeking to temper the message of national
pride with a reference to the solidity of British rule, he claimed that 'such an
enterprise as this, so entered upon, symbolizes the confidence of Indians in
themselves, their willingness to be associated with a project somewhat novel
in this country, and their assurance of the political stability which alone can
guarantee the continued advancement of India'.[36]

The hydroelectric works in Mysore and Bombay were trailblazers for the
development of water power in the colonial world at large. Together they
exemplified the advantages and disadvantages of state- versus private-led
approaches, and both became key reference points for colonial administrators, engineers and entrepreneurs elsewhere. But if these projects served as

---

36. Quoted in Rutnagur, *Electricity in India*, 39; see also Lanthier, 'L'électrification de
Bombay', 222–23.

models for hydropower development, they also presaged some of the social and political tensions that the future held in store. In the event, both raised thorny questions about the costs, benefits and side-effects of hydroelectric development – and how they should be apportioned.

Conflict arose on variety of levels: between the different users of rivers, between displaced locals and distant beneficiaries, and between different political units upstream and downstream. The Cauvery Falls scheme initially avoided most of these problems since its run-of-the-river design scarcely altered the overall hydrology of the river. But as demand for its power grew, so too did the need to modify the river. By the time the powerlines reached Mysore city in 1908, the seasonal fluctuations of the Cauvery precluded any further expansion of the plant's generating capacity. During the driest months from February to May, the normal discharge of the river was insufficient to cover the power needs of the goldmines alone. In fact, periodic inadequacies of water flow forced the Mysore government to pay the mining companies some £38,000 in compensation for failing to supply the contracted amount of power.[37]

As ever, the solution was to build a storage dam upriver. The task fell to Mokshagumdam Visvesvaraya, a prominent hydraulic expert who had become Mysore's chief engineer in 1909 (and was later appointed *dewan* in 1913). Renowned for both his technical skill and visionary ambitions, Visvesvaraya drew up plans for a huge multipurpose dam that would not only store water for the Sivasamudram plant but also generate an additional eighty thousand horsepower (sixty thousand kilowatts) of electricity and irrigate 150,000 acres (61,000 hectares) of land. In its original design, the Krishnarajasagar Dam was to be 8,600 feet long, 124 feet high (2,600 by 38 metres), and store 48 billion cubic feet (1.36 billion cubic metres) of water, making it the largest reservoir in India to date. But the problem with impounding such a vast amount of water in the upper Cauvery was that it affected the supply of water in the neighbouring state of Madras. More specifically, it directly impeded the Madras government's plans to build its own storage dam at Mettur about a hundred kilometres downstream from the Krishnarajasagar site.[38]

The ensuing confrontation turned into modern India's first major interstate water dispute. Madras and Mysore had already been at loggerheads over the Cauvery's waters during the irrigation boom of the late nineteenth century, and in 1892 they signed a treaty that only partially resolved the argument. The simultaneous proposals for the Krishnarajasagar and Mettur projects – both submitted in 1910 – once again brought the states into direct conflict. Although Madras agreed to the first stage of Visvesvaraya's dam (limiting it to a height of 80 feet and a storage capacity of 11 billion cubic feet), it objected to the second

37. Hettne, *Political Economy*, 238.
38. Visvesvaraya, *Memoirs*, 46–47; Barber, *Cauvery-Mettur Project*, 12–19.

FIGURE 7.3. The newly completed Mettur Dam, August 1934.
By permission of akg-images/British Library, photo 1123/10(7).

phase of construction, which would more than quadruple the reservoir's volume. The inability of the two sides to reach an agreement forced the government of India to step in as arbitrator. It took until 1924 for the two sides finally to reach a settlement, though the outcome satisfied neither party. In the short term, the agreement allowed both projects to go ahead: the Krishnarajasagar Dam was raised to 124 feet, thus enlarging its reservoir, and the Mettur Dam was completed in 1934 (at 5,300 feet long and 176 feet high, briefly the largest dam in the world). Yet over the longer term, the agreement merely marked a stage-post in a water dispute that rumbled on well into the twenty-first century, one of the most protracted and acrimonious of its kind in the entire world.[39]

While the governments of Madras and Mysore battled over their water rights in the courts, the Tata brothers became embroiled in a very different type of conflict. The dispute centred on the company's plans for a new hydropower project near Mulshi in the Pune district, the third and largest of the Tatas' installations in the Western Ghats. Like its predecessors, the Mulshi scheme essentially comprised a large dam (half a mile, or eight hundred

39. In 2018, the Indian Supreme Court temporarily resolved the dispute by establishing a fixed allocation of water for fifteen years and creating an independent regulator to manage the distribution of water from the Cauvery River. This paragraph is based on Rani's 'Historical Background' (1035–39), Barber's *Cauvery-Mettur Project* (19–21) and Visvesvaraya's *Memoirs* (48–52). See also Amrith, *Unruly Waters*, 161–63.

metres, in length) and a power plant to send electricity to Bombay. Also like its predecessors, it entailed the submergence of thousands of acres of land and dozens of rural villages.

The trouble started in summer 1919 when residents in the affected villages were informed of the plans. Local landowners and moneylenders were the first to raise the alarm, but by the end of the year thousands of farmers were attending meetings to figure out how they could avoid losing their land. Over the following years, they staged a series of sit-ins, rallies and demonstrations, often assembling in their hundreds at the dam site to stop construction work. In 1921, they became increasingly organized under the leadership of socialist firebrand and Indian independence activist 'Senapati' (commander) Pandurang Mahadev Bapat. By April that year the movement had achieved sufficient size and public sympathy – including an endorsement from Gandhi – to persuade local officials to call a temporary work stoppage.[40]

In response to the protests, the Tata Company tried to convince local people to accept compensation payments and move elsewhere. Under the Land Acquisition Act of 1894, the company was allowed to make compulsory land purchases covering a total of ten thousand acres (forty square kilometres), around half of it rice paddy. Altogether, around 7,500 people were to be displaced, but few agreed to accept the payments on offer. Levels of trust were low, with good reason. As the Bombay government itself recognized, expellees from the Tatas' previous dam projects had not been well compensated. The Valvan and Shirawta reservoirs displaced twenty-five villages and 4,700 people, but there were no coordinated efforts to resettle them. During the construction of the Andhra valley scheme, officials tried to find suitable land for those who asked for it, but most of the 'oustees' simply ended up moving to neighbouring villages, some with a cash payment and some without.[41]

When work on the Mulshi project resumed in early 1922, the clashes became more heated. Hundreds of protestors regularly disrupted the construction work, even at the risk of fines, occasional beatings and jail time. From autumn 1922 to spring 1923, they increasingly resorted to sabotaging the works rather than just delaying them, and many were arrested for unlawful damage. Yet despite all the protests and publicity, work on the dam proceeded apace. By autumn 1923, Gandhi advised the *satyagrahis*, or passive resistance movement, to call off the struggle, partly because its leader, Senapati Bapat, was not a firm believer in non-violence. As it turned out, Gandhi's withdrawal of support largely ended the popular movement. Although a group of diehards continued with a series of more violent attacks, most were eventually arrested, and Bapat himself was sentenced to seven years.[42]

40. Vora, *First Anti-dam Movement*, 3–9, 31, 42, 62–64.
41. Vora, 28–29, 71, 91–92.
42. Vora, 95–99, 104–5, 116–21.

In the end, the Tatas got their way. The Mulshi Dam was completed in 1927, submerging a total of twenty-seven villages and around 13,400 acres (54 square kilometres) of land. While most of the higher-caste families left the region entirely, many of the ousted farmers became wage labourers in nearby villages. Although some of them used their compensation money to pay off debts or purchase land elsewhere, most ended up worse off than before, not least because the sudden out-migration from the reservoir zone pushed up land prices in surrounding areas. Twenty years later, many of the expellees hopefully assumed that Indian independence would finally enable them to receive better compensation, but they were quickly disappointed. Neither the Tata Company nor the new independent government provided any facilities to nearby settlements, and it was only in 1970 that they finally even got a bus service. Perversely, as late as 1980 the mostly poor and illiterate residents of the resettlement villages still had no electricity from the dam that had displaced their families over half a century earlier. It was only in the 1990s, amid the broader proliferation of dam protests across India, that basic improvements were finally made.[43]

The Tata Company's infrastructure projects in the Ghats were thus landmarks of colonial hydropower in more than one sense. They not only represented a major engineering and commercial achievement; they also heralded a pattern of displacement and dispossession that recurred numerous times over the following decades, and that continued on an even greater scale after Indian independence.

Scaling Up, Spreading Out: Colonial Hydropower between the World Wars

In the history of hydropower, as in so many areas of life, the First World War was an important watershed. In Europe and North America, the exigencies of wartime economic mobilization led to an unprecedented level of economic and technological planning, and the electrical sector was no exception. Electricity was vital to the war effort, especially for the processing of mineral ores and the production of nitrates. On both sides of the Atlantic, belligerent states took a more directive approach towards the construction of large new power plants and distribution systems. In the post-war years, they generally retained a central role in the planning and supervision of electrical infrastructures. As demand for electricity continued to rise in the 1920s and 1930s – driven by escalating domestic consumption as well as new energy-intensive industrial processes such as electrolytic refining and fertilizer production – shortages of coal and oil for thermal electricity plants remained a nagging anxiety. While

43. Vora, 156–63.

government planners pointed to the inevitable depletion of coal reserves, periodic miners' strikes further underlined the risks of an over-reliance on fossil fuels.[44]

Against this backdrop, hydropower was increasingly seen as a vital strategic resource. Even in coal-rich Britain, officials concluded that 'we must look to water-power as a substitute for coal-power . . . as coal becomes scarcer and therefore more expensive'.[45] During the interwar years, technological improvements to turbines, generators and long-distance transmission made hydroelectricity an increasingly flexible and cost-efficient alternative to thermal electrical generation. It not only enabled governments to diversify their energy supplies but also promised to decrease their external dependence on other states. This was particularly attractive for countries that lacked abundant coal deposits (e.g., Italy) or that had suffered from wartime blockades (e.g., Germany), but the strategic advantages of hydropower were universally acknowledged. Amid the broader interwar shift towards economic autarky and state intervention, hydroelectricity represented not only an 'inexhaustible resource' but also 'an asset that one has oneself and that it is not necessary to acquire from abroad'.[46]

The crucial importance of electricity during and after the war prompted European governments to scrutinize both their own hydropower assets and those of their overseas colonies. For planners in France, Britain, the Netherlands and Belgium, the availability of cheap, reliable energy supplies in the colonies would greatly facilitate the development of their mineral and agricultural resources. Several colonial governments already began to take stock during the First World War. The South African government launched a hydrological survey in 1917, followed a year later by Kenya. India began a thorough examination of the subcontinent's hydropower resources at the behest of the wartime Industrial Commission (1916–18), while in the Netherlands East Indies, the government established a Bureau of Water Power and Electricity in 1917 for the purpose of exploring, surveying and developing suitable sites. In 1918, French and Belgian authorities in Central Africa began to emphasize the importance of the Congo's tributaries and their falls for power generation, and actively shared information with neighbouring colonies in view of the common interest in the hydraulic regimes of river systems that connected them across political borders. By far the most wide-ranging initiative was the Water Power Committee of the Conjoint of Scientific Societies, established by the British government in 1917 to conduct the first ever empire-wide survey of existing and potential hydropower resources.

44. T. Hughes, *Networks of Power*, 285–323; Lagendijk, *Electrifying Europe*, 39–44, 51–57; C. Jones, *Routes of Power*, 195–227; Mitchell, *Carbon Democracy*.

45. Clerk and Gibson, *Water-Power*, vi.

46. Cavaillès, *La houille blanche*, 215.

Its landmark report *Water-Power in the British Empire*, published in 1922, expressed the underlying rationale:

> The economic development of many of our tropical dependencies, whose latent wealth is practically untapped, is directly interconnected with the development of their water-power resources. Not only would an abundant supply of cheap power enable railroads to be operated, irrigation schemes to be developed, and mineral deposits to be tapped and worked, but it would go far to solve the labour problem, which promises to be one of some difficulty in the near future.[47]

What all of these surveys showed was that the hydropower resources of the colonies remained almost entirely 'wasted'. According to the 1922 Water Power Committee report, the development of hydropower in the British Empire compared 'unfavourably with that of its commercial competitors'. Whereas continental Europe exploited 18 per cent of its estimated potential and the United States just over 20 per cent, for the British Empire as a whole the figure was only 5 per cent. Moreover, nearly three-quarters of this capacity was in Canada alone, which meant that only a tiny percentage of available water power was harnessed elsewhere.[48] The situation was broadly similar in Europe's other colonial empires. Africa was thought to possess nearly half of the potential water power in the entire world, yet in French-ruled Africa there were only two small hydroelectric dams at the end of the 1920s, one in Morocco and one in Mali. The Congo basin alone was reckoned to possess over a quarter of the world's hydropower potential, yet the first hydroelectric installation in the Belgian Congo was built only in 1930. The Netherlands East Indies was estimated to have 6.6 million horsepower (4.9 million kilowatts) of hydropower potential, most of it in the 'outer isles', yet in 1928 only 120,000 horsepower had been developed, nearly all of it on Java. Indochina, despite its sizeable rivers and abundant rainfall, had no hydropower plants at all.[49]

Planners put forward a variety of proposals to remedy this situation. Among the key recommendations were greater imperial and regional coordination, enhancement of training opportunities for hydroengineers, and the provision of state assistance to lure private investment. In areas with extensive irrigation systems it was also suggested that feeder canals could serve as sources of hydropower, but in most places this proved impossible because of the overriding need to

47. Clerk and Gibson, *Water-Power*, 2. See also the discussion in Hoag's *Developing the Rivers* (141–47), Darnault's *Mission de prospection* (9–10, 236) and Donald Smith's 'Electrical Equipment Market' (7).

48. Clerk and Gibson, *Water-Power*, 13–14. Minus Canada, the entire British Empire had harnessed only 605,000 of an estimated 41 million available horsepower (1.7%).

49. United States Geological Survey, *World Atlas*, 3, 33; Showers, 'Electrifying Africa', 202–4; *Union minière du Haut-Katanga*, 150–52; Letcher, *South Central Africa*, 192–94; Donald Smith, 'Electrical Equipment Market', 10–12; Tertrais, 'L'électrification de l'Indochine'.

operate them according to the very different requirements of irrigation (see chapter 2).[50] The most urgent need was for more hydrological research. Even in India, whose nineteenth-century irrigation boom had generated a wealth of hydrographic data, it was possible only to make educated guesses about the most promising sites for hydropower. More common was the situation in Malaysia, whose hydropower potential was reportedly 'not possible to state even approximately'. There was similarly little information on the waterways of southern and eastern Africa, and for the Niger basin there were effectively 'no records of measurements or estimates' at all.[51] Although survey work accelerated during the 1920s and 1930s, the lack of reliable information about discharge rates and suitable generating sites remained a serious impediment for the development of hydroelectricity in the colonial world.[52]

The shortage of hydrographic data and trained engineers remained a problem for many years to come. Yet the biggest obstacle in most of colonial Asia and Africa was the absence of assured markets for electricity production. According to a widely used contemporary Indian manual for hydraulic engineers:

> It is not enough that the power be constant and sufficient in quantity, that the plant is well-designed, and that the cost of the same is reasonable. There must be a **market** in which the power can be utilized to advantage, and the price at which it can be sold in competition with all other sources of power, must be sufficient to . . . afford a fair return on the investment'.[53]

Wherever coal was readily available (as in parts of South Africa, Tonkin, northeastern India, or Southern Rhodesia) thermal generators usually presented a cheaper option. And even where other sources of energy were scarce, it was often difficult to justify investment in costly hydroelectric plants so long as demand (or, more specifically, the perceived prospect of a growth in demand) for electricity was low. The problem was typified by Nyasaland, whose acting chief secretary described the region's hydropower resources as 'greatly in excess of any development that can at present be foreseen and for which they could be used . . . Development has not yet reached a stage where it could be said that any considerable market for power is in sight'.[54]

50. Clerk and Gibson, *Water-Power*, 17–18, 50–51; Meares, 'Development of Water Power', 65.

51. Quotes from United States Geological Survey, *World Atlas*, 32. See also Clerk and Gibson, *Water-Power*, 21, 35, 38.

52. See Darnault, *Mission de prospection*; van Deuren, *Aménagement du Bas-Congo*; Kitson, *Outlines*, 41–50; Meares, *Hydro-electric Survey*; more generally J. Robbins, *Hydro-electric Development*.

53. B. Chatterjee, *Hydro-electric Practice in India*, 7 (emphasis in the original).

54. J. Robbins, *Hydro-electric Development*, 11. See also Hoag, *Developing the Rivers*, 143.

Much of the demand that existed, or that could readily be brought into existence, stemmed from mining and mineral processing. As the United States Geological Survey pointed out in its 1921 *World Atlas of Commercial Geology*, mining and hydroelectricity were inextricably linked:

> The development of the mineral resources of the world depends on the local availability of cheap mechanical or electrical energy. In many regions such energy must be obtained from water flowing in surface streams; in others it must be generated from fuels. The value of a mineral in the ground is intimately related to the source of the energy needed to recover it for commercial use. A knowledge of the water-power resources of the world is therefore essential to a proper study and utilization of the mineral resources.[55]

This was certainly the case in Southeast Asia. Malaysia's tin-mining industry – the largest in the world at the time – used around four-fifths of the colony's electricity in the early 1930s, including nearly all of the twenty-seven mega-watts generated by its first major hydroelectric dam at Chenderoh on the Perak River. On Sumatra, four of the five hydropower stations in operation in the late 1920s were built to power mining or cement operations. In India too, there was a close link between mines and hydroelectric development (as the Cauvery Falls scheme demonstrated).[56] But it was especially true in sub-Saharan Africa, where mineral exploitation long accounted for the bulk of capital investment. On Nigeria's Jos Plateau, the five-hundred-kilowatt Kwall Falls project was completed in 1925 to serve nearby tin mines, followed in 1930 by the Kura Falls scheme on the adjacent Bauchi Plateau. In Northern Rhodesia, the Prince of Wales himself opened the two-megawatt hydropower station on the Mulun-gushi River, built in 1925 to supply the Broken Hill lead and zinc mine fifty kilometres to the north-west. In Southern Rhodesia, the Rezende gold mine at Penhalonga operated the colony's only hydropower station. By far the larg-est installation in interwar Africa was the Mwandingusha Dam, completed in 1930 on the Lufira River in southern Belgian Congo. Built to supply power to the copper mines and refineries of Katanga, its initial sixty-eight-megawatt capacity – which was doubled by the end of the 1930s – dwarfed anything else in the region.[57] Although engineers dreamed of harnessing the enormous potential of Victoria Falls, its remote location hundreds of kilometres from

55. United States Geological Survey, *World Atlas*, 3.

56. Rennie, 'Chenderoh Water-Power Plant'; J. Robbins, *Hydro-electric Development*, 43–45; Clerk and Gibson, *Water-Power*, 38; Donald Smith, 'Electrical Equipment Market', 11–12.

57. Robert, *Le centre africain*, 140–41, 168; Birchard, 'Copper', 432; Melland, 'Natural Resources of Africa', 128; J. Robbins, *Hydro-electric Development*, 7–9, 17–18; Showers, 'Electrifying Africa', 198–99.

any mining operations made it impossible to sell the power that such a station could generate.

Where the limits of long-distance transmission put hydropower out of the reach of markets, it was nonetheless possible, at least in theory, to put markets within the reach of hydropower. The most grandiose attempt to do so was a Belgian scheme to dam the lower Congo at Inga Falls, a series of roaring cataracts where the river narrows, bends and drops its final ninety-six metres to the tidal zone. The colossal hydropower potential of the site was recognized as early as 1885, but it was only in the 1920s that the first detailed plans to harness it were drawn up. After surveying the falls, a Belgian reserve engineer named Pierre van Deuren calculated that they could produce an astounding five gigawatts, making them 'an inexhaustible source of wealth' that could transform the colony into a 'worldwide centre of activity of the first order'. In 1928, he submitted a proposal for developing the site, and in 1929 he established the Syndicat d'études du Bas-Congo (Syneba) to carry out further investigations. The basic idea was to use the power from Inga Falls to create a new industrial hub near the Congolese coast, including a 625-megawatt hydroelectric station, a series of metal processing works and a fertilizer plant. The Belgian Colonial Ministry was favourably inclined. In 1936, a special commission confirmed the technical feasibility of the scheme, but its economic viability was another matter. The financial constraints of the Depression years made it impossible to drum up the necessary investment, and with the outbreak of the Second World War, attention soon focused elsewhere. Like most of the visionary colonial hydropower proposals of the interwar years, the dream of creating a 'Congolese Ruhr' would have to wait.[58]

A more modest but perhaps more practical means of developing markets for hydropower was to boost local household consumption. Just as in the industrial world, the process of electrification in the colonies was not only a matter of building power grids but also involved the gradual 'absorption' of electricity into everyday life.[59] One common way to encourage this was to make electricity more affordable. In the 1920s, public utility companies in the Netherlands East Indies introduced cheaper rates for indigenous consumers in an effort to persuade them to install electricity in their homes. In India, Swarajist (supporting self-rule) politicians continually pressured electricity suppliers to reduce rates in order to encourage more uptake among small industries and ordinary households.[60] As it turned out, such early arguments for state intervention and the partial de-commodification of electricity

58. Van Deuren, *Aménagement du Bas-Congo*, 5–7, 232, 242, quotes at 34 and 242; Misser, *La saga d'Inga*, 20–21; Showers, 'Grand Inga Hydroelectricity Scheme', 33–35.

59. See, e.g., Nye, *Electrifying America*.

60. S. Sarkar, *Let There Be Light*, 177–78; Donald Smith, 'Electrical Equipment Market', 13–14.

eventually formed the basis of the much larger electrification programmes launched by nationalist governments after independence.[61]

Another way to increase electricity consumption in the colonies was to publicize it as a quintessentially 'modern', science-based form of energy, a marker of 'civilization' itself. Compared with other domestic fuels, it not only represented a cleaner alternative for lighting or cooking but could also power a range of other appliances that promised to make life easier. Electricity, remarked one French observer, 'can be the creator of new needs in a land where the forest native does not have any'.[62] According to H. G. Howard, chief engineer of the Madras Electricity Department, 'people must be educated to think electrically and realise that electricity is just as important to the community as railways, telegraphs, telephones, irrigation systems, and other social necessities'.[63] If hydroelectric dams and distribution systems were an archetypal 'big' technology dominated by state or corporate bureaucracies, they could also give people the chance to engage with a variety of new 'everyday technologies' that they could selectively adopt on their own terms.[64]

The main problem with boosting 'native uptake' was the fact that most people had little opportunity to use electricity even if they wanted to. One reason was that electrical grids were focused overwhelmingly on urban centres. In the princely state of Mysore, whose distribution network was the envy of most other Indian provinces, only a tiny proportion of its electricity was used in the countryside (mainly by small industries). In the Bombay Presidency, the rural share was practically zero. Madras was the only Indian state in which rural electrification was advocated from the outset, yet even here it accounted for only 9 per cent of the load at the end of the 1930s. In the Netherlands Indies, the availability of electricity was similarly skewed towards towns, while in Indochina the colonial government's electrification drive of the 1930s completely ignored the countryside, despite widespread calls to use electric water pumps for irrigation. Although officials sometimes cited technical difficulties (above all the violence of tropical thunderstorms) as a hindrance to rural electrification, the main reason for their disregard of rural areas was that they did not view them as viable markets.[65]

Even within the cities, electricity remained beyond the reach of most indigenous residents. In order to recoup their up-front infrastructure costs,

61. See E. Chatterjee, 'Asian Anthropocene'.

62. Guernier, *L'Afrique*, 264.

63. *Times of India*, 4 December 1930, cited in Kale, 'Structures of Power', 471.

64. See esp. Arnold, *Everyday Technology*. For similar dynamics in Central America, see Montaño's *Electrifying Mexico*.

65. See, e.g., Drouin, 'L'électrification du Tonkin'; Tertrais, 'L'électrification de l'Indochine', 600. On Madras: Kale, 'Structures of Power', 460–70. On India more generally: E. Chatterjee, 'Climate of Scarcity'. For the Netherlands Indies: Donald Smith, 'Electrical Equipment Market', 14. For a general overview of the issue: Hasenöhrl, 'Rural Electrification'.

electricity suppliers (much like the municipal suppliers of piped water and sewerage) naturally focused on areas inhabited by those who had the means to pay for it. Given the stark income discrepancies between different social and racial groups, domestic electricity supplies (again, like piped water supplies) were mainly concentrated in districts where Europeans and non-European elites lived. Fairly typical was the situation in Indochina, where the expanding interwar grid was celebrated for offering 'the European population infinite possibilities of increased comfort through various domestic appliances for ventilation, refrigeration, etc.', comforts otherwise enjoyed only by 'the native and especially the Chinese merchants in the larger cities'.[66] Rather than creating a mass market of consumers, electrification served to widen the gap between rich and poor, between colonizers and the vast majority of the colonized.

To a large extent, these discrepancies resulted from technological and market forces rather than an active attempt to prevent access to electricity among colonial subjects.[67] Yet in some territories – especially those in which a minority settler population exerted disproportionate political influence – they also reflected a deliberate strategy to privilege certain groups over others. In mandate Palestine, for instance, the hydropowered electrical network that was built in the 1920s and 1930s was expressly conceived to serve Jewish rather than Arab interests. Designed by the Russian-born Zionist engineer Pinhas Rutenberg, who acquired an electrical monopoly from the British authorities in 1921, the grid was vigorously opposed by Arab residents who – rightly, as it turned out – saw in it the infrastructural makings of a Jewish state.[68] Meanwhile, in the Southern Rhodesian industrial town of Bulawayo, electrification efforts focused almost exclusively on the homes of white settlers. In order to create a more reliable market for the municipal electrical plant, the town council subsidized the tariff rates for white suburban consumers and even introduced a hire-purchase scheme to encourage the acquisition of hotplates, radios, water heaters and other electrical appliances. By contrast, the town's African residents had only minimal access to electricity despite living next to the power plant, and also had to pay higher rates than most white households. As Moses Chikowero has shown, electrification in Southern Rhodesia 'was racially conceived and executed, accentuating the urban African's tenuous socio-economic and political condition'.[69]

At a more fundamental level, electrical inequalities were also rooted in contemporary ideas about racial and civilizational hierarchies. They reflected the widespread view that many colonial subjects were too 'traditional' or

66. Robequain, *Economic Development*, 286.

67. A point emphasized by Jonas van der Straeten in 'Measuring Progress in Megawatt' (670). See also Mchome, *'Blackout Blues'*, 27–46.

68. Meiton, *Electrical Palestine*.

69. Chikowero, 'Subalternating Currents', 306.

'primitive' to be potential consumers of electricity. Such stereotypes were particularly prevalent in sub-Saharan Africa, which Europeans tended to regard as distinctly backward in comparison to the civilizations of Asia. For many of the colonial officials based there, a paternalistic emphasis on upholding native 'custom' led them to regard the indigenous populace as uninterested in or unprepared for the arrival of electricity.[70] Even in a relatively electrified city such as Nairobi, over half of the two thousand customers in the early 1930s were European, the remainder Asian, with 'practically no Africans' having a connection. In areas where non-African residents were scarce, such as Uganda, public electricity supplies were deemed completely impractical despite the fact that Uganda's water-power resources were acknowledged to be substantially greater than those of Kenya. According to a 1931 survey, there was a simple reason why these resources remained undeveloped, even for lighting Uganda's towns: 'Their requirements are insufficient to make it feasible, for the preponderating majority of the people, the Africans, are not potential customers'.[71] When British engineers carried out a survey of the hydroelectric potential of Owen Falls in 1934, they consistently viewed Africans either as potential labourers or political troublemakers, but never as electricity consumers.[72] In effect, the perceived 'traditionalism' of Africans was assumed to conflict with the use of electricity, which in turn kept them in a state of backwardness that continued to prevent the expansion of electricity networks. Much like the disparities that shaped household water and sewerage availability, inequities of access to electricity both reflected and reinforced the social and racial hierarchies of colonial societies.

The upwelling of interest in colonial hydropower in the 1920s and 1930s was part of a broader tendency to view Europe's empire as a source of renewal after the traumas of the First World War. The idea that the tropical colonies possessed an abundance of idle land and resources – and that the overcrowded nations of industrial Europe suffered from a shortage of both – was a common theme of European political thought ever since the nineteenth century. As the economist Paul-Leroy Beaulieu remarked in 1891, 'it is neither natural nor just that Western civilized peoples amass indefinitely and suffocate within the limited spaces that were their initial home . . . and leave perhaps half of the world to ignorant and powerless groups of people'.[73] Such concerns intensified sharply after the First World War, which not only highlighted Europe's reliance on overseas resources but also stoked fears of inexorable economic decline. After all, the rising global powers of the interwar period – the United

70. Hoag, *Developing the Rivers*, 151–52.
71. J. Robbins, *Hydro-electric Development*, 13.
72. Shamir, 'Head-Hunters'.
73. Leroy-Beaulieu, *De la colonisation* (1891), 842.

States and Soviet Union – both had vast hinterlands that could be exploited to satisfy their appetites for energy and raw materials. The perceived contrast between these 'youthful', continent-sized states and the small, war-torn countries of Europe reinforced the view that the control of territory and the extraction of resources from peripheries to industrial cores formed the basis of economic and political power. In order to counter the threat to Europe's global dominance, it was more important than ever to transform its colonies into storehouses of material wealth and markets for European goods.[74]

Africa in particular was regarded as a land of opportunity. Ever since the 1870s, intellectuals and officials throughout Western Europe had come to see the vast continent across the Mediterranean as the key strategic frontier for European expansion, a kind of southern equivalent to the American West. For some onlookers, the huge expanses of seemingly underused land conjured visions of large-scale European settlement as an alternative to emigration to the Americas. For most, however, the chief prize was access to African labour and raw materials. The desire to control the outward flows of African resources – minerals, vegetable oils, cotton, rubber – was a key driver behind the European 'scramble' for African territory in the 1880s, and the extraction of these resources only grew in importance after the war. Throughout the late nineteenth century and the early decades of the twentieth, most attempts to 'develop' African colonies were conceived as national projects between rival powers. During the 1920s and 1930s, they were increasingly overlaid by a new idea: the exploitation of African resources as a cooperative pan-European project.[75]

The idea of a 'Eurafrican' union was not new in the 1920s, but it was during this period that it rose to prominence. Its most vocal champion was the Austrian aristocrat Richard von Coudenhove-Kalergi, author of the widely read 1923 book *Pan-Europa* and an early proponent of European integration. His fundamental aim was to create a large, unified European trading zone modelled on the United States in a bid to boost Europe's economic prosperity and global power. Africa was central to his vision. He regarded it as nothing less than 'the future granary and source of raw materials for Europe'.[76] For Coudenhove-Kalergi, the two continents were inextricably linked. Each could develop its full potential only through the other. Europe, he claimed, was 'the head of Eurafrica, and Africa its body'.[77] Coudenhove-Kalergi was by no means alone in advocating a pan-European domination of Africa during the interwar years. Politicians and academics in France, Belgium, Italy and Germany articulated similar visions of Africa as 'the salvation of Europe'

74. See Beckert, 'American Danger'.

75. Hansen and Jonsson, *Eurafrica*, 17–70; Ageron, 'L'idée d'Eurafrique'; Fleury, 'Paneurope et l'Afrique'; Beckert, 'American Danger', 1161–66.

76. Coudenhove-Kalergi, *Paneuropa*, 145.

77. Richard N. Coudenhove-Kalergi, 'Afrika', *Paneuropa* vol. 5, no. 2 (1929), 1–19, quoted in Beckert, 'American Danger', 1162.

and as 'the great reserve – reserve of raw materials, reserve of markets – for Europeans'.[78]

For many interwar observers in Europe, Africa constituted more than just a reserve of raw materials. It also represented an enormous reservoir of hydroelectric power. According to the French political economist Eugène Léonard Guernier – whose 1933 book *L'Afrique: Champ d'expansion de l'Europe* served as a programmatic statement for the Eurafrican idea – harnessing the energy of Africa's waterways was a key element in the 'economic penetration' of the continent. For several reasons, it was a task that was especially suited to pan-European solutions. Not only would supranational coordination help to avoid water conflicts between different colonial empires (for instance on the Niger, Congo and Zambezi); it would also help stimulate the emergence of new cross-border markets, above all in the form of electrified railways. It was only matter of time, Guernier suggested, before 'a policy of electrification will gain a foothold, as today in Europe'. Since Africa was a land supposedly 'without history', let alone an electrical history, it made sense to learn from European experience and build an integrated network from the outset, since 'it is infinitely easier to "paint on a new canvas than on an old one"'. Through joint supranational exploitation, Africa's rivers could eventually serve European interests both directly (in the form of electricity transmitted from vast African hydropower plants) and indirectly (in the form of energy-intensive export goods).[79]

This conceptual linkage between hydroengineering and Eurafrican integration was an enticing prospect, and it eventually inspired one of the most ambitious hydraulic projects of the twentieth century: the 'Atlantropa' scheme devised by the German architect Herman Sörgel. In the late 1920s and 1930s, Sörgel led an association of like-minded engineers and technicians who literally sought to give concrete expression to the idea of an integrated Eurafrican supercontinent. Their plans foresaw the creation of a transcontinental network of railways, pipelines and canals that together would open up Africa's interior, irrigate parts of the Sahara, and create new agricultural land for the production of food, fibre and oil crops. The centrepiece of the project was a gargantuan dam at Gibraltar, which would form a physical and metaphorical bridge between Europe and Africa. The purpose of the dam was to halt the flow of water from the Atlantic into the Mediterranean, while a pair of smaller barrages at Gallipoli and the mouth of the Nile would cut the Mediterranean's water supply from its two other main sources. Gradually, the process of evaporation would cause the level of the Mediterranean to drop, exposing more farmland along the new coastline. At the same time it would also create an artificial 'fall'

78. Schubert, *Afrika, die Rettung Europas*; Joseph Caillaux, *D'Agadir à la grande penitence* (Paris: Flammarion, 1933), 125, quoted in Ageron, 'L'idée d'Eurafrique', 463. For an excellent recent analysis, see Denning's 'Unscrambling Africa'.

79. Guernier, *L'Afrique*, 55, 263–64.

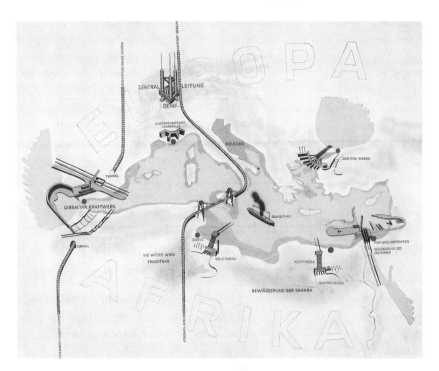

FIGURE 7.4. Herman Sörgel's Atlantropa scheme.
By permission of the Deutsches Museum Archive, ref. CD_78659.

between the Atlantic and Mediterranean, whose enormous energy potential could be harnessed by a battery of hydroelectric plants installed along the dam. In essence, the aim of Atlantropa was to turn the Mediterranean into a giant power plant.[80]

Although a hopelessly overambitious venture, Sörgel's utopian vision attracted many supporters. For this reason, it offers a useful insight into the diverse currents of thought about technology, politics, empire and environment that circulated in interwar Europe.[81] At one level, it reflected the powerful technocratic impulses of the period, which flourished amid the widespread sense of disenchantment with conventional politics (especially in the crisis-ridden atmosphere of interwar Germany). Sörgel himself possessed an almost unlimited confidence in the power of technology to overcome social, economic and political problems, and his proposals for reviving Europe's fortunes were very

80. Sörgel, *Atlantropa*. For detailed analyses of the project: Gall, *Das Atlantropa-Projekt*; Voigt, *Atlantropa*; Lehmann, 'Infinite Power' and *Desert Edens*, 72–91.

81. On Sörgel's world view, see esp. Lehmann's 'Infinite Power' (88–91) and *Desert Edens* (74–80).

much driven by engineers and scientists rather than politicians.[82] At another level, Atlantropa was also motivated by deep-seated anxieties about European economic, environmental and cultural decline, which gained widespread currency after the First World War. It was perhaps no coincidence that Sörgel was personally acquainted with the philosopher Oswald Spengler, a fellow Munich resident whose two-volume work *The Decline of the West* gained him international notoriety as interwar Europe's foremost cultural pessimist.[83] Like Spengler, Sörgel was profoundly concerned about the dangers emanating from the new global powers in the east and west, which together seemed to pose an existential threat to Europe's moral pre-eminence and material prosperity. He was equally alarmed by contemporary theories about resource shortages and the eventual 'desiccation' of Europe's climate, which posited an intimate connection between economic and cultural decline and a more general environmental crisis. As coal reserves would inevitably be depleted in an increasingly overcrowded Europe, the continent's insufficient land and energy resources would eventually doom it to a bleak future: 'at best it would still retain a fossilized culture, like Egypt or India today'.[84] Yet in contrast to those (like Spengler) who decried the soulless utilitarianism of technological civilization, Sörgel saw technology as the key to Europe's redemption. In his view, only radical technological solutions could avoid the all-encompassing crisis that he and others feared.

As one might expect, the specific solution that Sörgel proposed by no means convinced everyone. Many were dismissive of it; some were downright aghast. Critics of the Atlantropa scheme warned that lowering the level of the Mediterranean could have a range of catastrophically adverse consequences, from earthquakes and flooding to excessive salinization and the alteration of Europe's climate. Yet despite the often vehement condemnation that the project attracted, its technical feasibility per se was rarely called into question. What critics were most sceptical about were not the practical problems of such a grandiose project, but rather the political obstacles of European collaboration.[85] There was little doubt in the minds of interwar technocrats that Europe had to boost its hydropower supply to compete in the geopolitical contest for supremacy, and there was broad acceptance of the idea that it could do so on a sufficient scale only by harnessing the waters of Africa. Consequently, many observers concurred with the author Eugen Diesel, son of the famous inventor Rudolf Diesel, who remarked that 'Atlantropa is therefore not utopian, but accords with an inexorable course of development'.[86]

---

82. More generally on this theme: Graf, *Die Zukunft*; Rohrkrämer, *Eine andere Moderne?*.

83. Spengler, *Der Untergang des Abendlandes*; see also Farrenkopf, *Prophet of Decline*; Voigt, *Atlantropa*, 17–21.

84. Sörgel, *Atlantropa*, 78, quoted in Lehmann, 'Infinite Power', 81.

85. See Opitz, 'Atlantropa', 36; Gall, *Das Atlantropa-Projekt*, 53–54, 130–32; Voigt, *Atlantropa*, 47–52; Lehmann, 'Infinite Power', 92.

86. Quoted in Opitz, 'Atlantropa', 36.

Undeterred by his critics, Sörgel soon devised plans for an even more comprehensive replumbing of the African continent. In this second stage of the Atlantropa project, his focus shifted from the Mediterranean to the waters of the Congo basin. Together with the Swiss engineer Bruno Siegwart, a director at Royal Dutch Shell, he proposed the creation of a series of enormous dams that would transform the river's middle reaches into a vast inland sea that could eventually cover some nine hundred thousand square kilometres. Through the construction of a system of canals and hydroelectric plants, the resulting Congo Lake would not only facilitate internal shipping and supply irrigation water to arid regions around the basin but also, according to their calculations, generate up to forty-five gigawatts of power.[87] Beyond the Congo reservoir, Sörgel and Siegwart also sketched plans for an enlarged Lake Chad and a new inland sea on the Zambezi. The hope was that these lakes would produce a marked improvement in the regional climate, reduce tropical diseases such as malaria and blackwater fever, and ultimately open up millions of square kilometres of previously inhospitable terrain to European settlers in need of land. From a long-term geopolitical perspective, the 'opening up' (*Erschließung*) of the continent was nothing less than a 'matter of life or death' for the 'white race and culture of Europe'. As for the hundreds of thousands of Africans whose lands would be submerged, they barely registered as a matter for consideration. In fact, given the geography of disease in the region, there was a certain logic in 'destroying areas where only blacks can live' in order to facilitate the long-term domination of Africa by keeping their superior numbers over white settlers within certain limits. For Sörgel, as for many advocates of Eurafrican integration, Africa was 'like a full, untouched savings account', the 'only great extent of land in the world that still lies unexploited'. Insofar as he gave any thought at all to its inhabitants, their racial subordination for the benefit of Europeans was a taken-for-granted element of the entire scheme.[88]

Atlantropa attracted widespread attention in interwar Germany, but after the Nazi takeover in 1933 interest in the project gradually waned, and after the invasion of the Soviet Union in 1941 planning for a German-led Eurafrica effectively collapsed.[89] Although Sörgel, like so many Germans, sought to adapt to the new political situation, ultimately his focus on Africa was out of tune with the Nazis' plans to acquire 'living space' in the 'East'. After the Second World War, the scheme once again came into the spotlight amid calls for a 'Eurafrican' alternative to Europe's Cold War division into Eastern and Western blocs. But after 1945, neither the political, economic nor intellectual context were very

87. Sörgel and Siegwart, 'Erschliessung Afrikas'; Gall, *Das Atlantropa-Projekt*, 33, 57–59; Lehmann, 'Infinite Power', 82–84; *Desert Edens*, 84–87.

88. Quotes from Sörgel and Siegwart, 'Erschliessung Afrikas', 37–39; see also Lehmann, 'Infinite Power', 84 (which also discusses the overtly racist elements of the scheme); Gall, *Das Atlantropa-Projekt*, 56–61.

89. On the demise of wartime Eurafrica plans, see Denning's 'Unscrambling Africa'.

favourable for such a plan. Interwar apprehensions about a comprehensive cultural and environmental crisis seemed almost irrelevant amid the appalling wreckage of the immediate post-war years. Once the economic recovery of Europe took hold in the late 1940s and early 1950s, fears of imminent energy shortages were blunted by the rising tide of Middle Eastern oil and the promise of nuclear power. Nor did such a wide-ranging intercontinental scheme sit easily within the post-war geopolitical order, characterized as it was by Cold War partition, rising calls for African independence and a more limited form of European integration than what Sörgel had in mind. In 1952, at the age of sixty-seven, Sörgel was killed in a bicycling accident, and with his death the dream of Atlantropa died too.[90] Yet the fascination with technological mega-projects that animated Sörgel's vision – and the determination of politicians, scientists and engineers to harness the energy of Africa's rivers – remained very much alive.

Hydropowered Development

For Europe's colonial powers, the 1940s and 1950s were a period of both retreat and reinforcement. On the one hand, the loss of the majority of Asian colonies in the 1940s – first to Japanese troops, then to powerful independence movements – underscored the fragility of colonial rule and left little doubt that it would need to find new ways to justify itself in the post-war international order. Even where the European powers remained entrenched (mainly in Africa, the Caribbean and pockets of Southeast Asia), the pressures of wartime mobilization amplified demands for better social services, faster economic growth and higher living standards. On the other hand, the daunting task of economic reconstruction in war-torn Europe also highlighted the potential of colonial territories to serve as a source of revitalization. Amid the ongoing shortages and acute financial pressures of post-war recovery, the development and exploitation of colonial resources answered an urgent need for raw materials and foreign exchange.[91]

The overall result was an unprecedented programme of developmental imperialism, a surge of state intervention into the economies, societies and ecosystems of the colonial world. In some ways, this post-war development drive was hardly novel. There are good reasons why historians have sometimes referred to it as a 'second colonial occupation', for its primary aims broadly matched those of imperial reform efforts ever since the turn of the century: boosting exports, improving communications, increasing crop production and

90. Gall, *Das Atlantropa-Projekt*, 47–48, 166–69; Lehmann, *Desert Edens*, 103–11; 'Infinite Power', 92–98; Opitz, 'Atlantropa', 36. On the post-war resurrection of ideas of 'Eurafrica': Hansen and Jonsson, *Eurafrica*, 71–146; 'Another Colonialism'.
91. N. White, 'Reconstructing Europe'.

extracting raw materials. The difference was the sheer scale of such initiatives, which far surpassed anything that had been attempted before the Second World War.

This required, first and foremost, a whole new level of state investment. Whereas colonial states had previously operated on a shoestring budget, in the late 1940s metropolitan governments allocated record sums through new organizations such as the British Colonial Development Corporation (CDC, 1947), the French Fonds pour l'investissement en développement économique et social (FIDES, 1946), or within the framework of various five- or ten-year development plans.[92] It also required the systematic application of 'expert' knowledge. In order to maximize the effectiveness of their investments, British, French and Belgian authorities created an assemblage of new research agencies to study colonial resources and devise scientific plans for exploiting them.[93] Together, this unprecedented deployment of funding and know-how encouraged colonial technocrats to think big. After all, one of the key policy 'lessons' of the Second World War was that centralized state control, mass-production methods and large-scale technological projects could achieve dramatic results in a short space of time. The prevailing idea, in the words of one contemporary, was 'the bigger the scheme the better the results likely to be obtained'.[94]

Nowhere was the enthusiasm for large, high-tech projects greater than in the field of hydropower development. During the post-war years, the construction of dams accounted for much of the development funding spent by metropolitan governments, multilateral aid agencies and newly independent states. Among colonial officials and anti-colonial leaders alike, such projects were regarded as a powerful tool for economic transformation: stimulating industry, expanding transportation, boosting demand for manufactured goods and generally raising living standards. Hydropower dams thus became important, albeit ambivalent, political symbols. Depending on one's point of view, they were towering displays of the benefits of colonial rule or monuments to the promise of post-colonial economic emancipation.

The wave of dam building that swept across the post-war colonial world was closely bound up with the spread of 'integrated river basin planning'. The basic rationale of comprehensive river basin development was to coordinate the various uses of water across an entire watershed in order to avoid conflicts between upstream and downstream users and to ensure that the water was put to best use. The idea was pioneered by planners at the Tennessee Valley

92. See Havinden and Meredith, *Colonialism and Development*, 206–34; Afrique Occidentale française, *Le plan quadriennal*; *Bulletin agricole du Congo belge*, 109–10.

93. Hodge, *Triumph of the Expert*, 207–53; Bonneuil, *Des savants pour l'Empire*, 83–85.

94. Baldwin, *Niger Agricultural Project*, 1. On the role of the Second World War as a catalyst for the development of hydroelectricity, see Cohn, Evenden and Landry's 'Water Powers'.

Authority, one of the crown jewels of Franklin Roosevelt's New Deal. Established in 1933, the TVA was intended to modernize the economy of a rural southern region that that had long been regarded as backward and that was suffering acutely from the effects of the Depression. In order to coordinate water use across several different states, it was designed as a centralized federal agency with a broad array of responsibilities. Although its remit encompassed everything from transportation and irrigation to flood control, its main purpose was to electrify the region and attract new industries through the provision of cheap hydropower. Within a decade of its launch, the TVA had built over a dozen hydroelectric dams, whose combined output made it the single largest electricity supplier in the United States. Although it was less groundbreaking than has often been claimed (building in part on Indian, Soviet and other precedents), and less economically beneficial than its boosters liked to assert, by the 1950s the TVA was adopted by the United Nations as the global template for the development of water resources. With its emphasis on multipurpose dams and large-scale planning, it symbolized a new way of thinking about hydropower as a tool for economic growth.[95]

Colonial officials eyed this hydro-technocratic prototype with great interest. Although some elements of the TVA formula were of less interest to them than to their American counterparts – for example, the concern about watershed conservation and especially the emphasis on rural electrification – they shared a strong predilection for large-scale infrastructure projects and a commitment to closer state involvement in economic development. Above all, the TVA model of a centralized, autonomous public authority staffed with hydraulic engineers rather than bureaucrats spoke directly to the view that such matters were best left to scientific experts with minimal interference from other groups.[96]

It was precisely this vision of a state-led, hydropowered programme of economic development that inspired the first major post-war dam project in colonial Africa: the barrage at Owen Falls. Interest in the site spiked after the war amid plans to encourage the expansion of industry in Uganda. The newly appointed colonial governor Sir John Hall was a firm believer in hydropower as an engine of economic advancement. Cheap electricity, he argued, was the key to promoting African prosperity. By producing 'not copper ore but electrolytic copper, not bauxite but aluminium, not lime but cement, not raw cotton but piece-goods', an electrified Africa could move further up the value chains of the global economy. In 1946, he commissioned the engineer Charles

95. On the TVA: Downs, *Transforming the South*, 73–180; Phillips, *This Land, This Nation*, 83–107; Cater, *Regenerating Dixie*. On its status as international model: Finer, *TVA*; Lagendijk, 'From American South'. On its limited economic benefits: Kitchens, 'Publicly Provided Electricity'. On the global spread of US water engineering before the TVA, see generally Teisch's *Engineering Nature*.

96. Lagendijk, 'From American South'; Hoag, 'Transplanting the TVA?'. More generally on the transnational dimensions of New Deal initiatives like the TVA, see Patel's *New Deal*.

Westlake to conduct a feasibility study at Owen Falls, and the following year the government pushed forward with plans for a dam.[97]

In some ways, the Owen Falls project closely followed the TVA script. Planning was overseen by a new Uganda Electricity Board, an independent public corporation backed by government funds. In 1948, Westlake and several other engineers made a pilgrimage to the United States to study the TVA up close. Two years later, *Life* magazine breathlessly described the Owen Falls project as the keystone of an 'international super-TVA scheme' that would turn Lake Victoria into the world's largest reservoir, build a canal around the Sudd swamp in South Sudan, irrigate 1.5 million acres (6,000 square kilometres) of land, and 'create nothing less than a new civilization along a river that has cradled civilization since history began'. In 1952, the colonial government also established the Uganda Development Corporation, whose purpose was to lure overseas investment into the region by allowing the state to shoulder a share of the risk of industrial expansion.[98]

Yet in other ways, the Owen Falls scheme diverged from the TVA template. For one thing, it was never actually pursued as a multipurpose project, but solely as a means of producing hydroelectricity. In addition, its electricity was deliberately earmarked for industry and affluent urban households rather than rural consumers. Despite Westlake's vocal advocacy of general electrification as a basic public service, in practice the scheme disregarded Africans as potential customers.[99] Most importantly, despite all of the rhetoric about international coordination, in many ways the project signalled the *end* rather than the beginning of integrated river basin management along the Nile. As we saw in chapter 2, plans for a comprehensive transformation of the Nile basin reach back to the early 1900s, and conflicts over the precise shape this would take were by no means resolved by the 1929 Nile Waters Agreement. By the 1930s, the Egyptian Ministry of Works was studying proposals for projects all along the Nile, and by the 1940s such plans had culminated in the so-called Equatorial Nile Project, which envisaged massive storage works on East Africa's Great Lakes to regulate the river's flow.[100]

No sooner was planning for Owen Falls underway than the scheme became ensnared in the complexities of Nile basin politics. For the Ugandan administration, the aim of the dam was to generate hydropower, which was best pursued by ensuring a constant maximum discharge all year round. By contrast, officials in Cairo primarily wanted to raise the level of Lake Victoria (thus flooding low-lying shoreline areas of Uganda, Kenya and Tanzania) for

97. Quoted in Tvedt, *River Nile*, 212; see also Wilson, *Owen Falls*, 1–3.

98. 'Nile: Its Course', 119 (quote); Elkan and Wilson, 'Owen Falls Hydro-electric Project', 397–98; Hoag, *Developing the Rivers*, 161.

99. Westlake, Mountain and Paton, 'Owen Falls', 642–48; Hoag, *Developing the Rivers*, 158–61.

100. Blocher, *Der Wasserbau-Staat*, 277–89.

storing water to release during periods of shortage in Egypt. The Sudanese government was mainly worried about flood control and the implications of any hydrological alteration for the sprawling irrigation scheme at Gezira. Once again, the different water requirements that these various uses entailed made it impossible to serve so many different interests. In the middle of these clashing interests stood the British government, which had to act as mediator. Eventually it managed to broker an agreement whereby the Egyptian government paid Uganda £980,000 to construct a dam one metre higher than initially planned (thus boosting its storage capacity) and to operate it with a slightly lower discharge and power generating capacity than Uganda had originally proposed. In essence, the settlement gave Uganda most of what it wanted, Sudan some of what it wanted and Egypt considerably less than what it wanted. By failing to do much to satisfy Egypt's mounting water needs, it effectively marked the end of the long-standing British conception of the Nile basin as a hydrological system to be managed for the benefit of Egypt. In fact, the diplomatic battle over Owen Falls reinforced the belief among Egyptian nationalists that they would eventually have to find a solution to the country's water problems within its own borders. In this sense, the Owen Falls scheme was the direct prelude to the Aswan High Dam.[101]

On a more general level, the Owen Falls dam encapsulated the peculiar mixture of tenacity and fragility that characterized colonial power in the 1950s. On the one hand, it was celebrated as a symbol of Britain's determination to promote economic and social progress in the colonies. During its construction, officials regularly fed photos and information about the project to the international press. Upon its completion, the barrage was lavishly inaugurated by none other than Queen Elizabeth II herself. On the other hand, it also pointed to Britain's growing geostrategic frailties in Africa. Even as the queen officially opened the dam in April 1954, Prime Minister Churchill was engaged in a diplomatic struggle against a nationalist government in Egypt that was irked by the failure to get its way at Owen Falls. As a result of this stinging disappointment, the Egyptian government was more determined than ever to wrest control over the Suez Canal from Britain. Nearly fifty years after the unharnessed power of the falls first vexed Churchill's imagination, his thoughts were now vexed by the mounting threats to Britain's imperial power in Africa.[102]

For all the political wrangling over the Owen Falls dam, in the end its central purpose was to supply electricity to Uganda's growing mining industry. In this respect, it typified a more general trend across late-colonial Africa to combine hydropower and mineral extraction as a motor for economic development.

101. This discussion follows Tvedt's *Age of the British* (212–24) and *Exchanges of Notes between the Government of the United Kingdom . . . and the Government of Egypt*.

102. Tvedt, *Age of the British*, 223–24; Hoag, *Developing the Rivers*, 161–62.

The global mining boom that was triggered by the Second World War did not cease in 1945 but continued long after the fighting was over. As post-war reconstruction accelerated, and as the Cold War began to heat up, mining firms the world over increased their production and scoured the globe for new deposits. By and large, it was not very difficult to extract more minerals out of the ground. There were still plenty of untapped ore deposits strewn throughout the developing world. Even in areas that had been mined for decades, the deployment of new technologies and ever-larger machines allowed for the profitable exploitation of ever-lower grades of ore. The main bottleneck was the supply of power for smelting them. As European states sought to rebuild their war-torn economies, a combination of high electricity costs and spiralling demand threatened to create a shortage of much-needed metals.

During the immediate post-war years, European governments increasingly looked to their colonies to supply them both with minerals and with the energy required to process them. This was especially true of the all-important aluminium industry. Over the first half of the twentieth century, this light, non-corrodible, highly conductive metal had become an essential ingredient of modernity. Its indispensability for aircraft production had made it a key strategic resource ever since the 1920s. After the Second World War, demand for aluminium continued to soar owing to the rapid growth of the automotive, electrical and commercial aircraft industries. As bauxite reserves in France and North America were progressively depleted, several of Europe's colonies became major producers: Guyana, Suriname and Jamaica in the 1940s, followed by the Gold Coast and Guinea in the 1950s.[103] In the process, colonial hydropower resources became just as important as bauxite deposits.

The transformation of bauxite into aluminium is unusually energy-intensive even by the power-guzzling standards of the mineral processing industry. Raw bauxite is first converted into alumina (aluminium oxide) by milling it into a powder and subjecting it to high-temperature chemical treatment. The resulting alumina is then smelted into aluminium via electrolysis, which requires enormous amounts of electricity because of its high melting point ($2,072\,°C$). Consequently, the price of energy has always been the key component in the overall cost of aluminium production.[104] Ever since the late nineteenth century, aluminium companies had invested heavily in hydro-electric plants as a source of low-cost power. Once the best sites in Europe and North America were exploited, they increasingly competed for access to cheap hydropower overseas. The result was a sprawling commodity web linking bauxite-rich locations with hydropower-rich locations around the world.

103. See Sheller, *Aluminum Dreams*, 147–78, 194–202; Evenden, 'Aluminum'; R. Graham, *Aluminium Industry*, 80, 93–106; C. Davis, *Jamaica*; Larrue, *Fria en Guinée*; Campbell, *Les enjeux*.

104. R. Graham, *Aluminium Industry*, 85–86.

During the 1940s and 1950s, West Africa became increasingly enmeshed in this global commodity web. The first hydropowered aluminium complex in colonial Africa was the Edéa scheme in Cameroon, located around seventy-seven kilometres from the mouth of the Sanaga River. The idea was hatched in the late 1940s when a combination of sharply rising energy costs and dwindling bauxite supplies in southern France pitched the French aluminium industry into a state of crisis. The French government was eager to help find a solution. From 1950 to 1954, it used FIDES funds to support the construction of a hydro-electric dam at Edéa, and in 1954 it teamed up with Péchiney Ugine – Europe's largest aluminium firm – to form the ALUCAM corporation, which would build and operate a new alumina smelter on the site. In a parallel move, Péchiney Ugine also opened a new bauxite mine and alumina plant in Guinea to supplement French supplies of alumina destined for the ALUCAM smelter.[105]

When the Edéa project was completed in 1958, it was widely hailed as a model of mineral-based economic development. As one industry pamphlet triumphantly proclaimed, 'the moment of Africa's industrialization is also the moment of aluminium'.[106] According to its promoters, what made the Edéa scheme so important was not merely the economic benefit that it would purportedly bring to Cameroon. Equally if not more significant was its political symbolism. Instead of the usual colonial trading pattern whereby raw materials were shipped from Africa to be transformed into finished products in France, the dam and smelter at Edéa were built (at least in part) to convert a French raw material into a refined product in Africa. For contemporaries, Edéa thus marked the emergence of a 'kind of reverse colonial pact'.[107]

Underneath the rhetoric, however, there was nothing altruistic about this new colonial arrangement. If Edéa exemplified anything, it was not an inversion of imperial hierarchies but rather the tendency of 'colonial development' schemes to serve metropolitan interests. The Edéa complex was a textbook 'economic enclave', an island of industry more closely integrated with distant markets in France than with local economies. Nearly all of the dam's electricity was allocated to ALUCAM; the electrification of the local area scarcely entered the minds of project planners. Although a small number of local people benefitted by getting jobs at the smelter, the advantages for nearby communities were offset by the harsh labour conditions for workers who built the plant, and above all by the hundreds of thousands of tons of 'red mud' (a caustic alkaline waste product from bauxite processing, laced with toxic metals) that it released annually into the lower Sanaga River. The main beneficiary was Péchiney Ugine, which purchased Edéa's electricity at a cost of 0.8 francs per kilowatt-hour, compared to a price of 3 or 4 francs in France.

105. Laparra, 'Enelcam – Alucam'; Atangana, *French Investment*, 143–47.
106. *L'Afrique à l'heure de l'aluminium*.
107. 'Hydroélectricité et complexes économiques régionaux', 85.

Rather than representing a reversal of colonial economic relations, Edéa was built to tap cheap colonial hydropower resources for indirect 'export' to the industrialized world. As Martin Atangana has concluded, 'ALUCAM is not a Cameroonian problem solved by Péchiney. It is a problem of Péchiney solved in Cameroon'.[108]

In the meantime, even bigger problems within Britain's aluminium industry spawned an even grander scheme for exploiting African hydropower. Of all the major industrial economies, the United Kingdom was the least self-sufficient when it came to aluminium. In the early post-war years, the once-powerful British Aluminium Company produced only one-seventh of what UK fabricators needed. As a result, aluminium imports into Britain constituted a huge drain on the Exchequer at a time when the country could scarcely afford it. The main problem was not a shortage of bauxite (there were abundant deposits in various parts of the British Empire) but rather the lack of cheap power for smelting and manufacturing in the United Kingdom.

When British officials searched for suitable hydropower sites in the colonies, their attention soon focused on the Volta River in the Gold Coast.[109] The idea of damming the Volta was far from new. It was first proposed in 1915 by Albert Kitson, director of the Gold Coast Geological Survey, around a year after he discovered substantial bauxite deposits in the colony. In the 1920s and 1930s, engineers carried out further examinations and drew up increasingly ambitious plans for controlling the river. During the Second World War, the Gold Coast's bauxite output rose sharply, and by 1949 the British and Gold Coast governments were sufficiently interested in the Volta's hydropower potential to commission a full feasibility study. The final report, submitted in August 1951, called for the construction of an eighty-metre dam and power station at a total cost of around £40 million.[110] With energy costs in Britain prohibitively high, the Volta River Project quickly advanced beyond the planning stage.

One of its most enthusiastic backers was Kwame Nkrumah, whose pro-independence Convention People's Party had just won a landslide victory in the colony's February 1951 general election, the first in Africa to take place on the basis of universal suffrage. As the Gold Coast's first prime minister, Nkrumah not only pushed the Volta scheme up the political agenda but also transformed its place within the broader political context. Nkrumah was the epitome of a modernizing nationalist leader. He was a firm believer in the need for industrial development and he was convinced that colonial rule served to impede rather than facilitate it. Although the Volta River Project was initially conceived to serve British needs, for Nkrumah it was the cornerstone of Ghana's future economic independence, 'a scheme which can change the face

108. Atangana, *French Investment*, 147.
109. R. Graham, *Aluminium Industry*, 65–67.
110. Hart, *Volta River Project*, 13–16; Kitson, *Outlines*, 44.

of our land and bring wealth and a higher standard of living to our people'. In 1953, he chaired the project's Preparatory Commission, and during the election campaigns of 1954 and 1956 he made it a central plank of his party's programme.[111]

After Ghana achieved independence in 1957, the Volta River Project became very much 'Nkrumah's baby'.[112] What had started as a colonial enterprise became a nationalist initiative to overcome the legacy of colonial economic subservience. The problem was that the British and Canadian firms that had led the project to date quickly lost interest with the transition to independence. Undeterred by this setback, Nkrumah turned to the United States for assistance. In 1959, the American firm Kaiser Aluminum submitted a new design for the project that included a hydroelectric dam at Akosombo, an alumina plant and smelter at Tema, and secondary dams at Kpong and Bui. Over the next two years, officials from Ghana, the United States, Britain and the World Bank negotiated construction plans and financing arrangements. In 1961, the Ghanaian government set up the Volta River Authority – in conscious emulation of the TVA, and chaired by Nkrumah himself – to manage the development of the entire Volta River basin, including the dam and power station as well as the new reservoir, its fishery and inland navigation. Arguably the most challenging task for the Volta River Authority was to oversee the resettlement of some eighty thousand people who would be displaced by the reservoir (nearly 1 per cent of Ghana's entire population), whom Nkrumah insisted should be 'no worse off than before'.[113]

When the Akosombo Dam was finally completed in 1965, it ranked as one of the largest hydropower schemes in the entire world. The barrage itself was 600 metres long and 114 metres high, and the 8,500-square-kilometre Lake Volta (covering 3.6 per cent of Ghana's entire territory) was the world's largest man-made lake by surface area. The Volta River Project stood as the physical embodiment of Ghana's commitment to industrial modernization and future development. Nkrumah revelled in showing it off to foreign visitors, most of whom spent a night or two in the lavish Volta Hotel that was built on a hill overlooking the dam. Thousands of people visited the site each year, and during the construction phase the Ghanaian press continually ran stories about it.[114] At the formal inauguration of the dam in January 1966, Nkrumah hailed it as a major achievement not only for Ghana but also for the cause of international cooperation. In his words, it illustrated how the most technically

111. Quote from Miescher, '"Nkrumah's Baby"', 344–45; see also Hoag, *Developing the Rivers*, 179–82.

112. Miescher, ' "Nkrumah's Baby" '.

113. Hart, *Volta River Project*, 25–26, 76–84, quote at 88; more generally, Chambers, *Volta Resettlement Experience*.

114. See generally Miescher, ' "Nkrumah's Baby" '; figures from Hart, *Volta River Project*, 22–33.

FIGURE 7.5. Two Ghanian men conversing on the hotel terrace overlooking the Volta Lake, Akosombo, Ghana, late February 1962.
Source: NSAG Van Es Collection. CC BY-SA 4.0.

advanced countries – above all the United States – would be able to increase their own prosperity 'and at the same time assist in increasing the prosperity of the developing world' by providing poorer countries with financial and technical support. At a regional level too, the Volta River Project was to serve as a vehicle for pan-African solidarity through the export of much-needed electricity to neighbouring 'sister states'.[115]

Yet despite all of the post-colonial fanfare, in many respects the Volta River Project – like Cameroon's Edéa complex – was less a monument to economic independence than to the continuance of global power disparities, what one might call the 'neo-colonization' of African hydropower resources. In the late 1950s, while Nkrumah was discussing finance arrangements with the United States and the World Bank, the so-called 'big four' North American aluminium firms – Kaiser, Reynolds, ALCAN, ALCOA – jointly established the Volta Aluminium Company Ltd (VALCO) in a bid to pool their negotiating leverage in talks with the Ghanaian government. By creating what was essentially a mini-monopoly of interested parties, they managed to extract an eye-watering list of concessions from the government, including a heavily reduced tax rate, the ability to import alumina rather than mine and process it in Ghana itself, the right to transfer earnings and profits out of the country without restriction, a long-term

115. Quotes from Hart, *Volta River Project*, 41. See also Miescher, ' "Nkrumah's Baby" ', 363–64.

guarantee against expropriation, and, perhaps most importantly, an extremely low price for the electricity that they purchased from the state-owned Volta River Project. The perverse result was that the government of a developing country effectively took on additional debts to subsidize aluminium production by a group of wealthy multinational corporations, while simultaneously conceding to them much of its 'resource sovereignty' in the process.[116]

If the Volta River Project deal was a poor one for the Ghanaian government, ordinary Ghanaians also benefitted far less than they had been promised. Whereas the bulk of the dam's electricity went to VALCO, and a much smaller proportion to cities in Ghana, Côte d'Ivoire, Togo and Benin, the transmission wires completely bypassed the majority of rural-dwelling Ghanaians. Even those urban residents and businesses who received its electricity had to pay five times more for it than VALCO did. Despite all the publicity campaigns claiming that everyone would profit from the scheme, it in fact caused a series of social and environmental problems. Rather than stimulating industrial development in the region, it led instead to a sharp increase in waterborne ailments (especially malaria and bilharzia), overcrowding on resettlement schemes, rising levels of debt and severe damage to downstream fisheries.[117]

Against this backdrop, it is perhaps unsurprising that Nkrumah chose to omit any discussion of the Volta River Project from his widely read 1965 book *Neo-colonialism: The Last Stage of Imperialism*.[118] Although the scheme was very much his political 'baby', its overall outcomes reflected all too well the book's central thesis about the persistence of imperial economic dominance in Africa. In the end, even Nkrumah himself failed to benefit much from the Volta River Project, whose enormous costs exacerbated Ghana's ongoing economic difficulties. In February 1966, just one month after inaugurating the Akosombo Dam, he was swept from power in a military coup, never again to return to the country that he led to independence.

The disillusionments surrounding the Volta River Project were a variation on a common theme. Large hydropower projects, whether in the colonial world or elsewhere, rarely turned out to be as advantageous as initially claimed. The roots of the problem are not hard to find. Advocates of hydropower schemes often hyped the multiple benefits that they would bring – electrification, water supplies, flood control, irrigation – in order to convince government officials and win over public opinion. At the same time, they generally downplayed the social and ecological costs and disregarded the inevitable trade-offs between

116. R. Graham, *Aluminium Industry*, 179–82.
117. See Tsikata, *Living in the Shadow*; Hart, *Volta River Project*, 75–102; Akyeampong, *Between the Sea*, 178–82; Jobin, *Dams and Disease*, 272–83, 360–63.
118. Despite its manifest importance to Nkrumah, the project is mentioned only once in passing: Nkrumah, *Neo-colonialism*, 101.

the different uses that dams could theoretically serve. Once all the lobbying and publicity subsided, the cost–benefit ratio rarely proved as favourable as people had been led to believe. Invariably the distribution of advantages and disadvantages reflected hierarchies of economic and political power. While most of the rewards flowed to industrial and urban centres – or, indirectly, to affluent consumers thousands of miles away – the drawbacks landed overwhelmingly on local communities and ecosystems immediately above or below the dam.

The reconfiguration of the Zambezi River illustrates just how far-reaching and long-lasting these drawbacks could be. Measuring 2,500 kilometres in length, the Zambezi is the fifth-longest river in Africa and the largest system that empties into the Indian Ocean. During the twilight years of colonial rule, it was straddled by two of the biggest hydroelectric installations ever built on the continent, the Kariba and Cahora Bassa Dams. These two barrages shared much in common besides the Zambezi itself. They both epitomized the grand scale of late-colonial infrastructure projects and the science-led developmental discourse that animated them. They were heavily backed by modernizing bureaucrats eager to provide technological solutions to pressing political and social problems: in this case, a desire to delay or (more optimistically) avoid the eventual demise of colonial rule in the face of growing demands for independence. Both were putatively conceived to supply electricity for an entire region, yet ended up supplying mainly distant markets. And both had profound social and ecological consequences that lasted long after the end of colonialism.

The first to be built was the Kariba Dam, the largest infrastructural project ever launched by the British in colonial Africa. Straddling a remote stretch of the Zambezi, the 128- by 620-metre concrete structure ranked at the time as one of the engineering marvels of the world. After its initial closure in 1958, it gradually created the world's largest artificial lake by volume. Unlike most large dams of the era, Kariba served one main purpose: the production of electricity. Situated midway between Northern Rhodesia's copper mines and Southern Rhodesia's industrial centre of Bulawayo, it was designed to be the powerhouse of the newly incorporated Federation of Rhodesia and Nyasaland. What made it all possible was the development of 330-kilovolt lines that enabled the power plant to transmit electricity to consumer markets located over 550 kilometres away, farther than anything hitherto attempted in Africa. By the early 1960s, Kariba was annually sending over a billion kilowatt-hours to Central Africa's industrial hubs, and bypassing nearly everything in between.[119]

From an engineering perspective, Kariba was a major triumph of European science and technology. For advocates of the colonial federation it represented 'a monument to the white man's genius' and his 'physical struggle to master a

---

119. For a detailed account: Tischler, *Light and Power*; see also Showers, 'Electrifying Africa', 199, 207.

FIGURE 7.6. The Kariba Dam on the Zambezi River.
Source: Collectie Stichting Nationaal Museum van Wereldculturen.
CC BY-SA 3.0.

continent'.[120] Yet from a social and ecological perspective, it looked very different. For one thing, it forced around fifty-seven thousand Tonga people to vacate their riparian lands for higher ground. Most of the resettlement areas were far less fertile than the rich floodplain pastures inundated by the dam and therefore supported fewer livestock. Although the resettlement programme was initially pursued on a voluntary basis (at least by more paternalistically inclined officials), instances of Tonga resistance against the loss of their homeland eventually led to a more coercive approach. Predictably, most of the resettlement villages never received electricity from the dam that displaced their residents.[121]

To add insult to injury, the promises of abundant fish harvests from the new reservoir – a major benefit that was supposed to compensate the Tonga for the loss of livestock and dietary protein – turned out to be exaggerated. In the mid-1950s, the colonial fisheries adviser Fred Hickling conducted a study of the local ichthyofauna in order to estimate the future reservoir's fishery

120. Frank Clements, *Kariba: The Struggle with the River God* (London: Methuen, 1959), 13, quoted in D. Hughes, 'Whites and Water', 829.

121. Tischler, 'Cementing Uneven Development'. The literature on the resettlement is extensive: Colson, *Social Organisation* and *Social Consequences of Resettlement*; Scudder, *Ecology*; McGregor, *Crossing the Zambezi* and 'Living with the River'.

potential. Although he (like his scientific colleagues elsewhere in colonial Africa; see chapter 5) advised against any hasty stocking of exotic species, subsequent studies could find no local fish to feed on the profusion of zooplankton that would occur in the lake, so it was decided to stock it with various species of tilapia.[122] For a while, the plan appeared to work. As usually happens in new reservoirs, high nutrient and mineral levels from decaying vegetation and flooded soil led to an explosive rise in fish numbers. In turn, this burst of aquatic reproduction supported over-optimistic fishery forecasts among project supporters. After a few years, however, the gradual return to normal nutrient levels led to a steep fall in fish catches. In response, authorities introduced a small sardine species (*Limnothrissa miodon*, the same species that Belgian scientists released in Lake Kivu) from Lake Tanganyika in an effort to create a significant limnetic (open water) fishery on the lake. It proved to be a bad move. Unlike the relatively beneficial outcomes on Lake Kivu, at Kariba the exotic sardines did not spawn rapidly enough to sustain a sizeable fishery. In fact, their main effect was to displace the indigenous *Alestes* species that were already migrating into the limnetic region of the lake and were a favourite prey for the coveted tigerfish. All in all, the efforts to create a new fishery at Kariba did little to mitigate the losses of the Gwembe Tonga, and furnished yet another lesson in the dangers of meddling with aquatic ecosystems, especially those that are not very well understood.[123]

People were of course not the only organisms flooded out by the Kariba Dam. It also displaced large numbers of primates, elephants, hippopotamuses, antelope, leopards, and a host of smaller and less charismatic creatures. Altogether, the inundation of 5,580 square kilometres of the Zambezi plain is probably the largest single act of habitat devastation in colonial history. In response, conservationists and government officials launched the largest wildlife rescue campaign ever mounted up to that point: the fittingly named Operation Noah, which captured and relocated around seven thousand animals to the shores of the lake, mainly to the new Matusadona National Park in Southern Rhodesia. From 1958 to 1963, the rescue operation above Kariba became a focal point of the increasingly global wildlife conservation movement. But despite strong international support, there was no way that it could prevent vast numbers of animals from starving or drowning on disappearing islands.[124]

Meanwhile, around five hundred kilometres downstream, Portuguese authorities in Mozambique were drawing up plans for an even bigger dam at the Cahora Bassa rapids, the boundary between the middle Zambezi and its lower reaches. The idea first took shape in the mid-1950s while preparations

122. 'Prediction and Research on the Zambezi'.

123. For details: Balon and Coche, *Lake Kariba*.

124. Lagus, *Operation Noah*; E. Robins and Legge, *Animal Dunkirk*; Critchley, 'Operation Noah'.

for Kariba were underway. By the early 1960s, the project plans had evolved into a huge multipurpose dam designed to generate cheap energy for local industries, provide irrigation water for the production of commodity crops and attract tens of thousands of white settlers into planned agricultural settlements. As was so often the case, two of the main difficulties facing the project were a shortage of capital and the lack of a nearby market for electricity. In addition, Cahora Bassa was confronted by a more unusual threat: the acute security risk from guerrilla attacks by the Front for the Liberation of Mozambique (FRELIMO). To solve all three of these problems, Portuguese officials turned to South Africa's apartheid government, which provided both financial and military backing in exchange for the sale of cheap power to Johannesburg via new high-voltage transmission lines. According to the intergovernmental agreement, Cahora Bassa was redesigned as a single-purpose hydroelectric scheme without the irrigation and settlement facilities that were originally planned. Although Portuguese officials continued to claim that the dam would jump-start Mozambique's industrial development, its main purpose was to maintain colonial rule by enlisting South African support for the government's escalating war against the FRELIMO. Upon its completion in 1974, the $515 million mega-dam – the fifth-largest hydropower project in the entire world – exported over four-fifths of its electricity to South Africa.[125]

The Cahora Bassa Dam literally cemented the strategic military alliance of the Portuguese and South African governments against what they regarded as the 'black onslaught'.[126] Fixated as they were on the political and military aspects of the project, planners paid almost no attention at all to the effects it might have on local people or the environment. If it is possible to discern some benevolent intentions behind most colonial dam projects, and occasionally identify certain advantages that they brought, the Cahora Bassa scheme displayed few if any redeeming features. It was, as one observer has put it, 'a very bad dam indeed', one that was driven by an explicitly racist rationale that had become passé elsewhere in the late-colonial world and that amplified many of the problems that arose at Kariba.[127]

The most immediate and dramatic impacts were felt upstream. Despite government claims that the reservoir would displace less than half as many people as Kariba (around twenty-five thousand), it ultimately ousted over forty-two thousand, few of whom got much by way of compensation. Most of the expellees were rounded up into strategic settlements whose locations were chosen more on the basis of counterinsurgency concerns than their suitability for agriculture. Although the level of violence and intimidation varied from place to place, the process of resettlement was generally woeful. The planned

125. My discussion here is based on Isaacman and Isaacman's *Dams, Displacement.*
126. Quoted in Isaacman and Isaacman, 64.
127. Fontein, 'Damming the Zambezi', 429.

villages lacked even the most basic amenities and new arrivals were often left
to build their own dwellings out of whatever material they could find nearby.[128]

Moreover, the scant concern that colonial officials showed for the welfare
of people upstream was mirrored in an almost complete disregard for everything else that lived there. Like Kariba, the creation of the reservoir annihilated a huge area (over 2,700 square kilometres) of productive floodplains
and wildlife habitat. Yet in contrast to Kariba, the decision to fill the reservoir
(and therefore generate electricity) as soon as possible amplified the level of
environmental damage. Whereas Lake Kariba took nearly four years to fill,
Cahora Bassa's reservoir filled in a mere four months, which gave animals very
little time to adapt their movements and escape the rising waters. And unlike
Operation Noah, Portuguese wildlife rescue efforts above the dam amounted
to little more than a public relations exercise.[129]

This headlong rush to maximize electricity output also caused enormous
damage to livelihoods and ecosystems downstream. During the four months
when the lake was filling, engineers reduced the river flow to no more than a
trickle. The timing could not have been worse, for it coincided almost exactly
with the local rainy season (December to April) when peak flood levels would
normally inundate adjacent floodplains. The sudden termination of the annual
flood not only disrupted long-standing riverine agricultural cycles on which
thousands of households relied for subsistence; it also isolated the river from
its adjacent floodplain, thus depriving many fish species of their spawning
grounds. Worse still, concerns about abnormally heavy rains and technical
problems with the new turbines meant that the abrupt drying up of the river
was immediately followed by the deliberate release of huge amounts of reservoir water to safeguard the dam. Suddenly, the annual floodwaters that had
been withheld for several months surged down the valley with a vengeance,
inundating downstream fields and sweeping away large numbers of livestock.[130]

Few of these problems disappeared when Mozambique achieved
independence only a few months later in June 1975. In fact, no sooner was the
FRELIMO government installed than it abruptly reversed its earlier opposition
to Cahora Bassa and instead celebrated it as a source of prosperity and development. It was a stunning volte-face with long-term consequences. Over the following decades, the ongoing disruption of the Zambezi's natural inundation cycle
and the enduring habit of regulating reservoir levels solely in the interests of electricity production continued to wreak havoc downstream – hindering the growth
of vegetation, upending the reproductive cycles of fish, creating stagnant pools

128. Isaacman and Isaacman, *Dams, Displacement*, 91–114.

129. Isaacman and Sneddon, 'Social and Environmental History', 623–24; Isaacman
and Isaacman, *Dams, Displacement*, 65.

130. Isaacman and Isaacman, *Dams, Displacement*, 116; Isaacman and Sneddon,
'Social and Environmental History', 624–25.

for the breeding of disease vectors, and even altering the geomorphology of the lower Zambezi delta by depriving it of sediment and nutrients. The overall result was a marked decline in biodiversity, soil fertility and animal populations, all of which had profoundly negative effects on farming and fishing communities that had long depended on these resources. What's more, the ill effects of the dam on these communities were for many years aggravated by the violent campaigns of guerrillas backed by South Africa who sought to destabilize the new regime by sabotaging the project's power lines.[131]

In sum, the Cahora Bassa Dam did precious little to compensate for all the problems it caused. Few if any of its purported benefits ever materialized. It never provided irrigation water for farmers once the initial plans were overwritten by the agreement with the South African government. It certainly did not put an end to dangerous flooding along the lower Zambezi. In 1978, an exceptionally high flood left over ninety thousand people homeless, and similarly catastrophic flooding occurred again in 2000–2001 and 2007–8.[132] To top it all off, the people whose lives were upended by the dam did not even receive any of the electricity that it generated. Over thirty years after independence, the dam was still owned and operated by the Portuguese company Hidroeléctrica de Cahora Bassa (HCB), which continued to sell most of its electricity to South Africa. Even after Mozambique finally claimed legal ownership of the dam in 2006, Cahora Bassa was still managed primarily for the benefit of distant consumers or investors who did not have to live with its social and environmental consequences. As Allen and Barbara Isaacman have succinctly put it, 'South Africa received the energy, Portugal received the income, and the Zambezi valley residents paid the price.'[133]

At one level, the hydroelectric mega-dams on the Zambezi – like those on the Volta and Sanaga and at Owen Falls – can be regarded as products of a particular moment, artefacts of a heroic era of colonial developmentalism in which massive hydropower projects were built to maintain European political and economic influence in its colonies or soon-to-be ex-colonies. Yet like nearly all colonial hydropower projects, they outlasted the governments and political systems that created them. Long after the demise of Europe's empire, gigantic hydropower dams remained objects of fascination, even veneration, among politicians, engineers and government officials. Whereas European rulers had showcased them as evidence of their enlightened governance, for nationalist leaders they were icons of emancipation from imperial subjugation, concrete expressions of progress through science. Independence certainly changed their political valences, but it did little to diminish the attraction of hydropower as

131. Isaacman and Isaacman, *Dams, Displacement*, 117–39.
132. Artur and Hilhorst, 'Floods'; Isaacman and Isaacman, *Dams, Displacement*, 138–40.
133. Isaacman and Isaacman, *Dams, Displacement*, 141.

the key to a more prosperous future. Indeed, more hydropower dams were built in Africa and Asia in the 1960s alone than throughout the entire colonial period. It was only in the 1990s that the pace of construction began to tail off, partly because of local opposition and partly owing to the simple fact that the best sites were already exploited.

Even so, there was more to the colonial hydropower legacy than just an abiding captivation with high-tech schemes and state-led megaprojects. It also included a persistent set of economic interdependencies, knowledge hierarchies and management practices that profoundly shaped hydropower development and its socio-environmental consequences for decades to come. Even as post-colonial states looked to hydroelectricity as a path to prosperity, most depended on foreign investors or multilateral agencies to furnish the necessary capital and know-how. For many countries, especially in Africa, the result was not industrial 'take-off' but crippling debt. Nor did post-colonial planners and officials approach hydropower development very differently from their colonial predecessors. Although they rightly rejected older stereotypes of the 'backward native' who was uninterested in electricity – in Asia in particular governments built centralized grids to supply cheap electrical power to ordinary households[134] – many continued to prioritize the energy needs of export industries over local consumption. In order to justify the high costs of hydropower schemes, they routinely exaggerated the benefits and belittled or ignored the social and environmental downsides. And despite their denunciation of colonial governing practices, post-colonial leaders in Asia and Africa rarely shied away from using coercion to evict the thousands of people who were in the way. It is little surprise that hydroelectric dams have continued to elicit widespread protest from would-be 'oustees' and have numbered among the chief targets of environment justice campaigners throughout the Global South.[135]

None of this is to say that the legacy of colonial hydropower schemes has been unvaryingly harmful, or that the many subsequent dam projects that drew on colonial-era blueprints were all 'bad'. Most were conceived at least in part as a means of developing local and regional economies, and many provided at least some tangible advantages, at least for those domestic groups with the political or economic clout to capitalize on the electricity they produced, and certainly for the foreign corporations that designed and built them. Yet for the hundreds of millions of mostly rural people in the post-colonial world who remain without electricity, and especially for the tens of millions who have been displaced with scant compensation, efforts to harness the power of flowing water have continued to promise more benefits than they deliver, and to deliver more drawbacks than they promised.

134. E. Chatterjee, 'Asian Anthropocene'.

135. For overviews: Khagram, *Dams and Development*; McCully, *Silenced Rivers*, 281–311.

CHAPTER EIGHT

Ebb of Empire

DECOLONIZATION AND THE HYDRAULIC
REMNANTS OF COLONIALISM

THE COLLAPSE OF formal colonial rule was one of the most profound trans-formations in modern world history. Within the space of a few decades, once-mighty European powers ceded their control over the largest collective set of empires the world had ever seen, marking the end of nearly half a millennium of European overseas expansion. From the late 1940s to the early 1980s, nationalist movements in Asia, Africa and the Caribbean wrested power from their erstwhile political overlords, dozens of new constitutions came into force, and hundreds of millions of people were enfranchised as citizens of newly independent states. In many ways, the process of decolonization was as much a symptom as a cause of Europe's loss of pre-eminence on the global stage, an outcome rather than a driver of geopolitical change. Economically exhausted by the Second World War, European countries were no longer capable of maintaining their empires without the approval of the United States. Even after their economies had recovered, the shaping of an increasingly bipolar global order was mainly in the hands of the new superpowers, while efforts to 'develop' what was now called the 'Third World' became the prerogative of UN institutions and other multilateral agencies rather than the sole preserve of colonial states. Within the newly independent states, fledgling governments eager to overcome the legacies of colonialism looked to the United States or Soviet Union for inspiration, and broadly rejected the cautious development strategies of the colonial era in favour of large-scale industrialization and infrastructure projects. In all these ways, decolonization helped to forge a very different world.

Yet despite all the changes, the question of when – even whether – these empires truly 'ended' is a matter for debate. While it is easy enough to pinpoint the moment when external rule formally ceased in any given territory, this tells us nothing about the enduring marks it left on the politics, cultures, economies and landscapes of former colonies. Decolonization was not an event but a process, and it did not take long for contemporaries to realize that self-government did not put an end to economic dependence and political patronage, let alone to the deeply engrained attitudes that had been shaped for decades by the hierarchies of empire.[1] Kwame Nkrumah's vocal condemnation of 'neocolonialism' in the mid-1960s captured the ways in which the meaning of 'decolonization' itself changed in the wake of independence. During the years following formal independence, the chief task was no longer to achieve legal sovereignty but rather to liberate former colonies from continued economic and cultural subservience. In the event, many of these hopes were left unfulfilled. As political corruption spread and as economic prospects dimmed amid the economic crises of the early 1970s, much of the initial optimism surrounding independence turned into disillusionment. Furthermore, as Western agencies attached more strings to their aid packages in the 1980s and 1990s, the often-nominal political and economic autonomy of many former colonies was eroded still further. In many respects, Europe's empires never entirely disappeared.

These remnants of empire were as palpable in the hydrosphere as in any other realm of post-colonial life. Even over half a century after most colonies gained independence, the legacies still powerfully shape the waters of the Global South. The most obvious remains were the physical leftovers: the multitude of dams, dikes and diversions that continued to channel water flows to the benefit of some groups and territories over others. Less noticeable, but no less significant, were the many organizational continuities that underpinned these relics: a tightly interwoven set of management practices, institutions and bodies of expert knowledge that spanned the supposed caesura of independence. On a political level, nationalist states were every bit as eager as their colonial forerunners to consolidate their hold on territorial water resources and enhance their control over the communities that relied on them. Underlying all these continuities were the ideological holdovers of the colonial-era, above all a determination to tame nature for human designs and an enduring faith in modern science and technology as the best means to achieve it. Despite the radical transformation of the political framework, the fundamental ideas, practices and infrastructures of colonial-era water management survived decolonization more or less unscathed and continued to define the parameters within which the hydraulic efforts of post-colonial states tended to operate.

What most visibly changed after the demise of Europe's empires was not the overall direction of hydro-political travel, but rather the speed at which rivers, lakes and seas were altered for human purposes. In the wake of decolonization, hydraulic interventions generally intensified rather than subsided. One reason for this was the unprecedented rise in human numbers and the

---

1. On decolonization as process: J. Jansen and Osterhammel, *Decolonization*; Linstrum et al., 'Decolonizing Britain'.

consequent need for more food, energy and clean drinking water. Another factor was the rapid growth of global trade and the economic enticements that came with it. For ex-colonies in desperate need of revenue and under mounting demographic pressures, the booming post-war demand for foodstuffs and raw materials furnished a powerful incentive to harness their water resources to the fullest. Most important, perhaps, was the ardently developmentalist ideology of most nationalist governments, which reflected an abiding resolve to overcome what they regarded as decades of colonial underdevelopment, along with a more immediate political need to meet the expectations of millions of recently enfranchised voters. In January 1948, five months after Indian independence, Nehru remarked that the vast majority of the development plans that India had inherited 'unfortunately . . . still remain paper schemes. It is time that we gave effect to them'. Like his counterparts throughout Asia and Africa, he envisioned the creation of 'great river valley schemes which would not only irrigate the land, prevent floods, produce hydro-electric power and prevent malaria and other diseases' but also promote the 'rapid development of industries and the modernization of our agriculture'.[2]

For the rulers of newly independent states, the end of the colonial order represented a historic opportunity to remake nature to serve the needs of the nation. The sense of urgency surrounding this task, which was sharpened by the imperative to provide for the most basic needs of a rapidly growing population, only increased their enthusiasm for large-scale, high-impact, technology-driven hydraulic schemes. Over the following decades, they launched thousands of projects to regulate water flows, boost supplies for agricultural and domestic use, and harvest their aquatic resources. Many of these schemes were based on colonial-era plans, most were financially supported by Western-dominated lending agencies, and many were designed or directed by former colonial experts.

In this sense, the post-colonial transformation of the waterscape was very much a collective effort, one involving Western states and international institutions, as well as governments, businesses and end users throughout the Global South. Although relations among these groups were still marked by vast disparities of power and influence, their agendas for water development were often so aligned as to make it impossible to distinguish between colonial inheritances, neocolonial impulses and independent national initiatives. To explore the hydraulic legacies of empire is not, therefore, to focus solely on the imposition of external power over disadvantaged societies, however important these power differentials remained. The point of this chapter is rather to examine how the waters of the post-colonial world – their management, exploitation, reconfiguration and contestation – continued to be shaped by the material and ideological remnants of empire.

2. Nehru, *Independence and After*, 161.

Basins and Boundaries

The break-up of Europe's empires ushered in the greatest process of state-making in world history. During the late 1940s and early 1950s, the bulk of Europe's Asian empire was dismantled. India and Pakistan gained independence in 1947, Burma in 1948 and Indonesia in 1949, followed by Cambodia and Laos in 1953, and finally the expulsion of French troops from Vietnam in 1954. During the late 1950s and early 1960s, a similar wave of transitions swept Africa, starting with Sudan, Morocco and Tunisia in 1956, Ghana in 1957, Guinea in 1958 and then a surge of new African states from 1960 to 1964. Over the two decades that followed, there was a steady trickle of independence ceremonies across the Caribbean and sub-Saharan Africa, leaving only a handful of colonial holdouts by the early 1980s. Altogether, from 1945 to the end of the twentieth century, a total of ninety-six new states were created, most of them from the disbandment of Europe's colonial empires.[3]

With these new states came new (and thicker) borders, and with these borders came the challenge of rearranging older spatial configurations that no longer suited the new political circumstances. As post-colonial governments sought to control the traffic moving into and out of their territories, they weakened or severed many of the social, political and economic linkages that had previously spanned different colonies and tied them into wider imperial networks of exchange. After the upheavals of the mid-twentieth century, the great flows of external migration that had criss-crossed southern and southeastern Asia for at least a century were largely replaced by currents of internal migration from the countryside towards the cities or to large development projects in need of cheap labour.[4]

But it was one thing to regulate the movement of goods and people; it was quite another to govern the transboundary flows of water. Although post-colonial elites continued to regard control over water resources as a key element of state power, rivers did not respect the borders that decolonization created. At one level, the problems this presented were of course nothing new: the need to balance the interests of different water users has been around for millennia, and (as we have seen in previous chapters) it cropped up repeatedly throughout the colonial period. But with decolonization and the redrawing of the world map, the relationship between water and territory changed. What had previously been a matter of negotiation between colonial states and/or between colonial governments and local interests now became a matter of international diplomacy. In the wake of imperial dissolution, newly independent successor states either had to find new ways of managing

---

3. Figure from Christopher, 'Decolonisation without Independence', 213.

4. Amrith, *Migration and Diaspora*.

cross-border rivers or alter existing flows of water to conform to the borders they had created.

Perhaps the thorniest problems arose along the boundaries that partitioned the Indian subcontinent. Ever since the 1930s, tensions between the Indian National Congress and the Muslim League had raised questions about the future of a united India. As inter-communal violence escalated after the Second World War, it accelerated the drift towards division into separate Muslim- and Hindu-majority states. The British, racked by economic crisis at home, sought to extract themselves from the deteriorating situation as quickly as possible. In June 1947, they put forward a plan to separate the subcontinent into India and Pakistan. Two boundary commissions – one for Bengal and one for Punjab – were hastily established under the chairmanship of the lawyer and civil servant Cyril Radcliffe, who was charged with identifying a border that would leave as many Muslims in Pakistan, and as many Hindus and Sikhs in India, as possible. Time was absurdly tight; in the event, the commissions took little more than a month to determine the boundaries that would separate India from East and West Pakistan. So compressed was the timescale that the precise location of the border was announced only the day after formal independence was achieved on 15 August. What followed was a far cry from the 'orderly transition' that the British had hoped for. Over the following months, millions of refugees crossed the new borders, many of them falling victim to vicious assaults en route. Altogether up to twenty million people were displaced, twelve million of them in Punjab alone, and anywhere from two hundred thousand to two million people lost their lives in the violence.[5]

Partition not only separated the different religious communities in South Asia. It also severed the Indus River basin and the complex system of canals that for decades had sustained the largest irrigation scheme on Earth. As we saw in chapter 3, the Indus watershed was in many respects the birthplace of what later came to be known as integrated river basin planning. The Triple Canals project was the world's first system for transferring water between different rivers. During the early twentieth century, these inter-river transfers helped turn the Punjab into the breadbasket of the subcontinent. The problem after 1947 was that there was no neat way to disentangle the water flows that linked East and West Punjab, since the headworks and outlets of various water control schemes lay on different sides of the new border. In a single stroke, Partition threatened to sever a basin whose integration had taken half a century to achieve. Radcliffe himself despaired at the implications for the canal system, which he regarded as one of the greatest legacies of the Raj. Try as he might, there was no way to draw a border that allowed the irrigation systems of East and West Punjab to function effectively as discrete units. Although

5. On Partition generally: Khan, *Great Partition*; Zamindar, *Long Partition*.

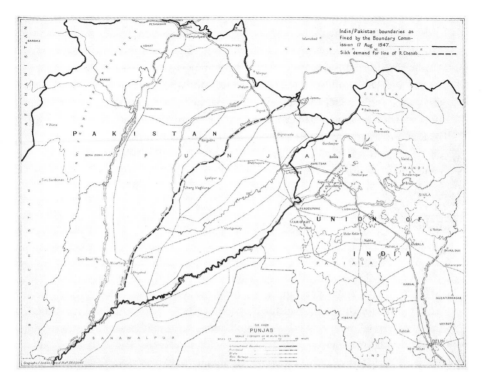

FIGURE 8.1. The India/Pakistan boundaries as fixed by the Boundary
Commission, 17 August 1947.
By permission of akg-images/British Library, IOR/X/12084.

he suggested that the two states should treat the irrigation system as a single
entity, in the wake of independence this appeared to both sides as an affront
to their claims of national sovereignty.[6]

The suddenness of Partition meant that, for the time being, there was little
that either side could do but improvise. Practicalities dictated a standstill agreement, but this was only ever an interim measure. When the standstill agreement
lapsed on 1 April 1948, Indian authorities in East Punjab unilaterally turned
off the tap to three major feeder canals flowing into West Pakistan. The implications were colossal. Overnight, India not only deprived water to over 5 per
cent of West Pakistan's cropland (indeed, at a vital moment at the beginning
of the planting season), but also denied the provincial capital of Lahore its
primary source of municipal water supplies. The decision to interrupt these
cross-border flows was a drastic step, and was based on several different motivations. The most immediate was the East Punjab government's determination to maximize its own water use – a policy that also repeatedly brought it

6. Gilmartin, *Blood and Water*, 204–6; Haines, *Rivers Divided*, 27–28, 40–42.

into tension with other Indian states and even the Union government after independence.[7] In turn, these tensions over water sharing were greatly exacerbated by the situation in Kashmir, which became a strategically important border province of India despite its Muslim majority. Clashes between Indian troops and Pakistani 'volunteers' flared up soon after Partition, and eventually prompted the UN to intervene since neither side was prepared to accept the accession of Kashmir to the other. Furthermore, the subsequent stalemate in Kashmir reflected the fact that some Indian politicians had never reconciled themselves to the very existence of a separate, independent Pakistan, and sought to undermine its viability however they could. Most fundamentally, the water stoppage expressed India's sovereign right to do what it pleased with its rivers. Although Nehru privately criticized the move as an 'inhuman act', he publicly defended it as a legitimate assertion of national control over India's water resources.[8]

The response in Pakistan was one of shock. The government immediately sent a delegation to New Delhi to negotiate a resumption of canal flows, but India, as the upstream riparian, imposed a harsh deal. It took nearly five weeks, until 4 May, for the Indian authorities to open the taps again, but only after Pakistan agreed to make payments and to recognize India's right to build projects that might reduce cross-border water flows in the future. As soon as the Pakistani delegation returned home, engineers in the Irrigation Department hastily started planning a series of major projects that would enable Pakistan to take control of its own water supplies. Although the 4 May water agreement overcame the immediate crisis, it failed to settle any of the underlying issues.[9]

Over the following years, the Indian and Pakistani governments engaged in an angry and protracted public battle over their proprietary rights to the waters of the Indus. At the heart of the dispute was a clash of opposing legal claims. India's case rested primarily on the principle of territorial control, or the notion that it exercised sovereign rights over every drop of water that flowed across its territory. The fact that Pakistan had already agreed to pay 'seignorage' charges according to the 4 May 1948 agreement was presented as tantamount to an admission that India 'owned' these waters. By contrast, Pakistan's claims rested on the concept of prior appropriation. According to this principle, West Punjab's historic use of water from what later became Indian sources entitled it to continue receiving the same river water in the same quantities as before. The corollary was that India, as the upstream user, had a legal duty not to harm existing water users downstream. Framed in this way, the dispute was not merely a matter of national sovereignty but instead

7. Haines, 'Disputed Rivers' and 'Development, Citizenship'.

8. Michel, *Indus Rivers*, 195–97; Haines, *Rivers Divided*, 42–48; Gilmartin, *Blood and Water*, 206–8, quote at 207.

9. Michel, *Indus Rivers*, 200–205; Gilmartin, *Blood and Water*, 210–14.

fell into the ambit of international law. In 1949, Pakistan tried to strengthen its claims by moving a UN resolution and bringing the case to the International Court of Justice, but neither of these efforts succeeded.[10]

All throughout the dispute, both governments pointed to the adverse effects of Partition to justify their actions, and both consistently cast themselves as the injured party. India contended that it had never wanted division in the first place, that it had lost its best irrigated land to Pakistan and that it therefore had to make the most of the water it controlled in order to survive. In response, Pakistan portrayed itself as the victim of bullying by a larger neighbour that abused its upstream position to undermine Pakistan's very existence as a sovereign state. The Pakistani position was summarized in the title of a government-issued booklet that it distributed in an attempt to cultivate international sympathy: *Pakistan: The Struggle for Irrigation Water – and Existence*. On both sides of the border, the sense of grievance over lost land or water gave an additional impetus to the development of hitherto unexploited water resources as a form of compensation. India's answer to Partition was the colossal Bhakra Nangal project, which tripled the amount of water available to the Indian portions of the Indus basin. Pakistan's was the Bambanwala-Ravi-Bedian-Dipalpur project, which transferred water from the Chenab and Jhelum Rivers to the Upper Bari Doab canal network (which had temporarily been deprived of its supplies in April 1948). The schemes were explicitly designed to free each country from dependence on the other. In effect, the integral management of the Indus basin that British engineers had begun over half a century earlier, and that Cyril Radcliffe had unsuccessfully sought to uphold, came to an end.[11]

This was the basic situation that David Lilienthal, the former director of the TVA, encountered when he arrived for a study tour of India and Pakistan in February 1951. As one of most renowned water engineers of the era, Lilienthal was particularly interested in the massive waterworks of the Indus basin and the ongoing quarrels that surrounded them. Like most outside observers, he regarded the current state of affairs as irrational, counterproductive, even dangerous. Against the backdrop of the escalating Cold War, he wrote a long article for *Collier's* magazine that described the Indo-Pakistani dispute as 'another Korea in the making'. In an effort to reduce geopolitical tensions in the region, he proposed that the problem of water management be removed from the political realm altogether. Echoing colonial officials such as Radcliffe, he contrasted the unifying developmentalist power of science with the parochial divisiveness of politics. He viewed Partition as an act against nature, a product of 'politics and emotion' rather than 'engineering or professional

10. Haines, *Rivers Divided*, 43–50; Michel, *Indus Rivers*, 198–200, 219.

11. Amrith, *Unruly Waters*, 186–87, 194–95, 198–202; Haines, *Rivers Divided*, 54–58; 'Development, Citizenship'; Gilmartin, *Blood and Water*, 212–13.

principles'. Whereas generations of engineers had treated the basin 'as a unit, as it is in nature', Partition had fallen 'like an ax' across the entire watershed. Although he was quick to acknowledge the separation of India and Pakistan as 'a final and permanent thing', the key challenge facing both countries was how to harness their 'now wasted waters' for the cause of development. Ever the technocrat, Lilienthal argued that 'this is not a religious or political problem, but a feasible engineering and business problem for which there is plenty of precedent and relevant experience'. Because the river 'pays no attention to partition', he called on both sides to develop it as a unit, much like 'the seven-state TVA system back in the US'.[12]

In essence, Lilienthal's vision elevated 'development' over 'sovereignty'. It was a classic example of a technical solution to a political problem, literally a means of engineering one's way around a difficult dispute. His proposal for cross-party talks was backed by Eugene R. Black, president of the World Bank, who offered to act as mediator. More importantly, it was also quickly accepted by the Indian and Pakistani governments, partly out of respect for Lilienthal's personal prestige, but also because it appealed to their own political aspirations at the time. In both countries, it enabled their central governments to portray themselves as the primary agents of rational development over and above the more sectarian regional interests that threatened national unity and that damaged their reputations on the global stage.[13]

Talks went on for over two years, but they did not get very far. Frustrated with the lack of progress, the World Bank proposed an entirely new solution in February 1954. Since it proved impossible to reach an agreement that reflected the unitary nature of the river basin, the only answer was to divide the river itself to reflect the separation of the two states. The proposal could hardly have diverged more sharply from Lilienthal's initial vision of an 'apolitical' development agency that transcended national divisions. According to the new plan, the physical environment would be re-engineered to conform to political realities, rather than the other way around. The entire flow of the basin's western rivers (Indus, Jhelum, Chenab) was assigned to Pakistan, apart from a small amount of the Jhelum's waters that went to Kashmir. In exchange, India gained control over the entire flow of the eastern rivers (Ravi, Beas, Sutlej), with the proviso that it would continue to supply historic deliveries to Pakistan for a specified transition period. Over the following six years of talks, Indian negotiators flexed their muscles as the upper riparian, while their Pakistani counterparts sought to maximize the compensation payments they received for the 'lost' waters of the eastern rivers. In the end, what facilitated the agreement was a massive funding package from the World Bank and

12. Quotes from Lilienthal, 'Another "Korea"'. For detailed discussions: Mehsud, 'Lilienthal's "Another 'Korea'"; Haines, '(Inter) Nationalist Rivers?'.

13. Michel, *Indus Rivers*, 219–22; Gilmartin, *Blood and Water*, 215–17.

Western governments (primarily the United States) that enabled Pakistan to launch its new Indus Basin Project, a series of barrages and canals that composed the world's single largest irrigation scheme.[14]

The resulting 1960 Indus Waters Treaty has often been hailed as a major success story of international water diplomacy. Despite the outbreak of several wars between India and Pakistan since it was signed, by and large the agreement has held up well. Throughout the 1960s and beyond, as decolonization movements continued to redraw the political map, it was widely regarded as a model for overcoming transboundary water disputes. But as some observers have pointed out, such claims of success are debatable. For one thing, the agreement was ultimately based less on cross-border 'cooperation' than on overcoming the need for any cooperation at all. By physically dividing the river basin and allocating its water to two sides, the treaty functioned not to transcend the divisions of Partition but rather – in many places quite literally – to cement them in place. The underlying political issues were therefore obscured rather than resolved, which meant that the unilateral construction of upstream hydro-projects by India inevitably led to more tensions over the following years. Moreover, these enduring political strains were aggravated by the mounting environmental fallout of the subsequent hydroengineering works. The race to expand irrigation and hydropower after the early 1960s led not only to a huge rise in waterlogging and salinization (especially in Pakistan) but also to a series of disease outbreaks and disastrous consequences for wetlands in the shrinking Indus delta. Although Pakistani, Indian and American hydroengineers took various measures to remedy these problems – the installation of tube wells, better drainage, the flushing of salts through excess irrigation – millions of hectares of farmland have been damaged or entirely ruined.[15]

Ultimately, the Indus Waters Treaty not only failed to overcome the competition for water in the region; it also exacerbated some of the same agricultural problems that made the development of these resources such a priority for Indian and Pakistani authorities in the first place. Whether the treaty can withstand the combined pressures posed by climate change, environmental degradation and rising expectations among the region's residents remains to be seen.

While decolonization on the Indian subcontinent led to a territorial separation of its rivers, in mainland Southeast Asia it gave rise to a more genuinely international approach. The main object of interest was the Mekong, the region's largest river and the world's most multinational waterway. Stretching some five thousand kilometres from its source on the Tibetan plateau to its outlet in the

---

14. Michel, *Indus Rivers*, 227–53.

15. On differing assessments of the treaty, see Haines's *Rivers Divided* (7–8). On environmental problems, see Kravtsova, Mikhailov and Efremova's 'Variations'; Hazell's 'Asian Green Revolution' (16); and Gilmartin's *Blood and Water* (235–40).

South China Sea, the Mekong flows through six countries: China, Burma, Thailand, Laos, Cambodia and Vietnam. In the mid-twentieth century, its watershed encompassed some of the least developed areas in all of Asia and was populated overwhelmingly by farmers engaged in rice cultivation. Although some parts of the lower basin were relatively fertile (e.g., the alluvial lowlands of Cambodia and the Mekong delta), large areas farther upriver had poor soils and were prone to violent flooding. Much of the region had long suffered from endemic poverty and social conflict, and after the collapse of French Indochina in 1954, struggles between communist and anti-communist forces left it highly unstable. For post-war planners, it epitomized the need for economic development. Harnessing the Mekong River was seen as the key for achieving this.

Much of the early impetus came from the UN's Economic Commission for Asia and the Far East (ECAFE), which was established in 1947 to promote post-war economic reconstruction. The commission's first survey of the Mekong in 1952, conducted by two officials from its Bureau of Flood Control, emphasized that the basin's resources 'have not yet been explored' but showed 'great potential for development' of irrigation and power-generation schemes. Following independence for Laos, Cambodia and Vietnam, the United States government became more actively involved in the region as well. In 1956, a team of specialists from the US Bureau of Reclamation conducted a survey of the river, whose main conclusion was that there were insufficient data to determine how best to develop it. Their report accordingly proposed a wide range of topographical, geological and hydrographical studies to support the construction of dams, ports and irrigation works, as well as to boost fish production along the river and especially on the great Tonlé Sap lake.[16]

International efforts to develop the Mekong began to crystallize in 1957 when a second UN-backed study listed five provisional sites for dam projects: Pa Mong, just upriver from Vientiane; Khemarat, several hundred kilometres downstream; Khone Falls, just above the Cambodia–Laos border; Sambor, around halfway between the Khone Falls and Phnom Penh; and at Tonlé Sap, just above Phnom Penh. It was estimated that this cascade of barrages would not only meet all the irrigation needs of the region but also protect two million acres (eight hundred thousand hectares) from flooding, generate thirty-two billion kilowatt-hours of electricity, and produce an estimated $300 million in exports annually – provided it was operated as 'an integrated system'. Towards this end, it was considered crucial to establish a mechanism for international control, preferably via a 'permanent body for the development of the basin'. The result was the Committee for Co-ordination of Investigations of the Lower Mekong Basin, or Mekong Committee for short.[17]

---

16. Quote from ECAFE, *Development of Water Resources*, 17; see also Schaaf and Fifield, *Lower Mekong*, 63, 83–86; Sneddon, *Concrete Revolution*, 106–9.

17. Schaaf and Fifield, *Lower Mekong*, 86–88; Lagendijk, 'Streams of Knowledge', 323–24.

Work got off to a quick start. The Mekong Committee's attention soon focused on three major projects. Chief among them was the 250-metre Pa Mong Dam spanning a narrow gorge on the main river between Thailand and Laos, which was designed to supply 1,800 megawatts of electricity and provide irrigation water to some 1.5 million hectares of land. Second on the list was the smaller Sambor Dam in Cambodia, which would generate a similar amount of power and irrigate around 150,000 hectares. Third was the Tonlé Sap works, which were designed to regulate the seasonal flow of water into and out of the great lake and thereby make it possible to irrigate or reclaim a further 3 million hectares of land. In the meantime, the committee also commissioned proposals for works on four of the Mekong's main tributaries: the Battambang in Cambodia, the Nam Ngum in Laos, the Nam Pong in Thailand and the Upper Se San in Vietnam.[18]

During these early years the Mekong Committee was buoyed by a powerful sense of optimism. Not only did it represent one of the first large-scale efforts to plan the economic, social and technical dimensions of river basin development in Asia; it was also the first time the UN had become directly involved in the long-term planning of an international river. With so much potential lying untapped, the Mekong seemed like a blank canvas on which technicians could design a better, more prosperous future for the forty million people who lived in the region. In a 1958 report on the river, Raymond A. Wheeler, former chief of the US Army Corps of Engineers, declared that 'wise conservation and utilization of its waters will contribute more towards improving human welfare in this area than any other single undertaking'. On the Mekong as on the Indus, engineers regarded the technical mastery of water as a mission that lay beyond political divisions or territorial boundaries. The Mekong Project, as it came to be known, was seen as a monument to the power of scientific rationality over partisan pettiness, a heroic example of 'how teamwork among courageous and far-seeing men is pitted against the rigors of an underdeveloped environment, the relentless pressures of government machinery, and the caprices of society in general'.[19]

For a while this apolitical vision seemed as though it might actually prevail. In stark contrast to the situation in the Indus basin, relations between the different riparian states were remarkably good. So too were their interactions with the major donor countries, which helped ensure that the committee received the financial and technical support that it required. Although the United States was the largest contributor of funds and know-how, Japanese and French agencies were also centrally involved, not least as a means of finding work for former colonial officials and landing lucrative contracts for flagship engineering companies

18. For a brief description of the projects: Schaaf and Fifield, *Lower Mekong*, 104–14.

19. J. Jacobs, 'Mekong Committee History', 139; quotes from Schaaf and Fifield, *Lower Mekong*, 4, 102.

such as Nippon Koei or the Société grenobloise d'études et d'applications hydrauliques. By 1963, the Mekong Committee enjoyed the support of over a dozen non-riparian governments, the full range of major international agencies, and a smattering of NGOs and multinational companies.[20]

But if the Mekong Project rested on a remarkably broad consensus, the underlying politics were never far from the surface. The anti-communist motivations behind it were evident from the beginning. As a 1956 ECAFE report noted, 'the entire project area is susceptible to outside subversive influence because it lies in close proximity to areas controlled or infected by Communist forces'. The great hope was that hydro-development would stabilize the area and 'forestall the expansion of subversion and chaos'.[21] One of the main reasons why so many Western officials were eager to develop the basin as quickly and thoroughly as possible was the geostrategic importance of the region after the Chinese Revolution in 1949. For US officials, big dams and other 'impact-type projects' were a potent geopolitical weapon – a means of demonstrating the country's technological prowess, rewarding friendly governments and reducing the attraction of communist movements. As US involvement in the region escalated, these strategic motivations came increasingly to the fore. Although the United States had not initially been the central player on the Mekong, preferring to leave matters mainly to regional and international actors, all of this changed after the 1964 Gulf of Tonkin incident. It was no coincidence that the 1965 speech in which President Johnson confirmed the commencement of bombing in North Vietnam was also the occasion where he announced a $1 billion plan to build a series of dams on the Mekong that would 'dwarf even our own TVA'. On the domestic front, the US government's hope was that such an ambitious campaign to modernize social and economic life along the Mekong – part of the so-called 'other war in Vietnam' – might assuage public opinion amid the growing unpopularity of US military involvement there. On the international front, the hope was that it might also win some credit with Asian states that had been antagonized by US actions in Vietnam. As it turned out, the results of Johnson's attempt to turbocharge plans for the Mekong were negligible. Regional and international actors broadly retained the initiative over the Mekong Project and resisted US attempts to force the pace. The only tangible outcome of US pressure was the completion of a hydropower dam on the Nam Ngum River in Laos, one of the committee's secondary projects, which the United States effectively bankrolled in order to have something to show.[22]

20. Biggs, 'Reclamation Nations', 230; *Quagmire*, 170–73; J. Jacobs, 'Mekong Committee History', 139; Schaaf and Fifield, *Lower Mekong*, 98–99.

21. ECAFE, *Final Report of the Mekong Planning Study* (Bangkok, 1956), 1–2, quoted in Tucker, 'Containing Communism', 159.

22. USAID, *Other War in Vietnam*; Biggs, 'Reclamation Nations', 234 (Johnson quote); Lagendijk, 'Streams of Knowledge', 325–26.

By the late 1960s, the fighting and political turmoil in the region had begun to erode the initial sense of optimism surrounding the Mekong Committee. On a practical level, the escalation of the war in Vietnam and the deteriorating security situation beyond its borders made it difficult to carry out surveying and data-collection work. On a political level too, the war strained relations between riparian states and caused major diplomatic headaches for donors, whose funding dropped sharply in the early 1970s. Given the enormous disruption caused by the war in Vietnam, it was ironic that the fallout from the end of the conflict was in some ways even more troublesome. For several years after the US withdrawal, the new governments in Vietnam, Cambodia and Laos were too consumed with internal affairs to appoint delegates to the committee. As the situation in Cambodia went from bad to worse under the Khmer Rouge, the country formally withdrew from the organization in 1977, prompting the other three riparian states to establish an Interim Mekong Committee in 1978. Compared with its predecessor, this new organization was severely restricted in what it could achieve, since any mainstream hydraulic works had to receive prior approval by all the other basin states, including Cambodia. Whereas the war had previously rendered large parts of the lower Mekong basin too unsafe for engineering operations, the post-war truncation of the committee now made it impossible to pursue mainstream development projects in any event.[23]

As the fallout from the Vietnam War took its toll, the Mekong Committee was also confronted by a chorus of concerns about the social and environmental implications of developing the river. Even during the confident early years of the committee, there was an element of anxiety that the rush to make progress was obscuring the need for careful social and economic analyses. A 1962 Ford Foundation study led by the river basin expert Gilbert White struck an early note of caution. Over the following years White's admonishments were echoed by the International Union for the Conservation of Nature (IUCN), which grew increasingly alarmed at the ever-growing scale of hydraulic plans for the Mekong, especially the gargantuan Pa Mong Dam. By the end of the 1960s, criticism of Pa Mong (and many other mega-dam projects around the world) became more public and more vociferous. As a *Washington Post* journalist put it in 1971, gone were the days when 'billion dollar dams like Pa Mong were a straightforward proposition', when 'there were no ecologists underfoot and almost everybody thought big dams meant instant progress'.[24] In a final attempt to salvage the project, the World Bank asked the Resources for the Future Institute to conduct an independent survey. Although the report endorsed the committee's plan to 'green-revolutionize' agriculture in

23. J. Jacobs, 'Mekong Committee History', 143.

24. Claire Sterling, 'Thai-Laos Dam Plan Is Perfect One – Except for Why?', *Washington Post*, 1 May 1971, A18, quoted in Sneddon, *Concrete Revolution*, 120.

the region (on which more below), it also broadly supported the sceptics' misgivings about the environmental consequences of such huge hydroengineering projects: above all the potential spread of disease (especially schistosomiasis), the unknown effect of irrigation on the region's soils, and the threat of severe soil erosion by displacing farmers from riverine tracts to more marginal upland areas. In the late 1970s, these findings were reaffirmed by a University of Michigan study, which suggested that the Pa Mong Dam would displace four hundred thousand people, unleash a devastating bout of deforestation and remain uneconomic as a power source for the foreseeable future.[25]

Eventually, the combined effects of political turmoil, socio-environmental criticism and mounting donor reluctance were too much to withstand. Although committee officials were loath to change course, they eventually rejected the construction of the showpiece Pa Mong Dam, arguably the 'greatest dam never built'.[26] For the next two decades, the Interim Mekong Committee continued to work on plans for the basin, but it was not in a position to undertake projects on the main run of the river. Nonetheless, despite the many setbacks of the 1970s and 1980s, in the end both the commission and its vision of large-scale river development survived intact. In 1995, Cambodia finally came back into the fold, and together with Laos, Thailand and Vietnam it co-established the independent Mekong River Commission. Since then, the commission's officials have revived plans to build a succession of dams on the main river, much to the delight of regional political leaders and multinational water-engineering firms, and much to the dismay of critics who maintain that the social, economic and ecological costs of such dams will far outweigh their benefits.[27]

In some ways, the return of relative political stability in the region since the 1990s has caused as many problems as it has solved. Given the patchy electrification of the area, there is certainly a need for more low-carbon electricity. But just as certain is the need to maintain its fisheries and agricultural productivity, both of which are threatened by barrages, which would disrupt the migration of spawning fish and reduce the flows of silt-laden water to downstream plains. As economies and populations in the region continue to grow, it will be harder and harder to juggle these different imperatives and keep diverging interests aligned, let alone to manage the multiple effects that hydropower development will have.[28] In this respect, the construction of the huge Xayaburi

25. G. White, *Economic and Social Aspects*; Tucker, 'Containing Communism', 160–62; Sneddon, *Concrete Revolution*, 112–13.

26. Quote from Sneddon, *Concrete Revolution*, 102; see also Tucker, 'Containing Communism', 162.

27. R. Stone, 'Mayhem on the Mekong'; Vaidyanathan, 'Dam Controversy'; Cronin, 'Hydropower Dams'.

28. On the multiple uncertainties generated by hydropower development and attempts by power corporations to rectify the unforeseen effects, see Whitington's *Anthropogenic*

Dam in northern Laos – the cornerstone of plans to turn the country into the 'battery of Southeast Asia' – has set an ominous precedent. In 2011, the Laotian government unilaterally proceeded with the project despite the opposition of the other riparian states and despite calls from the Mekong River Commission for a moratorium on mainstream dams in view of the irreversible environmental damage that they would likely cause. Many fear that this defiant action has paved the way for a rash of unilateral dam-building on the Mekong. Although the Mekong River Commission still counts as one of the world's most important transboundary river bodies, its actual ability to coordinate the development of the basin is set to be tested as never before.[29]

Of all the transborder water quarrels that followed the break-up of empire, none were more complex than those along the Nile. In part this was due to the sheer size of the river basin, which covers over three million square kilometres, around one-tenth of the entire African continent. Within this vast area, there are eleven riparian states (Rwanda, Burundi, Uganda, Tanzania, Democratic Republic of Congo, Kenya, Ethiopia, Eritrea, South Sudan, Sudan, Egypt), nearly all of them former European dependencies, and each one of them eager to assert its claims over the water that flows through its territory. In addition to the basin's size, a second complicating factor is its peculiar political geography, inasmuch as the Nile and its main tributaries do not form a border between any of these states. Instead, the Nile runs through their territory, which makes it relatively easy for any of the riparian states to build hydraulic infrastructure unilaterally on their stretch of the river. This alone creates ample potential for conflict, but what escalates it yet further is the extreme unevenness of water availability in the Nile basin. Whereas Egypt and Sudan account for 90 per cent of water usage, the vast bulk of their water resources originate beyond their national boundaries, above all in the Ethiopian Highlands, which contribute 80 per cent of the overall flow of the lower Nile. And to top things off, all of the ensuing tensions are exacerbated by the fact that the fundamental agreements that still shape different parties' claims on the Nile were forged by colonial governments rather than by independent states, which renders their validity a matter for debate.[30]

In many ways, the disputes stem directly from the colonial carve-up of the Nile basin. As Britain, France, Italy and Belgium expanded their influence throughout the region in the late nineteenth century, all recognized the importance of Nile water for the prosperity of their dependencies and quickly began

---

Rivers.

29. Giovannini, 'Power and Geopolitics', 66 (quote); Hirsch, 'Shifting Regional Geopolitics'; R. Stone, 'Mayhem on the Mekong'. For an excellent analysis of the exchanges between dam builders, environmental activists and local people, see Whitington's *Anthropogenic Rivers.*

30. I. Jacobs, *Politics of Water*, 107–11; Waterbury, *Nile Basin*, 1–6.

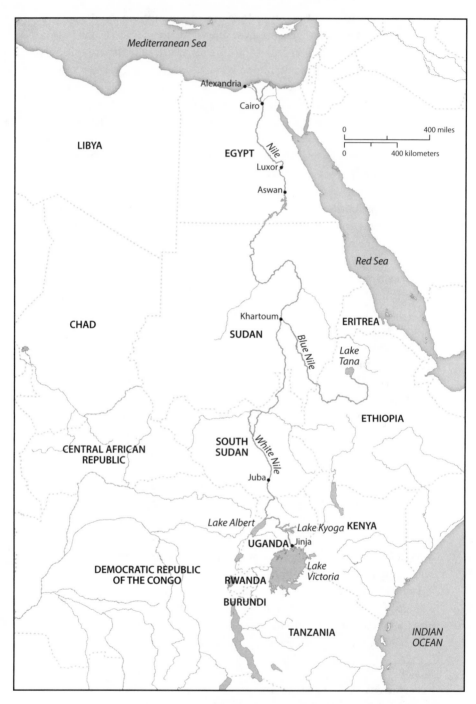

FIGURE 8.2. Map of the Nile River, with political boundaries.

to establish water-sharing agreements with one another. In April 1891, Britain and Italy drew up a protocol that delineated their spheres of influence in the Horn of Africa, part of which stipulated that no irrigation works would be built on the Atbara River that might affect its flow into the Blue Nile. In 1902, an agreement between Britain, Italy and Ethiopia demarcating the boundaries between Anglo-Egyptian Sudan, Ethiopia and Eritrea prevented Ethiopia from creating any structures across the Blue Nile, Sobat River or Lake Tana without the express agreement of the British government acting on behalf of Sudan. In 1906, the 'Tripartite Agreement' between Britain, France and Italy, which essentially maintained the existing territorial arrangements in Ethiopia, explicitly reaffirmed the precept that nothing should impede the flow of the Blue Nile, Atbara or Sobat Rivers. All of these pacts reflected an anxious recognition on the part of British officials that the bulk of the Nile's flow came from the Ethiopian portion of the basin, over which they had no formal control. Meanwhile, at the southern end of the Nile basin, Britain and the Belgian-ruled Congo Free State agreed to prohibit any structure that would impede the flow of the White Nile northwards. Over time, as the political influence of the colonial powers waned, the legal validity of all these settlements became more uncertain. Ethiopia, as the only formally independent state in the basin, never fully recognized any of them in the first place. According to the Ethiopian government, the 1891 protocol signed by Italy constituted a clear infringement of Ethiopian sovereignty, and in any event ceased effect with the end of colonial rule over the other states involved. It has likewise asserted that the 1902 agreement with Britain was plagued from the outset by disputes over different linguistic interpretations of key passages, and the 1906 Tripartite Agreement was of no consequence since the Ethiopian government was not a signatory.[31]

As noted in chapter 2, the core aim of these colonial-era agreements, at least from a British perspective, was to secure adequate water supplies for Egypt. Although works such as the Aswan Dam were also crucial in this respect, by the 1920s the development of water resources in Sudan – especially the huge irrigation scheme at Gezira – had begun to worry officials in Cairo. In 1925, a Nile Waters Commission was established to forecast the future needs of Egypt and Sudan and to apportion water on that basis. After a protracted set of exchanges between British and Egyptian officials, in 1929 the two sides finally signed the Nile Waters Agreement, which regulated water utilization between Egypt and Britain's Nile basin colonies. The agreement worked – and was designed to work – very much in Egypt's favour. Out of an average Nile flow of eighty-four cubic kilometres per year, Egypt received forty-eight (which included the entire river flow during the low-water season from January to July) and Sudan only four, leaving thirty-two cubic kilometres to flow unused into the sea. At the same time, it also gave Egypt the right to veto any

31. Okidi, 'History of the Nile'.

water projects in British territories upstream. The 1929 agreement thus sowed the seeds of future discord by disregarding the interests of Uganda, Tanzania and Kenya. And once again, Ethiopia was not party to it.[32]

For the next several decades, the potential for conflict over the inequitable distribution of Nile water was lessened by the dominant position of Britain throughout most of the basin. But as the riparian states achieved independence in the 1950s and 1960s, disputes over water rights became more clamorous and more complicated. It did not take long for the 1929 agreement to be called into question. After the Egyptian revolution in 1952, the British administration in Sudan called for a renegotiation of the treaty to increase its share of Nile water. After Sudanese nationalists achieved independence in 1956, the new government in Khartoum immediately issued similar demands. Given the crucial importance of Nile water to both countries, relations between them deteriorated quickly. While Sudan objected to plans to build the Aswan High Dam, Egypt refused to honour its previous pledge to help build a dam and reservoir at Roseires on the Sudanese stretch of the Blue Nile. When Sudan unilaterally repudiated the agreement, Egypt even dispatched army units to the border, though tensions eventually began to ease after a military coup in Khartoum installed a different government in 1958. In 1959, the two governments signed a new Nile Waters Agreement, which assigned the entire flow of the river at the time (eighty-four cubic kilometres) to the two states and altered the distribution ratio between them from 12:1 to 3:1. According to the agreement, Egypt was to receive 55.5 cubic kilometres of Nile water annually and Sudan 18.5, leaving 10 to be lost to seepage and evaporation behind the Aswan Dam. In essence, it allowed Egypt to build the Aswan High Dam (whose reservoir would extend 150 kilometres into Sudanese territory) and Sudan to build the Roseires reservoir and any other works that it needed to utilize its full share of Nile water. In addition, the two countries also agreed not to enter any unilateral negotiations with other riparian states and to establish a Permanent Joint Technical Committee for the purpose of pursuing cooperative projects. Overall, the 1959 Nile Waters Agreement, like its 1929 predecessor, once again disregarded the water needs of upstream states, which might want to divert a portion of Nile's flow for their own purposes.[33]

The stage was set for serious disagreements. As more riparian states gained independence, and as their desire and capacity to harness the Nile for their own purposes grew, so too did their resentment towards prior treaties that gave Egypt and Sudan the lion's share of Nile water. Tanzanian president Julius Nyerere was the first to argue that the two Nile Waters Agreements were incompatible with his country's status as a sovereign independent state.

32. Howell, 'East Africa's Water Requirements'; Blocher, *Der Wasserbau-Staat*, 268–73; R. Collins, *Waters of the Nile*, 156–57.

33. Okidi, 'History of the Nile', 333–35.

According to the so-called 'Nyerere doctrine', all treaties signed by the British on behalf of Tanganyika lapsed on Independence Day in December 1961, subject to a two-year grace period during which they would be either reaffirmed or modified. Over the following years, Uganda and Kenya adopted similar positions on the succession of treaties. Egypt's response to such arguments was that existing settlements remained valid and applicable in the absence of any further agreements, regardless of whether they were made by colonial or independent governments. In practice, none of this posed an immediate threat to Egypt's water supplies, but the fact that it potentially exposed them to the whims of upstream states certainly accelerated the momentum behind Egyptian plans for the Aswan High Dam.[34]

More worrying for the Egyptian government were events in Ethiopia. In 1958, while Egypt and Sudan were bilaterally dividing the Nile's water between themselves, the Ethiopian government launched an extensive study of the entire Blue Nile basin with a view to developing irrigation and hydroelectric power, all with the strong support of the US government. After five years of intensive research, water engineers from the US Bureau of Reclamation proposed four large hydroelectric dams with a combined storage capacity of fifty-one cubic kilometres, enough to hold the entire mean annual flow of the Blue Nile and eliminate its annual flood. In certain ways, these reservoirs presented possible advantages to downstream states insofar as they would greatly reduce losses to evaporation compared with the Aswan High Dam, and therefore be capable of releasing more water into the lower basin. But what alarmed Egyptian officials was the plan to divert six cubic kilometres of the Blue Nile's water to irrigation schemes in Ethiopia, which would reduce the total flow of the river by 8.5 per cent. Although the US-backed Blue Nile Project was at best a distant prospect, and seemed likely to remain a hypothetical one, for the Egyptian government any potential reduction of the Nile's precious water was a direct threat to the country's survival and therefore considered tantamount to an act of war. Egypt's abiding fixation on water security was not at all helped by the insistence of the Ethiopian government at the 1977 UN Water Conference that it was 'the sovereign right of any riparian state, in the absence of an international agreement, to proceed unilaterally with the development of water resources within its territory'. In 1979, when the Ethiopian government threatened to reduce the flow of the Blue Nile in order to thwart Egyptian plans to reclaim land in the west of the Nile delta, President Sadat warned that 'if Ethiopia takes any action to block our right to the Nile water, there will be no alternative for us but to use force'.[35]

At the heart of these arguments lay the same competing claims that framed the Indo-Pakistani dispute over the waters of the Indus. While Egypt

---

34. R. Collins, 'History, Hydropolitics', 122–23; Okidi, 328–29.
35. Quoted in Swain, 'Ethiopia', 687; R. Collins, 'History, Hydropolitics', 122–24.

and Sudan defended what they regarded as their historic rights to the Nile's waters (in Egypt's case, going back over five thousand years, and in both cases bolstered by colonial-era settlements), upstream riparian states asserted their territorial claims to a portion of the water that flowed within their borders. Whereas the dry downstream states made their case in the language of 'appreciable harm', arguing that any reduction in water supplies would cause catastrophic damage, upstream countries that had been disregarded by colonial-era agreements deployed a vocabulary of 'equitable use' that would logically entail a greater share for themselves. Fortunately for Egypt, throughout the 1970s and 1980s none of its upstream neighbours were in a position to execute any of their plans for water development. Although Sudan was a target for international irrigation investment, most projects were put on hold in the late 1970s as the country became engulfed in political and economic turmoil. Meanwhile, the Marxist junta that ruled Ethiopia from 1974 until 1991 was too busy fighting insurgencies and too unpopular with international lenders to make any headway, and the political and economic shambles presided over by the brutal dictator Idi Amin precluded any progress whatsoever in Uganda. As for Tanzania, Kenya and the other riparian states, they had little need for irrigation and minimal interest in developing the Nile's waters. For the time being, there was no immediate threat to Egyptian and Sudanese claims to the entire flow of the Nile.[36]

Indeed, Egypt and Sudan endeavoured not only to defend their water supplies but to augment them still further. In the late 1970s, the two governments agreed to build the Jonglei Canal, whose purpose was to divert part of the flow of one of the White Nile's major tributaries (the Bor River) to the mouth of another (the Sobat) in order to bypass the Sudd swamps in southern Sudan, where much of the water was lost to evaporation. The idea dated back to the colonial period, but it was given a new lease of life as recent droughts in upstream areas reduced the amount of water flowing into Lake Nasser (as the reservoir above the Aswan High Dam was named). Planning commenced in 1976, but the project was soon mired in public controversy. The seasonal floods of the Bor were crucial to the functioning of the Sudd ecosystem, and any diversion would likely undermine the livelihoods of all who lived there by drying out its grasslands, diminishing its fisheries and altering the water table. At a more general level, critics also warned that the project would have a damaging effect on the regional climate by reducing evaporation and rainfall. Although a French firm began work on the canal in 1978, the project was soon caught up in fighting between Sudanese government forces and South Sudanese rebels. Understandably, many in southern Sudan thought that the canal's benefits would be shared by Egypt and northern Sudan, while the damage would fall on them. In 1984, after completing 250 (out of a planned 360) kilometres of canal,

36. Waterbury, *Nile Basin*, 3–6, 27–32.

work was forced to a halt when the Sudan People's Liberation Army crippled the giant German-built excavation machine (whose rusting remains still stand near the southern end of the canal). Although technically an intra-state dispute, the clash over the Jonglei Canal both reflected and directly contributed to the growing secessionist dynamics that eventually redrew the initial postcolonial boundaries of Sudan.[37] Despite a joint attempt by the Egyptian and Sudanese governments to revive the project in 2008, all such plans ended with the achievement of independence by South Sudan in 2011.

It was only in the 1990s that any basin-level cooperation began to emerge. The Technical Cooperation Committee for the Promotion of Development and Environmental Protection of the Nile (TECCONILE), formed in 1993, was the first attempt to devise coordinated development plans for the Nile basin. After a series of multilateral conferences, the members adopted an action plan encompassing twenty-one different projects. In 1997, the World Bank agreed to provide financial support, but resentments about Egyptian domination and the failure to include representation from all the major riparian states blocked progress. Somewhat more promising was the Nile Basin Initiative launched in 1999. Involving all the states in the Nile basin (with Eritrea as an observer), its purpose was to forge a Cooperative Framework Agreement on matters of water utilization, conservation, the prevention of significant harm and conflict resolution, as well as data and information sharing, all of which was to be overseen by a permanent Nile River Basin Commission.[38]

Since its founding, the Nile Basin Initiative has been widely hailed as the first basin-wide mechanism for governing transboundary water issues in the region. Yet despite its promising potential, it has not entirely overcome the decades of mistrust and the fundamental clash of interests between upstream and downstream states. Disagreements have centred on the key article of the cooperative framework, which called on all member countries to work together to ensure that no actions would be taken that could 'significantly affect the water security of any other Nile Basin State'. Egypt and Sudan strongly objected to the word 'significantly' and insisted that the article should call on members 'not to adversely affect the water security and current uses and rights of any other Nile Basin State'. By 2011, the six main upstream states had all signed the agreement in its original wording, but Egypt and Sudan still refused. While upstream states were once again asserting their rights to develop the water resources within their borders – and were increasingly unwilling to wait for permission from Egypt and Sudan to do so – the latter continued to insist on their historic rights to the entire flow of the Nile. Since 2011, relations have

37. See generally R. Collins, *Waters of the Nile*. On the Sudd as a challenge to state authority: Schouten and Bachmann, 'Buffering State-Making'.

38. Ahmed, 'Principles and Precedents', 359–63; I. Jacobs, *Politics of Water*, 118; Swain, 'Ethiopia', 690–91.

further deteriorated as the Ethiopian government pushed ahead with plans for its massive Grand Renaissance Dam, which would create a reservoir capable of holding the bulk of the annual flow of the Blue Nile. Although it seems unlikely that Egypt would ever launch military action over the issue, and although international observers maintain that there is plenty of scope for a deal that could satisfy all parties, the problematic legacies of colonial agreements still persist, and consensus over sharing the waters of the Nile seems as elusive as ever.[39]

Dams and Development

The reason why post-colonial governments were so concerned about securing their water rights was because water was absolutely essential for their overall development plans. For newly independent states, the conquest of water was a precondition for growing their economies and improving people's living standards; indeed, for some it was the cornerstone of their very viability. All throughout the post-colonial world, the mastery of water lay at the heart of visions for a better, more prosperous future.

As one of the first such states to achieve independence, India was in a particular hurry to harness its waterways to the cause of national advancement. After decades of what they regarded as half-hearted colonial development efforts, India's nationalist leaders embarked on one of the most ambitious programmes of industrialization and economic modernization the world has ever witnessed. Among the main showpieces of this programme was a series of enormous hydraulic works that we have encountered in previous chapters: the Bhakra Nangal scheme in Punjab, the Hirakud Dam in Odisha, the Damodar Valley project in West Bengal and Jharkhand, and the Tungabhadra Dam in the Deccan. For Kanwar Sain, the chairman of India's Central Water and Power Commission, these huge multipurpose river valley projects were 'symbols of the aspirations of new India, and the blessings that stream forth from them are the enduring gifts of this generation to posterity'.[40] All of them promised a range of benefits – irrigation water for agriculture, power for industry, protection from flooding – but each was built with specific priorities in mind. Hirakud and Damodar were designed chiefly for flood control, Tungabhadra and Bhakra Nangal primarily for irrigation. Though based on colonial-era plans, all of these megaprojects were celebrated as nationalist monuments – or, as Nehru famously put it, as 'the temples of New India'.[41]

39. F. Lawson, 'Egypt, Ethiopia'; Badea, 'Water Conflicts'.

40. Quoted in Amrith, *Unruly Waters*, 196.

41. Nehru, *Modern Temples*, 40–49, quote at 40. On Bhakra: Michel, *Indus Rivers*, 316–40. On Hirakud: D'Souza, 'Damming the Mahanadi River' and *Drowned and Dammed*, 182–205. On Damodar: Klingensmith, *One Valley*.

India's national quest for water was soon mirrored elsewhere in Asia. Pakistan's Indus Basin Project centred on two gigantic dams – the Mangla across the Jhelum River and the Tarbela on the Indus – both of which were designed to store monsoon run-off for downstream release in periods of low flood. Like their Indian counterparts, they numbered among the largest dams ever built (both measuring nearly three kilometres long and over 140 metres high), and were feted as monuments to 'a great and glorious era in the history of Pakistan'.[42] Indonesia's nationalist leaders exhibited a similar passion for large-scale hydraulic works. Despite Sukarno's often strident anti-imperialist rhetoric, he was happy to allow Japanese agencies to finance half a dozen major projects on Java and Sumatra and in Kalimantan. His successor Suharto, who deposed Sukarno in a military-backed coup in 1965, was even more enthusiastic about dams. Drawing on Java's long tradition of indigenous hydraulic engineering, his 'New Order' government encouraged a strong association between dam construction and national prestige. For Sutami, Suharto's first and most influential minister of public works, feats of hydroengineering were 'patriotic acts' that demonstrated to the world Indonesia's status as the leading dam-building nation in Southeast Asia.[43]

When Africa emerged from colonial rule, it likewise witnessed a sharp upsurge in hydroengineering. In the early 1960s, while the Volta River Project was nearing completion, work began on the huge Kainji Dam across the Niger River in Nigeria. By the time it began operating in 1968, work had commenced on the Kafue Gorge Dam in Zambia and the Kossou Dam across the Bandama River in Côte d'Ivoire, both of which were inaugurated in the early 1970s. In Tanzania, Julius Nyerere launched a sequence of smaller hydroelectric projects in the Rufiji River basin. At the same time, he also commissioned plans for an enormous barrage at Stiegler's Gorge, which (had it been built) would have flooded a sizeable chunk of the Selous Game Reserve, a UNESCO world heritage site. In Zaire, Mobuto Sese Seko revived Belgian plans to dam the Congo at Inga Falls, completing 'Inga I' in 1972 and 'Inga II' in 1982, whose combined output of nearly 1,800 megawatts went mainly to European-owned copper mines located two thousand kilometres away in Katanga. Largest of all, of course, was the Aswan High Dam, which was finally finished in 1970 after eleven years of construction.[44]

All of these mega-dams had their roots in colonial-era plans, and all were designed for the twin purposes of water management and power generation. Nonetheless, the primary motive behind most post-colonial hydraulic works

---

42. Haines, *Rivers Divided*, 70–77, quote at 71; Michel, *Indus Rivers*, 268–316.

43. Aditjondro, 'Large Dam Victims', 29–34.

44. See generally Adams, *Wasting the Rain*, 131–37. On Stiegler's Gorge: Hoag and Öhman, 'Turning Water into Power'; Hoag, *Developing the Rivers*, 187–99.

was irrigation. Increasing agricultural production had been a central aim of colonial governments, and after independence it remained a more or less universal cornerstone of economic development plans. For national governments and international agencies alike, higher living standards were regarded as the key to solving the interconnected problems of poverty, inequality and political unrest in the so-called 'Third World'. Amid the neo-Malthusian fears of the post-war years, the imperative to grow more food also reflected rising concerns about runaway population growth and the prospect of food crises.[45] In order to increase output, it was necessary either to extend cultivation or to intensify it on existing farmland. Wherever water supplies were insufficient or unreliable, irrigation was a crucial precondition for agricultural intensification.

The pressure to expand irrigation was especially acute in the densely populated agricultural heartlands of South and Southeast Asia. India's first Five Year Plan, launched in 1951, called for a doubling of the irrigated area over the following fifteen to twenty years (totalling around forty to fifty million acres, or sixteen to twenty million hectares). In order to solve the country's 'food problem', it allocated 20 per cent of all expenditure to irrigation alone, plus a further 15 per cent to general agricultural development.[46] In 1958, Sukarno's 'Operation Prosperity', which aimed to achieve Indonesian self-sufficiency in rice production, was similarly predicated on a huge increase in water use. Echoing ideas long advanced by Dutch colonialists, it advocated a two-pronged solution to mounting food pressures on Java: more irrigation and fertilizers, and more state support for emigration to the 'outer isles' through the opening of new lands for irrigated rice farming.[47]

As it happened, the results of such programmes fell far short of expectations. In fact, both India and Indonesia became more rather than less reliant on food imports over the course of the 1950s. Matters came to a head in the mid-1960s as a succession of monsoon failures slashed yields across the region. Faced by the prospect of the first serious food shortages since the war, officials scrambled to distribute grain to areas that needed it. In the short term they managed to avert a major food crisis, but it was clear to all that such immediate aid measures were no substitute for longer-term solutions. Fortunately, it seemed, technology appeared to have an answer. By the mid-1960s, US-backed crop-breeding programmes in Mexico, Taiwan and the Philippines were beginning to register some astonishing results. When cultivated in the right conditions, the new hybrid strains of wheat, corn and rice that had been developed were capable of yielding up to four times more grain per hectare than most

45. E.g., Vogt, *Road to Survival*; Osborn, *Our Crowded Planet*; P. Ehrlich and Ehrlich, *Population Bomb*. For a detailed analysis: T. Robertson, *Malthusian Moment*.

46. Government of India Planning Commission, *First Five Year Plan*, 345–51; Government of India, *Review of the First Five Year Plan*, 2; Engerman, *Price of Aid*, 121.

47. Moon, 'Takeoff or Self-Sufficiency?', 195–97.

traditional crop varieties. Against the backdrop of recent food scares, these new 'miracle seeds' promised to achieve the kind of quantum leap in productivity that was necessary to keep food production ahead of demographic growth. After experimenting with high-yield wheat strains sourced from Mexico, Indian and Pakistani authorities soon began distributing the hybrid seeds throughout their irrigated provinces. By the late 1960s, officials in Indonesia and South Vietnam were encouraging farmers to adopt the IR-8 rice variety that had been developed at the International Rice Research Institute in the Philippines.[48]

Thus began the fabled 'Green Revolution' in Asia. Over the next three decades, the new crop varieties literally took root across dozens of countries in the Global South. By the 1980s, nearly half of the developing world's rice and wheat fields were sown with new strains. By the end of the twentieth century, high-yield rice accounted for over three-quarters of the crop in South and Southeast Asia, and high-yield wheat for well over 90 per cent.[49] It was here, along the southern rim of Asia, where the uptake of the new varieties was greatest and their impact most pronounced. This was mainly because the Green Revolution served multiple political interests across the region. For Western policymakers fixated on the Cold War, these new agricultural technologies were a useful tool for cementing key alliances and reducing communist influence in the backyard of the Soviet Union and China. For domestic elites in India, Pakistan, Indonesia and the Philippines, they promised not only to alleviate mounting food/population pressures but also to blunt unwelcome calls for land reform and generate much-needed revenue from crop exports and the reduction of imports.[50] By contrast, uptake of the new high-yield varieties in Africa was far more limited, partly owing to its lower geopolitical significance in Western eyes, partly as a result of environmental and infrastructural obstacles, and partly because of the cultivation of different staple crops (mainly sorghums, millets, yams, cassava) from those that had attracted the bulk of scientific attention to date. Yet in Africa too, governments and international agencies spent a considerable amount of effort and resources on crop breeding and agricultural improvement, spearheaded by the International Institute for Tropical Agriculture in Abadan and the Africa Rice Center in Abidjan.[51]

48. Cullather, *Hungry World*, 134–79; Perkins, *Geopolitics*, 183–86; Conway, *Doubly Green Revolution*, 48–52.

49. FAO, *Food for All*; Hazell, 'Asian Green Revolution', 4; Byerlee, 'Modern Varieties', 698–701. It is worth noting that hybrid maize followed a somewhat distinctive trajectory compared with wheat and rice, having been developed and shared earlier in the interwar period by public institutions in the United States: Byerlee, 'Globalization of Hybrid Maize'.

50. Angus Wright, *Death of Ramón Gonzalez*, 186; Cullather, *Hungry World*, 94–107.

51. R. Dumont, *Notes sur les implications*; P. Mosley, *Obstacles*; Conway, *Doubly Green Revolution*, 55.

The control of water was a key element of this entire agricultural trans-formation. The new high-yield crop strains could not perform any 'miracles' on their own, but were instead designed to respond to high doses of artificial fer-tilizers and carefully controlled water inputs. Across South and Southeast Asia, governments deliberately expanded irrigation facilities as a means of encouraging farmers to adopt them. Large-scale irrigation schemes were also planned in many parts of Africa – for example, along the Tana River in Kenya; the Senegal River in Mali, Mauritania and Senegal; and perhaps most notably in northern Nigeria, where a string of irrigation schemes was launched in the Sokoto, Kano and Borno states in the hope of eventually covering as much as two million hectares. Although the results of these efforts also fell far short of expectations, they nonetheless reflected the keen interest of post-colonial governments in building irrigation projects as a means of raising land and labour productivity and consolidating their control over regions far from the capital.[52]

Furthermore, it was not only surface waters that were harnessed to the cause of agricultural modernization. Across large swathes of Asia and Africa, farmers increasingly relied on massive withdrawals of groundwater. The use of wells for agriculture was an ancient practice, and it boasted numerous advan-tages over surface works. Not only were they much cheaper to build than dams and canal systems; they were also more reliable when the rains failed, and they lost much less water to evaporation than surface reservoirs. The chief drawback was the enormous amount of energy (usually human or animal energy) required to lift the water on to fields, which for centuries impeded the mobilization of groundwater at a large scale. All of this changed from the 1960s onwards with the spread of electric- and petrol-powered tube wells. In East and West Africa, where rural electricity was rarely available, groundwater pumps often relied on Japanese-built petrol engines, which were cheap to run and relatively easy to maintain since they were broadly similar to the engines of Japanese motorcycles that had become popular in the region. In India and Pakistan, the costs of tube-well installation and electricity were heavily subsidized by the state to encour-age more irrigated farming. By the early 2000s, groundwater accounted for no less than 70 per cent of India's irrigation. The result was a positive feedback loop of multiple-level water engineering: as demand for electricity rose accord-ingly, more and more of the subcontinent's surface flows were marshalled to produce power for exploiting subsurface waters.[53]

As the new package of high-yield seeds, irrigation and fertilizer spread, it proved remarkably effective at increasing agricultural productivity, at least for a while. From 1961 to 1991, average Asian maize yields rose from 1.2 tons per

52. Palmer-Jones, 'Irrigation'; Adams, *Wasting the Rain*, 162–71; Ertsen, *Improvising Planned Development*, 179–80; Aditjondro, 'Large Dam Victims', 30–33.

53. Adams, *Wasting the Rain*, 88–89, 145, 172, 192; Amrith, *Unruly Waters*, 256–58; Pomeranz, 'Great Himalayan Watershed'.

hectare to almost 3.2 tons, rice yields from 1.75 to 3.6 tons, and wheat yields from 0.6 to 3.2 tons.[54] In view of these results it is perhaps unsurprising that many observers hailed the Green Revolution as nothing less than a heroic achievement.

But there was an uglier side to these visions of abundance. As numerous critics had warned from the outset, the new agricultural technologies exacerbated social inequalities in the countryside. On a regional level, they widened discrepancies between irrigated and rain-fed areas, to the clear disadvantage of the latter. Even in well-watered areas the initial benefits fell overwhelmingly to affluent farmers who could most easily cover the costs of fertilizer, seeds, water fees or pumps. For poor smallholders who could not afford these external inputs, higher yields for their wealthier neighbours translated into lower prices, falling incomes and rising debts. In some areas – notably, the irrigated tracts of the Punjab – the resulting polarization fuelled not only intense social conflict but also a wave of suicides among hard-pressed farmers who could not get enough water. Just as in the colonial period, the deliberate intensification of agriculture also intensified struggles over access to local resources, above all water.[55]

The ecological impacts were equally profound, not least for the very water resources on which high-input agriculture depended. In an attempt to maximize per hectare yields, farmers often applied excessive doses of fertilizer, much of which ended up getting washed into waterways where it caused acute eutrophication. At the same time, the standard practice of planting the new crop varieties in monocultures exacerbated weed and pest problems, which in turn led to the use of more herbicides and pesticides, which likewise polluted surrounding water supplies and posed a significant health risk to local people. In semi-arid regions, the sharp increase in groundwater extraction from thousands of new tube wells depleted aquifers at an alarming rate, prompting farmers to dig deeper and more expensive wells to ensure adequate supplies. And wherever irrigation advanced too far ahead of drainage works, it was not long before the familiar problems of waterlogging and salinization began to appear.[56]

Despite all these social and environmental problems, and despite the ballooning scale of groundwater irrigation, dams continued to proliferate across the

54. Figures from FAO, 'Crops and Livestock Products', FAOSTAT, http://faostat.fao.org /site/567/default.aspx#ancor.

55. Corsi, 'Communalism'; Pomeranz, 'Great Himalayan Watershed'; Shiva, *Violence*, 23, 174–75. For a critical contemporary assessment: UNRISD, *Social and Economic Implications*.

56. On soaring fertilizer use and its effects: Hazell 'Asian Green Revolution', 3; Smil, *Enriching the Earth*, 116. On health impacts: esp. Angus Wright, *Death of Ramón Gonzalez*; Rola and Pingali, *Pesticides*; Adams, *Wasting the Rain*, 179–80. On waterlogging: Pomeranz, 'Great Himalayan Watershed'; Hazell 'Asian Green Revolution', 16; Smil, *Feeding the World*, 41–43.

Global South. During the decolonization decades, the construction of large dams acquired an almost irresistible momentum. The impetus behind dam-building was sustained by a powerful coalition of interests: governments keen on prestige projects, international agencies in search of major investment opportunities and domestic construction industries addicted to lucrative state contracts. In Asia and Africa alike, dam fever peaked in the 1970s and 1980s. Roughly half of all of Africa's dams were constructed during these two decades alone; so too were half of the four thousand or so dams built in India between 1947 and 2000.[57]

Although the consequences of all this dam building were by no means entirely negative – especially for city dwellers, landowners in drought-prone areas and industrialists – the advantages for local communities rarely offset the disadvantages. The problems were all-too familiar from the colonial era. One consequence was the increased incidence of water- and insect-borne disease, especially bilharzia and malaria, which commonly plagued communities near reservoirs or along irrigation canals. Another was the damage caused by the end of seasonal flooding, which often harmed flora and fauna as well as farming and fishing communities many kilometres downstream.[58] The most contentious problem was – or rather remained – the displacement of huge numbers of people, few of whom ever received sufficient compensation for what they lost. In Nigeria, the Kainji Dam displaced fifty thousand local residents, almost as many as Kariba had done a decade earlier (fifty-seven thousand). In Côte d'Ivoire, the Kossou Dam displaced eighty-five thousand, more even than the Volta River Project (around eighty-four thousand). In India alone, the best estimates indicate that dams have displaced or directly affected an astonishing forty million people since independence – more than all the state's other development projects put together – with the landless poor and so-called tribal groups by far the most likely to be evicted and least likely to receive any form of compensation.[59]

As a result, dams that were designed to be symbols of a more prosperous future instead became focal points of popular discontent. Displacement almost always provoked opposition. At Hirakud, India's first large barrage to be completed after independence, local resistance arose as soon as plans for the project went public in 1946. Although the opposition eventually culminated in a mass march of some thirty thousand people, local fury was no

57. Figures from Duflo and Pande, 'Dams', 611; Showers, 'Electrifying Africa', 204.

58. On disease: Jobin, *Dams and Disease*, 272–83, 360–63. On downstream effects: Richter et al., 'Lost in Development's Shadow'; Isaacman and Isaacman, *Dams, Displacement*, 126–35; Adams, *Wasting the Rain*, 137–54.

59. Chakravorty, *Price of Land*, 232–34; Scudder, *Future of Large Dams*, 194–95; Isaacman and Sneddon, 'Social and Environmental History', 618; Colson, *Social Consequences of Resettlement*; Chambers, *Volta Resettlement Experience*; Nixon, *Slow Violence*, 150–74; Adams, *Wasting the Rain*, 132.

match for the determination of the developmentalist state. When Nehru laid the foundation stone for the dam in 1948, he flatly told the assembled villagers that 'if you are to suffer, you should suffer in the interest of the country'.[60] Such large-scale protest was unusual at the time, but the outcome at Hirakud (see chapter 4) was not. From the 1940s through to the 1970s, governments generally ignored or repressed anti-dam protests in the name of the 'greater good', much as their colonial predecessors had done. From the 1980s, however, the tide began to turn as a combination of mounting public criticism of the social and environmental effects of large dams along with public campaigning by high-profile NGOs such as the International Rivers Network (established in 1985) helped dam opponents get better compensation for oustees. Indeed, on a few occasions they even managed to halt the construction of dam projects altogether. The most famous example was the gigantic Narmada Project, which consisted of 30 large, 136 medium and 3,000 small dams scattered throughout the Narmada River watershed in western India. Launched in the early 1980s with support from the World Bank, the scheme would have not only flooded out a large number of sacred sites but also displaced hundreds of thousands of people. In the late 1980s, a coalition of farmers, environmentalists and human rights activists joined forces to oppose the project and to mobilize international support. In 1993, the Save the Narmada movement scored a major success by pressuring the World Bank – the biggest financier of dam projects globally – to withdraw its funding for the scheme.[61]

As opposition to large dams continued to swell, the World Bank and IUCN responded by supporting the establishment of a World Commission on Dams in 1997. Consisting of representatives from academia, private enterprise, professional associations and civil society groups, its purpose was to conduct a comprehensive evaluation of the costs and benefits of large-scale dams to date. There was little doubt that the commission would cast a critical eye over such projects, but when its report was published in 2000, it offered a bleaker assessment than most had expected. Although it affirmed that dams had made 'an important and significant contribution to human development', it also concluded that 'in too many cases an unacceptable and often unnecessary price has been paid . . . by people displaced, by communities downstream, by taxpayers and by the natural environment'. On average, it found that large dams cost much more, took longer to build and delivered fewer benefits than promised. More fundamentally, it found that the inequitable distribution of whatever benefits they brought 'has called into question the value of many

60. Quoted in Viegas, 'Hirakud Dam Oustees', 53; see also Nayak, 'Big Dams and Protests' and 'Development, Displacement and Justice'; Khagram, *Dams and Development*, 36–37.

61. On the Narmada dispute generally: Nilsen, *Dispossession and Resistance*; Baviskar, 'Nation's Body, River's Pulse'. On the rise of anti-dam campaigning more broadly: McCully, *Silenced Rivers*, 281–311.

dams in meeting water and energy development needs when compared with the alternatives'.[62]

For a while, it seemed that the global dam-building juggernaut was finally being restrained. Amid growing criticism and closer international scrutiny, the pace of dam construction significantly slowed through the 1990s and early 2000s. Nonetheless, the slowdown proved to be only short-lived. By the mid-2000s, World Bank lending for dam projects was on the rise once again, starting with the $1.3 billion Nam Theun 2 Dam in Laos. Furthermore, even after the publication of the World Commission's report, many governments simply ignored its recommendations about environmental safeguards and stakeholder participation. Back in the Narmada valley, for instance, the Indian government pressed ahead with its plans despite the withdrawal of World Bank assistance and the persistence of strong local opposition. In 2017, some thirty years after the birth of the Save the Narmada movement, it inaugurated the enormous Sardar Sarovar Dam, which submerged 245 villages and displaced 127,000 people.[63]

India, as the second most 'dammed' country on the planet (behind China), may be especially susceptible to what Nehru once described as the 'disease of gigantism', but the syndrome has become endemic throughout most of the Global South.[64] In Pakistan, arguably the world's most irrigation-dependent country, interest in constructing more large dams has been just as intense as in India. As we saw above, Laos has blazed a trail for other mega-dams along the Mekong and has no shortage of plans for more. Along the Nile, the partially completed Jonglei Canal has continued to generate political interest and technical studies despite the inauspicious political context in South Sudan and despite the ongoing tensions between riparian states. In Central Africa, the gargantuan 'Transaqua Project' (also known as the Lake Chad Replenishment Scheme) proposes to dam several of the tributaries along the right bank of the Congo River and channel their water to Lake Chad through a 2,400-kilometre canal. Along the way, the canal will supposedly generate millions of kilowatts of electricity and provide irrigation water for thousands of square kilometres in the Sahel; the parallels with Herman Sörgel's utopian Atlantropa scheme are difficult to overlook. Further down the Congo, there are still live plans to create the world's largest hydroelectric station just above Inga Falls. Despite decades of setbacks stretching all the way back to Belgian initiatives in the early twentieth century (see chapter 7), the 'Grand Inga' scheme

62. World Commission on Dams, *Dams and Development*, xxviii.

63. Baviskar, 'Nation's Body, River's Pulse', 33; Goodland, 'Viewpoint'; Hay, Skinner and Norton, 'Dam-Induced Displacement', esp. p. 7.

64. Recent global statistics on large dams indicate a total of 9,215 for China, 6,785 for India, 5,366 for Brazil, and 4,602 for the United States: Mulligan, van Soesbergen and Sáenz, 'GOODD', 5; quote from a speech of November 1958, taken from D'Souza's 'Framing India's Hydraulic Crises' (112).

FIGURE 8.3. Protesters against the Sardar Sarovar project in the Narmada Valley, May 2015.
Source: countercurrents.org. Reproduced according to the organization's fair-use policy: https://countercurrents.org/fairuse.htm.

remains a tantalizing dream among hydraulic engineers, development agencies and regional governments; more recently it has also attracted the interest of Chinese authorities. If it is ever completed, the resulting disruption of the Congo River's hydrology – which includes a nutrient and sediment plume that stretches some eight hundred kilometres into the ocean – would have profound implications not only for regional societies and ecosystems but also for the biogeochemistry and marine food webs of the entire eastern equatorial Atlantic.[65]

Because of all the controversies that surround them, many of these mega-projects may never come to fruition. Whereas advocates insist that they are necessary to reduce poverty and increase supplies of renewable energy, opponents argue that they are not worth the costs and that resources would be better spent on other renewable power initiatives – not least because climate change is rendering river flows increasingly unpredictable in any event. Regardless of whether any of these plans are ever realized, it is already clear that the torrent of dam-building since the 1960s has been a major driver of global environmental change. Altogether, the fifty-eight thousand or so large dams that

65. On the Jonglei Canal: Ahmad, 'Post-Jonglei Planning'. On Transaqua: Sayan, Nagabhatla and Ekwuribe, 'Soft Power'. On Inga: Warner et al., 'Fantasy'; Showers, 'Grand Inga Hydroelectricity Scheme'.

had been built by the year 2020 stored the equivalent of around one-sixth of the world's total annual river flow.[66] Because much of this water is diverted into sprawling canal systems, some rivers now carry scarcely any water to the sea. The implications for downstream ecosystems are grim, including coastal estuaries that are important for marine life. Just as important as the reduction of water flows is the declining flux of sediments and nutrients, around half of which is trapped globally by human-made impoundments.[67] In recent decades, lower silt deliveries have caused many of the world's river deltas to shrink. As processes of erosion have outpaced their replenishment, millions of people have been placed at greater risk of coastal flooding, above all along the fringes of Asia.

Less widely appreciated, but no less important, is the way in which the decline in river flows and silt delivery is also altering the relationship between rivers, oceans and the planet's atmosphere. In tropical regions in particular, large reservoirs have been shown to emit large volumes of methane – a far more potent greenhouse gas than CO_2 – thus partially undermining the case for large dams as a means of combating climate change.[68] At the same time, obstructing the flow of sediment to the sea also affects the role of rivers in the global carbon cycle. By reducing the availability of trace nutrients such as iron, silicon, and phosphorus for consumption by marine phytoplankton, dams not only alter the foundation of marine food webs but also diminish the capacity of phytoplankton to 'fix' atmospheric carbon and transport it to the seabed.[69]

These links between dam-building and climate change, though not yet fully understood, highlight once again the fundamental interconnectedness of rivers, oceans and the atmosphere, even as they remind us that the water flows that current-day mega-dams seek to harness are not necessarily as dependable as one would like to think.

Water, Sanitation and the Post-Colonial City

Agriculture was by no means the only sector in which colonial-era problems of water shortage and uneven availability continued to cause problems in the post-colonial world. In cities too, unequal access to clean drinking water and sanitation remained an acute problem after independence. In some ways the two issues are linked. As the transformation of agriculture pushed millions of poor cultivators off the land, many flocked to the cities in search of work. From 1950 to 2018, the urban population of Africa grew more than sixteen-fold,

66. Mulligan, van Soesbergen and Sáenz, 'GOODD', 1.

67. Vörösmarty et al., 'Anthropogenic Sediment Retention'.

68. Deemer et al., 'Greenhouse Gas Emissions'.

69. N. Ward et al., 'Where Carbon Goes'; E. Thompson, 'Dams Alter Nutrient Flows'; Biddanda, 'Global Significance'.

from 33 million to 548 million. Over the same period, Asia's urban population rose ninefold from 246 million to 2.3 billion, with India alone counting
463 million urban dwellers. Although this unprecedented expansion of cities was part of a wider global trend, the growth rate in Africa and Asia was
higher than anywhere else in the world. And as this urban influx continued
to swell, municipal services and infrastructures were increasingly unable to
cope. The main outcome has been the creation of a 'planet of slums' throughout the Global South, a proliferation of shantytowns in which over a billion
people struggle to gain access to basic amenities, the most indispensable of
which is potable water.[70]

In many respects, this lamentable situation arose from the breakneck pace
of urbanization during the half century or so after independence, which would
have posed a challenge to municipal authorities even in the best circumstances. But at a fundamental level it also reflected deep-rooted colonial legacies. As we saw in chapter 6, urban water and sanitary systems formed part of
the ideological bedrock of the 'modern' city in the nineteenth and twentieth
centuries. Although the spread of these technologies in Europe's colonies was
couched in the rhetoric of civilizational uplift, in practice it tended to create
small enclaves of salubrity in which elites could lead what they regarded as
suitably hygienic ways of life, while the vast majority of urban residents had to
rely on increasingly polluted surface waters or the odd communal standpipe.
In the infrastructurally fragmented cities of empire, cleanliness rearranged
distinctions between the modern and the traditional, the hygienic and the
unhygienic. Sanitation and water supply thus became part of the broader discourse around race, civilization and modernity that reinforced the hierarchical
distinctions of colonial societies.

The colonial-era reordering of urban space and urban populations into
the sanitary and insanitary left an enduring imprint on the cities of the post-
colonial world. On a physical level, post-colonial authorities inherited urban
infrastructure systems that inscribed these inequalities into the very fabric
of the city. Piped water and municipal sewage systems lagged woefully behind
the expansion of urban populations, and even where governments boosted the
amount of water available to growing cities (through the construction of new
reservoirs, treatment plants, and the like), the distribution networks inherited from the colonial period often remained confined to central districts and
affluent garden suburbs where post-colonial elites now lived. In Lagos, the
new capital of independent Nigeria, the lack of colonial-era investment meant
that only 10 per cent of its residences had a municipal water connection in
the 1960s. In Jakarta too, only 12 per cent of the population had access to

---

70. M. Davis, *Planet of Slums*. Population figures from the United Nations Department
of Economic and Social Affairs's *World Urbanization Prospects* (24, 43).

household water connections even after the completion of a major surface water treatment plant in 1957.[71]

Just as important as the physical remains were the ideological holdovers of colonial sanitation policies. Long after the end of European rule, post-colonial patterns of water supply were still shaped by notions of 'civilizational differ-ence' and the 'hygienic citizen'. Although nationalist governments vehemently rejected the imperial rhetoric of racial and cultural inferiority, they continued to regard sanitation infrastructures as essential for the creation of an ordered, modern city. Like their colonial predecessors, they abhorred filth and disorder, and they sought to transform cities into clean, healthy spaces free from both physical disease and social degeneration.[72] Of course, nationalist strategies for urban improvement served somewhat different purposes and had different political inflections. Whereas colonial-era policies were mainly geared towards neutralizing the public health threat posed by poor people and unhygienic places, nationalist discourses of equality and social reform placed greater emphasis on enabling citizens to improve their own sanitation standards. From this perspective, urban improvement was as much about assimilating people into 'modern' ways of life as it was about upgrading the physical fabric of the city.

Yet this approach carried its own set of prescriptions, and in practice it served to perpetuate the same basic distinctions that had long underpinned colonial-era sanitation policies. In place of the 'backward native' came the poor rural migrant who needed to be educated about the importance of bet-ter hygiene. In place of the 'primitive habits' of 'native' city dwellers came the 'informal', unregulated water and sewage arrangements that flourished in shantytowns. For post-colonial governments gripped by runaway urbaniza-tion, the target for sanitary improvement efforts was not just the physical fab-ric of the city but also the 'ingrained habits and lack of desire as well as lack of training to use better accommodation'. As one urban reformer in India suc-cinctly put it in the 1970s, 'the real problem of the slums is not taking people out of slums but slums out of people'.[73] Although the vocabulary and motiva-tions differed from the colonial era, the poor were still faulted for their sani-tary shortcomings while wealthier residents retreated into enclaves of relative health and cleanliness. The post-colonial politics of urban water and sewerage continued to be as much about cultural symbolism, notions of citizenship and social differentiation as about public health.[74]

71. Gandy, 'Planning, Anti-planning', 378; Kooy and Bakker, 'Splintered Networks', 1851.

72. Chakrabarty, *Habitations of Modernity*, 65–79.

73. Jagmohan, *Island of Truth* (Delhi: Vikas, 1978), quoted in Sharan, 'In the City', 4909.

74. On links between water access, entitlements and 'hydraulic citizenship', see Anand's *Hydraulic City*. See also McFarlane, 'Governing the Contaminated City', 430–31; Engel and

One of the most conspicuous continuities was the persistence of colonial-era patterns of 'design demand', or the quantity of water regarded as the standard per capita allocation of any water delivery system. Water networks in colonial cities were, as noted earlier, designed to provide a certain volume of water per day to each user, with European and elite residents generally receiving a far larger share than other city dwellers. After independence these stratified design parameters were often retained, albeit with new economic groupings such as 'high-income', 'middle income' and 'low-income' replacing racial or ethnic categories. In Nairobi, for instance, the colonial design demand that provided the richest (mainly white) residents two or three times more water than low-income groups remained broadly intact for decades. Insofar as the ratio between different user categories changed in the wake of independence, it in fact became more polarized than ever. Whereas Nairobi's wealthiest inhabitants enjoyed a remarkably steady supply of more than two hundred litres per person between 1945 and 2005, over the same period the design demand for its poorest residents dropped from slightly over a hundred litres to a mere twenty litres. As the city's population exploded and water resources became stretched, the prioritization of high consumption by the rich meant that less water was available for the poor. While the wealthiest 10 per cent of residents nowadays consumes around half of Nairobi's water supply, the bottom third has no access to municipal water supplies at all.[75]

There were a host of reasons for these persistent inequalities. For one thing, the prohibitive capital costs of modern sanitary systems led many city authorities to focus on the most lucrative groups of customers. For a brief period after decolonization, it seemed that high levels of economic growth might make it possible to provide household water and sewer connections to the bulk of the urban population in many newly independent states. Unfortunately, it was not long before this vision fell afoul of economic realities. By the early 1970s, there was already little prospect that consumers would be able to pay enough to make such large, capital-intensive systems financially viable. In principle, governments could have turned to simpler, cheaper technologies as a means of improving sanitary conditions for more people. Some urban planners in India, for instance, advocated the alignment of neighbourhood services according to economic means rather than pursuing the more ambitious objective of universal equal access.[76] But the problem with such an approach was that it fell afoul of political realities. For nationalist leaders heavily invested in the idea of technology as a vehicle for modernization, any sinking of standards below colonial-era ideals ran completely counter to their promises of prosperity and advancement – a stance that was bolstered by the sanitation priorities of

Susilo, 'Shaming and Sanitation'.

75. Nilsson, 'Unseeing State', 492–96.

76. Sharan, 'In the City', 4907–8.

external donors and development agencies. Although most post-colonial governments lacked the financial means to achieve the dream of universal piped water, they nonetheless deemed it politically impossible to abandon it as their normative aim.[77]

The upshot of these practical and political pressures was a marked tendency towards 'showcase modernity' – that is, a strong affinity for prestige projects precisely because of (rather than in spite of) the ongoing inability to provide basic services.[78] The symbolic importance of centralized water and sewer systems, coupled with the lack of means to support their universal extension, prompted governments to focus their limited capacity for infrastructural investment on the most 'modern' parts of the city – mainly downtown areas that served as monuments to national progress and as hubs for attracting international business – at the expense of the majority of 'unmodern' areas, which were bypassed as symbols of the past. This was a common trend throughout the post-colonial world, but it was especially noticeable in the largest conurbations with the greatest pretensions to 'world city' status. In Jakarta, for instance, both Sukarno and Suharto consistently prioritized sanitation spending on the city centre in a deliberate bid to present the image of a modern nation to international visitors and Indonesians alike. Since the 1990s, efforts to transform Mumbai into a 'world class city' or to develop Delhi as a 'global city' have likewise focused on high-visibility projects and downtown areas rather than on more prosaic matters such as better sanitation in the hundreds of informal settlements that are scattered throughout their metropolitan regions. The continuing pattern of polarized services so common in cities of the Global South thus reflected more than just the socio-material hangovers of colonialism. It was also rooted in the emergence of new political strategies that sought to showcase the nation both at home and abroad as one that embraced a modern identity and modern lifestyles for its people. So long as policymakers were more concerned about cultivating the image of development rather than improving actual services, this approach made perfect sense.[79]

While city centres and affluent neighbourhoods aspired to 'first-world' hygienic status, improvements in water and sewage provision for poor districts came slowly if at all. In fact, sanitary conditions for poor residents in many cities deteriorated after independence as population growth outstripped infrastructural expansion, and especially as the imposition of neoliberal economic policies during the 1980s and 1990s led to drastic cuts in public services. The effects were particularly severe in sub-Saharan Africa, which has continued to

77. Nilsson, 'Unseeing State', 500–503.

78. I borrow the term from Gandy in 'Planning, Anti-planning' (378).

79. A point convincingly emphasized by Nilsson in 'Unseeing State'. On Jakarta: Kooy and Bakker, 'Splintered Networks', 1851–53. On Delhi: Dupont, 'Dream of Delhi'. On Mumbai: Björkman, *Pipe Politics*; McFarlane, 'Governing the Contaminated City', 428–29; Bombay First, *Vision Mumbai*.

FIGURE 8.4. Sanitation pipes bypassing the Dharavi suburb of Mumbai (considered to be one of the world's largest slums) en route to more prosperous quarters, December 2010.
Source: Wikimedia Commons. CC BY-SA 2.0.

suffer from lower levels of water and sewage provision than any other part of the world.[80] Lagos, by most measures Africa's largest city (with over twenty-three million residents in its wider metropolitan area), exemplifies the overall trend along the booming West African littoral. From the early 1960s to the early 2000s, its population grew from just under a million to well over ten million, while the proportion of its residents with piped water connections fell from around 10 per cent to under 5 per cent.[81] In East Africa too, both the accessibility and reliability of water services has generally deteriorated. Even for households fortunate enough to have a piped connection, water has often been available for only brief periods each day. In the early 2000s, some 90 per cent of the region's city dwellers regularly stored water in their homes to ensure adequate supplies (up from only 3 per cent in the late 1960s).[82] Although matters have improved somewhat since the turn of the century with the gradual recovery of investment and the widespread implementation of slum clearance and neighbourhood rehabilitation schemes, in 2017 it was

80. For an overview of the situation in Africa, see Chitonge, 'Cities beyond Networks'.
81. Gandy, 'Planning, Anti-planning', 383.
82. J. Thompson and Cairncross. 'Drawers of Water'; Nilsson, *Water for a Few*.

nonetheless estimated that around 2 billion people still lacked basic sanitation facilities and 785 million lacked access to clean drinking water. As a result, mortality rates have remained far higher in slums than in other areas (including among the rural poor), largely owing to diseases caused by contaminated water and poor sanitation.[83]

Lacking a dependable supply of piped water, poor city residents have all too commonly been forced to rely on wells, tanks, illegal taps or the army of private street vendors that have flourished since the 1980s and 1990s. 'Small-scale independent water providers', as they are called, have become especially prevalent in un-serviced informal settlements where connection rates are lowest, standpipes few and far between, and queues for clean water often prohibitively long. There are different types of providers offering different services: wholesalers who draw water from mains pipes to convey to areas with poor or intermittent supplies, paid water carriers for those who do not wish to queue at standpipes or cart their own supplies home, and retail vendors selling small plastic sachets or bottles of water directly to customers on the street. Collectively they serve as a kind of parallel water provisioning system, to some extent supplementing the coverage of public services and to some extent supplanting and competing with them. In many cities across Africa and Asia, they have become more of a hindrance than a help in the effort to improve public health. Because these informal 'water cartels' directly benefit from the inadequacies of municipal systems, they often deliberately undermine attempts by city authorities to expand water provision in poor areas through the use of threats, intimidation and occasional acts of sabotage. Another problem is the risk posed by unlicensed vendors selling water that is contaminated and/or laced with chemical additives in an attempt to sterilize it or mask the smell. When biologists tested water sachets on sale in Kumasi in 2003, they found that over four-fifths of them were unsuitable for drinking. Although governments have sought to regulate private vendors for the sake of public health, enforcement is often weak and patchy.[84]

Since the 1990s, the World Bank, International Monetary Fund and major donor countries have pushed to privatize the municipal urban water systems themselves as a means of attracting investment and enhancing their performance. All across the Global South, national governments and city authorities issued contracts to private (often multinational) water companies

83. Figures from World Health Organization, *Progress*, 7–8. It is worth highlighting that the situation is worse than the figures suggest, given that many 'improved' facilities are still unsafe. International health agencies place basic pit latrines under this category, and piped water sources are often hazardous owing to high levels of microbial contamination: Ezeh et al., 'History', 553; Lilford et al., 'Health of People', 565.

84. For an overview: Kjellén and McGranahan, *Informal Water Vendors*; A. Sarkar, 'Informal Water Vendors'; Venkatachalam, 'Informal Water Markets'. On Kumasi: McCaskie, 'Water Wars in Kumasi', 148–50.

to operate their systems and establish a supposedly more 'rational' market-based price structure that would promote efficiency and improve financial viability. Unsurprisingly, the reforms sparked concerted opposition from consumers, academics and activists, who argued that water was a public good and that access to clean water should be an inalienable right. Echoing the sentiments of colonial-era protesters, many were repulsed by the idea of commodifying a basic human need.[85] There was also a widespread sense that the acquisition of a country's water resources by foreign corporations was a glaring instance of neocolonialism. In the end, the impact of the privatization agenda was fairly negligible, partly because its opponents forced governments to backtrack, partly because of disappointing levels of investor interest, and partly because of the decades-old problem that water companies had little financial interest in serving low-income neighbourhoods.[86]

Yet amid all the furore over the rights and wrongs of privatization, it was easy to overlook a fundamental point: in practice, most water provision in poor urban settlements had always been informally 'privatized' because of the inadequacies of public provision.[87] Ever since the nineteenth century, neither colonial nor post-colonial governments have ever managed to offer a cheap, clean and reliable supply of water to all urban residents, many of whom consequently turned to other sources to meet their daily needs. Over a century and a half after engineers began to build new urban sanitation systems in Europe's colonies, the circulation of water in post-colonial cities remains decidedly unequal and fragmented.[88]

Decolonization and the Ocean Frontier

The post-independence rush to exploit natural resources played out on the seas as well as the land. In chapter 5 we examined how colonial officials regarded the offshore waters of Asia and Africa as a vast frontier of expansion. While many inland lake and river fisheries were already showing signs of stress from the effects of hydroengineering works or land conversion, the oceans appeared as an almost entirely untapped asset, and a practically inexhaustible one at that. During the first half of the twentieth century, colonial authorities sought to increase the catch in a variety of different ways: surveying the most promising fishing grounds, transferring boats and gear from the

85. On the complexities of distinguishing human rights from commodities in the context of water: Ballestero, *Future History of Water.*

86. Bakker, *Privatizing Water*; Mirosa and Harris, 'Human Right to Water'; Bayliss and Fine, *Privatization*; Bohman, 'Water and Sanitation Challenge', 102–10.

87. As highlighted at the time by Budds and McGranahan in 'Debates on Water Privatization'; see also McCaskie's 'Water Wars in Kumasi' (150–52).

88. For a recent overview: Gimelli, Bos and Rogers, 'Fostering Equity'; Anand, *Hydraulic City.*

industrial world, attracting metropolitan fishing boats through subsidies and financial incentives, and occasionally taking the unorthodox step of working with fishing communities to make gradual improvements to artisanal craft and fishing methods. Although the precise mixture of approaches varied from place to place, the overarching objective was to catch more fish by exploiting hitherto unused marine resources.

After independence this central aim was retained – indeed reinforced – by post-colonial governments and international agencies alike. During the post-war 'development decades', the exploitation of the seas became part of the wider campaign to modernize economies, boost food supplies and raise living standards across the 'Third World'. The surge of interest in fisheries development reflected the convergence of several different factors. One was the discovery of abundant and relatively unexploited fish resources off parts of Asia and Africa, which governments were determined to put to use. A second was the rising demand for seafood in affluent countries and the emergence of new market outlets for tropical species. A third was the acute balance-of-payment pressures felt by most newly independent states, coupled with the fact that fish exports constituted one of the quickest ways to earn significant amounts of foreign exchange. Underlying all of these factors was the mounting anxiety that rapid population growth in developing countries would outstrip the capacity of the land to meet human needs.[89]

The extent to which fisheries could supplement agriculture as a source of food was a matter of global concern, but it was particularly urgent in developing countries where demographic expansion was fastest and sea resources least exploited. For Georg Borgström, a prominent Swedish food scientist and economic geographer who became one of the post-war world's foremost authorities on hunger and population, the tendency to focus on humanity's caloric requirements and the capacity of agriculture to meet them was fundamentally misplaced. Although the sea contributed only 2–3 per cent of the world's food in the mid-1960s, it nonetheless provided a fifth of all the animal protein consumed globally (nearly as much as cattle), including roughly half of all animal protein in the developing world. According to Borgström, as soon as one factored in the importance of fats and proteins – especially so-called 'high quality' animal proteins containing all essential amino acids – it was impossible to overlook 'the true role of fish' in meeting the world's nutritional needs. To highlight the point, Borgström coined the notion of 'fish acreage', or the amount of land that would be required for a country to produce an amount of animal protein equal to its fish catch, based on prevailing agricultural methods and yields. For some wealthy countries like Norway or the Netherlands,

89. Platteau, 'Dynamics of Fisheries Development', 577; Hersoug, Jentoft and Degnbol, *Fisheries Development*, 36–37. On links between post-war population concerns and global fisheries: Locher, 'Neo-Malthusian Environmentalism'.

fish already accounted for the equivalent of around two-thirds of their entire cultivated acreage; in the case of Japan the figure was a whopping 154 per cent. For poor and populous countries in the Global South, where protein consumption was generally much lower, there was little chance that agriculture would ever realistically furnish enough protein to offset the need for more fishing, regardless of the productivity advances promised by the Green Revolution. In India alone, Borgström calculated that the entire world catch in the mid-1960s would provide each inhabitant no more than the protein equivalent of one average-sized herring per day.[90]

It was calculations like this that prompted the FAO to set ambitious short- and long-term targets for fish consumption in the developing world. According to data from its *Third World Food Survey*, meeting these targets would require no less than a sixfold increase on the 1960 global catch. By the early 1960s, the seas of the developing world became a crucial front in the UN's 'fight against hunger'.[91]

The key question was how best to increase supplies of fish, and for most observers the answer seemed as obvious as it did in the colonial era: namely, through the rapid modernization and industrialization of fisheries. Much like their colonial predecessors, most officials in Africa and Asia assumed that modern science and technology would be able to overcome all developmental obstacles so long as there was a sufficient influx of finance, equipment and technical assistance. The corollary of this assumption was that there was little to be gained from working with traditional fishermen, whom administrators still tended to regard as backward, conservative, and handicapped by illiteracy and superstition. As we have already seen, such prejudices against fishing communities had a long history in many parts of Asia and Africa. They were also widely shared by Western experts, who perceived artisanal fisheries as too backward to form the core of an effective development strategy, and who accordingly advised governments to replace them with more modern methods of capture, processing, distribution and marketing.[92] As far as actual fishing techniques were concerned, this involved the adoption of larger mechanized boats, power-assisted gear and modern harbour facilities, as well as new scientific infrastructures for surveying and monitoring fishery resources offshore. In the realm of processing and distribution, it meant the creation of refrigeration units, packaging plants and cold chain transport. For the purposes of marketing, it entailed a shift away from local consumption towards wider regional or international outlets that could absorb the envisaged increase in fish production. Altogether, these changes implied a radical shift away from small-scale,

90. Borgström, *Hungry Planet*, 25–34, 131–32.
91. FAO, *Fisheries*, 60–65; Parker, 'First Victories', 48–49.
92. Béné, 'Fishery Rhymes with Poverty'.

labour-intensive techniques towards a more centralized, capital-intensive fishing industry that could sell its catch to consumers far beyond the reach of the traditional artisanal sector.

During the heyday of planned development from the 1950s to the 1970s, this productivist approach prevailed throughout the seas of the post-colonial world. Echoing colonial-era arguments, fisheries experts working for international development agencies and advising Asian or African governments maintained that it was 'wasteful' to leave valuable stocks of fish unexploited though a lack of fishing.[93] Officials in India's central government, for instance, wasted little time in trying to modernize what they deemed as 'this very backward and neglected industry'. In the early 1950s, they requested assistance from the United States to acquire new boats, diesel engines, synthetic nets and refrigerated trucks. Several of India's provincial administrations followed suit: in West Bengal, for instance, around 40 per cent of the entire fisheries budget of 1951–56 was spent on the development of a deep-sea trawl fishery. From the late 1950s through the 1960s, the succession of government five-year plans allocated more and more funding to the mechanization of fishing craft and gear. Whereas India possessed only 13 mechanized boats at the beginning of the 1950s, by the early 1970s the number had leapt to over 10,500.[94]

Meanwhile, the rapid expansion of trawling in Philippine and Thai waters (supported by US and West German aid agencies) sparked parallel efforts to mechanize fleets across Southeast Asia. Over the course of the 1960s, trawling became the most important fishing technique off the shores of Peninsular Malaysia, while in Indonesia the New Order regime unleashed a surge of investment to promote mechanized fishing and the creation of fishing cooperatives.[95] In West Africa too, the adoption of industrial methods was broadly viewed as the most effective way to develop marine fisheries. In independent Senegal, the government continued on the same trajectory as the former French administration by initially neglecting its large canoe fishery as it sought to build a mechanized tuna fleet to supply French markets. Much the same applied to Ghana, where the fishing sector boasted some 384 mechanized craft by the end of the 1960s, most of them sailing out of new deep-water harbours built at Tema and Takoradi.[96]

Nonetheless, despite the predominance of such productivist development policies, this unquestioning faith in large-scale industrial fishing was not

93. Longhurst, *Mismanagement of Marine Fisheries*, 4.

94. Quote from *Report of the Fish Sub-committee*, 3; Liston, *Fishery and Aquaculture Programs*, 73–76; N. Rao, *Mechanisation and Marine Fishermen*, 23–26, 222–26; FAO, *Marine Small-Scale Fisheries*, 2.

95. Bee, *Development Problems*, 5–8; Semedi, *Close to the Stone*, 8–9; Butcher, *Closing of the Frontier*, 204–5, 209–10; Morgan and Staples, *Industrial Marine Fisheries*, 28.

96. Chauveau, 'L'essor thonier', 261–62; R. Lawson and Kwei, *African Entrepreneurship*, 19–21, 41.

universally shared, at least not at first. Just as in the colonial period, questions about rapid versus incremental and top-down versus community-oriented approaches continued to frame debates about how best to develop marine fisheries in former colonies.

Events in Kerala, on the south-western coast of India, illustrate both the attractions and limitations of pursuing a more gradual, people-centred approach. The state of Kerala was formed in 1956 out of the Malabar district of Madras and the recently merged states of Travancore and Cochin. As we saw in chapter 5, colonial-era administrations in the region had a record of working with fishing communities ever since the establishment of India's first fisheries department in Madras under Frederick Nicholson, and especially during the tenure of his successor James Hornell in the late 1910s and 1920s. For a decade or so after Indian independence, this general orientation in Kerala changed little, despite the push for industrial fisheries elsewhere on the subcontinent. In 1953, Travancore became home to the world's first UN-sponsored fisheries development scheme (the Indo-Norwegian Project for Fisheries Community Development, or INP), whose initial aims were clearly tailored to reflect those of the local administration: namely, to raise the productivity of artisanal fishermen, boost living standards among fishing communities, and improve the distribution and quality of fish products for domestic consumption. After 1957, the democratically elected communist government of Kerala (another world's first) continued to emphasize the gradual improvement of artisanal fishing methods and explicitly prioritized the harvest of fish as a source of rural livelihoods and cheap food. Instead of lavishing large sums on new industrial equipment, during the Second Five Year Plan of 1956–61 the Kerala government spent 86 per cent of its fisheries investment on practical improvements to traditional craft and the provision of cheap credit to artisanal fishermen.[97]

All of this changed during the late 1950s and early 1960s as the convergence of two different developments prompted a complete reversal of priorities in Kerala. First, Norwegian experts working for the INP swiftly abandoned their initial plans to motorize artisanal craft. Not only did they find it difficult to motorize the dugout canoes of Travancore fishermen, they also found that their preferred alternative – small, flat-keeled craft designed in Norway – offered few if any advantages over traditional canoes, especially for catching the abundant sardines and mackerel that schooled close to shore. Second, while the Norwegians were encountering unexpected problems, a handful of local merchants began to export small volumes of frozen penaeid prawns (hitherto of secondary importance in the area, and often used for fertilizer) to the United States. As the market for these prawns began to boom, a new INP-led marine survey confirmed that the waters off Kerala contained one of the world's richest

97. See Kurien, 'Technical Assistance', A-72–74; Pharo, 'Indo-Norwegian Project', 384–86.

prawn fishing grounds. Under pressure to make a success of the project, INP officials promoted the use of bottom trawling and new freezing methods to boost prawn exports. Although some Indian members of the project committee objected to the shift of emphasis away from community development and domestic consumption, the injection of large amounts of capital by powerful merchants in the area pushed project leaders and local officials towards a more 'modern', growth-oriented approach. By the mid-1960s, Kerala's fishery policy was focused almost entirely on industrial prawn trawling and the pursuit of foreign exchange. This remarkable U-turn was unusual but not entirely unique. In neighbouring Sri Lanka, where successive governments initially rejected FAO and World Bank recommendations to create an industrial fleet, the tide eventually turned after the mid-1970s with the expansion of export markets for high-value seafood products. In both Kerala and Sri Lanka, this eventual change of direction brought them broadly into line with the approach followed in most post-colonial states from the very beginning.[98]

Why did the industrial model of fisheries development prove so irresistible? One of its chief attractions was that it appealed to so many different interests, both internal and external. For Western policymakers and donor countries, it represented not only a rapid means of increasing food supplies in potentially unstable parts of the world, but also an opportunity for their own domestic firms to supply the necessary boats and equipment. The phenomenon of 'tied aid' (money that must be spent in the country donating it) was at least as common in the fisheries sector as anywhere else. Meanwhile, for the big international lending agencies, the accounting-induced tendency to focus on the volume rather than the social outcomes of financial aid likewise favoured an emphasis on shiny, expensive equipment that filled up the loan books. For officials in the FAO or in national fisheries agencies, it was much simpler to concentrate on a small number of large-scale projects than on a large number of small-scale projects, just as it was easier to deal with skilled expatriates than with often-illiterate fisherfolk. And for newly independent governments keen to burnish their electoral credentials, an industrialized long-distance fishing fleet seemed not only a fast way to earn much-needed foreign exchange but also a more prestigious political spectacle than an armada of improved canoes.[99]

Thanks in large part to the spread of mechanized trawling and purse seining, the post-war decades witnessed an explosion of fish catches throughout the Global South. The globalization of industrial fishing that had first

98. Kurien, 'Technical Assistance' and *Ruining the Commons*; Pharo, 'Indo-Norwegian Project', 386–89. On Sri Lanka: Alexander, 'Innovation'.

99. See R. Lawson and Kwei, *African Entrepreneurship*, 247; Cunningham and Neiland, 'African Fisheries Development Aid', 39–40; Hersoug, Jentoft and Degnbol, *Fisheries Development*, 166–67.

begun under colonial auspices made it possible not only to exploit offshore and demersal stocks that had previously been untouched but also to capture them more quickly and efficiently than was possible with traditional methods. In South Asia, the overall marine catch nearly trebled from around 700,000 tons in 1950 to 2 million tons in the mid-1970s. Landings shot up almost twice as fast in Southeast Asia, rising from around 1.6 million tons to 5.8 million tons between 1956 and 1980. Most spectacular was the upsurge off the coast of Western Africa, where the overall catch skyrocketed from 1.5 million tons in the late 1950s to around 10 million tons two decades later.[100] While much of the increase went to local or regional food markets, a large proportion was destined for export to the industrial world. For South and Southeast Asia, consumer demand in Japan, North America and Europe was an important driver of rising catches, especially for prawns and other high-value fish.[101] In West Africa in particular, the soaring catch was driven largely by the arrival of vast fishing fleets from Europe, North America, the Soviet Union and Japan, which immediately froze what they caught before hauling it directly back to home ports. In 1964, foreign fleets operating in the rich seas off the Saharan coast took around 400,000 tons; two decades later they annually took 2.3 million tons.[102]

As the fishing effort intensified, so too did the problems that it caused. In this respect, the technological transformation of fisheries showed some striking parallels with the agricultural changes wrought by the Green Revolution.[103] In both cases, the benefits were exceedingly skewed. As critics of the industrial fisheries model had long warned, most of the profits from increased catches went to local capitalists or merchants who owned or invested in new craft. By contrast, artisanal fisherfolk who lacked the means to acquire new boats and gear generally saw their incomes decline as fish prices dropped and near-shore catches fell under the additional fishing pressure. Although the industrial rigs could theoretically offer alternative employment opportunities for struggling fishermen, their capacity to catch more fish with fewer deckhands severely limited the amount of labour they could absorb, which in turn kept wages low. In Kerala, for instance, real incomes for trawler hands fell by 45 per cent from 1974 to 1982, while incomes for artisanal fishermen dropped by more than half. Over the same period, non-working boat owners (i.e., investors) increased their share of the total catch value from 27 to 43 per cent.[104]

100. Figures based on datasets from the Sea around Us (Pauly, Zeller and Palomares, Sea around Us): http://www.seaaroundus.org/data/#/fao; Butcher, *Closing of the Frontier*, 170; the figure for Western Africa includes the entire coast from Morocco to the Congo River.

101. Butcher, *Closing of the Frontier*, 171. From 1965 to 1975, Japanese imports of frozen shrimp rose from 21,000 to 110,000 tons, the bulk of them coming from Southeast Asia.

102. Troadec, 'Practices and Prospects', 99.

103. As noted by various contemporary observers, e.g.: E. Evans, 'Marine Scientific', 383; Allsopp, *Fishery Development Experiences*, 105.

104. Kurien, *Ruining the Commons*, 15–16.

While outcomes varied somewhat from place to place, this overall pattern of social polarization within fishing communities was common throughout much of the developing world.

Furthermore, the unequal social impacts of industrial fishing were inseparable from its ecological effects. The expansion of trawling and purse seining made it possible to catch enormous quantities of fish in a short space of time, but this also raised the risk of depleting fish stocks much faster than they could recover. The effects were becoming evident off West Africa by the mid-1970s, as the meteoric rise in landings suddenly levelled off despite a continuing increase in fishing effort. Though few could have imagined it at the time, the 10.5 million tons caught there in 1977 remains an all-time high.[105] In Southeast Asia too, the signs of overfishing were increasingly hard to overlook, especially in shallow inshore waters where fishing pressures were highest. Catch rates off the west coast of Peninsular Malaysia, for instance, dropped from 132 kg/hour in 1970 to 59 kg/hour in 1981, and off the east coast from 516 to 144 kg/hour. At the same time, there was also a marked increase in the catch proportion of so-called 'trash fish' in relation to commercially desirable species, another clear indicator of excessive fishing pressure. By the late 1970s, it was estimated that it took four times more effort and capital to catch a ton of fish than had been required a decade earlier.[106]

But if trawlers and purse-seiners were the main cause of overfishing, the consequences were felt by everyone. Indeed, they were particularly disastrous for small-scale fisherfolk, whose gear was no match for the trawl net or purse seine, and whose unpowered craft were unable to venture into more distant waters in search of new fish stocks. Although one of the main arguments for industrial fleets was their ability to exploit marine resources that small-scale fishermen could not reach, the problem was that many of the richest grounds – especially for shrimp – were found in the same shallow inshore waters that artisanal fishermen worked. When trawlers combed across these areas, they not only hauled in tons of fish that would otherwise have landed in the nets of artisanal fishers; they also wrecked many of their driftnets, traps and other gear. It was not long before tensions between the two groups boiled over into open conflict.

The coastal waters of Southeast Asia witnessed perhaps the most heated clashes. From 1964 to 1976, Malaysian authorities recorded a total of 113 disputes involving more than four hundred trawlers and over nine hundred artisanal boats. Many of these confrontations were violent: all in all, sixty-two boats were sunk, more than a hundred were destroyed, and over thirty-four

---

105. Figures from 'Catches by EEZ in the Waters of FAO Area Atlantic, Eastern Central (34)', http://www.seaaroundus.org/data/#/fao/34?chart=catch-chart&dimension =eez&measure=tonnage&limit=10 (Pauly, Zeller and Palomares, Sea around Us).

106. Bee, *Development Problems*, 36, 45.

people were killed in fights between trawler crews (many of them ethnic Chinese) and inshore fishermen (predominately Malays). It was no coincidence that nearly all of these incidents took place along the Penang and Perak coasts, where Malaysia's richest shrimp grounds were found.[107] Violent clashes were also widespread in Indonesia, especially along the Malacca Straits and the north coast of Java, where a favourite technique was to hurl Molotov cocktails into wooden-hulled trawlers.[108] Similar disputes flared up in Thailand, Vietnam and the Philippines, as well as off the coast of India and West Africa.[109] In an effort to quell the violence, governments introduced new regulations limiting the number of trawlers and prohibiting them from fishing within a certain distance of the shore. By and large, however, such measures were ineffective owing to the chronic inability of governments to enforce them, which allowed trawler crews to continue to fish inshore waters illegally. The most notable exception was the Indonesian government's unprecedented decision to impose a total ban on trawling in 1980–81 (first off Sumatra and Java, then covering most of the seas under its jurisdiction), which was relatively easy to enforce since most trawlers had to be based in large fishing ports, from which they could be monitored without going to the trouble of policing different fishing zones out at sea. In effect, the prohibition of trawling in Indonesian waters represented a wholesale reallocation of the country's demersal resources from trawler owners to small-scale fishers. As such, it proved highly popular among coastal communities and had a remarkably positive impact on employment and livelihoods, though its ecological implications were more ambiguous given the headlong rush of new entrants into what were already heavily worked artisanal fisheries.[110]

Overlaying these conflicts between trawlers and inshore fishers was a more general source of tension: the rising number of long-distance fishing boats operating off the shores of other countries. As we saw earlier, a small number of European boats had been fishing off the coast of West Africa ever since the nineteenth century, and indeed were encouraged to do so by French colonial authorities in the early part of the twentieth. During the interwar years, the presence of Japanese boats off the coasts of India, Malaysia, the Netherlands Indies, the Philippines and Indochina stoked animosity among locals and galvanized state efforts to exploit more of their 'own' marine resources before outsiders did. The phenomenon was by no means unique to tropical waters or

107. Ghee, 'Conflict over Natural Resources'; Bee, *Development Problems*, 8.

108. Bailey, 'Indonesia's 1980 Trawler Ban', 228–29.

109. Pomeroy et al., 'Fish Wars'. For India: Kurien, *Ruining the Commons*. For Africa: Belhabib et al., 'Fisheries Catch Misreporting', 3, 7; Koranteng and Pauly, 'Long-term Trends', 245–46.

110. See Bailey, 'Indonesia's 1980 Trawler Ban'; Ghee, 'Conflict over Natural Resources', 160–62.

colonial settings: during the 1950s, the presence of US boats off the western coast of South America led to major diplomatic rows, and from the late 1950s to the mid-1970s the 'cod wars' of the North Atlantic soured relations between Iceland and other European fishing nations (above all the United Kingdom). As developing countries slowly industrialized their fleets, they too got in on the act. Thai trawlers in particular became a common (and mostly unwanted) presence throughout Southeast Asian waters after they dramatically depleted stocks in the Gulf of Thailand in the late 1960s and early 1970s. Migrant fishers from Senegal and Ghana also began to fish all along the west coast of Africa, some going as far south as Congo.[111] Wherever these long-distance fishing boats went, antagonism with local fishers often followed.

In an attempt to curtail such incursions, governments increasingly expanded their jurisdictional claims over coastal seas. Up until the end of the 1950s, the international norm was for states to assert territorial rights three nautical miles from their coastlines. During the 1960s, most extended these claims to twelve nautical miles, thus denying foreign boats legal access to a large proportion of the best fishing grounds (not least for valuable species such as prawns). In the 1970s, access to the world's seas was radically reorganized with the introduction of Exclusive Economic Zones (EEZs) extending two hundred nautical miles from the coast (or, where there was insufficient space between different states, midway between their coastlines). Although it took from 1973 to 1982 for the United Nations Conference on the Law of the Sea to reach a final agreement on EEZs, most governments began to declare them before the conference was formally concluded, and most also recognized the resulting convention long before its formal ratification in 1994. While all coastal states were affected by the changes, they were especially significant for many developing countries whose waters had long been plundered by large numbers of foreign boats. Territorially speaking, the biggest winners were archipelagic states such as Indonesia and the Philippines, which gained vast marine jurisdictions. Economically, among the biggest potential winners were the countries adjoining the exceptionally rich coastal seas of north-west Africa (e.g., Senegal, Guinea, Sierra Leone), and in particular the countries just north of them with disproportionately long coastlines and small populations (Mauritania, Western Sahara).[112]

This national enclosure of the seas formed the basic framework in which the development of the world's fisheries took place from the 1980s onwards. It was generally thought that the establishment of EEZs would bring numerous benefits to developing countries. At most the fundamental level, their

111. Royce, *Fishery Development*, 95–100; R. Lawson and Robinson, 'Artisanal Fisheries', 281.

112. G. Moore, *New Law of the Sea*; Kaczynski, 'Foreign Fishing Fleets'. For a contemporary critique, see Ranganathan's 'Decolonization and International Law'.

FIGURE 8.5. Map of West Africa showing the exclusive economic zones of coastal states.

newfound 'ownership' of the seas enabled them to retain a far greater share of the proceeds of fishing than had previously been the case, whether through the sale of licences to foreign boats or the expansion of their own domestic fleets. At the same time, their ability to control the utilization of marine resources made it possible to implement alternative models of development such as the prioritization of small-scale fisheries for securing livelihoods and boosting rural incomes. A third advantage was that sovereign control over the seas would allow states to establish more effective forms of resource management by ending the free-for-all that had previously prevailed beyond the twelve-mile territorial limit (and often well within it). In order to capitalize on these perceived opportunities, the FAO launched the Comprehensive Programme for the Development and Management of Fisheries in Exclusive Economic Zones in 1979, which focused mainly on technical improvement, research and above all the expansion of scientific fisheries management in developing countries.[113]

The introduction of EEZs was also marked by a surge of interest in small-scale fisheries. This shift of emphasis away from the industrial model of the initial post-war decades was part of a wider trend in development thinking in the late 1970s and early 1980s, one that prioritized 'basic needs' over big infrastructure projects and that advocated technologies that were more sensitive to the different social, cultural and environmental contexts into which they were introduced. Under the banner 'small is beautiful', development agencies launched a series of artisanal fisheries projects that in many ways recalled the gradualist, people-centred approach that the Sri Lankan and Kerala governments had pursued in the 1950s and 1960s, and which unconventional colonial officials such as Hornell had advocated ever since the 1910s.[114] From 1978 to 1985, aid spending on small-scale fisheries projects more than doubled, from $35 million to over $80 million.[115] As the FAO optimistically declared, 'a revolution has occurred in the potential of fisheries to contribute to a new international order', one in which developing countries and even artisanal fishers would finally be able to 'secure their rightful place in world fisheries'.[116]

Unfortunately, things did not quite work out that way. For one thing, most coastal states quickly concluded that small-scale fisheries, however one might 'develop' them, would not be capable of fully exploiting the resources in their EEZs. By and large, national governments thus continued to subsidize industrial fishing. Among the international development agencies too, the growing interest in small-scale fisheries did not fundamentally alter the basic thrust of

113. FAO, *World Fisheries*; Biswas, 'FAO', 317–21; Garcia, 'Ocean Fisheries Management', 399–402.

114. Schumacher, *Small Is Beautiful*. On shifting development priorities in the 1970s more generally: Unger, *International Development*, 127–42.

115. Josupeit, 'Survey of External Assistance'; Biswas, 'FAO', 327–28; Thomson, 'Intermediate Technology'.

116. Royce, *Fishery Development*, 3.

FIGURE 8.6. Artisanal fisheries have persisted, albeit with difficulty, in many parts of West Africa: Senegalese pirogues at Saint-Louis, 2006.
Source: Wikimedia Commons. Public domain.

fisheries aid, around half of which still went to the industrial sector, with only a sixth going to the artisanal sector.[117] Furthermore, hopes that the demarcation of EEZs would lead to more effective forms of resource management were largely disappointed. Although the establishment of science-based fisheries management in developing countries certainly resulted in better data collection, better research institutions and better-trained personnel to staff them, it still failed on the key criterion of creating sustainable fisheries. The evidence was as clear as it was pervasive, above all in the form of stagnating, declining or locally collapsing catches caused by a combination of market pressures, management shortcomings and enforcement failures.[118]

Most importantly, perhaps, many of the fishery assets in the EEZs of developing countries were still siphoned off by others, mainly wealthy states in the Global North. Nowhere was the continued outflow of marine resources from poorer to richer countries more conspicuous than off the coast of north-west Africa. When the two-hundred-mile EEZ limits were first introduced in the region between 1976 and 1979, coastal countries managed to boost their share of the marine harvest from 35 to 52 per cent. After this initial realignment,

117. Josupeit, 'Survey of External Assistance', 10; Hersoug, Jentoft and Degnbol, *Fisheries Development*, 36–38; Robinson and Lawson, 'Some Reflections on Aid'.
118. Hersoug, Jentoft and Degnbol, *Fisheries Development*, 79–81.

however, the relative shares stayed roughly the same thanks to the signing of multilateral and bilateral fishery accords that secured continued access for long-range fishing countries.[119] In principle, the presence of foreign boats was not necessarily detrimental to the coastal states of north-west Africa, since most of them (with the exception of Senegal) remained incapable of fully exploiting their marine resources on their own – provided, of course, that the licence fees were priced appropriately and the volume of fish caught by foreign boats was not excessive. But the problem was that such deals were often highly skewed in favour of the more powerful party.

A classic example was the European Union's 'fishery cooperation agreements'. Although their proponents presented them as useful tools for promoting economic development and sustainable management in the waters of African signatory states, numerous analyses showed them to be highly unequal at best, and profoundly damaging at worst. African governments desperate for hard currency frequently allowed EU fishing boats to pay much less than the value of the fish they caught – even before taking account of the sizeable 'undeclared' catch. Despite the ability of EU fishing authorities to buy access at cut-rate prices, they customarily reduced their payments even further whenever African states revised their 'maximum sustainable yield' quotas downwards, thus undermining the incentive for prudent management in the face of overfishing. Although the outcome of these agreements varied from place to place – with Senegal deriving significantly more social and economic benefits than its neighbours – and although the governance arrangements gradually improved over the years, the overall result for most coastal states in north-west Africa was under-compensation and overfishing. It is thus little wonder that critics have condemned these agreements as vehicles for a 'neocolonial' exploitation of the seas and for entrenching African economic dependence on Europe.[120]

While offshore catches dwindled, these self-same patterns of unequal exchange also shaped the expansion of the aquaculture industry, by far the fastest-growing fisheries sector in the developing world. Ever since the 1970s, shrimp has been a favourite everyday delicacy of consumers in North America, Japan and above all in Europe, the world's leading importer of seafood. Soaring demand for shrimp has been the primary driver behind the explosive growth of aquaculture, and aquaculture has been the main source of global shrimp supplies. From 1975 to 2019, the production of farmed shrimp rose from 22,292 tons to 6.56 million tons, nearly all of which was exported from

119. Kaczynski, 'Foreign Fishing Fleets', 3–4.

120. There is a large literature on this subject. For recent analyses: Hammarlund and Andersson, 'What's in It'; Nagel and Gray, 'EU's Fisheries Partnership Agreement'; Kaczynski and Fluherty, 'European Policies'; Kaczynski, 'Foreign Fishing Fleets'; Goffinet, 'Development and Fisheries Management'; Iheduru, 'Political Economy'.

developing countries for consumption in developed countries.[121] South and Southeast Asia have long dominated global supplies, especially Thailand, Indonesia, Vietnam, India, Bangladesh and the Philippines.

In all these countries, multilateral lending agencies endorsed the 'Blue Revolution' as a tool for economic development. In some respects the strategy succeeded: since the 1980s, shrimp farming has indeed become a major source of jobs and export earnings in South and Southeast Asia. Yet the costs have been exceptionally high, both socially and ecologically. For one thing, the creation of tens of thousands of shrimp farms has destroyed vast swathes of coastal mangrove forests, which are among the most productive and diverse ecosystems on the planet. Not only has the industry wrecked crucial spawning grounds for marine flora and fauna – including the 'wild' shrimp that are caught and then fattened in the feeding ponds – it has also deprived local communities of a crucial source of land, fuel and timber. In some areas, the 'tragedy of enclosures' caused by the aquaculture boom sparked violent resistance by displaced coastal dwellers who had traditionally made a living from the mangroves and shorelines.[122] Meanwhile, another set of problems emanated from the ponds themselves, which polluted nearby wetlands through the outflow of organic wastes as well as the efflux of pesticides and antibiotics that are used to control disease in the densely stocked pools. Moreover, the effects also reverberated far offshore. Instead of reducing the overall fishing effort at sea (one of the purported benefits of aquaculture), the industry's voracious appetite for fishmeal actually intensified the strain on wild fish stocks, which were simultaneously being damaged by the loss of mangrove spawning grounds. In fact, the growing demand for so-called 'trash fish' has been a major reason for the continued trawling of areas where stocks of commercially valuable species have long been so depleted as to make further fishing there uneconomic.[123] In spite of various efforts to reduce the adverse social and environmental effects of the industry, shrimp aquaculture has continued to wreak havoc on the mangrove forests and inshore waters of South and Southeast Asia.

These imperceptible links between the seafood appetites of northern consumers and the destruction of aquatic environments in the Global South epitomize the ways in which the prevailing mechanisms of global trade detach

121. Figures from FAO Fisheries and Aquaculture: FishStatJ – Software for Fishery and Aquaculture Statistical Time Series (Rome: FAO Fisheries and Aquaculture Division [online], 2020), accessed 4 October 2023, https://www.fao.org/fishery/en/topic/166235 ?lang=en.

122. Martinez-Alier, *Environmentalism of the Poor*, 79–99; E. Collins, *Indonesia Betrayed*, 103–11; Hoanh et al., *Environment and Livelihoods*.

123. Bottema, Bush and Oosterveer, 'Beyond the Shrimp Farm'; Butcher, *Closing of the Frontier*, 281–87; Jayanthi et al., 'Impact of Shrimp Aquaculture'.

production from consumption, and consumption from its effects. The phenomenon is by no means unique to coasts and seas, and nor is it anything new. Like the interminable disputes over river basins and boundaries, the enduring fascination with large dams, or the persistent inequities of water access in cities and villages, it is in many respects a legacy of empire.

As independent states emerged from colonial domination, most found it difficult to shake off the subservient economic role they had inherited as producers of raw materials. In the circumstances, capitalizing on one's natural assets was an essential means of developing their economies, and for many countries the exploitation of their water flows and aquatic resources became a vital source of much-needed revenue and investment capital. In some ways, the strategy has paid dividends. Over the last half century or so, the enormous surge in agricultural output, hydropower generation and seafood exports has been a major source of earnings that has enabled at least some people in the Global South to increase their incomes and improve their living standards. Yet in the process it has also served to reinforce the same patterns of resource extraction, unequal exchange, and displaced social and environmental burdens that had disadvantaged these countries in the first place. More than sixty years after Europe's once-vast colonial empire was reduced to no more than a few remnants, the fundamental dynamics of global exchange still promote the flow of resource wealth from poor parts of the world to richer ones, with the bulk of ecological and social costs going in the opposite direction. To what extent the waters of the developing world can continue to absorb these costs is an open question, and one on which millions of livelihoods depend.

Water, Climate and the Legacies of Empire

IN MARCH 2023, THE Intergovernmental Panel on Climate Change (IPCC), the United Nations body charged with evaluating the science related to climate change, released the final synthesis of its Sixth Assessment Report. First established in 1988, the IPCC has been publishing these assessments ever since 1990, and in this sixth instalment it issues a series of warnings about the changes that have recently taken place and those we can expect in the coming years. Backed by reams of evidence, it concludes that climate impacts are already more widespread and serious than many had expected; that the risks will escalate rapidly as temperatures rise; that poverty, inequality and conflict heighten human vulnerability to these risks; and that it is already impossible to avoid more severe impacts from climate change in the short term.

Together, the six IPCC Assessment Reports have charted a lot of climatic upheaval during the past three decades. Even so, in many respects they have not changed very much over the years. The main problems, warnings and prescriptions conveyed in the Sixth Report closely echo those of previous assessments; the main difference is that they are based on a larger body of evidence and expressed with an even greater sense of urgency. The format of the reports themselves has also remained fairly constant. Although they have ballooned in scope to reflect the swelling body of research, each is made up of three main parts written by different working groups: one that evaluates the physical science of climate change; another that focuses on its social, environmental, and economic impacts; and a third that assesses various means of reducing greenhouse gas emissions and mitigating their effects. Within this recurrent pattern, each successive report varies in line with updated scientific datasets, evolving political and socio-economic contexts, and new methods for coping with the implications of a changing climate. Nonetheless, one particular novelty stands out in this sixth and latest instalment. For the first time in over thirty years, the word 'colonialism' has finally appeared in an IPCC Assessment Report.[1]

At first glance, the inclusion of a single word – 'colonialism' – may not seem especially important, but for a number of reasons it is. For one thing, it recognizes that many of the climate injustices we currently face are the product of deep-rooted historical legacies. According to the IPCC, colonial processes of dispossession, dislocation and exploitation not only number among the drivers of climate change in recent decades; they have also aggravated its impact by rendering certain people and places more vulnerable to it. Secondly, this acknowledgement reflects both the proliferation of recent literature connecting colonialism and climate change and the diversification of perspectives that fed into the latest Assessment Report. Whereas earlier reports were criticized for a lack of input from indigenous groups and scientists from the Global South, this time 44 per cent of the assembled experts came from developing and 'transitioning' countries. In addition to encompassing more viewpoints from around the globe, the group of experts for the Sixth Assessment Report also included more social scientists, historians and anthropologists than ever before. For the first time, it even included a technical paper on indigenous knowledge about (and adaptations to) climate change.[2]

A third reason why the inclusion of this single word is so significant is the very explicit way in which the IPCC has recognized the links between colonialism and climate change. References to 'colonialism' are by no means fleeting. The term appears dozens of times in the full report of Working Group 2 (on impacts, adaptation and vulnerability), and twice in its all-important summary for policymakers, by far the most widely read element of each report. As the summary plainly puts it, 'global hotspots of high human vulnerability are found particularly in West-, Central- and East Africa, South Asia, Central and South America, Small Island Developing States and the Arctic. . . . Present development challenges causing high vulnerability are influenced by historical and ongoing patterns of inequity such as colonialism, especially for many Indigenous Peoples and local communities'.[3] Statements such as this are important because the precise wording of the summary for policymakers is not only decided by the IPCC's teams of experts but also painstakingly agreed by government representatives from 195 different countries. In turn, the acquisition of official sign-off from participating governments matters for two reasons: it lends additional authority to the report, and (more importantly)

1. For brief but incisive discussions: Mercer, 'Link'; Funes, 'Yes, Colonialism'.

2. IPCC, 'Selection of Authors for IPCC Sixth Assessment Report', Newsroom, 6 April 2018, https://www.ipcc.ch/2018/04/06/ar6-author-selection/; Mustonen et al., *Compendium of Indigenous Knowledge*; Ford et al., 'Including Indigenous Knowledge'; Maldonado et al., 'Engagement with Indigenous Peoples'; Nakashima and Krupnik, *Indigenous Knowledge*; Mercer, 'Colonialism's Climatic Legacies'; Funes, 'Yes, Colonialism'.

3. IPCC, *Summary for Policymakers*, 12.

the summary for policymakers serves as the document of reference for the negotiations between world leaders at UN climate talks. By including such language, the IPCC has therefore made it crystal clear that contending with the unequal effects of climate change on different people and places requires policymakers to deal with the after-effects of colonialism.[4]

This welcome – and arguably overdue – international recognition of the climate-related legacies of colonialism is closely related to the story that has been told in these pages, for the effects of climate change are inextricably linked with the cascade of water-related crises that is currently affecting many parts of the world. Water is, and has always been, the main medium through which the effects of climate change are manifested in the environment and experienced in everyday life, generally in the form of too much or too little of it. Scientists have clearly established that even a slight rise in global temperature has significant effects on the water cycle, making rainfall less predictable and increasing the frequency and severity of floods, droughts and storms. According to the World Meteorological Organization, water-related threats have risen sharply since the turn of the twenty-first century. Between 2000 and 2019, droughts increased by 29 per cent compared with the 1980s and 1990s, affecting around 1.43 billion people. Over the same period, flood disasters have risen by a whopping 134 per cent compared with the preceding two decades, constituting 44 per cent of all disasters worldwide and affecting around 1.6 billion people. By and large, it is countries in the Global South that have borne the brunt of these changes. Together, they accounted for around 70 per cent of the deaths and roughly three-quarters of the economic losses caused by weather-related hazards over 1970–2019. During these five decades, around one-third of all flood disasters occurred in Asia, which accounted for well over half of the flood-induced economic losses worldwide. Meanwhile, 42 per cent of all droughts were recorded in Africa, accounting for over 99 per cent of drought-related deaths.[5]

These figures paint a stark picture of how global climate trends intersect with regional water vulnerabilities. But to make matters worse, certain parts of Asia and Africa now find themselves grappling with the double problem of too much *and* too little water at the same time. In densely populated coastal areas, especially but not exclusively along the southern and eastern fringes of Asia, rising sea levels threaten to inundate large swathes of fertile low-lying land (for example, in Bangladesh, India, Vietnam and Egypt), even as river deltas have been shrinking because of the excessive siphoning-off of silt-bearing river flows by dams upstream. In recent years, the Indus has joined the list of the world's major rivers (the Colorado, Yellow, Murray and Rio Grande) that

---

4. Mercer, 'Link'; Funes, 'Yes, Colonialism'.

5. World Meteorological Organization, *State of Climate Services*, 9–10, 19–20, 26. On the human experiences of such changes: Sultana, 'Unbearable Heaviness'.

regularly run dry before reaching the sea. Far away from the coast, inland river valleys are likewise threatened by the increasingly violent extremes of water surplus and deficit. As rising temperatures shrink the Himalayan glaciers that sustain most of the great rivers of South and East Asia, increased meltwater is set to make their flow more volatile than ever, fluctuating from unprecedented flooding in the wet season to record lows in the dry season. Over a decade ago, Kenneth Pomeranz made the point that 'for almost half the world's population, water-related dreams and fears intersect in the Himalayas and on the Tibetan plateau'. Given that temperature rises in the Himalayas are now around twice the global rate, and given that around half a billion people in South and Southeast Asia rely directly on the rivers that rise there, the sheer scale of the looming water crisis in the region is difficult to grasp.[6]

To what extent are these hydro-climatic problems themselves a legacy of colonialism? It is a question that permits no simple answers, and the arguments run in different directions. Many historical accounts draw attention to how the interrelated processes of European conquest, the expansion of commodity frontiers, and the mobilization of labour and natural resources in subjugated territories expedited the growth of the industrialized, fossil-fuelled economies of the Western world by supplying them with raw materials and keeping their prices artificially low, thereby encouraging a more rapid expansion of the carbon footprint of industrialized countries than would otherwise have been the case. By constructing markets that could draw in cheap goods from ever-more far-flung areas of supply, the global expansion of European power helped enable a minority of the human population in the West to live far beyond the resource constraints of their own surroundings. Moreover, there were always two sides to this unequal exchange between metropoles and colonies: a net influx of resources to Europe, and a net flow of social and ecological costs in the opposite direction. According to this logic, the long-term implications for the global climate were twofold: escalating greenhouse gas emissions produced by industrial countries, and lower rates of carbon sequestration elsewhere as more and more forestland was converted into fields and pastures – a trend that continued, even accelerated, after the colonial era.[7]

Meanwhile, other observers have highlighted the fact that the rapid uptick in global greenhouse gas emissions since the middle of the twentieth century coincided with the end of the colonial era, with some even suggesting that colonialism may actually have *delayed* the onset of the climate crisis. As Dipesh Chakrabarty has noted, 'the Anthropocene may stand for all the

6. Pomeranz, 'Great Himalayan Watershed', 5; A. Ghosh, *Great Derangement*, 89–90.

7. See, e.g., Ross, *Ecology and Power*, 14–16, 421–22; Bonneuil and Fressoz, *Shock of the Anthropocene*, 222–52; Mitchell, *Carbon Democracy*, 15–18; Beckert et al., 'Commodity Frontiers', 435–50; Hornborg, 'Footprints' and *Global Ecology*; J. Moore, *Capitalism in the Web*; Foster, Clark and York, *Ecological Rift*. On forest loss: M. Williams, *Deforesting the Earth*, 326–48, 420–83; J. Richards and Flint, 'Century of Land-Use Change'.

climate problems we face today collectively, but it is impossible for me, as a historian of human affairs, not to notice that this period of so-called great acceleration is also the period of great decolonization'. In the decades after independence, he argues, many countries that had been ruled by European powers made a decisive 'move towards modernization' and eventually 'towards a certain degree of democratization of consumption as well'.[8] Amitav Ghosh has taken this logic a step further by arguing that post-colonial Asia in particular 'played a pivotal role in setting in motion the chain of consequences that is driving the present cycle of climatic change', mainly through the rapid industrialization of its most populous nations from the 1980s onward. According to him, whereas 'the West's largest contribution to the accumulation of greenhouse gases came about through the continuous expansion of the carbon footprint of what was about 30 percent of the world's population at the beginning of the twentieth century', Asia's contribution came mainly through 'a sudden but very small expansion in the footprint of a much larger number of people, perhaps as much as half of a greatly expanded global population, late in the twentieth century'.[9]

The key question, as Ghosh puts it, is 'why did the most populous countries of Asia industrialize late in the twentieth century and not before?'[10] The conventional explanation is that the non-Western world lagged behind in the adoption of a carbon-based economy because the technologies that underpinned it were developed in the West and only gradually emanated outwards from there. The argument has some merit, inasmuch as a vastly disproportionate share of global greenhouse gas emissions to date is attributable to high historical levels of energy and resource consumption in the Western world. Nonetheless, the problem with this technological-diffusionist interpretation is that it disregards the ways in which colonialism actually restrained the spread of industrial technologies. For all the rhetoric about 'developing' colonial economies, the imperial powers sought to ensure that adequate amounts of raw materials were exported to Europe rather than consumed locally, which they likely would have been if, say, the early interest of Asian entrepreneurs to industrialize had been given the kind of state support that industrialists in Europe enjoyed. At the core of modern imperialism was a determination to ensure the dominance of Western capital over indigenous commerce, if necessary through the use of brute military force. And it is worth remembering that military force itself was partly a function of maintaining the West's technological advantage over other parts of the world. To be sure, there were other factors that also slowed the shift towards a carbon-based industrial economy in Asia and Africa, including strong intellectual and cultural currents of

8. Chakrabarty, 'Climate and Capital', 15.
9. A. Ghosh, *Great Derangement*, 91.
10. A. Ghosh, 93.

resistance to the consumerist brand of industrial capitalism that pertained in the West. But this does not negate the proposition that current-day atmospheric concentrations of greenhouse gases would have been reached long ago if the main empires of the modern era had been dismantled before the mid-twentieth century, and if Asian and African economies had thereby been allowed to accelerate earlier than they did. The upshot, as Ghosh suggests, is that colonialism 'may actually have retarded the onset of the climate crisis', along with all the water-related problems that accompany it.[11]

Despite the differences between these two sets of interpretations, ultimately they are not very far apart. The idea that colonialism may have delayed our contemporary climate crisis in no way denies the imperial exploitation of lands and peoples or the subsidies that it provided for the carbon-fuelled economies of Europe. Without the ability to transcend local resource constraints, industrial countries could never have achieved the levels of affluence or the global ecological footprint that they did. Nor does it ignore the fact that the ensuing flows of resources and socio-ecological costs (including but not limited to greenhouse gas emissions) disproportionately benefitted metropoles over colonies. As consumer appetites and demand for raw materials in industrial markets rose, they drew in resources faster than natural systems could replenish them and emitted wastes faster than natural systems could absorb them.

Furthermore, even if colonial rule delayed the spread of industrialism and higher material living standards in the Global South, it still provided norms, techniques and models for achieving a 'modern' economy and the lifestyles associated with it. Both during and after the era of high imperialism, most anti-colonial elites were determined to share in this bounty by rapidly developing their national economies through the technological subjugation of nature. Although this impulse certainly had its critics, few subscribed to Gandhi's famous warning about the implications of doing so: 'God forbid that India should ever take to industrialism after the manner of the West. . . . If an entire nation of 300 millions took to similar economic exploitation, it would strip the world bare like locusts.'[12] In the event, the dismantling of Europe's empire in Asia and Africa did not signal a turn away from dreams of an industrial future. Nor, for that matter, did it denote a disavowal of the colonizers' fixation on perpetual economic growth and habitual recourse to technological solutions to ensure that nature should continue to provide for it. Rather, it heralded a deliberate attempt to accelerate industrial and

11. A. Ghosh, 107–15, quote at 110. It is worth noting that recent research has shown how the roots of modern manufacturing in the developing world stretch back farther than is generally assumed (the early twentieth century for much of Asia, and the interwar period for parts of Africa and the Middle East), though the main upsurge undoubtedly occurred after 1950: O'Rourke and Williamson, *Spread of Modern Industry*.

12. 'Discussion with a Capitalist', *Young India*, 20 December 1928, in Gandhi, *Collected Works*, vol. 43, 412–13; A. Ghosh, *Great Derangement*, 111.

agricultural development as a means of liberating newly independent states from their subordinate role in the world economy once the political constraints of colonial rule were removed (albeit often, especially in Asia, by taking a more labour-intensive and resource-saving path than the one that was open to the early industrializers).[13] In this sense, perhaps the most consequential legacy of the colonial era was the proliferation of an 'imperial' view of nature as something to be conquered and remade to serve human ends.

This ambition to prevail over nature certainly applies to the hydrosphere. If the mastery of water flows and watery spaces formed a key element of the colonial drive for economic development, post-colonial states throughout Asia and Africa were even more determined to control them as a means of increasing agricultural output, generating power, controlling floods and harvesting aquatic resources. As the previous chapter has shown, colonial engineers may have built more and larger dams in Asia and Africa than anyone before them, but the number and scale of barrages ballooned over the years following decolonization. Likewise, although efforts to transfer industrial fishing methods to the colonial world made only limited progress, many independent coastal states in the Global South launched resolute campaigns to 'modernize' their fishing fleets or at least to exploit their marine stocks for revenue by charging foreign industrial fleets for the privilege of fishing their waters. Even if most post-colonial states made only limited headway in the provision of safe drinking water and sewage disposal for their growing populations – not least because of the infrastructural legacies they inherited from their colonial predecessors – here, too, the desire to use technology as a means of attaining 'modern' standards of sanitation was of paramount importance in guiding their investment decisions. Across all of these areas, regulating the hydrosphere has been, and remains, a critical factor for economic growth and prosperity. The great paradox is that the perpetual drive for growth that has animated these hydraulic interventions has served to exacerbate the very problem – anthropogenic climate change – that threatens to destabilize the water cycle yet further, with particularly deleterious consequences in the Global South.

Ultimately, this conundrum derives from the intimate interconnections between water, land, the atmosphere and the ways in which human activities are entwined with them. As anthropogenic climate change leads to more (and more severe) floods, droughts and storms, many ecosystems around the world – forests, wetlands, peatlands – get significantly more or less water than they have in the past, which in turn affects their capacity to sequester carbon from the atmosphere. Breaking this feedback loop is a crucial challenge for the future. Moreover, the effects of climate change are more than just a matter of water quantity; they also have consequences for water quality. In low-lying

---

13. See generally Austin, *Economic Development*. On the inadequacy of assuming the deliberate adoption of Western paths into the Anthropocene: Acker, 'Different Story'.

coastal areas, a combination of prolonged dry spells and rising sea levels is gradually turning many freshwater sources saltier, with grave implications for agriculture in the worst affected areas. Meanwhile, increasingly frequent downpours and floods regularly overwhelm waste-water systems and wash a variety of pollutants into nearby bodies of water, where they harm aquatic life and can even contaminate supplies of drinking water.

What confronts us, then, is a nexus of problems that encompasses water quality, health, agriculture, food security, disaster prevention, biodiversity and the atmosphere. And what this means in practice is that taking better care of the water cycle is important not only in and of itself but also for tackling climate change and mitigating its socio-economic effects. Towards this end, there are various things that can be done. Perhaps first on the list is protecting forests, mangroves and wetlands, which simultaneously store carbon, replenish groundwater, and shield coastal settlements and crop fields against storms, saltwater intrusion and rising sea levels. By the same token, it is vital to restore lost forest cover wherever possible, along with previously drained wetlands and peatlands to ensure that they function as sinks rather than as sources of atmospheric carbon. In many ways, such proposed solutions amount to returning former 'wastelands' back to their previously unruly state, a rewilding of land- and waterscapes that were often first domesticated during the colonial era. At the same time, making more space for 'nature' in cities, and supplementing these oases with raingardens, retention ponds, 'blue roofs' (which store rainwater and release it gradually) and permeable pavements helps both to moderate urban temperatures and to protect against floods by minimizing run-off and facilitating storm-water absorption. Equally important is reducing the level of water pollution from sewage, industrial wastes and agricultural fertilizers. Contaminated water bodies not only pose a threat to human health and wildlife but also emit large amounts of the three main greenhouse gases (CO_2, methane, nitrous oxide) from the breakdown of organic matter by aquatic microorganisms, especially when water bodies become deoxygenated by pollution-induced algal blooms.

As the Stockholm International Water Institute points out, many of these water-related measures are 'solutions that multi-task', indeed all the more so when applied in low-income countries where the need is most acute. Protecting forests, rewilding parts of cities and investing in waste-water management are actions that simultaneously serve to cut greenhouse gas emissions, improve societal resilience against the effects of climate change, boost economic growth and improve people's health – indeed, 'in a way that also helps reduce the gap between the rich and poor.'[14] Against this backdrop, we can take some encouragement from the fact that better water management is a top

14. Sköld, '5 Reasons'; Karlsson, 'Water and Climate'; see also World Bank, *Quality Unknown.*

adaptation priority for over four-fifths of the Nationally Determined Contributions submitted by countries that signed up to the 2018 Paris Agreement of the United Nations Framework Convention on Climate Change.[15]

These are all practical steps that we can take in the here and now. But in order to maximize their effectiveness and ensure sufficient investment behind them, it is critical that we overcome some of the legacies of colonial past. As we have seen at length in the preceding chapters, the history of efforts to control water in Asia and Africa is littered with top-down initiatives to re-channel flows or manage aquatic resources without seeking the consent – let alone input – of the people most directly affected. Alfred Deakin's criticisms of colonial water management in the 1890s as a form of 'despotic rule' whereby hydraulic bureaucrats executed schemes 'without regard to the individual wishes or interests of their constituents' may not be a fair description of all colonial-era projects,[16] and they hardly do justice to the more consultative approaches espoused by many development agencies today. Nonetheless, they by no means sound otherworldly to millions of people who have been at the sharp end of large-scale hydroengineering ventures over the past two centuries. The disjuncture between those making decisions about water and those affected by them is a deeply engrained pattern – especially across the Global South – and one that has nearly always entailed substantial costs. The massive dams, canals, sanitation systems and port infrastructures spearheaded by state-backed engineers or international funding bodies often solved the specific problems that political elites sought to overcome, but they often caused a host of new problems in the form of dispossession, displacement, detrimental impacts on livelihoods, social polarization, unintended ecological consequences, or new water-related risks upstream and downstream. If there is a central lesson to draw from these experiences, it is that water management efforts are often more effective in the long term, and nearly always more equitable in their outcomes, when they seek local participation and pay attention to local knowledge.[17]

This is in fact a lesson with broader applicability, for the question of equity and inclusion is one of the central issues that we face in dealing with a changing climate and its effects on the hydrosphere. The consequences are already affecting us all, and will do so more forcefully in the future, but they will obviously not affect us all equally. In order to adapt successfully, it is crucial that we focus not only on the global differentials of human vulnerability but also on what has created them in the first place. Part of the answer, of course, lies in the natural environment itself: the communities most at risk of increased flooding or water shortages are generally those situated along seasonal rivers, on low-lying coasts, in semi-arid regions and in areas that depend on monsoon rains. Even so, the

15. '2022 NDC Synthesis Report'.

16. Deakin, *Irrigated India*, 21.

17. For an overview: Selby, Daoust and Hoffmann, *Divided Environments*.

social dimensions of water vulnerability are at least as important as environmental factors. After all, there is nothing 'natural' about the fact that from 2010 to 2020 mortality rates from droughts, floods and storms were fifteen times higher in South Asia and sub-Saharan Africa than in wealthier regions.[18] Physical geography alone does not come close to explaining why just under 40 per cent of people in the least developed countries still lack even basic drinking water services and over 60 per cent are without basic sanitation, all of which has long been taken for granted in prosperous countries.[19]

Climate scientists have recently revised the widespread view that decades or even centuries of additional global warming are already 'baked in' to the climate system by the greenhouse gases that have historically been spewed into the atmosphere; the latest studies suggest instead that warming trends will level off fairly quickly if and when net emissions are reduced to zero.[20] Translated into the world of politics, these findings represent a firm rejection of 'climate fatalism' in favour of urgent, coordinated action. It is a message that applies not only to climate change itself but also to its unequal socio-economic impacts. Across the Global South, patterns of acute climate vulnerability have long been 'baked in' as a legacy of empire and colonialism, but there is no need to resign ourselves to this state of affairs.

Tackling the world's multiple water crises therefore demands more than just ingenious engineering and technological innovation (both of which are crucial). It also requires political solutions that operate on multiple scales; that is to say, actions that simultaneously take heed of local needs, historical rights and cultural values; that juggle the interests of different states that rely on common water resources; and that shift the bulk of the economic burden to those states and social groups most able to afford it. To borrow from the UN Framework Convention on Climate Change, the creation of a more water-resilient future is very much a matter of 'common but differentiated responsibilities'.[21] As *Liquid Empire* has sought to show, these obligations arise not only from the disproportionate responsibility of wealthy industrial societies for altering the Earth's climate and water cycle. They also derive from the fact that so many of our engrained habits of dealing with water, and so many of humanity's most acute water vulnerabilities, are deeply intertwined with the history of empire.

18. IPCC, *Summary for Policymakers*, 12.

19. World Health Organization and United Nations Children's Fund, *Progress*, 8–9.

20. See IPCC, *Global Warming of 1.5°C*; also Hausfather, 'Explainer'; Berwyn, 'Many Scientists'.

21. UNFCCC, United Nations Framework Convention on Climate Change.

Published Primary Material

Afrique Occidentale française, *Le plan quadriennal d'équipement et de modernisation de l'A.O.F.* ([Dakar]: Direction générale des Services économiques et du plan, 1953–57).

——, *Le port de Dakar en 1910* (Paris: Bibliothèque du journal *Les Annales coloniales*, 1910).

Agard, A., *La navigation maritime en Indochine française* (Hanoi: Imprimerie d'Extrême-Orient, 1935).

Allen, William, and T.R.H. Thomson, *A Narrative of the Expedition Sent by Her Majesty's Government to the Niger River in 1841*, vol. 1 (London: Bentley, 1848).

Arbelot, M. G., *Les ports français de l'Afrique occidentale* (Paris: Association française pour le développement des travaux publics, 1928).

Baikie, William Balfour, *Narrative of an Exploring Voyage up the Rivers Kwora and Binue, Commonly Known as the Niger and Tsadda in 1854* (London: Murray, 1856).

Baldwin, Kenneth D. S., *The Niger Agricultural Project: An Experiment in African Development* (Oxford: Blackwell, 1957).

Ball, John, 'Problems of the Libyan Desert', *Geographical Journal* vol. 70 (1927), 21–38.

Balls, W. L., *The Cotton Plant in Egypt: Studies in Physiology and Genetics* (London: Macmillan, 1919).

Baltzer, F., *Die Kolonialbahnen: Mit besonderer Berücksichtigung Afrikas* (Berlin: Göschen'sche, 1916).

Barber, C. G., *History of the Cauvery-Mettur Project* (Madras: Government Press, 1940).

Barlow, George Thomas, and J. W. Meares, *Hydro-electric Survey of India: Preliminary Report on the Water Power Resources of India* (Calcutta: Superintendent Government Printing, 1919).

Barois, Julien, *Les irrigations en Égypte* (Paris: Librarie Polytechnique, 1904).

Barrès, M. G., *Les ports de la côte occidentale d'Afrique* (Bordeaux: Pech, 1929).

Benas, J., 'Note sur la pratique de la carpiculture dans les étangs et rizières des environs de Bandoeng (Java)', *Comptes-rendus des sciences de l'Académie d'agriculture de France* (Paris, 1932), no. 7.

Bengal Hurkaru, *Account of the Great Bengal Cyclone of the 5th of October 1864* (Calcutta: Bengal Hurkaru, n.d.).

Bernard, P., *Le problème économique indochinois* (Paris: Nouvelles Éditions latines, 1934).

Birchard, R. E., 'Copper in the Katanga Region of the Belgian Congo', *Economic Geography* 16 (1940), 429–36.

Borgström, Georg, *The Hungry Planet: The Modern World at the Edge of Famine* (New York: Collier, 1967).

Borgström, Georg, and Arthur J. Heighway (eds), *Atlantic Ocean Fisheries* (London: Fishing News, 1961).

Bory, Paul, *La conquête du Soudan* (Tours: A. Mame, 1901).

Bouvier, René, *Richesse et misère du delta tonkinois* (Paris: Tournon, 1937), 65.

Brasseur, Gerard, *Le problème de l'eau au Sénégal* (Saint Louis, Senegal: IFAN, 1952).

Bréaudat, L., *Les eaux d'alimentation de la ville de Saigon* (Paris: Levé, 1905).

Brown, Robert Hanbury, *History of the Barrage and the Head of the Delta of Egypt* (Cairo: Diemer, 1896).

Bruzon, Étienne, *Le climat de l'Indochine et les typhons de la mer de Chine* (Hanoi: Imprimerie d'Extrême-Orient, 1930).

Buckley, Robert Burton, *The Irrigation Works of India* (London: Spon, 1905).

Bulletin agricole du Congo belge et du Ruanda-Urundi: Volume jubilaire (Brussels, Place Royale, 1960).

Burnett, A. W., *Report on the Colombo Waterworks* (orig. 1890), reprinted in *A Holiday Trip to Labugama: The Source of the Colombo Water Supply* (Colombo: Ferguson, 1891).

Buschkiel, Alfred L., *De teelt van karpers en de beginselen der visch teelt in Nederlandsch Oost-Indië* (Buitenzorg, Netherlands East Indies: Archipel Drukkerij, 1932).

Carle, Edmond, *Le riz en Cochinchine: Étude agricole, commerciale, industrielle, avec diverses notes concernant cette culture dans le monde* (Cantho, Vietnam: Imprimerie de l'Ouest, 1933).

Caty, R., 'L'amélioration des plantes de culture indigène aux colonies', *L'agronomie coloniale* vol. 25, nos 217-18 (1936), 34-42, 78-89.

Cautley, Proby T., *Report on the Ganges Canal Works: From their Commencement until the Opening of the Canal in 1854*, vol. 1 (London: Smith, Elder, 1860).

Cavaillès, Henri, *La houille blanche* (Paris: Armand Colin, 1922).

Chadwick, Osbert, *Report on the Sanitary Condition of Hong Kong* (London: Eyre and Spottiswoode, 1882).

Charles-Roux, François, *La production du coton en Égypte* (Paris: Armand Colin, 1908).

Chatterjee, Bhim Chandra, *The Hydro-electric Practice in India*, vol. 1 (Benares, India: Chatterjee, 1936).

Christie, G.F.S., *Report on Madras Fisheries* (Rangoon: Government Printer, 1919).

Churchill, Winston, *My African Journey* (London: Hodder and Stoughton, 1908).

Clemesha, William Wesley, *The Bacteriology of Surface Waters in the Tropics* (Calcutta: Thacker, Spink, 1912).

———, *Sewage Disposal in the Tropics* (London: Thacker, 1910).

Clerk, Dugald, and A. H. Gibson, *Water-Power in the British Empire: Reports of the Water-Power Committee of the Conjoint Board of Scientific Societies* (London: Constable, 1922).

Conybeare, Henry, *Report on the Sanitary State and Sanitary Requirements of Bombay* (Bombay: Bombay Education Society, 1855).

Cotton, Arthur, *Profits upon British Capital Expended on Indian Public Works, as Shown by the Results of the Godavery Delta Works of Irrigation and Navigation* (London: Richardson, 1856).

———, *Public Works in India: Their Importance, with Suggestions for Their Extension and Improvement* (London: Richardson, 1854).

Coudenhove-Kalergi, Richard N., *Paneuropa* (Vienna: Paneuropa-Verlag, 1923).

Cresswell, Ernest J. J., *Sponges: Their Nature, History, Modes of Fishing, Varieties, Cultivation, Etc.* (London: Pitman and Sons, 1922).

Darboux, G., J. Cotte, P. Stephan and F. van Gaver, *L'industrie des pêches aux colonies*, 2 vols (Marseille: Barlatier, 1906).

Darnault, Paul, *Mission de prospection des forces hydrauliques de l'Afrique Équatoriale française* (Paris: Larose, 1931).

Day, Francis, *Report on the Freshwater Fish and Fisheries of India and Burma* (Calcutta: Government Printer, 1873).

De, Kiran Chandra, *Report on the Fisheries of East Bengal and Assam* (Shillong, India: Eastern Bengal and Assam Secretariat Printing Office, 1910).

Deakin, Alfred, *Irrigated India: An Australian View of India and Ceylon, Their Irrigation and Agriculture* (London: Thacker, 1893).

Deasy, George F., 'The Harbors of Africa', *Economic Geography* vol. 18 (1942), 325-42.

De Bellefonds, L.M.A. Linant, *Mémoires sur les principaux travaux exécutés en Égypte depuis la plus haute antiquité jusqu'à nos jours* (Paris: Arthur Bertrand, 1872–73).

De la Blache, P. Vidal, *Principes de géographie humaine* (Paris: Librarie Armand Colin, 1922).

De la Tramerye, Pierre Paul Ernest l'Espagnol, *La lutte mondiale pour le pétrole* (Paris: Éditions de la vie universitaire, 1922).

Department of Industries, Bihar and Orissa, *Grow and Eat More Fish: Importance of Fish-Culture in Tanks and Other Confined Waters*, Bulletin no. 2 (Patna, India: Government Printer, 1932).

De Rouville, A., *L'amélioration des ports maritimes en Indo-Chine française* (Paris: Le Genie Civil, 1931).

De Vos, H.C.P., 'De strijd om en tegen het water', in: W. H. van Helsdingen (ed.), *Daar werd wat groots verricht: Nederlandsch-Indië in de XXste eeuw* (Amsterdam: Elsevier, 1941), 273–86.

Dickinson, Alfred, 'Water Power in India', *Journal of the Royal Society of Arts* vol. 66, no. 3417 (1918), 417–26.

Douie, James M., 'The Punjab Canal Colonies', *Journal of the Royal Society of Arts* vol. 62, no. 3210 (1914), 611–23.

Drouin, P., 'L'électrification du Tonkin', *Bulletin économique de l'Indochine* vol. 41 (1938), 481–85.

Dumont, René, *La culture du riz dans le delta du Tonkin* (Paris: Société d'Éditions, 1935).

Dutt, Romesh C., *Famines and Land Assessments in India* (London: Kegan Paul, 1900).

ECAFE (Economic Commision for Asia and the Far East), *Development of Water Resources in the Lower Mekong Basin* (Bangkok: United Nations, 1957).

Edelman, C. H., *Studiën over de Bodemkunde van Nederlandsch-Indië* (Wageningen, Netherlands: Veenman, 1947).

Elliott, John, *Report of the Vizagapatam and Backergunge Cyclones of October 1876* (Calcutta: Bengal Secretariat, 1877).

Escande, M. Léon, *Étude sur la navigabilité du fleuve Rouge: Voie de penetration commercial vers l'intérieur de la Chine* (Paris: Imprimerie nationale, 1894).

Everatt, Eric Launcelot, *Maintenance Dredging in the Bombay Harbour and Docks, and Upkeep of the Navigational Lighting of the Port* (London: Institution of Civil Engineers, 1926).

Exchanges of Notes between the Government of the United Kingdom of Great Britain and Northern Ireland and the Government of Egypt Regarding the Construction of the Owen Falls Dam, Uganda. Cairo, May 30, 1949 to March 20, 1950 (London: Her Majesty's Stationery Office, 1955).

Faulkner, P. Leo, *The Sundarbans of Bengal*, ed. by J. L. Gabbott (London: Camcot, 2017).

Ferrar, H. T., *Preliminary Note on the Subsoil Water in Lower Egypt and Its Bearing on the Reported Deterioration of the Cotton Crop* (Cairo: National Printing Department, 1910).

Figuier, Louis, *Les nouvelles conquêtes de la science*, vol. 2 (Paris: Librarie Illustrée, 1884).

Finer, Herman, *The TVA: Lessons for International Application* (Montreal: International Labour Office, 1944).

Firth, Raymond, *Malay Fishermen: Their Peasant Economy* (London: Routledge, 1946).

Fischer, Louis, *Oil Imperialism: The International Struggle for Petroleum* (New York: George Allen, 1927).

Franquet, Eugène, *De l'importance du fleuve Rouge comme voie de pénétration en Chine* (Paris: Charles-Lavauzelle, 1897).

Furnivall, J. S., *Colonial Policy and Practice: A Comparative Study of Burma and Netherlands India* (Cambridge: Cambridge University Press, 1948).

——, *Fisheries in Netherlands India* (Rangoon: Burma Book Club, 1934).

——, *Netherlands India: A Study of Plural Economy* (Cambridge: Cambridge University Press, 1939).

Gaitskell, Arthur, *Gezira: A Story of Development in the Sudan* (London: Faber and Faber, 1959).

Gastrell, J. E., and Henry F. Blanford, *Report of the Calcutta Cyclone of the 5th October 1864* (Calcutta: Military Orphan, 1866).

Gauthier, J., *Digues du Tonkin* (Hanoi: Imprimerie d'Extrême-Orient, 1930).

——, *Hydraulique agricole: Travaux de défense contre les inondations; Digues de Tonkin* (Hanoi: Imprimerie d'Extrême-Orient, 1930).

Goode, S. W., *Municipal Calcutta: Its Institutions in Their Origin and Growth* (Edinburgh: Constable, 1916).

Gourou, Pierre, *Les paysans du delta tonkinois: Étude de géographie humaine* (Paris: Moutons, 1965; orig. Éditions d'Art et d'Histoire, 1936).

——, *Le Tonkin* (Mâcon, France: Imprimerie de Protat Frères, 1931).

——, *L'utilisation du sol en Indochine française* (Paris: Hartmann, 1940).

——, 'Océanographie et pêche maritime en Indochine française', *Annales de géographie* vol. 221 (1930), 537–54.

Gouvernement général de l'AOF (Afrique Occidentale française), *Le port de Dakar: Ses origins, état actuel, extensions future* (Dakar: Grande Imprimerie Africaine, 1929).

Government of India, *Review of the First Five Year Plan* (New Delhi: Government of India Press, 1957).

Government of India Planning Commission, *The First Five Year Plan* (New Delhi: Planning Commission, 1952).

Graham, Michael, *The Victoria Nyanza and Its Fisheries: A Report on the Fishing Survey of Lake Victoria 1927–1928, and Appendices* (London: Waterlow, 1929).

Gruvel, Abel, *Les pêcheries de la côte occidentale d'Afrique* (Paris: A. Challamel, 1906).

——, *Les pêcheries des côtes du Sénégal et des rivières du sud* (Paris: A. Challamel, 1908).

——, *L'Indochine: Ses richesses marines et fluviales* (Paris: Société d'Éditions, 1925).

——, *L'industrie des pêches sur la côte occidentale d'Afrique* (Paris: Larose, 1913).

Guernier, Eugène Léonard, *L'Afrique: Champ d'expansion de l'Europe* (Paris: Armand Colin, 1933).

Harris, D. G., *Irrigation in India* (London: Humphrey Milford, 1923).

Harrison, Henry Leland, *The Bengal Embankment Manual, Containing and Account of the Action of the Government in Dealing with Embankments and Water-Courses since the Permanent Settlement* (Calcutta: Bengal Secretariat, 1875).

Hickling, C. F., *Production of Fish in the Colonial Empire*, Colonial no. 237 (London: His Majesty's Stationery Office, 1949).

——, *Production of Fish in the Colonial Empire* (London: His Majesty's Stationery Office, 1954).

——, *Tropical Inland Fisheries* (London: Longmans, 1961).

Hollings, M. A. (ed.), *The Life of Sir Colin C. Scott-Moncrieff* (London: John Murray, 1917).

Hope, Elizabeth, *General Sir Arthur Cotton, R. E., K. C. S. I., His Life and Work, by His Daughter Lady Hope* (London: Hodder and Stoughton, 1900).

Hora, S. L., 'The Use of Fishes for the Control of Mosquitoes', *Indian Medical Gazette* vol. 62 (1927), 187–88.

Hornell, James, *Bibliography of Scientific Publications by James Hornell* (Cambridge: Cambridge University Press, 1938).

——, *Fishing in Many Waters* (Cambridge: Cambridge University Press, 1950).

Houdaille, M., *Le chemin de fer et le port de la Côte d'Ivoire: Organisation d'une entreprise coloniale* (Paris: Berger-Levrault, 1905).

Houdemer, E., *Les poissons dulcaquicoles du Tonkin au point de vue de leurs relations avec l'hygiène* (Clermont, France: Thiron, 1934).

Howard, Alfred, *Crop Production in India: A Critical Survey of Its Problems* (Oxford: Oxford University Press, 1924).

'Hydroélectricité et complexes économiques régionaux', *Annales de Géographie* vol. 67, no. 359 (1958), 85.

Ibos, Pierre, *Le chemin de fer du fleuve Rouge et la pénetration française au Yunnan* (Paris: Charles-Lavauzelle, 1906).

Inglis, W. A., *A Review of the Legislation in Bengal Relating to Irrigation, Drainage, and Flood Embankments* (Calcutta: Bengal Secretariat, 1911).

Jackson, P.B.N., 'On the Desirability or Otherwise of Introducing Fishes to Waters That Are Foreign to Them', *Third Symposium on Hydrobiology and Inland Fisheries: Problems of Major Lakes* (Lusaka: Commission de Cooperation Technique en Afrique au sud du Sahara, 1960), 157–64.

James, C. C., *Drainage Problems of the East: Being a Revised and Enlarged Edition of 'Oriental Drainage'* (Bombay: Times of India, 1906)

————, *Drainage Problems of the East: Being a Revised and Enlarged Edition of 'Oriental Drainage'* (Bombay: Bennett, Coleman, 1917).

Jevons, William Stanley, *The Coal Question: An Enquiry Concerning the Progress of the Nation, and the Probable Exhaustion of Our Coal-Mines* (London: Macmillan, 1865).

Johnston, J., *Inland Navigation on the Gangetic Rivers* (Calcutta: Thacker, Spinck, 1933).

Johnston, James Henry, *Précis of Reports, Opinions, and Observations on the Navigation of the Rivers of India by Steam Vessels* (London: Cox, 1831).

Jojot, Charles, *Dakar: Essai de géographie médicale et d'ethnographie* (Montdidier, France: Grou-Radenez, 1907).

Khin, U., *Fisheries in Burma* (Rangoon: Government Printer, 1948).

Kidd, Benjamin, *The Control of the Tropics* (London: Macmillan, 1898).

Kitson, Albert, *Outlines of the Mineral and Water-Power Resources of the Gold Coast, British West Africa* (London: C. A. Terry, 1925).

Klunzinger, C. B., *Bilder aus Oberägypten, der Wüste und dem Rothen Meere* (Stuttgart: Levy and Müller, 1878).

L'Afrique à l'heure de l'aluminium: Centre de Documentation et de Diffusion des Industries Minérales et Énergétiques Outre-mer, Études et Documents no. 6 (September 1958).

Laird, Macgregor, and R.A.K. Oldfield, *Narrative of an Expedition into the Interior of Africa, by the River Niger, in the Steam-Vessels Quorra and Alburkah in 1832, 1833, and 1834*, vol. 1 (London: Bentley, 1837).

Lamminga, A. G., *Beschouwingen over den tegenwoordigen stand van het irrigatiewezen in Nederlandsch-Indië* (The Hague: van Langenhuysen, 1910).

Lavigne, Georges, *Le percement de l'isthme de Gabès* (Coulommiers, France: Brodard, 1876).

Lemasson, J., 'Aperçu général sur la pêche et la pisciculture dans les eaux continentales de l'Indochine et sur le programme des travaux projetés', in: Service de la pêche et de la chasse en Indochine, *Communications présentées aux 1re et 2e sessions du conseil indo-pacifique des pêches* (Phnom Penh: SPCI, 1950), 5–14.

Lemasson, J., and J. Benas, *Essais de mise au point de méthodes de rizipisciculture dans le delta et la moyenne region du Tonkin* (extract of *Bulletin économique de l'Indochine*) ([Paris], 1942).

Leroy-Beaulieu, Paul, *De la colonisation chez les peuples modernes* (Paris: Guillaumin, 1874).

————, *De la colonisation chez les peuples modernes*, 4th ed. (Paris: Guillaumin, 1891).

Les installations maritimes de Port-Bouet (Paris: Le Génie Civil, 1933).

Letcher, Owen, *South Central Africa* (Johannesburg: African Publications, 1932).

Lewis, Paul, *The Romance of Water-Power* (London: Sampson Low, Marston, 1931).

Lilienthal, David E., 'Another "Korea" in the Making?', *Collier's*, 4 August 1951, 56–58.

Ludwig, Emil, *Der Nil: Lebenslauf eines Stromes* (Amsterdam: Querido, 1935).

MacGeorge, G. W., *Ways and Works in India: Being an Account of the Public Works in That Country from the Earliest Times up to the Present Day* (London: Constable, 1894).

Mackenzie, Donald, *The Flooding of the Sahara: An Account of the Proposed Plan for Opening Central Africa to Commerce and Civilization from the North-West Coast, with a Description of Soudan and Western Sahara, and Notes of Ancient Manuscripts, &c* (London: S. Low, Marston, Searle and Rivington, 1877).

Madras Fisheries Bureau, 'Annual Report of the Madras Fisheries Bureau, 1915', in: *Annual Reports of the Madras Fisheries Bureau 1908–1917*, Bulletin 1 (Madras: Government Press, 1918).

——, *Papers from 1899 Relating Chiefly to the Development of the Madras Fisheries Bureau*, Bulletin 1 (Madras: Government Press, 1915).

Madras Fisheries Department, *Administration Report for the Year 1931–32* (Madras: Government Press, 1932).

——, *Administration Report for the Year 1936–37* (Madras: Government Press, 1937).

——, *Administration Report for the Year 1938–39* (Madras: Government Press, 1940).

Malengreau, G., *Vers un paysannat indigène: Les lotissements agricoles au Congo belge* (Brussels: Institut royal du Congo belge, 1949).

Martins, Charles, 'Le Sahara: souvenirs d'un voyage d'hier', *Revue des deux mondes* vol. 52 no. 2 (1864), 295–322.

Martins, Charles, and E. Désor, 'Observations sur le projet de la création d'une mer intérieure dans le Sahara oriental', *Comptes rendus des séances de l'Académie des sciences* vol. 87 (1879), 265–69.

Masani, Rustom Pestonji, *Folklore of Wells: Being a Study of Water-Worship in East and West* (Bombay: Taraporevala and Sons, 1918).

Maxwell, C. N., *Malayan Fishes* (Singapore: Methodist Publishing, 1921).

Meares, J. W., 'The Development of Water Power in India', *Journal of the Royal Society of Arts* vol. 71, no. 3656 (1922), 59–77.

——, Hydro-electric Survey of India. Triennial Report, With a Forecast of the Water Power Resources of India 1919–1921 (Calcutta: Government Printer, 1922).

Melland, F., 'The Natural Resources of Africa', *Journal of the Royal Africa Society* vol. 31 (1932), 113–32.

Ministère des Colonies, *Les ports autonomes de l'Indochine* (Paris, 1931).

Montel, Marie-George-Hippolyte, *La ville de Saigon: Étude de démographie et d'hygiène coloniales* (Bordeaux: Destout, 1911).

Morel, E. D., *Red Rubber: The Story of the Rubber Slave Trade Flourishing on the Congo in the Year of Grace 1906* (London: T. F. Unwin, 1906).

Morin, Henry G. S., *Utilisation des poisons à la lutte contre le paludisme* (Archives des Instituts Pasteur d'Indochine, October 1936).

Mouranche, R., 'Le développement de la pisciculture à Madagascar au cours de ces dernières années', in: Conseil scientifique pour l'Afrique au sud du Sahara, *Comptes-rendus du symposium sur l'hydrobiologie et la pêche en eaux douces en Afrique* (Bukavu, Belgian Congo: CSA, 1954), 45–59.

Nehru, Jawaharlal, *Independence and After: A Collection of the More Important Speeches of Jawaharlal Nehru, from September 1946 to May 1949* (New Delhi: Government of India, 1949).

——, *Modern Temples of India: Selected Speeches of Jawaharlal Nehru at Irrigation and Power Projects*, ed. by C.V.J. Sharma (Delhi: Central Board of Irrigation and Power, 1989).

Nicholson, F. A., *Note on Fisheries in Japan* (Madras: Government Press, 1907).

'The Nile: Its Course Unfolds Mighty Panorama of River Peoples and Civilizations', *Life*, 20 November 1950.

Nisbet, John, *Burma under British Rule* (London: Constable, 1901).

Nkrumah, Kwame, *Neo-colonialism: The Last Stage of Imperialism* (London: Nelson, 1965).

Normandin, A., *Étude comparative du problème de l'hydraulique agricole à Java, aux Indes britanniques, en Indochine* (Hanoi: Imprimerie d'Extrême-Orient, 1913).

——, *La question des inondations au Tonkin et ailleurs* (Hanoi: Imprimerie d'Extrême-Orient, 1923).

Notes on the Gezira Irrigation Project (no publisher, January 1926).

Pargiter, Frederick Eden, *A Revenue History of the Sundarbans, From 1765 to 1870* (Calcutta: Bengal Secretariat, 1885).

Parker, Frank W., 'First Victories: Positive Achievements in the Fight against Hunger', *Unesco Courier*, July/August 1962, 47–54.

Pearn, B. R., *A History of Rangoon* (Rangoon: American Baptist Missionary Press, 1939).

Peytavin, M., *Rapport sur la crue du fleuve Rouge et les inondations du Tonkin en 1915* (Hanoi: Imprimerie d'Extrême-Orient, 1916).

Pierron, Marcel, *Suggestion d'une solution pour l'irrigation et l'assèchement par pompage du delta du Tonkin* (Valence, France: Legrand, 1923).

Plehn, Friedrich, *Die Kamerun-Küste: Studien zur Klimatologie, Physiologie und Pathologie in den Tropen* (Berlin: Hirschwald, 1898).

Pouyanne, A. A., *Les travaux publics de l'Indochine* (Hanoi: Imprimerie Extrême-Orient, 1926).

——, *L'hydraulique agricole au Tonkin* (Hanoi: Imprimerie d'Extrême-Orient, 1931).

Public Works Department, *Godavari, Kistna and Cauvery Delta and the Penner Anicut Systems* (Madras: Government Printer, 1883).

Ramakrishna Mission, *Bengal and Orissa Cyclone Relief, 1942–1944* (Howrah, India: Ramakrishna Mission, 1945).

Regan, C. Tate, *Report on the Fishes of the Colonies* (London: His Majesty's Stationery Office, 1920).

Reitsma, S. A., 'De overwinning op den afstand: Te land', in: W. H. van Helsdingen (ed.), *Daar werd wat groots verricht: Nederlandsch-Indië in de XXste eeuw* (Amsterdam: Elsevier, 1941), 250–63.

Rennie, W.J.M., 'The Construction of the Chenderoh Water-Power Plant of the Perak River Hydro-Electric Power Scheme', excerpts 4974 and 4969, *Proceedings of the Institution of Civil Engineers* vol. 239 (1935), 313–55.

Report of the Calcutta Port Commissioners in Communication with the Bengal Chamber of Commerce on the Best Means of Extending the Accommodation for Shipping in the Port of Calcutta (Calcutta: Bengal Secretariat, 1883).

Report of the Committee on Fisheries in Madras 1929 (Madras: Government Printer, 1929).

Report of the Fish Sub-committee of Policy Committee No. 5 on Agriculture, Forestry and Fisheries (Delhi: Government Press, 1945).

Report of the Floods Enquiry Committee 1924–25 (Rangoon: Government Printer, 1927).

Report of the Indian Famine Commission. Part 1: *Famine Relief* (London: Eyre and Spottiswoode, 1880).

Report of the Indian Industrial Commission, 1916–18 (Calcutta: Superintendent of Government Press, 1918).

Report of the Indian Irrigation Commission, 1901–1903, vol. 1 (London: His Majesty's Stationery Office , 1903).

Report of the Orissa Flood Committee 1928 (Patna, India: Government Printer, 1928).

Report of the Special Commission on the Drainage and Sewerage of Bombay (Bombay: Times of India, 1878).

Reynaud, Gustave, *Hygiène coloniale* (Paris: Baillière, 1903).

Ribot, Georges, and Robert Lafon, *Dakar: Ses origines—son avenir* (Bordeaux: Delmas, 1908).

Richards, E. V., *Report on the Hydro-electric Resources of East Africa* (London, 1947).

'River Pollution in India', *Indian Medical Gazette* vol. 25, no. 2 (1890), 56–57.

Robbins, John E., *Hydro-electric Development in the British Empire* (Toronto: Macmillan, 1931).

Robequain, Charles, *The Economic Development of French Indo-China*, trans. by Isabel A. Ward (London: Oxford University Press, 1944).

Robert, Maurice, *Le Centre africain: Le domaine minier et la cuvette congolaise* (Brussels: Lamertin, 1932).

Robertson, Albert, *An Account of Some Recent Improvements in the System of Navigating the Ganges by Iron Steam Vessels* (London: Weale, 1848).

Roudaire, François Élie, *Rapport à M. le Ministre de l'Instruction publique sur la dernière expedition des chotts: Complément des études relatives au projet de mer intérieure* (Paris: Imprimerie nationale, 1881).

——, *Rapport à M. le Ministre de l'Instruction publique sur la mission des chotts: Études relatives au projet de mer intérieure* (Paris: Imprimerie nationale, 1877).

——, 'Une mer intérieure en Algérie', *Revue des deux mondes* vol. 44 no. 3 (1874), 323–50.

Rutnagur, Sorabji M., *Electricity in India: Being a History of the Tata Hydro-electric Project, with Notes on the Mill Industry in Bombay and the Progress of Electric Drive in Indian Factories* (Bombay: Indian Textile Journal, 1912).

Sandes, E.W.C., *The Military Engineer in India*, vol. 2 (Chatham, UK: Institution of Royal Engineers, 1935).

Schaaf, C. Hart, and Russell Hunt Fifield, *The Lower Mekong: Challenge to Cooperation in Southeast Asia* (Princeton, NJ: van Nostrand, 1963).

Schanz, Moritz, *Cotton in Egypt and the Anglo-Egyptian Sudan* (Manchester: Taylor, Garnett, Evans, 1913).

Schubert, Alfred Andreas, *Afrika, die Rettung Europas: Deutscher Kolonialbesitz—eine Lebensfrage für Industrie und Wirtschaft Europas* (Berlin: Deutsche Kolonialgesellschaft, 1929).

Schuster, Walter H., *Over de import en de transplantatie van vissoorten in Indonesia* (Bandung, Indonesia: Kementerian Kemakmuran, Djawatan Pusat Pertanian, 1950).

——, 'Provisional Survey of the Introduction and Transplantation of Fish Throughout the Indo-Pacific Region', *Proceedings of the IPFC* (1951), 187–96.

Schwarz, Ernest H. L., *The Kalahari, or, Thirstland Redemption* (Oxford: Blackwell, 1920).

Scott-Moncrieff, George, *Canals and Campaigns: An Engineering Officer in India 1877–1885* (London: BACSA, 1987).

Sennar Dam and Gezira Irrigation Works, Sudan (n.d. [1923–26]).

Sharpe, W.R.S., *The Port of Bombay* (Bombay: Port Trust, 1900).

'Short Account of the Ganges Canal', *North American Review* vol. 81, no. 169 (1855), 531–43.

Simms, F. W., *Report on the Establishment of Water-Works to Supply the City of Calcutta, with Other Papers on Watering and Draining the City* (Calcutta: Military Orphan, 1853).

Simpson, W.J.R., *First Survey of the Sanitary Condition in Singapore* (1906–7).

Singapore Municipality Waterworks, *Opening of New Works 26th March 1912* (Glasgow: Aird and Coghill, 1912).

Smith, David B., *Report on the Drainage and Conservancy of Calcutta* (Calcutta: Bengal Secretariat, 1869).

Smith, Donald, 'The Electrical Equipment Market of the Netherlands East Indies', *Trade Information Bulletin* no. 727 (Washington, DC: Government Printing Office, 1930), 10–11.

Smith, Richard Baird, *The Cauvery, Kistnah, and Godavery; Being a Report on the Works Constructed on Those Rivers for the Irrigation of the Provinces of Tanjore, Guntoor, Masulipatam, and Rajahmundry, in the Presidency of Madras* (London: Smith, Elder, 1856).

——, *A Short Account of the Ganges Canal* (Roorkee, India: Thomason College Press, 1870).

Sörgel, Herman, *Atlantropa* (Zurich: Fretz and Wasmuth, 1932).

Sörgel, Herman, and Bruno Siegwart, 'Erschliessung Afrikas durch Binnenmeere: Saharabewässerung durch Mittelmeersenkung', *Beilage zum Baumeister* vol. 3 (1935), 37–39.

Spengler, Oswald, *Der Untergang des Abendlandes: Umrisse einer Morphologie der Weltgeschichte* (Munich: Beck, 1919–22).

Stuart-Williams, S. C., 'The Port of Calcutta and Its Post-war Development', *Journal of the Royal Society of Arts* vol. 76, no. 3948 (1928), 890–906.

Thomas, H. S., *Report on Pisciculture in South Canara* (London: Eyre and Spottiswoode, 1870).

Thompson, G. A., 'A Plan for Converting the Sahara Desert Into a Sea', *Scientific American* vol. 107, no. 6 (1912), 114–125.

Todd, J. A., *The World's Cotton Crops* (London: Black, 1915).

Tulloch, Hector, *The Water Supply of Bombay: Being a Report to the Bench of Justices of that City* (London, 1872).

Union minière du Haut-Katanga: 1906–1956 (Brussels: Cuypers, 1956).

United States Geological Survey, *World Atlas of Commercial Geology*, Part II: *Water Power of the World* (Washington, DC: USGS, 1921).

Vageler, Paul, *Koloniale Bodenkunde und Wirtschaftsplanung* (Berlin: Parey, 1941).

Van der Heide, J. Homan, *Beschouwingen aangaande de Volkswelvaart en het Irrigatiewezen op Java in verband met de Solovalleiwerken* (Batavia, Netherlands East Indies: Kolff, 1899).

Van Deuren, Pierre, *Aménagement du Bas-Congo, projet du colonel du génie de réserve Pierre Van Deuren: Canalisation du fleuve dans les cataractes, houille blanche et développement industriel* (Paris: C. Béranger, 1928).

Verne, Jules, *L'invasion de la mer* (Paris: Hetzel, 1905).

Villarem, Georges, *Pêcheries du Tonkin* (Haiphong, Vietnam: Gallois, 1905).

Visvesvaraya, M., *Memoirs of My Working Life* (Bangalore: M. Visvesvaraya, 1951).

Walch, George T., *The Engineering Works of the Kistna Delta: A Descriptive and Historical Account* (Madras: Government Press, 1899).

'Water Power Resources of the Dutch East Indies', *Journal of the Royal Society of Arts* vol. 72, no. 3723 (1924), 320–21.

'Waterstaat', in: Paulus, J., D. G. Stibbe and S. de Graaff (eds), *Encyclopaedie van Nederlandsch-Indië*, vol. 4 ('s-Gravenhage: Nijhoff, 1921), 700–31.

Westlake, Charles Redvers, Reginald William Mountain and Thomas Angus Lyall Paton, 'Owen Falls, Uganda, Hydro-electric Development', *Proceedings of the Institution of Civil Engineers* vol. 3 (1954), 630–69.

Wiener, Lionel, *Les chemins de fer coloniaux de l'Afrique* (Brussels: Goemaere, 1930).

Willcocks, William, *Lectures on the Ancient System of Irrigation in Bengal and Its Application to Modern Problems* (Calcutta: University of Calcutta, 1931).

——, *Report on Perennial Irrigation and Flood Protection for Egypt* (Cairo: National Printing Office, 1894).

——, *The Restoration of the Ancient Irrigation of Bengal*, lecture to the British India Association, 6 March 1928 (Calcutta: Calcutta General Printing, 1928).

——, *Sixty Years in the East* (Edinburgh: Blackwood, 1935).

Willcocks, William, and J. I. Craig, *Egyptian Irrigation*, with an introduction by Sir Hanbury Brown, 2 vols, 3rd ed. (London: Spon, 1913).

Williams, George Bransby, *Sewage Disposal in India and the East: A Manual of the Latest Practice Applied to Tropical Conditions* (Calcutta: Thacker, Spink, 1924).

Worthington, E. B., *A Report on the Fisheries of Uganda Investigated by the Cambridge Expedition to the East African Lakes, 1930–31* (London: Crown Agents for the Colonies, 1932).

——, *Report on the Fishing Survey of Lakes Albert and Kioga* (London: Crown Agents for the Colonies, 1929).

——, *Science in Africa: A Review of Scientific Research Relating to Tropical and Southern Africa* (London: Oxford University Press, 1938).

Worthington, S., and E. B. Worthington, *Inland Waters of Africa* (London: Macmillan, 1933).

Wright, Arnold (ed.), *Twentieth-Century Impressions of Ceylon: Its History, People, Commerce, Industries and Resources* (London: Lloyds, 1907).

Zischka, Antoine, *La guerre secrète pour le pétrole* (Paris: Payot, 1933).

Secondary Literature

Abu-Lughod, Janet L., *Rabat: Urban Apartheid in Morocco* (Princeton, NJ: Princeton University Press, 1980).

Acciavatti, Anthony, *Ganges Water Machine: Designing New India's Ancient River* (New York: Applied Research and Design, 2015).

Acey, Charisma, 'Forbidden Waters: Colonial Intervention and the Evolution of Water Supply in Benin City, Nigeria', *Water History* vol. 4 (2012), 215–29.

——, 'Space vs. Race: A Historical Exploration of Spatial Injustice and Unequal Access to Water in Lagos, Nigeria', *Critical Planning* vol. 14 (2007), 48–69.

Acker, Antoine, 'A Different Story in the Anthropocene: Brazil's Post-Colonial Quest for Oil (1930–1975)', *Past & Present* vol. 249 (2020), 167–211.

Adams, W. M., *Wasting the Rain: Rivers, People and Planning in Africa* (Minneapolis: University of Minnesota Press, 1992).

Adas, Michael, *The Burma Delta: Economic Development and Social Change on an Asian Rice Frontier, 1852–1941* (Madison: University of Wisconsin Press, 1974).

——, 'Colonization, Commercial Agriculture, and the Destruction of the Deltaic Rainforests of British Burma in the Late Nineteenth Century', in: John F. Richards and Richard P. Tucker (eds), *Global Deforestation in the Nineteenth-Century World Economy* (Durham, NC: Duke University Press, 1983), 95–110.

——, 'Continuity and Transformation: Colonial Rice Frontiers and Their Environmental Impact on the Great River Deltas of Mainland Southeast Asia', in: Edmund Burke and Kenneth Pomeranz (eds), *The Environment and World History* (Berkeley: University of California Press, 2009), 191–207.

——, *Machines as the Measure of Men: Science, Technology, and Ideologies of Western Dominance* (Ithaca, NY: Cornell University Press, 1989).

Adelman, Jeremy, 'Mimesis and Rivalry: European Empires and Global Regimes', *Journal of Global History* vol. 10 (2015), 77–98.

Aditjondro, George J., 'Large Dam Victims and Their Defenders: The Emergence of an Anti-dam Movement in Indonesia', in: Philip Hirsch and Carol Warren (eds), *The Politics of Environment in Southeast Asia: Resources and Resistance* (London: Routledge, 1998), 29–54.

Agarwal, Anil, and Sunita Narain (eds), *Dying Wisdom: Rise, Fall and Potential of India's Traditional Water Harvesting Systems* (New Delhi: Centre for Science and Environment, 1997).

Agarwal, S. C., *History of Indian Fishery* (Delhi: Daya, 2006).

Ageron, Charles-Robert, 'L'idée d'Eurafrique et le débat colonial franco-allemand de l'entre-deux guerres', *Revue d'histoire moderne et contemporaine* vol. 22 (1975), 446–75.

Agnihotri, Indu, 'Ecology, Land Use and Colonisation: The Canal Colonies of Punjab', *Indian Social and Economic History Review* vol. 33 (1996), 37–58.

Ahmad, Adil Mustafa, 'Post-Jonglei Planning in Southern Sudan: Combining Environment with Development', *Environment and Urbanization* vol. 20 (2008), 575–86.

Ahmed, Samir, 'Principles and Precedents in International Law Governing the Sharing of Nile Waters', in: Howell and Allan, *Nile*, 351–63.

Ahuja, Ravi, *Pathways of Empire: Circulation, 'Public Works' and Social Space in Colonial Orissa (c. 1780–1914)* (Hyderabad: Orient BlackSwan, 2009).

Akyeampong, Emmanuel Kwaku, *Between the Sea and the Lagoon: An Eco-social History of the Anlo of Southeastern Ghana, c. 1850 to Recent Times* (Oxford: James Currey, 2001).

Alexander, Paul, 'Innovation in a Cultural Vacuum: The Mechanization of Sri Lanka Fisheries', *Human Organization* vol. 34 (1975), 333–44.

Ali, Imran, *The Punjab under Imperialism, 1885–1947* (Princeton, NJ: Princeton University Press, 1988).

Allsopp, W.H.L., *Fishery Development Experiences* (Farnham, UK: Fishing News Books, 1985).

Amrith, Sunil, *Crossing the Bay of Bengal: The Furies of Nature and the Fortunes of Migrants* (Cambridge, MA: Harvard University Press, 2013).

——, *Migration and Diaspora in Modern Asia* (Cambridge: Cambridge University Press, 2011).

——, 'South Asia's Coastal Frontiers', in: Gunnel Cederlöf and Mahesh Rangarajan (eds), *Nature's Edge: The Global Present and Long-Term History* (New Delhi: Oxford University Press, 2018), 210–28.

——, *Unruly Waters: How Mountain Rivers and Monsoons Have Shaped Asia's History* (London: Allen Lane, 2018).

Anand, Nikhil, *Hydraulic City: Water and the Infrastructures of Citizenship in Mumbai* (Durham, NC: Duke University Press, 2017).

Andersen, Casper, 'The Philae Controversy: Muscular Modernization and Paternalistic Preservation in Aswan and London', *History and Anthropology* vol. 22 (2011), 203–20.

Anderson, Katherine, *Predicting the Weather: Victorians and the Science of Meteorology* (Chicago: University of Chicago Press, 2005).

Anderson, Warwick, *Colonial Pathologies: American Tropical Medicine, Race, and Hygiene in the Philippines* (Durham, NC: Duke University Press, 2006).

——, 'Excremental Colonialism: Public Health and the Poetics of Pollution', *Critical Inquiry* vol. 21 (1995), 640–69.

Anh, Nguyen The, 'Japanese Food Policies and the 1945 Great Famine in Indochina', in: Paul H. Kratoska (ed.), *Food Supplies and the Japanese Occupation in South-East Asia* (Basingstoke, UK: Macmillan, 1998), 208–26.

Anker, Peder, *Imperial Ecology: Environmental Order in the British Empire, 1895–1945* (Cambridge, MA: Harvard University Press, 2001).

Armitage, David, Alison Bashford and Sujit Sivasundarum (eds), *Oceanic Histories* (Cambridge: Cambridge University Press, 2018).

Arndt, Erik, and Patrick J. Schembri, 'Common Traits Associated with Establishment and Spread of Lessepsian Fishes in the Mediterranean Sea', *Marine Biology* vol. 162 (2015), 2141–53.

Arnold, David, *Colonizing the Body: State Medicine and Epidemic Disease in Nineteenth-Century India* (Berkeley: University of California Press, 1993).

——, *Everyday Technology: Machines and the Making of India's Modernity* (Chicago: University of Chicago Press, 2013).

—— (ed.), *Imperial Medicine and Indigenous Societies* (Manchester: Manchester University Press, 1988).

——, 'Pollution, Toxicity and Public Health in Metropolitan India, 1850–1939', *Journal of Historical Geography* vol. 42 (2013), 124–33.

——, *The Problem of Nature: Environment, Culture and European Expansion* (Oxford: Blackwell, 1996).

——, *Science, Technology and Medicine in Colonial India* (Cambridge: Cambridge University Press, 2000).

——, *Toxic Histories: Poison and Pollution in Modern India* (Cambridge: Cambridge University Press, 2016).

——, *The Tropics and the Travelling Gaze: India, Landscape, and Science, 1800–1856* (Seattle: University of Washington Press, 2006).

Arsan, Andrew, *Interlopers of Empire: The Lebanese Diaspora in Colonial French West Africa* (Oxford: Oxford University Press, 2014).

Arthur, W. Brian, 'Competing Technologies, Increasing Returns, and Lock-In by Historical Events', *Economic Journal* vol. 99, no. 394 (1989), 116–31.

Artur, Luis, and Dorothea Hilhorst, 'Floods, Resettlement and Land Access and Use in the Lower Zambezi, Mozambique', *Land Use Policy* vol. 36 (2014), 361–68.

Astesiano, Gaston, Logan Byers, Johannes Friedrich, Tianyi Luo and Colin McCormick, 'Water Stress Threatens Nearly Half the World's Thermal Power Plant Capacity', World Resources Institute, 11 April 2018, https://www.wri.org/insights/water-stress-threatens -nearly-half-worlds-thermal-power-plant-capacity.

Atangana, Martin, *French Investment in Colonial Cameroon: The FIDES Era (1946–1957)* (New York: Peter Lang, 2009).

Austin, Gareth (ed.), *Economic Development and Environmental History in the Anthropocene: Perspectives from Asia and Africa* (London: Bloomsbury, 2017).

Ax, Christina Folke, Niels Brimnes, Niklas Thode Jensen and Karen Oslund (eds), *Cultivating the Colonies: Colonial States and their Environmental Legacies* (Athens: Ohio University Press, 2011).

Ayalov, Yaron, *Natural Disasters in the Ottoman Empire: Plague, Famine, and Other Misfortunes* (Cambridge: Cambridge University Press, 2017).

Badea, Cătălin, 'Water Conflicts: The Cast of the Nile River and the Grand Ethiopian Renaissance Dam', *Studia Universitatis Babes-Bolyai–Studia Europaea* vol. 65 (2020), 179–93.

Bailey, Connor, 'Lessons from Indonesia's 1980 Trawler Ban', *Marine Policy* vol. 21 (1997), 225–35.

Baillargeon, David, '"On the Road to Mandalay": The Development of Railways in British Burma, 1870–1900', *Journal of Imperial and Commonwealth History* vol. 48 (2020), 654–78.

Bakker, Karen, *Privatizing Water: Governance Failure and the World's Urban Water Crisis* (Ithaca, NY: Cornell University Press, 2010).

Ballantyne, Tony, *Between Colonialism and Diaspora: Sikh Cultural Formations in an Imperial World* (Durham, NC: Duke University Press, 2006).

——, 'Mobility, Empire, Colonisation', *History Australia* vol. 11 (2014), 7–37.

Ballestero, Andrea, *A Future History of Water* (Durham, NC: Duke University Press, 2019).

Balon, Eugene K., and André G. Coche (eds), *Lake Kariba: A Man-Made Tropical Ecosystem in Central Africa* (The Hague: Junk, 1974).

Bankoff, Greg, 'Aeolian Empires: The Influence of Winds and Currents on European Maritime Expansion in the Days of Sail', *Environment and History* vol. 23 (2017), 163–96.

———, *Cultures of Disaster: Society and Natural Hazards in the Philippines* (London: Routledge, 2003).

Bankoff, Greg, Georg Frerks and Dorothea Hilhorst (eds), *Mapping Vulnerability: Disasters, Development, and People* (London: Earthscan, 2004).

Barak, On, *Powering Empire: How Coal Made the Middle East and Sparked Global Carbonization* (Berkeley: University of California Press, 2020).

Barry, John M., *Rising Tide: The Great Mississippi Flood of 1927 and How It Changed America* (New York: Simon and Schuster, 1997).

Barth, Boris, and Jürgen Osterhammel (eds), *Zivilisierungsmissionen: Imperiale Weltverbesserung seit dem 18. Jahrhundert* (Konstanz, Germany: UVK, 2005).

Barth, Volker, and Roland Cvetkovski (eds), *Imperial Co-operation and Transfer, 1870–1930: Empires and Encounters* (London: Bloomsbury, 2015).

Bashford, Alison, 'Terraqueous Histories', *Historical Journal* vol. 60 (2017), 253–72.

Baskin, Yvonne, 'Africa's Troubled Waters', *Bioscience* vol. 42 (1992), 476–81.

———, *A Plague of Rats and Rubbervines: The Growing Threat of Species Invasions* (Washington, DC: Island, 2013).

Bassett, Thomas J., *The Peasant Cotton Revolution in West Africa: Côte d'Ivoire, 1880–1995* (Cambridge: Cambridge University Press, 2001).

Batchelor, John, *The Life of Joseph Conrad: A Critical Biography* (Oxford: Blackwell, 1994).

Baviskar, Amita, 'Nation's Body, River's Pulse: Narratives of Anti-dam Politics in India', *Thesis Eleven* vol. 150 (2019), 26–41.

Bayliss, Kate, and Ben Fine (eds), *Privatization and Alternative Public Sector Reform in Sub-Saharan Africa: Delivering on Electricity and Water* (Basingstoke, UK: Palgrave Macmillan, 2008).

Bayly, Christopher, *Indian Society and the Making of the British Empire* (Cambridge: Cambridge University Press, 1988).

———, *Rulers, Townsmen and Bazaars: North Indian Society in the Age of British Expansion* (Cambridge: Cambridge University Press, 1983).

Bayly, Christopher, and Tim Harper, *Forgotten Wars: Freedom and Revolution in Southeast Asia* (Cambridge, MA: Belknap Press of Harvard University Press, 2007).

Beasley, W. G., *Japanese Imperialism, 1894–1945* (Oxford: Oxford University Press, 1987).

Beattie, James, Edward Melillo and Emily O'Gorman (eds), *Eco-Cultural Networks and the British Empire: New Views on Environmental History* (London: Bloomsbury, 2015).

Beattie, James, and Ruth Morgan, 'Engineering Edens on This "Rivered Earth"? A Review Article on Water Management and Hydro-resilience in the British Empire, 1860–1940s', *Environment and History* vol. 23 (2017), 39–63.

Beck, Ulrich, *Risk Society: Towards a New Modernity*, transl. by Mark Ritter (London: Sage, 1992).

Beckert, Sven, 'American Danger: United States Empire, Eurafrica, and the Territorialization of Industrial Capitalism, 1870–1950' *American Historical Review* vol. 122 (2017), 1137–70.

———, 'Emancipation and Empire: Reconstructing the Worldwide Web of Cotton Production in the Age of the American Civil War', *American Historical Review* vol. 109 (2004), 1405–38.

———, *Empire of Cotton: A New History of Global Capitalism* (London: Allen Lane, 2014).

Beckert, Sven, Ulbe Bosma, Mindi Schneider and Eric Vanhaute, 'Commodity Frontiers and the Transformation of the Global Countryside: A Research Agenda', *Journal of Global History* vol. 16 (2021), 435–50.

Bee, Ooi Jin, *Development Problems of an Open-Access Resource: The Fisheries of Peninsular Malaysia* (Singapore: ISEAS, 1990).

Beinart, William, and Lotte Hughes, *Environment and Empire* (Oxford: Oxford University Press, 2007).

Belhabib, Dyhia, Viviane Koutob, Aliou Sall, Vicky W.Y. Lam and Daniel Pauly, 'Fisheries Catch Misreporting and Its Implications: The Case of Senegal', *Fisheries Research* vol. 151 (2014), 1–11.

Bender, Matthew V., *Water Brings No Harm: Management Knowledge and the Struggle for the Waters of Kilimanjaro* (Athens: Ohio University Press, 2019).

Béné, Christophe, 'When Fishery Rhymes with Poverty: A First Step beyond the Old Paradigm on Poverty in Small-Scale Fisheries', *World Development* vol. 31 (2003), 949–75.

Bennett, Brett M., and Joseph M. Hodge (eds) *Science and Empire: Knowledge and Networks of Science across the British Empire* (Basingstoke, UK: Palgrave Macmillan, 2011).

Bernal, Victoria, 'Cotton and Colonial Order in Sudan: A Social History with Emphasis on the Gezira Scheme', in: Allen Isaacman and Richard Roberts (eds), *Cotton, Colonialism, and Social History in Sub-Saharan Africa* (London: James Currey, 1995), 96–118.

Bernstein, Henry T., *Steamboats on the Ganges: An Exploration in the History of India's Modernization through Science and Technology* (London: Longmans, 1960).

Berron, Henri, 'Le littoral lagunaire de Côte d'Ivoire: Milieu physique, peuplement et modifications anthropiques', *Cahiers d'outre-mer* no. 176 (1991), 345–63.

Berwyn, Bob, 'Many Scientists Now Say Global Warming Could Stop Relatively Quickly after Emissions Go to Zero', *Inside Climate News*, 3 January 2021, https://insideclimatenews.org/news/03012021/five-aspects-climate-change-2020/.

Bhattacharyya, Debjani, *Empire and Ecology in the Bengal Delta: The Making of Calcutta* (Cambridge: Cambridge University Press, 2018).

——, 'Fluid Histories: Swamps, Law, and the Company-State in Colonial Bengal', *Journal of the Economic and Social History of the Orient* vol. 61 (2018), 1036–73.

——, 'A River Is Not a Pendulum: Sediments of Science in the World of Tides', *Isis* vol. 112 (2021), 141–49.

Biddanda, B. A., 'Global Significance of the Changing Freshwater Carbon Cycle', *Eos* vol. 98 (2017), https://doi.org/10.1029/2017EO069751.

Biggs, David, 'Managing a Rebel Landscape: Conservation, Pioneers, and the Revolutionary Past in the U Minh Forest, Vietnam', *Environmental History* vol. 10 (2005), 448–76.

——, *Quagmire: Nation-Building and Nature in the Mekong Delta* (Seattle: University of Washington Press, 2010).

——, 'Reclamation Nations: The US Bureau of Reclamation's Role in Water Management and Nation-Building in the Mekong Valley, 1945–1975', *Comparative Technology Transfer and Society* vol. 4 (2006), 225–46.

Bijker, Wiebe E., 'Dikes and Dams, Thick with Politics', *Isis* vol. 98 (2007), 109–23.

Bissell, William Cunningham, *Urban Design, Chaos, and Colonial Power in Zanzibar* (Bloomington: Indiana University Press, 2010).

Biswas, Margaret Rose, 'FAO: Its History and Achievements during the First Four Decades, 1945–1985', DPhil dissertation, Oxford University, 2007.

Björkman, Lisa, *Pipe Politics, Contested Waters: Embedded Infrastructures of Millennial Mumbai* (Durham, NC: Duke University Press, 2015).

Black, Jeremy, *Maps and History: Constructing Images of the Past* (New Haven, CT: Yale University Press, 1997).

Blackbourn, David, *The Conquest of Nature: Water, Landscape, and the Making of Modern Germany* (New York: Norton, 2006).

Blocher, Ewald, *Der Wasserbau-Staat: Die Transformation des Nils und das moderne Ägypten 1882–1971* (Paderborn, Germany: Schönigh, 2016).

Bloembergen, Marieke, and Remco Raben (eds), *Het koloniale beschavingsoffensief: Wegen naar het nieuwe Indië, 1890–1950* (Leiden: KITLV, 2009).

Boelens, Rutgerd, Jaime Hoogesteger, Erik Swyngedouw, Jeroen Vos and Philippus Wester, 'Hydrosocial Territories: A Political Ecology Perspective', *Water International* vol. 41 (2016), 1–14.

Bohman, Anna, 'Framing the Water and Sanitation Challenge: A History of Urban Water Supply and Sanitation in Ghana 1909–2005', PhD dissertation, Umeå University, 2010.

Bolster, W. Jeffrey, *The Mortal Sea: Fishing the Atlantic in the Age of Sail* (Cambridge, MA: Belknap Press of Harvard University Press, 2012)

Bombay First, *Vision Mumbai: Transforming Mumbai into a World Class City, A Bombay First–McKinsey Report* (Mumbai: Bombay First, 2003).

Bonneuil, Christophe, *Des savants pour l'Empire: La structuration des recherches scientifiques coloniales au temps de 'la mise en valeur des colonies françaises' 1917–1945* (Paris: Éditions de l'ORSTOM, 1991).

——, 'Development as Experiment: Science and State Building in Late Colonial and Postcolonial Africa, 1930–1970', *Osiris* vol. 15 (2000), 258–81.

Bonneuil, Christophe, and Jean-Baptiste Fressoz, *The Shock of the Anthropocene: The Earth, History, and Us* (London: Verso, 2016).

Booth, Anne, *Agricultural Development in Indonesia* (London: Allen and Unwin, 1988).

Bose, Sugata, *A Hundred Horizons: The Indian Ocean in the Age of Global Empire* (Cambridge, MA: Harvard University Press, 2006).

——, *Peasant Labour and Colonial Capital: Rural Bengal since 1770* (Cambridge: Cambridge University Press, 1993).

——, 'Starvation Amidst Plenty: The Making of Famine in Bengal, Honan and Tonkin, 1942–45', *Modern Asian Studies* vol. 24 (1990), 699–727.

Bosma, Ulbe, 'The Integration of Food Markets and Increasing Government Intervention in Indonesia: 1815–1980s', in: Jessica Dijkman and Bas van Leeuwen (eds), *An Economic History of Famine Resilience* (London: Routledge, 2019), 142–61.

——, *The Sugar Plantation in India and Indonesia: Industrial Production, 1770–2010* (Cambridge: Cambridge University Press, 2013).

Bottema, Mariska J. M., Simon R. Bush and Peter Oosterveer, 'Moving beyond the Shrimp Farm: Spaces of Shared Environmental Risk?', *Geographical Journal* vol. 185 (2019), 168–79.

Bourdillon, Jacques (ed.), *Les travaux publics français en Afrique subsaharienne et à Madagascar 1945–1985* (Paris: L'Harmattan, 1991).

Bray, Francesca, *The Rice Economies: Technology and Development in Asian Societies* (Berkeley: University of California Press, 1986).

Brecht, Henrike, Susmita Dasgupta, Benoit Laplante, Siobhan Murray and David Wheeler, 'Sea-Level Rise and Storm Surges: High Stakes for a Small Number of Developing Countries', *Journal of Environment & Development* vol. 21 (2012), 120–38.

Brocheux, Pierre, *The Mekong Delta: Ecology, Economy and Evolution, 1860–1960* (Madison: University of Wisconsin Press, 1995).

Brocheux, Pierre, and Daniel Hémery, *Indochina: An Ambiguous Colonization, 1858–1954* (Berkeley: University of California Press, 2009).

Broich, John, 'Engineering the Empire: British Water Supply Systems and Colonial Societies, 1850–1900', *Journal of British Studies* vol. 46 (2007), 346–65.

Brower, Benjamin Claude, *A Desert Named Peace: The Violence of France's Empire in the Algerian Sahara, 1844–1902* (New York: Columbia University Press, 2009).

Bryant, Raymond L. (ed.), *The International Handbook of Political Ecology* (Cheltenham, UK: Edward Elgar, 2017).

Buchet, Christian (ed.), *La mer dans l'histoire*, 4 vols (Paris: Boydell, 2017).

Budds, Jessica, and Gordon McGranahan, 'Are the Debates on Water Privatization Missing the Point? Experiences from Africa, Asia and Latin America', *Environment and Urbanization* vol. 15 (2003), 87–114.

Burbank, Jane, and Frederick Cooper, *Empires in World History: Power and the Politics of Difference* (Princeton, NJ: Princeton University Press, 2010).

Burton, Antoinette, 'Introduction: Travelling Criticism? On the Dynamic Histories of Indigenous Modernity', *Cultural and Social History* vol. 9 (2012), 491–96.

Büschenfeld, Jürgen, *Flüsse und Kloaken: Umweltfragen im Zeitalter der Industrialisierung (1870-1918)* (Stuttgart: Klett-Cotta, 1997).

Butcher, John G., *The Closing of the Frontier: A History of the Marine Fisheries of Southeast Asia, c. 1850-2000* (Singapore: Institute of Southeast Asian Studies, 2004).

——, 'The Marine Animals of Southeast Asia: Towards a Demographic History, 1850-2000', in: Peter Boomgaard, David Henley and Manon Osseweijer (eds), *Muddied Waters: Historical and Contemporary Perspectives on Management of Forests and Fisheries in Island Southeast Asia* (Leiden: KITLV, 2005), 63–96.

Butlin, Robin, *Geographies of Empire: European Empires and Colonies c.1880-1960* (Cambridge: Cambridge University Press, 2009).

Byerlee, Derek, 'The Globalization of Hybrid Maize, 1921-70', *Journal of Global History* vol. 15 (2020), 101–22.

——, 'Modern Varieties, Productivity, and Sustainability: Recent Experience and Emerging Challenges', *World Development* vol. 24 (1996), 697–718.

Campbell, Bonnie K., *Les enjeux de la bauxite: La Guinée face aux multinationales de l'aluminium* (Montreal: Presses de l'Université de Montréal, 1983).

Cariño, Micheline, and Mario Monteforte, 'An Environmental History of Nacre and Pearls: Fisheries, Cultivation and Commerce', *Global Environment* vol. 3 (2009), 48–71.

Carse, Ashley, *Beyond the Big Ditch: Politics, Ecology, and Infrastructure at the Panama Canal* (Cambridge, MA: MIT Press, 2014).

Cater, Casey P., *Regenerating Dixie: Electric Energy and the Modern South* (Pittsburgh: University of Pittsburgh Press, 2019).

Cederlof, Gunnel, *Founding an Empire on India's North Eastern Frontiers (1790-1840): Climate, Commerce, Polity* (New Delhi: Oxford University Press, 2014).

Chakrabarti, Pratik, 'Purifying the River: Pollution and Purity of Water in Colonial Calcutta', *Studies in History* vol. 31 (2015), 178–205.

Chakrabarty, Dipesh, 'Climate and Capital: On Conjoined Histories', *Critical Inquiry* vol. 41 (2014), 1–23.

——, *Habitations of Modernity: Essays in the Wake of Subaltern Studies* (Chicago: University of Chicago Press, 2002).

Chakravorty, Sanjoy, *The Price of Land: Acquisition, Conflict, Consequence* (Oxford: Oxford University Press, 2013).

Chambers, Robert, *The Volta Resettlement Experience* (London: Pall Mall, 1970).

Chambers, Robert, and Jon Moris (eds), *Mwea, An Irrigated Rice Settlement in Kenya* (New York: Humanities, 1973).

Chandra, G., I. Bhattacharjee, S. N. Chatterjee and A. Ghosh. 'Mosquito Control by Larvivorous Fish', *Indian Journal of Medical Research* vol. 127 (2008), 13–27.

Chatterjee, Elizabeth, 'The Asian Anthropocene: Electricity and Fossil Developmentalism', *Journal of Asian Studies* vol. 79 (2020), 3–24.

——, 'A Climate of Scarcity: Electricity in India, 1899-2016', in: Fredrik Albritton Jonsson, John Brewer, Neil Fromer and Frank Trentmann (eds), *Scarcity in the Modern World: History, Politics, Society and Sustainability, 1800-2075* (London: Bloomsbury, 2019), 211–28.

Chatterji, Joya, 'On Being Stuck in Bengal: Immobility in the "Age of Migration"', *Modern Asian Studies* vol. 51 (2017), 511–41.

Chattopadhyay, Swati, *Representing Calcutta: Modernity, Nationalism, and the Colonial Uncanny* (London: Routledge, 2005).

Chauveau, Jean-Pierre, 'Histoire de la pêche industrielle au Sénégal et politiques d'industrialisation. 1re partie: Cinq siècles de pêche européenne (du xv siècle au milieu des années 1950)', *Cahiers des sciences humaines* vol. 25 (1989), 237–58.

———, 'Histoire de la pêche industrielle au Sénégal et politiques d'industrialisation. 2ème partie: L'essor thonier et les limites d'une politique nationale d'industrialisation de la pêche (de 1955 aux premières années de l'Indépendance)', *Cahiers des sciences humaines* vol. 25 (1989), 259–75.

Chellaney, Brahma, *Water, Peace, and War: Confronting the Global Water Crisis* (Lanham, MD: Rowman and Littlefeld, 2015).

Chhabria, Sheetal, *Making the Modern Slum: The Power of Capital in Colonial Bombay* (Seattle: University of Washington Press, 2019).

Chiang, Connie Y., *Shaping the Shoreline: Fisheries and Tourism on the Monterey Coast* (Seattle: University of Washington Press, 2008).

Chikowero, Moses, 'Subalternating Currents: Electrification and Power Politics in Bulawayo, Colonial Zimbabwe, 1894–1939', *Journal of Southern African Studies* vol. 33 (2007), 287–306.

Chitonge, Horman, 'Cities beyond Networks: The Status of Water Services for the Urban Poor in African Cities', *African Studies* vol. 73 (2014), 58–83.

Chopra, Preeti, *A Joint Enterprise: Indian Elites and the Making of British Bombay* (Minneapolis: University of Minnesota Press, 2011).

Christopher, A. J., 'Decolonisation without Independence', *GeoJournal* vol. 56 (2002), 213–24.

Chu, Cecilia, 'Combating Nuisance: Sanitation, Regulation, and the Politics of Property in Colonial Hong Kong', in: Robert Peckham and David M. Pomfret (eds), *Imperial Contagions: Medicine, Hygiene, and Cultures of Planning in Asia* (Hong Kong: Hong Kong University Press, 2013), 17–36.

Cioc, Mark, *The Rhine: An Eco-Biography, 1815–2000* (Seattle: University of Washington Press, 2005).

Coclanis, Peter A., 'Metamorphosis: The Rice Boom, Environmental Transformation, and the Problem of Truncation in Colonial Lower Burma, 1850–1940', *Agricultural History* vol. 93 (2019), 35–67.

———, 'Southeast Asia's Incorporation into the World Rice Market: A Revisionist View', *Journal of Southeast Asian Studies* vol. 24 (1993), 251–67.

Cohn, Julie, Matthew Evenden and Marc Landry, 'Water Powers: The Second World War and the Mobilization of Hydroelectricity in Canada, the United States, and Germany', *Journal of Global History* vol. 15 (2020), 123–47.

Collins, Elizabeth Fuller, *Indonesia Betrayed: How Development Fails* (Honolulu: University of Hawaii Press, 2007).

Collins, R. O., 'History, Hydropolitics, and the Nile: Nile Control: Myth or Reality?', in: Howell and Allan, *Nile*, 109–36.

———, *The Waters of the Nile: Hydro-politics and the Jonglei Canal, 1900–1988* (Oxford: Oxford University Press, 1990).

Colson, Elizabeth, *The Social Consequences of Resettlement: The Impact of the Kariba Resettlement upon the Gwembe Tonga* (Manchester: Manchester University Press, 1971).

———, *Social Organisation of the Gwembe Tonga* (Manchester: Manchester University Press, 1960).

Conklin, Alice L., *A Mission to Civilize: The Republican Idea of Empire in France and West Africa, 1895–1930* (Cambridge: Cambridge University Press, 1997).

Conway, Gordon, *The Doubly Green Revolution: Food for All in the 21st Century* (Harmondsworth, UK: Penguin, 1997).

Cook, Ben, *Drought: An Interdisciplinary Perspective* (New York: Columbia University Press, 2019).

Cooke, Nola, 'Tonle Sap Processed Fish: From Khmer Subsistence Staple to Colonial Export Commodity', in: Eric Tagliacozzo and Wen-Chin Chang (eds), *Chinese Circulations: Capital, Commodities, and Networks in Southeast Asia* (Durham, NC: Duke University Press, 2011), 360–79.

Cookson-Hills, Claire, 'The Aswan Dam and Egyptian Water Control Policy, 1882–1902', *Radical History Review* no. 116 (2013), 59–85.

Cooper, Frederick, *Colonialism in Question: Theory, Knowledge, History* (Berkeley: University of California Press, 2005).

Cooper, Frederick, and Randall Packard (eds), *International Development and the Social Sciences: Essays on the History and Politics of Knowledge* (Berkeley: University of California Press, 1997).

Cornet, René, *La bataille du rail: La construction du chemin de fer de Matadi au Stanley Pool*, 3rd ed. (Brussels: Cuypers, 1953).

Corsi, Marco, 'Communalism and the Green Revolution in Punjab', *Journal of Developing Societies* vol. 22 (2006), 85–109.

Courtenay, Walter J., Jr, 'Biological Pollution through Fish Introductions', in: Bill N. McKnight (ed.), *Biological Pollution: The Control and Impact of Invasive Exotic Species* (Indianapolis: Indiana Academy of Science, 1993), 35–61.

Courtney, Chris, *The Nature of Disaster in China: The 1931 Yangzi River Flood* (Cambridge: Cambridge University Press, 2018).

Cresswell, Tim, *On the Move: Mobility in the Modern Western World* (London: Routledge, 2006).

Critchley, R. A., 'Operation Noah', *Oryx* vol. 5 (1959), 100–107.

Cronin, Richard P., 'Hydropower Dams on the Mekong: Old Dreams, New Dangers', *Asia Policy* vol. 16 (2013), 32–38.

Cronon, William, *Nature's Metropolis: Chicago and the Great West* (New York: Norton, 1991).

Crosby, Alfred, *Children of the Sun: A History of Humanity's Unappeasable Appetite for Energy* (New York: Norton, 2006).

———, *The Columbian Exchange: Biological and Cultural Consequences of 1492* (Westport, CT: Greenwood, 1972).

———, *Ecological Imperialism: The Biological Expansion of Europe, 900–1900* (Cambridge: Cambridge University Press, 1986).

Cullather, Nick, *The Hungry World: America's Cold War Battle against Poverty in Asia* (Cambridge, MA: Harvard University Press, 2010).

Cunningham, Stephen, and Arthur E. Neiland, 'African Fisheries Development Aid', in: Donald R. Leal (ed.), *Political Economy of Natural Resource Use: Lessons for Fisheries Reform* (Washington, DC: World Bank, 2010), 21–44.

Curtin, Philip D., *Death by Migration: Europe's Encounter with the Tropical World in the Nineteenth Century* (Cambridge: Cambridge University Press, 1989).

———, 'The End of the "White Man's Grave"? Nineteenth-Century Mortality in West Africa', *Journal of Interdisciplinary History* vol. 21 (1990), 63–88.

———, 'Medical Knowledge and Urban Planning in Tropical Africa', *American Historical Review* vol. 90 (1985), 594–613.

Cushman, Gregory T., *Guano and the Opening of the Pacific World: A Global Ecological History* (Cambridge: Cambridge University Press, 2013).

Cutler, Brock, 'Imperial Thirst: Water and Colonial Administration in Algeria, 1840–1880', *Review of Middle East Studies* vol. 44 (2010), 167–75.

Da Cunha, Dilip, *The Invention of Rivers: Alexander's Eye and the Ganga's Descent* (Philadelphia: University of Pennsylvania Press, 2019).

Daughton, J. P., *In the Forest of No Joy: The Congo-Océan Railroad and the Tragedy of French Colonialism* (New York: Norton, 2021).

Davis, B., Kenneth E. Wilburn and Ronald E. Robinson (eds), *Railway Imperialism* (Westport, CT: Greenwood, 1991).

Davis, Carlton E., *Jamaica in the World Aluminium Industry, 1938–1973* (Kingston: Jamaica Bauxite Institute, 1989).

Davis, Diana K., *Resurrecting the Granary of Rome: Environmental History and French Colonial Expansion in North Africa* (Athens, OH: Ohio University Press, 2007).

Davis, Mike, *Late Victorian Holocausts: El Niño Famines and the Making of the Third World* (London: Verso, 2001).

——, *Planet of Slums* (London: Verso, 2007).

Deb, Ritwika, *Kolkata, India: A Study of Increasing Water Insecurity and Deep-Rooted Spatial Division*, DEVP0024 Sustainable Infrastructure and Services in Development (London: University College London, 11 December 2020), https://doi.org/10.13140/RG .2.2.34769.25442.

Deemer, Bridget R., John A. Harrison, Siyue Li, Jake J. Beaulieu, Tonya DelSontro, Nathan Barros, José F. Bezerra-Neto, Stephen M. Powers, Marco A. Dos Santos and J. Arie Vonk, 'Greenhouse Gas Emissions from Reservoir Water Surfaces: A New Global Synthesis', *BioScience* vol. 66 (2016), 949–64.

De Iongh, Hans H., Petronella Spliethoff and Fritz Roest, 'The Impact of an Introduction of Sardine into Lake Kivu', in: Tony J. Pitcher and Paul J. B. Hart (eds), *The Impact of Species Changes in African Lakes* (London: Chapman and Hall, 1995), 277–97.

De Moncan, Patrice, *Paris inondé: La grande crue de 1910* (Paris: Mécène, 2009).

Denning, Andrew, '"Life Is Movement, Movement Is Life!": Mobility Politics and the Circulatory State in Nazi Germany', *American Historical Review* vol. 123 (2018), 1479–503.

——, 'Unscrambling Africa: From Eurafrican Technopolitics to the Fascist New Order', *Journal of Modern History* vol. 95 (2023), 627–67.

Derr, Jennifer L., *The Lived Nile: Environment, Disease, and Material Colonial Economy in Egypt* (Stanford, CA: Stanford University Press, 2019).

Dewan, Camelia, *Misreading the Bengal Delta: Climate Change, Development, and Livelihoods in Coastal Bangladesh* (Seattle: University of Washington Press, 2021).

Dewey, Clive, *Steamboats on the Indus: The Limits of Western Technological Superiority in South Asia* (New York: Oxford University Press, 2014).

Dossal, Mariam, 'Henry Conybeare and the Politics of Centralised Water Supply in Mid-Nineteenth Century Bombay', *Indian Economic and Social History Review* vol. 25 (1988), 79–96.

——, *Imperial Designs and Indian Realities: The Planning of Bombay City, 1845–1875* (Bombay: Oxford University Press, 1991).

Douglas, Mary, *Purity and Danger: An Analysis of Concepts of Pollution and Taboo* (London: Routledge and Kegan Paul, 1966).

Downs, Matthew, *Transforming the South: Federal Development in the Tennessee Valley, 1915–1960* (Baton Rouge: Louisiana State University Press, 2014).

Doyle, Martin, *The Source: How Rivers Made America and America Remade Its Rivers* (New York: Norton, 2018).

Driver, Felix, and Luciana Martins (eds), *Tropical Visions in an Age of Empire* (Chicago: University of Chicago Press, 2005).

D'Souza, Rohan, 'Damming the Mahanadi River: The Emergence of Multi-purpose River Valley Development in India (1943–46)', *Indian Economic and Social History Review* vol. 40 (2003), 81–105.

——, *Drowned and Dammed: Colonial Capitalism and Flood Control in Eastern India* (New Delhi: Oxford University Press, 2006).

——, 'Event, Process and Pulse: Resituating Floods in Environmental Histories of South Asia', *Environment and History* vol. 26 (2020), 31–49.

——, 'Framing India's Hydraulic Crises: The Politics of the Modern Large Dam', *Monthly Review* vol. 60 (2008), 112–24.

——, 'Mischievous Rivers and Evil Shoals: The English East India Company and the Colonial Resource Regime', in: Vinita Damodaran, Anna Winterbottom and Alan Lester (eds), *The East India Company and the Natural World* (Basingstoke, UK: Palgrave Macmillan, 2015), 128–46.

——, 'Water in British India: The Making of a "Colonial Hydrology"', *History Compass* vol. 4 (2006), 621–28.

D'Souza, Rohan, Pranab Mukhopadhyay and Ashish Kothari, 'Re-evaluating Multi-purpose River Valley Projects: A Case Study of Hirakud, Ukai and IGNP', *Economic and Political Weekly* vol. 33, no. 6 (1998), 297–302.

Duflo, Esther, and Rohini Pande, 'Dams', *Quarterly Journal of Economics* vol. 122 (2007), 601–46.

Dumont, Henri J., 'The Tanganyika Sardine in Lake Kivu: Another Ecodisaster for Africa?', *Environmental Conservation* vol. 13 (1986), 143–48.

Dumont, René, *False Start in Africa* (London: Andre Deutsch, 1966).

——, *Notes sur les implications sociales de la 'révolution verte' dans quelques pays d'Afrique* (Geneva: United Nations Research Institute for Social Development, 1971).

Dupont, Véronique, 'The Dream of Delhi as a Global City', *International Journal of Urban and Regional Research* vol. 35 (2011), 533–54.

Dusinberre, Martin, and Roland Wenzlhuemer, 'Being in Transit: Ships and Global Incompatibilities' (editorial), *Journal of Global History* vol. 11 (2016), 155–62.

Edgerton, David, *The Shock of the Old: Technology and Global History since 1900* (London: Profile, 2008).

Ehrlich, Joshua, 'The Meanings of a Port City Boundary: Calcutta's Maratha Ditch, c. 1700–1950', *Past & Present* vol. 257 (2022), 168–208.

Ehrlich, Paul R., and Anne H. Ehrlich, *The Population Bomb* (New York: Ballantine, 1968).

Eiden, Christian, *Versorgungswirtschaft als regionale Organisation: die Wasserversorgung Berlins und des Ruhrgebietes zwischen 1850 und 1930* (Essen, Germany: Klartext, 2006).

Elkan, Walter, and Gail Wilson, 'The Impact of the Owen Falls Hydro-electric Project on the Economy of Uganda', *Journal of Development Studies* vol. 3 (1967), 387–404.

Elliott, Rebecca, *Underwater: Loss, Flood Insurance, and the Moral Economy of Climate Change in the United States* (New York: Columbia University Press, 2021).

Elson, R. E., 'The Famine in Demak and Grobogan in 1848–1849: Its Causes and Circumstances', *Review of Indonesian and Malaysian Affairs* vol. 19 (1985), 39–85.

Elvin, Mark, *The Retreat of the Elephants: An Environmental History of China* (New Haven, CT: Yale University Press, 2004).

Engel, Susan, and Anggun Susilo, 'Shaming and Sanitation in Indonesia: A Return to Colonial Public Health Practices?', *Development and Change* vol. 45 (2014), 157–78.

Engerman, David C., *The Price of Aid: The Economic Cold War in India* (Cambridge, MA: Harvard University Press, 2018).

Epprecht, Marc, 'The Native Village Debate in Pietermaritzburg, 1848–1925: Revisiting the "Sanitation Syndrome"', *Journal of African History* vol. 58 (2017), 259–83.

Ertsen, Maurits W., 'Controlling the Farmer: Colonial and Post-colonial Irrigation Interventions in Africa', *Journal for Transdisciplinary Research in Southern Africa* vol. 4 (2008), 209–36.

———, *Improvising Planned Development on the Gezira Plain, Sudan, 1900–1980* (Basingstoke, UK: Palgrave Macmillan, 2016).

———, *Locales of Happiness: Colonial Irrigation in the Netherlands East Indies and Its Remains, 1830–1980* (Delft: VSSD, 2010).

Evans, Emmit B., Jr, 'Marine Scientific and Technological Assistance to Developing Countries: Science for Development or Technology for Malintegrated Growth?', *Economic Development and Cultural Change* vol. 24 (1976), 375–85.

Evans, Richard J., *Death in Hamburg: Society and Politics in the Cholera Years* (Oxford: Clarendon, 1987).

Evenden, Matthew, 'Aluminum, Commodity Chains, and the Environmental History of the Second World War', *Environmental History* vol. 16 (2011), 69–93.

Ezeh, Alex, Oyinlola Oyebode, David Satterthwaite, Yen-Fu Chen, Robert Ndugwa, Jo Sartori, Blessing Mberu, et al., 'The History, Geography, and Sociology of Slums and the Health Problems of People who Live in Slums', *Lancet* vol. 389, no. 10068 (2017), 547–58.

FAO (Food and Agriculture Organization), *Fisheries in the Food Economy* (Rome: FAO, 1968).

———, *Food for All* (Rome: FAO, 1996).

———, *Marine Small-Scale Fisheries of India: A General Description* (Madras: FAO, 1982).

———, *World Fisheries and the Law of the Sea: The FAO EEZ Programme* (Rome: FAO, 1981).

Farley, John, *Bilharzia: A History of Imperial Tropical Medicine* (Cambridge: Cambridge University Press, 1991).

Farrenkopf, John, *Prophet of Decline: Spengler on World History and Politics* (Baton Rouge: Louisiana State University Press, 2001).

Fasseur, Cornelis, *The Politics of Colonial Exploitation: Java, the Dutch, and the Cultivation System* (Ithaca, NY: Southeast Asia Program, Cornell University, 1992).

Fernando, M. R., *Famine in Cirebon Residency in Java, 1844–1850: A New Perspective on the Cultivation System*, Working Papers no. 21 (Melbourne: Centre of Southeast Asian Studies, Monash University, 1980).

Fernando, Tamara, 'Mapping Oysters and Making Oceans in the Northern Indian Ocean, 1880–1906', *Comparative Studies in Society and History* vol. 65 (2023), 53–80.

———, 'Seeing like the Sea: A Multispecies History of the Ceylon Pearl Fishery 1800–1925', *Past & Present* vol. 254 (2022), 127–60.

Fernando, Tamara, Felice Physioc and Alexis Rider, 'Flows of History', *Past & Present* vol. 260 (2023), https://doi.org/10.1093/pastj/gtad004.

Filipovich, Jean, 'Destined to Fail: Forced Settlement at the Office du Niger, 1926–45', *Journal of African History* vol. 42 (2001), 239–60.

Finley, Carmel, *All the Boats on the Ocean: How Government Subsidies Led to Global Overfishing* (Chicago: University of Chicago Press, 2017).

———, *All the Fish in the Sea: Maximum Sustainable Yield and the Failure of Fisheries Management* (Chicago: University of Chicago Press, 2011).

Fischer-Tiné, Harald, and Michael Mann, *Colonialism as Civilizing Mission. Cultural Ideology in British India* (London: Anthem, 2004).

Fleming, James Rodger, *Fixing the Sky: The Checkered History of Weather and Climate Control* (New York: Columbia University Press, 2010).

Fleury, Antoine, 'Paneurope et l'Afrique', in Marie-Thérèse Bitsch and Gérard Bossuat (eds), *L'Europe unie et l'Afrique: De l'idée d'Eurafrique à la convention de Lome I* (Brussels: Bruylant, 2005), 35–57.

Fontein, Joost, 'Damming the Zambezi: Light and Power for which Nation?', *Journal of Southern African Studies* vol. 43 (2017), 425–32.

Ford, James D., Laura Cameron, Jennifer Rubis, Michelle Maillet, Douglas Nakashima, Ashlee Cunsolo Willox and Tristan Pearce, 'Including Indigenous Knowledge and Experience in IPCC Assessment Reports', *Nature Climate Change* vol. 6 (2016), 349–53.

'Forum: Oceans of History', *American Historical Review* vol. 111, no. 3 (June 2006). Including: K. Wigen, introduction, 717–21; P. Horden and N. Purcell, 'The Mediterranean and "the New Thalassology"', 722–40; A. Games, 741–57; M. K. Matsuda, 'The Pacific', 758–80.

Foster, John Bellamy, Brett Clark and Richard York, *The Ecological Rift: Capitalism's War on the Earth* (New York: New York University Press, 2011).

Funes, Yessenia, 'Yes, Colonialism Caused Climate Change, IPCC Reports', *Frontline*, 4 April 2022.

Gall, Alexander, *Das Atlantropa-Projekt: Die Geschichte einer gescheiterten Vision; Herman Sörgel und die Absenkung des Mittelmeers* (Frankfurt a.M.: Campus, 1998).

Gallagher, Nancy E., *Egypt's Other Wars: Epidemics and the Politics of Public Health* (Syracuse, NY: Syracuse University Press, 1990).

Galpern, Steven G., *Money, Oil, and Empire in the Middle East: Sterling and Postwar Imperialism, 1944–1971* (Cambridge: Cambridge University Press, 2009).

Gandhi, *The Collected Works of Mahatma Gandhi*, ebook (New Delhi: Publications Division, Ministry of Information and Broadcasting, Government of India, 1999).

Gandy, Matthew, *The Fabric of Space: Water, Modernity, and the Urban Imagination* (Cambridge, MA: MIT Press, 2014).

——, 'Landscapes of Disaster: Water, Modernity, and Urban Fragmentation in Mumbai', *Environment and Planning A* vol. 40 (2008), 108–30.

——, 'Planning, Anti-planning, and the Infrastructure Crisis Facing Metropolitan Lagos', *Urban Studies* vol. 43 (2006), 371–97.

Gange, David, 'Unholy Water: Archaeology, the Bible, and the First Aswan Dam', in: Astrid Swenson and Peter Mandler (eds), *From Plunder to Preservation: Britain and the Heritage of Empire, c. 1800–1940* (Oxford: Oxford University Press, 2013), 93–114.

Garcia, S. M., 'Ocean Fisheries Management: The FAO Programme', in: Paolo Fabbri (ed.), *Ocean Management in Global Change* (London: Elsevier, 1992), 381–418.

Geertz, Clifford, *Agricultural Involution: The Process of Ecological Change in Indonesia* (Berkeley: University of California Press, 1963).

Gelvin, James L., and Nile Green (eds), *Global Muslims in the Age of Steam and Print* (Berkeley: University of California Press, 2014).

Ghassemi, Fereidoun, and Ian White, *Inter-basin Water Transfer: Case Studies from Australia, United States, Canada, China and India* (Cambridge: Cambridge University Press, 2007).

Ghee, Lim Teck, 'Conflict over Natural Resources in Malaysia: The Struggle of Small-Scale Fishermen', in: Lim Teck Ghee and Mark J. Valencia (eds), *Conflict over Natural Resources in Southeast Asia and the Pacific* (Oxford: Oxford University Press, 1990), 145–81.

Ghosh, Amitav, *The Great Derangement: Climate Change and the Unthinkable* (Chicago: Chicago University Press, 2016).

——, *The Hungry Tide* (London: HarperCollins, 2004).

Ghosh, Nabaparna, *A Hygienic City-Nation: Space, Community, and Everyday Life in Colonial Calcutta* (Cambridge: Cambridge University Press, 2020).

Ghosh, Sandipan, and Biswaranjan Mistri, 'Geographic Concerns on Flood Climate and Flood Hydrology in Monsoon-Dominated Damodar River Basin, Eastern India', *Geography Journal* vol. 2015 (2015), 1–16.

Ghosh, Tirtankhar, 'Floods and People: Colonial North Bengal, 1871–1922', *Studies in People's History* vol. 5 (2018), 32–47.

Gibson-Hill, C. A., 'The Steamers Employed in Asian Waters, 1819–39', *Journal of the Malayan Branch of the Royal Asiatic Society* vol. 27, no. 1 (1954), 120–62.

Gillis, John R., *The Human Shore: Seacoasts in History* (Chicago: University of Chicago Press, 2012).

Gilmartin, David, *Blood and Water: The Indus River Basin in Modern History* (Berkeley: University of California Press, 2015).

——, 'Models of the Hydraulic Environment: Colonial Irrigation, State Power and Community in the Indus Basin', in: David Arnold and Ramachandra Guha (eds), *Nature, Culture, Imperialism: Essays on the Environmental History of South Asia* (New Delhi: Oxford University Press, 1995), 210–36.

——, 'Scientific Empire and Imperial Science: Colonialism and Irrigation Technology in the Indus Basin', *Journal of Asian Studies* vol. 53 (1994), 1127–49.

Gimelli, Francesco M., Joannette J. Bos and Briony C. Rogers, 'Fostering Equity and Wellbeing through Water: A Reinterpretation of the Goal of Securing Access', *World Development* vol. 104 (2018), 1–9.

Giovannini, Gabriele, 'Power and Geopolitics along the Mekong: The Laos–Vietnam Negotiation on the Xayaburi Dam', *Journal of Current Southeast Asian Affairs* vol. 37 (2018), 63–93.

Goffinet, Thomas, 'Development and Fisheries Management: The Case of Northwest Africa', *Ocean & Coastal Management* vol. 17 (1992), 105–36.

Goodland, Robert, 'Viewpoint: The World Bank versus the World Commission on Dams', *Water Alternatives* vol. 3 (2010), 384–98.

Gordon, David M., *Nachituti's Gift: Economy, Society and Environment in Central Africa* (Madison: University of Wisconsin Press, 2006).

Goren, Menachem, Bella S. Galil, Arik Diamant, Nir Stern and Ya'arit Levitt-Barmats, 'Invading Up the Food Web? Invasive Fish in the Southeastern Mediterranean Sea', *Marine Biology* vol. 163, no. 8 (2016), 1–11.

Goswami, Manu, 'Imaginary Futures and Colonial Internationalisms', *American Historical Review* vol. 117 (2012), 1461–85.

Goubert, Jean-Pierre, *The Conquest of Water: The Advent of Health in the Industrial Age*, transl. by Andrew Wilson (Princeton, NJ: Princeton University Press, 1989).

——, 'La ville, miroir et enjeu de la santé: Paris, Montréal et Alger au XIXe siècle', *Histoire, économie et société* vol. 20 (2001), 355–70.

Goudswaard, Kees P. C., Frans Witte and Egid F. B. Katunzi, 'The Invasion of an Introduced predator, Nile perch (*Lates niloticus*, L.) in Lake Victoria (East Africa): Chronology and Causes', *Environmental Biology of Fishes* vol. 81 (2008), 127–39.

Graber, Frédéric, *Paris a besoin d'eau: Projet, dispute et deliberation technique dans la France napoleonienne* (Paris: CNRS, 2009).

Graf, Rüdiger, *Die Zukunft der Weimarer Republik: Krisen und Zukunftsaneignungen in Deutschland, 1918–1933* (Munich: Oldenbourg, 2008).

Graham, Ronald, *The Aluminium Industry and the Third World: Multinational Corporations and Underdevelopment* (London: Zed, 1982).

Greene, Julie, *The Canal Builders: Making America's Empire at the Panama Canal* (New York: Penguin, 2009).

Greenough, Paul R., *Prosperity and Misery in Modern Bengal: The Famine of 1943–1944* (Oxford: Oxford University Press, 1982).

Grinsell, Samuel, 'Mastering the Nile? Confidence and Anxiety in D. S. George's Photographs of the First Aswan Dam, 1899–1912', *Environmental History* vol. 25 (2020), 110–33.

Grove, Richard, *Green Imperialism: Colonial Expansion, Tropical Island Edens and the Origins of Environmentalism, 1600–1860* (Cambridge: Cambridge University Press, 1995).

———, 'A Historical Review of Institutional and Conservationist Responses to Fears of Artificially Induced Global Climate Change: The Deforestation-Desiccation Discourse in
Europe and the Colonial Context, 1500–1940', in: Yvon Chatelin and Christophe Bonneuil (eds), *Nature et environnement* (Paris: Orstom Éditions, 1995), 155–74.

Guha, Ranajit, *A Rule of Property for Bengal: An Essay on the Idea of Permanent Settlement*
(Durham, NC: Duke University Press, 1996).

Gunn, Geoffrey C., *Rice Wars in Colonial Vietnam: The Great Famine and the Viet Minh
Road to Power* (Lanham, MD: Rowman and Littlefield, 2014).

Habib, Irfan, 'Agrarian Relations and Land Revenue: North India' in: Tapan Raychaudhuri
and Irfan Habib (eds), *The Cambridge Economic History of India* vol. 1 (Cambridge:
Cambridge University Press, 1982), 235–49.

Haines, Daniel, *Building the Empire, Building the Nation: Development, Legitimacy, and
Hydro-politics in Sindh, 1919–1969* (Karachi: Oxford University Press, 2013).

———, 'Constructing State Power: Internal and External Frontiers in Colonial North India,
1850s–1900s', *Environmental History* vol. 20 (2015), 645–70.

———, 'Development, Citizenship, and the Bhakra-Nangal Dams in Postcolonial India,
1948–1952', *Historical Journal* vol. 65 (2022), 1124–44.

———, 'Disputed Rivers: Sovereignty, Territory and State-Making in South Asia, 1948–1951',
Geopolitics vol. 19 (2014), 632–55.

———, '(Inter) Nationalist Rivers? Cooperative Development in David Lilienthal's Plan for
the Indus Basin, 1951', *Water History* vol. 6 (2014), 133–51.

———, *Rivers Divided: Indus Basin Waters in the Making of India and Pakistan* (New York:
Oxford University Press, 2017).

Hall, S. R., and E. L. Mills, 'Exotic Species in Large Lakes of the World', *Aquatic Ecosystem
Health and Management* vol. 3 (2000), 105–35.

Halliday, Stephen, *The Great Stink of London: Sir Joseph Bazalgette and the Cleansing of
the Victorian Capital* (Stroud, UK: Sutton, 2001).

Hamlin, Christopher, *Cholera: The Biography* (Oxford: Oxford University Press, 2009).

———, *Public Health and Social Justice in the Age of Chadwick: Britain, 1800–1854* (Cambridge: Cambridge University Press, 1998).

———, *A Science of Impurity: Water Analysis in Nineteenth-Century Britain* (Berkeley:
University of California Press, 1990).

———, '"Waters" or "Water"? Master Narratives in Water History and Their Implications
for Contemporary Water Policy', *Water Policy* vol. 2 (2000), 313–25.

Hammarlund, Cecilia, and Anna Andersson, 'What's in It for Africa? European Union Fishing
Access Agreements and Fishery Exports from Developing Countries', *World Development*
vol. 113 (2019), 172–85.

Hanley, Susan B., 'Urban Sanitation in Preindustrial Japan', in: Lionel Frost (ed.), *Urbanization and the Pacific World, 1500–1900* (London: Routledge, 2017), 135–60.

Hansen, Peo, and Stefan Jonsson, 'Another Colonialism: Africa in the History of European
Integration', *Journal of Historical Sociology* vol. 27 (2014), 442–61.

———, *Eurafrica: The Untold History of European Integration and Colonialism* (London:
Bloomsbury, 2014).

Hardiman, David, 'Small-Dam Systems of the Sahyadris', in: David Arnold and Ramachandra Guha (eds), *Nature, Culture, Imperialism: Essays on the Environmental History of
South Asia* (New Delhi: Oxford University Press, 1995), 185–209.

Harley, John Brian, *The New Nature of Maps: Essays in the History of Cartography* (Baltimore, MD: Johns Hopkins University Press, 2001).

Harms, Robert, 'The End of Red Rubber: A Reassessment', *Journal of African History*
vol. 16 (1975), 73–88.

Harrell, Stevan (ed.), *Cultural Encounters on China's Ethnic Frontiers* (Seattle: University of Washington Press, 1995).

Harrison, Mark, *Climates and Constitutions: Health, Race, Environment, and British Imperialism in India, 1600–1850* (Oxford: Oxford University Press, 1999).

——, *Disease in the Modern World: 1500 to the Present Day* (Cambridge, UK: Polity, 2004).

——, *Public Health in British India: Anglo-Indian Preventive Medicine, 1859–1914* (Cambridge: Cambridge University Press, 1994).

Hart, David, *The Volta River Project: A Case Study in Politics and Technology* (Edinburgh: Edinburgh University Press, 1980).

Hasenöhrl, Ute, 'Rural Electrification in the British Empire', *History of Retailing and Consumption* vol. 4 (2018), 10–27.

Hausfather, Zeke, 'Explainer: Will Global Warming "Stop" as Soon as Net-Zero Emissions Are Reached?', *CarbonBrief*, 29 April 2021, https://www.carbonbrief.org/explainer-will-global-warming-stop-as-soon-as-net-zero-emissions-are-reached/.

Hausman, William J., Peter Hertner and Mira Wilkins, *Global Electrification: Multinational Enterprise and International Finance in the History of Light and Power, 1878–2007* (Cambridge: Cambridge University Press, 2008).

Havinden, Michael, and David Meredith, *Colonialism and Development: Britain and Its Tropical Colonies, 1850–1960* (London: Routledge, 1993).

Hay, Michelle, Jamie Skinner and Andrew Norton, 'Dam-Induced Displacement and Resettlement: A Literature Review', FutureDAMS Working Paper 004 (11 September 2019).

Hazell, Peter B. R., 'The Asian Green Revolution', International Food Policy Research Institute discussion paper 00911 (November 2009).

Headrick, Daniel R., *Power over Peoples: Technology, Environments, and Western Imperialism, 1400 to the Present* (Princeton, NJ: Princeton University Press, 2010).

——, *The Tentacles of Progress: Technology Transfer in the Age of Imperialism, 1850–1940* (Oxford: Oxford University Press, 1988).

——, *The Tools of Empire: Technology and European Imperialism in the Nineteenth Century* (Oxford: Oxford University Press, 1981).

Hedinger, Daniel, and Nadin Heé, 'Transimperial History: Connectivity, Cooperation and Competition', *Journal of Modern European History* vol. 16 (2018), 429–52.

Heffernan, Michael J., 'Bringing the Desert to Bloom: French Ambitions in the Sahara Desert during the Late Nineteenth Century—The Strange Case of "la mer intérieure"', in: Denis Cosgrove and Geoff Petts (eds), *Water, Engineering, and Landscape: Water Control and Landscape Transformation in the Modern Period* (London: Belhaven, 1990), 94–114.

Hernon, Ian, *Britain's Forgotten Wars: Colonial Campaigns of the Nineteenth Century* (Stroud, UK: Sutton, 2003).

Hersoug, Bjørn, Svein Jentoft and Poul Degnbol, *Fisheries Development: The Institutional Challenge* (Delft: Eburon, 2004).

Hettne, Björn, *The Political Economy of Indirect Rule: Mysore, 1881–1947* (London: Curzon, 1978).

Hill, Christopher V., *River of Sorrow: Environment and Social Control in Riparian North India, 1770–1914* (Ann Arbor, MI: Association for Asian Studies, 1997).

——, 'Water and Power: Riparian Legislation and Agrarian Control in Colonial Bengal', *Environmental History Review* vol. 14, no. 4 (1990), 1–20.

Hill, M. F., *Permanent Way: The Story of the Kenya and Uganda Railway* (Nairobi: East African Railways, 1950).

Hirsch, Philip, 'The Shifting Regional Geopolitics of Mekong Dams', *Political Geography* vol. 51 (2016), 63–74.

Hoag, Heather J., *Developing the Rivers of East and West Africa: An Environmental History* (London: Bloomsbury, 2013).

———, 'Transplanting the TVA? International Contributions to Postwar River Development in Tanzania', *Comparative Technology Transfer and Society* vol. 4 (2006), 247–67.

Hoag, Heather J., and M.-B Öhman, 'Turning Water into Power: Debates over the Development of Tanzania's Rufiji River Basin, 1945–1985', *Technology and Culture* vol. 49 (2008), 624–51.

Hoanh, C. T., T. P Tuong, J. W. Gowing and B. Hardy, *Environment and Livelihoods in Tropical Coastal Zones: Managing Agriculture-Fishery-Aquaculture Conflicts* (Wallingford, UK: CAB International, 2006).

Hochschild, Adam, *King Leopold's Ghost: A Story of Greed, Terror, and Heroism in Colonial Africa* (London: Macmillan, 1999).

Hodge, Joseph Morgan, *Triumph of the Expert: Agrarian Doctrines of Development and the Legacies of British Colonialism* (Athens: Ohio University Press, 2007).

Hoey, Brian, 'Nationalism in Indonesia: Building Imagined and Intentional Communities through Transmigration', *Ethnology* vol. 42 (2003), 109–26.

Hoffmann, Richard C., 'A Brief History of Aquatic Resource Use in Medieval Europe', *Helgoland Marine Research* vol. 59 (2005), 22–30.

Hofmeyr, Isabel, Uma Dhupelia-Mesthrie and Preben Kaarsholm, 'Durban and Cape Town as Port Cities: Reconsidering Southern African Studies from the Indian Ocean', *Journal of Southern African Studies* vol. 42 (2016), 375–87.

Holt, Emily (ed.), *Water and Power in Past Societies* (Albany: State University of New York Press, 2018).

Home, Robert, *City of Blood Revisited: A New Look at the Benin Expedition of 1897* (London: Collings, 1982).

Hopkins, Benjamin D., *Ruling the Savage Periphery: Frontier Governance and the Making of the Modern State* (Cambridge, MA: Harvard University Press, 2020).

Hornborg, Alf, 'Footprints in the Cotton Fields: The Industrial Revolution as Time–Space Appropriation and Environmental Load Displacement', *Ecological Economics* vol. 59 (2006), 74–81.

———, *Global Ecology and Unequal Exchange: Fetishism in a Zero-Sum World* (London: Routledge, 2012).

Hosagrahar, Jyoti, *Indigenous Modernities: Negotiating Architecture and Urbanism* (London: Routledge, 2005).

Hossain, Arif, and Sultana Shafeem, 'Frequency of Bay of Bengal Cyclonic Storms and Depressions Crossing Different Coastal Zones', *International Journal of Climatology* vol. 23 (2003), 1119–25.

Howell, Paul Philip, 'East Africa's Water Requirements: The Equatorial Nile Project and the Nile Waters Agreement of 1929; A Brief Historical Review', in: Howell and Allan, *Nile*, 81–107.

Howell, Paul Philip, and John Anthony Allan (eds), *The Nile, Sharing a Scarce Resource: A Historical and Technical Review of Water Management of Economic and Legal Issues* (Cambridge: Cambridge University Press, 1994).

Huber, Valeska, *Channelling Mobilities: Migration and Globalisation in the Suez Canal Region and Beyond, 1869–1914* (Cambridge: Cambridge University Press, 2013).

———, 'The Unification of the Globe by Disease? The International Sanitary Conferences on Cholera, 1851–1894', *Historical Journal* vol. 49 (2006), 453–76.

Huff, Gregg, 'Causes and Consequences of the Great Vietnam Famine, 1944–5', *Economic History Review* vol. 72 (2019), 286–316.

———, 'The Great Second World War Vietnam and Java Famines', *Modern Asian Studies* vol. 54 (2020), 618–53.

Hughes, David McDermott, 'Whites and Water: How Euro-Africans Made Nature at Kariba Dam', *Journal of Southern African Studies* vol. 32 (2006), 823–38.

Hughes, Thomas P., *Networks of Power: Electrification in Western Societies, 1880–1930* (Baltimore, MD: Johns Hopkins University Press, 1983).

Hundley, Norris, *The Great Thirst: Californians and Water, 1770s–1990s* (Berkeley: University of California Press, 1992).

Hunter, Louis, *Waterpower in the Century of the Steam Engine* (Charlottesville: University of Virginia Press, 1979).

Husain, Faisal H., *Rivers of the Sultan: The Tigris and Euphrates in the Ottoman Empire* (Oxford: Oxford University Press, 2021).

Huybrechts, André, *Transports et structures de développement au Congo: Étude du progrès économique de 1900 à 1970* (Paris: Mouton, 1970).

Iheduru, Okechukwu C., 'The Political Economy of Euro-African Fishing Agreements', *Journal of Developing Areas* vol. 30 (1995), 63–90.

IPCC, *Global Warming of 1.5°C: An IPCC Special Report on the Impacts of Global Warming of 1.5°C above Pre-industrial Levels and Related Global Greenhouse Gas Emission Pathways, in the Context of Strengthening the Global Response to the Threat of Climate Change, Sustainable Development, and Efforts to Eradicate Poverty*, ed. by Masson-Delmotte, V., P. Zhai, H.-O. Pörtner, D. Roberts, J. Skea, P.R. Shukla, A. Pirani, W. Moufouma-Okia, C. Péan, R. Pidcock, S. Connors, J.B.R. Matthews, Y. Chen, X. Zhou, M.I. Gomis, E. Lonnoy, T. Maycock, M. Tignor, and T. Waterfield (Cambridge: Cambridge University Press, 2018), https://www.ipcc.ch/sr15/chapter/spm/.

——, *Summary for Policymakers*, in: *Climate Change 2022: Impacts, Adaptation, and Vulnerability. Contribution of Working Group II to the Sixth Assessment Report of the Intergovernmental Panel on Climate Change*, ed. by H.-O. Pörtner, D. C. Roberts, M. Tignor, E. S. Poloczanska, K. Mintenbeck, A. Alegría, M. Craig, S. Langsdorf, S. Löschke, V. Möller, A. Okem, and B. Rama (Cambridge: Cambridge University Press, 2022), 3–33.

Iqbal, Iftekhar, *The Bengal Delta: Ecology, State, and Social Change, 1840–1943* (Basingstoke, UK: Palgrave Macmillan, 2010).

Isaacman, Allen F., and Barbara S. Isaacman, *Dams, Displacement, and the Delusion of Development: Cahora Bassa and Its Legacies in Mozambique* (Athens: Ohio University Press, 2013).

Isaacman, Allen F., and Chris Sneddon, 'Toward a Social and Environmental History of the Building of Cahora Bassa Dam', *Journal of Southern African Studies* vol. 26 (2000), 597–632.

Islam, M. Mufakharul, *Irrigation, Agriculture and the Raj: Punjab, 1887–1947* (New Delhi: Manohar, 1997).

Ismail, Shehab, 'Epicures and Experts: The Drinking Water Controversy in British Colonial Cairo', *Arab Studies Journal* vol. 26, no. 2 (2018), 9–43.

Jacobs, Inga M., *The Politics of Water in Africa: Norms, Environmental Regions and Trans-boundary Cooperation in the Orange-Senqu and Nile Rivers* (London: Continuum, 2012).

Jacobs, Jeffrey W., 'Mekong Committee History and Lessons for River Basin Development', *Geographical Journal* vol. 161 (1995), 135–48.

Jaenike, John, 'Comment on "Impacts of Biodiversity Loss on Ocean Ecosystem Services"', *Science* vol. 316, no. 5829 (2007), 1285.

Jakobsson, Eva, 'Industrialization of Rivers: A Water System Approach to Hydropower Development', *Knowledge, Technology and Policy* vol. 14, no. 4 (December 2002), 41–56.

Jansen, Jan C., and Jürgen Osterhammel, *Decolonization: A Short History* (Princeton, NJ: Princeton University Press, 2017).

Jansen, Marius B., *The Making of Modern Japan* (Cambridge, MA: Belknap Press of Harvard University Press, 2000).

Jayanthi, M., S. Thirumurthy, M. Muralidhar and P. Ravichandran, 'Impact of Shrimp Aquaculture Development on Important Ecosystems in India', *Global Environmental Change* vol. 52 (2018), 10–21.

Jennings, Christian, 'Unexploited Assets: Imperial Imagination, Practical Limitations, and Marine Fisheries Research in East Africa, 1917–53', in: Brett M. Bennett and Joseph M. Hodge (eds), *Science and Empire: Knowledge and Networks of Science across the British Empire, 1800–1970* (Basingstoke, UK: Palgrave Macmillan, 2011), 253–74.

Jennings, Eric T., *Curing the Colonizers: Hydrotherapy, Climatology, and French Colonial Spas* (Durham, NC: Duke University Press, 2006).

——, *Vichy in the Tropics: Petain's National Revolution in Madagascar, Guadeloupe, and Indochina, 1940–1944* (Stanford, CA: Stanford University Press, 2001).

Jerónimo, Miguel Bandeira, and António Costa Pinto (eds), *The Ends of European Colonial Empires: Cases and Comparisons* (Basingstoke, UK: Palgrave Macmillan, 2015).

Jobin, William, *Dams and Disease: Ecological Design and Health Impacts of Large Dams, Canals and Irrigation Systems* (London: E. and F. N. Spon, 1999).

Jones, Christopher, *Routes of Power: Energy and Modern America* (Cambridge, MA: Harvard University Press, 2014).

Jones, Eric, *The European Miracle: Environments, Economies and Geopolitics in the History of Europe and Asia*, 3rd ed. (Cambridge: Cambridge University Press, 2003).

Joseph, Sabrina, 'Islamic Law and the Management of Natural Resources in Seventeenth and Eighteenth Century Ottoman Syria', *Environment and History* vol. 21 (2015), 227–56.

Josupeit, Helga, 'A Survey of External Assistance to the Fisheries Sector in Developing Countries, 1978 to 1985', FAO Fisheries Circular no. 755, rev. 2 (1987), 8–10.

Kaczynski, Vlad, 'Foreign Fishing Fleets in the Sub-Saharan EEZ: The Coastal State Perspective', *Marine Policy* vol. 13 (1989), 2–15.

Kaczynski, Vlad, and David Fluherty, 'European Policies in West Africa: Who Benefits from Fisheries Agreements?', *Marine Policy* vol. 26 (2002), 75–93.

Kaika, Maria, *City of Flows: Modernity, Nature, and the City* (London: Routledge, 2005).

Kale, Sunila S., 'Structures of Power: Electrification in Colonial India', *Comparative Studies of South Asia, Africa and the Middle East* vol. 34 (2014), 454–75.

Kamissek, Christoph, and Jonas Kreienbaum, 'An Imperial Cloud? Conceptualising Interimperial Connections and Transimperial Knowledge', *Journal of Modern European History* vol. 14 (2016), 164–82.

Kander, Astrid, Paolo Malanima and Paul Warde, *Power to the People: Energy in Europe over the Last Five Centuries* (Princeton, NJ: Princeton University Press, 2013).

Karlsson, Andreas, 'Water and Climate', Stockholm International Water Institute, n.d., accessed 12 December 2022, https://siwi.org/why-water/water-climate/.

Keay, John, *Mad about the Mekong: Exploration and Empire in South East Asia* (London: HarperCollins, 2005).

——, 'The Mekong Exploration Commission, 1866–68: Anglo-French Rivalry in South East Asia', *Asian Affairs* vol. 36 (2005), 289–312.

Keene, Derek, 'Cities and Empires', *Journal of Urban History* vol. 32 (2005), 8–21.

Keeton, Charles Lee, *King Thebaw and the Ecological Rape of Burma: The Political and Commercial Struggle between British India and French Indo-China in Burma 1878–1886* (Delhi: Manohar, 1974).

Kelman, Ari, *A River and Its City: The Nature of Landscape in New Orleans* (Berkeley: University of California Press, 2006).

Kerr, Ian J., *Engines of Change: The Railroads that Made India* (Westport, CT: Praeger, 2007).

Khagram, Sanjeev, *Dams and Development: Transnational Struggles for Water and Power* (Ithaca, NY: Cornell University Press, 2004).

Khan, Yasmin, *The Great Partition* (New Haven, CT: Yale University Press, 2017).

Kim, Diana S., *Empires of Vice: The Rise of Opium Prohibition across Southeast Asia* (Princeton, NJ: Princeton University Press, 2020).

Kingsbury, Benjamin, *An Imperial Disaster: The Bengal Cyclone of 1876* (Oxford: Oxford University Press, 2019).

Kinloch, Robert F., 'The Growth of Electric Power Production in Malaya', *Annals of the Association of American Geographers* vol. 56 (1966), 220–35.

Kinsey, Darin, '"Seeding the Water as the Earth": The Epicenter and Peripheries of a Western Aquacultural Revolution', *Environmental History* vol. 11 (2006), 527–66.

Kirchberger, Ulrike, and Brett M. Bennett (eds), *Environments of Empire: Networks and Agents of Ecological Change* (Chapel Hill: University of North Carolina Press, 2020).

Kitchens, Carl, 'The Role of Publicly Provided Electricity in Economic Development: The Experience of the Tennessee Valley Authority, 1929–1955', *Journal of Economic History* vol. 74 (2014), 389–419.

Kjellén, Marianne, *From Public Pipes to Private Hands: Water Access and Distribution in Dar es Salaam* (Stockholm: Department of Human Geography, Stockholm University, 2006).

Kjellén, Marianne, and Gordon McGranahan, *Informal Water Vendors and the Urban Poor* (London: International Institute for Environment and Development, 2006).

Klein, Ira, 'Urban Development and Death: Bombay City, 1870–1914', *Modern Asian Studies* vol. 20 (1986), 725–54.

Klingensmith, Daniel, *'One Valley and a Thousand': Dams, Nationalism, and Development* (New Delhi: Oxford University Press, 2007).

Kolding, Jeppe, and Paul van Zwieten, *Improving Productivity in Tropical Lakes and Reservoirs* (Cairo: WorldFish Center, 2006).

Koncagül, Engin, Michael Tran and Richard Connor, *United Nations World Water Development Report 2020* (Perugia: UNESCO WWAP, 2020).

Kooy, Michelle, and Karen Bakker, '(Post)Colonial Pipes: Urban Water Supply in Colonial and Contemporary Jakarta', in: Freek Colombijn and Joost Coté (eds), *Cars, Conduits, and Kampongs: The Modernization of the Indonesian City* (Leiden: Brill, 2015), 63–86.

——, 'Splintered Networks: The Colonial and Contemporary Waters of Jakarta', *Geoforum* vol. 39 (2008), 1843–58.

Koranteng, Kwame Abu, and Daniel Pauly, 'Long-Term Trends in Demersal Fishery Resources of Ghana in Response to Fishing Pressure', in: Pierre Chavance, Moctar Bâ, Didier Gascuel, Jan Michael Vakily and Daniel Pauly (eds), *Pêcheries maritimes, écosystèmes et sociétés en Afrique de l'Ouest: Un demi-siècle de changement* (Luxembourg: Office des publications officielles des Communautés européennes, 2005), 243–52.

Kravtsova, V. I., V. N. Mikhailov and N. A. Efremova, 'Variations of the Hydrological Regime, Morphological Structure, and Landscapes of the Indus River Delta (Pakistan) under the Effect of Large-Scale Water Management Measures', *Water Resources* vol. 36 (2009), 365–79.

Kumar, Krishan, 'Colony and Empire, Colonialism and Imperialism: A Meaningful Distinction?', *Comparative Studies in Society and History* vol. 63 (2021), 280–309.

Kurien, John, *Ruining the Commons and Responses of the Commoners: Coastal Overfishing and Fishermen's Actions in Kerala State, India* (Geneva: United Nations Research Institute for Social Development, 1991).

——, 'Technical Assistance Projects and Socio-economic Change: Norwegian Intervention in Kerala's Fisheries Development', *Economic and Political Weekly* vol. 20 (1985), A-70–88.

Lacroze, Luc, *Les grands pionniers du Mékong: Une cinquantaine d'années d'aventures 1884-1935* (Paris: L'Harmattan, 1996).

Lagendijk, Vincent, *Electrifying Europe: The Power of Europe in the Construction of Electricity Networks* (Amsterdam: Aksant, 2008).

———, 'From American South to Global South: The TVA's Experts and Expertise, 1933-1998', in F. Trentmann, A.-B. Sum and M. Rivera (eds), *Work in Progress: Economy and Environment in the Hands of Experts* (Munich: Oekom, 2018), 79-101.

———, 'Streams of Knowledge: River Development Knowledge and the TVA on the River Mekong', *History and Technology* vol. 35 (2019), 316-37.

Lagus, Charles, *Operation Noah* (London: William Kimber, 1959).

Lahiri-Dutt, Kuntala, 'Large Dams and Changes in an Agrarian Society: Gendering the Impacts of Damodar Valley Corporation in Eastern India', *Water Alternatives* vol. 5 (2012), 529-42.

Lahiri-Dutt, Kuntala, and Gopa Samanta, *Dancing with the River: People and Life on the Chars of South Asia* (New Haven, CT: Yale University Press, 2013).

Landes, David S., *Bankers and Pashas: International Finance and Economic Imperialism in Egypt* (Cambridge, MA: Harvard University Press, 1958).

Landry, Marc, 'Europe's Battery: The Making of the Alpine Energy Landscape, 1870-1955', PhD dissertation, Georgetown University, 2013.

Lanthier, Pierre, 'L'électrification de Bombay avant 1920: Le projet de Jamsetji N. Tata', in: Dominique Barjot, Daniel Lefeuvre, Arnaud Berthonnet and Sopie Coeuré (eds), *L'électrification outre-mer de la fin du XIXe siècle aux premières décolonisations* (Paris: Société française d'histoire d'outre-mer, 2000), 211-33.

Laparra, Maurice, 'Enelcam – Alucam: L'énergie hydroélectrique du Cameroun à la rencontre de l'aluminium', *Outre-mers: Revue d'histoire* vol. 89 (2002), 177-200.

Larrue, Jacques, *Fria en Guinée: Première usine d'alumine en terre d'Afrique* (Paris: Karthala, 1997).

Latour, Bruno, *Reassembling the Social: An Introduction to Actor-Network-Theory* (Oxford: Oxford University Press, 2005).

Lawson, Fred H., 'Egypt, Ethiopia, and the Nile River: The Continuing Dispute', *Mediterranean Quarterly* vol. 27 (2016), 97-121.

Lawson, Rowena M., and Eric A. Kwei, *African Entrepreneurship and Economic Growth: A Case Study of the Fishing Industry of Ghana* (Accra: Ghana Universities Press, 1974).

Lawson, Rowena M., and Michael Robinson, 'Artisanal Fisheries in West Africa: Problems of Management Implementation', *Marine Policy* vol. 7 (1983), 279-90.

Le Coq, J. F., G. Trébuil and M. Dufumier, 'History of Rice Production in the Mekong Delta', in: Peter Boomgaard and David Henley (eds), *Smallholders and Stockbreeders: History of Foodcrop and Livestock Farming in Southeast Asia* (Leiden: KITLV, 2004), 163-85.

Lederer, André, *Histoire de la navigation au Congo* (Tervuren, Belgium: Musée Royal de l'Afrique Centrale, 1965).

Lehmann, Philipp, *Desert Edens: Colonial Climate Engineering in the Age of Anxiety* (Princeton, NJ: Princeton University Press, 2022).

Lehmann, Philipp, 'Infinite Power to Change the World: Hydroelectricity and Engineered Climate Change in the Atlantropa Project', *American Historical Review* vol. 121 (2016), 70-100.

Létolle, René, and Hocine Bendjoudi, *Histoires d'une mer au Sahara: Utopies et politiques* (Paris: L'Harmattan, 1997).

Lévêque, Christian, *Biodiversity Dynamics and Conservation: The Freshwater Fish of Tropical Africa* (Cambridge: Cambridge University Press, 1997).

Lévêque, Christian, J. Lazard and D. Paugy, 'Pêche et pisciculture continentales et marines au cours du XXe siècle', in: Philippe Bonnichon, Pierre Gény and Jean Nemo (eds), *Présences françaises outre-mer: XVIe–XXIe siècles* (Paris: Karthala, 2012), 91–118.

Lewis, Su Lin, *Cities in Motion: Urban Life and Cosmopolitanism in Southeast Asia, 1920–1940* (Cambridge: Cambridge University Press, 2016).

Ley, Lukas, *Building on Borrowed Time: Rising Seas and Failing Infrastructure in Semarang* (Minneapolis: University of Minnesota Press, 2021).

Ley, Lukas, and Franz Krause, 'Ethnographic Conversations with Wittfogel's Ghost: An Introduction', *Environment and Planning C: Politics and Space* vol. 37 (2019): 1151–60.

Li, Tana, '"The Sea Becomes Mulberry Fields and Mulberry Fields Become the Sea": Dikes in the Eastern Red River delta, c. 200 BCE to the Twenty-First Century CE', in: Greg Bankoff and Joe Christensen (eds), *Natural Hazards and Peoples in the Indian Ocean World: Bordering on Danger* (New York: Palgrave Macmillan, 2016), 55–78.

Lilford, Richard J., Oyinlola Oyebode, David Satterthwaite, G. J. Melendez-Torres, Yen-Fu Chen, Blessing Mberu, Samuel I. Watson, et al.,'The Health of People who Live in Slums 2: Improving the Health and Welfare of People who Live in Slums', *Lancet* vol. 389, no. 10068 (2017), 559–70.

Linstrum, Erik, Stuart Ward, Vanessa Ogle, Saima Nasar and Priyamvada Gopal, 'Decolonizing Britain: An Exchange', *Twentieth Century British History* vol. 33, (2022), 274–303.

Linton, Jamie, and Jessica Budds, 'The Hydrosocial Cycle: Defining and Mobilizing a Relational-Dialectical Approach to water', *Geoforum* vol. 57 (2014), 170–80.

Liston, John, *An Evaluation of Fishery and Aquaculture Programs of the Agency for International Development* (Washington, DC: US National Academy Press, 1982).

Locher, Fabien, 'Neo-Malthusian Environmentalism, World Fisheries Crisis, and the Global Commons, 1950s–1970s', *Historical Journal* vol. 63 (2020), 187–207.

Loftus, Alex, 'Rethinking Political Ecologies of Water', *Third World Quarterly* vol. 30 (2009), 953–68.

Long, Ngo Vinh, *Before the Revolution: The Vietnamese Peasants under the French* (New York: Columbia University Press, 1991), 122–33.

Longhurst, Alan, *Mismanagement of Marine Fisheries* (Cambridge: Cambridge University Press, 2010).

Lowe, S., M. Browne, S. Boudjelas and M. De Poorter, *100 of the World's Worst Invasive Alien Species: A Selection from the Global Invasive Species Database* (International Union for Conservation of Nature, 2004).

Lucassen, Jan, 'The Brickmakers' Strikes on the Ganges Canal in 1848–1849', *International Review of Social History* vol. 51 (2006), 47–83.

Ludden, David, 'The Process of Empire: Frontiers and Borderlands', in: C. A. Bayly and Peter Fibiger Bang (eds), *Tributary Empires in Global History* (New York: Palgrave Macmillan, 2011), 132–50.

Lynn, Martin, 'Change and Continuity in the British Palm Oil Trade with West Africa, 1830–55', *Journal of African History* vol. 22 (1981), 331–48.

——, *Commerce and Economic Change in West Africa: The Palm Oil Trade in the Nineteenth Century* (Cambridge: Cambridge University Press, 1997).

——, 'From Sail to Steam: The Impact of the Steamship Services on the British Palm Oil Trade with West Africa, 1850–1890', *Journal of African History* vol. 30 (1989), 227–45.

MacLeod, Roy M., *Nature and Empire. Science and the Colonial Enterprise* (Chicago: University of Chicago Press, 2000).

Macleod, Roy, and Milton Lewis (eds), *Disease, Medicine, and Empire: Perspectives on Western Medicine and the Experience of European Expansion* (London: Routledge, 1988).

Maier, Charles S., 'Consigning the Twentieth Century to History: Alternative Narratives for the Modern Era', *American Historical Review* 105 (2000), 807–31.

——— *Once within Borders: Territories of Power, Wealth, and Belonging since 1500* (Cambridge, MA: Belknap Press of Harvard University Press, 2016).

Maldonado, Julie, T. M. Bull Bennett, Karletta Chief, Patricia Cochran, Karen Cozzetto, Bob Gough, et al., 'Engagement with Indigenous Peoples and Honoring Traditional Knowledge Systems', in: Katharine Jacobs, Susanne Moser and James Buizer (eds), *The US National Climate Assessment* (Cham, Switzerland: Springer, 2016), 111–26.

Malm, Andreas, *Fossil Capital: The Rise of Steam Power and the Roots of Global Warming* (London: Verso, 2016).

Mani, J. S., 'A Coastal Conservation Programme for the Chennai Sea Shore, India: A Case Study', *Journal of Coastal Conservation* vol. 7 (2001), 23–30.

Mann, Michael, 'Delhi's Belly: On the Management of Water, Sewage and Excreta in a Changing Urban Environment during the Nineteenth Century', *Studies in History* vol. 23 (2007), 1–31.

Marçot, Jean-Louis, *Une mer au Sahara: Mirages de la colonisation, Algérie et Tunisie, 1869–1887* (Paris: Éditions de la Différence, 2003).

Markovits, Claude, *The Global World of Indian Merchants, 1750–1947: Traders of Sind from Bukhara to Panama* (Cambridge: Cambridge University Press, 2000).

Marks, Robert B., *Tigers, Rice, Silk and Silt: Environment and Economy in Late Imperial South China* (Cambridge: Cambridge University Press, 1998).

Marr, David G., *Vietnam 1945: The Quest for Power* (Berkeley: University of California Press, 1997).

———, *Vietnam: State, War, and Revolution (1945–1946)* (Berkeley: University of California Press, 2013).

Marsden, Ben, and Crosbie Smith, *Engineering Empires. A Cultural History of Technology in Nineteenth-Century Britain* (Basingstoke, UK: Palgrave Macmillan, 2005).

Marsh McLennan Ltd, *Sunk Costs: The Socio-Economic Impacts of Flooding* (2021).

Marsot, Afaf Lutfi al-Sayyid, *Egypt in the Reign of Muhammad Ali* (Cambridge: Cambridge University Press, 1984).

Martinez-Alier, Joan, *The Environmentalism of the Poor: A Study of Ecological Conflicts and Valuation* (Cheltenham, UK: Edward Elgar, 2002).

Masselos, Jim, 'Jobs and Jobbery: The Sweeper in Bombay under the Raj', *Indian Economic and Social History Review* vol. 19 (1981), 101–39.

Mauch, Christoph, and Christian Pfister (eds), *Natural Disasters, Cultural Responses: Case Studies Towards a Global Environmental History* (Lanham, MD: Lexington, 2009).

M'Bokolo, Elikia, 'Peste et société urbaine à Dakar: L'épidémie de 1914', *Cahiers d'études Africaines* vol. 22, nos 85/86 (1982), 13–46.

McCaskie, Tom C., 'Water Wars in Kumasi, Ghana', in: Francesca Locatelli and Paul Nugent (eds), *African Cities: Competing Claims on Urban Spaces* (Leiden: Brill, 2009), 135–55.

McCully, Patrick, *Silenced Rivers: The Ecology and Politics of Large Dams* (London: Zed, 1996).

McDougall, James, *A History of Algeria* (Cambridge: Cambridge University Press, 2017).

McDougall, James, and Judith Scheele, *Saharan Frontiers: Space and Mobility in Northwest Africa* (Bloomington: Indiana University Press, 2012).

McEvoy, Arthur, *The Fisherman's Problem: Ecology and Law in the California Fisheries, 1850–1980* (Cambridge: Cambridge University Press, 1986).

McFarlane, Colin, 'Governing the Contaminated City: Infrastructure and Sanitation in Colonial and Post-Colonial Bombay', *International Journal of Urban and Regional Research* vol. 32 (2008), 415–35.

McGregor, JoAnn, *Crossing the Zambezi: The Politics of Landscape on a Central African Frontier* (Oxford: James Currey, 2009).

———, 'Living with the River: Landscape and Memory in the Zambezi Valley, Northwest Zimbabwe', in William Beinart and JoAnn McGregor (eds), *Social History and African Environments* (Oxford: James Currey, 2003), 87–105.

Mchome, Emanuel Lukio, '"Blackout Blues": A Socio-cultural History of Vulnerable Electricity Networks and Resilient Users in Dar es Salaam, 1920–2020', PhD dissertation, Technische Universität Darmstadt, 2022.

McKittrick, Meredith, 'An Empire of Rivers: The Scheme to Flood the Kalahari, 1919–1945', *Journal of Southern African Studies* vol. 41 (2015), 485–504.

McLean, Stuart, 'Black Goo: Forceful Encounters with Matter in Europe's Muddy Margins', *Cultural Anthropology* vol. 26 (2011), 589–619.

McNeill, John R., *Something New under the Sun* (London: Penguin, 2000).

Medrano, Anthony D., 'The Edible Tide: How Estuaries and Migrants Transformed the Straits of Melaka, 1870–1940', *Journal of Southeast Asian Studies* vol. 51 (2020), 579–96.

Mehsud, Muhammad Imran, 'Lilienthal's "Another 'Korea' in the Making?" From the Cold War to the Indus Waters Treaty', *World Water Policy* vol. 6 (2020), 202–11.

Meiton, Fredrik, *Electrical Palestine: Capital and Technology from Empire to Nation* (Berkeley: University of California Press, 2019).

Melillo, Edward D., 'Making Sea Cucumbers out of Whales' Teeth: Nantucket Castaways and Encounters of Value in Nineteenth-Century Fiji', *Environmental History* vol. 20 (2015), 449–74.

Melosi, Martin, *Precious Commodity: Providing Water for America's Cities* (Pittsburgh, PA: Pittsburgh University Press, 2011).

———, *The Sanitary City: Environmental Services in Urban America from Colonial Times to the Present* (Pittsburgh, PA: University of Pittsburgh Press, 2008).

———, *Water in North American History* (London: Routledge, 2022).

Mercer, Harriet, 'Colonialism's Climatic Legacies', *On History*, 31 March 2021.

———, 'The Link between Colonialism and Climate Change Examined', *Week*, 25 April 2022.

Metcalf, Thomas R., 'Colonial Cities', in: Peter Clark (ed.), *Oxford Handbook of Cities in World History* (Oxford: Oxford University Press, 2013), 753–69.

———, *Imperial Connections: India in the Indian Ocean Arena, 1860–1920* (Berkeley: University of California Press, 2007).

Michel, Aloys Arthur, *The Indus Rivers: A Study of the Effects of Partition* (New Haven, CT: Yale University Press, 1967).

Miescher, Stephan F., '"Nkrumah's Baby": The Akosombo Dam and the Dream of Development in Ghana, 1952–1966', *Water History* vol. 6 (2014), 341–66.

Mikhail, Alan, *Nature and Empire in Ottoman Egypt: An Environmental History* (Cambridge: Cambridge University Press, 2011).

Miller, Peter N. (ed.), *The Sea: Thalassography and Historiography* (Ann Arbor: University of Michigan Press, 2013).

Minard, Pete, *All Things Harmless, Useful, and Ornamental: Environmental Transformation through Species Acclimatization, from Colonial Australia to the World* (Chapel Hill: University of North Carolina Press, 2019).

Mirosa, Oriol, and Leila M. Harris, 'Human Right to Water: Contemporary Challenges and Contours of a Global Debate', *Antipode* vol. 44 (2012), 932–49.

Mishra, Dinesh Kumar, 'The Bihar Flood Story', *Economic and Political Weekly* vol. 32, no. 35 (1997), 2206–17.

Misser, François, *La saga d'Inga: L'histoire des barrages du fleuve Congo* (Paris: L'Harmattan, 2013).

Mitchell, Timothy, *Carbon Democracy: Political Power in the Age of Oil* (London: Verso, 2011).

———, *Colonising Egypt* (Cambridge: Cambridge University Press, 1988).

———, *Rule of Experts: Egypt, Techno-politics, Modernity* (Berkeley: University of California Press, 2002).

Mizuno, Hiromi, Aaron S. Moore and John DiMoia (eds), *Engineering Asia: Technology, Colonial Development, and the Cold War Order* (London: Bloomsbury, 2020).

Montaño, Diana, *Electrifying Mexico: Technology and the Transformation of a Modern City* (Austin: University of Texas Press, 2021).

Montesano, Michael J., and Ian Brown, 'A Colonial Economy in Crisis: Burma's Rice Cultivators and the World Depression of the 1930s', *Journal of Southeast Asian Studies* vol. 40 (2009), 417–29.

Moon, Suzanne, 'Takeoff or Self-Sufficiency? Ideologies of Development in Indonesia, 1957–1961', *Technology and Culture* vol. 39 (1998), 187–212.

———, *Technology and Ethical Idealism: A History of Development in the Netherlands East Indies* (Leiden: CNWS, 2007).

Moore, Aaron S., *Constructing East Asia: Technology, Ideology, and Empire in Japan's Wartime Era, 1931–1945* (Stanford: Stanford University Press, 2013).

———, '"The Yalu River Era of Developing Asia": Japanese Expertise, Colonial Power, and the Construction of Sup'ung Dam', *Journal of Asian Studies* vol. 72 (2013), 115–39.

Moore, Gerald K., *The Implementation of the New Law of the Sea in West Africa: Prospects for the Development and Management of Marine Resources* (Halifax, NS: Dalhousie University, Dalhousie Ocean Studies Programme, 1985).

Moore, Jason W., *Capitalism in the Web of Life: Ecology and the Accumulation of Capital* (London: Verso, 2015).

Morgan, G., and D. Staples, *The History of Industrial Marine Fisheries in Southeast Asia* (Bangkok: FAO, 2006).

Mosley, Paul, *Obstacles to the Spread of the Green Revolution in Africa: Some Initial Thoughts* (Manchester: University of Manchester, Institute for Development Policy and Management, 1992).

Mosley, Stephen, 'Coastal Cities and Environmental Change', *Environment and History* vol. 20 (2014), 517–33.

Mosse, David, *The Rule of Water: Statecraft, Ecology, and Collective Action in South India* (New Delhi: Oxford University Press, 2003).

Mostern, Ruth, *The Yellow River: A Natural and Unnatural History* (New Haven, CT: Yale University Press, 2021).

Mukherjee, Janam, *Hungry Bengal: War, Famine and the End of Empire* (Oxford: Oxford University Press, 2015).

Mukherjee, Nilmani, *The Port of Calcutta: A Short History* (Calcutta: Port of Calcutta, 1968).

Mukhopadhyay, Amites, *Living with Disasters: Communities and Development in the Indian Sundarbans* (Delhi: Cambridge University Press, 2016).

Mukhopadhyay, Aparajita, *Imperial Technology and 'Native' Agency: A Social History of Railways in Colonial India, 1850–1920* (London: Routledge, 2018).

Mulligan, Mark, Arnout van Soesbergen and Leonardo Sáenz, 'GOODD, a Global Dataset of More than 38,000 Georeferenced Dams', *Scientific Data* vol. 7 (2020), 1–8.

Murray, Martin J., *The Development of Capitalism in Colonial Indochina (1870–1940)* (Berkeley: University of California Press, 1980).

Muscolino, Micah, *The Ecology of War in China: Henan Province, the Yellow River, and Beyond, 1938–50* (Cambridge: Cambridge University Press, 2015).

———, *Fishing Wars and Environmental Change in Late Imperial and Modern China* (Cambridge, MA: Harvard University Asia Center, 2009).

Mustonen, Tero, S. L. Harper, M. Rivera Ferre, J. Postigo, A. Ayanlade, T. Benjaminsen, R. Morgan and A. Okem (eds), 2021, *Compendium of Indigenous Knowledge and Local Knowledge: Towards Inclusion of Indigenous Knowledge and Local Knowledge in Global Reports on Climate Change* (Kontiolahti, Finland: Snowchange Cooperative, 2021).

Nagel, Philipp, and Tim Gray, 'Is the EU's Fisheries Partnership Agreement (FPA) with Mauritania a Genuine Partnership or Exploitation by the EU?', *Ocean & Coastal Management* vol. 56 (2012), 26–34.

Nair, Janaki, *Mysore Modern: Rethinking the Region under Princely Rule* (Minneapolis: University of Minnesota Press, 2011).

Nakashima, Douglas, and Igor Krupnik (eds), *Indigenous Knowledge for Climate Change Assessment and Adaptation*, vol. 2 (Cambridge: Cambridge University Press, 2018).

Nayak, Arun Kumar, 'Big Dams and Protests in India: A Study of Hirakud Dam', *Economic and Political Weekly* vol. 45, no. 2 (2010), 69–73.

———, 'Development, Displacement and Justice in India: Study of Hirakud Dam', *Social Change* vol. 43 (2013), 397–419.

Ngalamulume, Kalala J., 'Coping with Disease in the French Empire: The Provision of Waterworks in Saint-Louis-du-Senegal, 1860–1914', in: Petri S. Juuti, Tapio S. Katko and Heikki S. Vuorinen (eds), *Environmental History of Water: Global Views on Community Water Supply and Sanitation* (London: IWA, 2007), 147–63.

Nijman, Charles, *Irrigation Decision-Making Processes and Conditions: A Case Study of Sri Lanka's Kirindi Oya Irrigation and Settlement Project* (Colombo, Sri Lanka: International Irrigation Management Institute, 1992).

Nilsen, Alf Gunvald, *Dispossession and Resistance in India: The River and the Rage* (London: Routledge, 2010).

Nilsson, David, 'The Unseeing State: How Ideals of Modernity Have Undermined Innovation in Africa's Urban Water Systems', *NTM Zeitschrift für Geschichte der Wissenschaften, Technik und Medizin* vol. 24 (2016), 481–510.

———, *Water for a Few: A History of Urban Water and Sanitation in East Africa*, Stockholm Papers in the History and Philosophy of Technology (Stockholm: KTH Royal Institute of Technology, 2006).

Nixon, Rob, *Slow Violence and the Environmentalism of the Poor* (Cambridge, MA: Harvard University Press, 2011).

North, Michael, *Zwischen Hafen und Horizont: Weltgeschichte der Meere* (Munich: Beck, 2016).

Nyanchaga, Ezekiel Nyangeri, *History of Water Supply and Governance in Kenya (1895–2005): Lessons and Futures* (Tampere, Finland: Tampere University Press, 2016).

Nye, David E., *American Technological Sublime* (Cambridge, MA: MIT Press, 1994).

———, *Electrifying America: Social Meanings of a New Technology* (Cambridge, MA: MIT Press, 1990).

Ogle, Maureen, *All the Modern Conveniences: American Household Plumbing, 1840–1890* (Baltimore, MD: Johns Hopkins University Press, 1996).

O'Gorman, Emily, *Flood Country: An Environmental History of the Murray-Darling Basin* (Collingwood, Vic: CSIRO, 2012).

———, *Wetlands in a Dry Land: More-than-Human Histories of Australia's Murray-Darling Basin* (Seattle: University of Washington Press, 2021).

Okidi, C. O., 'History of the Nile and Lake Victoria Basins through Treaties', in: Howell and Allan, *Nile*, 321–50.

Oliver-Smith, Anthony, 'Peru's 500-Year Earthquake: Vulnerability in Historical Context', in: Anthony Oliver-Smith and Susanna M. Hoffman (eds), *The Angry Earth: Disaster in Anthropological Perspective* (New York: Routledge, 1999), 74–88.

Olukoju, Ayodeji, 'The Development of the Port of Lagos, c. 1892–1946', *Journal of Transport History* vol. 13 (1992), 59–78.

——, *Infrastructure Development and Urban Facilities in Lagos, 1861–2000* (Ibadan, Nigeria: Institut français de recherche en Afrique, 2013).

Opitz, Alfred, 'Atlantropa', *Kultur und Technik* vol. 3, no. 3 (1979), 33–36.

O'Rourke, Kevin Hjortshøj, and Jeffrey Gale Williamson (eds), *The Spread of Modern Industry to the Periphery since 1871* (Oxford: Oxford University Press, 2017).

Osborn, Fairfield H. (ed.), *Our Crowded Planet: Essays on the Pressures of Population* (London: Allen and Unwin, 1962).

Osborne, Michael A., 'Acclimatizing the World: A History of the Paradigmatic Colonial Science', *Osiris* vol. 15 (2000), 135–51.

Osterhammel, Jürgen, *Die Verwandlung der Welt: Eine Geschichte des 19. Jahrhunderts* (Munich: Beck, 2009).

Owen, Roger, *Cotton and the Egyptian Economy, 1820–1914: A Study in Trade and Development* (Oxford: Clarendon, 1969).

Pagden, Anthony, *Lords of All the World: Ideologies of Empire in Spain, Britain and France c. 1500–c. 1800* (New Haven, CT: Yale University Press, 1995).

Palmer-Jones, R. W., 'Irrigation and the Politics of Development in Nigeria', in: Michael Watts (ed.), *State, Oil and Agriculture in Nigeria* (Berkeley: University of California Press, 1987), 138–67.

Parnell, Susan, 'Sanitation, Segregation and the Natives (Urban Areas) Act: African Exclusion from Johannesburg's Malay Location, 1897–1925', *Journal of Historical Geography* vol. 17 (1991), 271–88.

Parrinello, Giacomo, 'Systems of Power: A Spatial Envirotechnical Approach to Water Power and Industrialization in the Po Valley of Italy, ca. 1880–1970', *Technology and Culture* vol. 59 (2018), 652–88.

Parrinello, Giacomo, Etienne S. Benson and Wilko Graf von Hardenberg, 'Estimated Truths: Water, Science, and the Politics of Approximation', *Journal of Historical Geography* vol. 68 (2020), 3–10.

Parthasarathi, Prasannan, *Why Europe Grew Rich and Asia Did Not: Global Economic Divergence, 1600–1850* (Cambridge: Cambridge University Press, 2011).

Patel, Kiran Klaus, *The New Deal: A Global History* (Princeton, NJ: Princeton University Press, 2016).

Paterson, J. A., and L. J. Chapman, 'Fishing Down and Fishing Hard: Ecological Change in the Nile Perch of Lake Nabugabo, Uganda', *Ecology of Freshwater Fish* vol. 18 (2009), 380–94.

Pauly, D., D. Zeller and M.L.D. Palomares (eds), Sea around Us: Concepts, Design and Data (2020). http://www.seaaroundus.org.

Pavé, M., and E. Charles-Dominique, 'Science et politique des pêches en Afrique occidentale française (1900–1950), quelles limites de quelles ressources', *Nature, sociétés* vol. 7, no. 2 (1999), 5–18.

Pearson, Chris, *Dogopolis: How Dogs and Humans Made Modern New York, London, and Paris* (Chicago: University of Chicago Press, 2021).

Pearson, M., 'Littoral Society: The Concept and Problems', *Journal of World History* vol. 17 (2006), 353–73.

Peet, Richard, 'Introduction to the Life and Thought of Karl Wittfogel', *Antipode* vol. 17 (1985), 3–21.

Peet, Richard, Paul Robbins and Michael Watts (eds), *Global Political Ecology* (London: Routledge, 2011).

Peluso, Nancy L., *Rich Forests, Poor People: Resource Control and Resistance in Java* (Berkeley: University of California Press, 1992).

Perdue, Peter C., *Exhausting the Earth: State and Peasant in Hunan, 1500–1850* (Cambridge, MA: Harvard University Press, 1987).

Perkins, John H., *Geopolitics and the Green Revolution: Wheat, Genes and the Cold War* (New York: Oxford University Press, 1997).

Peterson, Maya K., *Pipe Dreams: Water and Empire in Central Asia's Aral Sea Basin* (Cambridge: Cambridge University Press, 2019).

Pharo, Helge Ø., 'The Indo-Norwegian Project and the Modernisation of Kerala Fisheries, 1950–1970', in: Mike Shepperdson and Colin Simmons (eds), *The Indian National Congress and the Political Economy of India 1885–1985* (Aldershot, UK: Avebury, 1988), 382–99.

Phillips, Sarah T., *This Land, This Nation: Conservation, Rural America, and the New Deal* (Cambridge: Cambridge University Press, 2007).

Pietz, David A., *Engineering the State: The Huai River and Reconstruction in Nationalist China, 1927–1937* (New York: Routledge, 2002).

——, *The Yellow River: The Problem of Water in Modern China* (Cambridge, MA: Harvard University Press, 2015).

Pisani, Donald J., 'Beyond the Hundredth Meridian: Nationalizing the History of Water in the United States', *Environmental History* vol. 5 (2000), 466–82.

——, *Water and American Government: The Reclamation Bureau, National Water Policy, and the West, 1902–1935* (Berkeley: University of California Press, 2002).

Plageman, Nate, 'Colonial Ambition, Common Sense Thinking, and the Making of Takoradi Harbor, Gold Coast', *History in Africa* vol. 40 (2013), 317–52.

Platteau, Jean-Philippe, 'The Dynamics of Fisheries Development in Developing Countries: A General Overview', *Development and Change* vol. 20 (1989), 565–97.

Podobnik, Bruce, *Global Energy Shifts: Fostering Sustainability in a Turbulent Age* (Philadelphia, PA: Temple University Press, 2006).

Poloczanska, Elvira S., Michael T. Burrows, Christopher J. Brown, Jorge García Molinos, Benjamin S. Halpern, Ove Hoegh-Guldberg, Carrie V. Kappe, et al., 'Responses of Marine Organisms to Climate Change across Oceans', *Frontiers in Marine Science* vol. 3 (2016), 62.

Pomeranz, Kenneth, *The Great Divergence: China, Europe, and the Making of the Modern World Economy* (Princeton, NJ: Princeton University Press, 2000).

——, 'The Great Himalayan Watershed: Agrarian Crisis, Mega-dams and the Environment', *New Left Review* vol. 58 (2009), 5–39.

Pomeroy, Robert, John Parks, Richard Pollnac, Tammy Campson, Emmanuel Genio, Cliff Marlessy, Elizabeth Holle, et al., 'Fish Wars: Conflict and Collaboration in Fisheries Management in Southeast Asia', *Marine Policy* vol. 31 (2007), 645–56.

Poncelet, Marc, *L'invention des sciences coloniales belges* (Paris: Éditions Karthala, 2008).

Powell, Miles, 'Harnessing the Great Acceleration: Connecting Local and Global Environmental History at the Port of Singapore', *Environmental History* vol. 27 (2022), 441–66.

——, 'Singapore's Lost Coast: Land Reclamation, National Development and the Erasure of Human and Ecological Communities, 1822–Present', *Environment and History* vol. 27 (2021), 635–63.

Prashad, Vijay, 'Marks of Capital: Colonialism and the Sweepers of Delhi', *International Review of Social History* vol. 40 (1995), 1–30.

——, 'The Technology of Sanitation in Colonial Delhi', *Modern Asian Studies* vol. 35 (2001), 113–55.

'Prediction and Research on the Zambezi before Kariba: 1956–57', *Transactions of the Royal Society of South Africa* vol. 55 (2000), 21–27.

Pringle, Robert M., 'The Nile Perch in Lake Victoria: Local Responses and Adaptations', *Africa: Journal of the International African Institute* vol. 75 (2005), 510–38.

——, 'The Origins of the Nile Perch in Lake Victoria', *BioScience* vol. 55 (2005), 780–87.

Pritchard, Sara B., *Confluence: The Nature of Technology and the Remaking of the Rhone* (Cambridge, MA: Harvard University Press, 2011).

Putri, Prathiwi W., and Aryani Sari Rahmanti, 'Jakarta Waterscape: From Structuring Water to 21st Century Hybrid Nature?', *Nakhara: Journal of Environmental Design and Planning* vol. 6 (2010), 59–76.

Ramanna, Mridula, *Western Medicine and Public Health in Colonial Bombay* (Hyderabad: Orient Longman, 2002).

Ramasubban, Radhika, and Nigel Crook, 'Spatial Patterns of Health and Mortality', in: Sujata Patel and Alice Thorner (eds), *Bombay: Metaphor for Modern India* (Bombay: Oxford University Press, 1996).

Ranganathan, Surabhi, 'Decolonization and International Law: Putting the Ocean on the Map', *Journal of the History of International Law* vol. 23 (2020), 161–83.

Rani, Midatala, 'Historical Background of the Cauvery Water Dispute', *Proceedings of the Indian History Congress* vol. 63 (2002), 1033–42.

Rankin, William, *After the Map: Cartography, Navigation, and the Transformation of Territory in the Twentieth Century* (Chicago: University of Chicago Press, 2016).

Rao, B. Eswara, 'Taming "Liquid Gold" and Dam Technology: A Study of the Godivari Anicut', in: Deepak Kumar, Vinita Damodaran and Rohan D'Souza (eds), *The British Empire and the Natural World: Environmental Encounters in South Asia* (New Delhi: Oxford University Press, 2011), 145–59.

Rao, N. Subba, *Mechanisation and Marine Fishermen: A Case Study of Visakhapatnam* (New Delhi: Northern Book Centre, 1988).

Rao, Srinivasa, and John Lourdusamy, 'Colonialism and the Development of Electricity: The Case of Madras Presidency, 1900–47', *Science, Technology, and Society* vol. 15 (2010), 27–54.

Ravesteijn, Wim, 'Controlling Water, Controlling People: Irrigation Engineering and State Formation in the Dutch East Indies', *Itinerario* vol. 31 (2007), 89–118.

——, *De zegenrijke heeren der wateren: irrigatie en staat op Java, 1832–1942* (Delft: Delft University Press, 1997).

——, 'Irrigatie en koloniale staat op Java: De gevolgen van de hongersnoden in Demak', *Jaarboek voor ecologische geschiedenis* (1999), 79–106.

Ray, Indrajit, *Bengal Industries and the British Industrial Revolution (1757–1857)* (London: Routledge, 2011).

——, 'Imperial Policy and the Decline of the Bengal Salt Industry under Colonial Rule: An Episode in the 'De-industrialisation' Process', *Indian Social and Economic History Review* vol. 38 (2001), 181–205.

Reardon, Erik, *Managing the River Commons: Fishing and New England's Rural Economy* (Amherst: University of Massachusetts Press, 2021).

Redclift, Michael A., *Frontiers: Histories of Civil Society and Nature* (Cambridge, MA: MIT Press, 2006).

Reeves, Peter, 'Inland Waters and Freshwater Fisheries: Some Issues of Control, Access and Conservation in Colonial India', in: David Arnold and Ramachandra Guha (eds), *Nature, Culture, Imperialism: Essays on the Environmental History of South Asia* (New Delhi: Oxford University Press, 1995), 260–92.

Reeves, Peter, Bob Pokrant and John McGuire, 'The Auction Lease System in Lower Burma's Fisheries, 1870–1904: Implications for Artisanal Fishers and Lessees', *Journal of Southeast Asian Studies* vol. 30 (1999), 249–62.

Reeves, Peter, Bob Pokrant, John McGuire and Andrew Pope, 'Mapping India's Marine Resources: Colonial State Experiments, c. 1908–1930', *South Asia* vol. 19 (1996), 13–35.

Reid, Richard, 'Africa's Revolutionary Nineteenth Century and the Idea of the "Scramble"', *Past & Present* vol. 126 (2022), 1424–47.

Reinthal, P. N., and M.L.J. Stiassny, 'The Fresh-Water Fishes of Madagascar: A Study of an Endangered Fauna with Recommendations for a Conservation Strategy', *Conservation Biology* vol. 5 (1991), 231–43.

Revelle, Roger, and V. Lakshminarayana, 'The Ganges Water Machine', *Science* vol. 188, no. 4188 (1975), 611–61.

Reynolds, Terry, *Stronger than a Hundred Men: A History of the Vertical Water Wheel* (Baltimore, MD: Johns Hopkins University Press, 1983).

Richards, Alan, *Egypt's Agricultural Development, 1800–1980: Technical and Social Change* (Boulder, CO: Westview, 1982).

Richards, John F., *The Mughal Empire* (Cambridge: Cambridge University Press, 1993).

———, *The Unending Frontier: An Environmental History of the Early Modern World* (Berkeley: University of California Press, 2003).

Richards, John F., and Elizabeth P. Flint, 'A Century of Land-Use Change in South and Southeast Asia', in: Virginia H. Dale (ed.), *Effects of Land-Use Change on Atmospheric CO_2 Concentrations: South and Southeast Asia as a Case Study* (New York: Springer, 1994), 15–63.

———, 'Long-Term Transformations in the Sundarbans Wetland Forests of Bengal', *Agriculture and Human Values* vol. 7 (1990), 17–33.

Richter, Brian D., S. Postel, C. Revenga, T. Scudder, B. Lehner, A. Churchill and A. M. Chow, 'Lost in Development's Shadow: The Downstream Human Consequences of Dams', *Water Alternatives* vol. 3 (2010), 14–42.

Rijke-Epstein, Tasha, 'On Humble Technologies: Containers, Care, and Water Infrastructure in Northwest Madagascar, 1750s–1960s', *History and Technology* vol. 37 (2021), 293–328.

———, 'The Politics of Filth: Sanitation, Work, and Competing Moralities in Urban Madagascar, 1890s–1977', *Journal of African History* vol. 60, (2019), 229–56.

Robbins, Paul, *Political Ecology: A Critical Introduction*, 3rd ed. (Hoboken, NJ: Wiley, 2020).

Roberts, Callum, *The Unnatural History of the Sea* (Washington, DC: Island, 2007).

Roberts, T. W., 'Republicanism, Railway Imperialism, and the French Empire in Africa, 1879–1889', *Historical Journal* vol. 54 (2011), 401–20.

———, 'The Trans-Saharan Railway and the Politics of Imperial Expansion, 1890–1900', *Journal of Imperial and Commonwealth History* vol. 43 (2015), 438–62.

Robertson, Thomas, *The Malthusian Moment: Global Population Growth and the Birth of American Environmentalism* (New Brunswick, NJ: Rutgers University Press, 2012).

Robins, Eric, and Ronald Legge, *Animal Dunkirk: The Story of Lake Kariba and 'Operation Noah', the Greatest Animal Rescue since the Ark* (London: Herbert Jenkins, 1959).

Robins, Jonathan, *Palm Oil: A Global History* (Chapel Hill: University of North Carolina Press, 2021).

Robinson, M. A., and Rowena Lawson, 'Some Reflections on Aid to Fisheries in West Africa', *Marine Policy* vol.10 (1986), 101–10.

Rohkrämer, Thomas, *Eine andere Moderne? Zivilisationskritik, Natur und Technik in Deutschland, 1880–1933* (Paderborn, Germany: Schöningh, 1999).

Rola, Agnes C., and Prabhu L. Pingali, *Pesticides, Rice Productivity, and Farmers' Health* (Manila: International Rice Research Institute, 1993).

Rosenzweig, Michael L., 'The Four Questions: What Does the Introduction of Exotic Species Do to Diversity?', *Evolutionary Ecology Research* vol. 3 (2001), 361–67.

Ross, Corey, 'Confluent Narratives: Writing the History of Water and Empire', *Contemporanea* vol. 25 (2022), 162–67.

——, 'Constrained River, Constrained Choices: Seasonal Floods and Colonial Authority in the Red River Delta', *International Journal of Asian Studies* vol. 20 (2023), https://doi .org/10.1017/S1479591423000190.

——, *Ecology and Power in the Age of Empire: Europe and the Transformation of the Tropical World* (Oxford: Oxford University Press, 2017).

Royce, William F., *Fishery Development* (Orlando, FL: Academic, 1987).

Ruppenthal, Jens, *Kolonialismus als 'Wissenschaft und Technik': Das Hamburger Kolonia- linstitut 1908 bis 1919* (Stuttgart: Steiner, 2007).

Saha, Jonathan, *Colonizing Animals: Interspecies Empire in Myanmar* (Cambridge: Cam- bridge University Press, 2022).

Saikia, Arupjyoti, *The Unquiet River: A Biography of the Brahmaputra* (New Delhi: Oxford University Press, 2019).

Sarkar, Anindita, 'Informal Water Vendors and the Urban Poor: Evidence from a Nairobi Slum', *Water International* vol. 45 (2020), 443–57.

Sarkar, Suvobrata, *Let There Be Light: Engineering, Entrepreneurship and Electricity in Colonial Bengal, 1880–1945* (Cambridge: Cambridge University Press, 2020).

Sayan, Ramazan Caner, Nidhi Nagabhatla and Marvel Ekwuribe, 'Soft Power, Discourse Coalitions, and the Proposed Interbasin Water Transfer between Lake Chad and the Congo River', *Water Alternatives* vol. 13 (2020), 752–78.

Schiebinger, Londa, 'Forum Introduction: The European Colonial Science Complex', *Isis* vol. 96 (2005), 52–55.

Schivelbusch, Wolfgang, *The Railway Journey: The Industrialization of Space and Time in the Nineteenth Century* (Berkeley: University of California Press, 1986).

Schlichting, Kara Murphy, *New York Recentered: Building the Metropolis from the Shore* (Chicago: University of Chicago Press, 2019).

Schmidt, Jeremy J., 'Historicising the Hydrosocial Cycle', *Water Alternatives* vol. 7 (2014), 220–34.

Schmitthenner, Peter L., 'Colonial Hydraulic Projects in South India: Environmental and Cultural Legacy', in: Deepak Kumar, Vinita Damodaran and Rohan D'Souza (eds), *The British Empire and the Natural World: Environmental Encounters in South Asia* (New Delhi: Oxford University Press, 2011), 181–201.

Schnitter, Nicholas J., *A History of Dams: The Useful Pyramids* (Rotterdam: Balkema, 1994).

Schouten, Peer, and Jan Bachmann, 'Buffering State-Making: Geopolitics in the Sudd Marshlands of South Sudan', *Geopolitics* (2021): 1–19.

Schreyger, Emil, *L'Office du Niger au Mali 1932 à 1982: La problématique d'une grande entreprise agricole dans la zone du Sahel* (Wiesbaden, Germany: Steiner, 1984).

Schumacher, E. F., *Small Is Beautiful: A Study of Economics as if People Mattered* (London: Abacus, 1974).

Scott, James C., *Seeing like a State: How Certain Schemes to Improve the Human Condition Have Failed* (New Haven, CT: Yale University Press, 1998).

Scudder, Thayer, *The Ecology of the Gwembe Tonga* (Manchester: Manchester University Press, 1962).

——, *The Future of Large Dams: Dealing with Social, Environmental, Institutional and Political Costs* (London: Earthscan, 2005).

Segalla, Spencer, *Empire and Catastrophe: Decolonization and Environmental Disaster in North Africa and Mediterranean France since 1954* (Lincoln: University of Nebraska Press, 2021).

Selby, Jan, Gabrielle Daoust and Clemens Hoffmann, *Divided Environments: An Interna- tional Political Ecology of Climate Change, Water and Security* (Cambridge: Cambridge University Press, 2022).

Semedi, Pujo, *Close to the Stone, Far from the Throne: The Story of a Javanese Fishing Community, 1820s–1990s* (Yogyakarta, Indonesia: Benang Merah, 2003).

Sen, Amartya, *Poverty and Famines: An Essay on Entitlement and Deprivation* (Oxford: Clarendon, 1981).

Sen, Sudipta, *Ganges: The Many Pasts of an Indian River* (New Haven, CT: Yale University Press, 2019).

Sessions, Jennifer E., *By Sword and Plow: France and the Conquest of Algeria* (Ithaca, NY: Cornell University Press, 2011).

Seth, Suman, 'Colonial History and Postcolonial Science Studies', *Radical History Review* no. 127 (2017), 63–85.

Shamir, Ronen, 'Head-Hunters and Knowledge-Gatherers: Colonialism, Engineers and Fields of Planning', *History and Anthropology* vol. 29 (2018), 469–92.

Shankar, Devika, 'Water, Fish and Property in Colonial India, 1860–1890', *Past & Present* vol. 258 (2023), 79–114.

Sharan, Awadhendra, 'From Source to Sink: "Official" and "Improved" Water in Delhi, 1868–1956', *Indian Economic and Social History Review* vol. 48 (2011), 425–62.

———, 'In the City, Out of Place: Environment and Modernity, Delhi 1860s to 1960s', *Economic and Political Weekly* vol. 41 (2006), 4905–11.

———, *In the City, Out of Place: Nuisance, Pollution, and Dwelling in Delhi, c. 1850–2000* (New Delhi: Oxford University Press, 2014).

Sharma, Ashish, Conrad Wasko and Dennis P. Lettenmaier, 'If Precipitation Extremes Are Increasing, Why Aren't Floods?', *Water Resources Research* vol. 54 (2018), 8545–51.

Sharma, Sanjay, 'The 1837–38 Famine in U.P.: Some Dimensions of Popular Action', *Indian Economic and Social History Review* vol. 30 (1993), 337–72.

Sharman, J. C., *Empires of the Weak: The Real Story of European Expansion and the Creation of the New World Order* (Princeton, NJ: Princeton University Press, 2019).

Sheller, Mimi, *Aluminum Dreams: The Making of Light Modernity* (Boston, MA: MIT Press, 2014).

Shiva, Vandana, *The Violence of the Green Revolution: Third World Agriculture, Ecology and Politics* (London: Zed, 1991).

Showers, Kate B., 'Congo River's Grand Inga Hydroelectricity Scheme: Linking Environmental History, Policy and Impact', *Water History* vol. 1 (2009), 31–58.

———, 'Electrifying Africa: An Environmental History with Policy Implications', *Geografiska annaler B, Human Geography* vol. 93 (2011), 193–221.

Shutzer, Matthew, 'Energy in South Asian History', *History Compass* vol. 18 (2020), https://doi.org/10.1111/hic3.12635.

———, 'Oil, Money and Decolonization in South Asia', *Past & Present* vol. 258 (2022), 212–45.

———, 'Subterranean Properties: India's Political Ecology of Coal, 1870–1975', *Comparative Studies in Society and History* vol. 63 (2021), 400–432.

Sieferle, Rolf Peter, *The Subterranean Forest: Energy Systems and the Industrial Revolution* (Winwick, UK: White Horse, 2001).

Simonow, Joanna, 'The Great Bengal Famine in Britain: Metropolitan Campaiging for Food Relief and the End of Empire, 1943–44', *Journal of Imperial and Commonwealth History* vol. 48 (2020), 168–97.

Singaravélou, Pierre (ed.), *Les empires coloniaux xixe–xxe siècle* (Paris: Éditions Points, 2013).

———, *Professer l'Empire: Les 'sciences coloniales' en France sous la IIIe République* (Paris: Publications de la Sorbonne, 2011).

Singh, Nirmal Tej, *Irrigation and Soil Salinity in the Indian Subcontinent: Past and Present* (Bethlehem, PA: Lehigh University Press, 2005).

Singh, Praveen, 'The Colonial State, Zamindars and the Politics of Flood Control in North Bihar (1850–1945)', *Indian Economic and Social History Review* vol. 45 (2008), 239–59.

——, 'Flood Control for North Bihar: An Environmental History from the "Ground-Level" (1850–1954)', in: Deepak Kumar, Vinita Damodaran and Rohan D'Souza (eds), *The British Empire and the Natural World: Environmental Encounters in South Asia* (New Delhi: Oxford University Press, 2011), 160–78.

Sinha, Nitin, 'Fluvial Landscape and the State: Property and the Gangetic Diaras in Colonial India, 1790s–1890s', *Environment and History* vol. 20 (2014), 209–37.

Sköld, Maria, '5 Reasons Why the Climate Crisis is a Water Crisis', Stockholm International Water Institute, 20 March 2020, https://siwi.org/latest/5-reasons-why-the-climate-crisis-is-a-water-crisis/.

Smil, Vaclav, *Energy in World History* (Boulder, CO: Westview, 1994).

——, *Enriching the Earth: Fritz Haber, Carl Bosch, and the Transformation of World Food Production* (Cambridge, MA: MIT Press, 2001).

——, *Feeding the World: A Challenge for the Twenty-First Century* (Cambridge, MA: MIT Press, 2001).

Smith, Norman, *Man and Water: A History of Hydro-technology* (London: P. Davies, 1976).

Smith, Tim D., *Scaling Fisheries: The Science of Measuring the Effects of Fishing, 1855–1955* (Cambridge: Cambridge University Press, 1994).

Smith, Virginia, *Clean: A History of Personal Hygiene and Purity* (Oxford: Oxford University Press, 2007).

Sneddon, Christopher, *Concrete Revolution: Large Dams, Cold War Geopolitics, and the US Bureau of Reclamation* (Chicago: Chicago University Press, 2015).

Soens, Tim, Dieter Schott, Michael Toyka-Seid and Bert De Munck (eds), *Urbanizing Nature: Actors and Agency (Dis)Connecting Cities and Natures since 1500* (New York: Routledge, 2019).

Sreenivasan, A., 'Transfers of Freshwater Fishes into India', in: P. S. Ramakrishnan (ed.), *Ecology of Biological Invasion in the Tropics* (New Delhi: International Scientific, 1991), 131–38.

Stanley, Daniel Jean, and Andrew G. Warne, 'Nile Delta in Its Destruction Phase', *Journal of Coastal Research* vol. 14 (1998), 794–825.

Stein, Burton (ed.), *The Making of Agrarian Policy in British India, 1770–1900* (Oxford: Oxford University Press, 1992).

Steinberg, Theodore, *Acts of God: The Unnatural History of Natural Disaster in America* (Oxford: Oxford University Press, 2000).

——, *Nature Incorporated: Industrialization and the Waters of New England* (Cambridge: Cambridge University Press, 1991).

Stone, Ian, *Canal Irrigation in British India: Perspectives on Technological Change in a Peasant Economy* (Cambridge: Cambridge University Press, 1985).

Stone, Richard, 'Mayhem on the Mekong', *Science* vol. 333 (2011), 814–18.

Stott, Philip, and Sian Sullivan (eds), *Political Ecology: Science, Myth and Power* (London: Arnold, 2000).

Streets-Salter, Heather, and Trevor Getz, *Empires and Colonies in the Modern World: A Global Perspective* (Oxford: Oxford University Press, 2016).

Subramanian, Ajantha, *Shorelines: Space and Rights in South India* (Stanford, CA: Stanford University Press, 2009).

Sultana, Farhana, 'The Unbearable Heaviness of Climate Coloniality', *Political Geography* vol. 99 (2022), https://doi.org/10.1016/j.polgeo.2022.102638.

Sutter, Paul S., 'The Tropics: A Brief History of an Environmental Imaginary', in: Andrew C. Isenberg (ed.), *The Oxford Handbook of Environmental History* (Oxford: Oxford University Press, 2014), 178–204.

Swain, Ashok, 'Ethiopia, the Sudan, and Egypt: The Nile River Dispute', *Journal of Modern African Studies* vol. 35 (1997), 675–94.

Swanson, Maynard, 'The Sanitation Syndrome: Bubonic Plague and Urban Native Policy in the Cape Colony, 1900–1909', *Journal of African History* vol. 18 (1977), 387–410.

Tagliacozzo, Eric, *In Asian Waters: Oceanic Worlds from Yemen to Yokohama* (Princeton, NJ: Princeton University Press, 2022).

Taylor, Joseph E., *Making Salmon: An Environmental History of the Northwest Fisheries Crisis* (Seattle: University of Washington Press, 1999).

Taylor, Vanessa, and Frank Trentmann, 'Liquid Politics: Water and the Politics of Everyday Life in the Modern City', *Past & Present* vol. 211 (2011), 199–241.

Teisch, Jessica B., *Engineering Nature: Water, Development, and the Global Spread of American Environmental Expertise* (Chapel Hill: University of North Carolina Press, 2011).

Tertrais, Hugues, 'L'électrification de l'Indochine', *Outre-Mers: Revue d'histoire* vol. 89 (2002), 589–600.

Tessier, Olivier, 'Outline of the Process of Red River Hydraulic Development during the Nguyen Dynasty', in: Mart A. Stewart and Peter A. Coclanis (eds), *Environmental Change and Agricultural Sustainability in the Mekong Delta* (New York: Springer, 2011), 45–65.

Thévenet, Amédée, *La guerre d'Indochine* (Paris: France-Empire, 2001).

Thompson, Elizabeth, 'Dams Alter Nutrient Flows to Coasts', *Eos* vol. 101 (2020), https://doi.org/10.1029/2020EO148986.

Thompson, John, and Sandy Cairncross. 'Drawers of Water: Assessing Domestic Water Use in Africa', *Bulletin of the World Health Organization* vol. 80 (2002), 61–62.

Thomson, David B., 'Intermediate Technology and Alternative Energy Systems for Small Scale Fisheries', FAO Working Paper SCS/79/WP/87 (1979).

Tilley, Helen, *Africa as a Living Laboratory: Empire, Development, and the Problem of Scientific Knowledge, 1870–1950* (Chicago: University of Chicago Press, 2011).

Tischler, Julia, 'Cementing Uneven Development: The Central African Federation and the Kariba Dam Scheme', *Journal of Southern African Studies* vol. 40 (2014), 1047–64.

——, *Light and Power for a Multiracial Nation: The Kariba Dam Scheme in the Central African Federation* (Basingstoke, UK: Palgrave Macmillan, 2013).

Tønnesson, Stein, *Vietnamese Revolution of 1945: Roosevelt, Ho Chi Minh and de Gaulle in a World at War* (London: Sage, 1991).

Travers, T. R., '"The Real Value of the Lands": The Nawabs, the British and the Land Tax in Eighteenth-Century Bengal', *Modern Asian Studies* vol. 38 (2004), 517–58.

Troadec, Jean-Paul, 'Practices and Prospects for Fisheries Development and Management: The Case of Northwest African Fisheries', in: Brian J. Rothschild (ed.), *Global Fisheries: Perspectives for the 1980s* (New York: Springer, 1983), 97–122.

Tsikata, Dzodzi, *Living in the Shadow of the Large Dams: Long Term Responses of Downstream and Lakeside Communities of Ghana's Volta River Project* (Leiden: Brill, 2006).

Tucker, Richard P., 'Containing Communism by Impounding Rivers: American Strategic Interests and the Global Spread of High Dams in the Early Cold War', in: John R. McNeill and Corinna R. Unger (eds), *Environmental Histories of the Cold War* (Cambridge: Cambridge University Press, 2010), 139–64.

Tvedt, Terje, *The River Nile and Its Economic, Political, Social, and Cultural Role: An Annotated Bibliography* (Bergen: University of Bergen Press, 2000).

——, *The River Nile in the Age of the British: Political Ecology and the Quest for Economic Power* (London: I. B. Tauris, 2004).

——, '"Water Systems", Environmental History and the Deconstruction of Nature', *Environment and History* vol. 16 (2010), 143–66.

'2022 NDC Synthesis Report', United Nations Climate Change, 26 October 2022, https://unfccc.int/ndc-synthesis-report-2022#Adaptation-component.

Ulmen, G. L. (ed.), *Society and History: Essays in Honor of Karl August Wittfogel* (The Hague: Mouton, 1978).

UNFCCC, United Nations Framework Convention on Climate Change, FCCC/INFORMAL/84 GE.05-62220 (E) 200705 (Bonn: Secretariat of the UNFCC, 1992), https://unfccc.int/resource/docs/convkp/conveng.pdf.

Unger, Corinna R., *International Development: A Postwar History* (London: Bloomsbury, 2018).

United Nations Department of Economic and Social Affairs, *World Urbanization Prospects: The 2018 Revision*, ST/ESA/SER.A/420 (New York: United Nations, 2019).

United Nations World Water Assessment Programme, *Wastewater: The Untapped Resource* (Paris: UNESCO, 2017).

UNRISD (United Nations Research Institute for Social Development), *The Social and Economic Implications of Large-Scale Introduction of New Varieties of Food Grain: Summary of Conclusion of a Global Research Project* (Geneva: UNRISD, 1974).

USAID (US Agency for International Development), *The Other War in Vietnam: A Progress Report* (Washington, DC: USAID, 1966).

Vaidyanathan, Gayathri, 'Dam Controversy: Remaking the Mekong', *Nature* vol. 478 (2011), 305–7.

Van Bavel, Bas, Daniel Curtis, Jessica Dijkman, Matthew Hannaford, Maïka De Keyzer, Eline Van Onacker and Tim Soens, *Disasters and History: The Vulnerability and Resilience of Past Societies* (Cambridge: Cambridge University Press, 2020).

Van Beusekom, Monica M., *Negotiating Development: African Farmers and Colonial Experts at the Office du Niger, 1920–1960* (Oxford: Currey, 2002).

Van den Doel, H. W., *De stille macht: Het Europese binnenlands bestuur op Java en Madoera, 1808–1942* (Amsterdam: Bakker, 1994).

Van der Straeten, Jonas, 'Measuring Progress in Megawatt: Colonialism, Development, and the "Unseeing" Electricity Grid in East Africa', *Centaurus* vol. 64 (2021), 651–74.

Van der Straeten, Jonas, and Ute Hasenöhrl, 'Connecting the Empire: New Research Perspectives on Infrastructures and the Environment in the (Post)Colonial World', *NTM Zeitschrift für Geschichte der Wissenschaften, Technik und Medizin* vol. 24 (2016), 355–91.

Van Laak, Dirk, *Imperiale Infrastruktur: Deutsche Planungen für eine Erschließung Afrikas, 1880 bis 1960* (Paderborn, Germany: Schöningh, 2004).

Vann, Michael. 'Building Colonial Whiteness on the Red River: Race, Power, and Urbanism in Paul Doumer's Hanoi, 1897–1902', *Historical Reflections* vol. 33 (2007), 277–304.

Vann, Michael, and Liz Clarke, *The Great Hanoi Rat Hunt: Empires, Disease, and Modernity in French Colonial Vietnam* (Oxford: Oxford University Press, 2018).

Van Sittert, Lance, '"The Handmaiden of Industry": Marine Science and Fisheries Development in South Africa, 1895–1939', *Studies in History and Philosophy of Science* vol. 26 (1995), 531–58.

Venkatachalam, Lakhshmanan, 'Informal Water Markets and Willingness to Pay for Water: A Case Study of the Urban Poor in Chennai City, India', *International Journal of Water Resources Development* vol. 31 (2015), 134–45.

Verney, Sébastien, *L'Indochine sous Vichy: Entre révolution nationale, collaboration et identités nationales. 1940–1945* (Paris: Riveneuve, 2012).

Vernon, James, *Hunger: A Modern History* (Cambridge, MA: Harvard University Press, 2007).

Viegas, Philip, 'The Hirakud Dam Oustees: Thirty Years After', in: Enakshi Ganguly Thukral (ed.), *Big Dams, Displaced People: Rivers of Sorrow, Rivers of Change* (New Delhi: Sage, 1992), 29–53.

Viollet, Pierre-Louis, 'From the Water Wheel to Turbines and Hydroelectricity: Techno-logical Evolution and Revolutions', *Comptes rendus mécanique* vol. 345 (2017), 570–80.

Vogt, William, *Road to Survival* (London: Gollancz, 1949).

Voigt, Wolfgang, *Atlantropa: Welbauen am Mittelmeer, ein Architektentraum der Moderne* (Hamburg: Dölling und Galitz, 1998).

Von Hardenberg, and Wilko Graf, 'Knowing the Littoral: Perception and Representation of Terraqueous Spaces in a Global Perspective', *Isis* vol. 112 (2021), 108–10.

Von Simson, John, *Kanalisation und Städtehygiene im 19. Jahrhundert* (Düsseldorf: VDI, 1983).

Vora, Rajendra, *The World's First Anti-dam Movement: The Mulshi Satyagraha, 1920–1924* (Ranikhet, India: Permanent Black, 2009).

Vörösmarty, Charles J., Michel Meybeck, Balázs Fekete, Keshav Sharma, Pamela Green and James PM Syvitski, 'Anthropogenic Sediment Retention: Major Global Impact from Registered River Impoundments', *Global and Planetary Change* vol. 39 (2003), 169–90.

Walter, François, *Catastrophes: Une histoire culturelle (XVIe au XXIe siècle)* (Paris: Seuil, 2008).

Ward, Edward, *Sahara Story* (London: Robert Hale, 1962).

Ward, Nicholas D., Thomas S. Bianchi, Patricia M. Medeiros, Michael Seidel, Jeffrey E. Richey, Richard G. Keil and Henrique O. Sawakuchi, 'Where Carbon Goes when Water Flows: Carbon Cycling across the Aquatic Continuum', *Frontiers in Marine Science* vol. 4 (2017), 7.

Warner, Jeroen, Sarunas Jomantas, Eliot Jones, Md Sazzad Ansari and Lotje De Vries, 'The Fantasy of the Grand INGA Hydroelectric Project on the River Congo', *Water* vol. 11 (2019), 407.

Waterbury, John, *Hydropolitics of the Nile Valley* (Syracuse, NY: Syracuse University Press, 1979).

——, *The Nile Basin: National Determinants of Collective Action* (New Haven, CT: Yale University Press, 2002).

Whitcombe, Elizabeth, *Agrarian Conditions in Northern India: The United Provinces under British Rule, 1860–1900* (Berkeley: University of California Press, 1972).

——, 'The Environmental Costs of Irrigation in British India: Waterlogging, Salinity and Malaria', in: David Arnold and Ramachandra Guha (eds), *Nature, Culture, Imperialism: Essays on the Environmental History of South Asia* (New Delhi: Oxford University Press, 1995), 237–59.

——, 'Irrigation', in: Dharma Kumar and Meghnad Desai (eds), *The Cambridge Economic History of India*, vol. 2 (Cambridge: Cambridge University Press, 1983), 677–736.

White, Gilbert F., *Economic and Social Aspects of Lower Mekong Development* (Bangkok, 1962).

White, Nicholas J., 'Reconstructing Europe through Rejuvenating Empire: The British, French, and Dutch Experiences Compared', in: Mark Mazower, Jessica Reinisch and David Feldman (eds), *Post-war Reconstruction in Europe: International Perspectives, 1945–1949, Past & Present* Supplement 6 (Oxford: Oxford University Press, 2011), 211–36.

White, Richard, *The Organic Machine: The Remaking of the Columbia River* (New York: Hill and Wang, 1985).

Whitington, Jerome, *Anthropogenic Rivers: The Production of Uncertainty in Lao Hydro-power* (Ithaca, NY: Cornell University Press, 2018).

Wilberg, Michael J., and Thomas J. Miller, 'Comment on "Impacts of Biodiversity Loss on Ocean Ecosystem Services"', *Science* vol. 316, no. 5829 (2007), 1285.

Williams, Michael, *Deforesting the Earth: From Prehistory to Global Crisis* (Chicago: University of Chicago Press, 2003).

Wilson, Gail, *Owen Falls: Electricity in a Developing Country* (Nairobi: East African Publishing, 1967).

Wittfogel, Karl A., *Oriental Despotism: A Comparative Study of Total Power* (New Haven, CT: Yale University Press, 1957).

Wolf, Eric R., *Europe and the People without History* (Berkeley: University of California Press, 1982).

World Bank, *Quality Unknown: The Invisible Water Crisis* (Washington, DC: World Bank, 2019).

World Commission on Dams, *Dams and Development: A New Framework for Decision-Making* (London: Earthscan, 2000).

World Economic Forum, *The Global Risks Report 2021* (WEF, 2021).

World Health Organization, *Progress on Household Drinking Water, Sanitation and Hygiene 2000-2017: Special Focus on Inequalities* (New York: UNICEF, 2019).

World Health Organization and United Nations Children's Fund, *Progress on Household Drinking Water, Sanitation and Hygiene 2000-2020: Five Years into the SDGs* (Geneva: WHO and UNICEF, 2021).

World Meteorological Organization, *2021 State of Climate Services: Water* (Geneva: WMO, 2021).

Worm, Boris, Edward B. Barbier, Nicola Beaumont, J. Emmett Duffy, Carl Folke, Benjamin S. Halpern, Jeremy B. Jackson, et al., 'Impacts of Biodiversity Loss on Ocean Ecosystem Services', *Science* vol. 314, no. 5800 (2006), 787–90.

Worster, Donald, *Rivers of Empire: Water, Aridity, and the Growth of the American West* (New York: Pantheon, 1985).

Worthington, E. B., *The Ecological Century: A Personal Appraisal* (Oxford: Clarendon, 1983).

Wright, Angus, *The Death of Ramón Gonzalez: The Modern Agricultural Dilemma*, 2nd ed. (Austin: University of Texas Press, 2005).

Wrigley, E. A., *Continuity, Chance, and Change: The Character of the Industrial Revolution in England* (Cambridge: Cambridge University Press, 1988).

Yeoh, Brenda S. A., *Contesting Space: Power Relations and the Urban Built Environment in Colonial Singapore* (Kuala Lumpur: Oxford University Press, 2006).

Zamindar, Vazira Fazila-Yacoobali, *The Long Partition and the Making of Modern South Asia: Refugees, Boundaries, Histories* (New York: Columbia University Press, 2007).

Zeheter, Michael, *Epidemics, Empire, Environment: Cholera in Madras and Quebec City* (Pittsburgh, PA: University of Pittsburgh Press, 2015).

Zhang, Jiayan, *Coping with Calamity: Environmental Change and Peasant Response in Central China, 1736-1949* (Vancouver: University of British Columbia Press, 2014).

Zimring, Carl A., *Clean and White: A History of Environmental Racism in the United States* (New York: New York University Press, 2015).

Zimring, Carl A., and Steven H. Corey (eds), *Coastal Metropolis: Environmental Histories of Modern New York City* (Pittsburgh, PA: Pittsburgh University Press, 2021).

A NOTE ON THE TYPE

THIS BOOK has been composed in Miller, a Scotch Roman typeface designed by Matthew Carter and first released by Font Bureau in 1997. It resembles Monticello, the typeface developed for The Papers of Thomas Jefferson in the 1940s by C. H. Griffith and P. J. Conkwright and reinterpreted in digital form by Carter in 2003.

Pleasant Jefferson ("P. J.") Conkwright (1905–1986) was Typographer at Princeton University Press from 1939 to 1970. He was an acclaimed book designer and AIGA Medalist.